D1083463

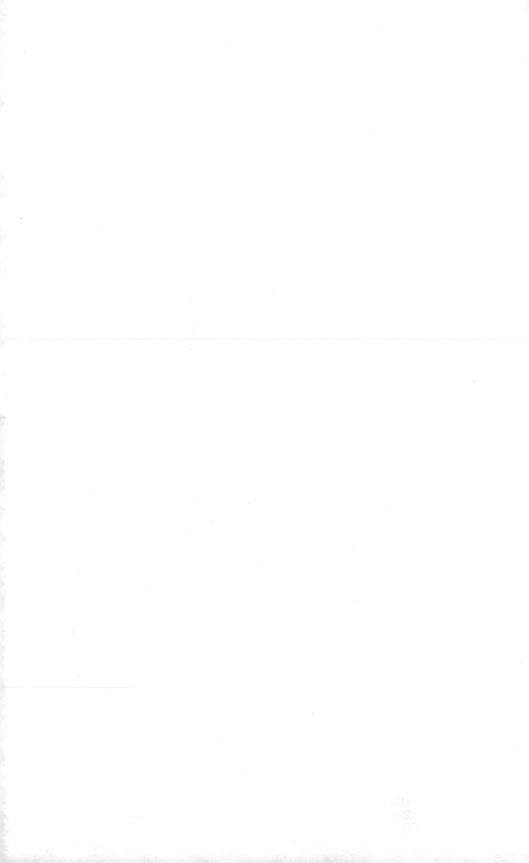

Locke in America

American Political Thought

Edited by

Wilson Carey McWilliams & Lance Banning

Locke in America
The Moral Philosophy
of the Founding Era

Jerome Huyler

 University Press of Kansas

Published by the University Press of Kansas (Lawrence, Kansas 66049), which was organized by the Kansas Board of Regents and is operated and funded by Emporia State University, Fort Hays State University, Kansas State University, Pittsburg State University, the University of Kansas, and Wichita State University

Library of Congress Cataloging-in-Publication Data

Huyler, Jerome.
   Locke in America : the moral philosophy of the founding era /
Jerome Huyler.
      p. cm. —(American political thought)
   Includes bibliographical references and index.
   ISBN 0-7006-0642-4 (cloth : alk. paper)
   1. Locke, John, 1632–1704—Contributions in political science.
I. Title. II. Series.
JC153.L87H89 1994 1995
320.5·12·092—dc20   94-26227

British Library Cataloguing in Publication Data is available.

Printed in the United States of America

10 9 8 7 6 5 4 3 2 1

Dedicated to the memory of my mother,
that noble, loving soul

Contents

Preface

For nearly a quarter century historical research has been effectively discounting the influence of John Locke on the founding of the American republic. Taken cumulatively, the landmark research of Caroline Robbins, J. G. A. Pocock, Bernard Bailyn, and Gordon Wood reshaped the map of American historiography. Working in various departments of intellectual history, they managed to weave together a strikingly resilient amalgam of concepts and concerns that stretched from eighteenth-century America all the way back to antiquity. Against Beard and the Progressives, the revisionists argued that the American Revolution owed more to ideas and ideology than to people's naked interests. But, against Becker and Hartz, they urged, the revolutionary ideology owed little to Locke.

The language of classical republicanism spoke of conceptions and concerns that were largely foreign to Locke's discourse, and vice versa. The fragmentation of society, the acquisitive quest for property, the emphasis on progress, prosperity, and the preeminent institutions of a capitalist political economy, all ostensibly Lockean recommendations, were, for the republicans, the embodiment of corruption and social ruin. Republicanism took an organic view of society, demanding civic virtue, political participation, and an overriding concern for the res publica, not the self. And it carefully studied the constitutional checks and balances and civic requirements needed to forestall corruption and preserve liberty. If the vocabulary of republicanism spoke of "Liberty" and "Property" (ostensibly Lockean formulations), this was not due to any ethos of individualism. Liberty was an attribute of republics, denoting the free, self-governing polity. And property, the freehold that conferred independence on a citizenry, was but the necessary means of resisting political dependence and tyranny.

The ideological school was easily able to document the republican influence on the American founding. Evidence was everywhere in the public prints, sermons, and orations of the revolutionary and constitutional periods. Thus, when

Gordon Wood raised the "discontinuity" claim, arguing in 1969 that the constitutional triumph of 1787–1788 signaled "the end of classical politics," scholars soon claimed otherwise. And they could point to a striking continuity of commitment to classical republican conceptions and concerns down to the nineteenth century.

But the Lockean influence would reappear as well. It was evident in what Joyce Appleby called "the aggressive individualism, the optimistic materialism, and the pragmatic interest group politics that became so salient so early in the life of the new nation."[1] The language of Lockean liberalism, in fact, can be discerned in a succession of political and religious controversies that embroiled America long before 1787, recently brought to light by Sandoz and Dworetz.

Some by now have grown resigned to the prospect that a multiplicity of ideological "tongues" could be speaking to us from a distant place and time and speaking at once. Is it that the founders were merely ideologically bilingual? Or were they speaking out of both sides of their mouths? If the ideological school is correct, if it must be believed that Americans took ideas seriously, then it behooves us to seriously treat both the Lockean and neo-Harringtonian languages they spoke. And therein lies the critical dilemma for the Pocock-Bailyn-Wood approach. If, as has been widely advertised, the core values supporting classical republicanism are inherently opposed to those that undergird classical liberalism, then the profusion of tongues signifies more than "confusion"; it suggests deep contradiction. Ideological revisionism renewed scholarly faith in the power of ideas (not simply humans' irrepressible interests) to shape the course of human events. But if the ideas these Americans expressed are so confused and contradictory, then how is it possible to ascribe authenticity to the purveyors of those ideas? Is not the entire ideological approach thereby suspect?

Or might the allegedly incompatible idioms of political discourse actually fit into a coherent and consistent ideological framework after all? It is this latter possibility that this book seeks to explore. The unifying aim of this study is to elaborate the view that the preponderance of American political thought between 1763 and 1800 reflected a remarkable continuity of commitment. And what the patriots of the Revolution, the Framers of the Constitution, the Federalists and anti-Federalists alike, and the Jeffersonian republicans in the Federalist era were most deeply committed to, all other influences notwithstanding, were the social and political principles nowhere more clearly enunciated than in the writings of John Locke.

Much of the confusion over assessing the extent of Locke's influence on the American founding, I will suggest, follows from a failure to come to terms with Locke's own social and political thought. His entire philosophy of nature has too frequently been reduced to such simple "sight-bytes" as acquisitiveness, interest-group pluralism, utilitarianism, or capitalist growth. But is Lockeanism really compatible with any of these modern conceptions? In sum, it will be necessary to say more precisely what Lockeanism is before we can hope to weigh its influence on the founding era.

Treating John Locke's corpus as a relatively comprehensive whole while taking into account recent studies that have shed much-needed light on Locke's historical context and social purposes, I shall seek to reconstruct a coherent picture of the Lockean worldview. Lockeanism, I shall conclude, is essentially individualist, as is commonly thought. But it represents a species of individualism that on the one hand comports well with the tenets of classical republicanism and on the other can philosophically oppose the very liberal trends and political practices that so worried the republicans and that we, two hundred years later, all too freely associate with liberalism and with Locke.

Ultimately, Lockeanism did not triumph in the United States. Challenged from the beginnings of American politics, it would succumb to forces that, however "liberal" they may appear today, were anathema to the theory and practice propounded by some important eighteenth-century British and American Lockeans. It is the saga of this civil war within liberalism, this "rise and fall," that I have tried to recapture here.

I should say something about the composition of this book. As one careful reviewer has observed, the project is "historical, interpretative, historiographic, conceptual, and methodological." In these pages the reader will revisit the work of a long line of commentators, and their views will often be discussed in much detail. I shall take exception to a variety of interpretive conclusions reached by such important writers as Appleby, Ashcraft, Pocock, Gordon and Neal Wood, Macpherson, Kramnick, Dunn, and Tully—students of the Western intellectual tradition who have made permanent contributions to scholarship. They have been my eyes and ears into a dimly lit past. My criticisms should not obscure my debt to them all but merely signify how much the political theorist can learn and benefit from the historian's tireless labors. It is the few but exceedingly important conceptual or philosophical confusions they take to their studies that I have tried to address. For all the fine efforts and contributions these scholars have made, that conceptual baggage has stood in the way of a proper understanding of both Locke and the character of the American founding.

I also devote perhaps more space than the reader will be accustomed to in presenting and quoting from a sizable number of recent historical and contextual studies with which I have no contention. This approach was dictated by two concerns. First, because I have traversed so much interdisciplinary ground I could not assume that the more theoretically minded reader would necessarily be sufficiently acquainted with the recent historical and contextual work that has been done, and vice versa, or that the eighteenth-century American historian would be sufficiently familiar with seventeenth-century European scholarship, and vice versa. And second, I understand that if I am to win the field for my substantive conclusions, my interpretation of Locke's thought and of the founders' labors will have to harmonize with and comprehend the widest possible array of historical and theoretical findings that have been reported and accepted by the community of scholars.

This book began as a doctoral dissertation I completed at the New School For Social Research in the spring of 1992. I wish to acknowledge and thank Margaret Jacob for chairing my dissertation committee and for devoting so much of her precious time and talent to reading and working out the problems I managed to work into earlier drafts of the dissertation. I also thank Patricia Bonomi for the words of encouragement she provided during the dissertation process (she cannot know how much they meant to me), as well as for her participation and many helpful recommendations. Steven Dworetz and Gordon Schochet have both made invaluable contributions to the book in its present form, and I am indebted to them both. I must thank Jacob Landynski for his effort on my behalf at a crucial moment of my career and acknowledge my debt to the late Elaine Spitz who was the inspiration for this project, long years ago. At the University Press of Kansas, Michael Briggs has been constant in his encouragement and support, and I shall be forever grateful to him. I must also thank Lance Banning for his thoughtful and constructive comments and recommendations and for allowing my work a place in his distinguished series. Closer to home, I want to express my appreciation to Gregory Bergamaschi for furnishing me the tools of my trade and to say to Dr. Marty Lewinter, thanks for all you have been and done. You have nourished my intellectual outlook and human spirit in more ways than I can count.

Introduction
Locke in America—
The State of the Debate

This is a book about Locke in America. For that very reason, I realized early on, it would have to be a book about America, and about Locke. To say what is "Lockean" about America, it is first necessary to say what "Lockeanism" itself is. It is not as obvious as it might appear. Those who have hotly debated the relative influence of Lockean liberal and classical republican influences on the American founding have only rarely and recently begun paying adequate attention to the strikingly complex body of thought that Locke left behind. Even those who have attested to the Lockean bearing on the origins of the United States (let alone the revisionists who have not) have a varied view of what is to be taken as evidence for their claim.

Many different "Lockes" have made their appearance in the United States at the hands of recent and distant American historians. Appleby's Locke is not Becker's Locke, who is not Kramnick's Locke, who is not Hartz's nor Diggins's Locke. As we shall see, even those scholars like Pangle and Dworetz, who have troubled to make a far closer acquaintance with Locke's major writings, have emphasized essentially two separate elements of Locke's thought and, in consequence, have rendered substantially different accounts of its historical influence.

A more careful examination of John Locke's writings will reveal that a lot of what has been portrayed as "Lockeanism" would not have been thought to be so by Locke himself and that what often passes for "Lockean" liberalism violates Locke's own deepest convictions and commitments. All too hastily Lockeanism can become associated (and confused) with Hobbesist hedonism (a la Strauss), with "possessive individualism" (a la Macpherson), with Benthamite utilitarianism (a la Appleby), and with the Protestant work ethic, narrowly (a la Dunn), or the policies and practices we associate with modern "capitalism," more broadly. Because each of these characteristics appears to oppose civic participation and the quest for a common and communal good, we situate Locke here, the republican thesis there, and endlessly wrangle over the impact of each on subsequent history. It will be useful at the outset to review the major contributions to the scholarly debate over Locke's influence on the American founding. Such a review will more concretely illustrate the conceptual weaknesses that have permeated that debate and demonstrate the need to delve more deeply and focus more sharply on Locke's own worldview before seeking to assess its significance for this nation's founding.

The Lockean Consensus

The question of Locke's influence on the American Revolution has been an abiding one. But it has been, as I say, a question fraught with conceptual difficulties. Thus those scholars who could locate a tangible connection between Locke and the American revolutionaries have addressed themselves to very different and arguably dubious notions of what Lockeanism really represents. And on each analyst's own terms, it is possible to question how authentic, consistent, and enduring a devotion to Lockeanism his or her Americans evidenced.

Carl Becker's influential treatment of *The Declaration of Independence* is a very good example of what I am trying to point out.[1] By carefully comparing the sentiments voiced by Jefferson in the second paragraph of the Declaration with the political philosophy of Locke, Becker was able to pronounce America's movement for independence an avowedly Lockean one. The common denominators, of course, were the shared commitment to natural rights, the social contract, and the legitimacy of resistance to despotic authority. The Declaration did not spell out in any great detail the Lockean philosophy of rights, Becker acknowledged, but it did not have to:

> Most Americans had absorbed Locke's works as a kind of political gospel; and the Declaration, in its form, in its phraseology, follows closely certain sentences in Locke's *Second Treatise on Government.*
> . . . The Americans did not borrow [this philosophy], they inherited it. The lineage is direct. . . . It was Locke's conclusion that seemed to the colonists sheer common sense, needing no argument at all. Locke did not need to convince the colonists because they were already convinced.[2]

Becker confirmed his conclusion with ample contemporary testimony, as when John Adams wrote in 1822, "There is not an idea in it [the Declaration], but what had been hackneyed in Congress far two years before." And Richard Henry Lee, who had moved for independence in the Second Continental Congress, "charged it as copied from Locke's treatise on Government." Jefferson, for his part, saw no need to deny the charge:

> I did not consider it as any part of my charge to invent new ideas altogether and to offer no sentiment which had ever been expressed before. . . . My aim was simply to place before mankind the common sense of the subject, in terms so plain and firm as to command their assent. . . . It was intended to be an expression of the American mind. . . . All its authority rests then on the harmonizing sentiments of the day, whether expressed in conversation, in letters, printed essays, or the elementary books of public right, as Aristotle, Cicero, Locke, Sidney, etc.[3]

And indeed, Becker pointed to numerous others who voiced the sentiments seemingly shared by Jefferson and Locke.[4] Yet by Becker's own account of the revolutionary developments, there is something troubling about this invocation of Lockean natural right. For Becker easily perceives that rather than a firm adherence to resolute principle it was the sheer "force of circumstances and the exigencies of argument . . . [that] prepar[ed] the minds of the colonists for the general theory which Jefferson was later able to take for granted as the common sense of the matter." What Becker discerned was how "step by step, from 1764 to 1776, the colonists modified their theory to suit their needs."[5]

The question, to borrow an idea from Margaret Jacob, is this: "Are discourses just rhetorical strategies used like shoes, depending if we are walking or running?" How can it be said that the American revolutionaries were devoted Lockeans when their arguments against parliamentary supremacy could shift with each passing exigency: from the artful distinction between "internal" and "external" taxation expressed during the Stamp Act crisis; to the distinction between taxation generally and regulation as such; to James Wilson's ultimate discovery that the American colonies were tied to the British Empire only through a common Crown but were independent of parliamentary law; to the rejection of all monarchical pretensions on the pages of Paine's *Common Sense;* to the affirmation of the natural and inherent rights of man by Jefferson in July of 1776?[6]

Was the revolutionary invocation of Lockean natural right a mere fortuitous expedient, a mere rationalization for a course of action the founders would have undertaken had there never been a John Locke? And what kind of commitment does that really represent, vis-à-vis the encompassing Lockean worldview? If

Jefferson's natural rights doctrine was "hackneyed" in Congress for two years, what had been the popular opinion (had there even been a popular opinion) for the prior ten years—and what would it be ten years later? In short, on Becker's own terms, a wealth of intellectual (not to mention social and political) evidence would yet be required to pronounce the American founding fully Lockean in character. Perhaps what really spurred the colonists to resistance and then revolution was the heavy yoke placed around their commercial necks by a far-off imperial ministry, not the "transcendent" principles that had accompanied the call to arms.[7]

Ironically, Louis Hartz, writing from a very different perspective, also purported to locate the Lockean character of the American founding. Seeking to understand not so much the origins of the American Revolution, however, as the absence in America of a revolutionary working-class movement and studying the contours of social relations rather than the intricacies of an elite's speculations, Hartz perceived an indomitable Lockean influence operating within American civilization. The idea of "equal creation," central to Locke's social teaching, figures prominently in Hartz's reflections as well; only it means something very different. For Locke (and Becker), it represented a fundamental moral law—the position of every individual standing in equal relation to his or her Maker. For Hartz, it signified the mere absence in America of Old World feudal relations.

Independence was not just something Americans declared; it was something they experienced. Equality was primarily a social, not a sublimely metaphysical, fact of life, at least for most of the white male population. In the fact that Americans were "born equal without having to become so" lies "the secret root from which have sprung many of the most puzzling of American cultural phenomena," including the phenomenon that modern political science has labeled "American Exceptionalism." As Hartz explained: "It is not accidental that America which has uniquely lacked a feudal tradition has uniquely lacked also a socialist tradition. The hidden origin of socialist thought everywhere in the West is to be found in the feudal ethos. The *Ancien Regime* inspires Rousseau; both inspire Marx." It is the study of comparative politics that holds the key to unlocking the American essence; for it is the sociological (not the intellectual) journey to Europe and back that ends in the discovery of the American liberal and Lockean world. "In Europe the idea of social liberty is loaded with dynamite; but in America it becomes, to a very remarkable degree, the working base from which argument begins. Here, then, is the master assumption of American political thought: . . . the reality of *atomistic social freedom*."[8]

What Locke described in his writings looked to the transplanted colonials "like a sober description of fact." The native conditions encountered by the common man "came as close to [Locke's images] as anything history has ever seen." European society for centuries had been held together by "an organic sense of structured differences." Not so America: "Amid the 'free air' of American life, something new appeared: men began to be held together not by the knowledge that they were different parts of a corporate whole, but by the knowledge that they were similar participants in a uniform way of life—by that 'pleasant uniformity of decent competence' Crevecoeur loved so much."[9]

From the fact of "atomistic social freedom" flowed the national consensus: "one of the most powerful absolutisms in the world . . . [For] when one's ultimate values are accepted wherever one turns, the absolute language of self-evidence comes easily enough."[10] Jefferson hardly needed an argument. The Hartzian thesis, as did Becker's, logically leads to its own denial. The universal compliance with the ethos of individualism in Hartz's view translates into a politics of pragmatism: "For the settlement of the ultimate moral question is the end of speculation upon it. Pragmatism . . . America's great contribution to the philosophic tradition, does not alter this, since it feeds itself on the Lockean settlement. It is only when you take your ethics for granted that all problems emerge as problems of technique."[11]

This position allows Hartz to immediately add that America's ardent Lockeanism constitutes no "bar in America to institutional innovations of a highly non-Lockean kind. Indeed, as the New Deal shows, when you simply 'solve problems' on the basis of a submerged and absolute liberal faith, you can depart from Locke with a kind of inventive freedom that European Liberal reformers and even European socialists, dominated by ideological systems, cannot duplicate."[12] The questions raised by Hartz are serious ones. How far may society "depart from Locke with a kind of inventive freedom" before it ceases being "Lockean" at all? Is Lockeanism really compatible with pragmatism in public policy, given its foundation in natural law? And when and how soon did the "inventive" and pragmatic departure from Lockeanism occur in America?

Like Becker and Hartz, the early Progressive historians also would link Locke to the American founding. In *An Economic Interpretation of the Constitution of the United States,* Charles Beard perceived not consensus, but social conflict in early America. Noticing the Framers' great emphasis on economic divisions during the Confederation period, Beard posed a telling hypothesis and suggested a large number of empirical questions that might confirm it. The ratification of the Constitution of 1787, he strongly suspected, signaled a defeat for lower-class agrarian and debtor interests and a triumph for the propertied elite: wealthy merchants, creditors, and the financial interest, generally. This thesis was carried into the post-Federalist period in his subsequent study, *The Economic Origins of Jef-*

fersonian Democracy. Once again, it was the division of Americans into capitalists and agrarians that, for Beard, figured most prominently in the disputes of the day.[13]

The point is that if one views Locke in Straussian or Macphersonian fashion as sanctioning the acquisitive impulses and capitalist interests held in check by an earlier Christian ethos, thereby fostering class drives and divisions within society, then the Progressive reading of the American founding can be depicted as essentially Lockean. In this case, the *Second Treatise of Government* could be tied to the founding not through the second chapter (on the state of nature and the rights of man), but through the fifth, "Of Property." Thus as Brown correctly summed it up, for Beard, the Constitution, "instead of being a document drawn up by patriotic men for the protection of life, liberty, and the pursuit of happiness . . . was the work of consolidated economic groups . . . that were personally interested in the outcome of their labors. . . . And the men who framed the Constitution benefitted directly from the government which they set up."[14]

Thus while they differed on innumerable points of analytical substance, Becker, Hartz, and Beard could all point to the Lockean foundations of American civilization. But they could do so only at the price of repudiating one or more aspects of Locke's own philosophic system and one another's analysis. For Becker, the Americans embraced the Lockean political ethic (man's rights), though they did so only gradually and on the basis of practical expedience, not original philosophic intent. Hartz even more categorically eschewed philosophy, making America's Lockeanism a matter of social experience and making pragmatism (not a resolute commitment to Locke's laws of God and nature) the operative principle of Lockean political organization. Beard found philosophy to be wholly superfluous to the historical project. He rejected philosophical principle as such, rejecting as well the portrait of consensus Hartz would paint and attributing naked commercial interest to the founders and their political project.

Republican Revisionism: The Demolition of the Lockean Myth

At any rate, by the 1960s a new approach to understanding the American founding would emerge. Reasserting a confidence in the power of ideas to move men, it would largely discount the power of *Locke's* ideas to move Americans. Instrumental in this shift was the work of Caroline Robbins. Following the publication of *The Eighteenth-Century Commonwealthman* in 1959, it became clear to students of American history that the "ideological" concerns and considerations voiced by the American patriots after 1763 were of a piece with views and sentiments that had been a commonplace feature of English radical thought for more than a century. In a breathtaking sweep of seventeenth- and eighteenth-century political thought, Robbins was able to trace no fewer than six generations of an "Old Whig" or "Commonwealthman" tradition, stretching from Harrington, Henry Neville, Marchamont Nedham, Milton, and Sidney in the Interregnum and Restoration periods, to Bolingbroke, Trenchard and Gordon, Toland, Tindal, Fletcher, Molesworth, and Moyle early in the eighteenth century, right through to the popular productions of James Burgh and John Cartwright in the revolutionary generation.[15]

Actually, for all her prodigious labors, Robbins had barely tapped the historical surface of this Commonwealthman, or republican, tradition. It was by finally tracing this discourse to its origins in antiquity that scholars began to appreciate how little it owed to Locke. As Quentin Skinner ably demonstrated in the second volume of his seminal study of *The Foundations of Modern Political Thought,* the natural law tradition within which Locke worked belonged to Reformation political theory. With its origins in the revival of Thomism in the counter-Reformation writings of Suarez, Bellarmine, Molina, and others, and its subsequent adoption by sixteenth-century antimonarchical Protestants, struggling to resist religious and political persecution in France, the Netherlands, and Scotland, this natural law discourse did indeed culminate in Locke's political work. But it was in volume one of his *Foundations* that Skinner outlined a very distinct tradition of discourse. Bearing little relation to Reformation resistance theories, it found its fullest expression in the Renaissance humanist writings of Machiavelli, Bruni, and Guiciardini, among others. Its roots ultimately could be traced to the ancient world and the thought of Aristotle, Cicero, and Polybius.[16]

Critical to the development of this "civic humanist" or "classical republican" model was the work of J. G. A. Pocock. He successfully tied the classical and Italian Renaissance authors to the Commonwealthman canon (and then to American political thought). In England, Pocock focused, first and foremost, on the writings of James Harrington, "who helped to make the eighteenth century what it notoriously is, the most classical-minded of English centuries. [Thus] did the humanist Renaissance come late to England."[17] After 1675, Pocock tells us, a group of "neo-Harringtonians" gathered around the opposition figure of Anthony Ashley Cooper, Lord Shaftesbury, further refined the "Radical" or "Real Whig" perspective. It was the efforts of these transmitters of the classical republican tradition that profoundly influenced the course of early eighteenth-century radical belief and in the course of time profoundly shaped the social outlook of colonial America. The conceptions contained in this classical republican paradigm may be easily enumerated and distinguished from the Lockean viewpoint.

The aim of classical politics is an eternal secular salvation: the continuance across time of the "free," meaning "self-governing" republic. As with all life forms, the aging process for the human polity, no matter how well conceived, was progressively degenerative. "The aim of politics," therefore, as Pocock writes, "is to escape from time; . . . [since] time is the dimension of imperfection and . . . change must necessarily be degenerative."[18] Two essential vehicles allow the res publica to escape the ravages of time. The first is institutional, contained in the theory of "mixed government." The "pure" forms (monarchy, aristocracy, and democracy, i.e., rule of one, few, or the many), as Aristotle taught, all contained the seeds of their own destruction. This is signified by a recurring cycle in which the polis careens between anarchy and tyranny. For Aristotle, the solution consisted of mixing the three pure forms in a single polity, enabling each to check and balance the others.

Now, the dividing of power among the democratic, aristocratic, and monarchical elements notwithstanding, the classical republic is conceived as one organic unit. There is a singular public good, and it was to be the focus of each citizen's attention. Herein lay the second vehicle designed to ward off the corrosive influence of time. It concerned the human personality itself: "Since association was in itself a good, and intelligent activity another, it followed that the highest form of active life was that of the citizen who, having entered the political process in pursuit of his particular good, now found himself joining with others to direct the actions of all in pursuit of the good of all."[19]

Here was virtue, active and civic. Its antithesis, *fortuna,* involved an abject submission before the natural and degenerative processes of time. Time's destructive influence was embodied in the term *corruption.* It denoted three interconnected aspects: first, the degenerative tendency to which all particular forms of government are prone; second, the specific cause of that degeneration, which is the dependence of some men upon other men; and third, the moral degeneration of the individual, who, in these circumstances, is prevented from developing his virtue by identifying his particular good with the good of all.[20] Only the independent citizen could freely participate with his voice, his vote, and his arms in the defense of the res publica. So preoccupied with stasis in human affairs, the classical paradigm would itself move and progress through time. Pocock witnesses such a pattern of transformation in Harrington's own thought and in the famous dictum that power must follow property.

In C. B. Macpherson's hands, this axiom of political life had been a declaration of independence for an emergent bourgeois consciousness.[21] For Pocock any economic implication becomes subordinated to the political requirement implicit in Harrington's larger, i.e., "classical," framework—in particular, the need to preserve civic independence. Property would be its purchase, the price of entrance into the civic life of the nation. "Harrington conveys what was to be perhaps his chief gift to eighteenth century political thought: the discovery of a means whereby the country freeholder could equate himself with the Greco-Roman *polites* and profess a wholly classical and Aristotelian doctrine of the relations between property, liberty and power."[22]

The neo-Harringtonians refined the classical teaching in two further respects. Whereas the classical tradition emphasized the role of an active citizen militia and saw professional standing armies (or worse, mercenary troops) as a direct, military threat, the neo-Harringtonians perceived the "standing army . . . as an instrument of corruption rather than of dictatorship."[23] The multiplication of military (in fact, all administrative) offices signaled an increase in patronage and ministerial influence over the beneficiaries of patronage, especially members of Parliament. Exerting such influence as patronage would allow, constitutional balance would surely fall victim to monarchical or ministerial will.

Further, the neo-Harringtonians departed from their mentor in their reading of history. Where Harrington saw in England's past "a record of instability," nothing to glorify or emulate, his disciples saw a once-glorious example of the Polybian mixed constitution. This gave the neo-Harringtonians an inestimable ideological advantage in their struggle to enlist country gentlemen in their campaign to deny a Catholic James Stuart the throne of England. For the gentry, "the antiquity of the constitution was the antiquity of their titles to estates and position."[24] Thus was a radical critique of court corruption tied to a conservative defense of property and privilege, in the hopes of mounting a successful resistance movement.[25]

We can already gauge the distance separating Locke and the republican writers by Pocock's light. Locke had stressed individual acquisitiveness; they emphasized civic participation and the quest for a public good. He appealed to natural law and reason; they appealed to prescriptive right and the ancient constitution. For Locke, reason was a tool of science and progress; they wished not to move forward but to stand still, to escape time. Progress, for Locke, encouraged the division of labor. "Specialization," in the classical view, "encouraged freemen . . . in pursuits which left them no time to be soldiers, judges or participants in government; . . . [and this] opened the way to the professionalized society which was virtually synonymous with corruption." The mechanics of politics likewise fell squarely within the humanist and republican, not the Lockean, tradition. And so Pocock concluded, "If one follows out the history of neo-Harringtonian ideas and their opposites, it is remarkable to observe how much could be said by their aid which did not necessitate reference to Locke at all."[26]

In *The Machiavellian Moment,* Pocock brought the civic outlook face-to-face with modernity. "At a very rapid pace, an entity known as Trade entered the language of politics, and became something which no orator, pamphleteer or theorist could afford to neglect." The rise of commercial society—of trade, credit, specialization, and, worst of all, "luxury"—endangered not just the polity, but the human personality. "What may be termed the ideology of the Country was founded on a presumption of real property and an ethos of the civic life, in which the ego knew and loved itself in its relation to a *res publica* or common good . . . but was perpetually threatened by corruption operating through private appetites and false consciousness."[27]

In this view, the human personality demanded association for its well-being. The economic imperative stood in fundamental conflict with the soul's own spiritual requirement: the fundamental human imperative. "We are at the point," Pocock writes, "where the classical concept of corruption merges with the modern concept of alienation, and the humanist roots of early Marxism become visible." And Pockock concludes:

> [Now] the individual . . . became more and more the dependent of those with whom he had contracted to perform specialized functions . . . less and less a personality immediately related to society in its undifferentiated form; and if here alone were the roots of individuality to be found, he parted with an essential component of self in proportion as he became progressively refined. The personality was impoverished even as it was enriched.[28]

The power of this perception for the eighteenth century meant that the debate over commerce would ultimately be decided on civic, not Lockean, grounds; the social good would have to be consulted. Those who would praise commerce propounded a "civic morality of investment and exchange. . . . It is when men realize that their well-being depends upon mutual support that credit is converted into confidence, into a mutual trust and a belief in one another; they realize that they cannot stand alone . . . [but] are members one of another." Pocock continues: "Credit is now being translated into virtue, in the entirely moral and societal sense of the word. The precondition of her health is the health of all society and the practice of all the moral activities which society entails."[29]

And when later that century under the influence of Mandeville and Hume the egoistic passions were unleashed and the moral "ought" driven out by a gripping, undeniable "is," the desideratum remained social. All that could be hoped was that, in Pocock's words, "the diversities of passionate and self-interested action might be manipulated and coordinated, or might magically or mechanically coordinate themselves, into promoting a common good no longer intimately connected with the inner moral life of the individual.''[30] Neither in the effort to reconcile the commercial society with the humanist ideal nor in the decision to discount moral ideals as such does Pocock espy the atomistic individualism that denotes Locke's deepest appeal.

Caroline Robbins exposed a tradition of political discourse that stretched across a century and a half of English history. Pocock rooted that discourse, first, in the Italian Renaissance, then all the way back to antiquity. But it was Bernard Bailyn who most directly found in this republican paradigm ''the ideological origins of the American Revolution.''[31] Looking afresh at the role of ideas in history, not presuming — as had the Progressive historians — that ideas merely mask the material interests of men, Bailyn came face-to-face with a veritable wealth of ''sources and traditions.'' In the public prints of eighteenth-century America, he encountered virtually every imaginable authority: from biblical prophets to pagan philosophers, from writers on English law (Fortescue, Coke, and Blackstone), to writers on natural law (Grotius, Pufendorf, and Locke), to writers on ancient history (Livy, Tacitus, and Plutarch). But how carefully had the Americans studied these writings? It varied, of course. Locke's view of natural rights, for example, was invoked, even before 1763. But too often it was ''defined in a significantly ambiguous way.'' Often, Locke could be ''cited . . . with precision on points of political theory, but at other times he is referred to in the most oft-hand way, as if he could be relied on to support anything the writers happened to be arguing.'' What gave the ideology of the American Revolution its distinctive character, what dominated the colonists' miscellaneous learning and shaped it into a coherent whole, Bailyn believed, ''was the influence of the 18th century Commonwealthmen and their Post-Restoration forebears. . . . From the earliest years of the century, this Opposition thought . . . was devoured by the colonists. . . . It nourished their political thought and sensibilities . . . [so that] there seems never to have been a time after the Hanoverian succession when these writings were . . . absent from polemical politics.''[32]

To this day, the preponderance of scholarly opinion has treated this opposition thought as essentially opposed not only to eighteenth-century English but to seventeenth-century Lockean politics, as well. In a work of enduring importance, Gordon Wood offered sound support for the Bailyn thesis as it related to the intellectual origins of the American Revolution. But on one critical point the two historians parted company. Although Bailyn clearly hoped to correct the view of Locke writ large over the revolutionary era, finding in eighteenth-century opposition thought a more vital motive for political resistance and revolution, his

American patriots were nonetheless attuned to the deeper Lockean goal of securing their inherent natural rights and liberties. In tying eighteenth-century opposition thought to more ancient or "classical" sources, Wood perceived a clear break with Locke's ideological program. As against a firm commitment to the sheer pursuit of self-interest and the assertion of individual rights and freedom from political interference, Wood's revolutionaries embraced an older and far more communal spirit. Following Aristotle, Polybius, and other ancient authors, the Spirit of '76 emphasized civic participation in and concern for the good of the res publica. "The sacrifice of individual interests to the greater good of the whole," wrote Wood, "formed the essence of republicanism and comprehended for Americans, the idealistic goal of their Revolution. From this goal flowed all of the Americans' exhortatory literature and all that made their ideology revolutionary."[33]

In that same work, however, Wood purported to discover the limits of republicanism in the American founding. While clearly finding a classical republican stamp on American revolutionary politics, Wood would concede that by the time the Constitution of the United States was ratified, classical politics had come to an end.[34] For Wood, the concession to factious divisions within society (so visibly pronounced in Madison's *Federalist* 10), signified not just the splintering of American society but a lamentable end to the hope of raising a cohesive, Polybian spirit of civic virtue in America. The American republic, the founders felt, would have to find a way to survive without it. Institutional checks and balances, a mutually offsetting leveraging of power, would now have to do the work that, it was formerly hoped, could be left to the public-spiritedness that had characterized the revolutionary struggle.

What did the Constitution of 1787 signify for civic humanism? For Wood, the answer is its demise in America, "the end of classical politics."[35] "By attempting to formulate a theory of politics that would represent reality as it was, the Americans of 1787 shattered the classical Whig world of 1776. . . . All sense of a graduated organic chain in the social hierarchy became irrelevant." From that time forward, "personal or private" liberty would be emphasized and the powers of government would be organized "to protect citizens . . . and their property even against the public will." Finally, the divorce of American and classical politics would be consummated in the fatal rejection of the civic metaphysics. Far from seeking to end or escape from time, America exalted in progress and improvement. The free researches of the human mind, working on the materials of experience, represented hope for future generations. Thus do Wood's Framers radiantly expect that "the illimitable progress of mankind promised by the Enlightenment could at last be made coincident with the history of a single nation. For the Americans at least, and for others if they followed, the endless cycle of history could finally be broken.''[36]

The ''end of classical politics'' thesis, however, would spark a great scholarly debate that endures to this day. Thus, as Pocock noted in his review of Wood's *Creation*, classical republicanism consisted of more than the organic conception of the polity and the effort to ''escape'' history. If some elements of classical politics would be defeated by 1787, others would yet command the attention of Americans. In fact, Pocock advised, ''the classical 'checks and balances' continued to exist . . . [after] the classical mode of conceiving 'the people' had passed away.'' Furthermore, ''virtue [which] consisted as much of the civic independence of the . . . freeholder . . . as of his membership in a [social chain or] hierarchy'' also informed the Framers' labors. And finally and most critically, ''there was the inveterate opposition between the agrarian man of independent virtue and the professionalized man of government and commerce.'' Thus though American politics would be built on ''an interest-group theory . . . a theory and practice of pluralism and consensus,'' a ''tension between working institutions and underlying values'' nevertheless persisted.

The Revolution, after all, had been a contest between America and England, Country and Court, and Virtue and Commerce, respectively, and the lines of battle were unequivocally drawn. Commerce, and all that flowed from it (banks, national debts, specialization, and luxury), remained the antithesis of virtue. For Pocock, the personification of commerce in America—the direct heir to Walpole—was Alexander Hamilton. The Jeffersonian response to Hamiltonian fiscal policy (and support for capitalism) represents a direct link to the classical past, ''to a quite remarkable degree, the great debate on his [Hamilton's] policies in the 1790's was a replay of Court-Country debates seventy and a hundred years earlier.''[37] This is quite correct. But its significance from a Lockean standpoint is not exactly clear. With whom would Locke side in the dispute between Country and Court, Cato and Walpole, Jefferson and Hamilton?

Insofar as the revisionists sought to post a civic or classical political language in competition with a Lockean one, so that Lockeanism is made to stand for what republicanism does not, the revisionist's Locke (certainly Pocock's), we could infer, would logically side with the policies of the Walpolean court and Washington's treasury secretary. That is not too outlandish a supposition to make, since so much of Lockean literature has been disposed to identify Locke with the fractious forces of acquisitiveness and the institutions of a liberal, capitalist order, or as Dworetz has appropriately phrased it, ''the bourgeois ethos—hedonism, materialism, self-interest.'' The disposition to define Locke in these terms largely issues from the interpretive findings of two widely read writers: Leo Strauss and

C. B. Macpherson. To the extent that this republican/Lockean dichotomy *is* a part of the revisionist project and rests, however implicitly, on the Straussian — Macphersonian appraisal, then that project is only as coherent and compelling as are these two mutually supportive but dated and decidedly unsympathetic interpretive reports. This alone should cause us to consider anew the veracity of revisionism and, more importantly, to consider much more carefully Locke's considerable corpus.[38]

The "Lockean"/Liberal Revival

At any rate, in defending their thesis of continuity, the revisionists were responding to the growing body of historians who, along with Wood, could glimpse avowedly liberal values and currents swiftly overtaking American politics by 1787. Some scholars, such as Joyce Appleby, went even further. Questioning the republican thesis at its root, she pointedly asked: "If a classical republicanism imbued with traditional notions of political authority dominated colonial thinking, where are the roots of that liberalism which flowed so quickly after independence? . . . Where and when are scholars to find the sources for the aggressive individualism, the optimistic materialism, and the pragmatic interest group politics that became so salient so early in the life of the new nation?"[39]

In an impressive series of articles Appleby expounded on the liberal roots of American civilization. Her central preoccupation was not with the natural conditions of a native wilderness society, a la Hartz, or a resolute natural law theory, a la Becker, but with the theoretical "foundry of modern utilitarianism." As she wrote in *Capitalism and a New Social Order*: "The capitalism in my title of course refers to a way of organizing the economy—a particular system for producing and distributing the material goods that sustain and embellish life."[40] The deeper question left unanswered by Appleby concerns the fundamental compatibility between her "utilitarian foundry" and the natural law foundations of Locke's social thought.[41] Would Locke knowingly open that political foundry?

Another scholar, J. P. Diggins, has also concentrated on the liberal basis of the American founding. In *The Lost Soul of American Politics* (1984), Diggins, like Appleby, found liberalism but, in a serious sense, lost Locke. Conceding the presence of certain elements of republicanism, Diggins nonetheless rejected the general revisionist thesis. Yes, fear of political corruption sparked American revolutionary fervor. But, he writes, "unless being suspicious is itself tantamount to being virtuous . . . we can only wonder why the American Revolution should be regarded as a virtuous political act." Clearly pointing at Locke's great influence as well as the role of the Calvinist work ethic, Diggins continued, "In American political thought it was work, not politics that enabled man to live an independent and productive life." And so there triumphed in America "an ideology of economic individualism. . . . The basically Lockean sense of property . . . became the *central faith* of the liberal consensus."[42]

Is Diggins following Hartz in seeing a hegemonic liberal and Lockean consensus in the soul of American politics? Liberal consensus, yes; Lockean consensus, I think not. In the first place, Diggins erroneously took Locke to be a majority-rule democrat. But, he says, the Framers by 1787 "sacrifice[d] the older Lockean principle of liberty as residing in the will of the majority, constraining that will by positive constitutional restraints."[43] Second and more fundamentally, the Framers rejected that "central faith" the American revolutionaries exhibited with respect to the rights of property. "In the Federalist," Diggins says, "property is treated as an 'interest' that requires protection by government, not primarily as a natural right the legitimacy of which lies in its historical origins, in the free act of labor. . . . Hamilton and Madison do not follow Locke and argue that man had a natural right to property because through labor man preserves life."

At the deepest level, *The Federalist* represents not just the discounting of particular paradigms (classical republicanism, majority rule, inalienable property rights, etc.), but the rejection of ideas as such. As Diggins would conclude: "Henceforth the Constitution represented not only what Gordon Wood has called the 'end of classical politics,' but also the end of the authority of political ideas — moral ideas . . . capable of commanding obedience because of their universal truth and not because they were contingent upon the immediate interests . . . of men. . . . Political ideas no longer enjoyed a 'transcendent requirement' that could obligate moral conduct." For Diggins this heralds the advent of "a Humean perspective that modifies both the Lockean and Whig paradigms." The "end of ideology" comes early to Diggins's America, where the dustbin of ideological history is filled to overflowing: "It is not the rational Lockean man, the benevolent Scottish communitarian, or the publicly responsive Machiavellian citizen that Madison has in mind when he describes man as possessed of some unalterable static core into whose nature the causes of faction have been planted."[44]

The theory of a natural market order postulated by Diggins's Framers, it should be emphasized, is not the same, sanguine model proffered by Appleby's Jeffersonians. Diggins's Americans were fearful of a world beset by ceaseless possessive striving. "The frantic love of money," as the French visitor Louis-Felix de Beaujour pointed out in 1806, which is "the result of . . . political equality which . . . leav[es] people with no other distinction except wealth [and] invites them to acquire it by every possible means,'' invites exploitation and social ruin.[45] But if the disease was wired into the American frame, so was its remedy. Diggins's America is a blend of two ''ideas'' — liberalism and Calvinism. The latter is the ever-present seed of redemption and renewal. It is the ''Soul'' America has lost but could (as in the labors of Lincoln) at times recover.

> Liberalism has given the American male the natural right to be free, become rich, and escape his marital vows, while Calvinism assured that he could do none of these without experiencing guilt. . . . Once we see the Calvinist foundations of liberalism . . . we are in a better position to see why . . . liberalism could carry the seeds of its own condemnation, particularly in its fostering of capitalism . . . as the nation threatened to sink into a morass of materialism.[46]

Thus while Appleby and Diggins began in earnest to challenge the republican revisionist thesis, finding a larger conceptual space in the American founding for Locke or, in Appleby's case, liberalism, more broadly, they diverged considerably on the precise character of liberalism and left unanswered important questions concerning Locke's relation to it. The insufficient attention they paid to Locke's body of thought diminished the usefulness of their otherwise considerable contributions, and we were left, yet again, wondering what *Lockean liberalism* really signifies.

Two more recent scholars, Thomas Pangle and Steven Dworetz, have devoted far more attention to Locke's important writings, also identifying significant Lockean sources in the American founding. It will be interesting and instructive (for pointing out the confusion that permeates the scholarly debate over Locke's meaning and influence) to compare Diggins's conclusions with their findings. A few brief observations will clearly point up the need to bring Locke's own thought into even sharper focus before venturing to assess his influence on eighteenth-century America.

More than any other writers who have sought to reassert Locke's influence on this nation's birth, Pangle and Dworetz have been the most studious in developing a detailed account of Locke's own philosophical and political thought. At their hands, the seventeenth-century thinker becomes far more sophisticated and interesting than the Locke who appears in Strauss or Macpherson (the ''straw'' Locke whom the revisionists all too casually targeted in their ''demolition'' of the Lockean myth).[47]

Yet for the importance of their respective contributions Pangle and Dworetz have, themselves, only provided two disconnected pieces of the Lockean puzzle.

While the former emphasized Locke the liberator of economic energy, the theorist of the commercial republic, the latter emphasized not Locke the apostle of "bourgeois" man, but Locke the "theistic" builder of a radical resistance theory. Similarly, while Pangle sees as evidence of American Lockeanism the strong commitment to "active," rather than "intellectual," virtue and commercial growth, Dworetz focuses largely on the New England clergy and their attachment to "theistic liberalism" and Locke's God-centered revolutionary ideology. In short, where Diggins finds America's Lockean acquisitiveness opposed and checked by America's Calvinist impulse (and Pangle sees that acquisitiveness extolled as an "active virtue"), Dworetz finds America's religious and revolutionary commitment to be squarely rooted in Locke's own Calvinist theology. If Pangle, Diggins, and Dworetz are added together what emerges is a Locke still sharply at odds with himself.

Pangle provides an additional and equally disturbing finding, for he ultimately is at a loss to account for Locke's own Lockeanism, as well as the founders'. Pangle's Locke is not a mere ideologist; he is a philosopher, concerned with truth and human understanding. But these are individual pursuits. They manifest what could be called a possessive intellectual individualism. Pangle thus asks: "How does Locke's concern with self-knowledge, self-possession, and comfortable self-preservation entail his public-spirited concern with enlightening his fellow men? Why should, why does, a philosopher write treatises on government and education? Until this question receives an adequate answer, we cannot say that we have found in Locke's rationalism a rational justification of his way of life."

This is a problem not just for Locke, but for the founders who followed him. Concluding his thoughtful study of Locke and the founding, Pangle wonders: How can the spirit of individualism and the legitimate activities of wealth-getting be squared with political sociability and the requirements of civic virtue? "Can the rational 'pursuit of happiness' (Locke's famous phrase) of a spirited and self-assertive being provide a compelling foundation for a noble conception of that being and of its politics? Or does the logic of the [Lockean] argument the Founders adopted and made the theoretical cornerstone of the new republic compel them, in the final analysis, reluctantly or unwittingly, to subordinate the high in mankind, as they conceive it, to the low?"[48]

It will be useful to situate my own project alongside those of Dworetz and Pangle. As I have intimated, despite the importance of their respective contributions Pangle and Dworetz have provided two disconnected pieces of an incomplete puzzle. For the former, Locke is the apostle of the active or bourgeois virtues and the commercial republic; for the latter he is the theistic architect of limited government and the theorist of political resistance. Pangle focuses on eighteenth-century America's embrace of Locke's bourgeois values, while Dworetz emphasizes the New England Calvinist clergy's attachment to John Locke's resistance theory. Dworetz is quite clear in separating Locke the writer on revolution from Locke the moral advocate of private property, economic accumulation, and the politics of laissez faire.

> The Revolutionists drew not at all from chapter 5 ("Of Property") of the *Second Treatise,* but primarily from chapter 11 ("Of the Extent of the Legislative Power"). The issue in dispute was not the right of the subject to appropriate from nature, but the right of the government to expropriate the subject. . . . The formal Lockean connection, then, was not an ideological rationalization for unlimited capital accumulation, it was, instead, a demand for constitutional politics and limited government; and when England failed to honor that demand, it became a justification for armed resistance and revolution.[49]

This formulation is unfortunate insofar as it diminishes Locke's emphasis on the moral worth of productive labor and even aggressive appropriation, as well as the call for a liberty that will allow for such wholly moral and material pursuits (i.e., the right of individuals to keep and enjoy the just products of their industry). I will argue that it is precisely because the Americans accepted the veracity of Locke's chapter 5 that they heeded the advice, as Dworetz correctly says, of chapter 2.

This book, then, shall theoretically couple the two aspects of Lockean thought that Dworetz and Pangle have correctly surveyed and trace their emergence and consolidation in the American experience. It shall locate the theological/ philosophical underpinnings of the spirit of commerce and enterprise and go on to expose the consequent need for limited (as opposed to arbitrary) government within the Lockean worldview, on the one hand, and in the eighteenth-century American experience, on the other.

There is a second weakness in the Dworetz account (one that is partially corrected by Pangle) that is central to my own project. Dworetz continues to ideologically separate the Lockean and republican traditions of discourse. He writes: "Lockean theory . . . [supplied] the concepts and categories in which the Revolutionists articulated their deepest concerns about liberty and property. . . . republican ideology could not furnish effective theoretical shelter against Parliament's new economic policies or, for that matter, against the dangerous principle of illimitable parliamentary sovereignty upon which those policies were based.

To defend liberty and property, then, the opposition to Parliament enlisted the services of Locke, not 'Cato.' ''[50]

Pangle more clearly perceives how a ''modern'' commercial republicanism could fuse the classical and Lockean worldviews, but only up to a point. In pinpointing the active, economic virtues and commercial liberties that most Americans cherished, Pangle partially compensates for Dworetz's omission. He readily sees the extent to which Locke's moral recommendation of economic ambitiousness is reflected in the lives and writings of the Americans. But it is precisely the Americans' emphasis on the ''active virtues'' that causes Pangle to raise some puzzling questions with respect to Locke and the American founding. Besides his difficulty in accounting for Locke's own ''Lockeanism,'' as well as the founders', there is a second critical difficulty that emerges from his study.

Given the triumph of the ''active virtues,'' the spirit of individualism, and the rise of the commercial republic, all extolled by Locke and embodied in the American founding, how are we to account for the bitter ideological distance that separated Federalist from anti-Federalist and, later, Jeffersonian republican? By what means are we to wall off what Pangle considers the ''little'' liberalism of a ''Cato'' or a Jefferson from the ''big'' liberalism of a Walpole or a Hamilton? On what grounds could the Lockean ''Cato,'' anti-Federalist, or Jeffersonian republican repudiate the commercial ''liberalism'' or ''state-centered'' capitalism implicit in the public policies of Walpole or Hamilton? Indeed, on what basis could the revolutionaries of 1776 consider the individualism seemingly inherent in colonial factionalism well before the Revolution to be a manifestation of political corruption, as Bailyn and Wood have assured us they did? These questions can be answered, I suggest, but the answer necessitates that the exact limits of Lockean law and the rational bounds of individual self-pursuit be located far more precisely than they have been.

A more recent contribution to the literature, one that undertakes a breathtakingly broad survey of the history of republicanism, reaches and reinforces Pangle's estimate of the founding era, yet invites, as well, many of the questions Pangle left unanswered. That worthy study merits some attention. In his magnum opus on *Republics Ancient and Modern* Paul Rahe did indeed study the transformation of republicanism at it moved from the Old World to the New World. Never neglecting the traditional republican concepts and concerns, he nonetheless managed to coherently sew into the seams of the American republic's founding a number of clearly discernible Lockean threads. The modern republic, epitomized by the American example, did indeed extol the individualist ethos (as Appleby, Hartz, and Pangle had urged). Eighteenth-century America was flush with an ebullient spirit of energetic and private enterprise. Self-made men, such as Franklin, ''were more plentiful than they had been anywhere in the world at any previous time in human history.'' Against the classical commitment to the civic life, Rahe found in the lives and letters of Jefferson, Paine, James Wilson, John Adams, and George Mason a veneration of the private life and, at times, a tiredness with the rigors and burdens of public service. ''Nowhere in the fledgling United States,'' Rahe emphasized, ''did anyone persistently and unambiguously assert the primacy of political life in the manner of the ancient Greeks.'' Like Pangle, he clearly discerned the zest for commercial adventure and the rejection of the bellicose and Spartan spirit of antiquity. Individual liberty was the Americans' goal. Its corollary, ''the natural equality of mankind,'' represented a truth ''hidden from the antients, and . . . one of the wonderful discoveries of modern times,'' as DeWitt Clinton had announced.[51]

A second discovery of the modern age was the idea that, as James Wilson phrased it at the Pennsylvania Ratifying Convention in 1787, ''the supreme, absolute and uncontrollable authority *remains* with the people.'' All republican sources aside, it was, as Wilson announced, ''the great and penetrating mind of Locke . . . [alone who] pointed towards even the theory of this great truth.'' Rahe found the theory of popular sovereignty, which logically led to a justification of popular resistance, everywhere in the revolutionary era. He found it, in fact, doing some very heavy lifting. To Locke's doctrine of popular resistance, as much as to the Old Whig tradition, Rahe attributed ''the ethos of jealous anticipation and political distrust that . . . [was] so typically American.'' ''The civic humanism which had so captured scholarly research,'' this well-versed student of republics, ancient and modern, could conclude, was ''by and large a figment of the scholarly imagination.''[52]

And yet, large portions of Rahe's discussion of the founding era are consumed with the conceptions and concerns of republicanism, a republicanism that would continue to rely on civic (and religious) virtue and on the importance, especially for Jefferson, of a citizenry educated in the history (the rise and fall) of republics and civically active. Jefferson's tireless push for public education bespoke the Virginian's clear commitment to the building of a well-trained aristocracy of virtue. In examining with great care *The Federalist Papers,* Rahe also emphasized the institutional aspects of republicanism: the need for a mixed and balanced constitution. Wrapped in ''the toga of Plutarch's Publius,'' Rahe wrote, Hamilton, Madison, and Jay ''rejected outright any great veneration for the far distant past.''[53] *The Federalist* would advertise a decisively modern republicanism, but what exactly was its relation to Locke? In the final analysis, there is no satisfactory effort to comprehensively harmonize the Lockean and republican themes that weave themselves through the tapestry of Rahe's otherwise near-encyclopedic narrative.

This problem is most evident as Rahe turns his attention to the constitutional and early national periods, at which point Locke might almost be reported missing. The discussion of the Confederation, constitutional, and Jeffersonian periods strongly emphasizes the republican side of his liberal republican synthesis, and that is, of course, understandable given the needs of the moment.[54] More specifically, from the standpoint of a triumphant Lockeanism, Rahe, like Pangle, failed to account for the deep divisions between Federalists and anti-Federalists and the subsequent animus that energized the Jeffersonian response to Hamilton's financial policies.

Rahe cited the weaknesses that Americans perceived in the 1780s vis-à-vis the actions of the state legislatures and the tumult that issued from the various and competing factions that filled the political fields, but he failed to adequately analyze those weaknesses from a Lockean standpoint or reveal how the constitutional revisions of 1787 reaffirmed the republic's commitment to Lockean natural right. In fact, Rahe's discussion of the Confederation period was all too brief. And his treatment of Jefferson's and Madison's "epic struggle" against Hamiltonianism emphasized the republican, not the Lockean, side of the equation. In combating the erstwhile treasury secretary the two Virginians stressed: (1) the need for a strict constitutional construction, (2) the encroachments of powers reserved to the several states, (3) the "ill effect" that Hamilton's fiscal plans could have on "the present temper of the southern states," and (4) the typically republican fear of Hamilton's candid sympathy with the Humean view that corruption was "an essential part of the weight that maintained the equilibrium" of his much admired British Constitution.[55]

In short, after the revolutionary period, Locke's name and deeper philosophy largely dropped out of Rahe's study, and an emphasis on republican institutions and even civic virtue, indispensable issues for the new nation to be sure, took center stage. Locke does make a reappearance, at places, but it is a single-issue Locke: Locke the theorist of popular resistance.

In what does Rahe locate "the *theoretical* foundation of Jefferson's opposition to Hamilton and his program"? In the "fear that the people would become inured to acquiescence and thus gently fall prey to servitude." In Jefferson's own easy acceptance of popular rebellion, a public evil that "is productive of good" insofar as it "prevents the degeneracy of government," Rahe finds Locke's continuing influence. That may well be so, but it is certainly a truncated Locke, and it begs the deeper questions: What in the Hamiltonian program could be construed as violative of Locke's deeper theory of political right? In what ways was it tyrannous, and why exactly did it invite Jefferson's and Madison's enmity, other than for the essentially republican-inspired concern over "Corruption"?[56] What, if any, were the Lockean evils that the Jeffersonians so energetically hoped to forestall? And what were the Lockean fears that just a few years earlier had so tormented the anti-Federalists in their hostility to the frame of '87? These are the striking questions that remain unanswered in the yet lively effort to come to terms with the American founding and that demand a stricter accounting of John Locke's own body of social and political thought.

The Lockean/Republican "Consensus"

Passing over the ambiguities and complexities that have hampered the work of those who posit a strong liberal and Lockean influence on the American founding, there is one further reason to revisit Locke's thought before assessing its influence on the founding. This is the misleading theoretical conclusion to which even stalwart upholders of the republican faith have recently been drawn.

The central premise that informs nearly all of the liberal *and* republican revisionist historians (from Pocock to Wood, to Appleby, to Diggins, to Dworetz) is that these two ideologies—the liberal and republican—stand in essential and mutual opposition.[57] The problem is that each side of this debate can point to a considerable body of historical evidence suggesting the operative power of its respective thesis. Consequently, that debate has most recently moved onto higher ground, i.e., onto the ground of scholarly consensus. There has indeed been something of a meeting of scholarly minds on the question of America's founding, only it has been purchased at a terrible price: a resolute concession to human self-contradiction.

Thus, striking an accommodating tone and denying a charge brought by Wood, Pocock, the revisionist, insisted he had not intended "to eliminate Locke as the patron saint of American culture and replace him with Machiavelli." Pocock goes on, "I treated the 'republican' discourse to a considerable degree in isolation, establishing its paradigmatic character by showing that it possessed the capacity to offer a comprehensive account of its world; . . . and I never concealed the fact of intimate competition between rival discourses . . . [whereby] any alternative 'paradigm' would . . . have to compete for paradigm status by means of an intensely contested dialogue with the pre-existing discourse."

Admitting the presence of what Daniel Rodgers, in a masterful recapitulation of the "career" of the republican concept, called "bits and pieces of all sorts of structurally incompatible languages," Pocock thus confessed to the presence not so much of paradigmatic languages, but rather of an emblematic multilingualism. Alternative "ways of talking," Pocock wrote, "do not typically succeed in excluding one another." They do, however, signify "debate, perplexity, and contradiction." Specifically, the language, or was it the mere "rhetoric," of republicanism "survived to furnish liberalism with one of its modes of self-criticism and self-doubt," so that "the persistence of a republican world-view continued to render commercial society, and the role of the self in it, problematic."[58]

Lienesch, too, conceded the simultaneous presence of disparate idioms of discourse operating on the minds of the founders, of thinking that was "ambivalent, contradictory and sometimes flatly paradoxical."[59] As for the Framers, Forrest McDonald wrote, "they were politically multilingual, able to speak in the diverse idioms of Locke, the classical republicans, Hume, and many others, depending upon what seemed rhetorically appropriate to the argument at hand." Speaking elsewhere of the Framers' "Principles and Interests," McDonald recognized two distinct factions informing the Convention of 1787: a court party, following the Hume-Mandevillian line and willing to work with the base material that was man, and a country party, adopting a Bolingbroke-Montesquieu path and holding out for virtue, or at least for mechanisms (such as a prohibition on dual office holding) that would hinder the rise of corruption. Speaking more generally of "court party nationalists" and "republican ideologues," McDonald failed to find any monolithic outlook: "It should be obvious . . . that it is meaningless to say that the Framers intended this or that; . . . their positions were diverse and, in many particulars, incompatible. Some had firm, well-rounded plans, some had strong convictions on only a few points; some had self-contradictory ideas; some were guided only by vague ideals."[60]

And Isaac Kramnick, who did much to uncover the liberal/Lockean roots of late eighteenth-century English radicalism, concurred: "The assumption that there is but one language—one exclusive or even hegemonic paradigm—that characterizes the political discourse of a particular place or moment in time" is dubious at best. He, in fact, found four "distinguishable idioms" in the discourse of 1787: "republicanism," "Lockean liberalism," "work-ethic Protestantism," and "state-centered theories of power and sovereignty." And he cautioned: "None dominated the field, and the use of one was compatible with the use of another by the very same writer or speaker. There was a *profusion and confusion of political tongues* among the founders. They lived easily with that clatter; it is we two hundred years later who chafe at their inconsistency."[61]

And why would we not chafe at the inconsistencies? If the founders were moved by their ideology, and not by their mere material interests, this "profusion and confusion" of ideological tongues and "rhetorical" moves would seemingly cause them to move in hapless circles. How can it be said that the founders were driven by their ideas when their ideas could only drive them in sundry and opposite directions at once? If the fundamental tenets supporting Lockean liberalism and classical republicanism stand in such stark opposition as has generally been supposed, and yet both "paradigms" could exert their influence on this founder or that, it is difficult to imagine that anything could have been founded at all, short of disorder and paralysis. How, then, are we to account for a nation conceived in confusion and dedicated to ideological discord?

It is not surprising that, in concluding a careful bibliographical overview of "Republicanism: The Career of a Concept" in 1992, Daniel Rodgers could point to the near dead end to which that career was leading. By the late 1980s, he wrote, "as republicanism was catching up the imagination of more and more historians, explaining so much, it was quietly coming apart at its core." The revisionists sought to locate a firm intellectual structure operating on the minds of the founders. But given this documentable "world of complex currents, interlaced strands, a handful of powerful texts and systematic thinkers, and beyond a loosely structured, confused, and altogether familiar muddle," all "structure — social and intellectual — was out; 'conceptual confusion' was in." The "accumulating anomalies" that haunted the republican enterprise (and that would pepper the literature of nineteenth-century "labor republicanism," "Southern republicanism," and feminist republican studies, which Rodgers ably cataloged) easily exhausted "the structuralist confidence of 1970's intellectual history. . . . Methodologically, that history had claimed too much; the post-structuralist reaction was already in full gear." The "structuralist mood in intellectual history had been unsustainable," Rodgers concluded; "its claims [were simply] too extravagant."[62] Thus in one sweeping bibliographical recapitulation of the debate over republicanism, Rodgers aptly summed up the quandaries into which scores of scholars were drawn by their intoxicating historical fetish. By essay's end, Rodgers's readers could understandably sense that he had brought his concept's career to the doorstep of retirement, if not exhaustion and expiration.

Yet, the careers of other leading historians were pointing to the prospect of a cyclical resurrection and renewal of republicanism's place in the founding era. Not every student of the American founding would so easily bend to the post-structuralist impulse. An effort would indeed be made to fuse together what Rodgers called a hybrid "liberal republicanism" or "republican liberalism." By the late 1980s stalwart students of the republican tradition were exploring the idea that both liberal and republican ideas could gel in the minds of the founders — and do so without leading them into confusion and contradiction. Responding to a host of critics and participating in a bicentennial forum devoted to a reconsideration of his deservedly esteemed *Creation,* Gordon Wood candidly rejected the "sharp dichotomy between two clearly identifiable traditions" that had gained prominence by the revolutionary era. "None of the Founding Fathers," Wood wrote, "ever had any sense that he had to choose or was choosing between Machiavelli and Locke." And he continued: "Jefferson, for example, could believe simultaneously and without any sense of inconsistency in the likelihood of America's becoming corrupt and in the need to protect individual rights from government. We ought to remember that these boxlike traditions into which the historical participants must be fitted are essentially our inventions, and as such are distortions of past reality."[63]

Lance Banning, too, would strongly suggest a historical meeting of ideological minds. In his influential work on *The Jeffersonian Persuasion* Banning gave an unmistakably republican spin to the events surrounding the founding of the American republic.[64] With a number of other students of republicanism, and despite Wood's original posting of an "end of classical politics" by 1787, Banning argued that principal elements of the republican ideology did indeed persist into and beyond the early national period or, to be more precise, that they coexisted with the more modern and liberal facets of American life and thought. But he was most emphatic in tracing a striking continuity of Commonwealthman concerns informing the Jeffersonian response to the program and policies of the Federalists.[65]

It was in his influential 1986 essay, "Jeffersonian Ideology Revisited: Liberal and Classical Ideas in the New American Republic," that Banning self-consciously set out to discover a common ground that liberal and revisionist historians could amicably share. Conceding the simultaneous presence of liberal and republican influences in late eighteenth-century America, he wrote, "While it is true that Jeffersonians were never strictly classical in their republicanism—no one has really argued that they were—neither were they merely liberal."[66]

Banning restated his ecumenical thesis in 1992 when he advised, "The republican hypothesis had always seemed to me to be an argument that Lockean or liberal ideas were only part of an inheritance." If the revisionists had emphasized the classical or civic components of the eighteenth-century mind, it was not to dispel or discard the liberal elements that, too, exerted their influence. "I do not now, nor did I ever, think of the republican tradition as a rival or alternative to a Lockean or liberal conceptions of the origins and limits of political authority," he urged. "These two distinguishable traditions [the liberal and republican] came into the English-speaking world together—and as allies, for the most part, rather than as foes. . . . [It would therefore be wrong to posit] an eighteenth-century war between competing classical and modern paradigms. . . . [The eighteenth century] combined two trains of thinking that are separable for analytical objectives of our own, but usually were mixed when eighteenth-century people thought about their current problems.''[67] The principal task for future scholarship, Banning realized, would be to somehow reconcile these ostensibly incompatible political idioms, to historically accommodate republicanism within the sweep of liberalism's rise while avoiding the pit of confusion and controversy into which earlier scholarship had so often fallen.

Reprising a view expressed in *The Jeffersonian Persuasion,* Banning sought to argue that Jeffersonianism represented an *"Americanization* of eighteenth-century opposition thought'' that could indeed find room for certain liberal propensities. Expressing ''Some Second Thoughts on Virtue and the Course of Revolutionary Thinking,'' in 1987, Banning clarified his idea of an ''Americanized'' and yet manifestly classical conception of virtue. Rebuffing the civic and Polybian view of virtue that Wood had worked into *The Creation,* i.e., the ''willingness of the individual to sacrifice his private interests for the good of the community,'' a conception of virtue that virtually ''obliterated the individual,'' Banning found ample space in the United States for wholly individualistic pursuits. ''Where Wood has emphasized the sacrifice,'' he responded, ''I would call renewed attention to the self who must perform it. . . . Revolutionary thinkers ordinarily assumed that citizens neither could nor should act selflessly.'' Nonetheless, there would still be ample room for sacrifice in Banning's liberal republic. For wholesale self-pursuit, ''if we understand that term to mean absorption in one's private goods to the neglect of public duty,'' *was* profoundly dangerous to a republic. Moreover, civic virtue could still be evidenced in acts of public participation, public service (i.e., office holding) and by a ''voluntary willingness to sacrifice one's private interests to community decisions, by obedience to laws, by consciousness of being ruled as well as ruling.'' For Banning, the commitment to private interest aside, all of these necessary and essential aspects of communal living testify to republicanism's firm imprint on the politics of the founding era. Devotion to liberal self-pursuit and republican civic-mindedness could thereby meet and merge.[68]

And yet, Banning continued to concede the logical and conceptual gaps that separated the liberal from the republican political discourse. As he wrote in 1986, ''Modern liberalism and classical republicanism . . . [bespeak] two distinguishable philosophies. . . . [They] begin with different assumptions about human nature and develop a variety of different ideas.''[69] Along with most other scholars in the field, Banning continued to distinguish ''a tradition emphasizing freedom *to* participate with others in an active public life from a tradition emphasizing freedom *from* encroachments on pre-governmental rights.'' These traditions, he reiterated in 1992,

> *do* begin with different assumptions about human nature [and] may be traced to different thinkers. Logically, if not historically, they seem to us to clash, and it is therefore necessary to explore the contradictions, tensions, and confusions in the thought of those who seem to have identified with both traditions. . . . My appeal in short, is for a reconsideration of the ways in which these two distinguishable traditions interpenetrated and entwined. . . . How did early Revolutionaries and their eighteenth-century sources manage so coherently to blend traditions which seem incompatible to us?[70]

Going beyond the ''eighteenth-century sources,'' Banning left his reader with a most illuminating and promising suggestion. To come to terms with ''that early Revolutionary blend of modern-liberal and neoclassical concerns,'' he appropriately advised, one ''would have to start with [a] further exploration of its origins in seventeenth-century England.''[71] This precisely captures the key to my own approach to deciphering the meaning of the American founding. For if, as Alan Craig Houston's recent work on Algernon Sidney clearly suggests, seventeenth-century republicanism could itself encompass the tenets of Lockean liberalism, then, conversely, Lockean liberalism could merge and meld into the concerns and conceptions that make up the ''language'' of republicanism.[72]

And if this is possible, then it will arguably turn out to be that it is our own anachronistic conceptions that have stood in the way of historical understanding. In conceiving of an ideological discontinuity between the Lockean and republican idioms have we simply misconceived and misconstrued the intellectual world inhabited by our forebears two hundred years ago? That is the striking possibility that demands deeper study and that necessitates a more penetrating reconsideration of John Locke's own social and political thought. For if by that careful reconsideration it can be determined that Lockeanism does not bar but rather admits and even informs the precepts we commonly associate with republicanism alone, then a much more penetrating grasp of the American founding itself will indeed be at hand.

More specifically, my own approach will emphasize not separate ''paradigmatic'' languages, but merely several compatible levels or layers of discourse. It is not so much, as Rodgers stated it, that the ''liberal and republican arguments were responses to fundamentally different problematics, that they organized distinctly different realms of experience . . . [and as per Pocock] were not fully on speaking terms.''[73] More precisely, I believe, Locke and the republicans addressed a single "problematic" (the just organization of civil government and society) but came at it from two distinct yet related paths, i.e., fundamental ends and necessary means, respectively. A republican science of politics, grounded in a particular appraisal of human history, in short, would be appended to the fundamental of politics rooted in Locke's essential estimate of human nature. Taken together, these two branches of human inquiry (the one belonging to political science, the other to moral philosophy) could comprehensively inform students of seventeenth- *and* eighteenth-century politics both of the necessary ends and sufficient institutional means of attaining and sustaining a legitimate and moral polity.[74]

This, ultimately, is why the liberal reader of the American founding can be right without rendering the revisionist wrong. And yet, as is also the case, both the liberal and republican students of the founding can be wrong in their appraisals, as well. In a most conciliatory (and Banningesque) essay, James Kloppenberg traced the liberal and republican lineages of the founding era. And he asked a most critical question: "What is to count as republicanism?"[75] If we are to adequately grasp the character of the founding era, however, it is just as important that we ask what is to count as liberalism, and, I think, still more important (as the above overview amply demonstrates) to inquire: What is to count as Lockeanism?[76]

1
Interpreting Locke's Thought and Assessing Its Influence

Ideological Origins vs. Philosophic Absolutes

Recent years have witnessed a rather dramatic change in the way that the "great works" are read. It is no longer satisfactory to treat a book, such as Locke's *Two Treatises of Government,* as a historically disembodied "masterpiece of political philosophy," providing universal recommendations for all people and periods. Emphasizing a contextual approach to textual interpretation, leading intellectual historians have persuasively argued that any intellectual production emerges out of a specific matrix of historical questions and conflicts that prevails in a particular place and time.[1]

Certainly in Locke's case the contextual labors have been proceeding at a near-feverish pace. Recent works have correctly examined Locke's prodigious thought against the backdrop of: (1) Shaftesbury's exclusion movement (e.g., Ashcraft), (2) the Baconian call for the advancement of useful knowledge for the purpose of temporal improvement (Neal Wood), (3) the economic thought of his age (Vaughn), (4) Protestant antimonarchical resistance theories (Skinner), (5) seventeenth-century natural law theory (Tully), (6) Sir Robert Filmer's assault on the populist paradigm in *Patriarcha* and other important writings (Schochet), and (7) the movement known as latitudinarian Anglicanism (Rogers and Marshall).[2]

There is, then, an embarrassing abundance of contextual settings within which John Locke's writings may be situated. But this need not lead to the despairing estimate suggested by Dunn: "The set of possible contexts which would be needed to exhibit the full meaning of Locke's intellectual life is so vast that there is no significant possibility that someone will ever be competent to grasp them all and, should such a paragon of learning and imagination exist, it is a little difficult to believe that he would choose to devote his talents to the elucidation of the intellectual achievement of John Locke."[3] Many of Locke's recent interpreters have indeed had to narrow their focus, attempting to master one set of contextual problems at a time. That is understandable, of course, and if any final integration of Locke's interests, aims, alliances, and commitments is ever to be had, it will be owing to the contributions of these fine scholars. But precisely because of the compartmentalized nature of the effort to date, the complete picture is just beginning to come into focus.

In the course of this work I will critically discuss the interpretative conclusions reached by those who have situated Locke's writings in these various historical and intellectual contexts, as well as those (such as Kendall and Strauss) who preferred to "go by the book." What I want to do here is to clarify my own approach to assessing the Lockean texts in the context of their author's historical and intellectual attachments and point to the contribution (as well as a peculiar pitfall) such contextual studies can make to the efforts to recover John Locke's social and political thought.

There is an issue raised by the contextualists that merits particular attention. In his own study of Locke's revolutionary politics, Ashcraft advised against reading a work such as the *Two Treatises* as a "Great Theory" of political philosophy. A political text, such as Locke's, is, for Ashcraft, a particular "set of structured meanings, serving a specific social aim and intended to effect a particular social outcome." The point is this: "Political theories represent a particular configuration of beliefs that appear meaningful to members of a specific society because they can be related to a set of socially constituted practices shared by an audience to whom the theorist has addressed himself."[4]

A political theory, in sum, is culturally specific, reaching no farther than the "social life world" inhabited by the author, his audience, and his adversaries. Thus Ashcraft urges, "In my view, a political theory is a set of structured meanings that are understandable *only* in reference to a specified context, wherein the concepts, terminology, and even the internal structure of the theory itself are viewed in relation to a comprehensive ordering of the elements of social life."[5] This position has been affirmed by a scholar who approaches contextual interpretation from a somewhat different avenue. Viewing a given text as more an intellectual than a social action, and therefore situating it within the broader stream of historical discourse from which it has emerged, Quentin Skinner nevertheless agrees with Ashcraft. "I wanted to get as far away as possible from the assumption that there is a canonical list of 'the problems of philosophy' . . . and that we only need to point to the list in order to explain the preoccupations of individual philosophers. . . . So I still remain the sworn foe of those who wish to write the type of history in which the [Great Theories of philosophy] on the 'nature of the just state' are compared."[6]

If such a view results in the necessary confinement of a given political or philosophical work to the specific temporal conditions, events, and problems that might have produced it, implying that no larger, broader, or deeper philosophic or cultural significance ought to be ascribed to such a work, then a response is indeed indicated. Thomas Pangle, in fact, has provided the beginnings of such a response. Ashcraft has indeed shed more than a modest measure of light on Locke's historical role, but, Pangle advises, "this light is purchased at the cost of an unprecedented obscuring of Locke's position as a philosopher."[7] More generally, Pangle observes, the very possibility of philosophy has been challenged by the twentieth century's tendency to submerge ideas in deeper economic interests (a la Marx), religious commitments (a la Weber), or even subconscious proclivities (a la Freud), or to reduce philosophic thought to narrow paradigmatic languages from which they cannot break out (a la the republican revisionists). With Pangle I would hope we could "truly open ourselves to the possibility that political debate or argument is not simply or entirely reducible to 'ideology' . . . [and] entertain seriously the hypothesis that some past statesmen, historians, and theorists may at times have been capable of liberating themselves, through critical thought, from the subtle blinders or limitations of class, religious indoctrination, and linguistic tradition or 'context.' "[8]

Preoccupied with locating ideological origins (in linguistic paradigms or social intentions), a historian ought not overlook the fact that ideologies are capable of transcending their temporal circumstances and transforming themselves into timeless, philosophic absolutes. Pressed to answer the challenges of their adversaries or challenged by their own curiosity, ideological craftsmen come to confront two relentless questions: Why is that so? and How do I know? They are thereby driven to ground their political assertions in a set of deeper moral postulates, and these in a still deeper conception of human nature and the nature of the universe all humans confront, past, present, and future. Those who are most careful with their assertions discover the need to construct a theory of knowledge (an epistemology) as well, to support the "purely" political claims they seek to press. As a result a comprehensive structure of philosophic thought emerges. Such structures do not diminish but, by lending rigor and intellectual force to the argument, radically enhance the persuasive power of the ideological case they are designed to support. Conversely, their submergence in partisan combat does not detract from their status as comprehensive structures of philosophic speculation.

The Structure of Locke's Philosophy

It should be acknowledged that this kind of approach to unlocking Locke's meaning would either have bemused or bedeviled Lockean scholars just a few short decades ago. One of the more persistent themes in Lockean scholarship has been the failure to find coherence, much less comprehensiveness, in his thought. Locke's political thought, for example, has generally been regarded as, in the words of one interpreter, "full of illogical flaws and inconsistencies."[9] Even more problematic has been the effort to integrate Locke's political thought into the full philosophic corpus he left behind. Neal Wood summed it up delicately when he wrote, "Scholars commonly view Locke as essentially a pluralistic thinker, and they consider each aspect of his thought—for example, the philosophical, political and economic—to be more or less self-contained and segregated with little mutual connection between them."

Less delicate was Charles Monson, who wrote "Locke is not a careful thinker" and offered solace in the possibility of "seek[ing] out the frequently repeated assertions and the broad outlines of the theory [to] escape the inconsistencies resulting from Locke's carelessness." Speaking directly to the relation between Locke's political and epistemological writings, Peter Laslett concluded: "It was written for an entirely different purpose and in an entirely different state of mind. None of the connecting links is present."[10]

Although more recent scholarship has begun finding somewhat greater "unity" and "coherence" in Locke's writings, the claim that Locke left an encompassing philosophic structure of speculation has not yet been advanced.[11] James Tully, for example, points to some important conceptual links between the *Essay concerning Human Understanding* and *The Two Treatises of Government*. They concern the examination of "mixed modes and relations" as a basis for arriving at normative truths, such as Locke posits in his political writings. This does not deny the basic point, however, for as Tully writes: "Laslett's primary intention . . . is to disabuse the reader of the notion that Locke's political theory might be a logical deduction from his philosophy, as for example, Hobbes' theory is. . . . With this I wholeheartedly agree."[12]

Disagreeing with that assessment are two more recent contributors: Ruth Grant and Richard Ashcraft. Ashcraft, in particular, makes a noteworthy comment when he claims "not only that Locke's presupposition about human nature is dependent upon his theological conception of God, but also that, were he to change his views on the former subject, the entire structure of his world view would be affected."[13] In this spirit and in opposition to the judgment of Laslett and Tully, I shall argue that Locke's political theory, in terms of broad fundamentals, follows directly from his deeper philosophy, i.e., the theory of human nature and reality presented in his philosophic writings. It is my strong contention that John Locke bequeathed to posterity just such a comprehensive worldview, furnishing answers and solutions to a staggering array of practical and theoretical problems that confronted his age. Just as Marx united in one formidable system British political economy, German idealist philosophy, and French socialism (with so great a historical impact), so Locke, working with the materials of his century, did likewise. What both men uniquely grasped is that only such a towering structure could have the power to move history—or effect immediate revolutionary reform.

The mark of comprehensiveness, then, is a thinker's capacity to address, satisfactorily answer, and logically and coherently integrate the full range of questions human ingenuity has thought to raise concerning a diverse range of speculative topics and fields. From metaphysics to epistemology, from ethics to politics, to economics and education, Locke indefatigably addressed the issues and arguments of churchmen and businessmen, political writers and radical reformers, scientists and philosophers, and ancients and moderns. Locke brought together, under one vast philosophic roof, a plethora of historical concerns, historiographical traditions, economic findings, and religious commitments. To omit any part of the whole is ultimately to miss the richness, the fullness, and the completeness of the intellectual structure that is "Lockeanism."

Locke's entire corpus, in short, also constitutes an important context by which we may grasp his intended meaning. And under the circumstances it is fair to suppose that the moral principles, say, or the theory of human nature postulated in certain works would bear directly on the political principles he would affirm in other writings. In the first place, a brief six years separate the publication of no fewer than six of his most notable compositions.[14] Beyond this, we know that Locke was a careful, cautious writer. He worked on his ideas not just over the years, but across the decades.[15] In fact, he was at work virtually simultaneously on his writings on theology, toleration, human understanding, economic policy, and politics. And he considered and returned to these questions over the course of his adult life.

Grounded not so much in seventeenth-century politics as in a specific metaphysical conception of human nature and natural (i.e., moral) law, John Locke's speculative system may be surgically separated from the immediate historical context he confronted. Taken together and treated as a comprehensive whole, his disparate writings can indeed be regarded a "great work" of philosophy, available for future generations confronted by similarly "unique" historical circumstances and challenges.

One methodological point, critical to the assessment of Locke's influence on eighteenth-century America, emerges from this understanding. The kind of structured philosophy that is discussed here and that I am attributing to Locke needs to be comprehended as an integrated whole and not a jumble of disparate doctrines. It is a hierarchically structured series of doctrines addressing and answering questions in each of the key fields of philosophy: metaphysics, epistemology, ethics, and politics. This means, on the one hand, that the political doctrine is intractably tied to the metaphysical and moral postulates from which it emerges and, on the other, that given the metaphysics and morals of the matter, the political teaching necessarily follows. Thus to deny, confound, or compromise those political principles is to discard and repudiate the fundamental principles from which they emerge. And, conversely, to deny or disparage the essential underpinnings of the philosophic structure is to cut off and set philosophically adrift the superstructure of belief—what Locke calls the fundamentals of politics.

A philosophy, such as the one just developed, in sum is a seamless whole. A dismissal or disavowal of any element of that structure, by either its author or its alleged adherents, will form a corrosive film penetrating and attacking every adjoining element. And that, I shall argue, points precisely to the conceptual difficulties that would affect the findings of many astute historians who genuinely found a Lockean influence at work in the founding era.

It is by treating his wide-ranging corpus as a powerfully interwoven philosophical sum that I can furnish a more comprehensive grasp of what Lockeanism represents—i.e., the kind of outlook and essential principles that need to be located before we can say of the events of 1776, 1787, or 1800 that they are "Lockean" in character, or are so to a greater or lesser extent. It was precisely the failure to contemplate the integrated structure of Locke's thought, and instead to focus on this or that particular element of his writings, that led to the varied and often mutually offsetting reports about Locke and the founding surveyed in the introduction.

Of Text and Context

Before I provide a brief overview of this book's structure and indicate what I take to be the cardinal elements of John Locke's philosophy of nature, man, and government, one question merits some consideration, for it points to the inestimable contribution that contextual inquiry can make to the interpretation of past thought. Am I claiming to have constructed a faithful reading of Locke's own social and philosophic worldview? Yes, I am. The intellectual structure I shall impute to Locke (by the close of Chapter 6) contains the essential elements of the Lockean speculative system (while sidestepping a wide range of issues that are not quite so essential). In that these elements directly address the fundamental questions raised by the fields of metaphysics, epistemology, ethics, and politics and therefore form a coherent and consistent worldview, I can claim that, in terms of broad fundamentals, I have gotten the whole Locke and that I have gotten him right. I would urge that the test of this rather ambitious claim will be in the number of Locke's intellectual positions and historical commitments this reconstruction is able to account for and the degree to which it is or is not contradicted by what we now know of Locke's life and thought. And therein lies the value and use of contextual analysis.

Those scholars who seek to interpret past political thought through the medium of historical context do indeed render an eminently valuable service to scholarship. And none of my remarks above was intended to be dismissive of the contextualist approach to Locke or any other past political thinker. On the contrary, not only do such contextual explorations enable us to gain ever deeper insights into the thinking of the past masters, but they enable us to verify or falsify a given interpretation of this or that intellectual "masterpiece." It is precisely by invoking what we have learned from one contextual exploration that we can often raise serious questions or doubts about a conclusion drawn from the narrow inspection of another particular text or context. This point deserves some elaboration.

In working with the text as well as the many contexts of an author's life one commits oneself to a comprehensive approach to the task of interpretation. To consider a great body of textual evidence while also weighing the full range of aims, interests, and commitments to which a given writer was attached is to furnish a massive amount of evidence with which to build, test, and verify an interpretive rendering. To construct such an interpretation in this comprehensive manner without falling into contradiction and error is indeed to lend strength and veracity to the intellectual assessment or reconstruction of a given thinker's thought. The requirements of an interpretive study, in this sense, are not dissimilar to the standards by which any general scientific theory may be tested. Such an interpretation should be as clear and simple as possible; it should endeavor to explain the widest possible range of relevant phenomena; and it should not contradict any clearly discernible or logically demonstrable facts currently known and accepted.

The interpretation of Locke's moral and political philosophy that I will develop in Chapters 3 through 6 will conform to these methodological requirements in large measure—taking into account a multiplicity of his biographical interests and attachments (i.e., his role as Christian apologist, exclusion Whig, Baconian natural philosopher, natural law theorist, devotee of the new mechanical philosophy, defender of private property and limited government, apostle of capitalism, and resolute champion of political resistance). All of these real-life commitments will be seen to be contained and noncontradictorily comprehended in a philosophy built from the following materials: (1) God as intellectual worker, (2) man as his workmanship, (3) the primacy of reason in matters of knowledge and valuation, (4) the ethic of industriousness, (5) the precept of "equal creation," hence (6) the natural and inherent rights and responsibilities of life, liberty, and property, (7) happiness as the purpose of private life, and finally, (8) the "public good" (i.e., the equal protection of life, liberty, and estate of all, but special privilege for none) as the chief end of government.

With an approach to Locke's social and political thought as an inextricably tied philosophic structure, it can be concluded that the moral precepts of reason, industriousness, and equal creation yield and demand a politics rooted in personal liberty, religious toleration, property, and equal protection. In keeping with the methodological position just outlined, I would again urge that the test of this rather ambitious claim will be in the number of Locke's intellectual positions and historical commitments this reconstruction is able to account for and the degree to which it is or is not contradicted by what we now know of Locke's life and thought. That test, ultimately, will be the reader's to make.

The General Plan of the Book: The Philosophy of Locke and the Founding of America

Because there is so very much on the plate, it will be useful to outline the general scope and organization of the book. Chapter 2 will lay out the general historical background that informs and inspires the Lockean project. It sets out what I take to be the central challenge Locke knew he would have to meet if he was to win the field for his political and ideological positions, namely, religious toleration, the sanctity of property, freedom of commerce, popular government, and the legitimacy of resistance to arbitrary power. Given the manifest trials and tribulations of the age and the multifaceted challenges posed to civil, ecclesiastic, and intellectual authority, seventeenth-century English society sorely needed to know what measure of human liberty (or repression) would be conducive to and compatible with social stability and civil (i.e., political) security. I believe it is the pressing need to furnish a clear and convincing answer to this demanding question that explains and unifies the disparate doctrines that constitute the structure of Lockean speculation. The High Church had one view of the matter, and it more often than not came down hard on the side of intolerance and repression. But the Low, or latitudinarian, wing of the Anglican church preferred an alternative approach. Locke's ties to latitudinarian Anglicanism, a movement of lay and clerical leaders who were generally far more accommodating toward dissent and the Dissenters' economic calling than was the High Laudian church, will be explored. In exposing Locke's ties to latitudinarianism, however, I do not mean to deny or disparage his perhaps closer attachment to England's Dissenters and radicals. Locke's basic philosophical values could accommodate and bridge a surprisingly wide measure of ideological space. As I have already indicated, my methodological premise here is that reconstructing Locke's historical purposes (and the purposes of those social groups with which he may be associated) lays the groundwork for a stronger case for the interpretative reading that follows.

The philosophical fundamentals of Locke's social thought are developed in Chapter 3. I essentially view the theory of human nature and human knowledge presented in Locke's epistemological and educational writings as an ideological case for emancipating English dissent (and the Dissenters' economic and intellectual energies) and stilling the forces of intolerance and repression in Stuart England. If mankind was rational and capable of moral and political prudence, then even non-Anglicans could be freed and permitted a wider latitude of belief and expression. Locke's conception of the Maker, God, and of his intent for us, his highest creation, provided the basis for asserting the essentially rational and prudential character of human nature. The philosophical doctrines of free will, the efficacy of reason, and the human capacity for rational self-discipline (the hedonist passions notwithstanding) make the case for toleration and trust.

Chapter 4 goes on to develop Locke's principal moral recommendation, which, again, springs from man's metaphysical nature and from the intent of man's supreme Maker. It may be summed up in the phrase *human industriousness*. For the bulk of mankind, this might well take the form of economic toil, production, and trade, but it encompasses all activity aimed at human understanding and improvement (in the Baconian tradition). It is not adequate to view Locke as extolling "bourgeois" accumulation, let alone human exploitation or conspicuous consumption. All is not a quest for unlimited appropriation, though some people naturally will work in the Lord's vineyard for their constant financial improvement. But Locke, for one, did not busy himself with commercial profiteering. He mainly wrote books, executed the duties of public office, invested here and there, and, for a time, pursued a peculiar patriotic business: resistance to what he and many others perceived to be an approaching Stuart absolutism.

The ethic of industriousness, in short, finds expression in an infinite variety of productive pursuits. Nature, to be commanded, must be obeyed, as the great Bacon said; but if it is to be obeyed, it must first be understood. Any human endeavor that can enlarge the store of knowledge and bring the troublesome forces of nature (or of arbitrary power) under control, thereby serving to fuel a more comfortable and commodious quality of life, qualifies as virtuous in Locke's book (regardless how well or poorly it pays).

Chapter 5 follows with a closer examination of John Locke's social ethic, i.e., the principles that ought to guide our conduct vis-à-vis our neighbors. By specifically cutting a path through the false dichotomy that pits Macpherson's "diabolic" Locke against Tully's more recent "angelic" Locke, I locate a moderate Locke, a seventeenth-century moralist who recommended a species of individualism and enterprise that comports well with civic, patriotic, and even philanthropic "sacrifice." Far from being isolated, self-possessed atoms, the inhabitants of Locke's world are beings who have every motive and incentive to socially "belong": to combine in scientific societies for the advancement of learning, in schools for the encouragement of youth, in common worship for the benefit of souls, and in political communities for the protection of everyone's just property. Individuals will essentially live for their own sakes; but living for oneself does not mean living by oneself, and it doesn't mean subjugating others *for* oneself. Anyone's arbitrary ends cannot be invoked to justify any ill-chosen means.

My aim in Chapter 6 is to reconstruct Locke's theory of government, or more precisely, to set forth the fundamentals of John Locke's politics. I shall answer the question: What is the limit of Lockean law—the limit that will allow individuals to live as nature and their Maker intend? Granted, there is a point at which a body of citizens can "lawfully" overthrow constituted authority. But that point comes only after a "long train of abuses" and "prevarications" have been visited on a people. The question is this: At what point does that peculiar train leave the station?

If the powers of government are derived from the people, then it is fitting to ask exactly how much power every person naturally possesses. Governments cannot acquire powers that the people who form and make up political societies, by their nature, never possessed. Locke begins his discussion by affirming that there is "nothing more evident than that Creatures of the same species and rank, promiscuously born to all the same advantages of nature, and the use of the same faculties, should also be equal one amongst another without Subordination or Subjection." And from that equal creation, I shall argue, there arises a principle of equal protection that society's laws must uphold and not violate. From all this it follows that civil government can go so only so far (Locke's own majoritarian doctrine notwithstanding). But just how far is so far? What is the legal architecture of a just society, as Locke defined it? That is the pressing question, which to this day has been insufficiently explored by Lockean scholars.

Chapters 7 through 10 go on to trace Locke's influence on the American founding. In fact, as I shall demonstrate in Chapter 7, long before the imperial crisis gets under way, in 1763, Americans (with some critical exceptions) adopted the tenets of Lockeanism as a daily routine. In daily practice they were living and enjoying the "Lockean" mode of life. Ultimately, I shall argue, it was the desire to preserve that quality of life that drove their ideological speculations, their political resistance, and their efforts at constitutional reconstruction.

Chapter 8 examines the "Spirit of '76," i.e., the revolutionaries' strong ideological attachment to John Locke's philosophy of nature, man, and government. This is not intended to diminish the influence of "republicanism" on the American founding in any major way. I will argue that there is surprisingly little in the eighteenth-century republican *science* of politics that compromises or contradicts the *fundamentals* of politics enunciated in the writings of Locke. It is not surprising that Pocock traced the important neo-Harringtonian reformulation of classical republicanism to the home of Anthony Ashley Cooper, Lord Shaftesbury — the very ideological and real estate on which Locke took up residence. And it is not surprising that Houston has very recently pointed out the strong similarities between the political theory of Sidney (the "republican") and Locke (the "Lockean").[16] In this connection, and expanding on the work of Hamowy, Pangle, and Dworetz (all of whom at least perceived a Lockean imprint on Trenchard and Gordon's writings), I shall treat *Cato's Letters* as a comprehensive synthesis of Lockean liberal *and* "classical" republican principles — a package readily available for colonial consumption during the political crises to come.

It is time, then, to discard altogether the essentially misleading Lockean/republican dichotomy. While Locke provided the "fundamentals" of politics, some among the eighteenth-century country party (e.g., "Cato," though not Bolingbroke) accepted those fundamentals and then appended to them: (1) a science of politics aimed at securing those fundamentals and (2) the grounds for suspiciously eyeing the slimmest assault on those fundamentals (i.e., the famous "Catonic" suspicion of political power rooted in the historical cycle of political decay that was itself rooted in the human craving for power and preferment).

Chapter 9 focuses on the constitutional period (1786–1788). All disputes over the mechanics of government notwithstanding (e.g., whether a small or a large and extended republic is more suited to a republican form of government, whether the powers of the departments of government ought to be strictly separated or overlapped, and so forth), I shall argue that the preponderance of Federalists (those who saw the need for stronger, centralized power to contain the "vices" of the confederate system) as well as the leading anti-Federalists (those who insisted that an invigorated national union would unavoidably invite those very "vices") concurred as to the fundamentals of government—i.e., the origins, aims, and limits of political authority. Both sides essentially sought to accomplish the same ends but differed profoundly on the safest and surest means of doing so. The central unifying aim, for Federalist and anti-Federalist alike, was the advancement of a civilization open to talent (though largely for the white, male population) and enshrined in the Lockean precept of "equal creation."

Chapter 10 heralds the vindication or "triumph" of the anti-Federalist fears and prophecies. It finds, in early national public policy, the abandonment of equal protection for a politics of special privilege. And it finds in the rise of Jeffersonian republicanism a striking effort to restore the equal protection that a vigilant devotion to equal creation demanded. Insofar as it was the fundamentals of government, nowhere more clearly articulated than in John Locke's social and political thought, that dominated this period I can ultimately portray the American founding as essentially Lockean. This assertion, however, necessarily raises a set of questions that need to be addressed. Is it my intention to argue that Locke's influence on the founders was immediate and direct? Is this what the founders took Locke to be saying? Did they even have a direct acquaintance with his principal writings, Dunn notwithstanding?[17] Frankly, I have not addressed these questions in any comprehensive manner, nor did I feel the need to do so.

My focus in Chapters 7 through 10 is not so much on Locke's influence per se, as on the peculiar principles that were embodied in his writings. Between 1763 and 1800 these were the preeminent principles that informed revolutionary, Federalist, anti-Federalist, and Jeffersonian republican activity, alike. They were not the only ones at work, however, as I have already intimated. The concern over corruption, the attention given to the historical cycles of ancient and modern political decay, the signs and symptoms of an approaching tyranny, the need for legislative checks on executive power, and other "republican" conceptions buttressed the case for resistance, rebellion, and political reconstruction throughout this period.

At the same time, these Lockean principles would be compromised and contradicted in large and small ways. Ultimately, the United States would veer considerably from its Lockean moorings. That, too, is part of the story I want to tell. In these pages the reader will not find a ubiquitous Lockean presence in the American founding (a la Hartz or Becker). The real feat for contemporary scholarship, I have long believed, is in detecting those points of the founding period in which "Locke" not only can be found, but was ultimately lost.

Did Locke himself "influence" the Americans in their foundational labors? Ultimately, the answer is, yes he did, even though some of Locke's principles are contained in the writings of his influential predecessors (e.g., Roger Williams, William Penn, and Samuel Pufendorf). Some, and in some notable cases *all,* of Locke's principles were transmitted to America in the writings of his disciples, eighteenth-century intermediaries (popular writers such as Trenchard and Gordon and serious theorists such as Burlamaqui). We shall see that the Lockean way of life, a moral code built on rational independence, industrious improvement, and social cooperation, was extolled and transmitted to the British colonials in many of the eighteenth century's most popular literary works, and they issue from Locke's pen as well.

There were, of course, other important factors. In many ways sheer circumstance contributed to the Lockean bearing of colonial society (e.g., the ease of obtaining land accommodated a wide franchise and broad political representation, the diversity of religious parties in a hostile environment encouraged religious toleration, etc.). But the main point, as Steven Dworetz has written in *The Unvarnished Doctrine: Locke, Liberalism, and the American Revolution,* is this:

> Establishing — or recovering — the Lockean connection neither includes nor requires a demonstration of Locke's "influence;" . . . the point is not who influenced whom, but that Revolutionary thought was of a certain character. Judging by the concerns and positions in Revolutionary thought, a vitally important element in that character was Lockean liberal. "Influence" is strictly an academic concern and ultimately a futile one. But we can show that the American Revolutionists [I include Federalists and anti-Federalists, as well as the Jeffersonian republicans] held liberal ideas about politics.[18]

Thus my focus is on Locke and just as importantly on a nexus of social and political recommendations (and in terms of essentials they are really few in number) that came to play a predominant role in eighteenth-century American life and thought and that were nowhere more systematically formulated than in the Lockean literary corpus.

2
Seventeenth-Century Background:
The Threat to Authority

Those who seek to examine the contextual settings out of which past political thought emerged render an eminently useful service to theoretical inquiry. They vastly enhance our capacity to view the world as our historical subjects viewed it, with all the social, cultural, and ideological issues he or she faced in far sharper focus. Once we have grasped the issues an author's age confronted and the kinds of conflicts those issues invited, once we have investigated the alliances and allegiances the writer formed and the social causes for which he or she fought, we can, with greater confidence, interpret the meaning of the political thought that thinker bequeathed. As Richard Ashcraft has written, "It is always relevant to raise questions concerning the meaning of a particular political theory that are referable to the actor's social life-world, the nature of the intended audience, and the purposes for which the political theory was formulated."

Locke did not pen his *Two Treatises* to persuade Adam Smith or Robert Nozick, or to launch the careers of Rousseau and Marx. He wrote to those individuals, then living, who would be willing and able to read him and who, if persuaded, would help accomplish the political (and other) ends for which he himself labored. Building on the work of Laslett and Cranston, Ashcraft thus wrote:

> Locke's political theory . . . arose within the context of a political movement in which he was a participant, along with thousands of others. The *Two Treatises* . . . was, in effect, the political manifesto of this movement. Much of the meaning of Locke's political theory is thus rooted not only in a particular perception of social reality, he shared with others in seventeenth-century England, but it is also tied in rather concrete terms to the specific political objectives around which large numbers of individuals organized themselves in the 1670's and 1680's.[1]

Locke's ideological aim in writing his essay on civil government, then, was not to justify to the world the throne of William III and the successful Revolution of 1688, but to enlist cadres in a political conflict that had gripped England seven to nine years earlier. By 1679, Locke, his patron Lord Shaftesbury (1621–1683), and many others in England would mount a parliamentary campaign to exclude James, Duke of York, a practicing Catholic, from succeeding his brother Charles II to the throne of England. By 1681, the actions of the king suggested to many in the exclusion movement that extraparliamentary means would have to be undertaken—and justified—if England's liberties were to be preserved. Toward this end, legions of "Exclusion" tracts were produced, urging the constitutional constraint of monarchical power—chief among them Locke's *Two Treatises of Government*.

I shall examine Locke's political theory in the context of that political movement in Chapter 4, but first I want to suggest that Locke's *epistemological* theory likewise arose within the context of a social movement of which he was an intellectually active participant. Far from being just another masterpiece of world philosophy, Locke's *Essay concerning Human Understanding* can also be read as a "tract" (albeit a philosophically rich and rigorously argued one) intended to achieve ideological objectives around which large numbers of Locke's contemporaries were organized.

The salient social and political conditions that informed ideological debate in Restoration England, then, merit careful attention, especially what can be considered the most fundamental and vexing problem of the age: the threat to authority in virtually all its guises. Also important to an understanding of the context within which Locke wrote is the ideological program pressed by one significant segment of English society: the latitudinarian Anglicans. They hoped to eradicate the sources of social unrest and unify the nation under God and sovereign, working not with force and repression, but with the tools of reason and toleration. Locke's relation to latitudinarianism merits some attention, because on a remarkable number of points, Locke's philosophy directly addresses the challenges taken up by these Low Churchmen and scientific "virtuosi."[2]

Locke the exclusion Whig and Locke the latitudinarian author were joined in common cause. In Locke, the epistemological and political theories stand in ideological union. The theory of knowledge and, even more important, the theory of human nature posted in the *Essay concerning Human Understanding* make possible and necessary the theory of civil society recommended in the *Two Treatises of Government*. What's more, the preponderance of contemporary scholarly opinion, which yet sees discontinuity in Locke's writings, and all questions of historical context aside, I shall ultimately show that the doctrines developed in

Locke's two towering works, when buttressed with ideas developed in his other writings, form a full-blown philosophy of nature—a worldview capable of "escaping" the time and place of its composition and exerting a considerable influence on the revolutionary events of the eighteenth century—and well beyond. Before the components of that philosophy can be pieced together, however, it is important to understand the stark social concerns such a theory would have to address and resolve if it hoped to attract and persuade its immediate audience.

The Dissolution of Authority

In accounting for the ideological dimensions of seventeenth-century debate, no factor, I think, is more fundamental (i.e., capable of explaining a greater range of issues raised and opinions expressed) than the century-spanning threat posed to authority. The challenge to political authority is, of course, manifest. From monarchy to commonwealth to monarchy, from personal rule (of king) to personal rule (of Cromwell), from regicide to Restoration within a single generation, the world wasn't just turned upside down, it was practically spinning like a top. It is not surprising that, as Margaret C. Jacob reports, "Restoration churchmen were obsessed with the problem of maintaining social and political stability." Obedience to authority and stability ultimately had to be a state of mind; a peculiar state that the church (among other institutions) would have to bring into being in every parish. In what H. T. Dickinson has called the "Ideology of Order," social and political peace were to be mutually reinforcing.[3]

The grounds of submission to authority would have to be internalized, made a part of people's affective life. To protect the order and property of the realm, doctrines of "nonresistance" and "passive obedience" were uniformly pronounced. These were deemed laws ordained by God and Nature, laws that people violate at their peril. For whatever calamities might befall a patriarchal society, it was *all in the family*. From king to commoner, the ideology of patriarchy held society together, though it did so by tying all its members into a hierarchical noose of ranks and stations. In the great chain, every being was linked by reciprocal bonds of privilege and obligation. For some, the privileges outnumbered the obligations. For most, duty and submission to authority formed the substance of daily life.

As a political theory, patriarchalism is most often associated with the name of Sir Robert Filmer (1590–1653).[4] In "Patriarcha" (1680), Filmer firmly identified paternal and political (i.e., monarchical) power. Unlike prior writers, Sir Robert saw "regal and paternal authority . . . as identical, not merely similar or in some way analogous." Filmer consummated a hearty marriage between a domineering social pattern and a pressing political need. In a final effort to secure the throne for the Stuart family he hitched patriarchal authority to royal sovereignty. As Schochet wrote, "Filmer insisted that the state was an extension of the natural hierarchy of the family and that political obligation was the same as the [scriptural] duty to obey fathers."[5]

The move made sense. Separation from the Church of Rome presaged a keen interest in the career of God prior to his sending his son, Jesus, to the dominion of sin. The spiritual message of the creation, the significance of the fall and of original sin would become a preoccupation of the age, as would the examples of the great Hebrew patriarchs — Adam, Noah, and others. If their authority could be pressed into the service of Stuart absolutism, all the better. Filmer's natural law theory allowed absolute patriarchal sovereignty, originally given by God to Adam, to be passed down from Adam, generation after generation in linear succession, directly to James I and, finally, to his son Charles Stuart, England's sitting sovereign.

But this having been said, the patriarchal political theory ultimately had its foundation in a dominant social reality. "It lay like a motionless log across the stream of human progress for more than a dozen centuries," wrote the historian Paul Johnson.[6] For him, it was Roman Christianity, as such; but this could be said of the patriarchal theory, as well. And it was the power of patriarchy in the sociology of early Stuart life that was the real glue, the gripping force that held English civilization together and kept it still.[7]

The typical Stuart family or household, as Gordon Schochet emphasizes, was the basic social and economic unit. The patriarch was the titular head of the family and the source of authority — the true ruler of all under his local dominion, including his natural offspring as well as all his servants, retainers, renters, and any others who expected to live off his lands. His was a family extended in space and time, rooted in long-standing traditions of fealty and exacting obedience, for it was "only as a member of a family," Schochet writes, "that one acquired any meaning or status in society . . . it was through the family that an individual came into contact with the outside world." What is significant, Schochet writes,

> is that the relationships they comprised — master and servant, employer and worker, landlord and tenant, clergyman and congregant, and magistrate and subject — were all understood as identical to the relationship of father and children. [The patriarchal outlook] was supported by . . . [a] regularly taught ideology that corresponded to,

justified and rationalized life as it was actually experienced by the illiterate and inarticulate masses of seventeenth-century Englishmen.

The chief ideological support for the patriarchal outlook came, of course, from the will of God, as expressed especially in the Fifth Commandment. It simply admonished mankind to obey the parent. By the standard interpretation of the day, "parent" included all one's "superiors." Whatever their doctrinal disagreements in other matters, "the natural bonds of obedience were the prescribed teaching of all the sects."[8]

The duty of obedience was endlessly affirmed in the several catechisms widely circulated during the period. The uniform invocation of the Fifth Commandment is evident in the similarity between the shorter catechism of the Westminster Assembly of Divines (proclaimed in 1648, at the height of revolutionary realignment) and the equivalent discussion contained in the Anglican Prayer Book (or Book of Common Prayer). It was anything but a Stuart invention. As far back as 1528, William Tyndale wrote in his important account of Christian duties:

> Honor thy father and mother (Exod. xx) . . . love them with all thine heart; and fear and dread them, and wait on their commandments; and seek their worship, pleasure, will and profit in all things; . . . remembering that thou art their good and possession, and that thou owest unto them thine own self, and all thou art able, yea and more than thou art able to do. . . . Understand also . . . when thou pleasest them, thou pleasest God; when thou displeasest them, thou displeasest God.

This was the message of the *Whole Duty of Man,* "a short and plain direction to the very meanest readers," as well as Richard Baxter's special catechism directed to "those who are past the common small Catechisms, and which grow to a more rooted Faith, and to the fuller understanding of all that is commonly needed to a safe, holy, comfortable and profitable life."[9]

Beneath the biblical injunction, of course, stood the economic imperative. The household was indeed the primary structure of production and exchange, as well as the locus of regulation and discipline. The authority of the patriarch did not ring hollow. He commanded all the offices, tools, waterways, and wildlife that inhabited his estates. Servants, sons, and tenants alike were dependent on his good graces for their keep and sustenance. It is hardly surprising that noted commentators, even those with little religious scruple, nevertheless championed the patriarchal cause. Eschewing scriptural authority, simply discoursing on the foundations of civil society, Hobbes carefully urges the power of patriarchy on his readers: "For to be a king, is nothing else but to have dominion over many persons, and thus a great family is a little kingdom, and a little kingdom a family."[10]

By 1640, Schochet confirms, the "paternal image had become an established symbol in Stuart thought." As important was its forceful role in Stuart life. It was all of a piece. The sovereign's authority had to be absolute, as absolute as the father's authority over his family. As early as 1598, in *The True Law of Free Monarchy*, James VI of Scotland (soon to become James I of England) gave political expression to the patriarchal theory. "By the law of nature," he urged, "the King becomes a naturall Father to all his Leiges at his Coronation." Richard Mocket's *God and the King*, published in 1615 by order of James, urges that "there is a stronger and higher bond of Duty between children and the Father of their Countrey, than the Fathers of private Families. . . . Where we are required to honour the Fathers of private families," Mocket concludes, "so much more the Father of our Countrey and the whole Kingdom."[11]

The problem, as Schochet concluded, was that the "children" of the royal patriarch "were themselves either patriarchs in their own households or adults who had long ago outgrown the habits of servitude and subordination. They were being asked to transfer their childhood experiences to the political realm and to see themselves viz a viz political authority as they had once been in relation to their fathers and masters and as their own servants now presumably saw them."[12]

Of all the factors working to loosen the patriarchal bonds of seventeenth-century society, none is perhaps more significant than the rise of literacy and learning. Ignorance gives to the traditional the quality of the inevitable. Learning broadens the horizons, affording men and women the inestimable advantage of distinguishing that which *is* from that which *could and ought to be*. It arms individuals with the confidence to question and challenge the dictates of authority, to point out contradiction and error, and to search for new means and alternative ends.

In the century leading up to the English Revolution, England witnessed a spectacular expansion of educational opportunity. This ranged from expanded openings for the upper ranks at the universities and the Inns of Court, to the endowment of grammar schools in parish and market towns by individual benefactors or local groups. Basic literacy was now being taught by traveling schoolmasters or local curates throughout England. Not all ranks benefited, of course, and it is not surprising that Keith Wrightson speaks of a "hierarchy of illiteracy," ordered, as all else, along the lines of wealth and status. Nonetheless, he reports, "by the 1630's, a more substantial proportion of the population than ever before was in receipt of higher education, while schooling of all kinds was available to an extent which had never before been experienced."[13]

England by then had an educated and dedicated graduate clergy as well, drawn increasingly from the ranks of the "upper and middling ranks of society: sons of the upper yeomanry, urban tradesmen, the gentry and increasingly, members of clerical dynasties."[14] Opportunity, in fact, was expanding in all directions. Most important, the word of God was itself available to the plain, literate believer. "It is difficult," writes John Lilburne's biographer, "to exaggerate the importance of the bible in English."[15]

By 1539, the Great Bible was ordered to be chained in every church for all to see or read. Yet another Bible was translated into English by the Marian exiles — "of excellent scholarship, handy in size, conveniently divided into verses, encouraging thought and questioning by its copious notes . . . it became the private man's Bible."[16] The Genevan Bible, Christopher Hill writes, "was published in pocketable editions, so that men could study it in the privacy of their homes, or could produce it in a church or an ale-house to knock down an argument with a text."[17] Finally, James's Authorized Version, published in 1611, brought the word of God into reach of Englishmen everywhere. The supply and demand for the Bible rose proportionately — and so did the number of individuals prepared to decipher and deliver its meaning. Pauline Gregg thus writes: "With an English Bible in his hand, it was natural for a man to believe that he could find God himself with few auxiliary aids, and easy for him to give a personal interpretation to every passage. More than any other single thing, the Bible in the vernacular contributed to the growth of religious independence."[18]

Understandably, much of the action took place on the teeming thoroughfares of London. The market for God's truth flourished. Congregations were so eager to hear the revealed word, that besides ministers, lay lecturers without the cure of souls were regularly invited to preach. Many would not be content merely to repeat the old formulations. In ever-increasing numbers laymen found the courage to interpret the Scriptures for themselves and to spread the word to large audiences.

Printed pamphlets and books also served to spread the word. Arthur Dent's *The Plaine Man's Pathway to Heaven* was released in 1601. By 1640, it had run to twenty-five editions. *The Practice of Pietie* by Lewis Bayly, with no fewer than thirty-six editions by 1636, may have begun a popular trend. Bayly told his simple reader "how to read the Bible with profit and ease once every yeere." Foxe's *Book of Martyrs,* the writings of Luther, Calvin, Cartwright, William Perkins, and later John Saltmarsh's *Divine Right of Presbyterie Asserted,* William Dell's collected sermons, and John Archer's *Personal Reigne of Christ upon Earth,* all enjoyed a wide circulation. With the breakdown of the monarchy in the 1640s, and the absence of church and Crown courts, "writers were free to speak openly and without fear of retribution.'' Richardson and Ridden thus report that ''9000 per cent more pamphlets were published in 1642 (or 1,966), than in 1640.''[19]

Scripture, however, was but one of many intellectual influences that would be exerted on the minds of literate and learned Englishmen. The entire scope of classical and pagan speculation would soon become accessible to the curious inquirer. The secular approach to moral and political speculation, typified by Aristotle, Polybius, the Stoics, and the Epicureans, easily entered the stream of discourse.

The sixteenth-century Catholic Counter Reformation writers, such as Bellarmine, Suarez, and Molina, who recoiled at all divine right pretensions, assigning to government purely mundane and temporal responsibilities, would now penetrate English thought, as would the ideas of the natural law and resistance writers. The histories of ancient Greece and republican Rome would be available, as would the ''new learning'' of the ''moderns,'' which Sir Francis Bacon had so proudly championed.[20] And it was not only political thought that would be given a secular spin. Moral life, too, could be construed as aiming at secular and temporal ends — such as natural happiness, so emphasized in the writings of Cicero, Seneca, Aristotle, and even Aquinas.[21] Nowhere were the frightening implications of materialist and hedonist speculation more ominously put on parade than on the pages of Thomas Hobbes's *Leviathan*. And perhaps nowhere was the challenge to the social and religious foundations of political life more keenly felt. It had been prepared by centuries of effort, but at long last the spread of literacy, the revival of classical learning, and the modern (yet Aristotelian) emphasis on empirical data and purely natural processes (combined in the Thomistic synthesis) had finally fashioned a materialist/realist philosophy that could challenge the very foundations of a devout and religious age. If man was essentially selfish, how could the common good and general interest ever be achieved? If existence consisted exclusively of matter in motion, what room was there for an immaterial deity, an all-powerful and all-demanding God?

But beneath the challenge to man's benevolent nature and God's divine presence stood an even more fundamental challenge — a challenge to authority itself. No longer would the cloistered Schoolman be able to rest his case on the unimpeachable testimony of this or that past master; not even Aristotle would withstand scrutiny. In short order, a fiery battle for epistemological independence would be joined, as exposure to so diverse a variety of intellectual currents would furnish freethinkers the ways and means to resist the sterility of scholastic disputation. Bacon, Boyle, and Newton would command on this field of combat, urging rational, empirical inquiry and experimentation — and promising substantial results. Nature could be commanded, and the natural and social diseases that had for so long afflicted humanity steadily conquered; but to be commanded nature would have to be obeyed—and that meant understood, which in turn meant that inquiry would have to be free and truth judged on the merits.

But if reason could challenge authority, then its own efficacy could also be called into question—as it had been centuries earlier. If Epicureanism and Stoicism largely shared an optimistic outlook on life, believing that the good life could be apprehended and lived, ancient skepticism bespoke a pessimistic outlook—and a rebuke to epistemological self-confidence. The skeptical doctrines of Pyrrho (c. 360–270 B.C.E.) were reintroduced into Europe with the fifteenth-century translation of Sextus Empiricus's writings. Greatly adding to the appeal of skepticism was the phenomenal popularity of Montaigne (1533–1592) and his challenge to epistemological self-reliance.

With materials like these filtering through the intellectual environment of seventeenth-century England, nearly anything was possible. But secular currents aside, it is still possible to argue that the English Civil War represented a contest between two clerical models: the episcopal and the presbyterian. Critical to the slide toward midcentury revolution was the clash between Anglicanism and what many a Puritan heralded as the "true" reformed church, far closer to Calvin's Genevan model. The Calvinist imprint on English Puritanism has visible origins. The contact with Calvinism, which many an English cleric enjoyed during the Marian reign and exile, and the depth of their faith in the Genevan program is integral to understanding the campaign of parliamentary resistance.

The first Stuarts asserted the divine right theory, against the liberty of Parliament or the people. James Stuart, already king of Scotland before ascending to the English throne, had proffered his views in *The True Law of Free Monarchies* (1698). He grounded his title in God's gift alone and had found that his will was supreme. But what if the king, in his wisdom, ordered his subjects to act so as to compromise their deepest religious needs? What if a sovereign stood in the way of "true" religion, his church consoling the unregenerate through elegant, if spiritually impotent, ritual? The ceremonial forms, the Presbyterian believed, contributed to a laxity of moral discipline and from his outlook provided the lone congregant a very false sense of security concerning his immortal soul. It was no way to save a sin-weary nation. Intimately tied to the Anglican sacrament, even more important, was the Arminian heresy. As Nicholas Tyacke explains:

> During the first decade of the [seventeenth] century, Arminius, (a Dutch theologian) elaborated a critique of doctrinal Calvinism so systematic as to give his name to an international movement, namely Arminianism. He was concerned to refute the teachings of divine grace associated with the followers of Calvin. . . . [Not long after],

English Arminians came to balance their rejection of the arbitrary grace of predestination with a new found source of grace freely available in the sacraments, which Calvinists had belittled.[22]

Another approach was suggested by William Perkins, a leading Cambridge theologian who also rejected Calvinist doctrine. Perkins affirmed that individuals, by the purity of their souls and the integrity of their acts (though not the rituals they perform), could know themselves to be saved. Herein lies a far more benevolent and classical conception of man—and God. If man was free and responsible, able to redeem his own soul through a lifelong course of good works (even hard, demanding toil), and if by this he would be judged saved—rewarded for his unremitting labors on behalf of the one, true sovereign—then the universe was just and God was indeed a good creator and keeper.

At any rate, Charles had, by the mid-1620s, "become the architect of an Armenian revolution" within the Anglican church. The Prayer Book was now interpreted as rejecting predestinarian Calvinism "on the ground that this was no part of the teaching of the thirty-Nine Articles."[23] The great issue here, as Francis Kous told Parliament on 26 January 1629 (the last session before Personal Rule), was the "right of religion" itself. And, he went on, "this right, in the name of this nation, I this day claim, and desire that there may be a deep and serious consideration of the violation of it." The Arminian error, he dutifully explained, "maketh the sheep to keep the shepherd, [an error] that maketh mortal seed of an immortal God."[24] The sides were drawn. From the Puritan standpoint, the nation was "living in the last days of the world. . . . Antichrist was loose . . . and the godly were enlisted in a cosmic war between light and darkness, Christ and the devil."[25]

Whig historians of the nineteenth century, such as Acton and Macaulay, were basically off the mark in proclaiming the Presbyterians and parliamentarians the advance guard of liberty in the West. The men who managed the early years of the revolution did appeal to constitutional principle and sanction a loosening of economic regulation (especially state-chartered monopolies). If they claimed liberty, however, it was "liberty for the gospel," not for error. They dreamed of a national church, run by a hierarchy of councils, or presbyteries, with the power to impose a strict uniformity of worship and conduct.

To accomplish this and draw up a plan for a new national church, the Westminster Assembly was convened in 1643. Here the authority of the Presbyterians would be challenged by the Independent presence in the assembly. Like the Presbyterians, they too were orthodox Calvinists. And they too were "alike in that each considered his ecclesiastical system ordained by Scripture and therefore of divine right.''[26] Both churches, moreover, believed in imposing a strict discipline on their congregants. But where the Presbyterians saw the whole nation as their congregation, the Independent churches would assert their authority on those who wished to join and who were deemed sainted enough to belong.

The Independents, therefore, saw the need to resist a national Presbyterian discipline, on the one hand, and an Erastian assertion of parliamentary sovereignty over ecclesiastical affairs, on the other. Their appeal to divine natural law and their determination to resist religious uniformity brought the Independents to the doctrine of liberty of conscience. The plain believer had it, as of right, to covenant with the congregation of his choosing, adhering to its theological conventions and discipline.[27] Too much should not be made of this, though, for William Lamont may well be correct when he writes: ''The dissidents came to toleration as a second best. Unmixed communion was the ideal. For want of a Geneva, the least bad alternative was a toleration which would be sufficient in its breadth to allow that ideal to be put into practice on a smaller scale, at the level of the congregation.''[28]

Stalwart Independents would, at the Restoration, file into the dissenting churches, feeding, as we shall see, a conflict in state and church that would kindle the Exclusion Crisis and call forth the politics of Locke. In the meantime, neither the Erastians in Parliament nor the Presbyterians in the assembly could abide the Independents' solution—or their religion. The Presbyterian party demanded a national church, with synodical assemblies and with power to excommunicate and sanction member congregations and individuals, so as to preserve a saintly discipline over the nation. The Erastians in the assembly rejected Independency and toleration no less vigorously. For them, as Pease explains, ''divine right in a system of ecclesiastical anarchy was even worse than divine right in a system of spiritual tyranny.'' Independence would be defeated in the assembly by 1646, but the Presbyterian plan would also be rejected. Power, Parliament reckoned, could not be shared; it must be whole and indivisible—and preserved in Parliament.[29]

By 1647, another independent voice was echoing through the towns and trading fairs of England. Influenced by the doctrines of Independency and consumed by the righteousness of their cause, large numbers of Levellers, many making up the army rank and file, intensified the plea for liberty. And they certainly demonstrated how politically destabilizing liberty of conscience could be.

The revolutionary events of the 1640s dramatically illustrate the logical power of historical precedent—and the menace posed by a liberated mind. In bucking the authority of the king, defenders of parliamentary sovereignty invoked the doctrine of higher law. Specifically, they alluded to the laws of God, the laws of nature, and the rules of right reason (the fusion of Stoicism and Christianity). The explosive question, of course, was this: Who shall have the authority to define these laws and determine those rules?

In 1646, moderate Independents, such as John Cook, writing in his *Vindication of the Professors and Profession of the Law,* grounded law in the rule of reason. He demanded, however, that the High Court of Parliament, and not the people, must be its final arbiter. The author of *The Case of the Army Soberly Discussed,* released a year later, informed his readers that the defenders of Parliament against the king considered the law of nature to be something determined by heads of families in a patriarchal society. If the nature of government and the grounds of loyalty must be decided by the people, ultimately the people would consist solely of the heads of England's households — not the commonality of England as such. The moderate Independents, as we have already seen, promulgated the view that subjection to church government could only arise in the context of a freely chosen compact between congregation and congregant.

Working with all these materials, the Levellers would raise the revolutionary stakes appreciably. Writing in *London's Liberty in Chains,* John Lilburne embraced these very conceptions. Without compunction, he declares the law of England to be

> the Perfection of Reason, consisting of Lawfull and Reasonable Customes, received and approved of by the people and of the old Constitutions, and modern Acts of Parliament, made by the Estates of the Kingdome. But such only as are agreeable to the Law Eternall and Naturall, and not contrary to the word of God: For whatsoever laws, usages, and customes, not thus qualified; are not the law of the land; nor are to be observed and obeyed by the people, being contrary to their Birth-rights and Freedomes, which by the Law of God, and the great Charter of Priviledges, they ought not to be.[30]

Surely, a king could forsake the "Eternall" and "Naturall" laws ordained by God and "Reason," as was all too apparent to many. Appropriately, England's Constitution provided for a balance of power between king, Lords, and Commons. But what if the Lords neglected their high duty, acquiescing under the tyrannical impositions of an unruly monarch? Then political power could devolve to the House of Commons alone. And in Commons, Lilburne would place his highest trust — for a time. In the end, however, it too would prove a distressing disappointment. With his own articles of impeachment in hand, Lilburne could declare that the Commons had forfeited its title to govern, for it had: (1) failed to

resist a lawless House of Lords in their prosecution of some of its own MPs—
including Lilburne, himself; (2) timorously invoked "ministerial responsibility"
when faced with the egregious violations of right perpetrated by a Norman tyrant,
the English king; (3) stubbornly resisted crucial political reforms, such as annual
elections and an expansion of the franchise; (4) imposed the bondage of common
law, which, for Lilburne, was a Norman invention that made the common law a
high mystery to the common man—but made professional lawyers wise and
wealthy; and (5) continued to impose monopolies of trade, thereby thwarting the
commercial energies of the plain and Protestant believer.

Having before them the model and theory of the Congregationalist church
covenant, eminently adaptable for their political purposes, the Levellers were
free to declare that "the kingdom was without government, and in a state of nature." The failure of Lords and Commons, the king, the city Independents, and
the army to safeguard the people's liberties had set the people "free to seek in the
dissolution of all established authority a new method of making the people's liberties the supreme law of the land. . . . Accordingly, every honest man was at
liberty to promote the kingdom's welfare, by what means seemed best to him."[31]

And so the Levellers came to *The Agreement of the People,* an ill-fated attempt
to erect a fundamental law designed to govern government itself. By 1649, the
idea, along with its chief purveyors, would be decisively defeated at Burford.
The deepest danger posed by the Leveller movement, however, was not political;
it was epistemological. It was embodied in the act of a single, reasoning mind
and in the conclusions to which such a mind could come. Lilburne is the perfect
case in point, as he declares:

> Every particular and individual man and woman, that ever breathed
> in the world . . . are, and were by nature all equall and alike in
> power, dignity, authority, and majesty, none of them having (by na-
> ture) any authority, dominion or magisteriall power one over or above
> another, neither have they, or can they exercise any, but meerely by
> institution, or donation, that is to say, by mutuall agreement or con-
> sent, given, for the good, benefit and comfort each of other, and not
> for the mischiefe, hurt or damage of any.

For it is "unnaturall, irrational, sinfull, wicked, and unjust" to imagine that
men can ever part "with so much of their power as shall enable any of their Parliament men, . . . ministers, Officers or servants to destroy and undue them."
And it is "sinful, wicked, unjust, devilish, and tyrannicall" for "any man whatsoever, spirituall or temporall, Clergy-man or Lay-man," to presume "to rule,

govern, or reign over any sort of men in the world, without their free consent." Those who attempt it "doe thereby, endeavour to appropriate & assume unto themselves the Office and sovereignty of God (who alone doth . . . rule by his will and pleasure) and to be like their creator."[32]

The radical idea of personal sovereignty, and its explosive implication for civil society, is forcefully expressed by Richard Overton, as he aims *An Arrow against All Tyrants:*

> To every individual, in nature, is given an individual property . . . not to be invaded or usurped by any: for every man . . . hath a selfe propriety, else could he not be himself, and on this no second may presume to deprive any of, without manifest violation and affront to the very principles of nature, and of the Rules of equity and justice between man and man; mine and thine cannot be, except this be, no man hath power over my rights and liberties, and I over no man.[33]

The implication for religious diversity could hardly be missed. Since the government's authority derived from the people, and since no person individually had an authority to impose his religious ideas on another, no such power could ever devolve to king, Lords, or Commons. The call for toleration was sounded. Thus, perceiving early that a toleration for diversity, rather than an enforced uniformity could conduce to civil order, William Walwyn advised, "If the government would once protect people without taking account of their differences in religion, it would have a much better chance of receiving their loyalty in return." Preceding Mill by some two hundred years, Walwyn then declares, "Every man ought to be protected in the use of that, wherein he doth not actually hurt another."[34]

Although the Levellers' political aims would be decisively defeated by 1649, their stirring claims on behalf of religious liberty would be put to the test. The rise of literacy and learning, along with the demise of church and court tribunals capable of imposing religious uniformity, fueled a spectacular growth of sectarian worship. Even in 1645 Thomas Edwards was cataloging in the various editions of his *Gangraena* "the hundreds of religious and political vagaries the time afforded — not omitting the political teachings of Lilburne."[35] "No man," wrote Edwards, prophetically, "knows where these sectaries will stop or stay, or what principles they will keep."[36]

What cannot be stressed too greatly, and what the foes of sectarianism never ceased stressing, was that all these terrible, anarchic forces that threatened the peace of England would be the consequence of nothing more nor less than, in Walwyn's words, "the giving and hearing and debating of reason."[37] It is why

Locke would have to compose not just *A Letter concerning Toleration,* but also a lengthy and comprehensive *Essay concerning Human Understanding.* There he would need to argue, among many other things, that a due allowance for rational self-assertion was not inherently destructive of social order. The following chapter will show how the specific doctrines Locke developed in the *Essay* served to answer this stark ideological requirement.

It was a dilemma implicit in the Protestant program per se. In awakening the English mind, the Puritan movement, however unwittingly, ushered in if not an age of reason, at least an age of personal confrontation with scriptural, spiritual, and temporal authority. By their very example, the founders of Protestantism imbued faith-filled, reasoning individuals everywhere with the epistemological self-confidence to question all things — and to demand satisfactory answers. Conrad Russell put it well when he wrote, "In this, Puritans were facing a dilemma which had faced all Protestants since the Reformation." The dilemma was this: "Protestants had rejected the authority of the Pope on grounds of truth; and in so doing, they did not want to destroy the unity of the church: . . . Yet, as they rejected authority on grounds of truth, they created an opening for those of their followers who did not agree with them to do the same."

What was good for Calvin and Cartright would be good for Hooker, or Perkins, or Walwyn, or (and I shall come to him shortly), Winstanley. As John Saltmarsh stoically advised, "All the same arguments which had justified the Presbyterians in resisting the authority of the bishops could be used to justify the Independents in resisting the authority of the Presbyterians."[38] And so on and so forth. As the army chaplain William Dell advised, he "who fears God is free from all other fear, he fears not men of high degrees." Ultimately, wrote one radical, "we have chosen the Lord God Almighty to be our King and protector." Such men had little need for masters.

The bonds not only of civil society, but of *patriarchal* society hung in the balance. Thus, in the fate-filled summer of 1647, just weeks before the convening of the army council at St. Mary's Church in Putney, a pamphleteer would lament the breakdown of authority generally. "The nobility and gentry had lost not only 'the power and command they formerly held over their tenants, but also the respect of all,' no man in these days valuing his lord of whom he holds his lands (his free rent being paid) more than another man, scarce anything at all."[39]

What Edward Countryman would say of America's War of Independence applies to England's seventeenth-century struggle for independence as well, to wit: "During the Revolution . . . people who had long enjoyed less freedom began asserting a claim to equal rights with people who had long enjoyed more."[40] The fundamental freedom Englishmen demanded was *epistemological* — it was the freedom to employ one's own mental energies, to come to one's own truth, and not to be subject to another's beliefs. For the plain believer, the basic freedom was the freedom to think, which, in reality, was the freedom to seek and to find.

Central to the Protestant experience was the notion of the inner light that burned brightly within the breast of the true believer. "All Protestants," writes Hill, "had emphasized that religion must be based on inner conviction." Ultimately, perhaps inevitably, it had to end in antinomianism, which Hill describes as "a democratization of the Calvinist doctrine of election, a logical extension of Protestant individualism." As William Penn caustically observed years afterward: "Where once nothing was examined, nothing went unexamined. Every thought must come to judgment, and the rise and tendency of it be well approved before they allow it any room in their minds."[41]

Throughout the 1640s and 1650s radical sectaries proliferated in rapid succession. There were Seekers and Ranters, Muggletonians and Grindletonians, Quakers and Diggers, Anabaptists and Fifth Monarchists, and more. The inner light seemed to shine everywhere, casting dark, ominous shadows across the social landscape. Under its auspices radicals could find grounds for: (1) abolishing the Sabbath and tithes, since "ministers [were] antichristian and of no longer any use, now [that] Christ himself descends into the hearts of his saints"; (2) seeing "magistrates as useless now that christ himself is in purity of spirit come amongst us and hath erected the kingdom of saints upon the earth"; (3) casting "the Bible, as beggarly rudiments, milk for babes, for now Christ is in glory amongst us and imparts a fuller measure of his spirit to his saints than the Bible can afford."[42] The significance, even the possibility, of sin itself was called into question. On Edwards's testimony, we learn that some sectaries taught that men cannot sin, but if they do, "Christ sins in them" and "that God is in our flesh as much as in Christ's flesh." This being so then, sin aside, "all shall be saved at last."

What cannot be emphasized too greatly is that such socially disruptive notions as these flowed from the deepest of metaphysical ("naturall" and "eternall") postulates. The basic doctrine of materialism, for example, was materially wrapped up in sectarian belief. The Leveller, Walwyn, and the Digger, Winstanley, along with Quakers and Ranters skeptically challenged the notion of eternal punishment. Walwyn was said to believe that "hell was nothing but the bad conscience of evil men in this life." Winstanley doubted that there was a heaven or hell. The social threat posed by such sublime doctrines should not be discounted. As Hill concludes: "Plebian materialist skepticism and anti-clericalism could express themselves freely, and fused [*sic*] with theological antinomianism. The result was a rejection of clerical control of religious and moral life, and a rejection of the whole concept of sin, *the great deterrent.*"

Perhaps, as Robert Greene writing in *Selimus* supposed, "sin had been invented by priests and rulers to keep men in subjection."[43] But nothing would prove as socially disruptive as the fusion of materialism and pantheism—as the career of Gerrard Winstanley certainly suggests. From this metaphysical base, it would be possible to challenge the hierarchical structure of society, as well as the status of property and every title to it in the realm. With Winstanley, "God and Reason become one; the Christ within our hearts preached secularism."[44] "The whole creation," Winstanley taught, "is the clothing of God." But reason is the spiritual fabric that is meant to cover man. "If you subject your flesh to this mighty governor, the spirit of righteousness within yourselves, he will bring you into community with the whole globe." If God was everywhere and within everyone and all were equal one with another, then what basis was there for an inequality of status, privilege, and property?

The Levellers had not called for a leveling of men's estates but merely for a broad franchise and liberty of conscience and commerce. On the whole, they respected labor in one's calling, along with the rightful property that flowed from such honest industry.[45] For Winstanley and all those who fashioned themselves "True Levellers," the world and every acre of property in England could be turned upside down. God and reason advised the act, as Winstanley writes:

> In the beginning of time the great creator, Reason, made the earth to be a common treasury, to preserve beasts, birds, fishes and man, the lord that was to govern creation. . . . Not one word was spoken in the beginning that one branch of mankind should rule over another. . . . But . . . selfish imagination . . . did set up one man to teach and rule over another. And thereby . . . man was brought into bondage, and became a greater slave to such of his own kind than the beasts of the field were to him. And hereupon the earth . . . was hedged into enclosures by the teachers and rulers and the others were made . . . slaves.

Directly anticipating Rousseau, Winstanley taught that property was instituted by force and therefore held by force—"the power of the sword." Reason and the affirmation of men's natural rights had brought the Levellers to the principle of political democracy. The True Levellers affirmed the same but then employed these principles in the service of economic democracy. Winstanley continues: "The poorest man hath as true a title and just right to the land as the richest man. . . . True freedom lies in the free enjoyment of the earth. . . . If the common people have no more freedom in England but only to live among their elder brothers and work for them for hire, what freedom then have they in England more than we can have in Turkey or France?''[46] For Winstanley, property did not proceed from the fall of man; the advent of property produced the fall. As the seventeenth-century radical explained, ''When mankind began to quarrel about the earth, and some would have all and shut out others, forcing them to be servants; this was man's fall.''[47]

The threat posed by such ideas from the property holder's perspective was anything but theoretical. Like most Protestants, Winstanley was passionately devoted to the doctrine of works. As he wrote, ''It is action whereby the creation shines in glory. . . . So that this is the great battle of God Almighty, light fights against darkness, universal love fights against selfish power; life against death; true knowledge against imaginary thoughts.''[48] If property was artificial and against reason, then it could be invaded without injury. The seventeenth century saw its good economic years and its bad. Few were as harsh and punishing as the one that bore witness to regicide. Hardship was rife through the lower ranks in 1649. This distress, together with the doctrines preached by Winstanley, resulted in an effort, limited to be sure, to appropriate common holdings for the common good. At St. Georges Hill and in nine other locations in England, radical communities seized parcels of land — declaring, in effect, a communal right of enclosure that superseded political grants and common custom. Radical pamphleteers spoke out in support of the effort. As the author of *The Light Shining in Buckinghampshire* demanded, ''All men being alike privileged by birth, so all men were to enjoy the creatures alike without property one more than the other.'' Another well-circulated piece, *Tyrancoprit Discovered,* published in the Netherlands in August 1649, likewise denounced the ''rich thieves'' and called upon the nation to ''give unto every man with discretion so near as may be an equal share of earthly goods.''

The stark threat posed by these desperate men and their dangerous ideas would not soon be forgotten. The deepest danger, however, did not merely emanate from the attack on property. It resulted from the breakdown of authority and discipline that epistemological independence had invited. Citing Francis Osborne's worry in 1656, Hill appropriately concludes: ''Once implicit faith in the creed authoritatively established by a state church was abandoned, then 'the unbiassed rabble . . . emancipated out of the fetters their former creed confined them to,' would question the existence of heaven and hell no less than the Divine Right of Kings of which the Puritan clergy had taught them to be skeptical.''[49]

Once the questioning commenced, once the rule of reason (or the more generic ''inner light'') was epistemologically enshrined and man made the measure of truth and righteousness, every structure supporting or defining civil society could be denounced and undone. In the end, only force would hold society together—until, that is, the mechanisms of social control and conformity could, once more, be implanted in the minds of men.

It is not surprising that Cromwell, the parliamentarian, should reach the same conclusion as Filmer, the arch royalist—or that the latter would preach and the former practice suppression. At Putney, Henry Ireton (Cromwell's son-in-law) rebuked the Leveller rank and file of the army. Among his great concerns was the protection of property. "To destroy the principle of property," he stated, "is a thinge evill in ittself and scandalous to the world." The Levellers had not proposed anything of the sort; they merely wanted a broadening of the franchise. One Colonel Rainborough protested immediately. Couldn't men be expected to abide by the fundamental commandment, "Thou shalt not steal"? Ireton would not be so trusting; for if power flowed from property, as all could agree, property could as easily flow from power. "Is itt by the right of nature that all the people should have right to Elections? If you will hold forth that as your ground, then I thinke you must deny all property too," Ireton demanded.[50] What earthly power could prevent the poor and lowborn from seizing, by political act, every title of land in the realm?

Sir Robert Filmer, no Parliament man, was even more contemptuous of the populist paradigm. The precepts of equality and natural liberty, he reasoned, had to end in anarchy. To avoid the dreaded monarchy, Filmer feared, "we shall run into the liberty of having as many kings as there be men in the world . . . [and in truth] every man would, notwithstanding his political compact, be left with natural liberty, which is the mischief the pleaders for natural liberty do pretend they would must avoid."[51]

Cromwell found the answer to the dilemma in successive bouts of repression. Pride's Purge rid Parliament of recalcitrant MPs. Mutinous army troops, under Leveller direction, were suppressed at Burford churchyard, also in 1649. The Rump would see to the abolition of the Lords and monarchy alike. Parliament itself would be dissolved by 1655, and England placed under the control of eleven army major-generals—with Cromwell as autocratic Lord Protector.

Restoration and Repression

At any rate, the Commonwealth went and the Stuart monarchy by 1660 was happily restored. The people of England rejoiced. Force was not needed, but in the ensuing years, a new campaign of repression descended upon the land. It would be in the context of that campaign that a resistance movement would arise, ultimately pitting the ideology of Locke against the divine right doctrine of

Filmer.[52] On one level, the issue concerned "the True, Original, Extent and End of Civil Government." In a deeper sense, however, the issue under debate concerned the character of reason and the reasonableness of man. On this question, Locke would share the Levellers' optimistic view of human nature, grounding a democratic ideal "in their faith in the dignity and worth of the individual."[53]

The restored church and Parliament would be far less tolerant and trusting. The Clarendon Code (consisting of the Corporation Act, 1661; the Act of Uniformity, 1662; the Conventicle Act, 1664; and the Five Mile Act, 1665) proceeded, generally, from the view that dissenting Englishmen — those taking an independent course — would take every "opportunity to distil the poisonous principles of schism and rebellion into the hearts of his majesty's subjects, to the great danger of the church and kingdom." By these combined acts, those who would not take oaths of allegiance and supremacy, forswear the unlawfulness "upon any pretence whatsoever . . . [of] tak[ing] up arms against the king," and accept, under oath, "the sacrament of the Lord's Supper according to the rites of the Church of England" were virtually barred from central and local office.

Such a person could not become, as the Act of Uniformity declared, "dean, canon, and prebendary, master, fellow chaplain [or] tutor at any college, hall, house of learning or hospital . . . public professor or reader at the universities . . . schoolmaster [at] any public or private school . . . parson, vicar, curate, lecturer . . . [or] schoolmaster."[54] Those who failed to conform, those who would stand in dissent, could carry on their business, and business opportunities in the teeming cities were expanding. But they would remain outside the bounds of clerical and political affairs. Many who were Puritans during the Interregnum would escape the Dissenters' fate, joining Charles II in the Church of England at the Restoration.

The view of human nature that would prevail in the Church of England and Cavalier Parliament was pessimistic and contemptuous in the extreme. What developed in the 1660s and intensified during the following decade was a willful political campaign against dissent, as such. Enforcement of the penal statutes, particularly the Act of Uniformity, would cost more than one thousand clergymen their livings. The keepers of conventicles were frequently fined and often forfeited their property.

Nowhere is the venomous campaign of persecution more hotly in evidence than in Samuel Parker's *Discourse of Ecclesiastical Polity* (1669).[55] Parker, chaplain to Archbishop Sheldon, later elevated to the Bishopric of Oxford, issued nothing less than, in Ashcraft's words, "a declaration of war against all religious dissidents. . . . The fundamental assumption underlying the vehemence and severity of Parker's language was that opponents of the absolute authority of the king in matters of Church and State were, quite simply, not rational beings. The object therefore was to 'silence them,' not to reason with them.''[56] Astute to the fundamental and epistemological basis of social tumult, Parker divided the world into two intractable camps. The one consisted of those who supported monarchy and regarded the king as "vested with an absolute and uncontrollable power." The other comprised souls who regarded their own wills as sovereign masters. Individual conscience and reasonable inquiry were but presumptuous invasions of the monarch's absolute authority. "Everything any man has a mind to is his conscience," wrote Parker, "and murder, treason, rebellion plead its authority." No questioning of authority could be tolerated. For if a single exception was allowed an endless train of appeals for reform would follow. "In a word," writes Ashcraft, summarizing Parker's position, "if one law falls, they all fall. Stripped of all the colorful metaphors that surrounded it, this was the gist of Parker's argument."[57]

By their nature, humans were anything but rational and peaceful, much less capable of being entrusted with political power. By Parker's estimate, "humanity is virtually devoid of reason." Dissenters were all "willful fanatics, whose religion flowed from and preyed upon the lusts, passions, and ignorance of individuals." They were all "enthusiasts," inspired souls driven by "mysterious, superstitious beliefs." Quakers, Fifth Monarchists, Baptists, Independents, and Presbyterians could all be "lumped together with any Christian who claimed to have seen a vision or a miracle."[58]

In defense of Nonconformity, but in support of reason and human dignity as well, a number of Independents entered the ideological lists. John Owen most prominently, along with Robert Ferguson, John Humfrey, and Richard Baxter, placed various pamphlets in circulation. The titles alone attest to the critical role reason would play in the course of Restoration combat. There is Ferguson's *The Interest of Reason in Religion* and *A Sober Enquiry into the Nature, Measure and Principle of Moral Virtue*. A group of ten Nonconformist ministers (including Baxter) pleaded *The Judgment of Nonconformists of the Interest of Reason in Matters of Religion*. Of their efforts Ashcraft writes, "The Dissenters proposed to distinguish themselves by employing the standard of reason as the measure of their Christian beliefs, and by wielding it as a critical weapon against the ritualistic practices of Catholicism or the Anglican church or the imaginative delusions of the sectaries."[59]

By the mid-1670s the Nonconformists had found a stalwart champion in one of the leading political figures of the age, Anthony Ashley Cooper—"the most important opposition politician in Restoration England." At his side for a decade already and intimately involved in his political activities was John Locke. Ashcraft appropriately argues that "what we have come to recognize as the impressive intellectual contribution made by Locke to our cultural heritage, arose out of

the political turmoil that surrounded him as . . . [Shaftesbury's] trusted adviser.
. . . As a defense against popery, arbitrary power, and tyranny, and as the means
for insuring the advancement of trade and the protection of civil liberties, toleration was the keystone of Shaftesbury's policy.'' Locke's epistemological treatise,
for very practical political purposes, necessarily had to address "a whole complex of issues that the debate over toleration provoked by Samuel Parker's *Discourse of Ecclesiastical Polity.*''[60]

The Latitudinarian Anglicans

What Ashcraft did not examine in his *Revolutionary Politics,* however, was
the influence of another important ideological movement on the development of
Locke's philosophic thought. This was the movement situated for the most part
within the established church and known as latitudinarianism. Herein lies yet another possible context in which to situate and better comprehend the thought of
John Locke. In the remainder of this chapter I want to examine the relevance of
latitudinarianism for Locke's ideological project—in the broader context of the
perceived threat posed by religious disunity and sectarian antinomianism to the
peace of the realm.

At the outset it should be said that scholars are only now beginning to come to
terms with the seventeenth-century "latitude-men," and considerable uncertainties about the "movement" remain to be cleared away (e.g., Who fits in? Who
doesn't? What should qualify one for membership?).[61] Against the rational, scientific, and secular emphasis given the movement by Jacob in her important and
influential examination of *The Newtonians and the English Revolution* (1976),
recent studies have focused on the divinity of the latitudinarian divines and on
their deeper commitment to a traditional and highly structured past. Nevertheless, much light concerning the real-life aims and aspirations of this prolific and
influential segment of Restoration society has already been shed; and it explains
much about Locke's own social and intellectual purposes.

Latitudinarianism would bring together a number of intellectual developments, including the new mechanical philosophy of the Royal Society, with its
emphasis on empiricism and its experimental approach to the study of (God's)
nature, and the rational theology most closely associated with the Cambridge
Platonists, Benjamin Whichcote (1609–1683), Ralph Cudworth (1617–1688),
Henry More (1614–1687), and John Smith (1618–1652). Leading latitudinarians, in fact, enjoyed membership in the Royal Society and at some time studied,
taught, preached, or held office at the colleges of Cambridge. By the turn of the

eighteenth century the movement could be described, in the words of John Gascoigne, as "Newtonian natural theology."[62]

It is clear that latitudinarians may be generally grouped around the proposition
of comprehension—the unfulfilled effort to bring a larger section of dissent into
the national church. Not every Anglican cleric concurred with the views of Samuel Parker and the Laudian High Church party—much of which had been cast
into exile with Charles II. A number of moderate divines were far more conciliatory toward dissent, seeking a comprehensive worship organized around a few,
essential points of Christian worship. These were the latitudinarians. Their history can be briefly traced.

Archbishop James Usher had put forth a plan for a moderate episcopacy, designed to accommodate dissent years earlier. It is this plan that attracted much
interest among the latitudinarians. As early as the 1650s, Robert Boyle and others
of his stamp hoped for "a church settlement based upon Archbishop James Usher's schemes for moderate episcopacy."[63] At the Restoration leading Dissenters,
including Richard Baxter (1615–1691), who had discussed the plan with Usher
in 1655, joined the effort to find a formula for comprehension. He entered ne-
gotiations with Bishop Wilkins (and later, Tillotson) to work out a moderate religious comprehension, while conferring with such leading Independent ministers as John Owen on behalf of a national church.[64]

The efforts proved wholly unfruitful. Dissent was destined to persist, and the
perceived threat it posed had to be addressed. Many of the leading latitudinarian
churchmen, such as John Wilkins, John Tillotson, Simon Patrick, and Edward
Fowler, along with such esteemed Royal Society fellows as Robert Boyle, John
Evelyn, and John Wallis, had begun their Interregnum careers as Puritans. However, in the proliferation of pantheistic, materialist, and antinomian doctrines advanced by so many uncensored sectaries, and in the call for leveling and other
radical social reforms to which those doctrines led, these moderates easily perceived a dire social threat. In defense of true religion and civil order they joined
the Anglican communion at the Restoration and, all efforts at comprehension
aside, proceeded to work out a cosmological worldview designed to smash the
debased doctrines that had gained currency during the Interregnum.[65]

The latitudinarian clerics and their lay colleagues, the famed virtuosi of the
Royal Society, were thus faced not just with a competing High Church party that
wished to rule England through suppression and intolerance, but with a century's
worth of dissension and instability as well. If social and political legitimacy were
ever to be restored and lasting peace achieved, sectarian excess and the doctrines
that informed it (materialism, atheism, socinianism, skepticism, pantheism, etc.)
would also have to be decisively defeated. What the latitudinarians would need,

and they knew it, was nothing less than an encompassing worldview: a theory of God and nature, of man and society that could withstand all intellectual and ideological challenge. The urgent, *practical* need, in short, was for deep philosophic synthesis and coherence.[66]

Jacob and Jacob provide a good example of how the new science could serve the cause of Anglican apologetics. Thus, its scientific value aside, Boyle's "corpuscular theory" was designed to refute the materialism of Descartes, Hobbes, and the radicals, which, Boyle felt, could easily end in a rejection of all spiritual forces (including God's power over the created universe). The atomism of Epicurus, reworked to answer Christian needs, would thus allow for a nonmaterial plenum, filled by God's spirit and providential design.[67]

The science of the Royal Society aside, the seat of latitudinarianism resided in the Church of England. However moderate and accommodating toward dissent the moderate divines might appear, they belonged to the established ecclesiastical and political order. Accordingly, they held fast to the doctrines of nonresistance and passive obedience and accepted the Revolution of 1688 only after it had been sealed and settled. As Bishop Burnet explained, "The doctrines of passive obedience and non-resistance had been carried so far, and preached so much, that clergymen either could not all on the sudden get out of that entanglement, into which they had by long thinking and speaking all one way involved themselves, or they were ashamed to make so quick a turn."[68]

For that reason alone it might appear questionable to link Locke to the latitudinarian divines. The latitudinarians formed no part of Shaftesbury's exclusion movement; Locke was an active participant in that movement from its inception—leaving England with the discovery of the Rye House Plot in 1683 and actively supporting the radical community in exile until the Revolution of 1688.[69] Margaret Jacob points to another important distinction between Locke and the latitudinarians. Locke's political theory hinges on a social contract and the ceding of certain powers to government that originally inhere in the contracting parties. However,

> Churchmen avoided any justification of the Revolution that rested on contract theory. To their minds the theories of Locke and the other contractualists disregarded the necessity of God's active participation in the affairs of men. . . . On the existence of a divine plan in history rested the entire fabric of latitudinarian natural religion. . . . Just as the providence of God had played a crucial role in latitudinarian thinking during the Restoration, the same providence provided a necessary and suitable explanation for the Revolution.[70]

We might wonder then if it is either useful or necessary to read Locke in the context of latitudinarian Anglicanism. I believe it is. But there are those who wonder if it is even possible to situate Locke alongside a moderate Anglican establishment.

Having decisively tied Locke to Lord Shaftesbury's exclusion movement and the radical cause in general, Ashcraft has recently cautioned against a too-easy identification of Locke and latitudinarianism. To the extent that the latitudinarians did work for the cause of comprehension, it was for reasons and in a fashion quite foreign to Locke's ideological project. Central to Ashcraft's argument is the distinction between ecclesiastical comprehension (something favored by the latitudinarians) and a firm religious toleration (something favored mainly by the Nonconformists and stalwartly defended by Locke in *A Letter concerning Toleration* [1689]).[71]

Preoccupied "with the dimensions of political conflict" in Restoration England, Ashcraft argues that those who view the latitudinarians as occupying some middle ground between High Church Anglicans and the Nonconformists have failed to "appreciate what the political struggle over the most important problem—toleration of religious dissent—in Restoration England was all about." Latitudinarianism, then, "is not a moderate middle ground between contending extremes, it is, rather, *part* of one of the extremes." It belongs to the essentially *intolerant* and persecutory Church of England.[72] For Ashcraft, the question of religious toleration was the pivotal ideological question of the day. If such latitudinarian clerics as Stillingfleet, Patrick, Fowler, Joseph Glanvill, and Wilkins and Tillotson sought to foster comprehension and rational theology in English society and politics, Ashcraft argues, this did not signal any taste for toleration toward dissent.[73]

Although the Revolution of 1688 would bring the latitudinarian wing of Anglicanism to the pinnacle of power within the church, it would not usher in a period of liberal enlightenment. The terms of the Toleration Act of 1689 signified but a legal indulgence granting parliamentary exemption from the persecuting statutes (which remained in force). It was anything but a "principled recognition of a 'right' to religious liberty." Indeed, James II's indulgence of 1687, which was defeated by the Glorious Revolution, represented a far more enlightened approach to toleration, since it suspended all penal laws for Dissenters and Roman Catholics alike.[74]

From the "movement's" earliest days, the latitudinarians would confront a suspicious and hostile High Church party and Anglican squirearchy.[75] The moderate divines repeatedly professed their devotion to the Anglican worship and episcopal authority.[76] In their sermons and books they often blasted the "Mischief" and "Unreasonableness" of religious dissent and the manifest dangers of allowing it to go unchecked. Such moderate divines as Glanvill, Patrick, Fowler, Stillingfleet, and Tillotson joined with Samuel Parker and Archbishop Sheldon in castigating the dissenting "enemies of our church and government." A fractured church had to end, as it had so recently ended, in a fractured society and then in chaos and ruin. Stillingfleet, Glanvill, and Tillotson all called for a sterner enforcement of the penal statutes against Nonconformity. With the Parkers of the church they agreed that the riotous passions of fallen man, if not checked by obedience to civil and ecclesiastical authority, would assure social disruption.[77] Ashcraft can thus conclude that the "latitudinarians, by stirring up animosities and hatred with their epithets and invectives directed against dissenters, often served as the shock troops of persecution in the war against nonconformity."[78]

It is true that the latitudinarians emphasized rational, as opposed to revealed, religion, to a greater extent than did their High Church brethren. But to the moderate Anglicans, rational religion proved the veracity of revealed religion, and both counseled a due obedience to ecclesiastical and political authority in matters that are "indifferent" to the believer and essential to the peace of the nation. If, as Tillotson urged, Protestants own a liberty "to judge for themselves in matters of religion," that liberty had to be confined to a "great submission and deference to our spiritual rulers and guides, whom God hath appointed in his church."[79]

As Ashcraft rightly explains, for the Nonconformists, such as Richard Baxter, John Owen, and Robert Ferguson, rational theology meant much more than "a general exhortation in favor of a positive role for reason in religion." It meant, above all, "a willingness to *rely* upon the judgment of the individual as a rational free agent."[80] In practical political terms, this resulted in the Nonconformists' strident plea for toleration, as against the latitudinarians' paramount insistence on uniformity. For this reason, Locke, England's leading exponent of religious individualism and toleration, should not be grouped with the latitudinarians, but with the English Dissenters.[81] As Ashcraft writes, "A cultural history approach that brackets political and social conflict in order to assume a homogeneous cultural consciousness . . . will never succeed in understanding the meaning of ideas for historical actors with a far more acute sense of the interrelatedness and structure of the social life-world and the significance of the struggle to realize group-defined practical objectives."[82]

Presumably, at the point that political conflict will be duly impressed into historiographical service the ties between Locke and the latitudinarians will be severed. And yet it will remain necessary to explain Locke's affinity not merely to the laymen and scientists of the Royal Society, such as Boyle and Newton, but to a number of outstanding latitudinarian clerics, as well—such as Isaac Barrow, whose death in 1677 left Locke mourning the loss of "a very dear friend," and

John Tillotson, of whose death in 1694 Locke complained: "There is now scarcely any-body I can consult about doubtful points of divinity. I have, indeed, been robbed, to my great injury and sorrow, of a friend . . . to whom I was endeared by the intercourse of many years."[83] A strange way for Locke to speak of his ideological foes?

Ashcraft has built a compelling case, but he left behind a piercing irony. It has been his chief methodological contention that past works must be read in the context of the real-life alliances and allegiances to which their authors devoted themselves and the audiences to whom they hoped to appeal. The biographical fact is that Locke was both attached and devoted to some important latitudinarian leaders and to several of their projects. These associations need to be assessed, as well, and their bearing on Locke's social thought duly considered, if an adequate appreciation of Locke's work is to be had.

After 1660 and under the direction of a hostile High Church a good number of those who were derisively referred to as "latitude-men" were driven from Cambridge and relocated to London.[84] Many of these men, including John Tillotson, Simon Patrick, John Wilkins, Benjamin Whichcote, and John Mapletoft, would take up positions in the pulpits of London. In the early 1670s an intellectual circle formed around John Wilkins. Members of that circle included such Church of England divines as Whichcote, Patrick, Tillotson, Stillingfleet, and Mapletoft, along with sympathetic laymen such as the Socinian Thomas Firmin and John Locke, who belonged "to the Latitudinarian wing of the Church of England."[85] Locke grew particularly close to John Tillotson (1630–1694), who would be named Archbishop of Canterbury by William III. Locke's secretive radical activities and exile during the 1680s would not place him in contact with his moderate church friends. But again in the 1690s old acquaintances were renewed. Von Leyden reports that Thomas Firmin, a mutual friend of Locke's and Tillotson's, was Locke's guest at the fateful meeting, in 1672, in which the project for an essay "on the understanding" was initially conceived.[86] By the 1690s, Spellman writes, "as Deism and atheism gained adherents among the upper classes and open debate over the nature of Christ both shocked and challenged the clerical community an apparently insensitive [Archbishop] Tillotson continued to cultivate his friendships with the likes of the heterodox Thomas Firmin and John Locke . . . present[ing a] clear target for non-juring critics."[87]

One further point bears emphasis. However vitriolic the sermons and tracts against dissent may have been, the quest for comprehension, for an encompassing national church built around a few essential Christian tenets, remained for the latitudinarians a work to be done. After 1688, Tillotson, Patrick, Stillingfleet, and Tenison were instrumental in drawing up a bill of comprehension, which they submitted to the Lords. A Tory-dominated Parliament would defeat the comprehension act, however, and only the weak indulgence contained in the Toleration Act of 1689 would result.[88]

Locke's acquaintance with the Cambridge Platonists is also worth noting. He kept up a correspondence with one of their number, Ralph Cudworth, becoming especially close to his daughter, Damaris Cudworth Masham, who had an active hand in propagating her father's ideas. Another Platonist, Benjamin Whichcote (to whom Tillotson was especially devoted) was inducted Vicar of St. Lawrence Jewry, London, in 1668. Locke's biographer reported that he "became a member of his congregation."[89] All ideological and philosophical dispositions aside, Locke, in the last twenty years of his life, devoted himself to the meaning and message of God's Scripture and its significance for human conduct. The latitudinarian influence on his theological inquiries is manifest. Commenting to the Reverend Richard King in 1703 on his researches concerning "the parts of morality," Locke wrote, "The sermons of Dr. Barrow, Archbishop Tillotson and Dr. Whichcote are masterpieces in this kind."[90]

Locke's relationship to the virtuosi of the Royal Society, of which he was a fellow, is even more widely acknowledged. He became particularly close to Robert Boyle (1627–1691), a leading exponent of the new mechanical philosophy and a lay latitudinarian. Upon Boyle's death, Locke was designated an executor of his estate and fulfilled a promise to his "chief scientific mentor" when, in 1692, he saw to the publication of Boyle's *History of the Air*. The manuscript, left to Locke in fragmentary form, was edited and largely rewritten by Locke himself.

Locke also enjoyed a friendship and lengthy correspondence with another renowned scientist and lay latitudinarian, Sir Isaac Newton (1642–1727). Papers recording one of Boyle's prized projects, an effort to make gold by combining red earth and mercury, were entrusted to but two fellow scientists in England: Locke and Newton.[91] Newton, despite a Socinian bent, can be linked to the latitudinarians through the efforts of such younger churchmen and Boyle lecturers as Richard Bentley, William Whiston, and William Derham. It was their express aim to enlist Newtonian natural philosophy in the service of Anglicanism and against the false doctrines of pantheists, atheists, and even the more mystical divine right theories preached by the High Church. It was this younger generation that Jacob credits with delivering "the first public presentation of latitudinarian natural religion based on Newtonian principles."[92]

How are we to account for Locke's latitudinarian associations? We do so by grasping not just what divided them, ideologically, but what united them in common cause. Locke's view of toleration was indeed more advanced than the view of the latitudinarian clerics. They held firm to the belief that religious uniformity held the key to social tranquillity. Locke, from an early point, came to appreciate that the enforcement of religious uniformity was more the cause than the cure of social and political unrest. And although Locke and the latitudinarians could disagree on many other important matters (not the least being the principle of resistance, generally, and resistance to two Stuart kings, specifically — long before 1688), his association and affection for those moderate Anglicans are grounded in a number of mutual intellectual commitments.

Despite the political problem of effecting a comprehensive reformation of the Anglican Church, the latitudinarians steadfastly believed "that Christians should unite on the broad common ground of essentials in religion, while agreeing to differ over non-essentials; they all believed that reason could be relied upon to determine what was and what was not essential."[93] This was precisely the theme of *The Reasonableness of Christianity*. Published in 1695, one year after his dear friend Tillotson's death, this book contains Locke's contribution to a wide range of theological questions that the latitudinarians had had to ponder. They concerned the meaning of Adam's fall and the message of the Messiah's great redemptive act. What did a Christian have to believe, what acts did he or she have to perform to be welcomed into the Christian cum Anglican communion?

On the question of comprehension, specifically, Locke urges that there is but one qualifying test for inclusion in the Protestant, or Anglican, communion: a belief in Jesus Christ, the Messiah sent by God to redeem the sins of man since the fall of Adam. "For that this is the sole doctrine pressed and required to be believed in the whole tenor of Our Savior's and his apostles preaching," Locke claims to have shown through his exegesis of Scripture. Locke challenges his detractors to "shew, that there was any other doctrine, upon their assent to which, or disbelief of it, men were pronounced believers or unbelievers; and accordingly received into the Church of Christ, as members of his Body. . . . This was the only gospel-article of faith which was preached to them."[94] But for Locke, as for the latitudinarians, this sole article of faith was pregnant with a pair of new corollaries: a "law of faith" and a "law of works." Calvinist theology, in issuing its saints with an irresistible faith-imbued grace, had issued a catalog of religious confusions and an orgy of antinomian bedlam. The moderate Anglicans asserted that faith alone was insufficient for redemption. One had to show express faith in practical, reformed, and self-willed action. Locke phrased it like this:

> Though the devils believed [they could be saved by grace, or faith, alone], yet they could not be saved by the covenant of grace; because they performed not the other condition required in it, altogether as necessary to be performed as this of believing: and that is repen-

tance. Repentance is as absolute a condition of the covenant of grace as faith; and as necessary to be performed as that.[95]

Ingeniously, Locke reasons that if there were "no law of works," there could be no "law of faith." Men would not need the grace that faith gives to redeem them if there were no law to violate and so no sins for which to atone; it is dereliction from one's duty to perform the necessary works that beget sin and hence faith in the possibility of grace and redemption. With the latitudinarians, Locke emphasized the "whole duty of man," which meant doing good works as a constant pattern of life. Locke finds the difference between faith and works to be only this: "The law of works makes no allowance for failing on any occasion. Those that obey are righteous; those that in any part disobey, are unrighteous, and must not expect life, the reward of righteousness. But by the law of faith, faith is allowed to supply the defect of full obedience; and so the believers are admitted to . . . immortality, as if they were righteous."[96]

Thus in their mutual desire for a moderate toleration for dissenting articles of religion and their common emphasis on the need to conform to God's moral law, Locke and the latitudinarians shared much common ground. The difference between comprehension and toleration aside, both he and they worked to keep Christianity itself alive. If the moderate Anglicans felt only religious uniformity (in allowing for the inculcation of Christian duties in the schools and churches of the whole nation) could conduce to civil order, and Locke (with the Dissenters) pleaded that a lawful toleration of private faith and belief would more surely accomplish that very end, he and they held fast to the belief that Christianity itself was necessary for social peace. Only a nation committed to Christian piety, to a saving faith and the steady performance of good works, could endure. Religious and moral degeneracy were of a piece, and no nation could avoid their awful effects. Locke would build his philosophical edifice on a foundation of reason and natural law. But nothing within natural law can disparage the authenticity of the higher law—i.e., God's revealed word. Locke will have no truck with those who would make Jesus Christ "nothing but the restorer and preacher of pure natural religion; thereby doing violence to the whole tenor of the New Testament." The word of God, as passed on by the Apostles, is for "the instruction of the illiterate bulk of mankind, in the way to salvation."[97]

For Locke and for the latitudinarians, reason was a God-given resource designed to be used. But at the fall it was made a frail and enfeebled tool. "The knowledge of morality by mere natural light," as Locke says and the moderate Anglicans had to agree, "makes but a slow progress, and little advance in the world." This is due to "men's necessities, passions, vices, and mistaken interests, which turn their thoughts another way.''[98] The "strains" of moral reasoning, "the greatest part of mankind have neither leisure to weigh, nor, for want of education and use, skill to judge of.''[99] It was necessary that a "King and lawmaker" be sent to "tell them their duties, and require their obedience." This Jesus did and mankind is obliged to obey.[100] This represented Locke's response to the Deists who threatened England's faith and, therefore, its peace. With Ashcraft, we can pit the Dissenters' enthusiasm for toleration against the moderate Anglicans' insistence on religious union and episcopal authority. On this point, as on innumerable others, Locke stands with the Dissenters. But there were other currents that divided the intellectual waters of Restoration England. Locke could easily attach himself to a latitudinarian program designed to foster the faith of a population that was being led, either by its own infamous apathy or the dangerous doctrines of competing faiths, away from piety and peace.

As we have already seen, in their emphasis on moral conduct, on the need for faith *and* works, Locke and the latitudinarians were defending against two disquieting contenders for the people's religious sympathies. While the predestinarian theology of Calvinism posted a wholly irresistible grace for the saint but irresistible reprobation for the bulk of humanity, Roman Catholicism would pardon the sins of the worst sinner for a mere ceremonial act of contrition. As Spellman has cryptically observed, "While the Dissenter and Catholic complacently put their trust in the promise of unmerited free grace and the idle show of ceremony respectively, the chief responsibility of the Anglican was *'to govern within,'* and not to make Laws for the World without us.''[101] Ostensibly, the issue was repentance, for Christians, "the business of our whole lives." But with great ease a religious discussion over the requirements of Christian salvation was transformed into a rigorous inquiry into the character of moral (i.e., Christian) conduct. It was but a brief leap to the doorstep of moral philosophy.

If the clash over religious doctrine could drive Restoration England into the study of moral philosophy, it could also open up all the complexities of epistemological inquiry. Questions abounded in this, perhaps, the most intellectually inquisitive and contentious of epochs. Nearly any question that could be thought, could be put: How do we know there is a God, a creator? How can we authenticate the authority of Scripture or comprehend its claims? How can we grasp and demonstrate the duties demanded by God of his highest creation? As Locke himself explained, the idea for writing his *Essay* "on the understanding" arose when a group of acquaintances gathered to discuss "a subject very remote from this [i.e., the theory of knowledge], found themselves quickly at a stand, by the difficulties that arose on every side." Locke's friend James Tyrrell, present at the gathering in Locke's chambers, recorded on a margin note of his copy of the *Es-*

say that the difficulties arose in the course of a discussion about "the principles of morality and revealed religion." Locke continues: "After we had a while puzzled ourselves, without coming any near a resolution of those doubts which perplexed us, it came into my thoughts that we took a wrong course; and that before we set ourselves upon inquiries of that nature, it was necessary to examine our own abilities, and see what objects our understandings were or were not fitted to deal."[102]

The question of the latitudinarian lineage of Locke's epistemological thought can be legitimately raised. To a considerable degree, Locke's theory of knowledge was born of the theological quandaries into which moderate Anglican clerics were drawn in their continuing contest with religious heterodoxy and apathetic impiety. Here, again, Locke and the latitudinarians were besieged on all sides. The all-too-easy theological certainties propounded by, first, the Papists in Rome and then the Enthusiasts whose pilgrimage began in Geneva, stood at one side; while the skeptical uncertainties and denials of sundry Deists and atheists stood at the other. Looking backward there appeared the specter of intolerance and repression, faith and force; looking forward there appeared the prospect of anarchy and chaos. The latitudinarian way was the via media (since at least the days of Richard Hooker). There had to be a middle ground between Rome and Geneva, between blind trust and blind faith, and between absolute certainty and absolute ignorance; for God had not created man without sense or reason.[103]

If Locke and the latitudinarians would proclaim the veracity of reason, neither he nor they would place illimitable confidence in its powers. Human understanding is frail, and there is much that is "above" reason—and therefore unnecessary to contest. Reason could be poetically viewed as "the candle of the lord," a light that shines, but not all that brightly. As Rogers has written, that favorite illusion "was an indication not only that the mind of man could reach truth, but also, since a candle gives little illumination, that the truths reached are likely to be limited."[104] Chillingworth and his colleagues at Great Tew employed a moderate skepticism, what Rogers appropriately calls an "argument from Ignorance," to resist the claims of infallibility that emanated either from Rome or the Genevan-minded zealots and enthusiasts dangerously situated closer to home. Oxford and Cambridge latitudinarians, such as Chillingworth, Hales, Taylor, Whichcote, More, Glanvill, and Stillingfleet, employed "the argument from ignorance" to defend moderate toleration of uninjurious dissent against an inirenic intolerance and haughty taste for oppression. Locke borrowed heavily, yet built originally upon this tradition. With Whichcote, Locke would agree: "Our Fallibility and the Shortness of our Knowledge should make us peaceable and gentle: because I *may* be Mistaken. I *must* not be dogmatical and . . . imperious. I *will* not break the certain Laws of Charity, for a doubtful Doctrine or of uncertain Truth."[105]

Locke would issue a sustained defense of reason in human affairs. Locke's monumental essay "on the understanding" is in good measure a latitudinarian-like assault on "enthusiasm" and on the wild and irreligious ideas propounded by so many radical sectaries. Distinguishing those statements that are "above, contrary, and according to reason,"[106] Locke averred only those propositions that could be demonstrated. All others must be either false or uncertain. If even the most devout of divines failed to defend a proposition on the basis of sensory experience or rational arguments reducible to it, he would have no basis for affirming it, let alone imposing it on those who differed with him. For Locke, skepticism, far from being the breeding ground for despair and consternation, constituted an appeal for quiet contentment, tolerance, and peace:

> If by this Enquiry into the Nature of the Understanding, I can discover the Powers thereof; how far they reach . . . I suppose it may be of use, to prevail with the busy Mind of Man, to be more cautious in meddling with things exceeding its Comprehension; . . . to sit down in a quiet Ignorance of those Things, which, upon Examination, are found to be beyond the reach of our Capacities. . . . If we can find out, how far the Understanding can extend its view . . . we may learn to content our selves with what is attainable by us in this State. . . . [For it is when] men, extend . . . their inquiries beyond their capacities, and let . . . their thoughts wander into those depths where they can find no sure footing . . . that they raise questions and multiply disputes, which never coming to any clear resolution, are proper only to continue and increase their doubts.[107]

But if Locke and the latitudinarians skeptically greeted the "Revealed" scriptural claims of so many popes and sectarian saints, they were far more confident in the power of reason to unlock the mysteries of nature (of God's natural creation). If men could not and need not agree on those things that were "above reason," perhaps they could be persuaded by the discoveries that were "according to reason." Knowledge was possible to man, and it could not only ameliorate his personal and social predicament, but point the way to an understanding of God's providential design. Thus latitudinarian and Lockean skepticism do not extend to all matters under heaven. Theirs is not a universal doubt. For his part, Locke tells us his business "is not to know all things, but those which concern our conduct." And with a full measure of optimism, he advises his reader: "If we can find out those measures, whereby a rational creature, put in that state in which man is in this world, may and ought to govern his opinions, and actions depending thereon, we need not to be troubled that some other things escape our knowledge."[108]

All this is most evident in their common preoccupation with the science of the Royal Society. The wondrous discoveries made in the fields of chemistry, physics, optics, agriculture, astronomy, and mathematics were verifiable and available to all who would but duplicate a published experiment or fiddle with an arithmetic formula. Knowledge was attainable; an inquisitive mind could fathom the once-dark mysteries of nature. But the new science could be put to theological purposes as well, countering the claims of religious enthusiasm and atheistic skepticism. The fanatical sects could not withstand the demand for empirical demonstration and rational inquiry. For, in the words of Thomas Sprat, author of *The History of the Royal Society*, "such spiritual Frenzies . . . can never stand long, before a clear, and a deep skill in Nature." The "inner light" might raise a claim for this or that doctrine in the mind of a true believer, but unless that believer could back his claim with evidence and argument, it remained gratuitous and arbitrary. Here was the answer to all the saints and the solution to all their socially divisive sins. "Sprat," Margaret Jacob concludes, "offers the moderation instilled by the pursuit of true experimental science as a force for political moderation." Reason, logically processing the material provided by the senses, could persuade; it would not need to compel. It could validate revealed religion, but just as importantly, it held out the promise of a natural religion.[109]

This impressive move was made possible by the acceptance of Plato's metaphysical postulate. As one leading latitudinarian and Cambridge student phrased it, "All this world below is but the image of the world above, and these corporeal things are but pictures (though pale indeed & dull), of things spiritual."[110] The Platonists of Cambridge, of course, were Christians, and their conception of the material universe was of a universe created and ruled by a divine and omnipotent creator. The study of nature—of God's work—was a crucial supplement to the study of Scripture—God's word.[111] Any interpretation of Scripture that contradicted the perceived or proven structure of nature could, therefore, be declared illusory and false. By the same token, any theory of nature that could lead to a denial of the deity would need to be swiftly countered by latitudinarian science (as in the researches of Boyle and Newton).

The new mechanical philosophy, with its reliance on reason and empiricism, promised to reveal not merely the nature of the natural world, but the providential plan of its creator and governor. By apprehending the principles that govern in nature, natural philosophy could discern the principles God intends to govern in human society. "The design and harmony in the material order, imposed by spiritual forces, provided a model or guide to show how social and political relations should work if Christians were to fulfill the providential plan."[112]

It will be fruitful to view the lessons the latitudinarians learned from the study of the material universe. Though Locke would take a significantly different route to moral and political philosophy, as we shall see, it will be instructive to see how his latitudinarian colleagues could employ the researches of natural philosophy to construct a grand cosmological synthesis—thus proclaiming God's providential plan for the organization of human affairs. For the scientifically minded latitudinarians, nature revealed a wondrous harmony, order, and regularity. Each constituent contained its own principles of motion, constantly revolving in its own path, but all worked together. This was the type of society the latitudinarians envisioned.[113] It would require a good measure of tolerance for the diversity of religious belief and practice, and freedom for the plain believer to righteously pursue his faith—and his calling.

It was a message ideally suited to the Nonconformist temperament, so imbued with the ethic of work, and one the latitudinarians eagerly delivered to the dissenting congregations of London.[114] In the doctrine of work (i.e., the useful employment of one's God-given talents and industry), the latitudinarians found not just the basis of social harmony (successful tradesmen when left to their labor are not likely to incite insurrection), but a universal principle found everywhere in nature: "Industry and work pervade nature and ensure its stability, and this the latitudinarians took for further proof of the validity of the work ethic. Similarly every plant, every animal, every planet has a place, and men, if they follow their callings, have a preordained and unalterable place in society." What's more, the new mechanical philosophy would furnish remarkable mechanical arts that could put generations of Englishmen to work.

God-fearing and productive, perhaps human nature, if left free to believe, would not turn villainous and wild (as the High Church opposition feared). Perhaps humans could be taught to distinguish between the moderate call for a "sober self-love" and that "fully developed possessive individualism . . . seen by modern historians in the writings of Locke and Hobbes. . . . Private interest . . . by the cultivation of socially useful virtues, [including] diligence in one's calling . . . [and] charity toward inferiors, [could conduce to] the public good."[115] Seeing so resplendent a design and order in nature, the latitudinarians dreamed of erecting a natural social order, i.e., a relatively free market economy (with Locke, they could rail against economic privilege and monopoly restraint).[116] Through a moderate reliance on reason and a due allowance for faith the nation could grow prosperous and strong, a prophecy that comported well with the providential plan the moderate Anglicans supported: the one that depicted English-men as God's chosen people, elected to consummate the Reformation and usher in a glorious millennium.[117]

Conclusion

Richard Ashcraft has urged that "latitudinarianism [and, by clear implica-tion, Locke's place in history] . . . will [not] be adequately conceptualized or accurately portrayed by historians until a prominent role is assigned to political conflict as an interpretive foundation of historiography, and the long-standing di-vorcement between intellectual and political history is finally ended."[118] But even if we are to accept "political conflict" as the grounds for organizing our conception of historical forces and contextually positioning political texts, it is necessary to acknowledge that history often records a concurrence of conflicts simultaneously dividing a given age. And it is often difficult to separate the moral, religious, or intellectual from the starkly political contests in which his-torical actors find themselves engaged. I agree with Ashcraft that the question of toleration and, more broadly, the allowance for religious dissent within a national state/church figured prominently in the political alignments of Restoration En-gland. But this was not the only bone of contention in those contentious times.

The seventeenth century marked the historical turning point of another, more enduring conflict, one that would take the West from the civilization of the Mid-dle Ages to the brink of modernity, from a stolid preoccupation with life ever-lasting to a fixation on a more temporal, if no less intractable, predicament. If we fix our attention on this larger conflict, part political, but, more acutely, cultural and philosophical, we can begin to appraise the logic of linking Locke to the lat-itudinarians. If he and they took up opposing sides on the questions of toleration or political resistance, they nevertheless stood side by side on some matters of considerable importance. The commitment to rational theology, for example, should not be minimized, for within this rising religious orientation there lay a declaration of epistemological independence that, in time, would free the reason-ing mind from its bondage to scriptural, ecclesiastical and, in due course, even political authority.

If Laudian and latitudinarian were joined at the political waist they neverthe-less were separated on the metaphysics of the Christian faith. The debates over toleration and resistance ultimately boiled down to two competing estimates of human nature and to a question of whether humans could be trusted with a mod-erate measure of ordered liberty. The Laudian High Church answered in the negative, believing that society could be saved only if individuals were bound and restrained in the use of their mental and moral energies. And so it demanded total submission to the spiritual and temporal powers that be. The moderates of the Low Church were somewhat more optimistic in their assessment of human nature, allowing a wider latitude for individual thought and action. It was a debate that pitted the cynicism of a Hobbes or a Calvin, who found in the bowels of humanity only unruly passions and everlasting enmity, against the optimism of a Cudworth, a Whichcote, or, in short order, a Locke, each of whom dared to trust in the power of reason to rule over human affairs.

The question of reason, i.e., the role it would play in human affairs, its capacity to discover the laws of nature (through rational and scientific inquiry), and ultimately to direct the will of individuals in accordance with natural—and moral—law was absolutely critical to the social, religious, and political disputes of the age. The prospect of toleration hinged on the outcome of that dispute. All pessimistic appraisals of fallen man's hapless condition notwithstanding, Locke and the latitudinarians saw at least the potential of reason to govern the course of human affairs. Their mutual devotion to this common longing alone is sufficient to affirm the historical and theoretical linkages between Locke and the moderate Anglican establishment. The proof, if I may say it, is in the pudding.

Locke, the radical revolutionary, published his resistance "tract," *The Two Treatises of Government,* anonymously and to a distressingly cool contemporary reception. But Locke, the contributor to a firm tradition of "*establishment*" discourse, steadily leaning on and often echoing the words and century-spanning work of prominent moderate church apologists and lay latitudinarians, enjoyed a remarkably enthusiastic reception for *An Essay concerning Human Understanding* and his very much related educational writings.[119]

3
The Philosophical Foundations
of Locke's Social Thought

John Locke, Lay Latitudinarian

The spread of literacy and learning, together with the lapse of censorship and the opportunities provided by an army that awarded rank to talent, did portend a New Model civilization, as Bacon had surmised it would. Many felt the rising spirit of independence and the release of human energy wrought by these historical forces would redound to the benefit of all England. What Bacon dared to imagine, Milton could see unfolding before his eyes. In the abolition of thought control and the outpouring of novel religious, economic, and political ideas he discerned "a nation not slow and dull, but of a quick, ingenious and piercing spirit, acute to invent, subtle and sinewy to discourse, not beneath the reach of any point the highest that human capacity can soar to. . . . Methinks I see in my mind a noble and puissant nation rousing herself like a strong man after sleep and shaking her invincible locks."[1]

What many prominent Anglican prelates and Tory squires saw in all this was the radical questioning of all legitimate authority and the sure and certain dissolution of civil order.[2] Those who still sought a sanction for economic liberty and religious toleration—Dissenters and moderate Anglicans alike—needed to show that these potent forces could be safely released and channeled into socially fruitful and benign human projects and that such social progress would be conducive to, not disruptive of, the peace and prosperity of England. Such an effort, already explored in English latitudinarianism, is reflected as well in John Locke's prodigious intellectual labors. It is in this broader social and ideological context that the *Essay concerning Human Understanding* (Locke's political speculations aside) shall be read.

While sharing a clear set of social aims, Locke and the latitudinarians diverged on numerous major and minor points. The latitudinarians, as I have already said, rejected the contract theory of the state and repudiated the right of resistance. Locke, situated away from church and court, his two feet planted firmly in the country politics of his patron, Lord Shaftesbury, was free to weigh the grave danger posed by a popish monarch and to resist all absolutist pretensions.

Other differences are also evident. Locke adopted Boyle's "corpuscular theory," incorporating it into his own doctrine of substance (viz., its "real essence") and thereby supplanting the older Scholastic/Aristotelian view.[3] One informed latitudinarian, Edward Stillingfleet (1635–1699), bishop of Worcester, attacked Locke in print. By his lights, the doctrine of substance presented in Locke's *Essay* went too far in reducing the fundamentals of Christian theology; Locke's reasoning, Stillingfleet feared, would end in the Socinian rejection of the Trinity itself.[4] In a series of lengthy exchanges, ending only with Stillingfleet's death, Locke and Stillingfleet debated the significance for the Christian religion of Locke's epistemological views. By Stillingfleet's reasoning, the doctrine of substance was necessary for the justification of the doctrine of the Trinity. Locke's doctrine of substance made it so indefinite and uncertain a postulate as to call into question Trinitarianism and, therefore, Christianity itself. Locke, then, could be condemned for his Socinianism. The basic idea was that because, for Locke, a substance's "real essence" consists of the atomic corpuscles of which it is ultimately composed, and because humans have no sensory experience and therefore no "clear and distinct ideas" of these corpuscles, it would be possible to suppose that matter alone thinks — and thinks within us. It is therefore possible to doubt or deny the existence of the Father, the Son, and the Holy Spirit and disclaim, as well, their abiding presence within the Christian believer.[5] Locke steadfastly denied the implication.

Locke's skeptical denial of "innate ideas" represents yet another issue on which he and the Cambridge-based latitudinarians would disagree. Latitudinarianism, as outlined earlier, was born at Oxford in the 1630s, in the Great Tew circle surrounding William Chillingworth (1602–1644), John Hales (1584–1656), and its patron, Lucius Cary, second Viscount Falkland (1610?–1643). These Oxford theologians, Cranston reports, "had been content with skepticism; the Cambridge Puritans by birth and breeding were not. They could not do without some metaphysical assurance"[6] (i.e., a belief in the "innate" goodness of men). Cranston credits a younger member of this circle, Jeremy Taylor (1613–1667), as being the greatest influence in Locke's conversion to toleration.[7] Locke opens his *Essay* with a frontal assault on the notion of innate ideas, speculative and practical. Cudworth, in fact, explicitly repudiated Locke's well-known doctrine:

The soul is not a mere *rasa tabula*, a naked and passive thing which has no innate furniture . . . of its own nor anything at all in it but what was impressed upon it without; for if it were so then there could not possibly be any such thing a moral good and evil, just and unjust. . . . the anticipations of morality spring [not] merely from intellectual forms and notional ideas . . . but from some other more inward and vital principle in intellectual beings as such; whereby they have a natural determination in them to do some things and to avoid others, which could not be if they were mere naked passive things.[8]

The Cambridge Platonists believed that God's grace and God's love inhere in the human personality, assisting it to know and do good and avoid evil. As C. A. Patrides has written, quoting from the works of the Platonist John Smith, "They regarded Love as a single entity 'which issuing forth from God centres itself within us, and is the Protoplastick virtue of our Beings.' " As Benjamin Whichcote advised, "The spirit of God in us is a living law, informing the soul; not constrained by a law without, that enlivens not . . . we act in the power of an inward principle of life, which enables, inclines, facilitates, [and] determines [the will]."[9] In repudiating innate ideas, and therefore the "moral sense" that enjoins people to follow God's law and do good, Locke logically bowed to the power of Hobbes's (and indeed Calvin's) portrait of human nature. The human proclivity for self-aggrandizement so vividly portrayed in the pages of *Leviathan* (and the history of the times) would have to be confronted and incorporated into any persuasive system of moral philosophy.[10]

Finally, Locke can be distinguished from the latitudinarians in his refusal to play the "cosmological" card—their effort to order social relations on the patterns found in material and sentient nature. Perhaps Locke appreciated that there could be as many interpretations of "Nature" as there could be of "Scripture." At any rate, finding other intellectual materials in his cultural environment, in particular the speculations of numerous natural law writers, Locke would ground his social and political philosophy directly in a theory of human nature and in a special natural law relation between each individual and his divine creator. All differences of tactics and doctrine aside, however, Locke and the latitudinarians were united in their fundamental social objectives.

Before discussing Locke's natural law teaching, the theory of human nature he presented and the several moral virtues to which that theory logically led must be examined with some care. As the historical survey in Chapter 2 and the latitudinarian program make clear, Locke's age demanded a comprehensive vision—at once liberating and restraining—if legitimacy and order were ever to be finally achieved.[11]

What was on trial was not merely the vagaries of popular consent theory, but human nature itself, i.e., the capacity of people to follow reason without falling prey to their riotous passions. Beyond this, there were the sheer exigencies of ideological debate. As Locke himself explained, "There cannot any one moral Rule be proposed [and 'moral philosophy,' in Locke's day, included political theory], whereof a Man may not justly demand a Reason . . . the truth of all these moral Rules plainly depends upon some other antecedent to them, and from which they must be deduced."[12] This is the train of thought that originally introduced the queries that would evolve into the sophisticated theory of knowledge Locke would present in *An Essay concerning Human Understanding*.

In the course of working out his epistemological theory, Locke developed a comprehensive account of human nature itself, so necessary for the defense of his political philosophy. It is to this theory of human nature and, more broadly, Locke's metaphysical worldview that I shall now turn.

The Metaphysical Foundations of Locke's Social Thought

A comprehensive philosophy proceeds from the understanding that ultimately questions of value rest on more fundamental matters of fact, that, David Hume to the contrary notwithstanding, it *is* the "is" that determines the "ought." It is because man is what he is and the universe is what it is that individuals ought to live as they ought, morally and politically. That is the conception upon which Plato's thought is built, as is Hobbes's, Augustine's, and Aquinas's. And the same, I believe, can be said for Locke. Locke's chief failing is not that he neglected to furnish a well-structured system of philosophic speculation, but merely that he failed to present his system in a systematic format. All the ingredients are there, but they must be carefully pieced together from the writings he left on a remarkable array of subjects. Fortunately, the philosophic structure is not all that complex and may be reduced to a manageable number of fundamental propositions.

The Primacy of Existence

By the "primacy of existence" I mean that the world we perceive exists independently of our perceptions of it; it is an objective absolute. Defying the authority not only of Cudworth but of Descartes as well, Locke begins by declaring that at birth, the mind is as "white paper, void of all characters, without any ideas." From where do our ideas come? How are all the materials of reason and knowledge furnished? "To this I answer, in one word, from EXPERIENCE." All of men's ideas, from the simplest notions of "round," "solid," and "red" to the most complex of "mixed modes and relations," such as "wealth," "justice," and "gratitude," are derived, ultimately, from "sensation" or "reflection." Locke is emphatic on the point: "The understanding seems to me not to have the least glimmering of any ideas which it does not receive from one of these two." Every idea an individual can form derives, then, from "observation employed either about external sensible objects or about the internal operations of our minds perceived and reflected on by ourselves, [this] is that which supplies our understanding with all the *materials* of thinking." The beginning of ideas, in sum, coincides with the beginning of "perception — having ideas, and perception, being the same thing."[13] What is it that produces the perceptions we experience? It can only be the things perceived — the actual objects existing in the material world. Appealing to common experience and common sense, Locke repudiates the radical skepticism upon which Descartes built his philosophy: "It is plain those perceptions are produced in us by exterior causes affecting our senses: because those that want the organs of any sense, never can have the ideas belonging to that sense produced in their minds. . . . The organs themselves . . . do not produce them; for then the eyes of a man in the dark would produce colours and his nose smell roses in the winter."[14]

Locke also notices that our senses, in many cases, "bear witness to the truths of each other's report, concerning the existence of sensible things without us." If we see a fire, we can place our fingers in the flame; that should convince us. But Locke's rejection of the Cartesian doubt cuts even deeper. In the first place, he strongly suggests that the entire demand for "proof" is inappropriate in this regard:

> How vain . . . it is to expect demonstration and certainty in things not capable of it; and refuse assent to very rational propositions and act contrary to very plain and clear truths, because they cannot be made out so evident as to surmount the least . . . pretence of doubting. He that, in the ordinary affairs of life, would admit of nothing but direct plain demonstration, would be sure of nothing in this world, but of perishing quickly.[15]

It is possible to take Locke's critique of skepticism one step further. Descartes believed he could begin speculation by "doubting" everything (save the faculty that is doing the doubting). But, Locke would inquire, what is this "idea" of "doubting"? And from whence does it arise? Locke, first, is sensitive to those "negative names" we apply to certain ideas. These, he says, "stand not directly for positive ideas, but for their absence, such as insipid, silence, nihil, &c; which words denote positive ideas, v.g., taste, sound, being, with a significance of their absence." What is doubt if not an "absence" in the belief of an idea's truth (in this case, its correspondence to an external object)? Just as there could be no such idea as silence if there were no prior perception of sound, so there could be no doubt without a prior perception of truth. To doubt everything, or to hold that all is "illusion," is to epistemologically "smuggle" true belief into the very process of doubting. It is to say, as Locke affirms in another context, that there can only be injustice (i.e., theft) while believing that there is no rightful property. In truth, if there was no property, there could be no injustice (i.e., theft).[16]

This is as far as Locke can go in establishing the independent status of the world we perceive with our senses, but for him it is not necessary to go any further. Axiomatic to Locke's philosophy is the proposition that the world of sensory experience is real and is as we perceive it.[17] Now there exists, in the universe, an object that is not open to our senses, yet is critical to the construction of Locke's philosophy of nature. This is God, the creator.

The Existence of God

Because God is not a material presence and because humans have no innate ideas by which they might experience a divine, immaterial being, there are no automatic means of apprehending such a deity. Nonetheless, Locke cannot doubt his presence in the universe. It is necessary that Locke therefore furnish sound arguments for his belief. Of the arguments available to Locke, it is noteworthy that he proffers those that are grounded, ultimately, in sensory experience. Two lines of argument are provided. In his *Essays on the Law of Nature,* Locke invokes the "argument from design." Since it is evident that this "natural world is constructed with wonderful art and regularity" and that "it could not have come together casually and by chance . . . there must be a powerful and wise creator of all these things, who has made and built this whole universe and us mortals, who are not the lowest part of it." A second argument, and the one relied on in the *Essay* of 1690, is the so-called anthropological argument. As von Leyden explains:

> Since man cannot owe his existence to any of the inanimate things or living beings, which are less perfect than he is, and since he cannot have created himself, because — with the exception of God — nothing is its own cause, and also because he is himself imperfect (e.g., de-

void of an everlasting life which he would certainly have endowed himself had he been his own maker), it necessarily follows that there exists some superior power which has created man and to which man is subject.[18]

John Locke's philosophy of nature will be built not merely on a "rational" belief in the existence of God but more specifically on the shoulders of the Christian faith and the view of Jesus as Messiah. Locke, then, will have to furnish an epistemological basis for accepting revealed as God's revealed word. He makes a brief foray into the subject in Book IV of the *Essay* where he allows "outward signs" to convince us of the authority of those revelations.[19] His fullest treatment of these "outward signs" is given in *The Reasonableness of Christianity* and *A Discourse of Miracles*. Essentially, he employs as rational grounds for Christian belief: (1) the longstanding prophecies concerning the Messiah, and (2) the testimony of numerous witnesses to Jesus's performance of those prophecies, including the many miracles that attended the Messiah's temporal visit.[20] I have already discussed the meaning of the Messiah's message and Locke's estimate of the role of faith and grace in human life. What is left to explore now is Locke's estimate of human nature itself. The revealed word of God aside, the study of God's glorious work, humans, will also reveal what the maker expects of his highest creation.

Locke's Theory of Human Nature

The "Hedonist Psychology"

At the outset it is important to note that in denying the doctrine of innate ideas, Locke did not intend to deny innate states of consciousness as such. "I deny not that there are natural tendencies imprinted on the minds of men." He readily concedes that humans experience such instinctual states as hunger and thirst, among many others. Besides these, there is the whole host of "passions" inherent in human nature. For Locke, consciousness has two basic functions to perform. It plays a cognitive role, looking outward (and inward) and thereby seeing what is in the world (or in the mind). But it also plays an evaluative role, sizing up the benefit or harm that the things it sees may signify for oneself.

Individuals experience this appraisal primarily through the automatic mechanism of pleasure and pain. Our ideas of these states are derived from acts of reflection, as our ideas of outward qualities (e.g., solid and round) are derived from acts of sensation. The particular pleasures and pains we experience are "simple ideas," as are the particular shapes and colors we perceive. As such they are irreducible. We must be content merely to point at the given quality (e.g., round, in the one case, hunger, in the other) in our experience. These states of consciousness, "like other simple ideas cannot be described, nor their names defined, the way of knowing them is, as of the simple ideas of the sense, only by experience—in their case, reflection." The important point is that the pleasures and pains we experience exert a profound motivational influence over our lives. "Things, then, are good or evil, only in reference to pleasure or pain. That we call GOOD, which is apt to cause or increase pleasure, or diminish pain. . . . And, on the contrary, we name that EVIL which is apt to produce or increase any pain, or diminish any pleasure in us."[21]

Pleasure and pain, "and that which causes them—good and evil," Locke admits, "are the hinges on which our passions turn." And it is these passions that give rise to our desires and aversions: "The uneasiness a man finds in himself upon the absence of anything whose present enjoyment carries the idea of delight with it . . . we call *desire;* which is greater or less, as the uneasiness is more or less vehement."[22]

Locke takes us on a tour of the "modes" or varieties of pleasure and pain we experience daily, including joy, sorrow, hope, fear, despair, anger, envy, and shame, and in every case indicates the ways in which they relate to the attainment of pleasure or the prospect of pain. "In fine, all these passions are moved by things, only as they appear to be the causes of pleasure and pain, or to have pleasure or pain some way or other annexed to them." The power of pleasure and pain is manifest for Locke. "Nature, I confess, has put into man a desire of happiness and an aversion to misery; these indeed are innate practical principles which (as practical principles ought) *do* continue constantly to operate and influence all our actions without ceasing; these may be observed in all persons and all ages, steady and universal."[23]

Sentiments such as these have naturally led commentators to see in Locke a purely utilitarian ethic.[24] Interestingly, there is a strong case to be made that Locke, on purely empirical grounds, rejects utilitarianism for an even crasser hedonism. The utilitarian is a calculator, but Locke's psychological portrait discounts sober reflection and calculation: "[Though it] seems so established and settled a maxim by the general consent of all mankind, that good, the greater good, determines the will, [it seems evident] that *good,* the *greater good,* though apprehended and acknowledged to be so, does not determine the will, until our desire, raised proportionately to it, makes us uneasy in the want of it."

And so, "let a drunkard see that his health decays, his estate wastes; discredit and diseases, and the want of all things, even of his beloved drink, attends him in the course he follows: yet the return of uneasiness to miss his companions, the habitual thirst after his cups . . . drives him to the tavern, though he has in his view the loss of health and plenty, and perhaps the joys of another life." Hobbes had said that a man will be moved by the last desire; Locke would award the prize to "the most pressing [uneasiness] . . . judged capable of being then removed." Locke's theory of human motivation, moreover, can easily be viewed as defending not merely hedonism, but subjectivism as well: "Now, let one man place his satisfaction in sensual pleasures, another in the delight of knowledge: though each of them cannot but confess, there is great pleasure in what the other pursues; yet, neither of them making the other's delight a part of *his* happiness, their desires are not moved, but each is satisfied without what the other enjoys; and so his will is not determined to the pursuit of it."

These practical principles, the desire for happiness and aversion to misery, are innate and can be "observed in all persons and all ages, steady and universal." Are they absolute and controlling? Not necessarily, for as Locke immediately adds, opening the door to a potential negative or veto, "these are *inclinations of the appetite* to good, not impressions of truth on the understanding."[25]

Liberty and the Pursuit of Happiness

Ever the empiricist, Locke will look out and see men who are ruled by their desires. It has been so since the fall of Adam. But beyond what is actual, there is the possible — the capacity of individuals to overcome their appetites and rule themselves. Do we not, he asks, "find in ourselves a power to begin or forbear, continue or end several (actions) of our minds, and motions of our bodies, barely by (a thought) or preference of the mind (ordering, as it were commanding, the doing or not doing such or such a particular action)[?] This power which the mind has . . . is that which we call the *Will*."[26]

Locke's political theory aside, we find in his very theory of human nature a doctrine of "Liberty," which he defines as "a power in any agent to do or forbear any particular action, according to the determination or thought of the mind, whereby either of them (doing or forbearing) is preferred to the other." Where such a choice is "not in the power of the agent to be produced by him according to his volition, there he is not at liberty; that agent is under *necessity*." Locke then invites his reader to consider, employing his historical plain method: "As everyone daily may experiment in himself, we have a power to suspend the prosecution of this or that desire. This seems to be the source of all liberty, in this seems to consist that which is . . . called *free-will*.'' Many may think themselves helpless to alter their conduct. Locke does not. ''Nor let any one say, he cannot govern his passions, nor hinder them from breaking out, and carrying him into action; for what he can do before a prince or a great man, he can do alone, or in the presence of God if he will.''[27]

Now Locke is not simply saying that a man, at this moment or the next, may struggle to ''suspend the execution . . . of any of his desires,'' implying that life, at best, is a ceaseless war of will against appetite. Destructive desires, even the strongest, may not only be suspended; they may be informed and corrected. He thus draws a distinction between ''natural'' and ''adopted'' desires. Those that are natural arise from ''the ordinary necessities of our lives'' and include ''hunger, thirst, heat, cold, weariness with labour and sleepiness.'' Such natural desires are, so to speak, biologically wired into the frame of man and thus are undeniable and unavoidable. As opposed to the ''natural wants,'' we come by ''acquired habits.'' Qua passions, they may be every bit as fierce and compelling as the natural variety. Some may ''need'' to drink, carouse, gamble, or fornicate as much as they desire good food and shelter. Hardly necessary, however, they are ''acquired by fashion, example or education.'' Among these Locke includes such ''fantastical'' wants ''as itch after honour, power or riches.''[28]

As long as an individual lives, he will need food and so feel hunger; there is no choice in the matter. But his acquired wants form no necessary part of his constitution. Very often, Locke observes, ''fashion and the common opinion . . . settle wrong notions, and education and custom [form] ill habits,'' thus rendering ''the just values of things . . . misplaced, and the palates of men corrupted.'' In such cases, ''pains should be taken to rectify these; and contrary habits *change our pleasures,* and give a relish to that which is necessary or conducive to our happiness.'' Or, again, ''it is in our power to raise our desire in a due proportion to the value of that good, where in its turn and place it may come to work upon the will, and be pursued.'' In failing to give ''due consideration'' to our desires, we may well feel impelled by ''necessity,'' or account ourselves helpless to improve our conduct.

What this signifies, however, is not so much a defect in human nature as the frailty of our judgment and/or the weakness of our will. ''From not using it right [i.e., the judgment or the will] comes all that variety of mistakes, errors, and faults which we run into in the conduct of our lives, and our endeavours after happiness; whilst we precipitate the determination of our wills, and engage too soon before due examination.'' Locke goes on to discuss a wide variety of factors that lead to poorly formed desires and self-destructive conduct.[29]

One point must be emphasized. What Locke is *not* recommending is that individuals avoid or deny themselves pleasure. Rather, he is urging humans to pursue pleasure in its widest and fullest measure. This he calls happiness: "As therefore the highest perfection of intellectual nature lies in a careful and constant pursuit of true and solid happiness, so the care of ourselves, that we mistake not imaginary for real happiness is the necessary foundation of our liberty."[30]

It should not escape notice that the famous formulation of *The Two Treatises of Government,* "life, liberty and estate" aside, "the pursuit of happiness," most often associated with Jefferson's immortal Declaration of Independence, also holds a special place for Locke.[31] We may note as well that "liberty," so critical to Locke's political theory, appears first as an integral component of his theory of human nature. Recommending utilitarian calculation after all and bringing together his doctrine of liberty and concern with happiness, Locke inveighs his audience:

> This is the hinge on which turns the liberty of intellectual beings, in their constant endeavours after, and a steady prosecution of true felicity —
> That they can suspend this prosecution in particular cases, till they have looked before them, and informed themselves whether that particular thing which is then proposed or desired lie in the way to their main end, and make a real part of that which is their greatest good.[32]

In sum, we can make a distinction between purpose and standard. Pleasure (in its widest sense) is man's proper purpose, but pleasure, itself, is not the standard by which an object's worth is to be measured. "Locke's discussion of pleasure and pain," as Ruth Grant has aptly concluded, "is not a discussion of a hedonistic ethics but a description of the mechanism of motivation in men."[33] And it is a mechanism in need of repair. Happily, Locke finds, repair is possible:

> We should take pains to suit the relish of our Minds to the true intrinsick good or ill, that is in things; and not permit an allowed or supposed possible great and weighty good to slip out of our thoughts, without leaving any relish, any desire of its self there, till, by a due consideration of its true worth, we have formed appetites in our Minds suitable to it, and made ourselves uneasie in the want of it, or in the fear of losing it.[34]

One further point emerges from the discussion so far. Although Locke clearly intends to recommend an enlightened assessment of human good, that good still appears to be pointing to no purpose or end higher or loftier than the individual's own well-being. And that well-being is still being defined in terms of pleasure, however "true" or "solid." This, however, is not the whole story.

The Laws of God and Nature

If Locke has furnished humans a purpose, he has not as yet provided a standard by which human desires and actions may be measured and that purpose fulfilled. What is yet wanting are the rules of conduct, or the laws of morality whose observance will lead humans to the true felicity they seek. Locke will locate those rules in man's special relation to his maker and in the power that a divine creator necessarily will exercise over his creation. Locke's guiding conception in his discussion of morality is that of "law," i.e., of a rule promulgated by a lawmaker, made known to his subjects, and backed by rewards and punishments. As Locke emphasizes in the *Essay*, "*Moral good and evil, then, is only the conformity or disagreement of our voluntary actions to some law, whereby good or evil is drawn on us, from the will and power of the lawmaker;* which good and evil, pleasure or pain, attending our observance or breach of the law by the decree of the law-maker, is that we call *reward* and *punishment*."[35]

From this assertion it would appear that obedience to God's moral law is still grounded in prudence—in the consideration of divine reward and punishment that follows from this or that course of action. There is much, however, to suggest this is not the case. Locke's most sustained discussion of natural law (i.e., the grounds of moral reasoning) occurs in an early series of questions he addressed while at Christ's Church, Oxford. Written in 1664 but never published by Locke, these *Essays on the Law of Nature* already incorporate themes and positions that would carry over into Locke's mature thought. The grounds of obligation, as numerous readers of these essays have argued, here arise from God's will alone, and from the duty he imposes on his creation. As Locke says in *An Essay concerning Human Understanding*, "He has a right to do it; we are his creatures."[36] Thus, as Tully concludes, man's essential nature is that of "an existentially dependent creature. . . . Locke shows that God as maker has a special right in man as his workmanship, and that this correlates with a positive duty or obligation on the part of man to God [to do his bidding]."[37]

This "voluntarist" model of obligation finds ample support in Locke's *Essays on the Law of Nature,* where he declares, "All things are justly subject to that by which they have first been made and also are constantly preserved." And again, "Since God is supreme over everything and has such authority and power over us as we cannot exercise over ourselves, and since we owe our body, soul, and life—whatever we are, whatever we have, and even whatever we can be — to Him and to Him alone, it is proper that we should live according to the precept of His Will."[38]

Human nature is thus constructed not merely with natural appetites and a capacity for volition; wired right into its frame is a natural and intimate tie of kinship and thus an irrepressible set of duties by which it is to be governed. But to be effective, those duties, i.e., moral law, must not only be promulgated by a lawmaker, they must be known, or at least knowable. Possessing volition, humans are free to practice moral virtue, but they must possess the capacity to discover it as well. That there is such a capacity implanted in human nature Locke has no doubt: "For God, the author of this law, has willed it to be the rule of our moral life, and He has made it sufficiently known, so that anyone can understand it who is willing to apply diligent study and to direct his mind to the knowledge of it."

What makes such knowledge possible? The faculty of human understanding.[39] What is it that may be studied to lead man to a clear comprehension of his duties? Man himself. A quality inherent in Locke's conception of God is his purposefulness. As Locke says, God "has not created this world for nothing and without purpose. For it is contrary to such great wisdom to work with no fixed aim." And so "it does not seem to fit in with the wisdom of the Creator to form an animal that is most perfect and ever active, and to endow it abundantly above all others with mind, intellect, reason and all the requisites for working, and yet not assign to it any work, or again to make man alone susceptible of law precisely in order that he may submit to none." There is, then, a law of nature decreed by God and given to man, who alone of all the created species is capable of knowing and following it. Giving final form to the conception, Locke states, "This law of nature can be described as being the decree of the divine will, discernible by the light of nature and indicating what is and what is not in conformity with rational nature, and for this very reason commanding or prohibiting it."[40]

Before I turn to a consideration of the specific moral duties (and virtues) inherent in human nature, there is a perplexity that should be addressed. The metaphysical foundation of Locke's moral teaching now appears to be a confusing mix of not two, but three considerations. The utilitarian desire for true, lasting felicity can be pitted against both the stern duty to obey the commands of an omnipotent authority and the capacity of "intellectual nature" to follow the dictates of nothing more sublime than human reason. Not surprisingly, many commentators have pointed to the eclectic and inconsistent character of Locke's philosophic teaching.[41] One scholar, however, has worked through the seeming difficulty, furnishing a refreshingly simple accommodation of these disparate metaphysical strands. For Locke, according to Ruth Grant, "the rationalist criterion of right must be distinguished from the theological grounds of obligation, but here both must also be distinguished from the hedonistic psychology of motivation. Reason can tell a man what is right; his relationship to God is the source of his obligation to do what is right; and he will be motivated to do what is right by his expectation of painful or pleasant consequences of his actions."[42]

Moral duty, rational enlightenment, and human happiness merge; out of the trinity comes unity. The formulation is compelling and almost convincing, certainly in its simplicity. But if nothing else, the larger question, the matter of Locke's influence on a less devout, more deistic eighteenth century, requires a closer look at the voluntarist thesis. Is this the exclusive grounds of moral obligation for Locke? Perhaps not. Granted, "we are the work of a most perfect and wise maker . . . [and] appear to be intended by Him for no other end than His own glory, and to this all things must be related." Our duty to obey God and attend to his glory may well follow. However, Locke immediately adds: "Partly also we can infer the principle and a definite rule of our duty from man's own constitution and the faculties with which he is equipped. For since man is neither made without design nor endowed to no purpose with these faculties which both can and must be employed, his function appears to be that *which nature has prepared him to perform.*"[43]

Pursuing this more naturalistic and Aristotelian train of thought and citing Book 1, chapter 7 of the *Nicomachean Ethics,* Locke casts his gaze at "the special sort of work that each thing is designed to perform." Approvingly, he recalls "having taken account of all the operations of the vegetal and sentient faculties which men have in common with animals and plants, . . . he [Aristotle] rightly concludes that the proper function of man is acting in conformity with reason, so much so that man must of necessity perform what reason prescribes." Locke's position grows more naturalistic, as he soon adopts a truly natural view of natural law:

> Since man has been made such as he is, equipped with reason and his other faculties and destined for this mode of life, there necessarily result from his inborn constitution some definite duties for him, which cannot be other than they are. In fact, it seems to be to follow just as necessarily from the nature of man that, if he is a man, he is bound . . . to fulfill [the duties] appropriate to the rational nature, i.e., to observe the law of nature, as it follows from the nature of a triangle that, if it is a triangle, its three angles are equal to two right angles.[44]

The law of nature and all its composite moral postulates, as this surely seems to suggest, flow as much from the nature of man as from the dependence of man on his sovereign maker. Natural law, Locke can finally write, is a fixed and permanent rule of morals, which reason itself pronounces, and which persists, being a fact so firmly rooted in the soil of human nature. Hence human nature must needs be changed before this law can be either altered or annulled. . . . Since therefore all men are by nature rational and since there is a harmony between this law and the rational nature, and this harmony can be known by the light of nature, it follows that all those who are endowed with a rational nature, i.e., all men in the world are morally bound by this law.[45]

Locke's Moral Philosophy

The Virtue of Reason

John Locke's purpose in examining "the original, certainty, and extent of human Knowledge, together with the grounds and degrees of Belief, Opinion and Assent," is, he tells us, "not to know all things, but those which concern our conduct." And repeatedly he assures us that the field whose task it is to discover the proper rules of conduct, namely, moral philosophy, ranks with the other sciences that are "capable of demonstration."[46] But what were the specific moral rules Locke wanted to have demonstrated? Early, in his *Essays on the Law of Nature,* Locke speaks of the task of forming in young people the "foundations of the moral virtues." He here cites as examples "sentiments of respect and love for the deity, obedience to superiors, fidelity in keeping promises and telling the truth, mildness and purity of character [and] a friendly disposition." Elsewhere, he speaks of the parents' natural law duties to their offspring and of the child's duties to his parents. Even obligations toward the poor and destitute are considered as duties.[47]

One moral virtue never included in Locke's listings or sufficiently emphasized by many of his interpreters, yet implicit in Locke's entire philosophic enterprise, is reason itself. From all that has been said it should be clear that reason is the source not only of moral knowledge, but of all virtuous living—capable of informing not just the understanding of men, but their desires and wills, as well. Indeed, it is not going too far to say that for Locke, the fundamental moral dictum may be reduced to two words: Follow reason. The doctrine of reason occupies a pivotal position in Locke's philosophy of nature. Its influence stretches to virtually every other facet of his philosophy—from epistemology, to education, to ethics, to politics. It therefore deserves careful scrutiny. Locke begins: "The word reason . . . stands for a faculty in man, that faculty whereby man is supposed to be distinguished from beasts, and wherein it is evident he must surpass them.'' With the lower animals, humans share the capacity for sensation and certain basic instincts. Yet, ''sense and intuition reach but a very little way. The greatest part of our knowledge depends upon deductions and intermediate ideas.'' The ''faculty which finds out the means, and rightly applies them, to discover certainty . . . and probability . . . is that which we call *reason.*''[48] We may define it as the mental processes (e.g., the rules of induction and logic) that fashion the material provided by sensory experience into conceptual knowledge, thereby affording humans a far greater scope of understanding than is afforded to species limited to mere sensory awareness.

The crucial point is that, for Locke, reason, the cognitive instrument, is itself the proper moral agent, i.e., the agency most fit to guide and direct human action. It can more acutely weigh the threat a given object of experience may pose or more accurately project the benefits a settled course of action will occasion than can the unexamined (if automatic) passions. It lights the human path, teaching us ''all that we can or ought to do in pursuit of our happiness'' — in ''our constant endeavours after, and steady prosecution of true felicity.'' But in following reason a man not only pleases himself, he pleases his maker as well. ''He that believes without having any reason for believing may be in love with his own fancies; but neither seeks truth as he ought, nor pays the obedience due to his Maker, who would have him use those discerning faculties he has given him, to keep him out of mistake and error.''[49]

But what of revelation? What of faith? They are important, but they do not diminish the authority of reason: ''Faith is nothing but a firm assent of the mind: which, if it be regulated, as is our duty, cannot be afforded to anything but upon good reason; and so cannot be opposite to it.''[50] More than a reliable tool of cognition, reason is man's proper guide to action. Epistemology and ethics come together. This, in fact, is precisely the theme of a recent contribution to Lockean scholarship. It was with great acuity that Neal Wood observed:

> Besides writing a philosophic treatise of a technical nature, Locke had devised a work for the practical guidance and orientation of men of his own size, to aid ordinary educated men in their daily lives and in the ''management'' of their ''great Concerns.'' Locke's intention was very matter-of-fact and pragmatic; he wished to show his readers how they could act more rationally in society, in religion and politics.[51]

It is important to have a clearer sense of what the life of reason entails. Three ''corollaries'' in particular follow from the decision to extol the rational way of life. Each is a separate aspect of moral virtue and plays a critical role in the commitment to it.

The Virtue of Self-Discipline

The desires furnish humans with what can be considered an automatic estimate of the beneficial or harmful relationship of some object to themselves, and those desires exert a powerful motivating influence on human conduct. But any such estimate may be in error. What I feel is good for me may, in fact, be deadly. Fortunately, I am free to suspend my desire and examine "the true intrinsick good or ill that is in things" and, by exerting an act of will, act in a manner consistent with my true interests. Locke says, "The forbearance of a too hasty compliance with our desires, the moderation and restraint of our Passions, so that our Understandings may be *free* to examine, and reason unbiased give its judgment, being that, wherein a right direction of our conduct to true Happiness depends."[52]

The critical role of self-discipline in the education of youth is underscored in Locke's educational writings. To parents and tutors, Locke writes: "The great principle and foundation of all virtue and worth is placed in this, that a man is able to deny himself his own desires, cross his own inclinations and purely follow what reason directs as best, though the appetite lean the other way."[53] And then Locke boils the whole business of child rearing down to a single, if not a simple, prescription. The child must be taught "to get a mastery over his inclinations, and submit his appetites to reason. This being obtained and by constant practices settled into habit, the hardest part of the task is over."[54]

The Virtue of Thinking Long-Range

Human actions invite consequences, not all of which appear at once. The near-term benefit must be carefully weighed against the longer term loss, and vice versa. Among the miscellaneous papers published by Locke's cousin, Peter King, is one depicting, with some poignancy, Locke's personal encounter with the issue of long-range thinking. Titled simply "Thus I think," Locke's essay affirms his own decision to "seek happiness and avoid misery." "But here I must have a care I mistake not; for if I prefer a short pleasure to a lasting one, it is plain I cross my own happiness. . . . For example, the fruit I see tempts me with the taste of it that I love, but if it endanger my health, I part with a constant and lasting, for a very short and transient pleasure, and so foolishly make myself unhappy, and am not true to my own interest."

Locke will partake of innocent diversions, but only sparingly; for while they may "refresh myself after study and business . . . preserve my health, restore the vigour of my mind and increase my pleasure," if he indulges in these to too great a degree, he knows they will "hinder my improvement in knowledge and useful arts, . . . blast my credit, and give me up to the uneasy state of shame, ignorance, and contempt, in which I cannot be very happy."[55] Mastering his passions will afford Locke not only the benefits of true pleasure, but "a constant pleasure greater than any such [momentary] enjoyments." In *Some Thoughts concerning Education,* Locke explicitly speaks of the virtue of "Self-denial," observing that "he that has not a mastery over his inclinations, he that knows not how to resist the importunity of present pleasure or pain, for the sake of what reason tells him is fit to be done, wants the true principle of virtue and industry."[56]

The Virtue of Independence

Independence, for Locke, is not primarily a matter of making one's way in the world alone or of escaping parental authority upon reaching the age of discretion (though these, too, are moral requisites). It is something far more fundamental. The basic expression of independence is epistemological in character. It denotes the individual's determination to examine the world through his own eyes and to reason with his own mind. Hence Locke's oft-spoken disdain for the tyranny of opinion, the command of "authority." In fact, among the various grounds of human error, he writes, the one "which keeps in ignorance or error more people than all the others together, is . . . the giving up our assent to the common received opinion, either of our friends or party, neighborhood or country. How many men have no other ground for their tenets, than the supposed honesty, or learning, or number of those of the same profession? As if honest or bookish men could not err, or truth were to be established by the vote of the multitude."[57] "A Mind free and Master of it self and all its Actions" is the vision Locke holds forth in his educational writings.[58]

Reason and Society: War or Peace

There is nothing more sacred and inviolate for Locke than the integrity and independence of an individual's honest judgment. Is this how he thinks most people form their convictions? No, Locke is not at all oblivious to the darker, or fallen, side of human nature. Too often people move, and think, in a herd. Of the average individual, Locke affirms, "it is enough for him to obey his leaders, to have his hand and his tongue ready for the support of the common cause, and thereby approve himself to those who can give him credit, preferment, or protection in that society."[59]

Of course, if some are eager to follow, others are just as eager to lead—as the proliferation of Interregnum sects and radical religious cults so ably demonstrated. Locke appreciates the danger of sectarian enthusiasm as well as any in the High Church party:

> The love of something extraordinary, the ease and glory it is to be inspired, and be above the common and natural ways of knowledge, so flatters many men's laziness, ignorance, and vanity, that, when once they are got into this way of immediate revelation, of illumination without search, and of certainty without proof and without examination, it is a hard matter to get them out of it. Reason is lost upon them, they are above it.[60]

The philosopher in Locke dreams of something better; the empiricist knows well of what materials mortal men are made. "The assuming an authority of dictating to others and a forwardness to prescribe to their opinions, is a constant concomitant of this bias and corruption of our judgments." Armed with divine illumination, touched by the holy spirit, each enthusiast for the "true" truth will rant, or seek, or shake, or quake until he has turned the world upside down and inside out.

> For if the light, which every one thinks he has in his mind . . . be an evidence that it is from God, contrary opinions have the same title to be inspirations; and God will be not only the Father of lights, but of opposite and contradictory lights, leading men contrary ways; and contradictory propositions will be divine truths, if an ungrounded strength of assurance be an evidence that any proposition is a Divine Revellation.

It is precisely

> to this crying up of faith in *opposition* to reason, [that] we may . . . ascribe those absurdities that fill almost all the religions which possess and divide mankind. . . . And what readier way can there be to run ourselves into the most extravagant errors and miscarriages, than

to set up fancy for our supreme and sole guide, and to believe any proposition to be true, any action to be right, only because we believe it to be so? . . . Whatever credit or authority we give to any proposition more than it receives from the principles and proofs it supports itself upon, is owing to our inclinations that way, and is so far a derogation from the love of truth as such.[61]

We are back to Cromwell and Ireton, to Filmer and Parker—and to the fundamental problem created by the spread of literacy, learning, and the uncensored mind. Locke grasps the dilemma clearly: "Who can reasonably expect arguments and conviction from [the enthusiast] in dealing with others, whose understanding is not accustomed to them in dealing with himself?" Locke confronts the dangerous phenomenon of sectarian enthusiasm head on. For him, it is the negation of reason, and, in fact, "it takes away both reason and revelation, and substitutes in the room of them the ungrounded fancies of man's own brain, and assumes them for a foundation both of opinion and conduct." It is a tempting human passion, and there are many enthusiasts for it—as Locke and the latitudinarians well appreciated.[62]

But the enthusiastic assertion of radical religious or political ideas marks the beginning of debate, not the end. It is never sufficient to merely affirm this or that dogma. Until they are supported by reasoned argument and the weight of evidence, such assertions are arbitrary and capricious. They lack epistemological support and ought not to command political support. Having discredited the notion of innate ideas (rejecting even the benignant mysteries of the Platonists), having confronted the specter of Hobbesian hedonism head on, Locke would not admit the power of irrationalism in human affairs. Thus he writes, "Though one cannot say there are fewer improbable or erroneous opinions in the world than there are, yet this is certain; there are fewer that actually assent to them and mistake them for truths than is imagined." What errors there are may be allowed; they pose no real threat, as such. "It would, methinks, become all men to maintain peace, and the common offices of humanity and friendship in the diversity of opinion."[63]

It was a lesson learned years earlier. During his brief diplomatic visit to the Elector of Brandenburg in 1665, he had seen Calvinist, Lutheran, and Catholic tolerated and at peace. As he wrote to his friend Boyle: "They quietly permit one another to choose their way to heaven; and I cannot observe any quarrel or animosities amongst them on account of religion."[64] In the final analysis, Locke would argue in *A Letter concerning Toleration*,

It is not the diversity of opinions (which cannot be avoided), but the refusal of toleration to those that are of different opinions (which might have been granted) that has produced all the bustles and wars that have been in the Christian world. . . . conventicles and nurseries of factions and seditions, are thought to afford the strongest matter of objection against this doctrine of toleration. But this has not happened by anything peculiar unto the genius of such assemblies, but by the unhappy circumstance of an oppressed or ill-settled liberty.

Factions arise in the natural course of human affairs; they cannot be avoided. "Some enter into company for trade and profit, others for want of business have their clubs for claret. Neighborhood joins some, and religion others. But there is only one thing which gathers people into seditious commotions, and that is oppression."[65]

But there is a cure for sedition even more efficacious than toleration; it is reason itself. The idea is not to lament human error but to enliven the human understanding. It is a work to be done. Invoking the authority of his judicious mentor, Richard Hooker (1554–1600), Locke imagines, "If there might be added the right helps of true art and learning, (which helps, I must plainly confess, this age of the world, carrying the name of a learned age, doth neither . . . know nor generally regard), there would undoubtedly be almost as much difference in maturity of judgment between men therewith inured, and that which men now are, as between men that are now, and innocents."[66]

What Hooker recommended, and what Locke, in very large measure, provided in his *Essay concerning Human Understanding,* was a manual for the improvement of the human intellect. One of Locke's correspondents easily appreciated the significance of Locke's effort. Of this production, Sir James Mackintosh wrote:

Few books have contributed more to rectify prejudice . . . to diffuse a just mode of thinking — to excite a fearless spirit of inquiry — and yet to contain it within the boundaries which nature has prescribed to the human understanding. An amendment of the general habits of thought is . . . an object as important as even the discovery of new truths. . . . the correction of the intellectual habits is probably the greatest service which can be rendered to science. In this respect the merit of Locke is unrivalled.[67]

Locke's studious thoughts concerning education were, of course, to the same effect, as was a posthumously published work, *On the Conduct of the Understanding* (1706). The book might rightly be viewed as the first "how-to" manual on the art of clear thinking. William Molyneux, to whom Locke wrote of the project, heralded it in his reply to Locke as nothing less than a "code of intellectual ethics."[68]

Reason, Locke and the latitudinarians hoped, however hesitatingly, could wipe aside the dark plague of ignorance and fanaticism of the past epoch. And as the towering achievements of "a Boyle or a Sydenham . . . the great Huygenius and the incomparable Mr. Newton" suggested, the dawning of a luminous new age was already gleaming just off the historical horizon.

The force of reason, not repression, would most effectively silence the clamorous "saints" and their frenzy-driven sects. If the human mind would be enlivened, not enslaved, if individuals could be encouraged to question the claims of the enthusiasts, to demand satisfactory answers, and to quietly acquiesce before differing religious opinion in matters that are "above" reason, then society could progress in peace and the High Church fears could finally be laid to rest. Locke and the latitudinarians shared that hopeful vision, but Locke's position is the more powerful. In rejecting the doctrine of "innate ideas," in relying on reason alone to fathom the mysteries of heaven and earth, the Oxford don went further than the Platonists of Cambridge. For that rejection undercuts the inspired claims of the enthusiasts at their root.

Reason is far from the last word in moral philosophy. Much more remains to be said concerning the duties of man to man and subject to sovereign (and vice versa). First, however, I need to say something about the lifestyle that reason recommends for the individual himself, i.e., the principles that are to direct human energy. For Locke, man is meant to live rationally, bowing neither to the authority of opinion nor the pull of the most pressing passion. But what is he to do, specifically, with the life he is given? That is the question to which I shall now turn.

4
The Virtue of Industriousness for the Benefit of Life

A good deal of the debate surrounding John Locke's political thought has focused on Locke's role as a theorist and apologist for an emergent capitalist order. That has been both understandable and unfortunate. It is understandable in that Locke's writings do indeed appear to support many of the facets of modern capitalist life. At the very least, for example, Locke's teaching on property assumes that individuals will naturally seek to enlarge their possessions, appropriating as many of the fruits of nature, acres of land, and products of human industry as their circumstances will permit. And they will do so by all imaginable means. The acquisitive impulse is implicit in Locke's estimate of human nature, as is the ethic of individualism. And while he will impose a few original restraints on individual accumulation, he seems to be intent on justifying the largeness of men's possessions, the unequal division of material riches, and, more fundamentally, the institution of private property per se.[1] If that explosive institution is fundamental to the liberal, capitalist order, and I think it is, then Locke can indeed be considered a progenitor of capitalist progress and an exponent of ethical egoism. But can it be said that material acquisitiveness, the steady accumulation of wealth, represents, for Locke, a cardinal moral virtue so that that system which sanctions the release of this peculiar human proclivity is the one, true moral social system? Yes and no. We shall soon see why. First, one revealing point should be aired.

The scholarly emphasis on Locke's relation to capitalism proceeds, in good measure, from a certain orientation, the modern predilection to view the past through the prism of material relations, rather than, say, deeper systems of moral belief. And it is historical materialism in particular, i.e., the conceptual tools and normative judgments implicit in Marxian analysis, that has until recently informed Lockean political studies. Having relegated ideas and ideals to the debased position of "superstructure," having come to regard the class struggle as the surer model for charting the contours of human "progress," and seeking to dissect the peculiar stage through which humanity (in the form of proletariat and bourgeoisie) is now progressing and struggling, Marxist scholarship has been able, by and large, to set the terms of debate.[2] And though that debate has surely been joined of late and the materialist bent roundly challenged, much controversy and confusion remain to be cleared away—precisely because the debate has been couched in these terms.[3]

The Marxist or materialist-centered approach to Locke has been unfortunate and, in several ways, unproductive. By working backward, i.e., by working not from Locke's deepest commitments, but from our own modern conceptions (e.g., our view of "egoism," "individualism," "class," "capitalism," and even "exploitation"), we have largely missed the critical distinctions and nuances that informed Locke's political and economic outlook.[4]

In his highly influential study of *The Political Theory of Possessive Individualism* C. B. Macpherson painstakingly revealed how by sweeping aside the traditional restraints on human acquisitiveness (the so-called spoilage and sufficiency qualifications placed on accumulation early in his chapter on property), Locke paved the way for the unlimited appropriation of land and wealth, thereby sanctioning gross social inequality. Rendering private property sacrosanct and assigning to government a full and complete responsibility for its protection, Macpherson's Locke thereby provided all the theoretical supports needed for capitalism's historical arrival. He went on to ascribe to Locke a nefarious scheme of "class differentials," whereby the working classes could be duly sacrificed and exploited on behalf of the propertied interests, all for the greater benefit of capitalist growth. Locke, Macpherson conceded, never explicitly justified the social exploitation of the laboring classes. He did not have to. "The common assumption was that the labouring class was something that was to be managed by the state to make it productive of national gain. It was not that the interests of the labouring class was subordinate to the national interest. The labouring class was not considered to have an interest; the only interest was the ruling class view of the national interest."[5]

Could this have been Locke's view? Was this stalwart seventeenth-century resistance writer and radical really the arch defender of the status quo, a conservative champion of the propertied classes? What, in fact, was the historical context in which Locke penned his *Two Treatises of Government*? It was in addressing this last question that Richard Ashcraft and Neal Wood rose to challenge Macpherson's broad analysis. Coming at Locke from two very distinct contextual avenues, however, these two eminent intellectual historians were led to dismiss not only Macpherson's findings, but each other's conclusions as well. Since both Ashcraft and Wood have contributed so much to our assessment of Locke's actual purposes and since both have put into place important pieces of the Lockean economic puzzle, I want to examine with some care their respective reports.[6]

Exploring more thoroughly than ever before Locke's role as a political activist, Ashcraft, as I have shown in Chapter 2, provided a clear methodological statement signifying the value of such an undertaking. If we are ever to understand the meaning of a political text, he argued, we had better come to terms with ''the nature of the intended audience, and the purposes for which the political theory was formulated.'' We had better be prepared, in short, to look into the author's ''social life-world.'' Building on the work of Laslett and Cranston,[7] Ashcraft defined that world and the work it called upon Locke to perform: Locke's *Two Treatises* was the ''political manifesto'' of a specific political movement. The meaning of the work is ''thus rooted . . . in a particular perception of social reality,'' as well as ''the specific political objectives around which large numbers of individuals organized themselves in the 1670's and 1680's.''[8]

By the mid-1670s large numbers of Englishmen began to view with grave alarm the course of political events in their nation. A new and invidious campaign against religious dissent, a treaty of alliance with King Louis XIV of France (that included perilous terms kept hidden from Parliament until their eventual discovery by Ralph Montague[9]), and the refusal of the Crown to hold parliamentary elections down to 1679 appeared as many dim signposts signaling darker dangers ahead. Easily reminded of the absolutist dispositions of the first two Stuart monarchs, many people in England could readily suspect that the sins of the father had descended to the sitting son, Charles II, and to a second son and lineal successor, James, Duke of York (a practicing Catholic). Nothing so worried seventeenth-century Englishmen as the specter of ''Popery.'' Catholicism, as the examples of Spain and France showed, was but another word for absolutism. ''In the Commons debates of 1680, it was argued with reference to a future government run by Catholics, that since 'we are heretics, they will burn us, and damn us. For our estates they will take our lands, and put monks and friars upon them.' Popery, therefore, meant slavery in the form of a loss of one's property rights.''[10]

Aside from the matter of property, there was the matter of conscience, something of inestimable value for those industrious middle classes bent on dissent from Anglican worship. As many a Whig would passionately plead, ''It is not only lawful for such a prince to destroy those of his subjects who disagree from him in faith and worship, but it is an indispensable duty upon him to do it.''[11] As early as 1675, the author of ''A Letter from a Person of Quality to His Friend in the City'' (thought to be penned by Shaftesbury and/or Locke) warned of a plan ''to establish a French-style absolute monarchy in England, the clergy's willingness to justify this absolutism with a theory of the divine right of kings, the danger of a popish successor to the crown, and the prospect that a standing army may be created, or is already in existence."[12]

By 1679, an organized opposition arose, having as its immediate purpose to legally exclude James from succeeding his brother to the throne of England. At the center of the opposition stood Lord Shaftesbury. At his side stood Locke, his closest adviser and confidant since 1667. If they hoped to attain their difficult objective, members of the opposition knew they would have to unite, under the banner of exclusion, a variety of social groupings. One constituency to whom the Whigs addressed their appeals, and therefore whose activities and interests they wished to defend, "was the industrious and trading part of the nation." The message they needed to deliver was plain: "Artisans, small gentry, yeoman farmers, tradesmen, and merchants were all productive members of society and ought, therefore, to unite in the pursuit of their interests against an idle and wasteful landowning aristocracy in order to establish that kind of society in which all sections of the social structure could work together for the realization of the common good."[13]

Commercial liberty, so dear to the artisanal and trading classes, would have to be upheld. But the gentry, with their stake in liberty and property, would also have to be persuaded that in a polity founded on popular consent, property relations would not be turned upside down by a leveling majoritarian tide. Ashcraft summed up the Whig challenge in this way: "If a practical alliance between the country gentry and the urban tradesmen was to be effected, . . . the theoretical problem of property rights had to be confronted and resolved in a manner that would satisfy both groups. The theoretical solution to the problem of property . . . was formulated by Locke . . . within the framework set by this political alliance."[14]

The recovery of Locke's ideological objective allowed Ashcraft to more clearly interpret the thrust of Locke's chapter on property and, important for our purposes, to dispute one of Macpherson's key conclusions. In asserting that Locke's aim was to defend unlimited appropriation and in equating rational behavior with unbridled acquisitiveness, Macpherson placed Locke on the side of the most conservative element of the English aristocracy. Seeing, however, that Locke needed to ideologically enlist the lower ranks of society "against the idle, unproductive, and Court-dominated property owners," Ashcraft countered, "Macpherson's statement that Locke's argument justifies 'unlimited appropriation' of property is an ill-chosen phrase, since it is not land nor its appropriation that Locke wishes to justify, but rather *the extension of trade*."[15]

This hardly settled the question. Ashcraft's own conclusions, in fact, would be called into question by Neal Wood, who essentially shared Ashcraft's methodological approach. But where Ashcraft saw in Locke's political writings "the radical political language and concepts common to a vast literature of Whig exclusion tracts and pamphlets written by lawyers, doctors, clerics, and journalists committed to the [exclusion] cause,"[16] Wood, after undertaking no less extensive a survey of seventeenth-century pamphlet literature, noticed a language and vocabulary Locke shared not with political activists, but with a long line of agricultural improvers. The recovery of this contextual link allowed Wood to render a very different interpretation of Locke's views on property and capitalism. For Neal Wood, Locke would be identified as a "theorist of early agrarian capitalism, *not* as a thinker who articulated the interests and aspirations of an incipient mercantile and manufacturing bourgeoisie."[17]

For evidence, Wood pointed to Locke's lifelong interest in husbandry and the extensive library he owned on the subject. Beyond this, there is Locke's consuming emphasis on the productivity of cultivated land and the derision he heaped on the great, uncultivated "wasts," be they English fens or the virgin territories of America. One common geographical denominator should serve to indicate the drift of Wood's argument. After all, it was not the great commercial city of London, but the simple farming country of Devonshire that was "extolled by Locke as an example of how industry and improvement could transform barren land into fertile acreage."[18] For years, agricultural improvers had been pointing to that very spot on the English map to advertise their bountiful accomplishments. Wood quotes the historian Mildred Campbell to that effect: "Devonshire was the shire most often referred to as a shining example of the way in which a naturally barren county could become one of the most productive through care and treatment of its soil. The husbandry innovators begged less industrious . . . sections to follow Devon's example."[19]

Significantly, Wood traced the seventeenth-century preoccupation with agricultural improvement to Sir Francis Bacon (1561–1626). Decades earlier, Bacon had called for "the application of science to agriculture and the writing of natural histories of husbandry as well as of trade." A good proportion of the text of his *Sylva Sylvarum* (1627), published the year after his death, "is devoted to plants, horticulture, sylviculture, agriculture and agronomy. . . . The work as a whole is conceived of as a natural history, a compendium of facts and observations gleaned from a number of popular writers."[20]

By midcentury the labors of such professed Baconians as John Evelyn and Samuel Hartlib assured that Bacon's call to inquiry would not go unheeded. Throughout the travail of civil war, Interregnum, and Restoration, the business of improvement went on. Enclosure of the vast forests and fens, while depriving many citizens of their common holdings, encouraged capital investment and intensive cultivation, thereby raising dramatically the productivity of the soil—as Locke certainly appreciated it would.

Besides enclosure, the keen interest paid to experimentation confirms the century's zest for agricultural improvement. Leading figures of the Royal Society were thus actively engaged in finding better methods and means of cultivation. They included Locke's friend and mentor Robert Boyle who, Wood points out, devoted far more time to the subject than is generally recognized. So too did Benjamin Worsley and John Wilkins, also devoted Baconians. Wilkins can be credited with being "the guiding light in the founding of the Royal Society." Besides Locke's friends and scientific bedfellows, there is the case of Shaftesbury who "planted fruit trees and laid out gardens, developed new strains of apples and plums, engaged in stock breeding and agricultural experimentation." As a Lord Proprietor of the Carolinas, in fact, Locke's great patron "energetically promoted agricultural innovation in the colony." Wood concludes: "Locke, a countryman by birth and upbringing, a Baconian and Fellow of the Royal Society, an associate of Shaftesbury, Worsley, Boyle and Wilkins, could hardly have failed to be interested in agriculture."[21]

As for Ashcraft's view of Locke's economic attachments, Wood, recalling Locke's economic writings, specifically answers: "Merchants, speculators and middlemen are criticized for being unproductive drones [and] for removing money from circulation." For Wood, then, "Locke was the classic theorist of landed society and the landholder, not of commerce and mercantile interests."[22] And yet other pertinent evidence casts considerable doubt on Wood's reading of Locke. There is, for example, the matter of his and Shaftesbury's other investments. As Locke's biographer reports:

> Ashley's [i.e., Shaftesbury's] "specialty" was trade. Though a considerable landowner, he was chiefly interested in stock-holding and colonial expansion; he was the leading member of the Committee for trade [in the CABAL] government, and when the province of Carolina was founded in 1663 and put under the control of a board of Lords Proprietors, Ashley seized most of the strings. . . . He was the complete progressive capitalist in politics; he might have been invented by Marx.[23]

As for Locke, he "was easily infected with Ashley's zeal for commercial imperialism, seeing as clearly as his patron saw the possibilities it offered for personal and national enrichment."[24] A partial list of Locke's commercial involvements is provided by Peter Laslett: "He followed his wealthy patron into his investments—the Africa Company, the Lustring Company and finally the Bank of England. He invested in mortgages, lent money all his life . . . and at interest;

although he protested that he 'never lov'd stock jobbing' there is, in his letters of 1700–01 a clear example of stock-market profiteering in the shares of the Old and New East India Companies."[25] Finding, however, that Locke also "profoundly mistrusted commerce and commercial men" and "suspected the motives of the founders of the Bank of England," Laslett was forced to conclude that "no simple conception of 'ideology' will relate Locke's thought with social dynamics. . . . The attempts to make his doctrine into a straight justification of capitalism has to be . . . too complex to be convincing."[26]

Was Locke so muddled a thinker that he could encourage the appropriation of land while denouncing his nation's most successful appropriators? Was he so polemical (if not hypocritical and dishonest) a writer that he could plead with "the trading part of the nation" to enlist in the cause of exclusion (then capitalize on its labors), yet denounce the activities of the purveyors of commerce: merchants and middlemen, bankers and brokers? How could Locke support capitalist progress while questioning the propriety of the capitalist proclivity? And how could two such fine intellectual historians as Ashcraft and Wood fall into so significant a division of opinion on this question?

The problem, as I have already suggested, is conceptual—reflecting the disparity between seventeenth- and twentieth-century economic notions. For it is we who impose on Locke and his century a meaning of "capitalism" broad enough to embrace all the activities of all the classes driven by the desire for material gain. Locke, I want to suggest, had no such conception. He did not entertain, as a common denominator of legitimate human activity, the profit motive (though he would not object to the making of profit per se).

With Locke, it is always essential to seek out the fundamental principles and not simply to drop all *philosophic* context and draw inferences from this aspect of his life or that element of his writings. And it is entirely unnecessary to imagine that there is a tension between the various contexts in which his politics can appropriately be placed. Critical to a balanced appreciation of Locke's intellectual labors, I believe, is the supposition that nothing he said or did as a political activist and exclusion Whig confounds or contradicts his interest in agricultural improvement. Ashcraft can be right without making Wood wrong—and vice versa. Once we consider the political and economic doctrines alongside the deeper moral and metaphysical premises upon which they are grounded, we can begin to appraise the vast integration of Locke's several alliances and allegiances.

For Locke, the categories of legitimate economic activity proceed from and depend upon a more basic category: an elusive *moral* category. Locke's deepest commitment is not to commerce or agriculture (or, for that matter, to exclusion or anti-Catholicism); it is to God and his human creation: *man qua man*. Locke's ultimate interest lies not in wealth per se (whatever its origin or extent), but in a peculiar duty derived from the special relationship that exists between man and his maker. Man's moral duties follow from his being "the Workmanship of one Omnipotent, and infinitely wise Maker; All the Servants of one Sovereign Master, sent into the World by his order and about his business."[27]

Since such a creator cannot create anything in vain, since "it is contrary to such great wisdom to work with no fixed aim," we, his creation, can discover his design and intent by examining our own God-given constitution. It cannot possibly be that God made man, giving him "an agile, capable mind . . . and a body besides which is quick and easy to be moved . . . by virtue of the soul's authority," for no purpose whatever or for any ill-chosen purpose one might depravely conceive, "that all this equipment for action is bestowed on him by a most wise creator in order that he may . . . therefore be more splendidly idle and sluggish." It is abundantly evident to Locke "that God intends man to do something."[28]

What is man to do? What work does God demand and human reason recommend? Once again, we learn of God's design for man by examining the material that he has fashioned. We look, that is, at man's essential nature and needs. It is in the *First Treatise* that Locke urges:

> God having made Man, and planted in him, as in all other Animals, a strong desire of Self-preservation, and furnished the World with things fit for food and Rayment and their Necessaries of Life, Subservient to his design, that Man should live and abide for some time upon the Face of the Earth, and not that so curious and wonderful a piece of Workmanship by its own Negligence or want of Necessaries, should perish again presently after a few moments continuance: God, I say, having made Man and the World thus, spoke to him, (that is) directed him by his Senses and Reason . . . to the use of those things, which were serviceable for his Subsistence and given him as means of his Preservation.[29]

In Chapter 3 I listed reason, or rationality, as Locke's first and foremost moral virtue. But reason alone will not furnish humanity with the means of its preservation. To survive people must first find and then process the food and fuel upon which their preservation depends. Industry, the productive employment of human talent and energy, can be regarded as the second cardinal virtue in the Lockean moral frame. As Locke understood it: "God when he gave the World in common to all Mankind, commanded Man also to labour, and the penury of his Condition required it of him. god and his Reason commanded him to subdue the Earth, i.e., improve it for the benefit of life, and therein lay out something upon it that was his own, his labour."[30]

It easily follows from this that the cultivation of the soil and, yes, arduous labor and experimentation to raise its productive powers are worthy employments of human energy. And it is no wonder that Locke's chapter on property is so uniformly preoccupied with detailing the stages of agronomic development. Since it is Locke's purpose there to expose the conditions that rationally dictate, first, the parceling and privatizing of land and, second, the formation of civil communities, and since both of these developments necessarily occur in a rude, undeveloped natural state, Locke's attention to agriculture and primitive forms of exchange is entirely appropriate. His inattention to the more advanced commercial and financial relations is similarly understandable.

But there is no earthly reason to imagine that all of life's "comforts and conveniences" can be provided for by agricultural labor alone. Accordingly, Locke, in his *Essay concerning Human Understanding*, strongly suggests that "whatsoever is necessary for the conveniences of life, and information of virtue," whatever will conduce to a "comfortable provision for this life, and [pave] the way that leads to a better," is suitable for human industry. Wholly comfortable with the practical arts and their useful applications, Locke says, "He that first invented printing, discovered the use of the compass, or made public the virtue and right use of quinine, did more for the propagation of knowledge, for the supplying and increase of useful commodities, and saved more from the grave, than those who built colleges, workhouses, and hospitals."[31]

This should not automatically be construed as an assault on reasoned inquiry, charity, or medical care. In *De Arte Medica,* an unfinished work generally attributed to Locke and his friend and medical mentor, Thomas Sydenham (1624–1689), "the happy discoveries . . . [of] new inventions" and their role in furnishing "the conveniences of human life" are again applauded. "Of this," the authors go on,

> the ploughman, tanner, smith, baker, etc., are witnesses. the great inventions of powder and the loadstone, which have altered the whole affairs of mankind, are undeniable instances; so that those who had read and writ whole volumes of generation and corruption knew not the way to preserve or propagate the meanest species of creatures; he that could dispute learnedly of nutrition, concoction and assimilation was beholding yet to the cook and the good housewife for a wholesome and savory meal.[32]

Man does not live by bread alone. There is the need for fuel and for fabrics, for furnishings for the home and tools for the workplace. Since human preservation depends on a limitless variety of material supports, since an infinite range of goods and services are conducive to commodious living, a galaxy of productive outlets are available for industrious application — some more remunerative than others, of course. But *profit* is not the governing principle; that principle is *preservation*. It is not a question of how much land or money a man might accumulate, but how usefully his land, money, and energies are employed. In serving the market, an individual serves his maker, for in this way he not only preserves himself, but makes full use of his God-given potential. What is crucial from a moral standpoint is not what a person does, but how he chooses to do it. Neal Wood has provided a sound list of virtues and vices culled from Locke's economic essay of 1691. The list is instructive once the necessary limitation Wood includes is appropriately discounted: " 'Industry,' 'frugality,' 'sobriety,' 'diligence,' 'thrift,' 'good husbandry,' 'good order,' 'well-ordered trade,' were the terms employed by Locke that summarized his agrarian prescription . . . as opposed to 'lazy,' 'idleness,' 'indigent,' 'extravagant expenses,' 'expensive vanity,' 'debauchery,' [and] 'mismanaged trade.' "[33]

But the prescription was not written just for the man at the plough. Merchants and even money lenders are revered as useful benefactors, for, as Locke advises in a single, sweeping dictum, "trade, then, is necessary to the producing of riches, and money is necessary to the carrying on of trade."[34] Locke speaks with even-toned sanguinity, in fact, of all the productive branches of industry.[35] He appreciates what it is that will diminish it. For an individual or a nation, the sure sign of preservation is a protracted bout of material progress — i.e., prosperity. Its precondition is a diligent application of industrious energy. Remove the cause and you will not long enjoy the effect: "For want, brought on by ill-management, and nursed up by expensive vanity, will make the nation poor and spare nobody."[36]

"Ill-management" and "expensive vanity" are the bane of bountiful living and the immediate targets of Locke's invective. This is what allows him to castigate certain members of the "capitalist" classes (be they merchants, money lenders, or country gentlemen) while still championing the cause of capitalist growth.[37] At once spelling out the economic basis of moral living and rejecting the artful contrivances urged on by certain political leaders, Locke warns, "And if the virtue and provident way of living of our ancestors (content with our native conveniences of life without the costly itch after the materials of pride and luxury from abroad) were brought in fashion and countenance again amongst us; this alone would do more to keep and increase our wealth, and enrich our land, than all our paper helps, about interest, money, bullion, etc."[38]

In modern terms, we can say it is an ethic of production, not a craven life ruled by "conspicuous consumption," that Locke wishes to recommend. There is something about this ethic of industry, certainly by Locke's time, that needs to be appreciated. No individual could possibly do (i.e., produce) it all. Preservation and prosperity demanded a good measure of specialization and a relatively complex structure of market relations or, more to the point, a division of labor. It would be necessary for each moral agent to pursue one line of work (or, at best a limited few), relying on his own surplus and his neighbors' moral energies and special talents to furnish the remainder of his "comforts and conveniences." What any individual needed, in seventeenth-century terms, was a chosen "calling."

I do not think that it was Locke's primary purpose, in either his chapter on property or his considerations on sundry economic proposals (such as the legal lowering of interest), to morally instruct his peculiar audience on the worthiness of work. On that question, Locke's Protestant audience probably needed no instruction. But to gain a deeper appreciation of the context within which Locke's economic ideas were set forth, it is important to take a closer look at the people to whom Locke addressed himself.

Locke's was an age of agricultural improvement and commercial adventure, of scientific experimentation and mechanical invention. In every field individuals were busy producing the requisites of life. But England's producers were England's believers. The men of trade were also men of deep faith.[39] It is not that the Puritans happened to be the businessmen, but that for the Puritan, business, industry, and work became the essence of religious devotion. Human energy, like the wondrous rational faculty itself, was a gift from God—a gift not to be squandered in aimless passage but productively invested in hard, unremitting toil. As R. H. Tawney explained many years ago, "It is will—will organized and disciplined and inspired will quiescent in rapt adoration or straining in violent energy, but always will—which is the essence of Puritanism, and for the intensification and organization of will every instrument in that tremendous arsenal of religious fervor is mobilised."[40]

"A godly discipline was . . . the very ark of the Puritan Covenant." Work was just another name for worship, and the market a solemn cathedral for these "thinking, sober, and patient men . . . such as believe that labor and industry is their duty toward God." Commercial enterprise represented both a show of devotion and a sign of grace—a very potent brew. "God," said the Puritan divine, "doth call every man and woman . . . to serve in some peculiar employment in this world, both for their own good and the common good." This is not just the dictate of God, but the dictate of reason as well: "God hath given to man reason for this use," Richard Steele cautioned, "that he should first consider, then choose, then put in execution; and it is a preposterous and brutish thing to fix or fall upon any weighty business, such as a calling or condition of life, without a careful pondering of it in the balance of sound reason.'' The approach to business was calculating, but it was not necessarily calm. ''The Puritan flings himself into practical activities with the demonic energy of one who, all doubts allayed, is conscious that he is a sealed and chosen vessel.''[41]

The ethic of industry naturally ran up against the more traditional ethic of charity. Business, from an earthly standpoint, was self-serving. Christianity commanded brotherly sacrifice and warned that ''money is the root of all evil.'' The examples of the saints and the commands of ecclesiastical authority at first hobbled the spiritual call. The early writings of the period are filled with prohibitions and proscriptions against ungodly avarice. Thus does Ames's *De Conscientia,* described by Tawney as ''the most influential work on social ethics written in the first half of the seventeenth-century,'' admonish the faithful never to ''sell above the maximum fixed by public authority. [He] must follow the market price and 'the judgment of prudent and good men.' [He] must not take advantage of the necessities of individual buyers, must not overpraise their wares, must not sell them dearer merely because they have cost . . . much to get.''[42]

Richard Baxter's *Christian Directory,* which Tawney hails as ''a Puritan *Summa Theologia* and *Summa Moralis* in one,'' likewise subordinated business profit to religious ethic. The Puritan was still ''bound to consider first the golden rule and the public good'' and comport himself so as to ''avoid sin rather than loss.'' Eventually, the man of commerce would depreciate much of his Christian liabilities. As the century wore on, more and more Puritans came to equate work and success with their own godly good; just as they came to view sloth and failure as the wages of sin, i.e., the devil's due.[43]

The Christian's calling would no longer be an assigned station on the social hierarchy of a patriarchal civilization. It would become ''a strenuous and exacting enterprise, to be . . . chosen by each man for himself, with a deep sense of his solemn responsibilities.''[44] Personal progress and improvement was not just anticipated; it was soon converted into a Christian duty. By century's end Richard Steele was carefully instructing his audience on *The Tradesman's Calling.* From now on, Steele explained, ''if God shows you a way in which you may lawfully get more . . . and if you refuse this, and choose the less gainful way, you cross one of the ends of your Calling, and you refuse to be God's Steward.''[45] To shirk one's awesome responsibility, ''the moral duty of untiring activity,'' and choose instead ''the evils of luxury and extravagance'' was to neglect not merely God's will, but one's own rational nature. For the ''tradesman's first duty is to get a full insight into his calling, and to use his brains to improve it.''[46]

The virtue of reason and the virtue of industry thus fuse in the Puritan psyche marking a watershed in religious and human history. "Virtues are often conquered by vices," Tawney aptly concluded, "but their rout is most complete when it is inflicted by other virtues, more militant, more efficient, or more congenial." The world had indeed been turned upside down. "Plunged in the cleansing waters of later Puritanism, the qualities which less enlightened ages had denounced as social vices emerged as economic virtues. They emerged as moral virtues as well."[47]

The ethic of work infected not just the urban tradesmen. The planting classes, too, were affected with its zeal — even if many a country gentleman neglected its pressing call. Most indicative of the changing times was the changing attitude toward land reform. The business of enclosure played a leading role in seventeenth-century life and thought. "Long the typical example of uncharitable covetousness, enclosure is now considered not merely economically expedient, but morally beneficial." The moral and economic knot cannot easily be untied: "The pursuit of economic self-interest, which is the law of nature, is already coming to be identified by the pious with the operation of the providential plan, which is the law of God. Enclosure will increase the output of wool and grain. Each man knows what his land is suited to produce, and the general interest will be best served by leaving him free to produce it."[48]

The old theory that understood property as "not merely a source of income, but a public function," that invoked the principles of Christian charity and social obligation to "protect the peasant by preventing enclosure" of the commons, was fast disappearing. The theory that took its place and that "was to become in the eighteenth century almost a religion," Tawney correctly concluded, "was that expressed by Locke."[49]

An intriguing curiosity emerges from Wood's persuasive study. For his part, Ashcraft was able to contextually situate Locke's political theory alongside a long line of exclusion Whig tracts. Ashcraft bolstered his claim considerably by going on to trace Locke's real-world behavior as assistant to Shaftesbury and political exile in the Dutch republic (1683–1689). In short, down to the Glorious Revolution, Locke wrote and acted like the radical revolutionary that he was. Can Wood make the same claim? On Wood's contextual terms, I think not. But on closer examination, i.e., by exploring a deeper, more fundamental aspect of seventeenth-century experience, we can grasp and comprehend the various causes and commitments to which Locke attached himself.

It is noticeable, in the context of Locke's prodigious lifelong labors, how little time and attention he devoted to the kind of economic calling Wood examined. Though he owned (by inheritance) a modest amount of land and scrupulously collected rent all his life, he did not toil in the fields or energetically seek to enlarge his landed possessions. Nor did Locke exemplify the call of commerce. Although he invested in commercial ventures and loaned money at interest, he could hardly qualify as a merchant prince or capitalist financier. In short, though he was by no stretch of the imagination a poor man, acquisitiveness did not play a pivotal role in Locke's own life. Mostly, he wrote books, kept journals, and carried on an avid correspondence. If he was socially active in his adult years, it was owing to his political principles and civic proclivities more than to any private material ambitions; Locke was, first, a radical, then a holder of public office.

Ought we to conclude that this great spokesman for the Protestant calling shamelessly shirked his own moral and religious responsibilities, writing about wealth, yet unwilling to work very hard for it? Not at all, for it was *work,* rather than *wealth,* that mattered most in the Protestant psyche. Labor was for the sake of improvement, not enrichment. The calling, in sum, must be understood in the broadest possible light to encompass any useful field that would serve to increase and extend the comforts and conveniences of temporal life. Any ''job description'' that could accomplish this end would constitute a fit outlet for human industry.

Certainly, tradesmen would bring the necessities of life to market, and financiers would furnish the fuel that turned the steady wheels of trade. Agricultural improvers could discover, and artful mechanics invent, ever-more-useful methods and machines of production. But for the seventeenth-century mind, awash in the discoveries of ''a Boyle or Sydenham . . . and the incomparable Mr. Newton,'' rational inquiry itself would serve the human quest for improvement. Scientific investigation too would itself become an exacting enterprise—a demanding calling—to be strenuously undertaken by anyone fit and prepared for its peculiar challenges. As Locke affirmed: ''I would not . . . be thought to disesteem or dissuade the study of *nature.* I readily agree, the contemplation of his works gives us occasion to admire, revere, and glorify their Author: and if rightly directed, may be of greater benefit to mankind than the monuments of exemplary charity that have at so great charge, been raised by the founders of hospitals and almshouses.''[50]

The historical root of this understanding deserves a little closer scrutiny. In *John Locke and Agrarian Capitalism,* Neal Wood ably revealed how Francis Bacon, in urging his audience to unlock the secrets of the soil, inspired successive generations of agricultural improvers to raise its productive powers for the benefit and use of life. But it was in his examination of *The Politics of Locke's Philosophy* that Wood exposed the Baconian roots that would blossom into the several important branches of seventeenth-century (and Lockean) natural philosophy.

Bacon was the arch exponent of the New Learning, the empirical approach to human understanding. Lord chancellor in the court of James I, he was among the first to fathom the sheer usefulness of properly directed human inquiry. Though his own record of scientific accomplishment was not substantial, Bacon's "great service to science," as Basil Wiley explained, was in giving "it an incomparable advertisement, by associating with it his personal prestige, his 'elizabethan' glamour, and his great literary power."[51] He really did much more than this. Before human curiosity could be fully awakened and the secrets of nature systematically explored, the human mind would have to be released from its bondage to scriptural dogma and a hegemonic church authority. In short, the first important battle waged in the struggle for human independence was not political, but epistemological. Bacon's task was to show that scientific inquiry was "Promethean and not Mephistophelean." Bacon's tactic was ingenious. The study of nature would be nothing more than the "study of God's Work, as a supplement to His Word. . . . God has revealed himself to man by means of two scriptures: first, of course, through the written word, but also, secondly, through his handiwork, the created universe. To study nature, therefore, cannot be contrary to religion; indeed, it is part of the duty we owe to the Great Artificer of the world."[52]

But there was more in Bacon's way than the word of God implanted in Scripture; there was the accumulated wisdom of all the venerated ancients. What passed for energetic inquiry in all the schools was the mere picking apart of logical incongruencies and wondrous paradoxes in the body of received opinion. Logical deduction from long-accepted, church-endorsed axioms, rather than careful observation and disciplined induction, was the method of the Old Learning.

If real inquiry was to get under way the authority of the ancients would have to be challenged no less than the authority of Scripture. Once again, Bacon would eagerly undertake the task at hand. Unable to abide the "dead hand" of scholastic learning, the empty laboratories of "hair-splitters," unwilling to countenance the "proud, puffed-up minds" laboring "to except ignorance from ignominy," Bacon sallied forth: "Sciences of this kind stand almost at a stay, without receiving any augmentations worthy of the human race; in so much that . . . not only what was asserted once is asserted still, but that what was a question once is a question still."[53]

What Bacon set himself to demonstrate is the folly of holding fast to the wisdom of the ancients when that meant closing one's eyes and ears to the sweeping discoveries of the moderns. Thus the emerging "mechanical arts," Bacon urges, "having in them some breath of life, are continually growing and becoming more perfect. As originally invented they are commonly rude, clumsy, and shapeless; afterwards they acquire new powers and more commodious arrangements and constructions."[54]

As a single invention progresses, develops, and is improved, as a keen-witted apprentice may invent a marvelous labor-saving procedure such as the master who gave him his trade could barely conceive, so all learning is cumulative. "No doubt," Bacon admits, "the ancients proved themselves in . . . abstract meditations, wonderful men." Nevertheless, "as in former ages when men sailed only by observation of the stars they could indeed coast along the shores of the old continent or cross a few small and mediterranean seas; but before the ocean could be traversed and the new world discovered, the use of the mariner's needle, as a more faithful and certain guide, had to be found out."[55] Received opinion was as a dead hand. The New Learning would be for the benefit and use of life: "In behalf of the business which is in hand I entreat men to believe that it is not an opinion to be held, but a work to be done."[56]

Here I stand, proclaims Bacon in his *Great Instauration,* laboring to lay the foundation "not of any sect or doctrine, but of human utility and power."[57] But it is in the *Nova Organon* that Bacon most clearly names the grand object of his desire: "Human knowledge and human power meet in one; for where the cause is not known the effect cannot be produced. Nature to be commanded must be obeyed; and that which in contemplation is as the cause is in operation as the rule."[58]

Knowledge is for power's sake: not the kind of power by which some men dominate and enslave others, but the kind that will enable mankind to rule nature for the betterment, the improvement, of the earthly estate. What a thing to contemplate. If nature could only be *obeyed*—i.e., studied by reason's purifying light, marking and measuring the material provided by the senses—it could then be *commanded*. Dreaded famines and floods, plagues and pestilence, storms and tempests might be stilled forever. The social condition, too, could be improved. Incessant war and civil conflagration could cease and civilization settle in peace, comfort, and quietude. Invention and exploration could go forward and the human condition steadily improved. It was a vision of progress and perfectibility that would haunt the Western imagination for generations to come.

Although not occupying a central position, the New Learning at least took up some space within the Puritan mindset. Thus Brownowski and Mazlish estimate that of the sixty-eight early fellows of the Royal Society about whom we have information, forty-two were clearly Puritans.[59] The Royal Society was founded in 1662 at Gresham College. Originally, it comprised two scientific groups: one, already occupying the grounds of Gresham, was headed by the mathematician John Wallis. Wallis during the Civil War had been busy decoding enemy messages for Cromwell. The second scientific group belonged to Robert Boyle, the chemist and physicist, whose family had also sided with Parliament against the king.

The preoccupation of the Royal Society fellows, whose thinking had been formed by the writings of Francis Bacon, was practical. Brownowski and Mazlish estimate that roughly 60 percent of the work done by the Royal Society in its first thirty years was prompted by practical concerns and only 40 percent by issues of pure science. Useful inventions and gadgets proliferated, and if an experiment did not prove functional overnight, the fellows "were tempted by morning to move on to another."[60] Summing up the outlook of "such dedicated christian virtuosi as Boyle, Newton, Wallis and Wilkins," but first pressed by Bacon, Wood aptly concluded: "While science cannot help us fathom the mysteries of religion it is crucial to praising god and ameliorating the lot of man. Our intellect is a gift from the Supreme Maker. By employing it in exploring nature and revealing the wondrous order and regularity of the world, we are at once . . . serving the Holy Architect . . . and forwarding His great design."[61]

Some of the most notable Baconian natural philosophers, as we have already seen, left the Puritan fold at the Restoration. Hence, as Margaret Jacob writes, "after 1660, Puritanism gave way to liberal Anglicanism, and the mantle of science passed to a new generation of intellectual leaders."[62] Among these we can count such virtuosi and latitudinarians as Robert Boyle, Thomas Sprat, John Wilkins, and Isaac Newton. Allowing that Locke, too, counted himself an Anglican and latitudinarian, one of Wood's interesting discoveries can nonetheless be appreciated. Seeing that "there was a definite affinity for Bacon among those of Puritan background and upbringing . . . Locke not the least of them," Wood was drawn to a most fascinating connection. Bacon had dreamt of a universal science, comprehending all useful objects of study. He compiled a listing of those branches in a lengthy "Catalogue of Particular Histories." Insightfully, Bacon grasped that if a full knowledge of nature was to be had, the faculty charged with *knowing* nature would also have to be investigated. Accordingly, the seventy-eighth item in Bacon's "Catalogue" is listed as a "History of the Intellectual Faculties, Reflexion, Imagination, Discourse, Memory, etc." "Locke's essay, *De Intellectu Humano,*" Wood imaginatively concludes, "was just such a natural history, one that would have satisfied Bacon's complaint that an analysis of the understanding in terms of sensation still remained to be done."[63]

But science would have to study more than the phenomena of nature and the phenomenal faculty of understanding. The social world, too, would need to be explored and explained, a realization amply reflected in the work of the Royal Society. Its scientists were not satisfied merely to chart the heavens and seas for the benefit of world trade. The whole universe of human commerce needed to be studied as well. And the thrust of inquiry was ever driven by practical considerations. Accordingly, the society "spent much of its time attempting to promote industry, empire and trade."

The marked interest displayed toward the New World is particularly notable. As J. R. Jacob explains in his study of *Robert Boyle and the English Revolution,* even before its incorporation in 1662 the Royal Society had been urged by the king to "survey the riches of the empire." Boyle was himself instrumental in "the preparation of a history of trades." Throughout the 1660s, the fellows, including Boyle, "continued to press . . . for surveys of the natural wealth of New England with a view to its systematic exploitation." Novel projects, based on a working knowledge of the mineral resources of the New World, would furnish employment for English emigrants, as well as America's native population. Science, and its commercial applications, would introduce the Protestant way of work and worship to the natives of the New World. In England and America, the "patient inquiry by which science proceeds" could present "a model of how men might behave and as such would serve as a healthy corrective of the religious enthusiasm" that was so destructive of social peace and progress. Thus were "the purposes of trade, empire, science, and religion . . . wedded together in the minds of the Fellows."[64]

But the first business of the Royal Society was science, i.e., rational inquiry into the natural laws governing the relations of all the objects of its study. Thus the laws of production and trade would, themselves, become fit objects of study. To that end, empirical tools and rigorous conceptual methods would have to be furnished. It fell to Sir William Petty (1623–1687), an early fellow of the society, to devise the statistical methods for that particular undertaking. Petty's *Political Arithmetick* (1691) and *Treatise on Taxes and Contributions* (1692) laid the foundations of modern economic science. Statistics could now be gathered and organized for study and policy recommendation. And beyond matters pertaining to political economy, questions relating to the laws and organization of the polity — the civil frame within which men would live and labor — would also have to be investigated. A science of politics, too, could serve a useful human purpose.

Certainly such speculation could degenerate into a fruitless, endless splitting of intellectual hairs. Bacon knew it, and so did Locke. The learned doctors of the schools might not advance human understanding by any appreciable measure, but then country gentlemen and certain commercial middlemen may also live idle, extravagant, and unproductive lives. In publishing *Some Considerations on the Consequences of Lowering the Rate of Interest and Raising the Value of Money* (and sundry other economic papers), and in publishing *An Essay concerning the True, Original, Extent and End of Civil Government,* as well as his epistemological and educational writings, John Locke revealed, in unmistakable terms, his steadfast devotion to *his* chosen calling. If, as Tawney wrote, "what is required of the Puritan is not individual meritorious acts, but a holy life—a system in which every element is grouped around a central idea, the service of God, from which all disturbing irrelevancies have been pruned, and to which all minor interests are subordinated," then Locke, as few who came before or after him, did what was demanded. Pangle's question can again be considered:

> How does Locke's concern with self-knowledge, self-possession, and comfortable self-preservation entail his public spirited concern with enlightening his fellow men? Until this question receives an adequate answer, we cannot say that we have found in Locke's rationalism a rational justification of his way of life. . . . Locke's apparent failure to explain his own civic spirit is only the most egregious instance of a more unanswered question that pervades his writings. . . . [How does] the Lockean moral reasoning provide . . . an adequate rational justification for the moral action that is required and expected in even a permissive Lockean civil society[?][65]

The rationale for Locke's civic deeds and intellectual outpourings should now be more clear. And Panglean dualism (the false dichotomy that pits the "active" against the "intellectual" sides of virtue) can be critically exploded. Once we begin to appreciate that so very much human activity, "high" intellectual and political activity as well as "low" economic activity, is necessary for the paramount Baconian goal of human improvement and that all such activity demands a profound measure of toleration and liberty, we can put Pangle's pressing question to rest. If the proper, God-directed, reason-dictated life is to be lived, it will be necessary to furnish, among other things: (1) the means of discovering the nature of that life (hence, the *Essay* on the understanding); (2) the methods by which children might, accordingly, be raised (hence the *Thoughts* on education); (3) a system of political economy suitable for the life they are to lead (hence the *Considerations* on interest, money, and trade); and (4) a frame of government that will enable humans to live as the maker intended (hence, *The Two Treatises* and the radicalism of Locke's life). If, as Bacon urged, the task was not in the knowing but in the doing, then the farmer and philosopher, the shopkeeper and scientist, the educator, economist, and political activist would all have to do it together.

5
A Benignant Egoism: John Locke's Social Ethic

From the discussion thus far Locke's moral teaching could be reduced to this: Be rational and industrious, i.e., think and work. It is an ethic well suited to an individual, socially isolated and living alone in a state of nature. Is it sufficient, however, for a social being living in society? Are there, for Locke, any moral duties that individuals owe to one another? Is the individual designed to live entirely for his or her own sake, going after and getting whatever he or she wants, regardless of the impact such behavior might have on others? Or is every person morally obliged to consider and care for the welfare of others, sacrificing oneself, when necessary, for their benefit? Does Locke uphold an unbridled egoism, or might he yet counsel altruism? In the secondary literature, both interpretations have been proffered.

The egoist reading was most aggressively advanced in C. B. Macpherson's *The Political Theory of Possessive Individualism*. There he ascribed to Locke not only an argument defending unlimited appropriation of land and riches and, therefore, a great inequality of wealth, but also a doctrine of "class differentials" that rendered the lower ranks of men devoid not merely of property, but of reason and rights as well. The sacrifice of these men's interests to the interests of the industrious appropriators, who alone were rational and enjoyed rights, signified, in Macpherson's estimation, Locke's allowance not merely for inequality, but for exploitation as well.[1]

At the other end of the interpretive schism stands the view of James Tully. Reading Locke's writings in relation to a host of earlier contributors to a discourse on property and natural law, Tully found anything but a system that emphasized egoism and exploitation. Tully's Locke defends nothing if not an ethic of altruism and sacrifice for the sake of others.[2] It will be the competing claims of these two commentators that I shall adjudicate here.

In penning his *Two Treatises of Governing,* Locke was doing his all for his patron, Shaftesbury, and the cause of exclusion. "In the face of the prevailing Whig convention of appealing to the prescriptive force of history" (i.e., the immemorial common law, Magna Charta, and the decisions of important English jurists, most notably Sir Edward Coke [1552–1634], Chief Justice of the King's Bench),[3] Locke's ideological task, as Tully notes, "is discharged in the language of natural law and rights."[4]

The move was made necessary by the reintroduction of the ideas of Sir Robert Filmer (1588–1653) into the ideological contest on behalf of Stuart absolutism. Bypassing all agreements between sovereign and subject, Filmer had founded sovereignty in the incontestable right of dominion that God gave to Adam and that, through Adam, had been passed on to each patriarchal successor. Transcending the compacts and common laws of nations, political right (for Filmer, absolute power) had thus come to be founded in an immutable, natural, and absolute law—the divine gift of God. If the Whigs were to win their ideological battle, they would have to assault Filmer on his own high ground and then construct a well-honed natural law argument of their own on behalf of popular sovereignty and limited government. Locke easily perceived the requirements of the contest. Addressing his readers—friend and foe alike—he candidly urged:

> 'Tis true, the Civil Lawyers have pretended to determine some of these Cases concerning the Succession of Princes; but by our A's Principles [i.e., Filmer's], they have meddled in a matter that belongs not to them: For if all political Power be derived only from Adam, and be to descend only to his Successive Heirs, by the *Ordinance of God and Divine Institution,* this is a Right Antecedent and Paramount to all Government; and therefore the positive laws of Men, cannot determine that which is it self the Foundation of all Law and Government.[5]

The problem, as Nozick noticed some time ago, is this: If it was Locke's avowed aim to put forward a powerful argument for limited government rooted in the laws of God and nature, how is it that he "does not provide anything remotely resembling a satisfactory explanation of the status and basis of the law of nature in his *Second Treatise*"?[6]

Nozick's remark invites two general replies. First, this discussion has shown that a comprehensive natural law philosophy is indeed suggested in the opening pages of Locke's *Second Treatise*. When Locke writes, "The State of Nature has a Law of Nature to govern it, which obliges every one; And reason, which is that

Law, teaches all Mankind, who will but consult it," he is very much discoursing on precepts of immutable, natural law. Moreover, he covers a great deal of philosophic ground when he immediately adds, "For Men being all the Workmanship of one Omnipotent, and infinitely wise Maker, All the Servants of one Sovereign Master, sent into the World by his order and about his business, [and that] they are his property whose Workmanship they are, made to last during his, not one another's Pleasure." Locke is certainly introducing into his social and political speculations the fundamental considerations he had developed in his early *Essays on the Law of Nature*. And though not spelled out in so fine a detail as in his philosophic writings, it is clear that Locke's social and political philosophy will hinge on the work of the maker and on his relation to his highest creation: man.

To gain a clear appreciation of Locke's social ethic, however, it will be necessary to become acquainted with a tradition of philosophic speculation to which Locke was self-consciously contributing, i.e., the seventeenth-century discourse on natural law. In countering Sir Robert Filmer's ideas on political right, Locke was issuing his own defense of natural law and popular sovereignty, as his readers well understood.

As Jacob and others have examined a tradition known as latitudinarianism, as Pocock and Robbins have exposed a language of republicanism with its special vocabulary and outlook, so a number of recent scholars have pointed to yet another paradigm that would occupy the attention of many leading seventeenth-century lights. Among those who figure most prominently in this discourse are Hugo Grotius (1583–1645), Samuel Pufendorf (1632–1694), John Selden (1584–1654), Richard Cumberland (1631–1718), and Locke's friend James Tyrrell (1642–1718).

Jean Barbeyrac (1674–1744), a French legal theorist, published the writings of Grotius and Pufendorf and provided a critical summation of natural law thought down to his day. In "An Historical and Critical Account of the science of morality, and the Progress it has made in the world, from the earliest times down to the publication of this work," an essay included in the annotated English edition of Pufendorf's *The Law of Nature and Nations,* Barbeyrac places Locke squarely in the tradition of these natural law writers. Granting to Grotius the honor of having virtually founded "the methodological Study of the Law of Nature," Barbeyrac nevertheless "grants Locke the honour of completing the theoretical reconstruction in a definitive manner."[7] Barbeyrac specifically asserts the superiority of Locke's philosophy of property over the views of earlier writers and tells us that the workmanship model, barely touched upon in the *Second Treatise,* forms the foundation of seventeenth-century natural law theory.

In what circumstances is this seventeenth-century natural law discourse rooted? What are its guiding and common conceptions? What are its aims? And with what conceptual materials was it to work out the solutions to the problems it encountered? Like the latitudinarians, the natural law writers began with a deep confidence in reason and with an assertion of a special relation binding man to his maker. Where the latitudinarians relied more heavily on a providential reading of God's unwritten work, i.e., nature, arguing by extrapolation from the behavior of physical and sentient objects to the proper organization of men in society, the natural law writers rooted their social teaching in a more immediate relation between every individual. The common commitment shared by the writers on natural law may be easily summarized: (1) the universe is God's creation, as is every man; (2) men are born equal and born into an original state of nature; (3) all things generously given by God are given to all men in common for their benefit and use; (4) God wills the preservation of all mankind; and (5) insofar as the state of nature contains grave inconveniences because of the fallen state of man, God enjoins all men to form civil bonds, i.e., to enter society and bind themselves under government.

From this basic condition and from the understanding that God gave all the fruits of the world to mankind generally for its benefit and use, the natural law writers sought to justify the division of property, the inequalities that existed in their respective societies, and the legal institutions under which people now lived. The central task was to show how the natural and original equal right to all the fruits of nature could legitimately end in the unequal division of wealth and status in civil society and, hence, (1) the justice of existing social relations and (2) the necessity of political obedience.

It was Sir Robert Filmer's aim to show that the premises of the natural law tradition could not support the conclusions—and social conditions—the natural lawyers were bent on defending. Filmer mercilessly pointed to the contradictions in the original postulates of natural law speculation, arguing that those postulates had to end in anarchy and ruin. What hung in the balance by 1680 was every freehold claimed by every Englishman in the land. And Shaftesbury's enemies never ceased warning that by the doctrine of natural equality, any popular cabal deprived of an equality of possessions, fired by envy, and feeding on a contentious demand for political rights and representation could freely level the property of every God-fearing subject of the realm.[8] Only a dismissal of the presumed natural equality and original liberty, only a steady devotion to absolute, patriarchal cum monarchical rule could protect the propertied from the clamorous mob. If you owned property then, given the historical force of Interregnum precedent, it would be difficult indeed to avow such a natural equality.

It is important to look a little closer at the natural law discourse concerning the principle of property, for it was by exhuming the seventeenth-century dialogue over property that modern commentators came to ascribe to Locke a salutary commitment to an ethic not of ribald egoism, but of altruism.

The essence of Filmer's attack on the populist or contractarian model proffered by the natural law theorists, as Gordon Schochet has written, centered on "the moral and logical impossibility of deriving government, private property, and the hierarchical arrangements that exist in society from the conditions of original natural freedom and equality predicated by contractual thinkers."[9]

Grotius, for example, posited a primitive communism in nature, whereby the fruits of the earth were given to all men in common for their preservation. He defended the principle of private property by sanctioning "seizure" or "first possession." What seizure entitled a man to, however, was merely the use of what he had seized (e.g., a parcel of land). Genuine property rights could only be conferred by common consent, or agreement. Grotius writes:

> Thus also we see what was the original of property, which was derived not from a mere internal act of the mind, since one could not possibly guess what others intended to appropriate to themselves, that he might abstain from it; and besides several might have a mind to the same thing, at the same time; but it resulted from a certain compact and agreement, either expressly, as by a division; or else tacitly, as by seizure. For as soon as living in common was no longer approved of, all men were supposed, and ought to be supposed to have consented, that each should appropriate to himself, by right of first possession, what could not have been divided.[10]

The crux of the dilemma is this. Grotius's conception was of a world originally "owned by everyone through their common rights. . . . [Thus] every time something was individually appropriated, everyone else lost what was once theirs."[11] The problem for Filmer consisted of the impossibility of ever obtaining a unanimous consent to relinquish any part of a common inheritance to any lone individual.

> Certainly it was a rare felicity, that all men in the world at one instant of time should agree together in one mind to change the natural community of all things into private dominion; for without such a unanimous consent it was not possible for community to be altered: for if but one man in the world had dissented, the alteration had been un-

just, because that man by the law of nature had a right to the common use of all things.[12]

A parallel argument could as easily be made for political obligation. As Filmer writes, "If it be imagined that the people were ever but once free from subjection by nature, it will prove a mere impossibility ever lawfully to introduce any kind of government whatsoever, without apparent wrong to a multitude of people."[13] As with property, so with political obligation; neither could be instituted without a unanimous, simultaneous agreement of all individuals in the world, for by nature all men are free and equal and enjoy a share in a common patrimony. No number of individuals, in sum, could give away the freedom or property enjoyed equally by all.

But there is more. Not only would it be physically impossible to ever obtain unanimous consent to parcel the earth or surrender natural freedom for political bonds, but even if such consent could be had, the agreements of the parent would have no bearing on the natural equality and freedom of the child. "Where children take nothing by gift or by direct descent from their parents, but have an equal and common interest with them, there is no reason . . . that the acts of the fathers should bind the sons."[14] The writers who followed Grotius made important alterations in natural law theory. And though many of these changes went undiscussed by Filmer, they too would have to be considered by Locke if he was to work through to a satisfactory natural law theory defining the limits of political obligation and authority and protecting the sanctity of property.

One issue, especially, deserves some consideration. Owing to the primal obligation of natural law to preserve mankind, Grotius posited what has been called "inclusive rights." In contrast to an "exclusive" right to one's own property, this consisted of everyone's right to be included in the goods and resources necessary for human preservation. As such it limited the "exclusivity" of individual property and placed upon the propertied a duty of charity. John Selden, however, denied the moral obligation to give charity, insisting on the exclusiveness of property. He went on, however, to grant to civil communities the final authority to provide for the welfare of the needy. As Horne has written: "The renunciation of common rights explains why the right of necessity [hence the obligation of charity] could not be invoked, but the ability of a people to make virtually any law they wanted opened the way for a nation to turn voluntary charity toward the poor into a system of poor relief financed by taxes."[15]

In the writings of Richard Cumberland, the concept of the common good took precedence. In or out of civil society, that which was deemed to be in the common interest could be enacted and undertaken. If the principle of private property served that end, as Cumberland and the others believed it did, then so be it. It was no part of his plan to level men's estates, and all of the natural law writers believed that only the preservation of the property relations existing in their day could contribute to the peace and preservation of society. But on the principle of the "common good," what would prevent the overturning of property should there be widespread distress over the division of land and wealth by an awakening populace? If it was ultimately the people, Filmer's democratic mob, who were to define what was and was not good for the common people of England, then what could not be countenanced under Cumberland's prescription? Cumberland went on to endorse Selden's political welfare provisions. And just what species of provision, given the tug and tempo of politics, could not be demanded given enough time?

By far, Samuel Pufendorf's *Of the Law of Nature and Nations* (1672) was the preeminent contribution to natural law theory down to Locke's day. Pufendorf would make one critical innovation in Grotius's postulates. Where the latter posited a "positive community" in the state of nature, whereby everyone owned everything, Pufendorf introduced a "negative community," insisting that originally nothing was owned as such. For him, no one was necessarily entitled to anything, and the goods of the earth "lie free for any taker."[16] This approach avoided the problem Filmer ascribed to Grotius, namely, showing how everyone could renounce their common rights and so invite the division of property. In making this move, however, he also had to renounce the principle of original, natural rights as such. Thus the advent of property for Pufendorf "necessarily presupposeth some human act, and some covenant either tacit or express." As Horne concludes: "The moral content of a property right . . . could be supplied only by agreements between individuals. . . . Only through an agreement could the physical act of taking become the moral act of owning."[17]

As with the other theorists of natural law, Pufendorf conceived of a God who enjoins the preservation of all, not the mere enrichment of some. The law of "necessity" is fully operative and even allows individuals to violate rights of property in times of extreme distress. The rich had a duty toward the downtrodden, and charity was morally obligatory. As with Selden, however, Pufendorf recognized that such violations could be obviated should civil society enjoin "a strict and perfect obligation" of charity, i.e., a system of public assistance. Insofar as the poor could be assured their subsistence, the right of necessity could not be demanded.[18] Invoking the common good with Cumberland, Pufendorf went on to defend a host of public interventions, including wage and price controls, guilds, and the right to regulate inheritance and marriage, charter commercial monopolies, introduce sumptuary laws, and compel people to work.

Notwithstanding such concessions to positive acts restricting rights or redistributing property in society, it was the singular object of the natural law writers to uphold the sanctity of property and defend against its wanton invasion. The question was that given these various concessions to "necessity," charity, and sacrifice, could property be adequately defended? Or could Filmer's weighty challenge be expanded to all of these variations on the populist, equalitarian theme?

Locke, of course, asserted the original liberty and equality of all men and went on to build a theory of property and civil government from that metaphysical base — all the while working with the conceptual tools bequeathed by the natural law theorists. As with the latitudinarians, however, Locke did not agree on all points with his predecessors. Most important, where Grotius, Pufendorf, and the others employed their theories in the service of absolutism, Locke ended up advocating the rights of resistance and revolution. But to start from the beginning and to fill in the phrases already cited:

> The State of Nature has a Law of Nature to govern it, which . . .
> teaches all Mankind, who will but consult it, that being all equal and
> independent, no one ought to harm another in his Life, Health, Liberty, or Possessions. For Men being all the Workmanship of one Omnipotent . . . Maker, All the Servants of one Sovereign Master . . .
> [and] being furnished with like Faculties, sharing all in one Community of Nature, there cannot be supposed any such Subordination
> among us, that may Authorize us to Destroy one another, as if we
> were made for one another's uses.[19]

Reason, as we have seen, has several meanings for Locke. It is an instrument of cognition through which we come to understand the nature of the universe, including human nature. But it is also an instrument of evaluation, through which we discover our moral duties and responsibilities. To follow reason in its fullest sense is to acknowledge the essential equality of every individual and to follow whatever principles flow from that inherent equality. This is best captured in the ancient idea of "right reason."

Locke's challenge was to answer Filmer's objections and show that this original equality of all men, including the equal right to the fruits of nature, was compatible with the preservation of property, security under law, and, when necessary, political resistance. Locke had to persuade his readers that in resisting James's succession to the throne on the basis of natural equality and popular consent (rather than patriarchal appointment), English property relations would not be overthrown and anarchy visited on the nation, Filmer's protestations notwithstanding.

What Locke sets out to show is "how Men might come to have a *property* in several parts of that which God gave to Mankind in common . . . without any express Compact." For "if such a consent as that was necessary, Man . . . [would have] starved, notwithstanding the Plenty God had given him."[20] To discharge his assignment Locke makes a number of important theoretical moves. Most important perhaps, he grounds property in nature, and not, as the earlier rights theorists were wont to do, in social convention or contractual arrangement. And he does so while avoiding no fewer than three traps Grotius fell into vis-à-vis Filmer.

First, while allowing that in the state of nature the whole world is owned in common, i.e., adopting the "positive community" plan, he will need no unanimous consent of the world's shareholders to divide this common property. This is because, though the whole world is owned in common, each owner is entitled to only that share that is necessary for his own preservation. The idea is clearly elaborated in a useful, if simple, example: "Though the Water running in the Fountain be every ones, yet who can doubt, but that in the Pitcher is his only who drew it out?" This is buttressed by what Macpherson has called the "spoilage" and "sufficiency" qualifications. An individual is entitled to the property he has labored to extract, so long as there is as much and as good left for others to appropriate through their own labor, and as long as what he extracts is not left to spoil uselessly in his possession. As Locke affirms: "For he that leaves as much as another can make use of, does as good as take nothing at all. No Body could think himself injur'd by the drinking of another Man, though he took a good Draught, who had a whole River of the same Water left him to quench his thirst." What's more, "the case of Land and Water, where there is enough of both, is perfectly the same."[21]

Second is the question of what it is that makes the water (or anything else) one's own. For Locke, it is neither a question of "seizure," nor "first possession," nor common consent; it is simply one's own labor. By mixing industrious energies with the fruits of the earth, be it in the act of picking a wild berry, extracting coal, or planting a row of corn, one mixes something that is *his alone* with the resources of nature, thereby adding something to the natural product and so making it one's own.[22] Locke clearly intends to apply this theory to more than mere "use rights," for the same analysis is made with respect to the enclosing of land and the products that follow from its improvement. Locke thus emphasizes, *"As much Land* as a Man Tills, Plants, Improves, Cultivates, and can use the Product of, so much is his *Property."*[23] This property, Locke assumes throughout his entire discussion, is what makes it possible for the individual to fulfill his moral duty to God and practice the second cardinal virtue: industriousness. God and reason, as we have already seen, command man to labor, to improve the earth for his benefit and use. This alone requires rights of ownership. "And hence subduing and cultivating the Earth, and having Dominion, we see are joyned together. The one gave title to the other. So that God, by commanding to subdue, gave Authority so far to *appropriate*. And the Condition of Humane Life, which requires Labour and Materials to work on necessarily introduces *private possessions*."[24]

The third important innovation concerned the contract that formalized property relations. Filmer had wondered when and how such a compact could ever have been concluded. Locke was able to elude the entire dilemma by making the contract not an agreement to respect divisions of land, but merely an agreement among men to use money.[25] The introduction of this medium of exchange obviated the natural law limitations on accumulation and ushered in an era of, in Macpherson's well-chosen words, "unlimited individual accumulation."[26] Since individuals now sell the product of their labor to buyers who will use them before they spoil, since gold and silver themselves cannot spoil, and since the labor that is applied in the process of accumulation radically enhances the value of the earth's produce (an acre of cultivated land being equivalent to an enormity of land left fallow), men may indeed accumulate as much as their industry, ambition, and talent will allow without injuring others.[27]

Macpherson's reading of Locke's allowance for unlimited appropriation has been generally accepted, though the more general conclusion that Locke therefore supports an unbridled egoism has, of late, been roundly criticized. Having placed Locke squarely within the natural law discourse of his age, and having tied Locke's moral teaching to its Christian roots, an impressive number of recent interpreters have vigorously rejected the individualist or egoist reading of Locke's writings. Dunn, Ashcraft, Tuck, Horne, and, above all, Tully have emphasized the altruist and collectivist bearing of Locke's social thought. It is to this reading that I shall now turn, placing the greatest emphasis on James Tully's significant interpretative study of the *Two Treatises of Government*.

As early as 1969, John Dunn was urging that while Locke did indeed appear to sanction "vast but altogether just differentials in the ownership of property" resulting from the "relations of capitalist production and monetary exchange," there is entirely "no reason . . . to suppose that he believed the life of unlimited capitalist appropriation to exemplify a greater level of moral rationality than the life of the devout peasant."[28] Tully went much further, finding nowhere in Locke's political writings the requisite institutions of capitalism: banking, investment, stock incorporation, or industrial wages. In fact, says Tully, echoing Keith Tribe, "it is not only wage labour which is absent from Locke's writings; the capitalist finds no space there either."[29] As for "money," it is not so much the means of exchange, for Tully's Locke, as it is the "Root of all evil." Its acceptance "outside of civil society" may be natural; it may even be inevitable. But by Tully's lights, it is no blessing. "The acceptance of money," he takes Locke to say, "brings with it the fall of man."[30]

In a serious sense, capitalism is but the social expression of a philosophic egoism. And that philosophic base, too, Tully claims is missing. The spiritual dimensions of Locke's thought are powerful enough to smash the "Adamite" claims of Filmer without falling into the "Atomite" trap that claimed Hobbes. Locke was not a capitalist; he was a Christian and, therefore, an altruist. And Tully is not alone in this opinion. After carefully placing Locke's social thought in the context of the natural law discourse of his age, Tuck forthrightly concluded: "It is the clear tenor of Locke's argument that the industrious poor are always *entitled* to the wherewithal with which to make their livelihood. . . . It is also true that societies can make explicit and positive agreements about the distribution of property, as about any other matters, and that the distribution can be altered thereby."[31]

In similar fashion, Horne found Locke "explicitly enjoin[ing] the political community to organize relief." He thus quotes Locke to this effect: "The first and fundamental natural law, which is to govern the legislative itself, is the protection of the society, and (as far as will consist with the public good) of every person in it."[32] And Ashcraft in his weighty examination of Locke's *Two Treatises of Government,* concurs, stating the categorical imperative this way:

> Locke's notion of morality is firmly rooted in the assumption that individuals bear a collective responsibility towards others, defined for them by the precepts of natural law. . . . whatever degree of emphasis one wishes to attribute to the individualism of Lockean thought it cannot be allowed . . . to override the importance of Locke's conception of the universe in terms of the collective and communal responsibilities of mankind.[33]

But the most comprehensive casting of the collectivist spirit of Locke's social thought remains James Tully's *A Discourse on Property.* As Tully points out, and as the discussion in Chapter 3 explained, for Locke, man is inherently *dependent,* not, as Strauss and Macpherson claimed, independent and metaphysically alone. Strauss had gone so far as to argue that Locke was really a wolf named Hobbes, dressed in sheeps' clothing, masking his immoral meaning behind well-accepted Christian pieties.[34] This is the view Tully most profoundly rejects.

Hobbes, the arch materialist, looked at man interacting in his natural habitat; he could not find "society." The human condition, for him, was not all that different from the physical condition: it was all matter in motion. For Hobbes, the original state was composed of individuals, socially isolated and in competition, one with another, for scarce resources and for reputation and glory (upon which each one's preservation depended). It was a state of "warre: and such a warre, as is of every man, against every man." And in this state, "the life of man, [is] solitary, poore, nasty, brutish, and short."[35] But Tully's Locke "never considers a congeries of presocial and isolated individuals. He cannot because society is an irreducible datum of man's existence."[36] In his *Essays on the Law of Nature,* Locke appears to reject the egoist impulse outright. Is it true, he inquires, "that what each individual in the circumstances judges to be of advantage to himself . . . is in accordance with natural law . . . and that nothing in nature is binding except so far as it carries with it some immediate advantage?"[37]

"It is this we deny," Locke answers. Certainly men may turn themselves into beasts, caving in to their craven urges and eschewing all self-restraint. But these are "degenerate" men, those who surrender reason to blind passion, as the discussion in Chapter 3 argued. For, Locke explains, "an Hobbesist with his principle of self-preservation, whereof himself is to be the judge, will not easily admit a great many plain duties of morality."[38] And it is precisely these "plain duties of morality," these "natural positive duties toward others" that draw Tully to his pivotal interpretive reading of Locke's social thought. Man is not an "atom," existentially isolated and alone. Man is God's creation, the product of his workmanship, and is therefore dependent, not independent, floating in a vast moral vacuum. As Tully concluded, human "obligations arise from the acts which constitute various relations . . . [so that] God as maker has a special right in man, his workmanship, and . . . this correlates with a positive duty on the part of man to God."[39]

As we have indeed seen, for Locke "all things are justly subject to that by which they have been made and are also constantly preserved." And "Preservation" is man's duty and responsibility. However—and here is the chief conception around which the collectivist reading of Locke is drawn—what God intends is the preservation not merely of this lord or that master, but of all mankind. As Locke himself states, "Every one as he is bound to preserve himself, and not to quit his Station wilfully, so by the like reason when his own Preservation comes not in competition, ought he, as much as he can, to preserve the rest of mankind."[40]

From the principle of preservation, Locke is inextricably drawn into the controversy over property. It could not be otherwise. For it is only by appropriating property, by fashioning the raw products of nature (given by God for the benefit and use of all), that humans are able to preserve themselves. If there were no rightful means of dividing the earth and its fruits, no means of individuating the "common inheritance," humans would perish for want of sufficient opportunity to feed and shelter themselves. And so Locke takes on the challenges that so vexed the seventeenth-century natural law writers who preceded him. Well attuned to the contours of that discourse, with its emphasis on "inclusive" rights and the provisions it made for charity and distributive justice in civil society, Tully could counter the Macphersonian emphasis on unbridled acquisitiveness and limitless appropriation. Locke's theory of property, given the commitment to natural law and God's commandment, had to be worked out "within a context of positive duties to others and equal claims to common goods."[41]

Tully's key move is to depict Locke's property not as private, but as something held "in usufruct." It consists of "the right to use and enjoy God's property for God's purposes." What Tully's Locke grants is a severely limited title to property. One may properly exclude others from the land one tills and on which one works and lives, but only so long as one is working or living upon it, only so long as one has left "enough" and "as good" for others, and only so long as the product of one's land and labor does not spoil uselessly in one's possession. Should a person fail to keep any of these qualifications, then he or she immediately forfeits any claim to that property. Tully explains: "The cultivated field and its products are both property because they cannot be taken without the proprietor's consent; the definition obtains only because these are his property as objects of use. The moment they cease to be objects of use, they cease, by definition, to be his property and so the inclusive rights of others apply."

The "inclusive" right to be preserved, moreover, is always operative in Tully's view. Thus do positive duties toward the poor arise: "Since a person has a property for the sake of preserving himself and others . . . charity is a right on the part of the needy and a duty on the part of the wealthy. [Where] a case of need arises . . . one man's individual right is overridden by another's claim, and the goods become his property."[42]

Beyond this, Tully tells us, Locke's insistence on the right of an heir to his father's inheritance also represents a serious restraint on private property. Tully locates a communal-use right, as it were, that places property in the patriarch's trust and care but does not make it his. The family, in short, "becomes a communal organization with common property." For Tully, this nonpatriarchal model of the seventeenth-century family really mirrors "a human society of community of goods, mutual assistance and maintenance." In fact, it is the English Commons (also involving communal ownership) that Tully sees as Locke's ideal "model" of property. "All the exclusive rights which Locke's commoners possess were present on the English Common and called 'properties.' "[43]

We must, for a moment, step out of the wilderness and move into the civil state; it is from this abiding moral base that Tully derives the true origins and character of government. Men do indeed quit the state of nature to redress the real grievances that invariably arise therein, but those grievances consist not in the wanton violation of anyone's exclusive rights, but in the untoward deprivation of people's *inclusive* rights. What is it that so compromises human felicity and impels mankind to unite politically? "The institution which serves to create the requisite state of affairs, *is money.*"[44]

Before the introduction of money—essentially any nonperishable commodity serving as a medium of exchange—individuals had no reason, no incentive to "hoard" more land than they could productively use. What would they do with the surplus? Why would they spend their precious hours planting, raising, and gathering crops they could never consume? Some surplus could be expected, allowing individuals to barter with others for goods they could not themselves produce. But the earth's product being perishable, humans would be disinclined to appropriate more and more land to the disadvantage and discomfiture of others.

"Money ends the golden age." It is something a man may hoard without limit, since "the exceeding of the bounds of his just property . . . [lies not] in the largeness of his Possession, but the perishing of anything uselessly in it." Money, Tully concludes, "caters to and extends the unnatural desire to accumulate more than one needs." And it does this to the distress of many. "The acceptance of money brings with it the fall of man." Far from approving unlimited acquisitiveness, Locke inveighs, "Covetousness, and the desire of having in our Possession, and under our Dominion, more than we have need of . . . [is] the Root of all Evil." It is at this juncture that "the pravity of mankind" comes to bloom. It is now we witness the "Covetousness of the Quarrelsom and Contentious."[45]

With the introduction of money we reach, to paraphrase Adam Smith, a "full complement of land" stage—the natural outgrowth of admitting unlimited appropriation and production for exchange. All this is natural, but it is also problematical. Though all the land may now be appropriated, it is clear that not every individual will be fortunate enough to come by a strip of land to call his own. All "inclusive" rights notwithstanding, many people will have to do without land and without the means of preservation. This, though, is something that God never could have intended. What is the remedy? Government! "Money disrupts

[the] natural order, and government is required to constitute a new order of social relations which will bring the actions of men once again in line with God's intentions."[46]

God's resolute intent for mankind and the implacable moral duty that intent places on every individual do not disappear with the introduction of money and the full enclosure of the land. The natural law injunctions governing "spoilage" and "sufficiency" still obtain. Morally, money changes nothing, in Tully's view. People are very much their brothers' and sisters' keepers, charged with preserving all mankind. Once money is accepted natural individuation becomes dysfunctional and, with the formation of civil society, property becomes wholly conventional. It is all necessary if every individual's inclusive right to property and preservation is to be respected. From here, the entire aim and end of civil society is easily elaborated. Each member hereby relinquishes the power "of doing whatsoever he thought fit for the Preservation of himself, and the rest of Mankind. . . . [This] he gives up to be regulated by laws made by the Society, so far forth as the preservation of himself and the rest of that Society shall require."[47]

And since it is not merely his person, but also "those Possessions which he has, or shall acquire" that each member "submits to the Community," it is clear, to Tully, that property becomes conventional (no longer natural) and that individuals "have such a right [only] to the goods, which by the Law of the Community are theirs."[48] The precepts of natural law are eternal and unconditional. The only thing that is conditional is any person's claim to his or her own property. In society, all such claims are handled conventionally, and individuals may possess only as much and as good as God's natural law allows. "Community ownership of all possessions," Tully thus asserts, "is the logical consequence of the premises of Locke's theory in the *Two Treatises*." Property in society is public, not private. The "proprietor" is but custodian, and Macpherson is stood on his head. Tully concludes, "Private and common ownership are not mutually exclusive but mutually related: private ownership is the means of individuating the community's common property and is limited by the claims of all other members."[49]

One might imagine that Locke would discuss the process by which these "claims" are adjudicated and "land reform" effected. It is, oddly enough, a subject he never addresses. Undaunted, Tully surmises that "whatever particular legal form this might take in a given commonwealth is not a problem of theory but of prudence."[50] The claim that, for Locke, property in civil society is purely conventional and so subject to political redistribution shall be taken up in the succeeding chapter. Here, I want to raise some objections to Tully's strictly moral claim, i.e., the altruistic reading of Locke's ethical theory. First, however, I want to raise a few intriguing historical questions that naturally arise from Tully's interpretation of Locke's moral meaning.

From Ashcraft's methodological perspective, one may genuinely wonder when in his life Locke ever attached himself to the cause of "redistributive justice." Is this what Shaftesbury was proposing as a solution for the problems that confronted every popish-fearing Englishman? What really were the problems Locke and Shaftesbury perceived, and what were the arguments they advanced to solve those problems? Who was Locke's likely audience, and in what ways were their interests being threatened?

Do you suppose Shaftesbury suspected for a single second what Tully thinks his closest friend and adviser was philosophically plotting? Could Locke's patron have imagined that the man living under his roof, enjoying his largesse, and sharing in his political plans really regarded every surplus shilling in his patron's London account, every surplus acre in the Shaftesbury estate, as the common inheritance of all Englishmen—subject to appropriation by a socially aroused Parliament? Certainly there was no shortage of needy Englishmen whose difficulties could have been eased by a due restitution of the "misappropriated" lands in the possession of every duty-defying lord and baron in the realm.

Needless to say, this was not the cause for which the Earl of Shaftesbury was fighting and risking everything. Nor was it Locke's cause. In fact, there was not in England any discernible movement at that time anxious to effect such a transfer of landed wealth. Earlier, during the Civil War years, as we've already seen, numerous radicals, the "True Levellers," had harbored such aspirations.

To see how historically incongruous Tully's moral reading of Locke is, it is necessary to look more closely at the opposition movement to which Locke belonged. A clearer understanding of Locke's existential context—the practical and theoretical problems he would have to address in order to win the field—is necessary to reconstruct his intellectual intentions as a spokesman for that opposition party.

I have already pointed out how Locke, in composing his *Essay concerning Human Understanding,* needed to counter the assault on reason hurled by the High Church Anglicans (particularly Samuel Parker's blistering assault on the reasoning, dissenting mind). But as in the debates at Putney Church in 1647, now, too, the question of property was also on the table. Only now, with respect to the defense of property, Shaftesbury hoped to put the court on the defensive.

A French-leaning Charles II put fear into many Englishmen, but he would eventually pass.[51] His Catholic brother—and heir—signaled calamity. It was as dark and dangerous a prospect as many could imagine. The imminence of the succession was finally enough to bring together a broad amalgam of social forces. Englishmen, standing on nearly every rung of the socioeconomic ladder, could easily perceive the threat this posed. At the hub of the opposition stood Shaftesbury, furiously laboring to hold the loose spokes of the movement in place. At his side stood Locke. The resistance, as always, was centered and seated in Parliament, the ancient bastion of private property and free thought. But the glue that held the Exclusion party together was not the rabid thirst for laissez faire, either on the pulpit or in the market. It was not so much what Shaftesbury's loose coalition was for, in that there could be little in the way of consensus; it was a question of what every good Englishman had to rally *against*.

As I have said, it was a virtual premise of life for the English that Catholicism was tantamount to absolutism. And if that was the premise, the conclusion was all around them, especially in the hated tyrannies of France and Spain. The argument for a "natural" succession had to be resisted at all costs. The focus of the exclusion campaign, as we have already seen, was a simple exclusion bill that would effectively bar James from succeeding his brother to the English throne. The battle over exclusion remained a battle of ideas, down to the dissolution of Parliament in 1681. Men were being asked not to take up arms, but to cast their ballots. As always, the arguments had to be directed to the head and the heart. People's ideas had to be changed and their deepest interests aroused. An able body of English writers rallied to the Whig cause, a cadre of intellectual activists that included James Tyrrell, Algernon Sidney, Henry Neville, and John Locke, who asked: "Can anyone say, the king . . . may . . . take away all, or part of the land [or] the goods or money [from any one of his subjects] at his pleasure? If he can, then all free and voluntary Contracts cease, and are void, in the World. . . . And all the Grants and Promises *of Men in Power,* are but mockery and collusion."[52]

Property was indeed the pressing problem of the day — but only the property good Englishmen already had and desperately hoped to hold onto. The great threat to that property, as Locke and his party believed, emanated most immediately from the prospect of a "lawless" and Catholic king reigning absolutely from above. In addition to this threat from above was a well-perceived threat to property emanating from the clamorous social classes below. We are right back to Putney, Cromwell and Ireton, and Filmer. The Tories countered that the greatest danger to property lay not in allegiance to a sovereign monarch, but in a concession to popular rule and the Whig's vaunted consent theory.

It was indeed a complex challenge that Locke had to confront. A successful resistance theory, such as the one Shaftesbury sorely needed (following the final dissolution of Parliament in 1681), would have to declare property invincible outside civil society and within the bounds of the law of nature, and then, without overturning anyone's property rights and without falling into contradiction and error, gingerly bring all the property claimed into civil society — affording it the full measure of protection it demanded. If Locke hoped to reach his intended audience, he knew he would have to take absolute power away from the tyrant without inviting, in its stead, the sure and certain tyranny of the "Mob." Tully's emphasis on duty, sacrifice, and the primacy of charity would render property subject to redistribution and play directly into the hands of Locke's ideological foes. It was precisely this outcome that Locke needed to block.[53]

And so, starting from the natural law supposition most familiar to his audience — the view that the world and all the inferior creatures were given to all people equally for their preservation — Locke explains how a due division of the common inheritance could proceed without injury and violation. After all, he writes, "being given for the use of Men, there must of necessity be a means *to appropriate* them some way or other before they can be of any use or at all beneficial to any particular Man. The fruit or Venison, which nourishes [a man] . . . must be his . . . [so] that another can no longer have any right to it, before it can do him any good for the support of his Life."[54]

Locke's ingenious move, as we have seen, was to redefine the character of the Commons. Upon closer scrutiny, he realizes, God could not have given every inch of the earth to everyone in common. Rather he gave to each the liberty to possess and use as much as that individual required for his own preservation. This much one could appropriate without anyone's approval, since the great fount of individuation lay not in another's approval, but in his or her own person: in one's "Labour." Moreover, one's own acquisition need not embarrass or deprive any neighbor who, having a like power and property in labor, might do likewise.

The original condition of mankind is such as to provide a sufficient supply of nature's fruits to clothe and feed all comers. It was a commonplace for Whig writers to assert the ease of meeting the natural law demands at a time when population was sparse and the extent of territory vast. Ashcraft thus summarizes, borrowing liberally from Locke's own text: "The population was small," people "wandered freely up and down," possessions "would not be very large," human needs and desires were confined, "so that it was impossible for any man, this way, to encroach upon the rights of another or acquire to himself, a property to the prejudice of his neighbor."[55]

Locke does not equivocate; and the "use" right, which Tully finds in earlier natural law writings, is of little value to Locke: "As much land as a Man Tills, Plants, Improves, Cultivates, and can use the Product of, so much is his Property. He by his Labour does, as it were, inclose it from the Common." And once money, a nonperishable medium of exchange, is introduced, anyone "might heap up as much of these durable things as he pleased, the exceeding of the bounds of his just Property not lying in the largeness of his possession, but the perishing of anything uselessly in it.''[56]

This is how Locke looks at property; always and everywhere it is that which is already owned. And that property is so far from alienated upon people's entering political society that it is "only with an intention in every one the better to preserve himself, his liberty and property . . . that Men . . . enter into Society [and] give up the Equality, Liberty, and Executive Power they had in the State of Nature." And who would do otherwise? Who among Locke's audience would join civil society (or follow Shaftesbury) if it necessitated the surrender of 25 percent or 75 percent of their estates, or however much a popular majority could decide natural law and the needs of others might demand, in any year. If that is all a man could expect from society, he would be better off remaining out of it; at least he would be left with a power of self-defense and not be forced to pay for his own dispossess notice. "For no rational creature can be supposed to change his condition with an intention to be worse [off].''[57]

Admittedly, though, all of this begs the question—the deeper and more fundamental question raised by Tully in his *Discourse*. How can this ascription of absolute private property and acquisitive self-interest comport with the moral duties recognized by the natural law writers, Locke included? Never mind Shaftesbury's intentions, what about God's intentions? What about every person's duty to preserve not just himself or herself, but all mankind?

The real questions is this: What exactly does the "preservation of all mankind" require, for Locke? For Tully, the answer is land. And it is man's continual dependence on there being "enough" and "as good" land available for every person that persuades Tully to reject Macpherson's strong conclusion, vis., the elimination of the natural law restraints on appropriation following the introduction of money. Tully sees "no evidence . . . that the great productivity of the appropriated land more than makes up for the lack of land available to others.''[58] And the moral obligation to see that those "others" are preserved necessitates the strict observance of those obligations. But with all due respect, if Tully sees no evidence here, then it can only be that he is not looking very hard. There is, in fact, every evidence for the removal of the natural law limits; it is as plain as arithmetic.

The crucial point is that man, living in peace, under a rule of law, applying his labor as he pleases, will infinitely improve the productive powers of the earth. It is not "raw" nature but the products fashioned by human labor that allow mankind to thrive in comfort and convenience, since "he who appropriates land to himself by his labour, does not lessen but increases the common stock of mankind." Locke says:

> The provisions serving to the support of humane life, produced by
> one acre of inclosed and cultivated land, are . . . ten times, more
> than those which are yielded by an acre of land of an equal richnesse,
> lyeing wast in common. And therefore he, that incloses land and has
> a great plenty of the conveniencys of life from ten acres, than he
> could have from an hundred left to Nature, may truly be said to give
> ninety acres to mankind.[59]

And it is not at all surprising that the "*Property of labour* should be able to over-ballance the Community of land," for "tis Labour indeed that puts the difference of value on every thing." Finally computing what part of human subsistence is "owing to Nature, and what to labour, we shall find, that in most of them 99/100 are wholly to be put on the account of labour." With utmost clarity, Locke summarily says, "From all which it is evident, that though the things of Nature are given in common, yet Man . . . had still in himself the great Foundation of Property; and that which made up the great part of what he applied to the Support or Comfort of his being, when Invention and Arts had improved the conveniences of life, was perfectly his own, and did not belong in common to others."[60]

But hadn't Locke railed against covetousness? Hadn't he denounced in the *Essay* such "adopted" passions as the "itch after power or riches"? Hasn't he bowed to the corrupting and degenerate effects of money and condemned the "Pravity" of human nature unleashed by the agreement to trade shiny metals for the produce of the earth? Yes, Locke has done all these things, and yet it is all consistent with his special advocacy of strenuous labor and material acquisitiveness. Recall Tully's admonition: "The acceptance of money brings with it the fall of man." It is now that "a state without quarrels or contentions becomes one of contention for more ground, trespassing and enlargement of possessions. . . . Instead of the meek inheriting the earth through their Christian labour, the covetous people whom Locke inveighs against threaten to engross it."[61] Taking notice of Locke's "Letter concerning Toleration," Tully endeavors to bolster his case. As Locke does clearly warn: "[The] pravity of mankind being such that they had rather injuriously prey upon the fruits of other men's labour than take pains to provide for themselves, the necessity of preserving men in the possession of what honest industry has already acquired . . . obliges men to enter into society with one another."[62]

Clearly, the incentive and opportunity men now have to enlarge their possessions invite trouble. But the wickedness that may now arise is no reflection on money, only on those who become wicked. Locke surely does distinguish between two classes of men: the one good, the other not. God "gave the World . . . to the use of the Industrious and Rational," he urges, "not to the Fancy or Covetousness of the Quarrelsom and Contentious."[63] The introduction of money and the allowance for a largeness of possessions need not reduce people to violence and violation. "He that had as good left for his improvement, as was already taken up, needed not complain, ought not to meddle with what was already improved by another's Labour: If he did, 'tis plain he desired the benefit of another's Pains, which he had no right to."[64]

The bane to human preservation is not money; and it is not acquisitiveness, per se. It is the individual who would turn himself into a burden on mankind, becoming a beast and preying on the honest industry of the innocent. It is up to every person to discover the limits of liberty and restrain his or her lawless appetites, as Locke believed we could. It is because many may not so comport themselves "that governments are instituted." But we should not get ahead of ourselves.

If we may speak of a duty to preserve mankind, its significance may have been spelled out in a journal entry of Locke's, dated 15 July 1678. In this entry, under the heading *Lex Naturae,* fittingly enough, Locke forms an analogy between the duties of children to fathers, creatures to their creator, and the duties that bind all persons to one another. "[If one] finds it reasonable that his children should assist and help one another and expects it from them as their duty, will he not also by the same reason conclude that God expects the same of all men one to another?" One would suppose so; but what exactly is the nature of the assistance Locke has in mind here? He immediately answers the important question: "If he finds that God has made him and all other men in a state wherein they cannot subsist without society and has given them judgement to discern what is capable of preserving that society, can he but conclude that he is obliged and that God requires him to follow those rules which conduce to the preservation of society?"[65]

Thus it is the act of uniting into civil society itself, and establishing settled and known laws, that satisfies the mandatory requirement of preservation, according to Locke. And there is another, but very much related, sense in which this duty to preserve mankind may be understood. Once again, the text that is critical to Tully's interpretation appears to point to the altruist requirements of life: "Every one as he is bound to preserve himself, and not to quit his station wilfully, so by the like reason when his own Preservation comes not in competition, ought he, as much as he can, *to preserve the rest of Mankind.*'' Once again, however, we must ask: what obligations does this injunction actually impose on individuals, and how substantially has Tully taken Locke out of context? For Locke continues immediately: ''and may not, unless it be to do Justice to an Offender, take away, or impair the life, or what tends to be the Preservation of the Life, Liberty, Health, Limb or Goods of another.''[66]

Against Tully's repeated invocation of Locke's commitment to ''the public good'' as the end of social and political activity, it may be that the ''public good'' demands nothing more strenuous than a due respect for private property and individual industry.[67] Given the ethical injunction of labor and the Protestant's already well-developed commitment to its call, a steady output of the goods and services necessary for commodious living could be expected to follow in due course.

Morally implicit in this entire conception is a peculiar obligation that all people by nature possess. Tully's general dictum may be accepted, to wit: ''Men have natural rights *because* they have natural duties.''[68] The duty to preserve oneself begets the duty, and therefore the right, to live productively. But for Locke, individuals also have natural responsibilities. Locke holds individuals accountable for their conduct—and for their own preservation. Having come to terms with the power of the appetites, but nonetheless embracing the doctrines of free will, i.e., volitional self-regulation, John Locke will expect individuals to exercise their willpower and judge the propriety of their desires before being carried to act on them. Failing in this, it may well ''come to pass that a man may justly incur punishment.'' It will be worth quoting Locke on this at length:

> For though his will be always determined by that which is judged good by his understanding, yet it excuses him not; because, by a too hasty choice of his own making, he has imposed on himself wrong measures of good and evil; which, however false and fallacious, have the same influence on all his future conduct, as if they were true and right. He has vitiated his own palate, and must be answerable to himself for the sickness and death that follows from it. *The eternal law and nature of things must not be altered to comply with his ill-ordered choice.* If the neglect or abuse of the liberty he had, to examine what would really and truly make for his happiness, misleads him, the miscarriages that follow on it, must be imputed to his own election.[69]

Perhaps, in society everyone cannot be a landowner or even the owner of a thriving mercantile concern. But the means of preservation are, nonetheless, available. The market in land aside, what emerges is an expansive market for labor. Being without property, many people may have to "alienate" their labor in return for a wage; and though that wage may be sufficient for little more than a bare subsistence, it will enable many people to subsist. This does not, for Locke, signify a condition of slavery: "A Freeman makes himself a Servant to another, by selling him for a certain time, the Service he undertakes to do, in exchange for wages he is to receive; And though this commonly puts him into the Family of his Master, and under the ordinary Discipline thereof; yet it gives the Master but a Temporary Power over him, *and no greater, than what is contained in the Contract between 'em.*"[70]

I do not want to make too much of this. Life, for the laboring classes, was harsh in the extreme. Yet, as the proposals for Poor Law reform certainly suggest, Locke did not evidence the keen sensibilities toward the hard-pressed poor that, say, Rousseau would a century later. The lower ranks are indeed handicapped (though given the emphasis on individual responsibility Locke would not, in Marxian fashion, consider them to be exploited). Living, as Locke says, "from hand to mouth," and "their share [of the national income] being seldom more than a bare subsistence [these classes] have not the time or opportunity to raise their thoughts above that, or struggle with the richer for theirs."[71] It is not, as Macpherson seemed to say, that the laboring classes are not rational per se, but that having no property and being economically bound to a life of servitude and drudgery, they have no opportunity to develop or employ their rational capacities. The faculty of reason for these people is somewhat of a vestigial organ—of little use or consequence.[72]

Still, certain facts should be considered. In the first place, Macpherson counted in England's "labouring classes" 85 percent of the adult males living in Locke's time. It was on their shoulders that the remaining 15 percent—the owning classes—would place the heavy burden of life. Macpherson's figures, however, have come under question. Ashcraft, for one, has strenuously faulted him for his overly broad definition of "servants" to include wage laborers and beggars. The seventeenth century, Ashcraft argues, had no such pat conceptualization. Decades earlier, in fact, the Levellers had excluded from the category of servant: "the thousands of miners, the weavers receiving piece-rate wages, seamen, or soldiers, or the forty-thousand laborers working in the shipyards; it was the personal servant within a household they had in mind." The Whigs expressly addressed their appeals to "all freemen." That included laborers of every description: "coopers, tallow-handlers . . . [and] other manual occupations." Consequently, the class Macpherson wants to count an underclass did not approach the number he estimated. "At most, these individuals represented not two-thirds of the male population, but approximately fifteen percent, including beggars."[73]

The more important point, however, is that although Locke may have been unable to envision the measure of unparalleled opportunities that would await even the lowliest of laborers in the climate of natural abundance that was eighteenth-century colonial America, he did support enthusiastically the heroic efforts of lowborn men (such as his friend Thomas Firmin) to raise themselves up by their own efforts. As Neal Wood has appropriately written: "Locke extended hope to the socially inferior among his readers that through their own efforts they might climb the ladder of prestige and preferment. Knowledge is power, and those willing to lead the strenuous rational life do not necessarily labor under an inborn handicap in acquiring either."[74]

Spurning undeserved privilege and the unproductive waste of human talent (especially among the highborn), Locke hoped, above all, to "encourage the efforts of talented persons of lesser station" in a civilization opened, or at least gradually opening, to the talents—the vision bequeathed by Bacon. Wholly prepared to countenance inequality in the distribution of riches, he nevertheless labored to effect an egalitarian distribution of opportunity or something as close to it as circumstances would allow.

In rejecting Tully's altruistic reading of Locke it is not at all necessary to reassert Macpherson's brutal egoistic rendering. And that is so for more reasons than the one just raised. Writing from a Marxian perspective, Macpherson was intent on interpreting seventeenth-century social thought against the history of an emergent political economy of capitalism. He could thus reduce Locke's moral teaching (as well as the writings of Hobbes, Harrington, and the Levellers) to a rudimentary calculation of economic self-interest. The conception that dominated his thinking was that of "possessive individualism," a concept that was easily able to generate a postulate of "class differentials" and, not surprisingly, a doctrine of class exploitation. Acquisitiveness, in Macpherson's view, was the sum and substance of moral living. Thus he wrote with respect to Locke: "The essence of rational conduct is private appropriation of the land and the materials it yields. . . . The industrious and rational is he who labours and appropriates. . . . those who are left with no land cannot be industrious and rational in the original sense; they cannot appropriate and improve the land to their own benefit, which was originally the essence of rational behavior."

Therefore those who owned no land and so could not labor for themselves were spiritually dispossessed. "At the point where labouring and appropriating become separable," Macpherson writes, "full rationality went with appropriating rather than with labouring." Possessing no land, the laboring classes would now be subject to the will and welfare of those who did.[75] This reading, however, cannot be sustained. In the first place, certainly for Locke, the making of money (i.e., acquisitiveness) is not the measure of morality. Industrious activity is a crucial moral virtue, yes, but it cannot be reduced to a matter of acquisitiveness. Such appropriation was but one expression of applied human energy and far from the only one available. The production of useful knowledge or inventions could certainly place one among the ranks of the rational and moral. As I observed in Chapter 4, improvement, not enrichment, was the truer test of a person's moral accomplishment. The measure of virtue would be not the accumulation of wealth per se, but the fullest employment of one's moral talents and energies. A great scientist could die a pauper; this would not diminish his achievement or stature in Locke's eyes. On the other hand, a great landed gentleman could be a useless wastrel, squandering his inheritance in debauchery and idleness. He would not warrant a footnote in a volume patterned after Plutarch but entitled "The Lives of Locke."

Beyond this, the radical "individualism" ascribed to Locke on the pages of Macpherson's book must also be rejected. For the collectivist reading of Locke, while overblown in the writings of Tully and others, is not entirely without merit. By no stretch of the imagination are individuals portrayed by Locke as Macpherson imagined: as isolated atoms, socially cut off from fraternal and communal bonds. Those who point to the communal character of Locke's social thought can make a good case.[76] As I have shown and as Locke succinctly states in the opening of Book Three of the *Essay concerning Human Understanding,* "God having designed Man for a sociable Creature, made him not only with an inclination, and under a necessity to have fellowship with those of his own kind, but furnished him also with Language, which was to be the great instrument, and common Tye of Society."[77]

There is, moreover, ample room in Locke's social thought for other directed action. In the first place, Locke places at least some emphasis on charity. For those who are in dire need of assistance, those whose very survival is in question, he demands charitable assistance, "since 'twould always be a Sin in any Man of Estate, to let his Brother perish for want of affording him Relief out of his Plenty." And Locke goes on, "As *Justice* gives every Man a Title to the product of his honest Industry, . . . so *Charity* gives every Man a Title to so much out of another's Plenty, as will keep him from extream want, where he has no means to subsist otherwise."[78]

Locke made a clear and dramatic statement on the subject of charity in a brief essay he titled "Venditio." Although the essay was intended as a justification of unregulated market prices, a critical caution is nevertheless inserted: If a seller "extorts so much from . . . [his buyers'] present necessity as not to leave them the means of subsistence afterward he offends against the common rule of charity . . . and if any of them perish by reason of [his] extortion *is no doubt guilty of murder.*"[79]

Nor would charity be confined exclusively to those in extreme need. He recommended and practiced charity for those who generally deserved it, i.e., those who were in need through no fault of their own. The person who perhaps knew Locke best offered testimony to Locke's benevolence in this regard. As Damaris Cudworth Masham remembered,

> He was naturally compassionate and exceedingly charitable to those in want. But his charity was always directed to encourage working, laborious, industrious people, and not to relieve idle beggars, to whom he never gave anything. . . . People who had been industrious, but were through age or infirmity passed labour, he was very bountiful to . . . [believing not] that they should be kept from starving or extreme misery . . . [but that] they had, he said, a right to live comfortably in the world.[80]

The charitable impulse does indeed find expression in Locke's writings. But the effort to argue, from citations such as these, that Locke recommended a general duty to yield one's property or profit to any needy claimant cannot be made. The obligation of charity, strictly speaking, obtains only in extremis. The critical question of whether government possesses the power to enforce that obligation will be taken up in the following chapter.

Beyond the question of charity, the evidence of Locke's sociability extends to his attitude toward human relations generally. That attitude is particularly pronounced in his educational writings, where Locke stresses continually the inculcation of a liberal and benevolent temperament. It is apparent to Locke that "children, who live together, often strive for mastery, whose wills shall carry it over the rest." But Locke is not content with such a style of life. Children, on the contrary, "should be taught to have all the deference, complaisance, and civility one for the other imaginable." Instead of this "insolent domineering," children should be shown that a benevolent care for others will "procure them respect, and that they lose no superiority by it, but on the contrary, they grow into love and esteem with every body."[81] Locke then enjoins parents and tutors to instill the virtue of "Liberality" in their charges. "As to the having and possessing of things, teach them to part with what they have easily and freely to their friends;

and let them find by experience, that the most liberal has always most plenty, with esteem and acommendation to boot."[82]

It is in this context that Locke, as Tully noticed, speaks of "covetousness and the desire of having in our possession, and under our dominion, more than we have need of" as "being the root of all evil." It is not Locke's intent to recommend altruistic sacrifice here, but merely a generous temperament that really costs a person nothing. He immediately continues, "Let [the child] sensibly perceive, that the kindness he shows to others is no ill husbandry for himself, but that it brings a return of kindness, both from those that receive it, and those who look on."[83]

Thus, "by a constant practice" of generous acts, Locke expects that "good-nature may be settled . . . into an habit, and [maturing children] may take pleasure, and pique themselves in being kind, liberal, and civil to others."[84] And so Locke advises parents to instill in their progeny a "natural temper of benignity and compassion" toward others. The whole point here is that in rejecting Tully's version of altruism one need not accept Macpherson's unadulterated egoism.

One final issue concerning the sociability of Locke's moral teaching deserves some attention. This is his attitude toward public service. I have already shown in the preceding chapter that Locke, though by no means a poor man, did not devote his considerable energies to the making of money per se. He lived the life of an intellectual; and he did so in the belief that the knowledge individuals were capable of coming to would be of benefit and use to mankind generally. The point I want to make here is that as his lifelong practices confirm, Locke well understood that the accumulation of knowledge could best be pursued in cooperation with others.

It is in this context that we can appreciate Locke's membership in the Royal Society, his collaboration with others in innumerable study and scientific groups, as well as the vociferous correspondence to which he devoted so much of his time and energies. Locke's public-spiritedness, in fact, is evidenced in the positions he accepted on behalf of his nation. His early diplomatic mission to the Elector of Brandenburg, the posts he held under Shaftesbury's offices, and his stint on the Board of Trade in the 1690s all attest to Locke's zest for public service and the public good. Indeed, his active participation in Shaftesbury's resistance campaign alone should persuade us that "Lockean liberalism" stands for something other than an obsession with personal acquisitiveness, as Macpherson would have it. It was not, after all, an itch for riches that persuaded Locke to defend England from Stuart absolutism.

The significance of this public-spiritedness for our larger inquiry should not go unnoticed. The question of Locke's bearing on the founding of the United States is one that pits two competing paradigms against one another: the "liberal" (or Lockean) and the "civic humanist" (or classical republican). If, as Lance Banning has written, liberalism "posits a society of equal individuals who are motivated . . . by their passions of self-interest" and is to be contrasted with a "republicanism . . . concerned with the individual's participation with others in civic decisions . . . [and which] regards this merely economic man as less than fully human," then what are we to do with Locke? Not only did John Locke contribute mightily to public affairs in his day, he self-consciously advertised the importance of a civic consciousness, as well as a keen working knowledge of historical and political practices. As Robert H. Horwitz has rightly noted, it was Locke's intent in his educational writings: "to provide, among other things, an understanding of civic virtue. Locke believed that this kind of virtue was compatible with—and even indispensable for—the maintenance and well-being of legitimate republics or commonwealths."[85]

In sum, it is possible to count among the seventeenth century's most devoted civic humanists, or classical republicans, the person of John Locke. Why would Locke implore parents and tutors to instill in the young an acquaintance with history and civil law, going so far as to write, "This general part of civil law and history, are studies which a gentleman should not barely touch at, but constantly dwell upon and never have done with"? In part, because mastery of these subjects will afford one ample "employment and esteem every where." But beyond this, and as Locke's own life amply indicates, individuals must be concerned with the maintenance and well-being of their commonwealth and kingdom, as such. Why is that? As Horwitz properly noted, "[Though many] men would not [themselves] pursue the highest political honors and offices . . . they would understand that their long-term *self-interest* was inextricably bound up with the welfare of the commonwealth."[86]

As we shall now see, only in a well-maintained polity could the individuals who make up civil society live the lives that the moral laws of God and nature enjoin. People need to be rational in the sense discussed earlier,[87] and they need to be industrious as well. But only a certain type of society, one distinguished by certain characteristics, will enable them to live the rational, industrious lives their maker intends them to live. To build and maintain such a society, a stringent measure of civic participation and virtue will indeed be required.

Conclusion: The "Angelic/Diabolic" Dichotomy

Before moving on to the "True, Original, Extent and End" (in sum, the nature) of such a society, a concluding comment on the colloquy between Macpherson and Tully should be considered. Despite their broad area of disagreement, these two commentators do see eye-to-eye on at least one point. Human intercourse, they imagine, demands human sacrifice. Apparently, there is no other path. Some must be made to live for the sake of others; the only dispute is over details, over who shall be the object of sacrifice. Macpherson's Locke insists that the "meek" exist solely for the sake of the mighty (hence his notion of class differentials), while Tully's Locke insists that the "greedy" and covetous humbly bow before the "just" claims of the "needy" (and so indulge in self-sacrifice).

Believing that the price of one man's gain must be another man's loss, embroiled in the dichotomy that pits an "unbridled egoism" against the ethic of altruism, Christian piety against capitalist accumulation, both scholars seem to be engaged in a kind of high-brow name-calling. They browse through the pages of intellectual history, searching for saints and sinners, "angels" and "devils." And so they each failed to glimpse the honest meaning and extraordinary significance of John Locke's social ethic.

What John Locke did was to make an unprecedented philosophical recommendation. What he recommended was that the sacrificing stop. Let every individual live *for his or her own sake*—neither sacrificing (i.e., politically exploiting) others for one's own benefit, nor depriving oneself for the benefit of others. Let individuals live in society and under law, but let them live freely, secure in person and property, dealing with others by mutual agreement to mutual advantage. We shall now see how that recommendation plays out politically.

6

The True, Original, Extent, and End of Civil Government

As a number of commentators have explained of late, Locke drew an important distinction between matters of theory and matters of prudence in his discussion of political affairs. In offering "Some Thoughts concerning Reading and Study for a Gentleman" in 1697, he thus wrote that "Politicks contains two parts, very different the one from the other. The one, containing the original of societies, and the rise and extent of political power; the other the art of governing men in society." In similar fashion, writing on "Wisdom" in 1672, he had separated politics into two distinct categories: the "Fundamentals," or "the form of the State," and "Administration." Since, as Locke believed, the purpose of the study of politics was to discover "the art of conducting men right in society," he could view "true politics . . . as a part of moral philosophy."[1]

Before one could fashion the institutional arrangements by which civil society would be governed, it would be necessary to comprehend the fundamental ends for which such societies are formed. One must grasp the purposes of things before one can discover the most effective and efficient means for their accomplishment. Moreover, various individuals fully concurring on the legitimate ends of government could differ greatly over the most appropriate means for achieving their common objectives. Historical practices and policy approaches could be raised and debated on prudential grounds, without signifying any fundamental disagreement over ultimate or fundamental conceptions. This distinction, one that will figure prominently in the discussion of a future eighteenth-century political discourse, should be noted.[2]

Leaving aside questions of policy and prudence, what I want to do here is to confine myself to the first and fundamental branch of politics, and then only to the most fundamental questions with which it is concerned. It is the question of the origins and ends of government, and the implication of these for the limits of political power, that is most relevant here. Less fundamental matters, though matters still belonging to the philosophical and not the prudential part of politics, will not need to be raised. These would include, for example, the intricate problems associated with Locke's theories of consent, obligation, prerogative, resistance, conquest, and legislative preeminence. There has been surprisingly little written about the extent and limits of political authority in the secondary literature on Locke. And those commentators who have taken up positions on this important question (either from a Christian or a capitalist framework) have uniformly seen Locke as allowing for a scope of political power that, to me, appears greater than his fundamental moral and political premises would permit (though, characteristically, the specific powers allowed by these interpreters are largely left unenumerated).

In short, it is not sufficient to say merely that Locke wrote his *Two Treatises* to counter the ascendancy of Stuart absolutism. Unless I am mistaken, he intended to counter far more than what he saw as an egregious usurpation of political authority by a would-be tyrant. Or, to put it in other words, I think there is a line to be drawn regarding the bounds of political power that, though falling well short of usurpation and tyranny, will nonetheless limit the scope of public power. In attempting to draw this line, I shall have to confront once more the theories proffered by Tully and Macpherson, for both commentators, implicitly at least, will assign to the Lockean polity an expanse of power that I cannot find.

The key move, for Macpherson, is to read Locke's political theory as "provid-[ing] a moral basis for a class state." Beginning with the accepted foundations of natural equality, he was able to argue for "differential class rights and so . . . the justification of a class state." This allowed Locke to reconcile the need to protect individual property and to defend majority rule. Since only the rational and propertied could be counted full members of society and possess full political rights, no danger could be posed to property. Macpherson thus writes: "The individuals who have the means to realize their personalities (that is, the propertied) do not need to reserve any rights as against civil society, since civil society is constructed by and for them, and run by and for them. All they need do is insist that civil society, that is, the majority of themselves is supreme over any government."[3]

To what lengths a majority may go in the "defense," "protection," or "promotion" of their property interests is unfortunately not spelled out by Macpherson. Certainly the "rights" of alienated labor will pose no insuperable obstacle to state expansion. What is spelled out, at least, is the theoretical irony that Locke's vaunted individualism ultimately ends in "collectivism." Macpherson writes: "The notion that individualism and 'collectivism' are the opposite ends of a scale along which states and theories of the state can be arranged . . . is superficial and misleading. Locke's individualism, that of an emerging capitalist society, does not exclude but on the contrary demands the supremacy of the state over the individual.''[4]

Tully, and others who emphasize the religious foundations of Locke's thought, perceive, with Macpherson, the collectivist bent of his political theory. Collectivism may be thought to signify any system that, as Macpherson says, "demands the supremacy of the state over the individual," rather than one that sees its fundamental mission as protecting the individual's liberty and property against the demands of other social groups. As I concluded in the previous chapter, both Tully and Macpherson read Locke as sanctioning the subjection of certain individuals for the benefit of certain others in society (the laboring classes or capitalist classes, respectively).

Tully's reading is informed, first, by the implacable will of God enjoining "the preservation of society," and of every member in it, and, second, by the powers lodged in the hands of political society upon its formation. Individuals in civil states give up the liberty they originally possessed "to be regulated by Laws made by the Society . . . which Laws . . . in many things confine the liberty [they] had by the Law of Nature." And it is not merely liberty that the individual gives up; for one also "submits to the Community those Possessions which he has, or shall acquire. . . . For it would be a direct Contradiction, for any one, to enter into Society with others for the securing and regulating of Property; and yet to suppose his Land whose Property is to be regulated by the Laws of the Society, should be exempt from the jurisdiction of that Government."[5]

Property, Tully reasons, is therefore wholly conventional in civil society and so subject to regulation for the "Public Good." Civil society, generally, and government, specifically, have a certain mission—as well as the rightful authority to carry it out. As Locke states: "By the same Act therefore, whereby any one unites his Person, which was before free, to any Commonwealth; by the same he unites his Possessions, which were before free, to it also; and they become, both of them, Person and Possession, subject to the Government and Dominion of that Commonwealth."[6]

By what mechanism is the preservation of society to be secured? What is it, ultimately, that the individual submits his person and possessions to? The answer is the will of the majority, "which have a Right to act and conclude the rest," for if this, "in reason, not be received, *as the act of the whole,* nothing but the consent of every individual" would be necessary, something "next impossible ever to be had." And so "every one is bound by that consent to be concluded by the majority."[7]

The majority have a power over the persons and possessions residing in civil society and a purpose for which to exercise it, namely the preservation of the whole society and of every member within it. Such, then, are the views of the Christian commentators and those who take the opposed, capitalist, approach to reading Locke's political thought. What I want to suggest is that both approaches (and more important, both sets of conclusions) contain certain difficulties. Such arguments, I think, are largely taken out of context and, at any rate, do not comport well with explicit expressions clearly enunciated by Locke in his political and philosophical writings. In this chapter I hope to reconstruct a more coherent reading of Locke's politics, showing how the difficulties encountered by both sets of interpreters can be avoided. Such a reading, I believe, must proceed from and comport with the portrait of human nature and the theory of natural law morality developed earlier.

Any examination of Locke's political thought, of course, must begin in the state of nature—a most perplexing state, judging from the controversy surrounding it in the contemporary literature. The first question that presents itself is whether Locke intends or needs to argue that the state of nature is a historical condition that existed sometime in antiquity. Although various commentators have argued that such a state needs to have existed if Locke's politics is to be anchored in reality, and although Locke himself spends considerable time discussing the natural condition that precedes the formation of civil societies, I take the view that the question is largely inconsequential. What is critical for the development of Locke's political theory is not so much the state of nature, but a knowledge of the nature of man as such. For the state of nature, whatever else may be said of it, fundamentally falls "within the bounds of the Law of Nature."[8]

All individuals naturally possess certain physical capacities and certain moral obligations. They experience a host of passions, yet, being by nature rational, have the capacity to question their inclinations and project the consequences of pursuing any one of them. They have the capacity of volition and so can restrain and even educate their destructive passions. Moreover, their power to reason can instruct them in the existence of a most powerful and perfect being, who is their creator and to whom they are morally wed. "Reason," in short, is but "the common Rule and Measure, God hath given to Mankind."[9] What reason recommends, as we have seen, is an ethic of industriousness and a respect for property—the essential precondition and just reward for industrious labor. What labor and land have joined together, Locke would affirm, let no one tear asunder. The concept that formalizes the moral relations between individuals is that of "rights."

It will be necessary, now, to go over some much-covered ground, showing how Locke brings individuals from the state of nature to the state of civil society. Such a rehearsal is necessary, I believe, because there are certain implications of that fateful move, namely the limits of political authority, that have been all but overlooked in the secondary literature to date. Locke thus begins: "To understand Political Power right, and derive it from its Original, we must consider what State all Men are naturally in, and that is a *State of perfect Freedom* to order their Actions, and dispose of their Possessions, and Persons as they think fit, within the bounds of the Law of Nature, without asking leave, or depending upon the Will of any other Man."[10]

Invoking the law of nature, Locke arrives at the fundamental moral status enjoyed by all persons: it may be seen as a state of equal creation. For, "being all equal and independent, no one ought to harm another in his Life, Health, Liberty, or Possessions. . . . [Hence] there cannot be supposed any such *Subordination* among us that may Authorize us to destroy one another, as if we were made for one another's uses."[11]

There are of course several senses in which the concept of "equality" can be understood. For Locke, human beings are equal in the sense that they all possess like needs and like capacities and so should be left free to exercise their individual capacities for the satisfaction of their needs (hence their preservation). Given his understanding of economics (the productivity of improved acreage and the condition of plenty following the agreement to exchange nonperishable metals), this will conduce to the preservation of all. But all this implies nothing about how fully any particular individual will exploit his natural endowments or how excellently endowed he or she may be:

> Though I have said . . . that all Men by Nature are equal, I cannot be supposed to understand all sorts of Equality: Age or Virtue may give Men a just Precedency: Excellency of Parts and Merit may place others above the Common Level; . . . and yet all this consists with the Equality, which all Men are in, in respect of Jurisdiction or Dominion one over another . . . being that equal Right that every Man hath, to his Natural Freedom, without being subjected to the Will or Authority of any other Man.[12]

Locke clearly intends to fashion this doctrine of equal creation (Locke speaks of "common Equity") into a juridical construct—albeit one existing prior to the formation of political society. He explicitly refers to this natural condition of liberty and equality as a "Right" inhering in every person. Moreover, the fundamental rights of life and liberty immediately suggest, to Locke, a corollary right, that of self-defense. "And that all Men may be restrained from invading others Rights, and from doing hurt to one another, and the Law of Nature be observed . . . the *Execution* of the Law of Nature is in that State, put into every Man's hands, whereby every one has a right to punish the transgressors of that Law."[13] As Locke correctly observes, "the *Law of Nature* would . . . be in vain, if there were no body that in the State of Nature, had a *Power to Execute* that Law, and thereby preserve the innocent and restrain offenders."[14] Locke describes this corollary right as the "Executive power," and it consists in the punishing of offenders of the law of nature and procuring just reparations to the offender's victim.

Before proceeding to a discussion of civil society, one critical issue must be raised. It would not be entirely correct to reason that people's rights arise exclusively from the principle of "equal creation," i.e., the natural equality of every individual. More fundamentally, the rights of life and liberty, with the corollary executive power that arises therefrom, are inherent in the human personality per se. Rights, in sum, spring from man's essential nature as a rational being. They are, so to speak, wired right into the human frame and so cannot be surgically separated. Individuals are born with two eyes, two arms, two legs, a capacity to reason, and, of necessity therefore, not merely the duty, but also the right and responsibility to exercise their reason for the proper guidance and preservation of their lives. One of the most profoundly significant statements enunciated by Locke, therefore, and one inextricably linking Locke's metaphysical moral and social speculations, reads this way: "The *Freedom* then of Man and Liberty of acting according to his own Will, is *grounded on his having reason,* which is able to instruct him in that Law he is to govern himself by, and make him know how far he is left to the freedom of his own will."[15]

This understanding, I believe, applies not merely to property relations, but to religious relations as well. In addition to preservation in this life, every individual must gravely consider the prospect of salvation in the life to come. Hence the sanctity of individual judgment is the fundamental basis for Locke's defense of toleration. As Locke states it:

> All the life and power of true religion consist in the inward and full persuasion of the mind; and faith is not faith without believing. Whatever profession we make, to whatever outward worship we conform, if we are not fully satisfied in our own mind that the one is true, and the other well-pleasing unto God, such profession and such practice, far from being any furtherance, are indeed great obstacles to our salvation.[16]

The questions of salvation and preservation, moreover, cannot be separated. God enjoins every person to value both and to pursue both by fully exercising his or her rational, volitional, and industrious powers. One saves oneself through worship and preserves oneself through work. That is, one worships in the church of one's choice and preserves oneself by laboring in one's chosen calling (expecting and enjoying the just fruits of one's labor). To interfere with individual freedom, in either realm, is to rob individuals not just of their freedom, but of the right and responsibility they have to reason. And in the process, it is to cross God's commandment enjoining the salvation and preservation of his creation.

This understanding is sufficient to clear up another long-standing difficulty — "the ambiguous state of nature." Numerous commentators have attempted to show that Locke's very teaching on the state of nature is riddled with contradictions, that while he wishes to say that people in that state are rational and peaceful, they apparently are nothing of the sort. For that state is so precarious and insecure that they must rush from it into the civil state, surrendering their natural claims to liberty and property into its hands. For Macpherson, "This is the central contradiction in the explicit postulates on which Locke's political theory is built."[17] And it is precisely in working out this "contradictory" view of the state of human nature, if you will, that Macpherson purports to locate two types of human being (one having reason, property, and rights, the other possessing none of these). From this discussion, the entire question of "ambiguity" should be easily set aside. All humans are rational by nature, but the exercise of reason is volitional. At any time or place, a majority may be rational, industrious, and respectful of the rights of others, and only a small minority may be moved by a lustful urge to violate the persons and properties of their neighbors. Or, on the contrary, only a minority of humans may choose reason, the bulk of the inhabitants of a given territory turning themselves into wild beasts and preying on the just deserts of other people's labors.

The critical point is that, *in either case,* in Locke's state of nature or Hobbes's precarious state of war, all humans will realize the necessity of more completely protecting themselves by forming political bonds. In fact, even in a state where everyone was normally peaceful and rational, honest disputes could be expected to arise. And since "self-love will make Men partial to themselves and their Friends," even the most innocent of disputes may flare into disorder and end in a cycle of violence and reprisal. Hence given human nature, where any natural community did exist it would be likely, even inevitable, that the need for an agency of government and law would be recognized. Peace and preservation could not be maintained without it. Thus does Locke conclude, "*Civil Government* is the proper Remedy for the Inconveniences of the State of Nature which must certainly be Great, where Men may be Judges in their own Case."[18]

What every individual requires but the state of nature cannot possibly offer is this: "an establish'd, settled, known law, received and allowed by common consent to be the Standard of Right and Wrong . . . a known and indifferent judge, with Authority to determine all differences according to the established Law . . . and the Power to back and support the Sentence when right, and to give it due execution.''[19] In short, to protect and preserve their natural rights and liberties, individuals must submit to objective laws, impartial judges, and upstanding peace officers. Together, the civil functions performed by these institutions signify the state's legal power to provide for the common defense. These are powers that governments may rightfully acquire, since they emanate from rights that those who form civil society naturally possess.

In placing themselves under the protection of government individuals give up ''the Equality, Liberty and Executive Power they had in the State of Nature, into the hands of the Society, to be so far disposed of by the Legislative, as the good of the Society shall require.'' They agree never to take the law into their own hands but instead to rely on the prevailing rule of law to settle all disputes and right all wrongs. ''The . . . power . . . of doing whatsoever he thought fit for the preservation of himself, and the rest of Mankind,'' Locke says, ''he gives up to be regulated by Laws made by the Society . . . which Laws . . . in many things confine the Liberty he had by the Law of Nature.''[20] There are essentially three aspects of power that Locke discusses.

First, having delegated to government the function of defense, a citizen must simultaneously yield to government certain powers it must have if it is to fulfill this vital function and provide for the common defense. ''The power of punishing he wholly gives up, and engages his natural force (which he might before imploy in the Execution of the Law of Nature, by his own single Authority, as he thought fit) to assist the Executive Power of the Society, as the Law thereof shall require.''[21] Though the forms of assistance (perhaps a better word would be cooperation) are not specifically enumerated, in context they may be thought to include such things as the granting of subpoena powers, search and seizure, jury duty, and the power to arrest, detain, try, and (upon a finding of guilt) sentence a defendant and make an innocent victim whole through compensation from the estate of an offending party, in a civil action. The execution of the law and the enforcement of justice simply require such ''police powers'' and societal cooperation.

Second, having granted to government the power to enact and enforce the laws that shall govern society, a person must naturally be expected to obey the laws once they are enacted. If every individual reserved for himself the right to decide what laws he or she would and would not obey, there could be no rule of law and so no protection under law. However, since unanimous consent to laws could never be expected, the will of the majority has to be deemed sufficient for the enactment of such laws. Obedience to majority rule is requisite.[22]

Third, having authorized government to protect their lives and preserve their properties, a people must furnish it with the means of financing its vital protection services. The state requires the power to procure the materials, personnel, and facilities that will allow it to perform its proper functions. Governments do not grow in nature. Naval vessels, coastal installations, and military outposts do not come without cost. Anyone who expects, and who indeed enjoys, the protection of the law (having consented, at the very least, by his or her residence within a society to be bound by it) must be expected to support it. "'Tis true," says Locke, "governments cannot be supported without great charge, and 'tis fit every one who enjoys his share of the Protection, should pay out of his Estate his proportion for the maintenance of it."[23] The power to tax, Locke would argue, is the power to protect.

I do not think it is possible, however, to start from the premise of the powers ceded by Locke to government and arrive at the kinds of redistributive or "welfare" powers clearly implied in the commentaries of Tully and the others steeped in seventeenth-century natural law. For Locke, as for many an architect in society, form follows function. The function of government determines the form (i.e., the legal framework and limits of authority). For Locke, "the great and chief end of Men's uniting into Commonwealths and putting themselves under Government" is not the collecting of tax revenue or the compliance with majority opinion; it is "*The Preservation of their Property.*"[24] In the state of nature individuals acquire property, as well as implacable rights to what, by their labor and free exchange, is theirs. They bring their property with them into civil society, submitting both to be regulated by laws. It would be impossible if a highwayman could rob at will, retreating to his estate each dawn, declaring sanctuary and keeping the authorities from pursuing or apprehending him. The civil authority must have access to property and person if the cause of justice is to be served. And it must have a "taking" power not merely to support its operations, but to punish offenders, redress grievances, and compensate injured parties.

The chief power is placed by Locke in the legislative function. Of it he writes, "This Legislative is not only the *supream power* of the Commonwealth, but sacred and unalterable in the hands where the Community have once placed it." Apparently approaching a doctrine of legislative supremacy, in fact, Locke adds: "Nor can any Edict of any Body else, in what Form soever conceived [have any force], which has not its *Sanction from* that *Legislative,* which the publick has chosen and appointed. For without this the Law could not have that, which is absolutely necessary to its being a *Law, the consent of the Society,* over whom no Body can have a Power to make Laws, but by their own consent."[25]

Locke cedes this generous gift of power to the legislature, but he does so immediately after he advises, "The *first and fundamental positive Law* of all Commonwealths, *is the establishing of the Legislative power* . . . [yet] the *first and fundamental natural Law,* which is to govern even the Legislative it self, is *the preservation of the Society,* and (as far as will consist with the public good) of every person in it.''[26] Securing the laws of nature against a rapacious legislative power is uppermost in Locke's mind. In fact, Locke entitles this chapter on the supposed supremacy of law: *"Of the Extent of the Legislative Power."*

The power ceded by society to its legislature is strictly limited. A legislative body may not seize the property or restrain the liberty of some citizens for any purpose it might deem worthy of public encouragement, not even if a popular majority approves of that worthy purpose. The laws of God and nature sanction private property and even gross economic inequality, and neither can be overturned in society. It is wholly misleading to assert, as Tully, Tuck, Horne, and others have, that in society the right of property is conventional. Rights are not created by society but merely given formal and legal recognition there. It is Locke's purpose to deny the view that *"by being born under any Government we are naturally Subjects to it,* and have no more any title or pretence to the freedom of the State of Nature."[27] On the contrary, as Locke declares, "the Obligations of the Law of Nature, cease not in Society but only in many Cases are drawn closer, and have by Humane Laws known Penalties annexed to them, to inforce their observation. . . . Thus the Law of Nature stands as an Eternal Rule to all Men, Legislators as well as others."[28]

In pledging to cooperate with the authorities, abide by majority rule, and pay one's taxes, Locke's citizen does not sign his life over to the state; on the contrary, it is only to better preserve his life and liberty that he enters it at all. "But though Men when they enter into Society, give up the Equality, Liberty, and the Executive Power they had in the State of Nature, into the hands of the Society; . . . yet it being only with an intention in every one the better to preserve himself his Liberty and Property; (For no rational Creature can be supposed to change his condition with an intention to be worse)."[29]

Civil society, in sum, "is obliged to secure every ones Property by providing against those three defects above mentioned, that made the State of Nature so unsafe and uneasie."[30] Locke's argument respecting the limits on political power, in fact, cuts even deeper. It is not just that government cannot deprive some of their liberty and property for the benefit of others because that is not what it is meant to do; it is that, as no single person has a right to "take away, or impair the life, or what tends to the Life, Liberty, Health, Limb or Goods of another,"[31] so no society can ever come by such a power—not a single despot and not a duly constituted legislative majority. The powers of government, after all, are derived from powers delegated to it by the people; the people are the sole source of political authority. If they never had such a power to cede to government, no government could lay claim to it.

> For nobody can transfer to another more power than he has in himself; and no Body has an absolute Arbitrary Power . . . over any other, to . . . take away the Life or Property of another. . . . and having in the State of Nature no Arbitrary Power over the Life, Liberty or Possessions of another, but only so much as the Law of Nature gives him to the preservation of himself; . . . this is all he doth, or can give up to the Commonwealth . . . so that the Legislative can have no more than this.[32]

It is in the final analysis only the "Executive Power," i.e., the power that allows individuals to punish transgressors and make restitution for injury inflicted that is ceded to government. Thus, though individuals in or out of civil society may benevolently part with as much of their own goods as their charitable instincts may incline them to, they have no power to seize the goods of others for purposes they may deem worthy. And as Locke holds each individual morally responsible for his own welfare (having the native capacity for rational and industrious conduct), so he does no more or less in civil society. In sum, I can find no basis for ascribing to Locke's politics a social welfare function, as Dunn, Tuck, and Tully appear to do. In fact, in discussing the limits of political authority in his *Letter concerning Toleration*, Locke explicitly bars the prospect. Joining the threads of spiritual and material self-responsibility, Locke thus demands:

> The care of every man's soul belongs unto himself, and is to be left unto himself. But what if he neglect the care of his soul? I answer: What if he neglect the care of his health or of his estate, which things are nearlier related to the government of the magistrate than the other? Will the magistrate provide by an express law that such a one shall not become poor or sick? Laws provide, as much as possible, that the goods and health of subjects be not injured by the fraud and violence of others; they do not guard them from the negligence or ill-husbandry of the possessors themselves. . . . it is not in the magistrate's power to repair my loss, to ease my suffering, nor to restore me in any measure, much less entirely, to a good estate. . . . And therefore the magistrate cannot take away these worldly things from

this man or party and give them to that, nor change propriety amongst fellow subjects (no, not even by a law), for a cause that has no relation to the end of civil government.[33]

Once again, this should not be construed as a mean streak in Locke's personality. In his writings on toleration Locke reaffirms the role of benevolence and charity: "We must not content ourselves with the narrow measure of bare justice; charity, bounty, and liberality must be added to it. This the Gospel enjoins, this reason directs, and this that natural fellowship we are born into requires of us."[34] But Locke draws a sharp distinction between what is morally admirable and what is politically permissible:

> Covetousness, uncharitableness, idleness, and many other things are sins, by the consent of men, which yet no man ever said were to be punished by the magistrate. The reason is because they are not prejudicial to other men's rights, nor do they break the public peace of societies. Nay, even the sins of lying and perjury are nowhere punishable by laws, unless in certain cases in which the real turpitude of the thing and the offense against God are not considered, but only the injury done unto men's neighbors and to the commonwealth.[35]

What I have been attempting to argue is that although Locke is not quite the possessive egoist Macpherson made him out to be, though he advises charity, liberality, and benevolence in the moral sphere and councils civic-mindedness generally, his politics, nonetheless, affords the widest scope to individual self-pursuit and industrious acquisitiveness (barring, that is, violations of others' equal rights). Moreover if this analysis is correct, Locke's teaching will not countenance the enactment of legislation and the collection of taxes for the giving of relief to the hard-pressed poor—even if such measures proceed from the clear will of the majority. The majority may indeed decide which laws are most appropriate for the preservation of property, but it may not overstep the bounds of its authority by effecting a redistribution of property—giving to Peter what naturally and rightfully belongs to Paul. From the metaphysical and moral foundation of *equal creation,* Locke will build a political edifice formed from the materials of *equal protection!*

The next question is this: Despite the clear commitment Locke makes to Christian natural law and the religious basis for political association, is Locke, after all, the preeminent theorist and apologist for an emerging culture of capitalism? As it turns out, this is a deeply complex question. It requires us not only to ferret out the economic implications of Locke's political doctrine, but also to relate these implications to Locke's economic teachings. Even more fundamentally, it challenges us to come to conceptual terms with the colossus—capitalism itself.

Several considerations offered by Tully point to the difficulty of the matter. As far as he can see there are a host of features, common to capitalism, that are missing in Locke's treatment. Tully writes, "It is incorrect and anachronistic to impute the assumption of capitalist wage-labour to Locke." Technically, he points out, a "social division of labour, in which a labourer is hired to do a complete service, was the dominant and *non-capitalist* mode of production in England until at least the late eighteenth century." Thus Tully agrees with Marx, who "treats this as a distinct organization of work which had to be dissolved before a capitalist mode of production could supplant it." Tully immediately goes on to argue that "it is not only wage labour which is absent from Locke's writings; the capitalist finds no space there either." This is because he sees "no evidence in the *Two Treatises* that money functions as capital; it is simply hoarded." And where does Locke look to find the origin of economic value? To labor, not capital. As Tully explains:

> If Locke were to justify the capitalist anywhere in the *Two Treatises,* one would think that he would say capital played at least some role in creating valuable and useful things. But the capitalist is absent here as elsewhere, along with the landowner and the master. The ploughman, reaper, thresher, baker, ovenbreaker, planter, tiller, logger, miller, shipbuilder, clothmaker and tanner alone make things useful to the life of man and create value. The products are theirs, and any non-worker . . . has no title to them.

There is, in short, "no economic analysis [here]," but rather an "indistinction of economy and polity in the transitional epoch which produced mercantillist theories."[36]

Locke, as detailed in Chapter 4, had a sophisticated appreciation of the capitalist process. He lent money at interest and well knew that in investing in commercial companies, what he was investing was capital. Moreover, his major economic essay, *Some Considerations on the Consequences of Lowering the Rate of Interest and Raising the Value of Money,* was specifically concerned with the effects of economic regulation on capital formation (i.e., on the businessman's ability to borrow money).[37]

The details of Locke's life aside, it is the deeper, conceptual issue that is of first concern. For his part, Tully considers as crucial to capitalism a number of institutional arrangements: a ''subdivided'' mode of production, wage labor, and capital investment. Failing to find these arrangements in Locke's political writings, he fails to see how Locke could be saying anything about the subject of capitalism at all. Clearly, capitalism is a moving target, signifying different things to different theorists. All Werner Sombart needed to date its origins was the invention of bookkeeping by double entry, introduced by Leonardo of Pisa in 1202.[38]

The question is this: Are these various features *essential* to capitalism, or are they merely ''accidents,'' in the Aristotelian sense? Consider a simple analogy, something as ordinary as a chair. In modern terms, a chair is something that is made with commodity labor and mass produced following an initial capital investment in plant, machinery, and raw materials. Does this mean, though, that a three-thousand-year-old object, hand-crafted from a fallen tree, whittled into shape by a patriarch's primitive knife, and tied together by jungle vine cannot be a chair? Clearly it can, if it is a man-made object, designed to support the weight of a person when he is sitting. To deny its ''chairness'' on the basis of its lacking some salient features of the modern chair is to define one's subject by nonessentials. And that appears to be precisely what Tully has done.

Leaving aside for the moment the social relations of production and the class divisions into which members of a society are distributed under capitalism, there is a certain social institution so essential to the operations of a market economy that it may arguably be regarded as the fundamental fount from which so many other characteristics flow. This is the principle of private property. If property is private and is broadly construed as including the ''property'' every person has in his or her liberty and labor and if the chief function of government consists in the protection of property in this broad sense, then that is sufficient to fashion all the historical and evolutionary arrangements recorded in all the ''stages'' of capitalist growth. If all individuals share equally the capacity to exchange their labor and to gain, keep, use, and dispose of the fruits of their honest industry (however much, however modest), then with the passage of time and the multiplication of new industries and technologies, all of the salient features of mature capitalism could be expected to follow.

One colossal caveat, however, must be considered. The modern conception of capitalism has been very greatly influenced by Marxist historical analysis and, more precisely, the doctrine of historical materialism. This has meant that of primary focus in the examination of capitalism has been the relations of the various classes living under that political economy. And that relation has largely been seen as inegalitarian and exploitative. The inhabitants of the capitalist political economy are divided into two camps: the owners of the tools of production and those whose lives and labor are subject to the domination of those owners. What is more, liberal egalitarian doctrine (and ideological superstructure) notwith-standing, the government of a capitalist state has very often been viewed as being ruled by and for the bourgeoisie (as opposed to the working classes). It is con-sidered, in short, a state of special privilege for the owners of the tools (capital included) of production.

Historically, of course, Marxist historians can point to innumerable examples of capitalist economies engaging in this type of practice. The governments of capitalist nations could actively promote the interests of capital, and even protect capitalist interests from an aggrieved and agitated social "underclass," by un-derwriting social welfare measures (e.g., protective labor legislation or the pro-vision of public assistance).[39]

The critical point I want to make is that the Lockean political framework—and a civil society founded upon it—cannot allow such social "relief" for *any* of its classes or their members. If Locke is to be taken seriously, if his metaphysics, his moral philosophy, and the political principles that proceed from these are to be respected, then all species of special privilege (for rich and poor, owner and la-borer) have to be proscribed. Any measure whose intent or effect would be not to protect all, but to provide advantages for the few is one that confounds and com-promises the precepts of equal protection and equal creation. Insofar as "capi-talist" states have engaged in such practices, and they surely have, from a Lock-ean standpoint (i.e., the standpoint of his philosophical frame) we may regard these as being "mixed" or compromised political economies, rather than strict expressions of *Lockean* liberalism.

The effort by London merchants to legally lower the rate of interest from 6 percent to 4 percent illustrates the point. The act, Locke understood, would, for the sake of reducing by one-third the cost of money for one group, reduce the profits derived from the lending of money for another. Well aware of the pruden-tial impact of the measure, Locke was also aware of its moral meaning: "To fine men one third of their estates, without any crime, or offence committed . . . [to] give to Richard what is Peter's due, for no other reason, but because one was borrower, and the other lender [is lamentable]." For this would "impoverish a great and innocent part of the people, who having their estates in money, have as much right to make as much of the money as it is worth . . . as the landlord has to let his land for as much as it will yield."[40]

From the Lockean standpoint the capitalist who petitions government not for redress of grievances, but for commercial subsidies and special privileges, *is no capitalist.* Strictly speaking, in fact, he is a *socialist,* for he regards liberty and property (albeit other people's liberty and property) not as private and something to be protected, but as public, something to be seized or suppressed for his benefit. It is not so much that the ruling ideas are the ideas of the ruling classes, but that the "capitalist" classes have very often been willing to discard the very idea and premise of capitalism to advance their immediate commercial interests. What Locke presents is a theory of capitalism rooted not in class exploitation, but in certain intractable moral and metaphysical postulates that forbid the political practice of political exploitation. Examining Locke's political and economic thought, Vaughn summed the point up well:

> If in the course of Locke's arguments he provides a justification for capitalism, it is only incidental to his major purpose of asserting the right of free men to provide for their own well-being to the best of their ability. If capitalism is justified, it is only because it is a consequence of men's asserting that right through their ownership of private property. To Locke, private property is completely moral in that it grows from men's application of natural law, operates to reward industry and punish sloth, and has the effect of benefiting the entire commonwealth.[41]

Locke left a number of essays on subjects directly relating to the organization of England's economy, and it will be fitting to examine the economic doctrines he advanced in the light of the interpretation I have given to his political thought. Is there any discernible tension between the political ideas as just interpreted and the nascent economic objectives Locke sought to advance? Several issues will have to be taken up. They include Locke's position with respect to the setting of interest rates, recoinage, and the effecting of a favorable balance of trade for his country. An opposing point of view, that of Joyce Appleby, will also need to be considered.

The question of legally lowering the rate of interest was first raised in the 1660s and then again by 1690 in the writings of Sir Josiah Child (1630–1699).[42] Child, a director of the East India Company, was directly representing the interests of English merchants who on both occasions wanted lower rates of interest on the money they borrowed. Locke, who had answered Child in an unpublished essay of 1668, now expanded and published his *Considerations* in 1691, again repudiating the designs of the merchant capitalists in favor of an unregulated and unfettered market rate of interest.[43] And Locke exhibited the same propensity in his considerations on raising the value of money, a scheme pressed by William Lowndes (1652–1724), the secretary of the treasury.[44] England's silver coins, though accepted for purposes of domestic trade, had been badly "clipped" over the course of the seventeenth century. The silver content of the coins, therefore, had been substantially reduced. And because of this they were not accepted at their face value for purposes of foreign trade. The problem rose to crisis proportions by the 1690s, and a strong demand for recoinage resulted. The Lowndes plan called, essentially, for devaluation. The problem was that if the "clipped" coins would be recalled and recast at the prevailing value of silver, far fewer coins would be issued and the circulating medium dramatically reduced. Lowndes thus called upon the Privy Council to reissue coins with 80 percent as much silver as the old standard and with fluted edges that could not be clipped. Although silver bullion retained a value of five shillings, the new coins would be valued at six shillings, three pence.

Locke strenuously objected to the plan. The value of gold and silver, he insisted, should not be artificially set by government but instead reflect the esteem conferred upon them by universal consent. It is important to point out that the recoinage debate, similar to the debate over interest rates, brought contending economic interests into ideological confrontation. Englishmen perceived that a public policy favored by one interest, say merchants, could easily embarrass the interests of others, say landlords or manufacturers. The competition among the various economic interests would play a sizable role in the economic writings of Malthus, Ricardo, and Smith in the next century. And Locke's reasoning too could be seen in this light, i.e., as a conservative defense of certain landed and propertied interests and as harming the interests of others.

But more fundamentally, Locke in defending "hard money" was asserting a fundamental moral relation that he believed should prevail in human affairs. As Joyce Appleby writes, Locke believed that "a government devaluation would *rob* all the creditors and landlords of the kingdom who had lent money or established rents when shillings bore a different denomination."[45] The issue was not economic so much as it was moral—concerned with the protection and preservation of individual property rights. Moreover, Locke's insistence that the value of coin be tied exclusively to the going market rate, not the desires and dictates of sitting magistrates, signified, more generally, "a limitation of government in economic affairs." And, as Appleby concludes, looking ahead, "Locke's definition of money made way for the nineteenth-century belief in natural economic laws beyond the reach of political authority."[46]

All of this notwithstanding, Appleby would follow Letwin in rejecting the view that Locke consistently adopted laissez-faire positions on economic matters. For, she writes, "in truth, if English mercantilist policies date from 1696," as she argues, "he [Locke] must be considered their principal architect."[47] How is this conclusion reached and how persuasive is it?

Like Letwin, Appleby rests her case for Locke's mercantilist bent on his insistence that only a favorable balance of trade will increase the wealth of a nation. Contrary to Locke's opponents, who, while favoring government intervention on the question of money vociferously defended policies of free trade in the domestic and international arenas, Locke advocated governmental action to ensure a favorable trade balance, hence national prosperity.[48] With Neal Wood and David McNally, Appleby insists on associating Locke with England's landed interest and the problems that befell it during the 1690s.[49] As it turned out, a vigorous advocacy of free trade swiftly receded by the turn of the eighteenth century, and Appleby can point to "England's swift conversion to protectionist legislation and balance-of-trade thinking" and an attendant decline of "a vigorous assertion of liberal sentiments" in the 1690s. Locke, she finds, stands in the forefront of this historic shift: "Locke's economic reasoning strengthened a new sovereign, the class of landed and industrial employers who seized the initiative in 1696 and replaced the invisible hand of the market with the official hand of mercantilist regulation."[50] Appleby writes:

> Behind the balance-of-trade theory there lay a model of the national economy linking all classes in England to a common goal. Since the theory stipulated that wealth accrued from the net gain from foreign trade, the whole economy could be viewed of as of a kind of national joint stock trading company. In this concept, the members of society did not compete with each other but rather participated jointly in England's collective enterprise of selling goods abroad.[51]

Allowing, for the moment, that Locke did indeed recommend public interventions for the purpose of enhancing the nation's trade balance, would this necessarily confound his position on property, sanctity of contract, and freedom of trade (as evidenced in his admonition against currency and interest rate tampering)? Perhaps not. Notice that while forcefully defending the principle of toleration, Locke could, nonetheless, bar Catholics and atheists from practicing their faith. This is not a contradiction in his position on toleration as much as it is a limitation based on another critical societal value: security. The Catholic whose primary allegiance is to a foreign power (the pope), or an atheist who, owning no religion, could not be expected to respect his sworn oaths of obedience to civil authority, simply had to be excluded from civil affairs. Appleby herself seems to appreciate the deeper interest that was involved in the debate over interventionism: "Tying wealth to power, the balance of trade theory offered a justification for protectionist legislation firmly grounded on national security."[52]

As it turns out, England had been at war with its continental rivals since 1689, and the European wars had taken a terrible toll on English commercial life. The result had been an outflow of specie, exacerbating the coin shortage. French privateers preyed mercilessly on England's commercial vessels, eroding much of the capital that had been accumulated in the previous period of commercial activity. The channels of trade naturally narrowed, shrinking trade and employment throughout the kingdom. Under such circumstances, and with the clear understanding that economic prosperity alone could finance military prowess—and save the nation from its enemies—a measure of interventionism could well be defended.

It is true that various interests, having benefited from wartime interventionist measures, might argue for a continuation of protectionist policies long after the national emergency had passed. And a political regime willing to consolidate its power by winning those interests over to its side could indeed be expected to accede to their wishes by granting a variety of special privileges and subsidies. These policies could not, however, be defended from Locke's fundamental moral and political postulates. But there is no very compelling evidence that, under such pacific conditions, Locke favored such a policy of privilege.

Clearly, Locke does emphasize the importance of achieving a surplus of trade. And in his *Considerations* he often alludes to government's need to ensure such a favorable balance. But can such a broad generality be construed as to afford Parliament or a sitting ministry the mercantilist measures Appleby's analysis implies? We have seen Locke in another context enjoining the ''preservation of all mankind.'' Far from implying a blanket endorsement of an altruist ethic, as I argued in the previous chapter, all this required was a due respect for others' rightful property and a willingness to form civil bonds for the self-same end. Locke, in similar fashion, taught that in forming social bonds, individuals submit their properties to be regulated by standing laws. But this did not signify government's power to regard property as purely conventional, subject to any chance regulation a majority might deem convenient. Government's power, like the individual's duty to sacrifice, was restricted, subject to the fundamental moral and metaphysical precepts of Locke's natural law/natural rights doctrine.

With respect to Locke's economic doctrine, much the same can be said. A favorable balance of trade, he believes, is the sole basis for raising a nation's material standard of living; and indeed government must play an important role in effecting such a favorable trade balance. But by what means is it to accomplish this task? From the entire tenor of Locke's discussion, it becomes clear that the policies Locke will recommend are restricted to those that conform well with his position on the sanctity of property and contract and his view of government as impartial umpire. A favorable trade balance consists, above all, of an energetic trade flow. And such a flow results from a steady output of produced goods (industrial and agricultural).

Well appreciating the importance of money to trade, Locke noticeably argues *against* the bullionist's proscription on the transfer of gold and silver out of the country.[53] Government can indeed stimulate or impede a nation's productivity and trade. It can do so, not through mercantilist interventions, but by affording appropriate protection—but only insofar as it affords protection to property and wisely rules on matters respecting interest rates and the value of money, the whole subject of Locke's *Considerations*. For Locke, it is by strictly respecting the rights of property, including the sanctity of contract and the liberty of individuals to exchange their property at "the free and market value" of things, that government will encourage the production of industrial and agricultural goods and stimulate national and international commerce. If English government fails to protect merchant ships, for example, merchants will not venture their capital in world trade, and the trade balance will languish. This certainly is a proper task for government.

The protection of property domestically is equally to be sought after. As more people purchase land, for example, more produce can be anticipated for the channels of trade. And so, Locke advises, what "makes a scarcity of buyers of land, are doubtful and ill titles: where these are frequent and fatal, one can no more expect that men, who have money, should be forward to purchase, than ships, richly laden, to venture themselves amongst rocks and quicksands" (or preying privateers).[54] Security in the value (the worth) of money in fact is itself a precondition of vigorous trade. "Money is the measure of commerce, and the rate of every thing, and, therefore, ought to be kept . . . as steady and invariable as may be," Locke writes. But its value is to be set by the consent of the market, not the variable and inconstant designs of government. For, Locke writes, "it is very unfit and inconvenient that gold, or any other metal, should be made current, legal money, at a standing settled [i.e., legally imposed] rate. This is to set a rate upon the varying value of things by law, which justly cannot be done; and is . . . as far as it prevails, a constant damage and prejudice to the country, where it is practised."[55]

And the same pertains to the setting, i.e., the artificial lowering, of interest rates. The merchants want cheap money, expecting to reap higher profits from it, and Child's plan would reduce the interest on hired money from 6 percent to 4 percent. But from whom will they borrow it? Will the *supply* of capital be increased by a diminishing of return on investments? Locke does not believe so.

"And that it will not bring in more of our neighbour's money upon loan, than we have at present amongst us, is so visible in itself, that it will not need any proof." Moreover, those ventures deemed to be more risky will also go wanting if the return on capital is legally diminished. For all these reasons, the regulation of interest is incompatible with the expansion of trade and the building of favorable trade balances.[56]

Thus the sound laws Locke allows for the encouragement of favorable trade balances are comprehended in the very laissez-faire solutions (and the need to protect property and contract) contained in his *Considerations on the Consequences of Lowering the Rate of Interest and Raising the Value of Money,* and not in the sundry mercantilist recommendations for which others in England may have been lobbying.

One further point, already suggested, should be more strongly emphasized. If Locke's economic recommendations flow from considerations of prudence (i.e., the maximization of trade and wealth), they nevertheless are wholly consistent with the juridical conceptions adumbrated in his natural law and political writings. The principle of equal creation, enshrined in the political postulate of equal protection, in fact, forms no small part of Locke's overall argument. The protection he would afford is not to narrow classes of individuals, but to liberty and property as such.

Thus, he reasons, the market rate of interest should float as freely as the rate fetched by any other market commodity, such as land. The taking of interest and the taking of rent are morally equivalent and just.[57] And public interference in the market's allowance for interest taking, or rent taking, is a denial of justice. Nor is Locke solely concerned with the rights of the well-to-do. For, as Locke says,

> it will be a loss to widows, orphans, and all those who have their estates in money . . . [and who] have as much right to make as much of the money as it is worth (for more they cannot), as the landlord has [to] let his land for as much as it will yield. To fine men one-third of their estates [by imposing a 4 rather than a 6 percent rate], without any crime or offense committed . . . [and] transfer a third part of the moneyed man's estate, who had nothing else to live on, into the merchant's pocket; and that without any merit in the one, or transgression in the other, seems very hard.[58]

Locke does indeed acknowledge the diversity of competing interests within society and the disparate demands those interests may make on government. But he rails against the type of demand that will benefit some at the expense of others. "This pulling and contest," he writes, "is usually between the landed-man and the merchant . . . with whom I may here join the monied man." Often, he goes on,

> the landed-man finds himself aggrieved, by the falling of his rents, and the strengthening of his fortune, while the monied-man keeps up his gain and the merchant thrives and grows rich by trade. These, he thinks, steal his income into their pockets, build their fortunes upon his ruin, and ingross more of the riches of the nation than comes to their share. He, therefore, endeavours, by laws, to keep up the value of lands which he suspects lessened by the others' excess of profit.[59]

Sir Josiah Child had argued that by reducing the rate of interest, there would be more buyers of land and so its value would rise (along with the profits of trade). "But all this," Locke urged, is "in vain. The cause is mistaken and the remedy too." So far is Locke from siding with the conservative landed-interest, as some have argued, that he spends a good deal of time in his *Considerations* castigating them for their profligacy and ill-husbandry. If the value of land is low, it is more likely because there are too many sellers. Why? It is due to a "general ill-husbandry, and the consequence of it, debts." And he goes on, chiding the habits of government and individuals alike:

> If a neglect of government and religion, ill examples and depraved education, have introduced debauchery: and art, or chance, has made it fashionable for men to live beyond their estates; debts will increase and multiply, and draw with them a necessity on men, first of encumbering, and then selling their estates. . . . It is with a kingdom as with a family. Spending less than our own commodities will pay for, is the sure and only way for the nation to grow rich. Til then, we in vain, I fear, endeavour with noise, and weapons of law, to drive the wolf from our own to one another's doors. . . . For want, brought in by ill-management, and nursed up by expensive vanity, will make the nation poor and spare nobody.[60]

Throughout his writings, Locke professes his commitment to the public good and general welfare. But it is not correct to conclude that this consists in whatever the public, or a majority, or any interested segment of society decides will be good or will conduce to its welfare. From both a moral and practical standpoint the public good consists in the protection and preservation of property, which includes "life, liberty and estate." It is comprehended in the conception of natural and immutable rights, because in Locke's view, rights do inhere in human nature, and they cannot be denied or abridged. "Man, being born, as has been proved, with a Title to perfect Freedom, and an uncontrouled enjoyment of all the Rights and Privileges of the Law of Nature, equally with any other Man, or Number of Men in the World, hath by Nature a Power . . . to preserve his Property, that is, his Life, Liberty and Estate, against the Injuries and Attempts of other Men."[61]

But what about the individual who, being without real property, must continually "alienate his labour" in return for a bare subsistence wage? The crucial point is that it is *only* his labor that he alienates. To repeat: "A Freeman makes himself a Servant to another, by selling him for a certain time, the Service he undertakes to do, in exchange for wages he is to receive; And though this commonly puts him into the Family of his Master, and under the ordinary Discipline thereof; yet it gives the Master but a Temporary Power over him, *and no greater, than what is contained in the Contract between 'em.*"[62]

Whatever property a man could acquire, whether it was the tools of his trade or just the clothes on his back, this was his. The meanest wage laborer in England had an absolute right to his wages, if nothing else. And what if those wages were withheld? That is why there is government whose task it is "to govern by promulgated established laws, not to be varied in particular Cases, but to have one Rule for Rich and Poor, for the Favorite at Court, and the Country Man at Plough."[63]

Conclusion: Epilogue and Prologue

John Locke was not just a man with a mission, he was an intellectual missionary singularly devoted to spreading a multiplicity of secular and religious gospels. But whether one looks at Locke, the agricultural improver, or Locke, the revolutionary conspirator, the moral educator, or the epistemological innovator, the moralist or the economist, the patron of piety and free thought or the partisan of property and free trade, whether one situates Locke's thought within the context of Grotian natural law, latitudinarian natural theology, or Baconian natural history, Reformation resistance theory, or the Renaissance's humanist philosophy, one will not find in Locke's writings the splintered, fractured, and contradictory thought that too many, for far too long, have mistakenly thought they had found.

To understand the scope and scale of this man's intellectual achievement it is necessary to situate his writings within each and all of these contextual settings at once. The prodigious contextual researches of a long line of keen and penetrating modern minds (from Ashcraft to Goldie, Spellman to Schochet, Tully to Tuck, Horne to Vaughn, and Yolton to Wood, etc.) have finally enabled the important project of contextual integration to begin. And those researches have furnished the methodological means of contextually cross-checking the veracity of any given interpretive finding or variable reading that could be advanced in the project to reconstruct Locke's meaning and message.

But this Restoration writer did much more than contribute to the various dialogues, discourses, and "paradigms" of his age. He is not just a polemical or dialectical contributor; above all he is a philosopher! And though he did not present his philosophy in a systematic form, the system is nonetheless there. If one approaches Locke with sufficient patience and sympathy (of which, until recently, there has been a noticeable lack), one will find it. Because Locke was a philosopher, and a very careful one at that, his many texts are themselves an important context by which to assess the merits of any reconstructive reading — including my own.

A philosophy is an ordered structure of thought concerning the nature of reality, man, and society (civil and political). It is a hierarchically arranged and logically interdependent sequence of doctrines that stand or fall together. The more basic principles form the foundation of and rationally entail the subsequent tenets, which in turn may be seen as logical expressions or implications of those fundamentals. Further corollaries and deductions follow until a complete system of thought (comprising answers to the important questions of metaphysics, epistemology, ethics, and politics) is at hand. Such a system is as weak or as strong as the number of questions it can answer and the number of contradictions it does (or does not) contain.[64]

The reconstruction of Locke's thought presented to this point, I believe, faithfully conforms not only to the individual doctrines presented in the various Lockean texts, but to the many political, religious, social, and scientific alliances Locke formed over the course of his long and lustrous life. From his interest in agricultural improvement to his many commercial investments, from his attachment to the moderate Anglican divines to his activities on behalf of Shaftesbury's exclusion Whigs, from his defense of human industry and private property to his blasts against the wasted lives of the idle and indolent gentry *and* the sacrificial privileges demanded by the "Moneyed," all may be understood in terms of Locke's single-minded commitment to natural law and natural right.

Locke, indeed, allied himself with a vast variety of seventeenth-century causes and crusades. But his affiliation with one complements rather than contradicts his attachment to another. That is because, at root, those social and scientific movements shared so much in common. All aiming at preservation and peace, in an age dominated by insecurity, suffering, and strife, they dedicated themselves to: (1) rational inquiry and Baconian improvement—hence Locke's links to the agricultural improvers and the labors of Locke's Royal Society fellows—and/or (2) the social conditions (e.g., tolerance toward diversity and security of property) necessary to make inquiry and improvement, peace and prosperity possible—hence Locke's latitudinarian attachments and revolutionary leanings. Locke's own intellectual productions, as we have seen, pointed in all these directions at once.

It is now possible to say what will be required of the American founding before it can be portrayed as Lockean, un-Lockean, or Lockean up to a point. A nation's founding is a political event (or series of events). At the center of such a founding there can rest a fundamental and far-reaching premise powerful enough to inform and comprehend the structure of law and the precise powers of the civil authority that is built into that founding. At the heart of Locke's political theory rests the principle of ''equal creation.'' It signifies the individual's fundamental independence before all others in the sight of God and in the very nature of things. Grounded in the deeper Lockean metaphysics (i.e., Locke's theory of human nature), it forms the moral guide to the entire political project and immediately begets the principle of ''equal protection'' (in the broad sense already discussed). What is protected is the individual's liberty of conscience and commerce. A society grounded in the precept of ''equal protection'' leaves him (it is difficult in the Lockean context to speak of ''her'') free to follow whatever path his rationality, religion, and chosen ''calling'' command—and free to keep, use, and dispose of the just fruits of his honest industry (tax contributions aside). Most importantly, it issues an equal measure of liberty and independence to all and thereby bars the granting of special privileges to the few at the expense of the many—or vice versa. In short, it accords individuals not only the right, but the responsibility to determine the course of their lives. And it admits every opportunity for social cooperation and mutual assistance.

Although it is possible to argue that such an arrangement will conduce to the ''greatest good of the greatest number'' (and Locke did so argue), the principle of equal protection is not a utilitarian instrument. Fundamental political arrangements are not the province of prudence; they occupy a peculiarly ethical province. They proceed from the nature of things and the moral implications of human nature. The legitimate powers of government are determined by the ''true, original, end and extent of government'' as such. Many pragmatic decisions remain to be made (involving the crafting of objective laws to more clearly define and subsequently enforce the inherent and equal rights of citizens), and representative majorities must meet to make those decisions. Innumerable choices and options are possible. But if the fundamental tenets of the Lockean system are to be honored, many choices and options will fall outside the realm of possibility. Any particular decision needs to be measured against the fundamental standard of natural right. Thus a "Lockean" political architecture, rooted in the principle of free trade and free expression, for example, but built on a base of utility or majority will (and subject to change at any time by that majority upholding a more "progressive" view of utility), lacks the foundation needed to characterize that edifice as Lockean. Bentham's or Mill's justification for these social structures is not Locke's.

On the other hand, a whole host of concerns and considerations never touched upon by Locke (but belonging to a separate ideological idiom or related area of inquiry) may inform a nation's social or political outlook without necessarily undercutting the Lockean character of that nation's political commitments. Principles belonging to the *science* of politics, for example, need not collide with principles belonging to the branch of moral philosophy that inquires into the *fundamentals* of politics. It is the task of historiography to determine whether two such idioms actually can cohere or whether they are compelled to compete for the attention of a political nation.

In the next four chapters I shall argue that, all other influences notwithstanding, the fundamental political principles that America's founders enunciated and for which they fought formed, for Locke, the "true, original, extent and end of civil government." Again, I shall not argue that Locke's influence was necessarily immediate and direct—i.e., that America's founders were preoccupied or even largely acquainted with Locke's political and philosophical speculations. My aim, rather, is to determine whether and to what extent the values and principles the founders embraced were constitutionally Lockean. Lest the reader feel disappointed by this disclaimer, I should add that, as I turn to the formative, pre-Revolutionary period in colonial history to look for Locke, there will be ample opportunity to discover the various ways and means by which a philosopher's most sublime notions can move through space and time and settle in the soil of largely unsettled and virgin political territories.

7
Eighteenth-Century Background: Locke in America

For earlier students of the American founding, such as Becker and Hartz, the basic faith that Locke was America's guiding influence could almost be taken for granted. Beneath this easy acceptance there rested a formidable assumption—the understanding that Locke was the dominant political theorist of his age. His great fame proceeded not just from his philosophical and educational writings but from the pivotal role he was thought to have played in England's Glorious Revolution. For a long time scholarship accepted Locke's word when he announced in his preface that his intent in penning the *Two Treatises of Government* was "to establish the throne of our Great Restorer, Our Present King William; to make good his Title, in the Consent of the People . . . And to justifie to the World, the People of England whose love of their just and natural rights, with their resolution to preserve them, saved the Nation when it was on the very brink of Slavery and Ruine."

For some time now scholars examining both shores of the eighteenth-century Atlantic community have been taking another look at the measure of Locke's influence there. The once-enshrined view of Locke writ large across the pages of eighteenth-century Anglo-American history has come under continuing assault. Concerning the reception of Locke's anonymously published *Two Treatises of Government,* Ashcraft, Nelson, Thompson, Plumb, J. P. Kenyon, and H. T. Dickinson, from varying perspectives, all attribute to Locke a much-diminished role in the political discourse of the times.[1]

Dunn, too, has shared in this reassessment. Turning his attention to America specifically, he found that before 1745 the "men whom we can show to have read [Locke's politics] with any care were few."[2] In fact, "there is no evidence that the *Two Treatises* figured in the set curriculum of any American college before the revolution." In addition, Dunn wrote: "Its academic standing had never been all that high; it never held the unimpeachable eminence of the works of Grotius or Pufendorf. Its subject matter was too limited."[3] Locke's speculations did, Dunn admits, enter into the deliberations of some colonists, as when the Reverend John Bulkley, borrowing liberally from Locke's thoughts on property, sought to divest American Indians of their claimed territories. Thus was the "moral dignity of labour," and not the older tenet of "first occupancy," enlisted in the service of "expropriation of the Indians by the laborious and God-fearing people of New England."[4] Jonathan Boucher, the Anglican Tory, also evidenced an awareness of Locke and so issued a frontal attack on his dangerous ideas.

Most important for Dunn, those who came to adopt Locke during the revolutionary crisis were already predisposed toward their course. As he wrote, echoing Hartz, "The Adamses and Jefferson, Dickinson and Franklin, Otis and Madison, had come to read the *Two Treatises* with gradually consolidated political intentions and they had come to it to gather moral support for these intentions." Having come to the point of exasperation, the Americans saw their course clearly. "There existed a legal order, and the political moves of the English government, or the governor of Massachusetts were in breach of that order. Endlessly the work of Locke was summoned to expound the tautology that illegality was not legal." In fact, Dunn concludes: "There is no reason to suppose that anything Locke ever wrote caused the least deflection of their political behavior from the paths it would otherwise have followed. The use of his name was more a feature of their affective life than a guarantee of any energetic conceptual exploration. It belonged to the rhetoric not to the analysis of politics."[5]

Moreover, for Dunn, Locke's politics had even less of a bearing on the Framers in 1787. "For the most part Americans found no need . . . to ascend to a level more theoretical than that of the *Federalist,* and by the time that they did . . . Locke's work had become a historical curiosity. . . . the book was never again to be an emotional or conceptual focus in the discussion of the politics of the nation." It was Benjamin Rush who summed up Locke's role, such as it was. In Dunn's view, Rush dismissively advised: "It is one thing to understand the *principles,* and another thing to understand the *forms* of government. The former are simple; the latter are difficult and complicated. . . . Mr. Locke is an oracle as to the *principles,* Harrington and Montesquieu are oracles as to the *forms of government.*"[6] Most significant for Dunn's analysis of the American Revolution was the appreciation that "to most men in America, by 1774, the affective force which attached to the duty to obey social norms, the internalized structure of social control, had become irrevocably detached from the Legal order of the English polity."

If that is so, it still remains to explain why it was so. By what process, by virtue of what combination of influences or circumstances had these North American colonists liberated themselves from the "affective force," the "social control" of the English legal order? And what role may Locke have played in that liberating experience? What values did the transplanted colonists come to internalize? And to what degree could they said to be Lockean in character?

In discussing the seventeenth-century background to Locke, I tried to lay out the salient historical problems a serious writer would have to address to win an audience for his philosophic ideas. My aim in laying out the eighteenth-century background to the American founding is somewhat different. I proceed from the view that any particular philosophy may or may not be reflected in the life and times of any particular people. A philosophy might say "Be Honest," or "Be Industrious," or "Be Tolerant toward Diversity." The inhabitants of a remote prairie wilderness may have never encountered a philosophy of this, or any other, description. Yet those inhabitants, in their daily lives and as a result of ancient custom or the example of a revered forefather, may live honest, industrious, and tolerant lives. In short, a philosophy of life may or may not, to a greater or lesser degree, reflect a people's actual life-style and shared value commitments.

The question here is this: To what extent can we find in eighteenth-century colonial life the kinds of human commitments and social relations enshrined in Lockean liberalism that under a certain political circumstance (e.g., the prospect of an oppressive absolutism) might bring thirteen North American colonies to assert in Lockean fashion the inherent and indefeasible rights of mankind? To what measure were Americans living in daily experience the enlightened philosophy of life Locke so exuberantly endorsed, and in what not very obvious ways could Locke's ideas have been transmitted to eighteenth-century America? These are the questions I shall explore in the remainder of this chapter. The answers will prove useful as we go on to confront the question of Locke's bearing on the next chapter of the nation's founding, the American Revolution.

Hartz's early emphasis on environmental influences would continue to figure in historical research. As Bernard Bailyn correctly noted, the free soil and social climate of the New World were more conducive for the planting and reaping of a liberal and enlightened stock-seed than was the socially confining and, in many respects, exhausted ground of the Old. "Many, indeed most, of what these leaders considered to be their greatest achievements during the Revolution—reforms that made America seem to half the world like the veritable heavenly city of the eighteenth-century philosophes—had been matters of fact before they were matters of theory and revolutionary doctrine."[7]

The practices of primogeniture and entail (i.e., political restraints preventing property owners from dividing their estates or leaving them to anyone other than the first-born son) were duly criticized by Locke.[8] Jefferson considered the Virginia acts abolishing these practices critical to the overthrowing of Old World, aristocratic privilege and the founding of a truly democratic government. But primogeniture and entail, as Bailyn notes, "had never taken deep roots in America, not even in Tidewater Virginia."[9] A cheap and abundant mass of land available for settlement had rendered such ancient restrictions obsolete. The institution of chattel slavery did, of course, take deep root in the southern planting colonies. And while as the century wore on growing numbers of Americans would, often in Lockean tones, come to damn and disown the practice, in the meantime the black population certainly owned no Lockean natural rights.[10] Nonetheless, the point to bear in mind is that American slavery, however dreadful and repugnant a practice, need not blind us to many of the more enlightened aspects of colonial culture, certainly when viewed in relation to a European culture that would long remain so much less free and enlightened.

A second such aspect concerned the broadening of the franchise. Writing on late eighteenth-century English radicalism, Isaac Kramnick noted the ardent demands of England's disenfranchised dissenters for "a full and fair representation." Of this controversy Kramnick noted, "In a most striking case of historical oversight, few who have written on this period have noted that this formulation . . . is lifted directly from Locke."[11] The point Bailyn pressed was that in America there was entirely no need for "cries for universal manhood suffrage" or "popular theories claiming, or even justifying, general participation in politics." Circumstances here too obviated the need for any such protest. As Bailyn reports, "The traditional English laws limiting suffrage to freeholders of certain competencies proved in the colonies, where freehold property was almost universal, to be not restrictive but widely permissive."[12] Moreover, given the absence of a hereditary aristocracy or long-established corporate constituencies, representation had to be actual and direct, not "virtual." Government was designed to act for the sake, and often under the instruction, of the governed for the common good. Again, this was not high theory, it was daily practice. Implicit in all this was what would become, and remain, one of the most explosive of all democratic suppositions. Bailyn explains: "Surrounding all of these circumstances and in various ways controlling them is the fact that that great goal of the European revolutions of the late eighteenth century, *equality of status before the law—the abolition of legal privilege—*had been reached almost everywhere in the American colonies at least by the early years of the eighteenth century."[13]

The metaphysics of the matter (i.e., the question of equal creation) aside, the dint of circumstance enabled colonial Americans to expect an ample measure of equal protection from their governing bodies. How Americans would respond once these expectations were dashed and special privileges politically doled out (as, in many respects, they would be) we shall begin to see in the succeeding chapter.

Other values, also affirmed by Locke, found expression in the social patterns of America. The question of religious liberty, certainly one that is critical to the Lockean worldview, merits attention. Only recently, in fact, have we begun to reassess the significance of religion for colonial America. The long-standing view that projected a steep trend toward secularization in the Age of Enlightenment has now been called into question. As Bonomi and Sandoz have recently argued, religious belief and practice continued to occupy a central position in colonial life throughout the period.[14]

With Bailyn, Bonomi also perceived that "the Old World traditions of a single church establishment and intolerance toward dissenters were being eroded . . . [but that] in most cases such changes had far more to do with force of circumstance than with principle."[15] Maryland is a good case in point. Awarded to Cecilus Calvert, a Catholic, by Charles I in 1632, the colony enjoyed no religious establishment. This was largely owing to the fact that Maryland Protestants formed a numerical majority from the start, outnumbering Catholics by ten to one. Though the Catholic leaders took charge, they easily perceived the necessity of following Calvert's injunction "to do justice to every man without partiality." Given the unruly conditions of the 1640s and the subsequent assault on Catholicism on both sides of the Atlantic, a bare majority of Catholics succeeded in enacting an "Act concerning Religion." Turning on its head the traditional prescription for civil peace, it urged that "the inforceing of the conscience in matters of Religion hath frequently fallen out to be of dangerous Consequence." The act went so far as to forbid residents of the colony from labeling any neighbor a "heretick, Schismatick, Idolotor, puritan, Independent, Prespiterian . . . popish pr[i]est, Jesuite, Jesuited papist, Lutheran, Calvenist, Anabaptist, Brownist, Antinomian, Barrowist, Roundhead, Sep[ar]atist, or any other name."[16]

Necessity, not principle, certainly appears to have counseled prudence. This tolerance, however, would end for Catholics with Maryland's conversion to a royal colony following the Glorious Revolution. In New York as early as 1663 and in the proprietary colonies founded during the Restoration period, the pressing need to build population, secure boundaries, and enlarge, in mercantilist fashion, the wealth of the nation, urgently recommended a policy of toleration for dissent. The Carolinas, in particular, faced the hostile French and Spanish on their frontier flanks, "making prompt settlement crucial to the colony's stability." The Carolina proprietors, establishing Anglicanism in the colony, nevertheless "granted liberty of conscience to the Baptists, Huguenots, Quakers, and Presbyterians who offered the likeliest prospects as settlers."[17] As the experience of the Middle Colonies suggests generally, the great diversity of religious congregations and sects not only stimulated competition and interest in religion among the colonists, but rendered uniformity an impossible prospect.

This "toleration-by-circumstance" thesis, however, should not be taken too far. In the first place, toleration was not a uniform practice in colonial America. Well into the eighteenth century much of New England successfully resisted the trend. And, on the other hand, from the start, impressive American leaders counseled toleration on principle. This of course is true of Roger Williams, who succeeded in gaining a patent for the colony of Rhode Island in 1644. It is also true of William Penn and those of Quaker persuasion who settled in New Jersey, Delaware, and Pennsylvania. And it is true of several principal participants in the founding of the Carolinas, including Lord Shaftesbury and John Locke.

But many who hoped to build free and tolerant communities continually faced stiff competition from those who, on principle, stood against tolerance and freedom of conscience (especially the New England clergy). In the ensuing contest over toleration, we can discern important Lockean roots planted in the soil of colonial America. The battle lines in the war for religious independence were drawn, fundamentally, around the question of human nature itself. At the root of the religious controversy there stood two very different sets of answers to some abiding philosophical questions. How far could individuals be trusted with liberty? What measure of control and discipline could they exert over themselves without falling into conflict and confusion? What room was there for human improvement or educational progress? To gauge the extent and limit of Locke's influence on America it will be useful to consider some of the features of the eighteenth-century debate over toleration—a debate that, at bottom, pitted the cynical view of Hobbes against the optimism of Locke.

There is no more fitting place to begin this exposition than in the Puritanical soil of seventeenth-century New England. With some notable exceptions, the religious and political leaders of early New England were men of stern discipline. If they believed in liberty, it was the liberty to live according to God's gospel. Presbyterianism in England was still in its ascendancy (protesting the Laudian High Church) when those who would steer the course of New England life made the transatlantic voyage. The Puritans who settled in Massachusetts Bay were steeped in the strict, theocratic doctrines of Calvin and the Calvinist conception of man's fallen state. Theirs was a God of wrath, not love. Of these leaders, Vernon Parrington wrote: "They loved power quite as much as did the ungodly, and accounting themselves God's stewards they reckoned it sin not to use it in his name. God did not speak in the Scriptures through majority votes; his chosen were a minority, the remnant in Israel."

Although eschewing a unitary Presbyterianism for a more "democratic" Congregationalism, Massachusetts Bay ceded a power to the state "to intervene in ecclesiastical matters and require the magistrate to enforce uniformity in creed and worship." In the adoption of the Cambridge Platform, along with the Westminster Confession of Faith, "the work of creating the organism and creed of an authoritative state-church was completed." Under the eighth and ninth articles of the Cambridge Platform,

> Idolatry, Blasphemy, Heresy, Venting corrupt and pernicious opinions, are to be restrayned and punished by civil authority. . . . [And] if any church one or more shall grow schismaticall, rending it self from the communion of other churches, or shall walk incorrigibly or obstinately in any corrupt way of their own, contrary to the rule of the word; in such case, the Magistrate is to put forth his coercive power, as the matter shall require.[18]

To such as John Cotton, among the most intellectually able of Puritan divines, the laws of God were to be found in Scripture alone. He could accept "the Bible as a rule of universal application, perfect and final." As there was no recognition of natural law, so there was no recognition of natural rights; there was only ethical stewardship. "Freedom," Parrington aptly concluded, "was the prerogative of righteousness; the well-being of society required that the sinner should remain subject to the Saint." The desire for liberty of conscience or democracy in the state could be considered "the sinful prompting of the natural man, a denial of the righteous authority of God's chosen rulers."[19] In his long dispute with Roger Williams, Cotton had ample opportunity to hone his argument. To Williams's charge that after running from England to escape persecution, the persecuted had become the new persecutors, Cotton could reply: "There is a vast difference between men's inventions and God's institutions; we fled from men's inventions, to which we else should have been compelled, we compel none to men's inventions. . . . [For] if the worship be lawful in itself, the magistrate compelling him to come to it, compelleth him not to sin, but the sin is in his own will that needs to be compelled to a Christian duty."[20]

As John Cotton was the minister, so John Winthrop was the civil manager, the magistrate, of the theocratic order. Both reared in strict Calvinism, accepting God's call to stewardship, and so opposed to the democratic principle, minister and magistrate alike inferred the pravity of mankind. This attitude is perhaps nowhere more clearly exposed than in Winthrop's "Little Speech" on liberty (1645). And nowhere is the Hobbesian notion of human nature more in evidence.

"The great questions that have troubled the country," Winthrop appreciates, "are about the authority of the magistrate and the liberty of the people." Here are his answers:

> There is a twofold liberty, natural (I mean as our nature is now corrupt) and civil or federal. The first is common to man with beasts and other creatures. . . . [It is a] liberty to do what he lists; . . . a liberty to evil as well as to good. This liberty is incompatible and inconsistent with . . . and cannot endure the least restraint of the most just authority. The exercise and maintaining of this liberty makes men grow more evil, and in time to be worse than brute beasts. . . . This is that great enemy of truth and peace, that wild beast, which all the ordinances of God are bent against, to restrain and subdue it.

Certainly this is not John Locke's estimate of the human condition. Where is the ameliorating activity of reason and a rational willpower? Where is the emphasis on learning and improvement? For Winthrop, the depravity of mankind is paramount. The corruption of the human soul must ever confound the civil peace. The awful propensities of mankind can be checked only by a "subjection to authority." Only in such submission will subjects enjoy an authentic "civil liberty," which is but the "liberty to do that only which is good, just and honest." Nor is it possible to straddle the two forms of liberty; it is either/or. "If you stand for your natural corrupt liberties, and will do what is good in your own eyes, you will not endure the least weight of authority, but will murmur, and oppose, and be always striving to shake off that yoke; but if you will be satisfied to enjoy such civil and lawful liberties such as Christ allows you, then will you quietly and cheerfully submit unto that authority which is set over you."[21]

Though it is possible within a decade of Winthrop's speech to speak of the "Twilight of the Oligarchy," it is also true that the Puritan cum Presbyterian ideal found able defense in the succeeding generations, especially in the tireless labors of the Mather clan: Richard, Increase, and Cotton. Cotton Mather's (1663–1728) *Magnalia Christi Americana,* which has been described as "the *magnum opus* of the Massachusetts Theocracy," might also be described as the post mortem of a failing culture.

It would be little match for the rising tide of liberalism. The stirrings of liberalism, in fact, come early, even to New England. And though they are, in part, the product of the native conditions (i.e., the wide distribution of freehold land), these socially divisive impulses sprang most immediately from the minds of some very gifted men and at least one influential woman. In the labors of Roger Williams, Anne Hutchinson, and the Quaker disciples of George Fox, the religious patterns of seventeenth-century New England would be rigorously challenged.

The career of Roger Williams (1604–1683) begs attention here. Immigrating to New England two years before Locke's birth (1630) and founding a democratic polity at Providence, Rhode Island, by Locke's fourth birthday, Williams opposed uniformity and defended toleration in strikingly "Lockean" terms. A protégé of Lord Coke, the great English jurist; graduate of Cambridge; and teacher to Cromwell, Milton, and Sir Harry Vane (whose assistance at Court helped procure the Rhode Island patent), Roger Williams struck a powerful blow for liberty of conscience and the separation of church and state. Turning the Puritan worldview upside down, he argued that it is religious uniformity, not diversity, that sparks enmity between individuals and disturbs the civil peace of society. Political society, he held, was indeed divine in origin in that it is a natural condition decreed by God in his very creation of man. But it is a mundane state, designed for purely mundane ends, viz., the protection of people's "Bodies and Goods." The magistrate's power is a commission from the people and has only as much strength as the people can and do give it. One can find no more fitting text supporting the "joint-stock-company" theory of the church than in the writings of Roger Williams. Replying to the theocratic thinking of Master John Cotton, he advises:

> The church, or company of worshippers, whether true or false, is like unto a body or college of physicians in a city—like unto a corporation, society, or company of East India . . . or any other . . . company in London; which companies may hold their courts, keep their records, hold disputations, and in matters concerning their society may dissent, divide, break into schisms and factions, sue and implead each other at the law, yea, wholly break up and dissolve into pieces and nothing, and yet the peace of the city not be in the least measure impaired or disturbed; because the essence or being of the city, and so the well being and peace thereof, is essentially distinct from those particular societies, the city courts, city laws, city punishments distinct from theirs.[22]

Coming in a time when inferences drawn from religious experience and association could easily spill over into discussions of civil association, such attitudes toward the church would soon find expression in the "joint-stock" conception of the state. For Williams, "A Civill Government is an ordinance of God, to conserve the Civil peace of the people, so farre as concerns their Bodies and Goods." From a Lockean perspective, his language is indeed striking:

> The *Soveraigne, originall,* and *foundation of civill power* lies in the
> *People* . . . [who] may erect and establish what *forme* of *government*
> seems to them most meete for their *civill condition;* It is evident that
> such *Governments* as are by them erected and established have no more
> power, nor for no longer time, then the *civill power* or people consenting
> and agreeing shall betrust them with This is cleere not only in *Reason,*
> but in the experience of all *commonweales,* where the people are not
> deprived of their naturall freedom by the power of Tyrants.

From this it is clear that ultimate sovereignty lies in the people, that the magistrate is but the people's servant, and that "every lawful Magistrate whether succeeding or elective . . . goes beyond his commission who intermeddles with that which cannot be given him in commission from the people."[23]

What could not be surrendered to the commonwealth was one's liberty of conscience. As Williams wrote, let "None bee accounted a Delinquent for *Doctrine.*" When, at the Restoration, Rhode Island petitioned and received a Royal Charter (1663) religious liberty was for the first time enshrined into American constitutional law. For this charter decreed that

> noe person within the sayd colonye, at any tyme here-after, shall bee
> any wise molested, punished, disquieted, or called in question, for
> any differences . . . in matters of religion [as long as he or she does]
> not actually disturb the civil peace of our sayd colony. [And this shall
> prevail over] any lawe, statute or clause . . . usage or custome of this
> realme, to the contrary hereof, in any wise, notwithstanding.[24]

What I am most concerned with, however, is that Williams's commitment to political democracy and the immutable right of religious liberty proceed from his basic conception of human nature. Unlike Cotton, Winthrop, and the Mathers, he steadfastly upheld the dignity and worth of the individual believer—regardless of what he happened to believe (Quakers and Jews would find welcome in his commonwealth). Individuals were essentially rational, peaceful, and good and could be trusted with civil and religious liberty. Vernon Parrington, with characteristic grace, summarized Williams's estimate of humankind:

> It was the spirit of love that served as teacher to him; love that exalted
> the meanest to equality with the highest in the divine republic of
> Jesus, and gave an exalted sanction to the conception of a Christian
> commonwealth. He regarded his fellow men literally as the children

of God and brothers in Christ. . . . he sought to adjust his social program to the determining fact that human worth knows neither Jew nor Gentile, rank nor caste. . . . With this spirit of Christian fellowship, warm and human and lovable, repudiating all coercion . . . he went forth.[25]

The Reverend John Wise of Ipswich struck another critical and early blow against the Puritan theocratic orthodoxy and its pessimistic outlook on human nature. As Roger Williams had countered the doctrine of John Cotton, Wise rejected Increase Mather's 1705 proposal to confer greater power on the central council over individual congregations and ministers. By the so-called consociation scheme, the authority of the central synod would be "final and decisive." Wise was successful in defeating at least this element of the Mather plan. His greater importance, however, lies first in the fact that he based his own arguments on natural law doctrine (though leaning more on Pufendorf than Locke), and second, in the influence he exerted on subsequent American political thought. His two main works, *The Church's Quarrel Espoused* (1710) and *A Vindication of the Government of New England Churches* (1717), had a deep and lasting impact on his contemporaries. These two works, reissued in 1772, enjoyed a subscription of 1,130 copies.[26]

It was Wise's purpose to vindicate the independence of the individual congregation against theocratic supremacy but, even more profoundly, to vindicate and defend the independence of the individual conscience against any form of ecclesiastical (or civil) tyranny. He would make his stand on the unshakable ground of natural law, exuding the most profound confidence in the capacity of humans to discover and do good. Interestingly, he patterned his conception of church government on his argument concerning the rise of civil government and rooted both forms in a singular perception of human nature. In a spirit that is unmistakably Lockean, John Wise writes, "The original of civil power is the people," and the "end of all good government, is to cultivate humanity, and promote the happiness of all, and the good of every man in his rights, his life, liberty, estate, honor, etc., without injury or abuse to any."[27] Wise infuses humanity with three immutable "immunities." They are worth quoting in full:

The prime immunity in man's state is that he is most properly the subject of the law of nature. He is the favorite animal on earth; in that this part of God's image, viz. reason is congenate with his nature, wherein by a law immutable, instampt upon his frame, God has pro-

vided a rule for men in all their actions, obliging each one to the performance of that which is right.

The second great immunity of man is an original liberty *instampt
upon his rational nature*. He that intrudes upon this liberty, violates
the law of nature. The native internal liberty of man's nature implies
a faculty of doing or omitting things according to the direction of his
judgment.

Wise does not mean by this a license to give vent to the first, last, or strongest
ill-passion one might experience. He quotes Plutarch to the effect that "those
persons only who live in obedience to reason, are worthy to be accounted free.
They, alone live as they will who have learnt what they ought to will." True and
natural liberty consists in being "guided and restrained by the ties of reason, and
laws of nature." This being so and being universally applicable to all, Wise is
drawn to the last inherent feature "instampt" on human nature:

> The third capital immunity belonging to man's nature, is an equality
> amongst men; which is not to be denied by the law of nature. . . .
> [Thus] it follows . . . that every man esteem and treat another as one
> who is naturally his equal, or who is a man as well as he; . . . it is a
> command of nature's law, that no man . . . shall arrogate to himself
> a larger share than his fellows, but shall admit others to equal privi-
> leges with himself . . . [with, quoting Ulpian] 'no servitude or sub-
> jection.'[28]

Human reason for Wise, as for Locke, is the root of human liberty and equality. With all of the natural law writers, Wise affirms the inherent sociability of
human nature and the need to quit the condition of natural liberty and equality for
the greater security of the civil estate. Having "resigned himself with all his
rights for the sake of a civil state," however, it is nevertheless the case that "his
personal liberty and equality is to be cherished and preserved to the highest degree."

> So that though man is inclined to society, yet he is driven to [it] by
> great necessity. For that the true and leading cause of forming gov-
> ernments, and yielding up natural liberty, and throwing man's equal-
> ity into a common pile to be new cast by the rules of fellowship, was
> really and truly to guard themselves against the injuries men were
> liable to interchangeably; . . . [And, therefore] in a civil, as well as

in a natural state of being a just equality is to be indulged so far, as that every man is bound to honor every man, which is agreeable both with nature and religion. . . . otherwise a man in making himself a subject, he alters himself from a freeman, into a slave, which to do is repugnant to the law of nature.

Wise went on to discuss the three basic forms of government—democracy, aristocracy, and monarchy—clearly favoring the democratic as "being most agreeable to the just and natural prerogatives of human beings." Abruptly shifting the grounds of discussion from temporal to spiritual affairs, Wise questions the very legitimacy of the theocratic discipline. "How can it consist with the honorable terms man holds upon here on earth; that . . . when they enter into charter-party to manage a trade for heaven, [they] must *ipso facto* be clapt under a government, that is arbitrary and dispotic yea that carries the plain symptoms of a tyranny in it?"

This the laws of God and nature cannot allow, since "man . . . is under God, the first subject of all power, and therefore, can make his own choice and by deliberate compacts, settle his own conditions for the government of himself in a civil state of being." Wise warns those who would overturn the natural laws that should they succeed, the people have a right to free themselves from bondage and begin government anew. He therefore concludes: "That a democracy in church or state is a very honorable, and regular government according to the dictates of right reason. And therefore That these churches of New England, in their ancient constitution of church order, it being a democracy, are manifestly justified and defended by the law and light of nature."[29]

Here, at the virtual dawn of American civilization, in the writings of Williams and Wise, stands a conception of human nature at strict variance with the Puritanical impulse carried over by English Presbyterianism. Ostensibly, the issue was toleration. But as I have tried to point out, critical to the debate over free religious expression were two diametrically opposed perceptions of human nature. One, cynical and pessimistic, affording little liberty or responsibility to the plain believer, decreed that people must be led to a life of piety by the strong dictate of authority. The other, quietly confident in the human potential, affirmed the reasonableness of human nature and the capacity of individuals to make their own way in the world without turning it upside down in disorder and upheaval.

John Wise, it is true, did not carry the day in Massachusetts. His was a holding action, and though it did hold the Presbyterian influence in Congregationalism at bay, Anglicans and dissenters (largely Baptists and Quakers) in that colony had to fight long and hard for religious liberty. In Connecticut, the consociation movement, as it was called, gathered even more momentum. By 1708, the Congregational clergy in that colony drew up the Saybrook Platform, instituting, in Bonomi's words, "a presbyterial form of church government . . . for the management of ecclesiastical discipline." Despite passage of a Toleration Act in the same year and future laws exempting Anglicans, Quakers, and Baptists from paying Congregational church rates, Bonomi could report, "So potent was the combined power of church and state in the colony that by 1730 officials had recognized but one Baptist congregation, one Anglican church, and no Quaker meetings."[30]

If we turn to the Middle Colonies, however, the experience is very different. Here, owing largely to the great diversity of religious denominations and a relatively late arrival of Congregational (largely Lutheran and German Reformed) churches, uniformity could not easily be had. Moreover, lacking a Harvard or a Yale, which trained hundreds of young men for the ministry in New England, the settlers here had to rely more heavily on lay leaders for religious instruction. This, in turn, resulted in a greater empowerment of congregations in choosing their ministers and controlling church affairs. This voluntarism, again largely the result of the natural and native conditions of the region, militated against the imposition of any strict religious discipline.[31] But there was more to it than that. Especially in the Jerseys and in Pennsylvania, the *idea* of tolerance found powerful voice, in large part from the influence of Quakers generally, and their leading inspiration and light, William Penn, in particular. In Penn's Pennsylvania, liberty of conscience was asserted as a fundamental right. Penn's 1682 *Frame of Government* thus declared:

> That all persons living in the province; who confess and acknowledge the one Almighty and eternal God, to be the Creator, Upholder and Ruler of the world; and that hold themselves obliged in conscience to live peaceably and justly in civil society, shall, in no ways, be molested or prejudiced for their religious persuasion, or practice, in matters of faith and worship, nor shall they be compelled, at any time, to frequent or maintain any religious worship . . . or ministry.

The sanctity of the individual conscience is again confirmed in the Quaker tenets of humility, pacifism, and tolerance. It is "force [that] makes hypocrites; 'tis persuasion only that makes converts." Like Williams in Rhode Island and Wise in Massachusetts, Penn would place his trust in the people, affirming the dignity and reasonableness of human nature and therefore the worth of democratic self-rule. In the preface to his *Frame of Government,* he proclaimed, "Any government is free to the people under it . . . where the laws rule, and the people are a party to those laws, and more than this is tyranny, oligarchy, or confusion.''

The opening paragraph of the 1682 *Frame* reveals Penn's estimate of human nature and the basis for the coercive authority of the state. God fitted his rational creatures with "skill and power, [and] with integrity" that they may rule "justly." But men are, in the final analysis, free and given to passions that can pull them off the path of righteousness. It was thus necessary that he who "would not live conformable to the holy law within, should fall under the reproof and correction of the just law without, in a judicial administration." The law of society "was not made for the righteous man, but for the disobedient and ungodly." What is it the law is meant to do? Writing on "England's Present Interest Considered" (1675) and addressing "the basis of reasonable societies," Penn urges people "to live honestly, not to hurt another, and to give every one their right." From this he derives "those rights and privileges which I call English, and which are the proper birth-right of Englishman:"

> I. An ownership, and undisturbed possession: that what they have is rightly theirs, and no body's else. II. A voting of every law that is made, whereby that ownership or propriety may be maintained. III. An influence upon, and a real share in, that judicatory power that must apply every such law, which is the necessary, and laudable use of juries.

On the principle of property and the importance of representation in the matter of taxation, Penn's 1682 *Frame* asserts: "That no money or goods shall be raised, upon, or paid by, any of the people of this province by way of public tax, custom or contribution, but by a law, for that purpose made; and whoever shall levy, collect, or pay any money or goods contrary thereunto, shall be held a public enemy to the province and a betrayer of the liberties of the people thereof."[32]

But it is not the political principles of Penn I want to emphasize here. At bottom stands a perception of human nature. It is one that is benevolent and optimistic and would place great trust in the power of the people to do good. What is the root of this confidence? Although the doctrine of the "inner light" is central to the Quaker experience (one that in the hands of the radical sectaries of Interregnum England could end in civil confusion), Penn clearly associates that light with a far more benign and pacific instrument: reason itself. In *Some Fruits of Solitude in Reflections and Maxims Relating to the Conduct of Human Life* (London, 1693), Penn developed this understanding. "Man being made a Reasonable and so a Thinking Creature," there is nothing "more worthy of his Being, than the right Direction and Employment of his Thoughts.'' Reason proclaims truth and is an objective measure of it. ''It is for want of examining it by the same light and measure that we are not all of the same mind.''

As with Locke, so with Penn: reason was a natural faculty, but one that had to be employed by a diligent exertion of the will. It required work, but it was a work that should be done. ''A reasonable Opinion must ever be in Danger, where Reason is not judge.''[33] Let reason and free expression prevail, allow human ingenuity to question, seek, and persuade, and the minds of men and women (and Quakers afforded women far more freedom and respect than did the Congregational churches) and all society would benefit.

Here in the ''free air'' of the Middle Colonies the ideas of Roger Williams, John Wise, and William Penn could be put to the test. The results were impressive, for here and now individuals could experience the personal power of choice, exercise discretion, and rely on their own independent judgment in matters affecting their faith and salvation. Religion did not suffer for the absence of discipline, but flourished. The result ''was a kind of free market for theistic beliefs and practices that reflected almost every color in the spectrum of Western Christendom.'' Vigorous religious competition, the product of a voluntary faith, stimulated rather than discouraged church growth. Noting the significance of all this for America's future, Bonomi appropriately suggested that a flourishing religion spurred by ''voluntary participation . . . may have fortified Americans of the Revolutionary generation as they embarked on a still new experiment that rested heavily on the uncoerced virtue of its citizens.''[34]

Before America would enter upon the business of revolution, however, it would pass through a phase of intense religious self-examination. The Great Awakening of the 1740s (along with the antecedent revivals of the prior decade) certainly appears to contradict the thesis of an ascendant liberal or latitudinarian religious order. Surely it casts grave doubt on the notion that Americans by then were firmly committed to the precepts of natural theology or an optimistic vision of human nature.

The Great Awakening was, in good measure, a reaction against the secularization of society and a spreading Arminianism (with its emphasis on works, rather than the surrender to faith alone). This reaction is most easily evident in the case of Jonathan Edwards (1703–1758) and the events surrounding his ministry at Northampton, Massachusetts. As early as 1662, the Massachusetts synod had adopted the ''Halfway Covenant.'' By this arrangement people not currently professing their faith would be counted ''halfway'' members of the visible church provided they had received baptism in infancy and lived in an upright fashion. Such people could not vote in church affairs, however, or partake in the

Lord's Supper. Edwards's grandfather, Solomon Stoddard, during his tenure loosened the reins of discipline still further. By his lights, all members of the community who were not outwardly immoral in their conduct were entitled to all the sacraments of the church, including the Lord's Supper. All those who would seek grace through worship and communion (in Arminian fashion) were entitled to full membership in the visible church since, as he held, the "saints" are invisible, no matter how much they may profess. Perry Miller spoke to the significance of Stoddard's teaching:

> [Stoddard] henceforth baptized not merely the children of members, but all the children in town, he took into the communion not merely the professing adults, but all adults. At one fell swoop he cured the evils of the Half-Way Covenant by going beyond it; . . . and identif[ying] the visible church no longer with the community of saints, but with the town meeting — where he himself was dictator and lawgiver. [35]

It was the Halfway Covenant and the doctrines of Stoddard that Jonathan Edwards rejected upon succeeding his grandfather at Northampton in 1729. And it was the example and theological doctrines posted by Edwards in his revival ministry of the 1730s that played no small role in shaping the course of the Great Awakening after 1740. Contrary to earlier views, the spirit of the Awakening was indeed pervasive in America, affecting the religious outlook of persons of every social rank scattered throughout the Middle and New England colonies. [36] Now, it is not at all difficult to discern the fundamental breach between the Awakening and the rational theology of a Penn, a Williams, or a Wise. Splitting the Congregational churches throughout the colonies, the antirevival part could well be considered "synonymous with rationalism in theology and with the substitution of morality for religion." Indeed, it is Charles Chauncy, the revivalists' most articulate and outspoken foe, who extols a liberal and Lockean outlook. His notable election sermon, delivered before Governor William Shirley of Massachusetts on 27 May 1747, is an exuberant exposition of limited government and the rights of individuals in matters of conscience. As he warns:

> Justice in rulers should be seen likewise in their care of the religious rights and liberties of a people. Not that they are to exert their authority in *settling articles of faith*, or *imposing modes of worship*. . . . Nor are penal laws at all adjusted in their nature to enlighten men's minds, or convince their judgment. This can be done only by good reason . . . the only proper way of applying to reasonable creatures. [37]

It was not the reasonableness or innate goodness of God's highest creature to which the great preachers of the revival addressed themselves and appealed. There is little that is Lockean in the Awakening's emphasis on the "conversion experience." What it demanded was the confession of one's utter sinfulness and depravity. It further demanded the acknowledgment that in justice, one deserved the slings and sorrows of eternal damnation. If one was to be saved, it would be through God's grace alone—and not the work of artful sacraments. Edwards dutifully described a three-stage process in his *Narrative of Surprising Conversions*. In it, he clearly harks back to a grimmer Calvinistic assessment: "Persons are first awakened with a sense of their miserable condition by nature, the danger they are in of perishing eternally. . . . Those that before were secure and senseless, are made sensible how much they were in the way to ruin in their former courses . . . till a sense of their misery, by God's Spirit setting in therewith, had had fast hold of them."

In the second phase, the convert learns how utterly helpless he is to save himself and so how deserving of damnation he—and all mankind—truly is. Finally, a few fortunate souls enjoy the third stage, "a calm of spirit" that comes with the "special and delightful manifestation" of God's saving grace.[38] This conception, then, leans on "innate ideas" throughout and casts human nature in its dimmest light. Appealing to the deepest sense of sin and pravity, not only in the depraved but in every man, the great revivalists couched their appeals in the language of emotions, not reason. In this, too, we see a deeply antirational commitment. "If the fundamental principle of the Great Awakening was insistence on personal conversion," Goen writes, "its most striking characteristic was religious excitement."[39] In many places, "people would cry out, in the time of public worship, under a sense of their overbearing guilt and misery, and the all-consuming wrath of God, due to them for their iniquities; others would faint and swoon under the affecting views which they had of God and Christ; some would weep and sob."[40]

The "New Light" itinerants who followed in Edwards's train spread the gospel of human depravity with great zeal and much success. George Whitefield, Gilbert Tennent, and a legion of successive itinerants preached before huge crowds, converting wherever they went. But it was the fiery James Davenport (1716–1757) who typified the emotional extravagances of the revivalist movement. Making his evangelical mark on Connecticut, he would, by 1742, be arrested for violating "An Act for Regulating Abuses and Correcting Disorders in Ecclesiastical Affairs." Upon the conclusion of his trial, the assembly found that "the said Davenport is under the influence of enthusiastical impressions and impulses, and thereby disturbed in the rational faculties of his mind, and therefore to be pitied and compassionated, and not to be treated as otherwise he might be."

Expelled from Connecticut, Davenport made his way to Massachusetts. Being barred from the church pulpit, he took to the fields, conducting himself so as to once more find himself under arrest. Once again, he was found innocent by virtue of being deemed "non compos mentis." Undaunted, he took up the Lord's work in New London, "his mind," according to one historian, "in a state of fervid exaltation, amounting to frenzy."

> He first ordered his devotees to burn all their wigs, fine clothes, and jewelry, in order to cure them of "idolatrous love of worldly things." He then demanded that they bring all their "unsafe" religious books, and on Sunday evening, March 6 [1743], he led the company down to the wharf, where they set fire to [the] works. . . . They marched around the pyre shouting "Hallelujah!" and "Glory to God."[41]

By 1743, the battle lines were firmly drawn. The "Old Lights," as the antirevivalists were called, took up ecclesiastical arms against the awakened "New Lights." Though the movement had largely subsided by 1745, it is not difficult to understand how some could characterize the Great Awakening as "a tempest of ungoverned passions that swept over the colonies, leaving wreckage everywhere, in the alienations and divisions in families, neighborhoods, and churches, the undermining of cherished institutions, and a relapse into indifference, debauchery, and irreligion."[42]

If painfully little in all this appears to be Lockean in character, then appearances can indeed be deceiving. From the 1730s, much more was awakened than American's lowly estimate of human nature. Though large numbers would now account themselves sinners in the sight of God, they would, one by one, learn to count on themselves, not the force of a mediating authority. "This," concludes Goen, "made the whole movement essentially democratic, and gave a tremendous new importance to the common man. Eventually it was to weaken the autocratic parish system and exalt local church autonomy in an unprecedented way."[43] Actually, the story is more complicated and interesting than that.

The Great Awakening did indeed spawn divisions within families, neighborhoods, and churches. As itinerant preachers and lay exhorters railed against the established, though "unconverted" Old Lights, and as the Old Lights countered the "schismaticall" interlocutors rancor and confusion spread. Nevertheless, as Bonomi explains, "The internecine spectacle that ensued, the loss of proportion and professional decorum, contributed to the demystification of the clergy, forced parishioners to choose between competing factions, and overset traditional attitudes about deference and leadership in colonial America."[44] Thus the influence of the Awakening was felt well after its decline, by 1745, in the continuing proliferation of separatist churches.

The revivalists may not have gloried in the spirited quest for human independence, or what would follow from it, and "they may not have been deliberate social levellers, but their words and actions had the effect of emphasizing individual values over hierarchical ones." By dint of the controversy they brought on, original intentions aside, they needed to "insist that there were choices, and that the individual himself was free to make them." The logic of the historical circumstance was inexorable. Capturing the "new spirit of defiant individualism," Bonomi concludes: "No longer were consensual values to prevail over individual ones, at least in matters concerning the soul. Now private judgment and intuitive understanding had equal if not superior claim on the conscience. In a word, decision making had been internalized. . . . the individual, standing alone in the sight of God, was the primary vessel of salvation."[45]

And looking ahead, Bonomi correctly observed: "Once having taken part in the dismantling of old institutions and the shaping of new ones, Americans at every social level would find themselves less hesitant to do it again."[46] For Locke, human virtue consisted of the fullest use of reason. Its immediate corollary was "independence," which I characterized as, first and foremost, an epistemological state. It is precisely this independent cast of mind that was unleashed by the unsettling midcentury revivals.

Moreover, this fierce spirit of epistemological independence, given the exigencies of religious conflict, spilled over into the social arena, pitting the principle of liberty against the power of authority. The New England separatists were intractably led to justify their independent course. Presbyterian and Congregational separatists would now revisit the hallowed ground pioneered by William Penn, Roger Williams, and John Wise. In marshaling their arguments they harked back, as well, to the ideas of Chillingworth, Tillotson, and Locke. Solomon Paine of Connecticut invoked each believer's "unalienable Right in matters of the worship of God, to Judge for himself as his Conscience receives the Rule from God, who alone hath Right to challenge this Sovereignty over and property in them."[47] Elisha Williams, even more attuned to the intricacies of natural rights argument, demanded, "The Rights of Magna Charter depend not on the Will of a Prince, or the Will of the Legislature, but they are the inherent natural Rights of Englishmen."

Reproducing virtually verbatim Locke's theory of government rooted in "equal creation," Williams goes on to assert the individual's inherent right to property and liberty of conscience. "The members of a civil state *do retain their natural liberty or right of judging for themselves in matters of religion.* Every man has an equal right to follow the dictates of his own conscience in the affairs of religion.'' Most important, Williams, as Locke, locates the foundation of people's rights in their inherent constitution as rational beings. The understanding is critical:

> The rights of conscience are sacred and equal in all, and strictly speaking unalienable. This *right of judging every one for himself in matters of religion* results from the nature of man, and is so inseparably connected therewith, that a man can no more part with it than he can with his power of thinking: and it is equally reasonable for him to attempt to strip himself of the power of reasoning, as . . . [to vest] another with this right.[48]

One question clearly emerges at this point. What was so rational a theologian as Elisha Williams doing defending this separatist impulse, presumably rooted in a Great (neo-Calvinist) Awakening? Or, in other words, how does the scriptural literalism of a Jonathan Edwards together with the entire revivalist worldview comport with the natural theology thereafter employed to justify religious purity? Are individuals depraved, helpless sinners, saved by faith and grace alone? Or are they rational, self-directed creatures, capable of self-assertion and spiritual improvement?

The first point that must be made is that the Awakening should not be too closely identified with fundamentalist Calvinism—if that is taken to embrace a pure biblical literalism. By the time it commenced more than a few New England clergymen had become supporters of reason, even sponsors of rational theology. As great a Calvinist as Cotton Mather, in fact, could be heralded as ''the leading champion of modern science in Massachusetts.'' In *The Christian Philosopher* (1721), Mather affirmed ''that *Philosophy* is no *Enemy*, but a mighty and wondrous *Incentive* to *Religion;* . . . What we call NATURAL *philosophy*, is what I must encourage you to spend much more Time in the Study of.'' The spirit of Francis Bacon haunts the pages of the work. Mather thus points to a ''*Twofold Book of God;* the Book of the *Creatures*, and the Book of the *Scriptures;* God having taught first of all us by his *Works*, did it afterwards . . . by his *Words*.''[49]

Another influential minister, Benjamin Coleman of the Brattle Street Church in Boston, preached that ''the Law of *Nature* is a very *Sacred* Law, and the Light of Nature a very *great light*.'' In another sermon, entitled ''God Deals with Us as Rational Creatures'' (1723), Coleman advised that ''there is a Soul in man endued with a principle and power of reasoning.'' Upholding the doctrine of innate ideas, i.e., of God's commands implanted in the human conscience, Coleman said, "This is *essential* to a rational Creature to have the *Law of God* written on his mind and Conscience; for Reason in us is this Law; and it is given man for his Government and Conduct."[50]

The infusion of reason and natural theology, it must be said, was intended to assist, not replace revealed religion. The study of God's work was meant to append the teaching contained in his word. Moreover, the essential tenets of Calvinism did not come under attack, despite the spread of reason, natural theology, Newtonian mechanics, and what was called a "Catholick Spirit" of toleration for religious diversity.

Nonetheless, by the 1730s it was becoming increasingly clear to many Calvinist ministers that the spreading spirit of reason and rational theology did pose a somber threat to Calvinist theology. Anyone attuned to developments back home could perceive how, in a Toland or a Tindal, a Deist affirmation of nature could obviate any need for the revealed word. Reason's study not just of nature, but of the pagan authors of antiquity could only exacerbate the deterioration of religious commitment. Worst of all from the Calvinist perspective was the Arminian heresy that lurked just beneath the surface of rational self-assertion. A believer, enticed by the power of his rational faculty, daily improving his understanding and perfecting his faith or conduct, could well discount his sinfulness or innate depravity. Self-reliance and self-abnegation, many correctly perceived, would make strange pew-fellows.

Addressing *New England's Lamentations* (1734), John White of Gloucester thus warned of the New Learning and so many new books that appealed to our brave, young men, "suiting their Proud and self conceited Hearts, by extolling *free* Will and *self Sufficiency.*" Samuel Johnson, the New England Anglican, too, foresaw the corruption of religion in the progress of a rational outlook. Himself a devoté of the New Learning, he nonetheless warned "that Arianism and Latitudinarianism so much in vogue often issued in Socinianism and that in Deism and that in atheism and the most dissolute living; that the more gentlemen pretended to reason and deep speculation the more they dwindled in faith . . . the more irreligious and immoral they grew, and that in proportion as they grew more conceited and self-sufficient." In particular, he lamented how "melancholy [it was] to observe the gradual but deplorable progress of infidelity and apostasy in this age of mighty pretense and reasoning from the well meaning but too conceited Mr. Locke, down to Tindal, and thence to Bolingbroke, etc. etc."[51]

It was against this background—a great decay in the beliefs of vital religion, a spread of free and rational inquiry, a clamorous demand for reason and argument and "Proof of Doctrines," and the fear that, by this course, "the Calvinistical Principles" would "subside and die away"—that the cry for a New Rebirth spread. Ironically, it was the rationalist Benjamin Coleman of Brattle Street who invited the "Grand Itinerant," George Whitefield, to New England to restore the faith.[52] And it was Whitefield who castigated the colleges for introducing young minds to the latitudinarians, such as Samuel Clarke and John Tillotson. Of Harvard and Yale, Whitefield said, "Their light is become darkness." In any case it was not too long before darkness descended over the Awakening. By the fall of 1745, Newlin reports, it "came to an end as an affective movement." Beginning as an effort to reinvigorate faith and discourage reason, it ended up a wholesale flight into frenzied emotionalism. And it was largely perceived, and rejected, as such.

To be sure, diehard revivalists continued to pitch their wares. But the more sober, including Jonathan Edwards himself, admitted to the excesses and labored to show that it was nonetheless the work of God that had been done. Edwards, for his part, penned a number of works defending the role of the affections in the work of revival. In 1741, he preached a sermon entitled *Distinguishing Marks of a Work of the Spirit of God*. Expanded and published as a small book in the same year, it attempted to argue that the many emotional excesses — the physical agitations or mental excitements — were a reflection on the human spirit, not the divine. A second effort, *Some Thoughts concerning the Present Revival of Religion in New England* (1743), continued the defense. Here, Edwards sought to justify the affections against those who would extol reason and will at their expense. He argued that the affections were an integral component of the will, indistinguishable from it. The task was to distinguish between genuine and fake religious affections. This line of inquiry resulted in a book entitled *A Treatise concerning Religious Affections,* which has been called "the most significant theological outcome of the Great Awakening."[53]

At any rate, Edwards's effort to defend, or revive, the revival failed dismally. "In the interval between his *Distinguishing Marks* and his next book, two thirds of the pamphlets and three-fifths of the newspaper articles dealing with the revival were wholly or largely unfavorable to it."[54] By then, Edwards's chief antagonist, Charles Chauncy, was fast gaining the high ground. Directly responding to Edwards, and recognizing both the sovereignty of reason and the importance of independence in judgment, he advised:

> The plain Truth is, an *enlightened Mind* and not *raised Affections,* ought always to be the Guide of those who call themselves Men: and this, in the Affairs of Religion, as well as other Things. . . . If we would act up to our Character as Men, or Christians, we must not submit blindfold to the Dictates of others. . . . Nor can we be too

solicitous, so far as we are able, to see with our own Eyes, and believe with our own Understandings.

Chauncy, as Newlin concludes, "became the outstanding example of a ratio-
nalistic liberalism which completely repudiated Calvinism."[55] He championed
the cause, eventually posting a doctrine of universal salvation (owing to the benevolence of God) and rejecting the doctrine of original sin, until his death in
1786. Innumerable other clergymen shared Chauncy's estimate of human nature
and human reason. The *Seven Sermons* of Jonathan Mayhew (1749) explicitly
relied on Locke to justify the life of reason, the freedom of the will, and religious
and moral self-determination. The Dudleian lectures inaugurated at Harvard in
1755 were largely devoted to the spread of natural theology. Typical of the tenor
of the lectures were the views of Ebenezer Gay, who, delivering the second of the
series, advised:

> Whoever observes the divine Workmanship in Human Nature, and
> takes a Survey of the Powers and Faculties with which it is endowed,
> must needs see that it was designed and framed for the Practice of
> Virtue. . . . Man hath a principle of Action within himself and is an
> Agent in the strict and proper sense of the Word. The special Endow-
> ment of his Nature . . . is the Power of Self-determination, or Free-
> dom of Choice.[56]

There is abundant evidence that Locke's epistemological view had by the third
quarter of the eighteenth century gained a wide circulation. As Gad Hitchcock
said in his Dudleian lecture of 1779, "The opinion of innate ideas and principles
which prevailed for so long a time, is now almost universally given up; and that
of the human mind receiving them afterwards distinct and simple; comparing,
compounding and disposing of them . . . is adopted in its room, as the original of
knowledge."[57]

Confidence in reason's power as both a cognitive and motivational mechanism
and hence confidence in the individual's capacity for self-government and steady
improvement are two of the most salient features of the American worldview at
the dawn of the imperial crisis. And the assertion of reason and natural religion
was not confined to the Congregational or Separatist churches of New England.
As Bonomi has pointed out, "The Anglican church represented the pinnacle of
rational religion in eighteenth-century America. The scientific revolution, Enlightenment humanism, Locke, and the Scottish sense writers—all admired by

the southern gentry—had shifted the emphasis from an interventionist God to one whose greatest gift to humankind was natural reason."[58]

But it is in the work of a northern Anglican, Samuel Johnson, that we can see the implications of a rising reliance on reason and rational religion for thirteen colonies heading toward revolutionary ferment. Originally steeped in Calvinist doctrine, Johnson while at Yale came across the writings of Bacon, Boyle, Locke, and the latitudinarians. His conversion to the New Learning was sudden, and he soon became a converted and ordained clergyman of the Church of England. Signing on as a tutor at Yale in 1716, he and another colleague introduced Locke and Newton to the curriculum "as fast as they could."[59] Johnson apparently kept silent during the period of the Awakening, though in letters to English churchmen he did note the "dreams and visions, ecstasies, trances, revelations and conversions attended with fallings, swoonings convulsions, terrors, joys, assurances and I know not what, together with endless confusion, lying and misrepresentation."[60] Then, in 1746, he issued a short treatise entitled *A System of Morality*. It was his aim to present a code of ethics "to be founded in the first principles of reason and nature; in the nature of God and man, and the various relations that subsist between them; and from thence to be capable of strict demonstration."[61]

Easily perceiving the manifest harmony and order in nature and convinced that the natural order springs from a supreme and benevolent governor, "the great Almighty Mind," Johnson rejected the Calvinist doctrines of original sin and predestination. There was neither benevolence nor justice in such principles. Seeing that he who "evidently governs the natural world . . . must much more govern the moral world," Johnson was obliged to conclude that the individual can expect to be treated "as a reasonable and moral agent" and judged on the basis of his "use of the abilities and talents" that have been placed in his care. "For as sin consists in a free and voluntary disobedience, so duty consists in a free and willing obedience to the known will of God. So that without a power of liberty or free agency, there could have been no such thing as either virtue or vice, praise or blame . . . rewards and punishments."[62] Elegantly capturing John Locke's fundamental conception of free will as well as Locke's plain method, Johnson writes:

> I can excite imaginations and conceptions of things past or absent, and recollect them in my mind at pleasure, and reject or keep them under my consideration as I please . . . and am at liberty to suspend judging till I have carefully examined them, and to act, or not to act, in consequence of my deliberations, as I think fit. In the impressions

of sense indeed I am passive, but in all these I am evidently active, and can choose or refuse, will or nill, act or forbear, from a principle of self-exertion; which are all truly great and noble powers.[63]

For Johnson, as for Locke, passions are not good or bad in themselves. They can incline individuals toward the one or the other. Too often they come to rule when they are thoughtlessly given their lead and when self-restraint is lacking. But the rightful governor of human conduct is reason. Again, the tool of cognition is the appropriate guide to action. "Our reason . . . is manifestly given us to make a just estimate of things, and to preside over our inferior powers, and to proportion our several appetites and passions, to the real nature, and intrinsic value of their respective objects so as not to love or hate, hope or fear, joy or grieve, be pleased or displeased at any thing beyond the real importance of it to our happiness or misery."[64]

From this the cardinal virtue in human affairs is easily elaborated: "From what hath been said, it is plain, that the first duty incumbent upon me, as a reasonable active creature, in order to answer the end of my being, is, to cultivate and improve the reason and understanding which God hath given me, to be the governing principle and great law of my nature, to search and know the truth, to find out wherein true happiness consists, and the means necessary to it." Accordingly, Johnson realized it was incumbent upon himself to inquire "whether I am what I ought to be," and if not, "what I ought to do, as a means in order to be and do what I ought . . . in order finally to answer the end of my being." Addressing the "Subordinate Duties," he recommended the practice of daily self-examination and constant improvement.[65]

Six years after the publication of his *System,* Johnson issued a still more comprehensive treatise: *Elementa Philosophica: Containing Chiefly, Noetica, Or Things Relating to the Mind or Understanding: and Ethica, or Things relating to the Moral Behavior.* Lockean in substance and style, this work embraced "the Art of Reasoning . . . from the first Dawnings of Sense to the highest Perfection, both Intellectual and Moral." It was, indeed, characteristically Lockean for, as Newlin writes, "it was specifically designed as a textbook for young students, and it contains not only material for educational use but also what may be considered as a philosophy of education." Touching on the aim and end of the educational process, Johnson thus urged, "One of the chief concerns in culture and education is, to discipline and moderate the passions, and to inure them to a ready submission to the dictates of reason and conscience."[66]

Samuel Johnson's intellectual contribution, it is important to say, did not go unnoticed by his countrymen. The *Elementa Philosophica* was published on the press of Benjamin Franklin. Making full use of the *Elementa* in the Philadelphia Academy, which he had founded, the public-spirited Franklin tried, but failed, to persuade Johnson to serve as the school's founding president.[67] Johnson's stature in the eyes of his countrymen, moreover, is further attested to in his promotion as the first president of King's College (now Columbia University) in 1755.

Johnson's elevation, in fact, should come as no surprise, for as is now evident, his (and Locke's) pedagogical philosophy by midcentury had so swept across the colonial landscape as to allow one recent scholar to notice a virtual "transformation" of family life in America. In his study entitled *Prodigals and Pilgrims: The American Revolution against Patriarchal Authority, 1750–1800,* Jay Fliegelman ably documents the sweeping changes that were being effected in the colonists' social outlook. What he sees is a diminution in the traditional conception of the father as lord and master over his maturing children and, in its place, an emphasis on guiding the maturing child along the path of rational development and self-reliance.

Thus the patterns just traced in the period's religious life are aptly mirrored in its family life. The principle of voluntarism, so characteristic of the American church, would as well become the defining characteristic of the American hearth. Concentrating not so much on what the colonists produced as on what they consumed—i.e., not the sermons they preached and penned, but the bestsellers they purchased and read—Fliegelman exposed a definite Lockean influence on early America's social development.

If, as Dunn advised, few Americans evidenced any real acquaintance with Locke's political writings, by midcentury Locke's educational writings were well advertised. Locke's *Thoughts concerning Education,* itself reprinted more than nineteen times before 1761, formed the principal influence on a legion of literary transmitters. The works on education by such luminaries as Isaac Watts, Phillip Doddridge,[68] and James Burgh, the fictional writings of Samuel Richardson *(Pamela or Virtue Rewarded, Clarisa or The History of a Young Lady),* Daniel Defoe *(Robinson Crusoe),* Oliver Goldsmith *(The Vicar of Wakefield),* Jean Francois Marmontel *(Moral Tales),* and Lawrence Sterne *(The Life and Adventures of Tristram Shandy,* a favorite of Jefferson's), as well as the popular guidebooks of the period, such as Lord Chesterfield's *Letters to His Son* and John Gregory's *A Father's Legacy to his Daughter,* all develop avowedly Lockean moral themes. And it was to these transmitters that countless Americans turned for entertainment, inspiration, and moral guidance.[69] "In summary," Fliegelman writes,

> the new model of [family] government transmitted to America by these writers . . . insisted that force and imperiousness be surren-

dered in favor of guidance. . . . It imagined as its ideal product a man made independent of all authority but that of the introjected voice of his educated reason, moral sense, or guided inclination. What the seventeenth and eighteenth centuries anxiously called a masterless man need not be feared if he had become his own master.

The new value structure, while reflecting Scottish sentimentalist as well as Rousseauean influences, was fundamentally Lockean in character. "Filial independence" was its cornerstone. And that independence "permitted the family to organize on a voluntaristic, equalitarian, affectional, and, consequently more permanent basis. Indeed, the point most reiterated in Locke's *Education* is that the parent who provides his child with the proper education and access to experience will be revered long onto his child's adulthood."[70] This was the message hammered home in an ever-expanding literary corpus. Indeed, as Fliegelman writes, "the volumes Americans chose to read on the eve of Revolution constituted virtually a crash course on rational pedagogy, in general, and the ideal redefinition of parenthood and generational relations, in particular."[71] The question of Locke's influence on the development of America's political ideas aside, it is very much Fliegelman's aim to argue that the influence exerted by Locke over Americans' educational and familial patterns, the emphasis on independence and its consequent rejection of a passive submission to authority, played a cardinal role in shaping the Spirit of '76.

Of course, one could easily peruse the historical record for evidence demonstrating how backward and *dependent* colonial social relations remained down to the dawn of the imperial crisis. In *The Radicalism of the American Revolution,* Gordon Wood has indeed projected a provincial society bound up in the ancient traditions of monarchy, hierarchy, and patriarchy as it entered upon the stage of revolutionary history.[72] Rarely if ever has an entire society moved in lockstep *up* or *down* a particular social path. What the findings of Bonomi, Fliegelman, and others reveal are some of the important forces that helped to give some elements within that society the courage to psychologically free themselves from the traditional social and religious dependencies, to adopt a more autonomous and *self-governing* way of life, and to prepare to more self-reliantly meet their historical destiny.

Before turning to the revolution that would, indeed, alter the course of human events, one further theme ought to be developed. It concerns the goal or end of human living, i.e., the purpose for which Americans asserted their independence, exerted their labors, applied their talents, and deployed their understandings.

Again, it is Samuel Johnson who most ably advertised the chief signpost on the turnpike most Americans hoped to travel. Believing, as we have already seen, in a benevolent deity, he had to avow: "It is plain that His primary intention must have been so far from making them [human beings] to be miserable, that He did undoubtedly make them with a design that they might be, in some good degree, happy, in the participation and enjoyment of His goodness, in proportion to their several capacities and qualifications." Ethics, then, "is the art of living happily, by the right knowledge of ourselves, and the practice of virtue; our happiness being the end, and knowledge and virtue, the means to that end." What is happiness? It is "that pleasure which ariseth in us from the enjoyment of ourselves, and all that is really good for us, or suitable to our natures." And what is really good for us?

> Inasmuch . . . as God hath made us to be intelligent, free, active creatures; and since our happiness must immediately depend upon the right use of these powers, and must consist in the free and vigorous use of them, in conformity to the great law of our nature, which is the inward sense of our own reason and consciences; it must accordingly be His design, not only that we should be happy, but that we should be so by means of our own activity, and by always freely acting reasonably, and consequently that we should cultivate and improve our reason in the best manner we can . . . in order to make a right judgment how we ought to . . . conduct ourselves to the best advantage for our own happiness.[73]

Whether theist, like Johnson, or Deist, like Franklin, Americans, to one degree or another, answered nature's call. The same native conditions that bred the spirit of tolerance and religious diversity offered ample opportunity for the employments of human industry. With unmatched energy, Americans labored to unlock the mysteries of nature, to build the stores of human understanding for the benefit of life and the improvement of the human condition. Enlightenment in America was a work to be done. And it was a work done by countless pioneers of science and invention. By century's end, every aspect of the natural and moral universe would come under exploration in a vast laboratory that could indeed be heralded "The Empire of Reason." As Commager aptly wrote of this "Empire," "The Old World imagined, invented, and formulated the Enlightenment, the New World—certainly the Anglo-American part of it—realized . . . and fulfilled it."[74] This is not to suggest that all Americans fancied themselves learned scholars and scientists. That is not the point. The cultivation of human understanding was but one of many avenues of industry available to the North American colonists. Nor was happiness reserved only for the scientific elite of the country.

By the mid-eighteenth century America was a nation in the making. And, as it was widely preached, God himself commended the great act of making, of improving. "If it were true, as Locke and other economic writers had long maintained," write Sachs and Hoogenboom, "that divinely-sanctioned labor was the source of all value, then riches were surely heavenly-inspired returns for outstanding diligence." Such was the lesson learned in schoolhouses and colleges throughout the colonies. "Harvard professors pronounced with unction that wealth was more conducive to virtue than poverty."[75] With tireless zeal, Benjamin Franklin published on his presses lessons for personal advancement and economic self-sufficiency. In a virtual paraphrase of Locke's own life, Franklin sternly admonished: "The Way to Wealth, if you desire it, is as plain as the Way to Market. It depends chiefly on two Words, INDUSTRY and FRUGALITY: i.e., Waste neither Time nor Money, but make the best Use of both. He that gets all he can honestly, and saves all he gets (necessary Expences excepted) will certainly become RICH."[76]

Franklin's advice concerning the way to wealth was endlessly reproduced in the literature of the period. A cottage industry gradually emerged, pointing out the how-to's of money management and accumulation. A steady demand for books relating to the conduct of business was met by enthusiastic publishers.[77] To the colonials, money and material gain meant a comfortable enjoyment of life's necessities, freedom from the stresses of penury and debt, self-advancement, God's favor, and, at least to James Murray of North Carolina, "a vital ingredient of nuptial bliss"—as it could set a couple "above the cares of the world."

None of this, it may be added parenthetically, was intended as an endorsement of luxury and fine living per se. Always and everywhere the moral emphasis was on work, as it was for Locke. Idleness and extravagance were twin evils sanctioned nowhere under the cope of heaven.[78] Of course heaven was rapidly receding from view, and reality would not always live up to moral propriety. As it turned out, sumptuary laws, legally prohibiting many luxuries and entertainments, fell into disuse. And many began to pragmatically insist that the demand for luxury goods could bolster industry and provide new jobs for the steady immigrant flow. Through it all, however, the reigning ethic was one of production, not consumption. Hearty consumption was widely regarded as the just and happy reward for honest industry and initiative, but for most it was not an end in itself.

The Enlightenment ideal consisted of the employment of human ingenuity and industry for the improvement of the human condition. It was an ideal at least as old as Francis Bacon, and it was ably buttressed by the Protestant emphasis on unrelenting toil in the vineyard of each individual's chosen calling. But the Enlightenment ideal called as well for a due liberation of human talent and a sharing of opportunity among all ranks and stations. Here, too, Bacon had led the way, recommending that England "countenance and encourage and advance able men, in all kinds, degrees and professions."[79] The ideal was of a civilization open to the talents. Largely thwarted in Europe because of the deeply embedded traditions of a civilization rooted in class privilege and hierarchical structures of authority, that ideal flourished in the colonies of North America. The "great goal," namely, "equality of status before the law [and] the abolition of legal privilege," as Bailyn remarked, "had been reached almost everywhere in the American colonies."[80] It was, as Commager confirmed, a vision dreamt of in Europe but only realized in American life.

The vision itself aside, it was largely owing to the favorable conditions of a virgin wilderness and the opportunities it afforded. "In this emerging . . . commercial culture," Jack Greene has recently written in *Pursuits of Happiness,* "the central orientation of people . . . became the achievement of personal independence, a state in which a man and his family and broader dependents could live 'at ease' rather than in anxiety, in contentment rather than in want, in respectability rather than in meanness, and perhaps most important, in freedom from the will and control of other men." And he continues, quoting from the work of J. R. Pole, "The ideal of the masterless man became associated with a variety of other values . . . [including] a jealous regard for personal autonomy; 'a hearty confidence in the individual['s] . . . ability to manage his own affairs'; a growing 'respect for the integrity of individual character' and . . . 'a profound attachment to private property' . . . and high expectations for one's children."[81]

The bottom line is that in the colonies of North America, philosophy and reality met, and in the meeting a hitherto unrealized measure of exuberance and promise was historically released (all compromises and contradictions notwithstanding). Innumerable observers noted the happy condition of the North American colonists. Comparisons with the motherland were frequent. As one anonymous writer exalted, hinting at the hapless impact of land policy back home, in America, the "great ease of gaining a farm renders the lower class of people very industrious which . . . banishes everything that has the least appearance of begging, or that wandering, destitute state of poverty, which we see so common in England. . . . Poor, strolling and ragged beggars are scarcely ever to be seen; all the inhabitants of the country appear to be well fed, cloathed and lodged."

Could it have been a coincidence that this traveler found nowhere on earth "a greater degree of independency and liberty . . . [or a more total absence of] that distinction of the ranks and classes . . . which we see in Britain, but which is infinitely more apparent in France and other arbitrary countries.''[82] To the provincial American, as Ver Steeg reported, progress and improvement were happily self-evident: ''In his lifetime, he witnessed vast changes: the indentured servant in Pennsylvania who became a small farmer; the storekeeper in Boston who became an adventurous and prosperous merchant; and the immigrant in New York who acquired land sufficient for a barony. The world of the provincial American was filled with evidence of almost unbelievable successes. Why should he not believe in progress?''[83]

And why should he not be happy? No explorer of the American psyche, certainly before Tocqueville, better captured the ebullient confidence and radiant promise of eighteenth-century American life than the French visitor J. Hector St. John de Crevecoeur. An aristocrat by breeding, Crevecoeur would take up a position on the Tory side of the revolutionary debate. A romanticist at heart, he painted a portrait that graphically captured in luminous hues the emotional excitement that settled over the brave new immigrant as he or she passed from the Old World to the New.

> No sooner does an European arrive, no matter of what condition, than his eyes are opened upon the fair prospects. . . . Has he any particular talent or industry? He exerts it in order to procure a livelihood, and it succeeds. Is he a merchant? The avenues of trade are infinite. Is he eminent in any respect? He will be employed and respected. Does he love a country life? Pleasant farms present themselves. Is he a laborer, sober and industrious? He need not go many miles, nor receive many informations before he will be hired, well fed at the table of his employer. . . . Does he want uncultivated land? Thousands of acres present themselves. . . . Whatever be his talents or inclinations, if they are moderate, he may satisfy them.

But Crevecoeur did not merely catalog the ample varieties of opportunity that awaited the lowliest sojourner in the free soil of America. More fundamentally, he depicted the opportunity-fed transformation that took root in the soul of the immigrant voyager.

> [He] no sooner breathes our air than he forms schemes and embarks in designs he never would have thought of in his own country. . . . He begins to feel the effects of a sort of resurrection. Hitherto he had not lived, but simply vegetated. He now feels himself a man, because

he is treated as such. . . . Judge what an alteration there must arise in the mind and thoughts of this man. He begins to forget his former servitude and dependence. His heart involuntarily swells and glows. . . . If he is a good man, he forms schemes of future prosperity. He proposes to educate his children better than he has been educated himself. He thinks of future modes of conduct, feels an ardor to labor he never felt before. Pride steps in and leads him to everything that the laws do not forbid. . . . He sees happiness and prosperity in all places disseminated. He meets with hospitality, kindness, and plenty everywhere. . . . From involuntary idleness, servile dependence, penury, and useless labor, he has passed to toils of a very different nature, rewarded by ample substance—This is an American.

"The state of incessant excitement," wrote the Austrian settler Francis Grund early in the succeeding century, "gives to the American[s] an air of busy inquietude . . . which, in fact, constitutes their principal happiness."[84]

If, as Dunn advises, Locke's political speculations played no significant role in America during the first half of the eighteenth century (and even this proposition is problematical), it is nonetheless true that Locke's deeper understanding of human nature (from which that political teaching emerged) was fast becoming a staple of colonial culture. Locke's emphasis on science and improvement, on epistemological independence and industrious self-exertion, on labor and property, and on a single social corollary implicit in each of these fundamental tenets, i.e., the precept of "equal creation," is roundly reflected in the lifestyle of eighteenth-century America.

It was not Locke alone who helped shape the consciousness of Americans. The natural law writers, such as Grotius and Pufendorf, the latitudinarians, such as Clarke and Tillotson, and the natural philosophers, such as Boyle and Newton, also exerted a significant influence. The literary transmitters played their part, and so did circumstance. The ample opportunity afforded by a vast and fertile continent, far removed from the stifling constraints of a class order and happily "suffering" from a salutary imperial "neglect," must indeed be factored into the colonial equation.

Not everyone benefited, it hardly needs to be pointed out. But if large segments of the population, African slaves and Native Americans most significantly, were systematically denied the liberty, property, and opportunity afforded to most white settlers, if women generally were chained to traditional patriarchal patterns, if natural disasters and economic downslides cast their dark shadows over human felicity, it was nonetheless true that a larger portion of humanity found in these North American colonies more avenues for advancement and a freer form of life than had ever before been experienced or imagined. It is as Wood has written, in *The Radicalism of the American Revolution:* "To focus, as we are today apt to do, on what the Revolution did not accomplish—highlighting and lamenting its failure to abolish slavery and change fundamentally the lot of women—is to miss the great significance of what it did accomplish; indeed, the Revolution made possible the anti-slavery and women's rights movements of the nineteenth-century and in fact all our current egalitarian thinking."[85]

It is, I believe, the significance of this fact, and all the shared conflicts, values, and felicitous circumstances that had made it possible, that must be appreciated if the meaning of the American founding is ever to be mastered. The significance of John Locke's political philosophy for the United States aside, the British colonists, to paraphrase Margaret Jacob, were living the Lockean Enlightenment as a matter of daily experience. The key to this enlightened life lay more and more in the colonists' profound confidence in reason and in the possibilities it presented to all who would consult it. "Fix reason firmly in her seat," Jefferson advised his nephew, "and call to her tribunal every fact, every opinion. Question with boldness even the existence of a God; because, if there is one, he must more approve of the homage of reason, than that of blind-folded fear." Reason, "which is the glory of our nature," advised the Deist Reverend Elihu Palmer, invites "a full scope . . . to the operation of intellectual powers" and furnishes man "an unqualified confidence in his own energies." If one need not fear to question the might of God, how less fearful would he be of questioning that of a far-removed government, should the need arise? For, as it has been said, in capturing the spirit of Locke and of early America, "if man [or government] is not yet perfect . . . he [it] is at least perfectible. Just as there are objective, natural laws in science, so there are objective, natural laws in ethics; and man," armed with the confidence that reason can inculcate, "is capable of discovering such laws and of acting in accordance with them."[86] Could a people so bountifully endowed and dutifully and happily employed bow to the will of an oppressive Parliament or imperious prince or, for that matter, countenance an even closer, more insidious and factious challenge to their way of life? And to whom could they turn for ideological relief? It is to these questions that I now turn.

8
The Spirit of '76

John Locke's moral philosophy was reflected in the aspirations, controversies, and daily way of life of the American colonists. Confidence in reason, with its immediate corollary, cognitive independence, and its social corollary, voluntary human relations (at home and in church), all helped to loosen the religious and familial bonds that had bound earlier generations. A strong commitment to labor, intellectual and manual as well, signified America's devotion to the Lockean cum Baconian tenet of industriousness and improvement, as well as to self-improvement and personal happiness. Finally, resistance to imperious authority—whether ecclesiastical or patriarchal—marked the people's fundamental attachment to individualism. All of these traits of character, considered alongside the opportunities offered by a hospitable wilderness environment would, it was hoped, be sufficient to produce the happiness these Americans were looking for.

The millennium, however, was hardly in view. Midcentury wars with Spain and France posed a stark threat to the colonists' good fortune. Britain defeated its foes, and that, in time, resulted in new fiscal impositions, a tightening of regulatory enforcement, and, eventually, crisis and rebellion. Beginning with the issuance of writs of assistance, the proclamation restricting settlement west of the Alleghenies in 1763, and the Sugar and Currency Acts of 1764, American colonists everywhere began to feel the imperial pinch. Seaport merchants, southern planters, and consumers generally could not help but notice the impact of these and subsequent parliamentary enactments. The Stamp Act of 1765 was particularly irksome, adversely affecting virtually every American.[1] Devoted to an ethic of industry and material improvement, the people of British North America quickly began protesting the imperious measures enacted from afar, until, on 4 July 1776, an independent-minded people declared their sovereign independence from an intrusive motherland.

As we have seen, Bonomi and Fliegelman each perceived how resistance to social authority (at church and at home) prepared the colonists for their mature resistance to political authority. Insofar as Fliegelman's pedagogical revolution was inspired by Locke's *Thoughts concerning Education* or the epistemological revolution was assisted by Locke's *Essay concerning Human Understanding* (and its literary transmitters), and insofar as these social developments fostered a spirit of independence and a propensity to resist untoward authority, then Locke's influence on the Revolution itself, political principles aside, could be said to be significant.

Yet despite all this, the preponderance of recent scholarly opinion is not at all persuaded that the Spirit of '76 was in any fundamental sense Lockean. Locke, as Bailyn advised in his pathbreaking study of *The Ideological Origins of the American Revolution*, "could be "cited . . . with precision on points of political theory, but at other times he is referred to in the most oft-hand way, as if he could be relied on to support anything the writers happened to be arguing."[2] What gave the ideology of the American Revolution its distinctive character, "what dominated the colonists' miscellaneous learning and shaped it into a coherent whole," Bailyn urged, "was the influence of the eighteenth-century Commonwealthmen and their Post-Restoration forebears. . . . From the earliest years of the century, this Opposition thought . . . was devoured by the colonists. . . . It nourished their political thought and sensibilities . . . [so that] there seems never to have been a time after the Hanoverian succession when these writings were . . . absent from polemical politics."[3]

No single volume of opposition thought played a larger role in shaping the colonial outlook than John Trenchard and Thomas Gordon's *Cato's Letters*. And it was precisely by linking the conceptions and concerns of the eighteenth-century *Cato* to the ideological idiom of classical republicanism that at least some revisionists seemed to assign Locke a much-diminished role in the American founding. In this chapter I shall examine in fine detail the several elements of the "Catonic" worldview, demonstrating how virtually all of *Cato's* concerns and conceptions were reproduced in the colonial campaign against British imperial policy. I will, however, go on to demonstrate how the "republican" principles enunciated by Trenchard and Gordon were self-consciously built on a foundation of Lockean natural right. In short, the "science" of politics bequeathed by a long line of republican writers could easily and noncontradictorily be appended to the "fundamentals" of politics bequeathed by Locke. *Cato's Letters*, in short, represented a comprehensive synthesis of republican *and* Lockean thought that would inform the American struggle for political independence.[4]

To understand the Lockean character of the Spirit of '76 it is necessary to look in detail at the important "republican" concerns taken up by Trenchard and Gordon, the context within which those themes emerged, and the relevance they had for the colonists of British North America.[5] Equally important is a discussion of the peculiarly Lockean themes that are reproduced in the various letters of "Cato." Finally, we shall see how both the Lockean and republican elements could coalesce in the writings and speeches of the North American colonists.

Cato's Letters

The 144 "Essays on Liberty, Civil and Religious," collected and called *Cato's Letters* by Trenchard and Gordon held a particular fascination for eighteenth-century America.[6] With Cato, Bailyn reports, the colonists "studied the processes of decay and dwelt endlessly on the evidence of corruption they saw about them. . . . Everywhere, they agreed there was corruption—corruption technically in the adroit manipulation of Parliament by a power-hungry ministry, and corruption generally, in the self-indulgence, effeminizing luxury, and gluttonous pursuit of gain."[7]

Before turning to the "Catonic" vision, as it is reflected in American revolutionary ideology, we would do well to examine a little more closely the character of Cato's assault on British politics, the circumstances that called it forth, and the requirements for restoring balance in government and virtue to the people of Britain.

Cato's Letters is a complex though clearly written political text. Informing the concerns and complaints of Trenchard and Gordon are, first, a dark and disturbing portrait of human nature and, second, a series of circumstances that could not help but confirm that somber and distressing portrait. "A great philosopher," Cato wrote,

> call[s] the State of Nature, a State of War; which Definition is true
> . . . were all Men left to the boundless Liberty which they claim
> from Nature, every Man would be interfering and quarrelling with
> another; every Man would be plundering the Acquisitions of another;
> the Labour of one Man would be the Property of another; Weakness
> would be the Prey of Force; and one Man's Industry would be the
> cause of another Man's Idleness.[8]

This may be inferred not merely from the experience of all human societies, which experience Trenchard and Gordon, under the guise of Cato, could ably recite, but from the very motor of human motivation. "The World is governed by Men, and Men by their Passions; which being boundless and insatiable, are always terrible when they are not controuled: Who was ever satiated with Riches, or surfeited with Power, or tired with Honours?" And again: "Men are never satisfied with their present Condition, which is never perfectly Happy and perfect Happiness being their chief Aim, and always out of their Reach, they are restlessly grasping at what they can never attain." That this drive after power naturally yields up a war of all against all, Cato had no doubt: "There is nothing so terrible or mischievous, but human Nature is capable of it. . . . [Men] seldom or never stop at certain Degrees of Mischief, when they have Power to go further; but hurry on from Wickedness to Wickedness, as far and as fast as human Malice can prompt human Power." "Power," is the devil, in the Catonic worldview. Its nemesis is "Liberty": "Power is naturally active, vigilant and distrustful; which Qualities in it push it upon all Means and Expedients to fortify itself. . . . It would do what it pleases and have no Check. Now, because Liberty chastises and shortens Power, therefore Power would extinguish Liberty; and consequently Liberty too much cause to be exceeding [*sic*] jealous, and always upon her Defence."[9]

Cato dwells endlessly on the loss of liberty in lands near and far. Much like Machiavelli, he discusses in endless detail the cunning practices of corrupt princes and ministers. The effects of power were readily apparent: "Let us look round this Great World, and behold what an immense Majority of the whole Race of Men crouch under the Yoke of a few Tyrants, naturally as low as the meanest of themselves, and by being Tyrants, worse than the worst."[10] "Let us therefore grow wise by the Misfortunes of others," Cato counseled. "Let their Virtues and their Vices, and the Punishment of them, too, be an example to us; and so prevent our Miseries from being an Example to other Nations. . . . In fine, let us examine and look narrowly into every Part of our Constitution, and see if any Corruptions or Abuses have crept or galloped into it."[11]

By what means are the people's rights and liberties to be preserved? This, Cato could answer. Rejecting all simple political orders, he calls for the maintenance of a "Mixed Regime." For it is only here that

> the Interest of the Magistracy, which is the Lot and Portion of the Great, is to prevent Confusion, which levels all Things; the Interest of the Body of the People, is to keep Power from Oppression, and their Magistrates from changing into Plunderers and Murderers; the Interest of the standing Senate, which is, or ought to be composed of Men distinguishable for their Fortunes and Abilities, is to avoid ruin and Dissolution from either of these Extremes.[12]

It is only by making power a check on power that liberty may be protected from the ravages of time. This, in fine republican fashion, can only be accomplished with free and frequent elections, a mandatory "Rotation of Magistracy" (since even the most honest men will succumb to the temptations of power if permitted to hold office for indefinite periods), and, above all, the ceaseless vigilance of every freeholder, seeing to it that public men "never have an Interest detached from the Persons entrusting and represented, or never the means to pursue it."[13]

England, Cato conceded, was better suited for the preservation of liberty than most nations of Europe. But the cracks in the political foundations were beginning to widen. On the surface, all was well. The Crown would not veto acts of Parliament or create prerogative courts. Judges did not serve at the pleasure of the king. Parliament had to be convened at least once every three years, and elections held once every seven. In fact, following the glowing review that would flow from Montesquieu's visit, Britons could bask in the brilliance of their republican Constitution and the stability it had brought.[14] But, Cato knew, there was a secret Constitution that had to alarm any true defender of the public liberty. "The Crown, acting through its chief officers of state, far from being distinct in interest from the Commons and the Lords, and no more than an equal co-partner with them in the legislature, operated with elements of both in both Houses to achieve in effect a mastery of the whole government which it maintained with rare interruptions through the century."[15]

The executive achieved this dominance through what was technically called "influence." By the granting of public offices (members of Parliament could simultaneously hold other offices in government), places, pensions, outdoor posts, public contracts, and other forms of patronage, the executive was able to control the votes cast in Parliament and thereby achieve its will. It was this "influence," cast as a cancerous corruption within the body politic, that Cato relentlessly attacked. For here was the end of mixed government in England. Here was the subversion of political checks and balances—and political liberty.

And then there was the matter of the public debt. Critical to the preservation of a free Parliament was the Crown's reliance on it for funds. While a British king, in the wake of the Revolution Settlement of 1689, would not dare to raise taxes unilaterally, monarchical independence was being prepared by the Crown's capacity to borrow money and sustain a progressively larger load of debt. A succession of late seventeenth- and early eighteenth-century wars provided the need and the opportunity. Begun in 1693 with a £1,000,000 loan from private subscribers, the debt soon ballooned dramatically. The first transaction of the Bank of England (founded in 1694) was a £1,200,000 loan to the government at 8 percent interest. It had been written into the terms of the founding charter. A £2,000,000 loan followed soon thereafter.[16]

Taxes and loans from the bank and private subscribers were eminently useful but hardly adequate to fund the expenses of government. In 1710, a new scheme, employing a very old device—the trading company—was preferred. A charter was issued granting a monopoly on trade with all of Spanish South America. Under the terms of the charter, stock in the South Seas Company could be acquired by turning in government debt certificates. The company, in fact, went on to take over nearly the whole of the national debt through the issuance of stock. And, in fact, as long as the value of South Sea stock rose on the London exchange, more debt could be summarily issued and converted. The certainty of monopoly profits, along with government interest payments on bonds held by the company, went a long way in bolstering shareholder confidence and the value of South Sea stock.

For a while, all went well. The scheme was so successful that speculative fever soon overtook the whole country. Between September 1719 and September 1720, 190 "bubble" companies were organized "or at least attempted to sell stock." Everyone, it seemed, was rushing to get in on a good thing. South Sea stock, which had sold for £129 on 30 January 1720, climbed to £200 by March, then jumped to £415 in May. On June 24 it was trading at £1,050. And there it peaked. Within three months the stock plummeted to under £400, and by year's end, a single share could be had for £120.

The crash, when it came, occurred with a force that had never before been experienced (except in France, where the Mississippi bubble had burst earlier that same year). Fortunes were wiped out overnight, savings destroyed in a flash. It was, in fact, the entire panoply of fiscal interventions—the monopoly charters, the subscription loans, the bank, and the public debt, all culminating in the South Sea scheme—that occasioned Trenchard and Gordon's fiery production and three-year project. "What ruin . . . [and] Devastation of Estates!" cried Cato. "What Publick Misery, and Destruction of Thousands, I may say Millions have we seen by the Establishment and wicked Intrigues of the present South Sea Company."[17] Nine of the first ten letters were devoted to exposing the principals and directors of the company.

But it was not merely economic misfortune that these great monopolies projected; there was the political mischief they performed as well: "The Influence and Violence that they bring upon our Constitution." "Exclusive companies," Cato stormed, "alter the Ballance of our Government, too much influence our Legislature, and are ever the Confederates or Tools of ambitious and designing Statesmen."[18] The process had been gathering momentum for some time, for by

11 March 1720, Trenchard and Gordon, in characteristic tones, desperately
warned:

> Public Corruptions and Abuses have grown upon us: Fees in most, if
> not in all Offices, are immediately increased: Places and Employ-
> ments, which ought not to be sold at all, are sold for treble Values:
> The necessities of the Publick have made greater Impositions un-
> avoidable, and yet the Publick has run very much in Debt; and as
> those Debts have been encreasing, and the People growing poor, Sal-
> aries have been augmented, and Pensions multiplied.[19]

Hysterical hyperbole? Of the South Sea disaster, the economic historians
Clough and Cole write: "The crash rocked London with scandal and dismay. It
was found that in its dealings with the government the company had resorted to
corruption and had bribed most of the ruling Whigs, including thirty members of
Parliament, the chancellor of the exchequer, and the postmaster-general, not to
mention two of the King's mistresses."[20]

Here, in the conduct of these commercial lords, lay the stock-seed of corruption and the fatal threat to English liberty. What was its essence? Cato answered,
"the gratifying of private Passion by Publick Means." For once it got under way,
the spirit of party and faction would not stop until all power was put into the
hands of the brokers "and the constitution itself . . . changed into a Stock-
Jobbing Cabal."[21] It was a critique and a worldview rooted squarely in the classical republican tradition. To paraphrase Pocock, it is remarkable to observe how
much could be said about the English opposition press in the early eighteenth
century that does not necessitate reference to Locke at all. What for most interpreters is Locke's wholesale endorsement of capitalist growth and individual acquisitiveness apparently finds no shelter in the Catonic outlook. For the opposition writers, "Luxury," "Venality," and "Corruption" were of a piece, the
bane of civil liberty and human felicity.

What would be the solution? Vigilance and virtue. Englishmen must attend to
the public good and not be bribed by alluring temptations of short-range and ef-
fort-free riches. They must learn to curb their private passions, to submerge their
private interests in a singular common interest. No nation could long endure a
cacophony of so many private interests out for personal gain at public expense.
Cato sternly exhorted his countrymen:

> Consider, my dear Friends, what I have said, and think what you are
> doing, while you are raising Hue and Cry after Men who will betray

you; while you are fending afar for Courtiers, for Directors of bubbles, for Companymen, and public Pick-pockets, to represent you; while you are giving up, perhaps for ever, to the Mercy of Blood-Suckers, your honest Industry, and the just Profits of your Trade, for a poor momentary Share of their infamous Plunder.[22]

Cato's, however, was hardly the only voice crying in the English wilderness. In addition to other "Old Whigs," such as Robert Molesworth whose *Account of Denmark* was an account of liberty lost, many on the political right joined in opposition to the politics of corruption and the engines of a worrisome financial revolution. Hardly republican in his principles, the English Tory owed more to Filmer and Parker than to Locke or Harrington. The Tory voice wished for a conservative order rooted in absolute monarchical authority and the principles of passive obedience and nonresistance. Moreover, since taxes fell disproportionately on the conservative landed interest, that voice naturally decried the tax-driven, debt-driven engines of commercial and financial growth. None on the right were more vocal in denouncing the modern trends than Henry St. John Viscount Bolingbroke. *The Craftsman,* which he published for ten years (1726–1736), relentlessly exposed the "system of government where a single minister turns sovereign and through patronage, influence, corruption," and the distribution of "honours, titles, preferments, pensions . . . hopes and promise[s]" works his will "in all matters of state."[23] Herein lay the root of public excess.

The Politics of Republicanism in America

It was within this framework of opposition thought in the age of Walpole that Bernard Bailyn was first able to glimpse the ideological origins of the American Revolution. As he explained:

> It would be difficult to exaggerate the bitterness, the virulence, the savagery of the attacks on Walpole's ministry by the opposition press—and difficult also to exaggerate the importance of these attacks in the origins of American politics. . . . For these ideas, these beliefs, fears and perceptions became primary elements of American politics in its original, early eighteenth-century form; primary in the sense of forming assumptions and expectations, of furnishing not merely the vocabulary but the grammar of thought, the apparatus by which the world was perceived.

After carefully examining the vast outpouring of pamphlet and periodic literature produced during the imperial crisis, Bailyn concluded: "It was primarily this opposition frame of mind through which the colonists saw the world and in terms of which they themselves became participants in politics. . . . It was in terms of this pattern of ideas and attitudes . . . that the colonists responded to the new regulations imposed by England on her American colonies after 1763."[24]

If the seed of corruption is sown into the very constitution of the civil state by virtue of the power it possesses, if the thirst for riches and the hunger for power grow insatiable in those who once possess them and if, therefore, the passions of the powerful had always to be suspiciously eyed and vigilantly guarded against, then the people of British North America by 1776 had, indeed, to be alarmed. The evidence had been mounting for more than a decade.

But they counted themselves fortunate, these Americans. They knew that the English Constitution had been fashioned over long centuries and that it afforded them ample prescriptive protection against the abuse of power. They could not be taxed but with their consent. They would be tried by a jury of their peers in all legal cases brought against them. They would be governed by their own legislative bodies. Their property would be stoutly protected. They were, after all, Englishmen.

Except that writs of assistance were being routinely issued against merchant vessels. Vice Admiralty courts, unencumbered by local juries, were being established to try and execute cases in matters relating to commerce, property, and taxation. A Declaratory Act had ruled the English Parliament supreme and authoritative in all matters whatsoever. Westward migration had been restricted, thereby holding down the number of electors and legislators a British minister would have to control, or purchase. A standing army had been stationed in America, and colonial offices were being rapidly multiplied. Internal taxes had been imposed with the consent of no one who enjoyed representation in Parliament. The financially troubled East India Company was granted a rebate of customs duties, which some colonials feared would give it a virtual monopoly in their markets. Ports had been closed and trade outlawed, colonial assemblies had been dissolved, and colonists had been shot.

A classical case of corruption, indeed. And the Americans, as educated and literate a people as any there was, investigated and advertised the case at every turn. In fact, it did not take the imperial crisis for Americans to discover or testify to the sorry state of corruption in their mother country. As Bailyn reports: "How widespread the fear was in America that corruption was ripening in the home country, sapping the foundations of that most famous citadel of liberty, may be seen not only in the general popularity of periodicals like *The Craftsman* and *Ca-*

to's Letters . . . but in the deliberateness with which some of the most vituperative of the English jeremiads were selected for republication in the colonies.''[25]

And then there was the growing testimony of many American visitors to Britain by midcentury. Lewis Morris of New York, Dickinson, Franklin, and the Carrolls (Charles Sr. and Jr.), among others, wrote or returned from England, informing their countrymen of the fallen state of affairs in Britain. More than £1,000,000, Dickinson wrote his father from England in 1754, had been spent in efforts to decide the general election that year. ''Bribery is so common that it is thought there is not a borough in England where it is not practiced.'' Election reform was on the lips of public men, he duly reported, ''but it is ridiculous and absurd to pretend to curb the effects of luxury and corruption in one instance or in one spot without a general reformation of manners. . . . Heaven knows how it can be effected.''[26]

Freely acknowledging his ''incalculable'' debt to Bailyn, Gordon Wood made a sizable contribution of his own to the republican thesis.[27] Again, republican conceptions and concerns would form the context within which the Revolution of 1776 would be explained. Critical to Wood's account, however, was not just the corruption of manners, morals, and politics abroad, but what many in America perceived to be the spreading cancer of corruption at home. Republican government demanded civic virtue of its citizens. But everywhere there was evidence of its surrender to private passions. Not untypical was the lament of John Adams: The ''Times of Simplicity and Innocence'' are fading from memory. ''Elegance, Luxury and Effeminacy begin to be established. . . . Venality, Servility and Prostitution, eat and spread like a Cancer.'' For David Ramsay writing in 1778, it was America's growing ''imitation of British extravagance, idleness and false refinements'' that the Revolution, alone, could end. Many saw ''an artificial intercolonial aristocracy,'' built on unmerited honors, dignities, and offices bestowed by the Crown, that was ''entrenching itself, consolidating and setting itself apart from the mass of American yeomen by its royal connections and courtier spirit of luxury and dissipation.'' Too many were attempting to emulate the lavish, if idle, lifestyle of these morally ruined sycophants. Continually, local factions and families vied for the spoils of public power in every colony.[28]

But the revolutionary crisis, especially after 1774, brought hope for a real moral reformation. Here, it appeared, was the promise, or at least the prospect, of virtue resurrected. Madison, James Iredell, and even the realist John Witherspoon could marvel at the rekindled spirit of self-sacrifice and public service — as evidenced in the colonists' compliance with nonimportation agreements and nonconsumption pacts and their participation in committees of correspondence and continental conventions.

On the eve of revolution, republican polemicists and Calvinist clergymen alike voiced their alarm over the people's fallen state. They demanded a reformation of manners, a return to rustic simplicity, devout repentance, and an end to extravagance and selfishness. It was the prevalence of "vice and corruption that many Americans saw in their midst . . . [that] became in fact a stimulus, perhaps in the end the most important stimulus, to revolution." Accordingly, the patriotic call in 1776 was for an end to private self-seeking. "The sacrifice of individual interests to the greater good of the whole," wrote Wood, "formed the essence of republicanism and comprehended for Americans, the idealistic goal of their Revolution. From this goal flowed all of the Americans' exhortatory literature and all that made their ideology revolutionary."[29]

Far from a socially divisive excursion into an unrepentant individualism, Wood considered the American Revolution "one of the great utopian movements in American history. . . . To make the people's welfare—the public good—the exclusive end of government became for the Americans . . . their 'polar star,' the central tenet of the Whig faith. . . . No phrase except 'liberty' was invoked more often . . . than the 'public good.' " Here was a resounding call "to discover somehow above all the diverse and selfish wills the one supreme moral good to which all parts of the body politic must surrender." The colonists could see the festering of individualism in the free soil of North America, and they were not better off for it. "Independence thus became not only political but moral. Revolution, republicanism and regeneration all blended in American thinking."[30] And little in all this seemed to relate to Locke's political vocabulary.

The Politics of Locke in America

Such is the argument that sees in the American Revolution a stirring repudiation of Lockean liberalism, in Macpherson's terms, of an aggressive and "possessive" individualism. That individualism, Wood conceded, would swiftly reassert itself in the aftermath of revolutionary triumph; he could thus speak of "the end of classical politics" in America—a depiction that has embroiled historical scholarship in controversy from that time forward.[31] Recent writers, such as Kramnick, Pocock, Banning, and McDonald, now perceive a multiplicity of political languages operating on the American mind during the constitutional period. But this theme or thesis of "multiplicity" may as easily be applied to the earlier revolutionary period as well. For if the literature of the Revolution is filled with allusions to civic humanism, as it surely is, it is also filled with conceptions and concerns that are unmistakably Lockean. What is more, one frequently encounters in that literature, to borrow Kramnick's language, "the use of one [ideological idiom] and the use of another by the very same writer or speaker" — often within a few paragraphs or pages, or at least the writings of the same period. As we soon shall see, the language of republicanism and the language of Locke meet, as well, on the pages of *Cato's Letters.*

Jefferson's *Declaration,* it should not be forgotten, comprises a compendium of classical republican concerns appended to a theory of resistance rooted in the language of natural right. Or consider the case of John Dickinson, who could rail against the effects of luxury and corruption afflicting England in his "London Letters," then implore Americans to weigh carefully "the welfare of their country . . . for the cause of one is the cause of all," in his "Farmer's Letters." And yet, in "An Address to the Committee of Correspondence in Barbados" (1766), speaking as a private individual, he candidly writes:

> KINGS or Parliaments could not give the rights essential to *happiness,* as you confess those invaded by the Stamp Act to be. We claim them from a higher source—The King of kings and Lord of all the earth. . . . It would be an insult on the divine Majesty to say, that he has given or allowed any man or body of men a right to make me miserable. If no man or body of men has such a right, I have a right to be happy. If there can be no happiness without freedom, I have a right to be free. If I cannot enjoy freedom without security of property, I have a right to be thus secured.[32]

Even more pronounced are the "multiple" views of Samuel West, as he expounded them in 1776. West believed that a "factious, seditious person, that opposes good government, is a monster in nature; for he is an enemy to his own species, and destitute of the sentiments of humanity . . . [and that] we ought to submit cheerfully to obey . . . and submit to all such regulations of government as tend to promote the public good." West nonetheless cites and quotes Locke to the effect that all men enjoy "a perfect freedom to order their actions, and dispose of their possessions and persons as they think fit, within the bounds of the law of nature, without asking leave or depending upon the will of any man."[33]

In the previous chapter, I showed that Americans were indeed attuned to the human desire for cognitive independence and self-assertion and to liberation from religious and patriarchal authority. These were causes championed by many who would fill the revolutionary ranks. Besides the steady emphasis on self-improvement, material advancement, strenuous labor in a chosen calling, and that commonplace depiction of the "just fruits of honest industry," there is the ever-present assertion of the individual's "inherent," "unalienable," "indefeasible," "necessary," and "natural rights," most often expressed as those of "life, liberty and property" (but often expanded to include, as Abraham Williams said, "The Rights of Conscience, [which] are unalienable, inseparable from our Nature"). Frequently accompanied by allusions to the fundamental ends and just limits of political authority and the blunt warning to would-be usurpers that such rights are not given to, and so cannot be taken from, the people, the principles enunciated are clearly Lockean in tone, emphasis, and, very often, attribution. Thus does Abraham Williams announce as early as 1762:

> As in a *State of Nature prior to Government,* every Man has a Right to the Fruits of his own Labour, to defend it from others, to recover it when unjustly taken away, or an Equivalent, and to a Recompence for the Damage and Trouble caused by this unrighteous Seizure. . . . So when civil Societies are formed, the *Community is naturally possessed of all the civil Rights of its Members.* . . . The Law of Nature . . . is the *Law* and *Will* of the *God of Nature,* which all Men are obliged to obey.[34]

In many instances, protesting colonials fused the constitutional rights of Englishmen with the natural rights of man, thereby merging the views of such legal luminaries and former chief justices of England as Coke, Hobart, and Holt, and the natural law views of Pufendorf, Burlamaqui, and Locke. In such fashion did James Otis, one of the most well-respected men of his day (until the recantation of his advanced views), protest the issuance of general writs of assistance in 1761. Borrowing from Dr. Bonham's dictum, decided by Lord Coke decades earlier, Otis, as John Adams reported, declared all acts against the Constitution void.[35] In a more developed, natural law defense of American liberties, Otis would later argue: "In order to form an idea of the natural rights of the Colonists, I presume it will be granted that they are men, the common children of the same Creator with their brethren of Great Britain. . . . Nature has placed all such in a state of equality and perfect freedom, to act within the bounds of the laws of nature and reason without consulting the will or regarding the humor, the passions or whims of any other men."[36]

"The colonists," Otis concludes, "are by the law of nature free born, as indeed all men are, white or black." And if "life, liberty and property could be enjoyed in as great perfection in *solitude,* as in *society,* there would be no need of government." But as men definitely do need "a common, indifferent, and impartial judge," men do form government—its "*end* . . . being the good of mankind, points out its three great duties: It is above all things, to provide for the security, the quiet, and happy enjoyment of life, liberty and property.'' Most enlightening is Otis's examination of the four commonly considered sources of civil authority. A government may be founded on ''grace . . . force . . . compact and property.'' He rejects all four, and his rejection of government-by-compact is particularly noteworthy, from a Lockean perspective. If compact is the basis of political power, he reasons, then

> when and where was the original compact for introducing govern-
> ment into any society, or for creating a society, made? Who were
> present and parties to such a compact? . . . Is not every man born as
> free by nature as his father? Has he not the same natural right to think
> and act and contract for himself? . . . What will there be to distin-
> guish the next generation of men from their forefathers, that they
> should not have the same right to make original compacts as their
> ancestors had? If every man has such right, may there not be as many
> original compacts as there are men and women born or to be born?

In effect sidestepping the original Filmerian challenge to the populist model, Otis founds civil society ''on the necessities of our nature.'' It is the constitution of man that sets out the fundamental ends and extent of civil authority.[37] Such were the views of many individual colonists, some well known and revered, others more obscure. It is when we turn to the important proclamations, declarations, and resolves of public conventions that we see just how greatly these legal and natural law ideas ordered people's thoughts and guided their conduct during the revolutionary period. Thus, within the compass of a few brief sentences, the Massachusetts Circular Letter of 1768 blends the legal and philosophical thoughts of Coke and Locke into a singular American protest. ''It is,'' the letter asserts, ''an essential, unalterable Right in nature, grafted into the British Constitution, as a fundamental Law, & ever held sacred & irrevocable by the Subjects within the Realm, that what a man has honestly acquired is absolutely his own, which he may freely give, but cannot be taken from him without his consent: That the American Subjects may, therefore . . . assert this natural and constitutional right.''[38]

In 1772, Samuel Adams drafted ''A State of the Rights of the Colonists'' on behalf of the Boston Town Meeting. It is Lockean through and through and, indeed, liberally quotes from Locke's *Second Treatise*. Affirming ''the *absolute rights* of Englishmen, and all freemen in or out of Civil society . . . [to] *personal security, personal liberty* and *private property,''* Adams asserts, ''all positive and civil laws, should conform as far as possible, to the Law of natural reason and equity.'' Appended to the Lockean theory of government was a sizable list of grievances against the British. The significance of the report, six hundred copies of which were printed for circulation throughout Massachusetts, was that by the time the Massachusetts legislature met in January 1773, more than a hundred Massachusetts towns had appointed committees of correspondence and adopted the Boston declaration or resolves very similar to it.[39]

Far more formally and officially, the ''Declarations and Resolves of the First Continental Congress'' (14 October 1774) insist: ''The inhabitants of the English colonies in North America, by the immutable laws of nature, the principles of the English constitution, and the several charters or compacts. . . . are entitled to life, liberty and property, & they have never ceded to any sovereign power whatever, a right to dispose of either without their consent.'' Clearly this language hints at the republican requirement of a free and (materially) independent citizenry. But, repeatedly, Americans alluded to the individual's right to the bounty of his or her exertions. Thus in an address to the inhabitants of Canada, the Second Continental Congress urged, ''By the introduction of your present form of government, or rather . . . tyranny. . . . You have nothing that you can call your own, and all the fruits of your labour and industry may be taken from you, whenever an avaricious governor and a rapacious council may incline to demand them.''[40]

As critical to the Lockean bearing of American revolutionary sentiment prior to the call for independence are the views expressed in common council following secession. In Virginia, George Mason crafted a stunning Bill of Rights. Adopted and grafted onto the fundamental law of the state of Virginia on 12 June 1776, it affirms ''that all men are by nature equally free and independent and have certain inherent rights, of which when they enter into a state of society, they cannot, by any compact, deprive or divest their posterity; namely the enjoyment of life and liberty, with the means of acquiring and possessing property, and pursuing and obtaining happiness and safety.''

In Massachusetts, that stalwart student of history and republicanism, John Adams, speaking for his state, declared, ''All men are born free and equal, and have certain natural, essential, and unalienable rights; among which may be reckoned the right of enjoying and defending their lives and liberties; that of acquiring, possessing and protecting property; in fine, that of seeking and obtaining their safety and happiness.''[41]

The "Old Whig" Synthesis

It should be clear by now that the revolutionary period evidences a deep and abiding commitment to both Lockean and republican conceptions and concerns. The problem, for modern scholarship, lies in the shared sense that these two political idioms are mutually incompatible. Fundamentally, where Lockeanism is seen as upholding the rights, liberties, and properties of individuals against government, republicanism is preoccupied with the common good of the res publica and sees such individualist proclivities as tending to the breakup or breakdown of social cohesion and a spreading cancer of corruption. Could this be a confusion that was simply missed by a generation rushing headlong into revolutionary upheaval? Or could this be a conceptual quandary entirely of our own making? Philip Greven offers a promising lead when he posits a bifurcation in the radical Whig ranks. He thus distinguishes between "moderate" Whigs, of whom he writes: "The point of the conspiracy that so many people believed to be directed against themselves was nothing less than the deprivation for individuals of their own liberty and their personal enslavement—that is, the prospect that they would be placed in a state of being without wills of their own. The central issue thus became the issue of personal autonomy or the freedom of a person's self and self-will."

The Lockean bearing on such concerns is manifest. As discussed in Chapter 3, reason and "self-will," or volitional responsibility, are critical to Locke's moral and social system. But along with the "moderates" Greven posits an "evangelical" party. Its vision was "of a perfected polity, virtuous, pure, and unanimous," united in "the belief that real liberty required the total suppression of the self for the good of the whole."[42] The problem is that important "evangelicals," such as John Adams and Samuel Adams, who longed for moral reformation and a common concern for the public good, frequently repaired to the principles of Locke in their revolutionary writings.

How could as astute a thinker as John Adams entertain so "obvious" a contradiction of basic values as in his pronouncement that "each individual of the society has a right to be protected by it in the enjoyment of his life, liberty and property. . . . And government is instituted for the common good . . . not for the profit, honor or private interest of any one man, family, or class of men"?[43] And how could so many of Massachusetts's leading lights ratify this ideologically incoherent passage as the Tenth Article of their state's constitution (1780)? To help guide us through this difficulty we should revisit the writings of Trenchard and Gordon, for all republican echoes aside it is possible to discern a distinctly Lockean voice in Cato's influential letters.[44] And a closer consideration of Cato's estimate of the human condition will be the starting point.

Cato certainly held a pessimistic estimate of human nature, seeing humans as irredeemably aggressive (not rational and peaceful). The passion for power and every awful thing that flowed from it seemed to be wired into the human constitution. But Locke, to no lesser degree, suspected people's unchecked passions. That is largely why the powers of governments and governors must be first established and then carefully proscribed. As good republicans, Trenchard and Gordon inquired into the methods and techniques of subverting the true purposes of government. This brought them to the mechanisms of public corruption they saw all around them. The republican solution was the restoration of a balanced constitution, a mixed government and an independent Parliament, and a virtuous citizenry intent on guarding against the growth of power.

These are not critical considerations for Locke, it is true. But Locke distinguished between the "fundamentals" of politics and the "science" of politics. The latter was chiefly concerned with the constitutional mechanics of the matter; the former, with the *main* matter, that is, the basic purpose politics was to serve. This was John Locke's primary interest and contribution. The real question is whether Locke and "Cato" disagreed over government's fundamental origins and ends. We know Locke's answer; Cato's is remarkably similar. To determine the limits of government, Cato advises it is necessary, first, "to ascertain . . . the Measure of Power which men in the State of Nature have over themselves and one another. . . . for no Man can give to another either what is none of his own, or what in its own Nature is inseparable from himself."

"All Men," Cato continues, "are born free; Liberty is a Gift which they receive from God himself; nor can they alienate the same by Consent." What is the end or purpose of human liberty? It is human preservation. This is the primary occupation of people, the activity that consumes human labor. Thus Cato also retraces the processes of economic growth. Finding an insufficiency in the "spontaneous Productions of Nature," people eventually take up "tillage and Planting," a vast improvement in productivity, since "an Hundred Men thus employed, can fetch from the Bowels of our common Mother, Food and Sustenance enough for Ten Times their own Number." But it is not until the "Invention of Arts and Science; that is, the finding out of more Materials and Expedients to make life easy and pleasant," that the quality of the human condition can be materially improved. These, in turn, depend in part on the division of labor and on "what we call Trade; which is the Exchange of one Commodity for another, or for that which purchases all Commodities, Silver and Gold."[45]

Since productivity ultimately depends upon industry and since "Men will not spontaneously labour but for their own Advantage," industry depends upon a due protection of its fruits. "To possess, in Security, the Effects of our Industry, is the most powerful and reasonable incitement to be industrious." But industry is still the second motor of human action; reason is its fuel: "True and impartial liberty is therefore the Right of every Man to pursue the natural, reasonable, and religious Dictates of his own Mind; to think what he will, and act as he thinks, provided he acts not to the Prejudice of another; to spend his own Money himself, and lay out the Produce of his Labour his own Way."[46]

Here is the principle of "equal creation," appropriately tied to its necessary root: the individual's reasoning mind and resolute will. But self-willing cannot, in reason, become a matter of other-destroying, for that other has a reasoning mind and will of his own, which commands equal respect. We each enjoy "the Privileges of thinking, saying, and doing what we please, and of growing as rich as we can without any other restriction, but that by all this we not hurt the Public, nor one another." The fundamental moral and social imperative follows directly. As every man desires to "enjoy the fruits of his own Acquisitions, arising from his Labour or Invention . . . [but will not] unless he allows it to others, who have *equal Reason* to expect it from him, it is the *Common Interest* of all who unite together in the same Society, to establish such Rules and Maxims for their mutual Preservation, that no Man can oppress or injure another, without suffering by it himself."[47]

If, given the rapacious passions of people, individuals cannot hope to enjoy such peace and reciprocity, they then will discover the need to form civil bonds. Cato's government is one instituted *by* men, deriving its just power *from* men— who originally have a peculiar power to cede to government. "Every Man in the State of Nature, had a Right to repel Injuries, and to revenge them; that is, he had a Right to punish the Authors of those Injuries, and to prevent their being again committed." Hence, Cato can advise, "That Right which in the State of Nature, every Man had, of repelling and revenging Injuries, in such Manner as every Man thought best, is transferred to the Magistrate." Once again it is Locke's "Executive Power," the power of punishing offenders that forms the sanction for the laws and rights of nature, that is thereby surrendered. "The Right of the Magistrate arises only from the Right of private Men to defend themselves, to repel Injuries and to punish those who commit them." Without ambiguity, Cato sums up: "Mutual Protection and Assistance is the only reasonable purpose of all reasonable Societies. To make such Protection practicable Magistracy was formed, with Power to defend the Innocent from Violence and to punish those that offended it; nor can there be any other Pretence for Magistracy in the World."

The laws of nature inform and delimit the authority of government. And "the Nature of Government does not alter the Natural Right of Men to Liberty, which in all political Societies is alike their Due." Indeed, urges Cato in language nearly identical to Locke's, "the sole End of Mens entering into political Societies, was mutual Protection and Defence; and whatever Power does not contribute to those Purposes, is not Government, but Usurpation."[48] Cato comes forward as unabashedly Lockean in his commitment to individual liberty and private self-pursuit.

The radical Whig voice in the age of Walpole, it must be emphasized, belonged to a highly vocal but politically inconsequential minority, sitting far to the right and left of the political mainstream.[49] In the main, British politics proved remarkably stable, and despite incessant war and a dramatically rising debt, the British economy flourished.[50] The radical voice was never silenced, however. English Nonconformists, allowed to ply their trades in freedom, were barred from attending the universities and from holding public office or enjoying the franchise. As Kramnick, Robbins, Bonwick, and others have shown, in the prospering circles of religious dissent, in the careers of Richard Price, Joseph Priestly, Anna Baubauld, John Wilkes, James Burgh, John Cartwright, and others, the republican *and Lockean* pleas for "a full and fair representation," for private and public careers open to talent and industry, and for the recognition of mankind's equal station and government's responsibility for affording equal protection are repeatedly raised. Thus does Kramnick, surveying English middle-class radicalism in the late eighteenth century, explain, "The praise of achievement and talent, the ideology of equal opportunity, and the cult of industry and productivity, all wrapped in doctrines of natural equality and independence [are at its base]."[51]

Americans knew these British radicals. In the "Club of Honest Whigs," for example, Franklin grew close to Price, Priestly, and Burgh. Virginia's Arthur Lee, Pennsylvania's Benjamin Rush, and Henry Laurens (who would become president of the Continental Congress), Andrew Eliot, and Jonathan Mayhew all either befriended or corresponded with leading English radicals. The influence of such important English radicals as Burgh, Priestly, and Price on Thomas Paine's development while still in London and in Lewes is also significant.[52] But in a deeper sense, the biographical meeting of transatlantic minds was superfluous. For in the early production and widespread circulation of *Cato's Letters,* the colonists found a well-formulated fusion of the science of politics bequeathed by classical republicanism and the deeper fundamentals of politics, as handed down by Locke. It was this prepackaged synthesis that became readily available for American consumption at a very early date.[53]

The critical question remains, however: how is it possible to render the Lockean and republican paradigms harmonious and consistent? How could so many astute scholars have so erred in seeing the two ideological languages as fundamentally antagonistic in terms of core values and assumptions? What allowed Pocock, Wood, and others to largely dismiss Locke from the historical account?

The republicans were alarmed by the rapacious passions of mankind. But so too was Locke as long as those passions remained unchecked by an exertion of the will, informed by reason. Both Locke and Cato accounted mankind responsible for suspending their passions until, after an act of judgment, a true and just course of action could be determined. Cato, far more than Locke, emphasized the need for constitutional balance and dwelled on the modern mechanisms by which the British Constitution was being corrupted and balance in government undermined. But these are issues belonging to the "science" of politics. They could easily be appended to the basic understanding of government's fundamental and unalterable origins and ends. The stark compatibility between Lockeanism and republicanism is now coming into clearer focus.

Thus Alan Craig Houston has recently provided a most informative and valuable study of *Algernon Sidney and the Republican Heritage in England and America*. Houston has carefully chronicled the ease with which Sidney, a resolute republican if ever there was one (he literally lost his head for his principles), could build his republicanism on a cornerstone of Lockean natural law. Rejecting, with Locke and James Tyrrell, the Filmerian precept of patriarchal subjection, Sidney started "with an ethic of individual freedom and a politics of consent." As Sidney said, "God in Goodness and Mercy to Mankind, hath with an equal hand given to all the benefit of Liberty, with some measure of understanding how to employ it." Combining the several critical aspects of liberty to which Locke was committed, Houston identifies Sidney's four-sided figure of liberty: it comprehends "the freedom of having power over one's own life, versus slavery to the commands of another; the freedom of conscience, versus slavery to the religious beliefs of another; the freedom of following reason, versus slavery to the passions; and the freedom of a nation to direct its own affairs, versus slavery to the dictates of foreign powers."[54]

Sidney's political theory, as well, is grounded in the verities of Lockean right, though as Houston contends, no developed theory of natural law. For Sidney governments were created "for the good of the People, and for the defence of every private man's Life, Liberty, Lands and Goods. . . . If the publick Safety be provided, Liberty and Propriety secured, Justice administered, Virtue encouraged, Vice suppressed, and the true interest of the Nation advanced, the ends of Government are accomplished."[55]

In the case of both Cato and Sidney, a man martyred for his irrepressible republicanism, Whiggish concerns could be attached to notions of Lockean right. What does this portend for an older revisionism that was constructed on a Lockean/republican fault line? Perhaps different things for different builders. As Michael Zuckert has most recently pointed out, Cato's "thorough-going individualis[m], methodological and ontological" must demolish the frame of an "organic . . . common good" upon which Wood built his creation, while at the same time annihilating the political soul of the Aristotelian citizen (ruling and being ruled, in turn) who resided in Pocock's civic temple.[56]

Zuckert's important study of *Natural Rights and the New Republicanism* clearly confirms the Lockean foundation supporting Trenchard and Gordon's republican project. Finding in *Cato's Letters* a solid endorsement of the private life, of natural rights, indeed, of all of the essential political doctrines Jefferson would work into his immortal Declaration, Zuckert appropriately concluded, "Cato does not stand for the triumph of republican over Lockean or liberal thought, but rather for the development of a genuine and immensely powerful synthesis between Lockean political philosophy and the earlier Whig political science."[57] Importantly, Zuckert raises the "equalitarian" doctrine, quoting Cato to the effect that "Nature is a kind and benevolent parent; she constitutes no particular favorites with endorsements and privileges, above the rest; but . . . seeds all her offspring into the world furnished with the elements of understanding and strength to provide for themselves." Such is the human condition in the Catonic state of nature. And because that state is so insecure, given the passionate nature of humans and the constant craving for power, preferment, and riches it must give way to the political state so that individuals will be protected in their just liberty and equality.[58] But it is only to protect that natural liberty that states are brought into being.

And yet, as revisionism has rightly pointed out, the eighteenth-century republican writers worried over the individualist impulse, easily perceiving the ever-present dangers to the common interest that *self-interest* historically and invariably unleashed. They candidly conceded its socially corrosive and politically corruptive tendencies.[59] The crux of the argument that seeks to bifurcate Lockeanism and republicanism, I believe, to a large extent hinges on the republicans' resolute campaign against "Corruption," which, in turn, appears to modern eyes as a campaign against private acquisitiveness and the engines of capitalist growth (which to an extent, but *only* to an extent, it was). It is the republican assault on "Luxury," "Idleness," and the individual's untrammeled pursuit of "Riches" and "Power" that seems to depart from the Lockean outlook.

How, indeed, is it that Cato could sit sanguinely by, granting us all the right "to possess, in Security, the Effects of our Industry" and affording us the chance "of growing as rich as we can" at the same time that he railed against the very public institutions—the bank, the debt, stock speculation, and the great chartered trading companies—that fueled capitalist growth and offered individuals the inestimable outlets and opportunities for the profitable employment of their industry, their talents, and their capital? What is it that allows Cato to admit some but toss aside other features of the nascent capitalist order? More immediately, all interest in industrious labor and private acquisitiveness aside, how is it that Cato could so assiduously counsel concern for public affairs and the common good and plead for virtuous participation in the political process of his day?

The Republican Lexicon in Lockean Context

The republican revisionists perceive in the language of the Revolution all of the ancient and classical conceptions: "public virtue," "the common good," the call for patriotic "sacrifice," and the endemic concentration on "corruption," "corrosion," and "decay." "Americans creating a new society could not conceive of the state in any other terms than organic unity." Running from the individualist idea, Wood added: "This common interest was not, as we might today think of it, simply the sum of consensus of the particular interests that made up the community. It was rather an entity in itself, prior to and distinct from the various private interests of groups and individuals."[60]

What the revisionists fail to see is how these conceptions can take on new connotations across time—how, that is, they can be enlisted in the service of deeper and more modern values, such as personal autonomy and industry, private property and commercial prosperity. What I propose to do is reassess the significance of the linguistic components of the republican lexicon for a people steadfastly devoted to the Lockean outlook on life.

Consider the colonists' commitment to the "common good." In what sense could this idea be identified with Lockean individualism, with private acquisitiveness and the preservation of "life, liberty and property"? First, it should be recalled that the pamphlet war against Parliament began in 1764 as a defense of America's commercial or economic interests, not as a protest against British taxation. Those complaints continued to be pressed to the end. From Stephen Hopkins's first foray to Thomas Jefferson's "Summary View," Americans were keenly sensitive to the economic impact of imperial policy.[61] Hopkins, the governor of Rhode Island, begins by precisely identifying the private and common interests of Americans. "In things which concern the interest of our native country in general, every person seems to have a right to give his sentiments." In describing how the British navigation acts were impeding American commerce generally, Hopkins clearly grasped that he was speaking out for every particular individual who would be adversely affected by the acts. In this sense he understood himself to be "serving" his "country" and "serving the public" to the best of his ability.

It was not difficult for astute Americans to see that the combination of trade restraints, prohibitions against colonial manufacturing, provisions of the Currency Act of 1764 (barring the colonies from issuing paper money or bills of credit), and, certainly by the time of the Stamp Act, the nefarious tax levies was producing an ever-deepening balance of trade deficit and causing a subsequent chronic shortage of specie. There was, in sum, a climate that every branch of colonial commerce required if it was to operate profitably, and a host of imperial laws and policies were swiftly and surely eroding that climate. This, indeed, worked to undermine the "common interest," the interest every honest merchant or manufacturer had in employing his talents and industry and enjoying the just rewards of his and her labor.

But in the acts of the British Parliament and Crown, Americans perceived not just a threat to their material interests; their spiritual interests were thought to be in jeopardy as well. Thus Bailyn and Bonomi have both pointed to the colonists' anxious anticipation of an Anglican bishop after 1767 and an eventual crackdown on religious dissent. Bonomi has written "that the threat of episcopacy alarmed provincials of every rank and section demonstrates how widespread was the fear of a combined church and state in colonial America." Here was an issue that could indeed unite Americans of all backgrounds in common cause and in opposition to a singular external threat. John Adams would later write that "the apprehension of Episcopacy" on American soil stirred the suspicions "not only of the inquiring mind, but of the common people" and contributed as much to the American Revolution as any other factor.[62]

But above all it was the apprehension of tyranny, as such, that stirred the American mind. If, as the lessons of history counseled, the thirst for "Power" once whetted was unquenchable and could be historically detected in the intrusion of standing armies, in nonrepresentative tax levies, in executive control of judicial salaries and tenure, and in the denial of home rule and the suspending and dissolving of local legislatures, then, certainly by 1776, the wake-up call had been sounded. Liberty of conscience, liberty of trade, and the political liberties proclaimed by generations of heroic martyrs would indeed be sufficient to circumvent whatever centrifugal forces may have been operating in the free soil of

America. Americans indeed hoped their countrymen would evince a high-minded "public spirit" and unite on behalf of the "common good." No less would be required if the singular imperial threat was to be repulsed.

If republicanism placed great emphasis on "public" or "civil" liberty while Locke stressed "private" liberty, again there is no necessary contradiction. If "Power," in the process of smashing "Liberty" in the republican sense, would inevitably strike at "liberty" in the Lockean sense, seizing property through confiscatory measures of taxation, extirpating individual industry, and commanding conformity of conscience, then public liberty could indeed be counted the first line of defense for a Lockean order. "To put the point somewhat baldly," writes Alan Craig Houston, "self-interest was the strongest possible foundation for civic virtue."[63] It should not be surprising that Locke, like so many American patriots, devoted so much of his time and energies to civically and patriotically opposing the absolutist designs of "Papist" power.[64]

The danger demanded as well a goodly measure of personal sacrifice, which the revisionists all too casually identify with the denial of Lockean self-interest. But what this signified, really, was a short-range sacrifice for the sake of securing the long-range and more permanent interests every Lockean patriot possessed: *liberty in both its private and public applications.* To sustain it, nonimportation and nonconsumption agreements would have to be respected (whatever hardship they might impose). Time taken out from the chores of daily life would also be required if committees were to meet and militia posts were to be manned. Not the least of the sacrifice involved the risk of confronting imperial authority, as in the case of tax resistance generally, and the Tea Party of '73, or Concord and Lexington specifically. None of this, however, departs very far from Locke's teaching or the example of his own life. On the contrary, one need only recall Locke's own patriotic sacrifices, including his exile in France (1675–1679) and Holland (1683–1689) and the perpetual risk in which his participation in Shaftesbury's affairs placed him.

But the Lockean bearing of such "public sacrifice" cuts even deeper. Locke urged individuals to suspend their immediate interests or passions and weigh, in the court of reason, the full implications of their desires and actions — and this, in the pursuit of a true and lasting felicity. Cato counseled the same and candidly lamented individuals' often deficient deference to the long-range view. "A very small Part of Mankind have Capacities large enough to judge of the Whole of Things; but catch at every Appearance, which promises present Benefit, without considering how it will affect their general interest; and so bring Misfortunes and lasting Misery upon themselves, to gratify a present Appetite, Passion, or Desire."[65]

The patriots determined they would not succumb to the weakness of evasion. Britain, playing to the colonists' short-range, material interests, actually reduced the tax on molasses in 1764, for example, from 6 percent to 3 percent. The Tea Act of 1773 did much the same. Repeatedly, however, the colonists looked not to short-run economic benefits, but to the longer-range political effects of imperial policy. John Dickinson, for one, noted the language of the Revenue Act of 1764, which called for the raising of revenue in America, rather than the accepted practice of regulating the trade of the empire through the navigation laws. Writing of the Townshend Act of 1767, he urged his countrymen:

> ROUSE yourselves, and behold the ruin hanging over your heads. If you ONCE admit, that Great-Britain may lay duties upon her exportations to us, *for the purpose of levying money on us only,* she then will have nothing to do, but to lay those duties on the articles which she prohibits us to manufacture — and the tragedy of American liberty is finished . . . [and] we are as abject slaves as France and Poland. . . . [The] whole . . . question is . . . whether the parliament can legally take money out of our pockets, without our consent. If they can, our boasted liberty is but . . . A sound and nothing else.

The Sugar Act reduced the tariff on molasses. The sums to be raised by the Stamp Act, Dickinson imagined, might not be very oppressive, and many in America might "be inclined to acquiesce under it." But, he urged, "a conduct more dangerous to freedom [could not] be adopted. Nothing is wanted at home but a PRECEDENT, the force of which shall be established, by the tacit submission of the colonies." If once this precedent is allowed, he feared "the parliament will levy upon us such sums of money as they chuse to take, *without any other* LIMITATION, *than their* PLEASURE."

Nor could a planter or merchant afford to selfishly confine his or her attention to his or her own colony's borders. Concerning himself with the 1765 act suspending the legislation of New York for that colony's failure to fully comply with the Quartering Act, the Pennsylvanian duly reasoned:

> A dreadful stroke is aimed at the liberty of these colonies. I say of these colonies, for the cause of *one* is the cause of *all*. If the parliament may lawfully deprive New York of any of her rights, it may deprive any, or all the other colonies of *their* rights; and nothing can possibly . . . encourage such attempts, as a mutual inattention to the interest of each other. . . . He certainly is not a wise man, who folds

his arms, and reposes himself at home, viewing with unconcern, the flames that have invaded his neighbour's house, without using any endeavour to extinguish them.[66]

It was as Burke, in his plea for reconciliation before the House of Commons on 22 March 1775, reported: "In other countries, the people . . . judge of an ill principle in government only by an actual grievance; [in America] they anticipate the evil and judge of the pressure of the grievance by the badness of the principle. They augur misgovernment at a distance, and snuff the approach of tyranny in every tainted breeze."[67]

In Lockean fashion, the American colonists considered their interests and welfare *in the long range*. The examination of the past informed their estimate of the future. Above all, they were guided by what they conceived to be, at once, their commercial welfare *and* their indefeasible rights. Did Americans act on behalf of their ideas or their interests? It is not an either/or situation. To defend their interests in this broad sense, Americans would have to repair to ideas—Lockean *and* republican; only ideas in the end would secure their vital interests.

One important matter demands some attention. This is the manner in which Lockean individualism fits into the republican concept of "civic virtue" and the "communal" character of eighteenth-century "civil society." Americans, not merely in their polemical productions but in their daily lives, I argued in Chapter 7, were devoted to personal industry and material self-advancement. It is a pattern that may well be identified with Lockean self-interest. It should not, however, be viewed in Macphersonian terms as an unbridled selfish acquisitiveness. This emphasis on the "self" certainly bespeaks a commitment to the individualist ethos. But as I urged with respect to Locke, the individualist ethic need not automatically be associated with a Hobbesian atomism. In the Lockean environment of eighteenth-century America there was ample room for human benevolence and social cooperation of every conceivable variety.

Thus it was most Lockean of Samuel Johnson to locate, within the compass of human nature, a profound principle of sociability. "I find we were evidently made for society, being furnished with the power of speech as well as reason, whereby we are capable of entering into the understanding of each other's minds and sentiments . . . and jointly conspiring to promote our common well-being; to which we are naturally led by a principle of benevolence, and social dispositions and affections, founded in the frame and condition of our nature."[68] For Johnson this, most immediately, "lays us under a necessity of mutual dependence one upon another, which obligeth us to enter into compacts for our defense and safety, and for maintaining both private right and public order." But it also allows for "promoting the common good . . . in the several communities to which we belong.''[69]

Nowhere is the spirit of sociability more in evidence than in the life of Johnson's publisher, Benjamin Franklin. Assiduously devoted to his own self-improvement and ever laboring to further his own fortunes, Franklin tirelessly devoted himself to projects of civic importance. Besides the private academy already mentioned, he also brought to fruition a volunteer fire company, a subscription library, a plan for paving, cleaning, and lighting the streets of Philadelphia, a Philosophical Society, the first Masonic lodge, and, given the threat posed by Spain and France, by 1744, a colonial militia (of, by Franklin's estimate, ten thousand strong).

Franklin's Junto, organized in 1727 for the mutual improvement of its members, gathered to discuss points of "Morals, Politics or Natural Philosophy." Eventually, each member formed junior juntos. As Franklin wrote in his *Autobiography,* "The advantages proposed [for this expansion] were, the improvement of so many more young citizens . . . [and the] better acquaintance with the general sentiments of the inhabitants on any occasion." Franklin's sociability is further attested to in the numerous printing houses he set up and sold to his workmen. Upon completing six years, his apprentices were permitted "to purchase the types of me and go on working for themselves." He profited by the deal, but his workmen could be said to have gotten the better of the bargain. Franklin was an individual who delighted in teaching others how to find and be themselves: industrious, honest, and frugal individuals in their own right. His great service to society notwithstanding, Benjamin Franklin never advised neglect of self-duty. Relentlessly, he pounded out on his presses the keys to personal success and fortune in life, the sure and simple "ways to wealth" discussed earlier.[70]

Although the example of one life does not an entire civilization make, it must be acknowledged that Franklin ranked among the most highly esteemed citizens of his republic, a moral paradigm in his own right.[71] What he most exemplifies for us is the "uncanny" ease with which the ethos of individualism and a spirit of civic-mindedness could merge without sacrifice of self *or* society. In the life of colonial America the paths of communal brotherhood and personal success could point in a single and singular direction.

And yet the fact remains, as the republican revisionists properly note, that Americans during the revolutionary period opposed great accumulations of wealth. They deplored the "Luxury" and "Extravagance," the "Venality" and "Dissipation" they saw overtaking their society everywhere. Above all, they condemned the "Corruption" that was corrosively eating away the virtuous core not only of British, but of their own civilization. This, in the final analysis, is the most telling article in the revisionists' indictment, the clearest evidence of Americans' moral effort to rid their society of the individualist ethos. And indeed, as Bailyn has noted, many Americans saw in the emergence of novel financial institutions the source of their troubles. Thus, in attempting to explain to themselves the reasons for Britain's imperious turn after 1763, many colonists would point to the ''greed of a 'monied interest' created by the crown's financial necessities and the power of a newly risen, arrogant, and irresponsible capitalist group, that battened on wars and stock manipulations.''[72]

To effect their schemes of enrichment, this ''capitalist'' class depended on the Crown's favor while, at the same time, the Crown depended on the connivance of Parliament to finance its wars and sustain its rising debt—hence the proliferation of lucrative places, posts, public pensions, and the like, and the assault on the balanced British Constitution. Far from signifying the revolutionaries' disenchantment with Lockean liberalism, however, this very assault on ''capitalism'' and ''corruption''—at home and abroad—constitutes the most stunning evidence yet of eighteenth-century America's principled embrace of Locke's fundamental moral and social categories: individualism, independence, equal creation, and equal protection. For the aspects modernity sees as so alarming to the virtuous Americans (national banks, public debts, monopoly charters, and financial speculation) represented not individual expressions of, but a blanket *repudiation* of those very categories. This is what has for too long been largely overlooked.

In their denunciation of the new financial institutions and the ''monied interest,'' the Americans were merely repeating the plaintive appeals voiced decades earlier in the productions of Trenchard and Gordon. Pangle, acutely conscious of the Catonic character of the emerging commercial republic, nevertheless saw the ground dividing Cato and the ministerial advocates of the new financial measures as fundamentally unbroken. Speaking of Trenchard and Gordon, he writes: ''Their battle with the Court party is best understood as a battle within the liberal tradition, between a more statist and aristocratic liberalism, on the one hand, and a more individualistic and populist liberalism, on the other.''[73]

For John Trenchard, Thomas Gordon, and their American disciples embroiled in that political ''battle,'' everything hung in the balance. For them, it was a battle of good versus evil. It was a contest that pitted ''Virtue'' against ''Corruption,'' ''Liberty'' against ''Power.'' And the fortunes and fate of Anglo-American civilization depended on the outcome. It seems somehow to trivialize a most weighty matter to view that contest as a debate among ideological comrades-in-liberal-arms. For the radical Whig mindset, there must have been something fundamentally incompatible between ''a more statist and aristocratic'' and a ''more individualistic and populist'' liberalism. It is that something that demands deeper exploration.

Zuckert, too, from his careful reading of *Cato's Letters,* appreciated the centrality of these developments for the British opposition. In the magnificent schemes of the South Sea directors, in the buying and selling of votes on the floor of Parliament, he appropriately perceived the sacrifice of the public interest to so many petty and partial interests awash in bribery and corruption. And he perceived in the Catonic response a clear civic plea for public virtue. But like Pangle, Zuckert left one question essentially unanswered: What exactly did all of this signify for the new (or liberal) republicanism?

From the revisionist perspective the answer was clear. Here lay the fruit of liberalism, the final and fatal flowering of the individualist/acquisitive ethos. The Machiavellian Moment had arrived. In the moments to come any keen student of history could anticipate the subversion of civic independence, the upsetting of the balanced constitution, and inevitably, the end of political liberty itself. Was this synthesized liberal republicanism an unstable element, after all? And was that all there was to it? Or was there more? The question that begs consideration is this: All allusions to liberalism aside, what did the events that occasioned the outpouring of Trenchard and Gordon's essays on civil liberty signify from a more narrowly *Lockean* perspective? The answer is not the logical *expression,* but the confounding *rejection* of moral and political right. Let us consider the American case.

Americans indeed believed in the individual's right to enjoy the just fruits of his ''honest industry'' (and to grow as rich as industry and circumstance would allow). But those dependent on Crown patronage who would do a minister's bidding for their own profit were, by the patriots' lights, neither industrious nor honest. As one alarmed American demanded:

> The present state of the British nation, the rapacity and profuseness of many of her great men, the prodigious number of their dependents who want to be gratified with some office which may enable them *to live lazily upon the labor of others,* must convince us that we shall be taxed so long as we have a penny to pay, and that new offices will be constituted and new officers palmed upon us until the number is so great that we cannot by our constant labor and toil maintain any more.

Locke's was an ethic of industry. It signified an emphasis on production, not idle dissipation and extravagant consumption. Locke, in his economic writings, roundly condemned the profligate owners of great estates who squandered their inheritance in luxury and gaming; Cato did likewise, and so did the Americans. More to the point, one man's labor could not be the excuse for another's luxuriant laziness. This was not independence, but crass servitude—the sacrifice of the able to the galling indolence of the idle. And it could never conduce to the industry, improvement, or happiness of the nation. Perhaps nowhere was the corrupted practice more evident than in Britain's promulgation of the Tea Act of 1773. It was Dickinson, that reluctant revolutionary, who expressed the sentiment best. Here, under the guise of regulation, lay a cynical and desperate scheme to award special privilege to a few at the expense of many.

> Five ships loaded with TEA, on their Way to America, and this with a View not only to enforce the Revenue Act, but to *establish a Monopoly for the East-India Company,* who have espoused the Cause of the Ministry; and hope to repair their broken Fortunes by the Ruin of American freedom and Liberty! No Wonder the Minds of the People are exasperated. . . . Pray have you heard, whether *they* and their *Ministers* have not made a Property of us, and whether we, OUR WIVES AND CHILDREN, together, with the HARD EARNED FRUITS OF OUR LABOUR, are not made over to this almost bankrupt Company. . . . The Rights of free States and Cities are swallowed up in Power. Subjects are considered as Property.

If, as Jefferson would assert in a rough draft of the Declaration, "all men are created equal and independent, [and] that from that *equal creation* they derive rights inherent and inalienable, among which are the preservation of life, and liberty and the pursuit of happiness," then as Locke had taught nearly a century earlier, none are entitled to any species of special (i.e., political) privilege. "The whole art of government," therefore, as Jefferson had explained two years earlier, "consists in the art of being honest. . . . *No longer persevere in sacrificing the rights of one part of the empire to the inordinate desires of another; but deal out to all equal and impartial right.*"

Or, as Samuel Adams wrote two years earlier still, reproducing Locke's own formulation: "*There shall be one rule of Justice for rich and poor; for the favorite in Court, and the Countryman at the Plough.*"[74] A people devoted to "equal creation," moreover, could not easily countenance the pretensions of their "social superiors," whose claim to superiority rested on the suppression of that people's honest aspirations. As James Otis proclaimed in 1762, "I am forced to get my living by the labour of my hand, and the sweat of my brow, as most of you are, and obliged to . . . [work] for bitter bread, earned under the frowns of some who have no natural or divine rights to be above me, and entirely owe their grandeur and honor to grinding the faces of the poor, and other acts of ill gotten gain and power."[75]

But what of the corruption Americans complained of at home? And what about the moral transformation they thought might be effected as a result of the revolution? It was not imperial policies alone that they had in mind as they pleaded for what Wood describes as "the duty of a republic to control 'the selfishness of mankind.' "[76] And it was not Tory haughtiness alone, the pretensions of would-be "American Lords" living off the labors of honest colonial taxpayers, that signified sin and corruption for the republicans and revolutionaries. Above all, moral transformation meant civic unity, as against the endemic factionalism that had run rampant in colonial America. Was this attack on faction not a singular rebuke to a self-serving individualism? On the contrary. The moral condemnation of factionalism in American society on the eve of revolution bespeaks an enlightened affirmation of individualism and Lockeanism as perhaps nothing else does.

In innumerable ways, the patterns of colonial life reflected the Lockean philosophic frame. In one respect, however, the colonial pattern sharply departed from that demanding vision. This divergence involved the factionalism that the revolutionaries would so vigorously oppose. What it signified, for Americans, however, was not "crass selfishness," at least not in the sense of self-improvement or self-enrichment, but rather a granting of privilege to some at the expense of others. Factionalism was judged a violation, not an expression of equal protection. As Wood himself advised, "To eighteenth-century American and European radicals alike . . . it seemed only too obvious that the great deficiency of existing governments was precisely *their sacrificing of the public good to the private greed of small ruling groups.*"[77]

John Locke and revolutionary America appealed for equality, as Thomas Shippen phrased it, "an equality, which is adverse to every species of subordination beside that which arises from the difference of capacity, disposition, and virtue." In the modern republic, unlike the old monarchies, where "favor is the source of preferment," David Ramsay declared, no one would "command the suffrages of the people, unless by his superior merit and capacity." "In a republican system," Wood adds, "only talent would matter." But that is precisely what colonial factionalism assiduously discounted. "As long as politics remained such a highly personal business, essentially involving bitter rivalry among small elite groups for the rewards of state authority, wealth, power, and prestige, the Whig distinction between country and court, legislature and executive, people and rulers, remained a meaningful conception for describing American politics.''[78]

The problem, however, was not with individualism, rightly understood, but with American politics as then practiced. The solution lay not in everyone's willingness to sacrifice for some organic ideal, disembodied from the interests and welfare of ordinary citizens, but in Americans' determination to stop sacrificing the interests and welfare of others to their own schemes of enrichment. It could be effected only if these "ruling elites," acknowledging the equal creation of all, would cease doling out those special privileges.

The perks of provincial office could take the form of monopoly privileges in the lucrative Indian trade, as in New York, or of control of timber resources (used in the production of ship masts), as in Massachusetts. The exigencies of war necessitated the awarding of public contracts throughout the colonies. And patronage, the awarding of lower offices, was yet another time-worn gift that ruling factions had at their disposal. Above all, however, Bailyn points to "the power of controlling the initial distribution of the primary resource of the society: land." To the political victors went the economic spoils, leaving "much of colonial politics" little more than "the efforts of individuals and groups to gain the benefits of these bestowals." In fact, Bailyn continues, "immunities and benefits had to be bestowed—to build wharves, roads, ferries, public vessels, civic buildings—in numbers and with a suddenness that had no parallel in the settled society of England."[79]

In most colonies and for much of the time competing families and factions vied for public power and private gain. It was an ambition that demanded executive control of the colonial assemblies, a control that, given the competition for power and the power of assemblies to block the executive will, resulted in often endless factional conflict. Of the situation in New York during one riotous period, Bailyn writes:

> The anti-Leislerians, favored by the avaricious Governor Benjamin Fletcher, rioted in the spoils of office and plundered their defeated enemies; when the side turned under the governorship of Lord Bellomont they were attacked with equal violence. Neither side in office could control the popular forces in the Assembly. . . . Both sides when in control of the administration went so far beyond the usual claims of prerogative as to attempt judicial murder; both sides out of office championed the cause of liberty, sought to extend representation, to bind representatives . . . to their constituencies and to enlarge the power of the House.[80]

One colony, New Hampshire, managed to avoid the avaricious competition for power. This however did not result in any meaningful measure of equal protection for its citizens. Speaking of the quarter-century reign of Benning Wentworth, Sachs and Hoogenboom explain: "During his tenure in office he handed out more than two hundred townships to friends, supporters and speculators. At the same time he filled his own coffers, for with each grant he reserved for himself five hundred acres of choice timberland. His relatives were cared for with political appointments and inside deals."[81]

The stability accomplished by the Wentworths in New Hampshire was the exception; the rule was a strenuous competition for power and for the benefits it conferred. In this lay the significance of factionalism for the American founders. Bailyn thus writes, "Parties and factions—their destructiveness, the history of the evils they brought upon mankind, their significance as symptoms of disease in the body politic—are endlessly discussed in the public prints; they are endlessly condemned and endlessly abjured."[82] For Bailyn, it was this real-world situation that allowed all of the Catonic concerns with "Power," "Corruption," and the sorry cycle of civic decay to become so prevalent and powerful an influence on the colonial imagination.[83]

If, by 1776, many Americans dreamed they could unite on behalf of a common interest and defend the public good against the private and selfish passions of men, it was not because they wished to extinguish individualism, but rather that they hoped to defend individualism from the petty squabbling for power, patronage, and privilege that factionalism at home and the tyrannous acts of Parliament and the Crown abroad came to signify for them. The concerns for industrious self-interest and the common good, in sum, are singular and indivisible. They stand as means to an end so that in providing for the former a polity promotes the latter.

The ease with which the Lockean and the republican paradigms could blend in the minds of Americans is perhaps nowhere better illustrated than in the series of essays that appeared, between 30 November 1752 and 22 November 1753, in the *Independent Reflector*.[84] "Patriotism, or public Spirit," one essay urged, "is so essentially necessary to the Prosperity of Government, and the Welfare of Civil Society, that without some Portion of the *former,* the *latter* . . . cannot long exist . . . [indeed] can have no Existence." The "Declension and Dissolution" of civil societies, in fact, may be measured "in Proportion to their Decay of Public Spirit: And that when selfish Principles and sordid Views become predominant." Selfishness is clearly abhorrent: "That we are not born for our selves alone, is the Voice of sound Philosophy—the Dictate of unerring Nature. . . . to coil ourselves up within the dirty Shell of our own private Interest and Conveniency, careless of the common Good; is denying our Title to Humanity, and forfeiting the Character of rational beings."[85]

The author goes on to distinguish a true from a false or hypocritical patriotism. For it is "under the Disguise of Patriotism, that first-rate virtue, [that] *Faction, Self-Interest,* and private Ambition are frequently concealed." Virtue must ever be on its guard against the false patriot: "The Coward, the Flatterer, the Wretch whose sordid Soul pays Obeysance to the splendid Insolence of Power and Fortune, [he who] can never feel the generous Warmth of honest Patriotism."

Must we infer from this, as Wood presumably would, that the author "could not conceive of the state in any other terms than organic unity"? Not at all, since he realizes that "the Good of the Public, includes the Life and Happiness of Thousands" of individual men and women. The wickedness presented by the "Spirit of Party and Faction" consists in "an Agreement . . . between the Rulers *to advance their private Interest, at the Expence of the People.*"[86]

And of what does the people's interest consist? For what are men and women made? Surely, echoing Locke, not "Indolence and Inaction . . . [for] the Creator of the Universe was too wise to form his Creatures for such insignificant Purposes. No Man can pretend a Charter of Indulgence, for a Life of absolute Ease and Inactivity." Reprising the latitudinarians' cosmological outlook, the *Independent Reflector* advises: "If we look around us, we see not only the whole material Universe in Motion, but the whole Animal System of the Universe incessantly active. Shall Man then who claims an Alliance with the sublime Intelligences above, who are Activity itself, by a Life of Idleness and Sloth, defeat the Intention of his and their common Creator?"[87]

Under what form of government is human industry and improvement most encouraged? Not one in which "the tyrant riots in the Spoils of his People . . . drains their Purses, to replenish his insatiate Treasury" and believes "a Vindication of the natural Rights of Mankind, is Treason." And not one in which invidious factions, under the cloak of patriotic goodwill, mimic the monarch's evil designs. The happy state is the "Condition of a free People." It is here that

> every Thing looks cheerful and happy, smiling and serene. Agriculture is encouraged, and proves the annual Source of immense Riches to the Kingdom: The Earth opens her fertile bosom to the Ploughshare, and luxuriant Harvests diffuse Wealth and Plenty thro' the Land: The Fields stand thick with Corn: The Pastures smile with Herbage: The Hills and Vallies are cover'd with Flocks and Herds:

Manufactures flourish: the unprecarious Plenty recompenses the Artificer's toil.[88]

Inveighing against the "slavish Doctrines of *Passive Obedience* and *Non-Resistance* the *Reflector* locates the Origin, Nature [and] Use . . . of Civil Government" in Locke's own deepest understanding. Men are born with a full "Title to Liberty," and

> had Man been wise from his Creation, he would always have been free. . . . It is the Depravity of Mankind, that has necessarily introduced Government. . . . Who can deny, that we have ceded a part of our original Freedom, to secure to us the rest, together with the other Blessings of Life? Without this Prospect, it is plain, no Man would ever subject himself to the Dominion and Rule of another. And therefore, tho' Government is necessary to our Well-being, it must be such as is consistent with it.

And what, fundamentally, is most "necessary to our well-being . . . [and] consistent with it"? "The Study of human Nature will teach us, that Man in his original Structure and Constitution, was designed . . . and created solely for the Enjoyment of his own Happiness."[89]

If an individual is to attain and enjoy that happiness, he must, in reason, be free to discover and pursue it. Reason holds the key to human happiness. It is, as it was for Locke, the ultimate source of liberty and the guide to true and lasting felicity. "For how little would avail our reasoning Faculties, were it possible for us to resign our native Right to a Freedom of Action." Every individual is subject "to the Laws prescribed to him by his omnipotent Creator," and

> being a rational Creature, [this] necessarily implies in him a Freedom of Action, determinable by the Dictates of his own Reason [and] the self-resolving Exertions of his own Volition. The Liberty of the human Will, and a Power of acting in Conformity thereto, are not only his indisputable Right, but also constitute his very Essence as a rational Creature; and cannot therefore, by any means whatever, be alienated from him in a social state.[90]

But the rights that derive from reason, including the pursuit of happiness, are not something that may be purchased at others' expense. What colonial factionalism represented for the *Reflector*'s contributors was not an expression of rationality or freedom, but their abject denial. "From the moment that Men give themselves wholly up to a Party, they abandon their *Reason,* and are led Captive by their *Passions.*" In that process, they abandon the objective affirmation of every individual's equal right in order to gain a nefarious advantage for their own party's avarice. They thereby surrender "their Zeal for the common Good," for a blind worship of special privilege, which is "the predominating Fervor of Faction."[91]

Equal protection was the great desideratum; it was rooted in the precept of equal creation. The rise of a contentious factionalism denied that equality and, in the end, would leave all society stripped of the law's protection. Once whetted, the covetous craving for power and preferment would spread until it devoured every principle and protection upon which free government rested. The great evil was not the aim or act of growing rich, but in doing it with government's help and at the expense of others: of using public power for private advantage.

There is, as it were, one further way of confirming the American commitment to a Lockean individualism. As with the pattern of factionalism, it too reveals the rule through a critical examination of a notable exception. What factionalism represented was a political attack on individual industry and equal opportunity from above. During the revolution an effort was mounted from *below* the social hierarchy, as well, to limit, if not industry, at least its fruits: individual wealth. Many in revolutionary America hoped they could effect a more equal distribution of America's resources through positive political measures.

Lockean individualism afforded all God's creatures the right, as well as the responsibility, of self-preservation. It was, by modern standards, a harsh and demanding ethic, mitigated only by the belief that those who suffered through no fault of their own, the innocent victims of life's circumstances (allusions to God's providential design notwithstanding), were deserving of compassion and aid. Damaris Cudworth, Lady Masham, as we saw much earlier, attested to Locke's own generosity toward the deserving poor. The distinction was by no means peculiar to Locke. It was one drawn by eighteenth-century Americans as well. As Sachs and Hoogenboom write, "Colonials imitated the English in drawing a distinction between the 'deserving poor' and 'sturdy beggars.' The first group, including helpless infants, widows, cripples and old people, was deemed deserving of state aid. The second group, encompassing all other persons without visible means of support, was deemed deserving of the workhouse." The essential idea was that "if prosperity was a reward for diligence, then poverty was the penalty for improvidence, and the poor had only themselves to blame for their misfortunes. To tax the rich to benefit the poor would corrode the substance of the rich without in any way helping the poor."[92]

As a number of "New Left" historians have noted, that view was not universally shared. Beneath the great merchants and planters, below the upwardly mobile middle ranks, there lay a genuine underclass. Nowhere did this social stratum rise to greater political prominence than in revolutionary Pennsylvania. There the militant Privates Committee of the colonial militia became "the foremost carrier of [an authentically] radical ideology." As Gary Nash has written, only here, "where a combination of artisans, shopkeepers and small traders captured control of the political process and then were themselves pressured from below by a highly policitised militia composed mainly of lower artisans, was the franchise given to all taxpayers, regardless of whether they owned property."[93]

The goals of artisanal life were modest: "a decent competency, dignity and economic independence." A conflict of values could be avoided as long as these goals could be gained. In the 1720s and then again in the 1760s, under the strain of dire hardship, deference to authority and to rugged individualism lost out to what E. P. Thompson has termed the more traditional "moral economy," a conception very much related to James Tully's understanding of God as intending the preservation not of this or that individual, but of all his human creation. It was this conception that emerged in the 1776 Pennsylvania Convention charged with drafting a state constitution. Among the proposals the radicals sought to include in that constitution was one sharply egalitarian and un-Lockean in substance and tone: "An enormous proportion of property vested in a few individuals is dangerous to the rights, and destructive to the common happiness of mankind, and therefore every free state hath a right by its laws to discourage the possession of such property."[94]

There is no question but that honest patriots appropriately worried over the civic distraction that could so easily accompany the blind pursuit of self-interest and material riches (even where there is no attempt to politically sacrifice the interests of others). Private "virtue" (i.e., personal industry) carried to a point beyond moderation could well extinguish the civic "virtue" that was deemed so essential to the maintenance of republican liberty. But I think it is a different conception that the New Left historians mean to raise here.

In the radical ranks of the Philadelphia militia, Nash writes, "a genuine counter-ideology, stressing egalitarianism and communitarianism, resonated with greatest force." The proposal, however, was defeated by a "liberal economic outlook" shared by "large numbers of property-owning, modestly prosperous mechanics in the more lucrative trades." Economic distress did not abate on 4 July 1776. Until 1779, the radicals pressed their demands for price controls, antimonopoly measures, land banks, and paper money. Then, fed up by the failure to remedy their distress, they marched on the home of James Wilson, a strong foe of the democratic measures. The "Fort Wilson riot," Eric Foner reports, "marked a major turning point in the history of popular radicalism in revolutionary Philadelphia. . . . [It] irrevocably split the artisan-intelligentsia radical leadership from mass crowd activities. What remained of the popular radicalism . . . was a set of stubbornly egalitarian ideas, which lacked both articulate leadership and organized political expression."[95]

Pennsylvania radicalism, for the New Left historians, signifies the limits of the Lockean, individualist consensus in revolutionary America and the persistence of an older, communitarian ethic. Considering the paltry accomplishment of this limited movement, however, and the failure of other colonial groups to raise similar demands to any effect, the New Left research seems more to support, than confound, the thesis of consensus, as regards America's commitment to Lockean individualism.

Conclusion

Such were America's moral and fundamental attachments in the revolutionary era. Reason counseled industry and improvement, and begot property — the protection of which provided the industrious the just fruits of their honest labors, as well as the "necessaries and conveniences" of life. The active, productive life, moreover, was deemed elemental in the pursuit of human happiness. And since, as Jefferson wrote on behalf of the white male population, "all men are created equal," government needed to treat them as such, providing equal protection and tossing out all vestiges of special privilege and corruption.

If these were America's stated principles, it must be said they were principles violated in many particular instances — in the instance of every black man, red man, woman, or religious sectarian who would not be counted equal or protected by equal laws.[96] Nevertheless, they were principles more clearly conceived and universally shared than at any prior time or place in human history. That, too, should not escape notice.

Contradictions and compromises notwithstanding, America by 1776 was at least aiming at an equalitarian social order. It may be summed up most directly in the Lockean conception of independence. Fundamentally epistemological, it signified every individual's indefeasible right to look at the world through his or her own eyes, to rationally pursue a self-willed course and thereby seek happiness, however it might be conceived. One might do this so long as one afforded all others an "equal and inherent right" to do no less. "I have sworn upon the altar of God," Jefferson proclaimed, "eternal hostility to all forms of tyranny *over the mind* of man."[97]

It is not surprising that the children of the Age of Reason would so highly prize the independent, reasoning mind. Reason, which belonged to each individual and constituted the appropriate motor of human conduct, was the root of virtue; happiness was its reward. These "thinking revolutionaries," to borrow Ralph Lerner's recent and apt phrase, displayed a philosophically rich and well-woven estimate of human nature. Between reason and happiness stood all the subsidiary individual virtues and social obligations that the laws of nature and nature's God counseled: industrious improvement in one's chosen calling and a due respect for the rights of property (and its corollary, the obligation of contract). Not very much need be made of Jefferson's decision to substitute "the pursuit of happiness" for Locke's own formulation: "life, liberty and property." It was, as John Dickinson explained, all of a piece. "Let these truths be indelibly impressed on our minds—that we cannot be happy without being free—that we cannot be free, without being secure in our property—that we cannot be sure in our property, if, without our consent, others may, as by right take it away."

Elsewhere, Dickinson wrote very much to the same effect: "I have a right to be happy. If there can be no happiness without freedom, I have a right to be free. If I cannot enjoy freedom without security of property, I have a right to be thus secured."[98] The relation between the rights of happiness and property was even more carefully explored in Morton White's *The Philosophy of the American Revolution*. For White, the critical influence on American thought was the work of an eighteenth-century Swiss philosopher, Jean Jacques Burlamaqui (1694–1748). His principal work, *The Principles of Natural and Political Law* (1747), enjoyed a wide American audience. James Wilson and Jefferson each owned copies of the work in the original French, and, as William Bradford reported to Madison, the English translation, brought out in 1748, was in great demand by the participants of the First Continental Congress.

Burlamaqui generally follows Locke closely. There is a God who has created and who rules over the universe. That God is omnipotent and omniscient, all-wise and all-good, so that what he does is not done for any evil purpose and is not done in vain. It is by grasping the God-given essence of human nature that we can clearly determine the purposes for which mankind is created. Hence, from the *essence* of man as a created being, we come to discover the *duties* of man and, from there, the *natural rights* that are essential to the performance of those duties. White sums up Burlamaqui's view:

(1) since God gave us life as part of our essence, put us into the same species and into society with our fellow-men, and gave us as part of our essence, a desire for happiness, God proposed at least three ends for us: the preservation of life, the preservation of liberty and the pursuit of happiness; and (2) since God proposed these three ends for us, He imposed on us three corresponding duties to attain those ends. From these two statements Burlamaqui inferred that from God's equal creation of man as a being with a certain nature and in a certain state, man derived the duty to preserve life, the duty to preserve liberty and the duty to pursue happiness.

Burlamaqui made a few significant modifications in Locke's political formulation that, nevertheless, lean heavily on the teaching contained in his *Essay concerning Human Understanding*. These modifications, for White, most influenced Jefferson's switch from "property" to the "pursuit of happiness." "(1) Burlamaqui denied that the right to property was expressed in a primary natural law and hence denied that it was an inherent natural right, given directly by God to man. . . . (2) Burlamaqui also thought that the duty to pursue happiness *was expressed in a primary natural law and therefore implied an inherent right to pursue happiness*."

Burlamaqui sharply distinguished what he called rights that are "unalienable" and those that are merely "adventitious." Primary, unalienable rights arise from "the primitive and original states . . . in which man finds himself placed by the very hand of God independent of any human action." Adventitious or secondary rights, though still "natural," arise not as the direct decree of God, but from the "great modifications" men effect as they fulfill their duties to him. These latter rights are "properly the work of man."

The argument is that for Jefferson and the signers of the Declaration, "the right of property," although natural and inviolate, "was not in the same exalted position as the duties duly mentioned" there. These latter rights were put on a pedestal; they were preeminently the rights that, when invaded by a government, gave people the right to make a revolution. They were God-given, inherent, unalienable, and not adventitious. They were moral powers no man could transfer to any person or government.[99]

This, of course, was not the Tory estimate. While I am not suggesting that every colonial foe of the revolutionary cause was a Tory—many, if not most, were honest Whigs who simply could not see a concerted design to reduce the British subjects of North America to slavery—it will be instructive to compare the premises that guided the patriots with those that informed the Tory. The latter's was an outlook shrouded in "subjection and subjugation." "Therefore," wrote "Massachusettensis," the Boston lawyer Daniel Leonard, "let the parliament lay what burdens they please on us, we must, it is our duty to submit and patiently bear them, till they will be pleased to relieve us." Jonathan Boucher, the Tory priest and self-confessed disciple of Sir Robert Filmer, concurred: "If the form of government under which the good providence of God has been pleased to place us be mild and free, it is our duty to enjoy it with gratitude and with thankfulness. . . . If it be less indulgent and less liberal than in reason it ought to be, still it is our duty not to disturb the peace of the community, by becoming . . . rebellious subjects, and *resisting the ordinances of God*."

"To suffer nobly indicates more greatness of mind than can be shown by acting valiantly," Boucher believed.[100] If your estimate of human nature was not much better than Hobbes's or Filmer's or Samuel Parker's, as explored in Chapter 2, then you could not trust people with the liberty to improve their political or social predicaments. The patriots, having far fewer reservations, chose to be valiant. God made man to be rational, free and happy, not to suffer in silent subjection and subjugation. They would be no less. Examining the breakdown of deference to religious authority at the time of the Great Awakening, Bonomi appropriately foretold how this rise of religious independence made it easier for Americans to declare their political independence three decades later—given the perceived prospect of a reinvigorated episcopal discipline. Examining the breakdown of patriarchal authority in approximately the same period, Fliegelman, similarly, saw how this experience made it easier for Americans to contemplate the prospect of separation from the political "father" at the time of the revolution.

Both inferences, I believe, have been appropriately drawn. The lessons of history, i.e., the rise and fall of republics, ancient and modern, informed the colonists of their fate, if they passively succumbed to a paternal and imperial will. So informed and so fitted by their familial and clerical experiences, Americans chose, as it were, to leave home and to lay the foundation for a new civil hearth. What the American people declared on 4 July 1776 was not just their "separate and equal station" among nations, but the equal and independent status of people, as such; not just the separation of thirteen North American colonies from an imperious motherland, but the independence of the human spirit itself. This did not make of Americans a congeries of social atoms, and it certainly did not signify the breakup or breakdown of civil society, as Macpherson might have it. Every species of social and civic bond would continue to bind individuals, in daily practice and in common revolutionary cause. Only now the bonds would be of their own making. In church and in market, in family life and philanthropic service, individuals would be drawn together by mutual choice and for mutual advantage.[101]

But, as John Adams urged as early as 1765, a ''direct and formal design . . . to enslave all America'' was being hatched. It would be necessary to think long and hard about the affairs of state. And it would be necessary to consult those great and learned thinkers who, themselves confronted with a rising oppression, had pursued these matters to their ''bottom.'' Adams said, in his *Dissertation on the Canon and the Feudal Law:* ''Let every slice of knowledge be open'd and set a flowering. The encroachments upon liberty, in the reigns of the first James and the first Charles, by turning the general attention of learned men to government, are said to have produced the greatest number of consummate statesmen, which has ever been seen in any age, or nation.''

He cites the examples of Harrington and Hampden and includes Sidney and Locke, who ''owed their eminence in political knowledge to the tyrannies of those reigns.'' And he urges his countrymen ''in the same manner to engage the attention of every man of lerning . . . that we may be neither led nor driven blindfolded to irretrievable destruction.''[102] Seeing more clearly than ever the consequences and costs of corruption, they would from this moment forward cease sacrificing the equal rights of others and the good of all to their own private interests but, instead, patriotically pledge themselves to the uniform common interest—a singular interest shared by every liberty-loving colonial. Such was the Spirit of '76 and such, at least for a while, was the hope.

9
The Constitution of '87

Against Dunn, and with Pangle and Dworetz I would conclude that Locke's influence on eighteenth-century America, broadly, and on the American Revolution, more narrowly, *"was massive."* And I reach this conclusion without diminishing by any meaningful measure the role of "republicanism" on the opening act of the American founding: the American Revolution. As the previous chapter amply demonstrated, the language of republicanism and the language of Lockeanism could indeed be posted side by side. What this dualism signified, however, was not "confusion," much less "contradiction" on the part of the revolutionaries, but merely a split focus of attention. John Dunn appropriately raised Benjamin Rush's counsel, and it is worth repeating: "It is one thing to understand the *principles,* and another thing to understand the *forms* of government. The former are simple; the latter are difficult and complicated. . . . Mr. Locke is an oracle as to the *principles*, Harrington and Montesquieu are oracles as to the *forms of government*."[1]

Dunn was mistaken, however, in dismissing the significance of both Locke and Locke's principles of government for the founders. And if this is true for the revolutionary period, it is so for the constitutional period as well. If Americans by 1787 "found no need . . . to ascend to a level more theoretical than that of the *Federalist*," as Dunn urged, it *was not* because "Locke's work had become a historical curiosity . . . never again to be an emotional or conceptual focus in the discussion of the politics of the nation."[2] On the contrary, it was because by 1787 there was *near total consensus concerning the authority of Locke's moral and political teaching*. Locke's views would inform not merely the movement for constitutional reform, but the views of those Americans who would stake positions on both sides of the ensuing ratification debate. That is the theme and argument of this chapter.

One point demands emphasis. I heartily concur with McDonald and those who divide the Framers into two (or more) competing camps. It is entirely appropriate to pit the traditional political science of Montesquieu against the more novel researches of David Hume. Most of the "great" questions that would be debated in and after the Convention of '87 pertain to just that: the science of politics. These interesting queries (e.g., whether a small or a large and extended republic is more suited to a republican form of government, whether the powers of the departments of government ought to be strictly separated or overlapped, and so forth) need not concern us. What will concern us are the "fundamentals" of government—the beliefs Americans had regarding the basic values at which civil government should aim and, more immediately, the ways in which down to 1787 American governments were falling well short of the mark.

The Vices of the System and the Need for a More Perfect Union

Against both Gordon Wood, who found in the politics of '87 discontinuity with the republican and revolutionary past, and those stalwart revisionists who emphasize a continuity with the classical republican tradition, I shall argue that in fundamental terms, the debate over the Constitution represented a profound continuity of commitment to John Locke's liberal politics and, in particular, to the precepts of "equal creation" and "equal protection."

Actually, it is remarkable how little had changed. Absent a common and imperious foe, American politics quickly reverted to familiar, factional form. Appleby views this shift as merely the emergence of "pragmatic interest group politics," while the nation's founders, both before and after 1776, viewed it as an unconscionable abuse of power. Diggins is profoundly mistaken in his theory of ideological declension, i.e., in seeing in the constitutional debates the discounting of "moral ideas that were capable of commanding obedience because of their universal truth." Certain political ideas, as I now hope to show, certainly did "enjoy . . . a 'transcendent requirement' that could obligate moral conduct."[3]

The so-called Critical Period, which was considered "critical" by many who were living through it, was a time of growing discontent and dissatisfaction. Under the Articles of Confederation, there was much cause for complaint, though the greatest part of the protest concerned not the actions of Congress, but the democratic measures undertaken in the various statehouses and the kinds of people who were pulling the democratic strings of power. It was the perceived inequities, primarily within the several states, that resulted in the convening of the

Constitutional Convention. It is important to see how deeply the alarm, sounded throughout America by 1787, was rooted in Locke's moral and political teaching.

To a degree, Locke's steady influence is evidenced in the continued outcry over factionalism and the abuse of public power for private advantage examined in Chapter 8. Thus, in Pennsylvania during the 1780s, many deplored the species of special privilege that went to the Bank of America, the College of Philadelphia, and other corporate entities. In fine Lockean fashion it was asserted that

> equal liberty and equal privileges are the happy effect of a free government. They are in fact convertible terms: neither can subsist without the other. A popular government . . . holds out *this equality* to its citizens. . . . The unequal or partial distribution of public benefits within a state, creates distinctions of interest, influence and power, which lead to the establishment of an aristocracy. . . . [something] contrary to the equal and common liberty which ought to pervade a republic.

Since it was "the characteristic of free-men [and] the object of the present revolution" that individuals "cannot be affected in their rights of personal security, personal liberty and private property . . . [a legislature has no right] to give monopolies of legal privilege—to bestow unequal portions of our common inheritance on its favourites."[4]

On the whole, however, the standing complaint voiced by most of America's political elite by the mid-1780s did not involve the aristocratic grab for power and privilege. It was a question of democratic excess that perplexed leading Americans. Before turning to the paramount concerns of the day, however, one issue ought to be addressed concerning the drive for national reform.

Some scholars have questioned the proportions of the crisis of the 1780s, seeing in the cries of crisis the typical and tactical hyperbole of ardent nationalists intent on effecting their dream of a strong national union.[5] And there is much evidence to support the view that this was a generally prosperous and bustling time for most white males in America.[6] Nonetheless, as Gordon Wood has urged after undertaking an exhaustive examination of the periodic literature and correspondence of the period, the alarms raised over the direction of American politics were an unrelenting feature of the public prints in every state. "The want of a decided tone in our government in favor of the general principle of justice," as one American described it, was "a continuing complaint in the press throughout the 1780's." I concur with Wood, who concluded, "No more appropriate term than 'crisis' could have been used to describe what was happening."[7]

The questions relevant here are these: What was the nature of the crisis as it was perceived by contemporaries? How does it relate to Locke's theory of human nature and government? And what enables us to accept it as a sincere and serious expression of contemporary educated opinion as opposed to mere conspiratorial rhetoric?

The predominant complaint, of course, was not singular, but plural. Part of the problem revolved around the relations between the states themselves. Discussing various "Trespasses of the States on the Rights of Each Other" in 1787, Madison pointed to the practice of some states "in restricting the commercial intercourse with other states" for the benefit of local manufacturers and merchants. Thus did the laws of Maryland, New York, and his own Virginia impose port restrictions in favor of vessels belonging to their own citizens. Such regulations tend "to beget retaliating regulations, not less expensive and vexatious in themselves than they are destructive of the general harmony." Under the same head, Madison included "paper money, instalments of debts, occlusion of Courts [and] making property a legal tender," which "may likewise be deemed aggressions on the rights of other States." Not specified, however, was the practice of several states that had imposed tariffs on articles imported from abroad, a cause of great umbrage. Of this practice, the historian John Miller wrote:

> Some states began . . . levying duties upon [Britain's] shipping and manufactures. As a result, the people residing in states that had few ports and ships complained that, as consumers, they were being taxed — without benefit of representation — by the commercial states. In self-defense, they opened their ports to British ships and goods. thus each state seemed bent upon creating a navigation system, complete with tariffs, bounties, and other governmental regulations of its own. The interests of the nation as a whole were almost wholly forgotten.

Citing the impositions levied by New York on goods ultimately consumed in New Jersey and Connecticut, Miller continues: "In their efforts to squeeze profits from their neighbors, New Yorkers went too far: the farmers of New Jersey and Connecticut attempted to throw off their 'bondage' . . . boycotting merchandise imported from that state; and New Jersey declared that it would not comply with the requisitions laid by Congress until New York had reduced its tariff." Alarmed over the spreading evils and anticipating the action that would be taken at the Constitutional Convention, Trench Coxe, the intrepid promoter of American manufacturers, warned:

Desultory commercial acts of the legislatures, formed on the impression of the moment, proceeding from no uniform or permanent principles, clashing with the laws of other states, and opposing those made in the preceding year by the enacting state, can no longer be supported, if we are to continue one people. . . . Commerce is more affected by the distractions and evils arising from the uncertainty, opposition and errors of our trade laws, than by the restrictions of any one power in Europe.

His solution, and Madison's, consisted of "a negative upon all commercial acts of the legislatures." If Coxe foresaw economic chaos and paralysis arising from the restrictions placed on trade, Hamilton was to make an even graver prophecy: "We may reasonably expect from the gradual conflicts of State regulations that the citizens of each would at length come to be considered and treated by the others in no better light than that of foreigners and aliens. . . . The infractions of these regulations, on one side, the efforts to prevent and repel them, on the other, would naturally lead to outrages, and these to reprisals and wars."[8]

More immediately, these animosities led aggrieved states to refuse compliance with requisitions of revenue called for by the confederated Congress. And that, in turn, resulted in the failure of Congress to retire the debt incurred during the War of Independence. Public creditors, at home and abroad, along with revolutionary war veterans who held promissory notes (scrip) were being systematically denied payment of the sums that had in good faith and credit been borrowed from them.[9] Equally galling was the condition of private creditors in the various states.

By the mid-1780s a sizable number of Americans had fallen into debt for a variety of reasons. As far as many in America were concerned, it resulted from the nefarious seduction "of a life of ease and pleasure." The corruptions of wealth and luxuriant living were fast overtaking the American population, it was widely asserted. *"An immoderate desire of high and expensive living,"* many began to say, was causing their countrymen "to contract debts which they have no rational prospect of discharging. All they seem to wish, is to obtain credit to figure away, and to make a brilliant appearance at the expence of others."[10] The Revolution for all its promise had failed after all to stem the spread of corruption, dissipation, and disease among the people. Where was the virtue, many asked, that alone could sustain America's noble experiment in republican government?

The inexorable link between private and public corruption could hardly be overlooked. To "manage" their personal problems Americans began to press for political solutions. Gaining control over various state legislatures, debtors soon succeeded in enacting "stay" legislation—measures designed to prevent creditors from removing property or personal belongings from those who were in arrears in their debt payments. Debtors found a second solution in the issuance of paper money. By causing an inflation, farmers could create a greater demand for their produce, raise their earnings, and thereby pay their creditors. In Rhode Island, the process was even more direct. There the state legislature simply loaned the freshly printed money to debtors on easy terms. This solved the problem for one group, but at the expense of another: the creditors. Debtors were paying their bills in full with money that was worth but a fraction of its original value. Not surprisingly, creditors began demanding specie as payment. That would prove no insurmountable barrier for the debtors, who went back to their statehouses to pass "legal tender" laws, thus making it an offense, punishable by fine or imprisonment, to refuse to accept the established, if depreciated, "coin" of the realm.

Even more directly, state legislatures were acting as judicial bodies, deciding individual cases. Thus in Vermont the legislature had virtually become "a court of chancery in all cases over £4,000 interfering in causes between parties, reversing court judgments, staying executions after judgments, and even prohibiting court actions in matters pertaining to land titles or private contracts involving bonds or debts, consequently stopping nine-tenths of all causes in the state."[11] Pennsylvania's legislature was acting similarly.

What has all this got to do with Locke's philosophy? To what could public and private creditors appeal, philosophically speaking, besides their interest in having their debts repaid? The answer lies in Locke's principle respecting the sanctity of property. As we have seen much earlier, having sanctioned a vast inequality in the possession of wealth, men having agreed to make a nonperishable commodity—gold or silver—a store of value and medium of exchange, Locke freely allowed individuals to exchange the products of their labors (be these in the form of goods or gold), or labor itself, for goods and services that others had to offer. It is, in fact, the prospect of trade that forms the incentive for people to enlarge their possessions.[12] But the act of exchange is a contractual act, a mutual agreement to give up something to get something else. This obtains whether the giving and getting occur simultaneously or whether specified terms of credit are agreed to. A creditor is a party to a contract (as is a debtor). He does not give away his property (be it a mortgage loan for land, or produce, or manufactured goods), but gives (or lends) it on certain specified terms. And he is entitled to payment under the terms to which he and his debtor have mutually agreed. To violate the terms of the contract was to violate the right he had to the property he had been promised and to commit an unjust act of theft against him.

If Lockean society is instituted for the protection and preservation of people's property and if such a society is fundamentally rooted in the "equal protection" of all to their just rights and properties, then the debtor-relief measures enacted in the several states during the Critical Period must be adjudged violative of Lockean right. From a moral and Lockean standpoint, it is of no consequence whether the violation of property is committed by a lone thief, a monarch's minister, or a majority faction sitting in a democratic legislature. Are these the terms on which America's political elite viewed the matters at hand?

It certainly would appear so. The public prints of the period are filled with outrage over the actions of the states: "The representative body," wrote one American, "are not authorized to ascertain the value of the property of individuals; and to decide on what terms (excepting by equal taxation) they shall part with it. In that case there could be no private property; but all property would in fact be a joint stock, and the property of the representative body." Have the people or their representatives, another asked, "the right to suspend, supersede or render void by *extemporary decrees,* the established standing laws, by which the payment of debts were secured?" No, he answered, such enactments "could not have the force of law." An entire town in New Jersey declared debtor relief legislation, generally, to be "founded not upon the principles of Justice, but upon the Right of the Sword, because no other Reason can be given why the Act . . . was passed than because the Legislature had the Power and Will to enact such a Law." The *Providence Gazette* on 5 August 1786 bemoaned the fate of Americans. "Woe to that people, whose laws legitimate crimes and vice." The attorney-general of North Carolina, James Iredell, and Chancellor Robert Livingston of New York denounced the legislative enactments of their respective states. And Noah Webster spoke against "so many legal infractions of sacred right—so many public invasions of private property—so many wanton abuses of legislative powers." Summing up the situation, another staunch defender of property and contract stormed:

> My countrymen, the devil is among you. Make paper as much as you please. Make it a tender in all future contracts, or let it rest on its own credit—but remember that past contracts are sacred things—and that legislatures have no right to interfere with them—they have no right to say, a debt shall be paid at a discount, or in any manner which the parties never intended. . . . To pay bona fide contracts for cash, in paper of little value, or in old horses, would be a dishonest, attempt in an individual; but for legislatures to frame laws to support and en-

courage such detestable villainy, is like a judge who should inscribe the arms of a rogue over the seat of justice. [13]

It has been frequently written that Shays's rebellion of 1786 in western Massachusetts, far from being the final outrage that awakened America to the need for constitutional reform, was merely an inconsequential tax revolt. Henry Knox's heated letter to Washington, wildly exaggerating the extent of the danger posed by Daniel Shays and his supporters, need not have precipitated the convening of the 1787 Philadelphia Convention had not interested and conspiring parties used the opportunity of the rebellion to effect their nationalist designs. The Massachusetts insurgents did lawlessly interfere with court proceedings, even destroying legal records on behalf of debtors. The deeper retort, however, as Wood notes, is that Shays's lawlessness was essentially irrelevant to the real problem Americans faced, which was "legal tyranny." [14] As Chief Justice John Marshall, reflecting on the events leading up to the drafting of the Constitution of 1787, remarked years later: "The power of changing the relative situation of debtor and creditor, of interfering with contracts . . . had been used to such an excess by the state legislatures" as to "impair commercial intercourse . . . threaten the existence of credit . . . [and] sap the morals of the people, and destroy the sanctity of private faith." To put a stop to "the evil" was the desire of "all the truly wise, as well as virtuous, of this community." [15] It naturally fed the movement for constitutional reform.

Or, as Madison himself professed: "The mutability of the laws of the States is found to be a serious evil. . . . I am persuaded I do not err in saying that the evils issuing from these sources contributed more to that uneasiness which produced the Convention" than any other concern of the time. "A reform, therefore, which does not make provision for private rights must be materially defective." [16]

Property or Principle: The Foundations of Federalism

The "vices of the system" down to 1787 were all addressed and remedied by the U.S. Constitution. To secure the people's rights of property and contract against the willful acts of state legislatures and to effect a more steady equality, viz., the consumers, tradesmen, and taxpayers of every state, the frame of 1787 specifies:

> No state shall . . . coin money; emit bills of credit; make any thing
> but gold and silver coin a tender in payment of debts; pass any bill of

attainder, *ex post facto* law, or law impairing the obligation of contracts. . . . No tax or duty shall be laid on articles exported from any
state. No preference shall be given by any regulation of commerce or
revenue to the ports of one state or those of another; nor shall vessels
bound to, or from one state, be obliged to enter, clear, or pay duties
in another. (Article I, Section 9)

Private creditors would hereby be afforded the legal protection to which they
were contractually and politically entitled. And the taxing powers ceded to the
new federal government (a power never granted to the confederated Congress)
would allow for retirement of the public debt, hence provide relief to the public
creditors.

The progressive historians viewed these constitutional provisions as a victory
for the interests of property (i.e., the moneyed as opposed to the agrarian or
debtor interest) more than the objective rights of individuals.[17] It would appear
that one modern historian shares the view. At the very least, J. P. Diggins is skeptical of the claim that these historical events can be explained in terms of professed ideas, rather than people's interests. "To describe what ideas do, how they
shape and focus attitudes and emotions, is to mistake a function for a cause. . . .
to explain . . . [an] event by the language that the event itself had generated is not
necessarily to explain what it was that caused the event or the language through
which it was expressed."

Directly challenging the ideological approach of Bailyn and Wood, Diggins
goes on to say that "the problem of ideology — whether it can be demonstrated
that man is capable of obeying ideas, apart from interests — remains unresolved.
Granting the pervasiveness of Lockean liberalism . . . [on] America's political
culture," he finds that "liberalism merely provided the means through which
property and interest came to be represented in the form of an idea."[18]

Perhaps, but perhaps not. I suggest that with respect to the entire debate surrounding the drafting and ratifying the U.S. Constitution, there is a good deal of
evidence to suggest that many in America were acting out of an authentic affinity
for what Madison called, at one point, "the voice of an enlightened reason," and
at another, "reason, justice and truth."[19] This is to say, as I shall throughout this
discussion, that it was reason and philosophic scruple, not merely personal acquisitive interests, that recommended the principles of liberty and property to
America's founders, i.e., that it was equal protection for all that they sought. I
would not quarrel with the idea that large numbers of Americans could be selfishly motivated, i.e., driven to seek legislative means to serve their own interests
at the expense of others, thereby discarding the principle of equal protection.

"Principle" may indeed be adopted for purposes of expediency, then neglected when it suits one's private purpose. Individuals, moreover, may genuinely change their minds over the course of time with respect to their principles; or they may fail to grasp certain logical or moral implications of the principles they profess; or they may with duplicity profess certain principles for the advantage that those professions may yield. All such possibilities present themselves. The point is that there may be means of ascertaining just how principled the participants to a particular moral or political debate were. There are several matters worth considering.

In the first place, the leaders who drafted the Constitution and who argued the need for political reform were not, by any stretch of the imagination, *all* aggrieved parties. Indeed, as Forrest McDonald and Robert E. Brown have both demonstrated taking up the Beardian challenge, there is at best a very tenuous link between the divisions within the Convention and the personal economic interests of the disputants.[20] Then, too, there is the fact that Americans found, at the root of the vices of the system, the forlorn acquisitive impulse itself. In "Catonic" fashion, the public prints blasted the "immoderate pursuit of gain," or the "luxury, dissipation and extravagance" that ended in runaway indebtedness and, in consequence, the decay of a public-spirited virtue (the hallmark of republican liberty) and a virtuous fulfilling of contracted debts.[21]

And this raises the most crucial point in the debate between "interests and ideas." A post-Marxian age looks back at history seeking out the economic determinants that have driven it. But the age in question had for its central and guiding preoccupation a critical *political determinant*. Material relations certainly mattered, as we have seen, but for the eighteenth-century constitution-crafters, the matter of the moment was not capitalism, but republicanism.[22] If relations of power commanded the universal attention of the period, that power was conceived in a political, not a narrowly economic fashion. For all their alarm over "the vices of the system" and the assault on property, the Framers' focus stood fixed on the question of containing public power and so confirming the viability of popular government.

What permeates the debate over every proposed mechanical feature of the Constitution is the perceived tendency of these features to preserve or encroach upon the liberties of the people as individuals and citizens of a new-modeled republic. This is particularly evident in the most contentious article debated in the Convention, the one that found the large states urging proportional representation and the small states insisting upon equal representation for each state. But it is true of virtually every other matter taken up in Philadelphia in 1787 as well. The protection of property was certainly one object with which the national government would be charged. But no less critical for the Framers were the matters of religious liberty, habeas corpus, jury trials, unreasonable searches and seizures, cruel and unusual punishments, and so forth.

Moreover, insofar as economic interests and liberties came under discussion, they arose out of a deeper moral commitment—a commitment to industry, improvement, and, above all, justice. The allowance for a secure enjoyment of all Americans (including, to an extent, American slaves) to the fruits of what honest industry had provided bespoke this deeper moral commitment. And it was a commitment that was punctuated by a still-deeper perception: a view of individuals as created equal and so deserving of equal protection under law. The awarding of special privileges, exemptions, and immunities to particular interests or classes, always at the expense of others wherever situated in the great economic chain, was the evil that the enlightened polity hoped to avoid.

That general commitment is particularly, but by no means exclusively, evident in James Madison's labors. His views merit some consideration. Madison, perhaps more than any other American of his day, saw the need and prepared for the task of constitutional reform. At his request, Jefferson sent from France the encyclopedic knowledge accumulated on the Continent pertaining to the history of ancient and modern republics. With this in hand, Madison prepared for the historic role he would play in 1787. I am not aware of any personal injuries he suffered, however, at the hands of Daniel Shays or the legislatures of Vermont and Rhode Island. Nor can it be said that he materially prospered from the securities afforded to property by the U.S. Constitution. Essentially, he devoted his life to public service and the cause of popular government. Moreover, he enlisted into the service of his country the philosophy of government bequeathed principally by John Locke and summed up in the precept of ''equal protection.'' This may be seen once we place the views he expressed in *The Federalist* alongside the ideas he voiced in essays he wrote at roughly the same time. What this shows is his steady commitment to the principle of property but not to the awarding of political advantage to any particular propertied class in his society.

Society, Madison appreciated, would ever be composed of competing interests. Thus he wrote: ''Those who hold and those who are without property have ever formed distinct interests in society. Those who are creditors, and those who are debtors, fall under a like discrimination. A landed interest a manufacturing interest, a mercantile interest, a moneyed interest, with many lesser interests, grow up of necessity in civilized nations.'' And while all sorts of distinctions emerge in society, ''the most common and durable source of factions has been the various and unequal distribution of property.'' It is precisely ''the regulation of these various and interfering interests [that] forms the principal task of modern legislation.'' That principal task follows from the sanctity that Madison assigns to the principle of property. Individuals do and must have the liberty to acquire, possess, and use it (though it invariably results in the fracturing of society into competing social groups). Why must society countenance the ''rights of property,'' which prove so ''insuperable [an] obstacle to a uniformity of interests''? Because the rights of property, for Madison, ''originate . . . in the faculties of men . . . [and] the protection of these faculties is the first object of government.''[23] Property is by no means primary in political speculation; it rests on a long chain of reasoning and some deeper, more fundamental values.

For Locke, the principle of property rested on the right and duty of every individual to act as to preserve himself or herself and the need to acquire and use property for the sake of preservation. Preservation depended, as well, on the liberty to will the course that would reward one with temporal and eternal salvation. ''The *Freedom* then of Man and Liberty of acting according to his own Will, is *grounded* on his having *Reason,* which is able to instruct him in that Law he is to govern himself by.''[24] Finally, ''being furnished with like Faculties, sharing all in one Community of Nature, there cannot be any *Subordination* among us, that may Authorize us to destroy one another.''[25]

Madison, like Locke, understood property in the broadest sense, to include one's ''life, liberty and estate.'' Writing on the subject of property in the *National Gazette* on 29 March 1792, Madison fleshed out his views. Besides

> that dominion which one man claims and exercises over the external things of the world, in exclusion of every other individual . . . [i.e.,] land, merchandise or money . . . a man has a property in his opinions and the free communication of them . . . [in] his religious opinions, and in the profession and practice dictated by them. He has a property very dear to him in the safety and liberty of his person. He has an equal property in the free use of his faculties and free choice of the objects on which to employ them. In a word, as a man is said to have a right to his property, he may be equally said to have a property in his rights.[26]

The nature, responsibility, and limits of government follow immediately from this Madisonian (cum Lockean) base. ''Government,'' therefore, ''is instituted to protect property of every sort, as well that which lies in the various rights of individuals. . . . This being the end of government, that alone is a *just* government which *impartially* secures to every man whatever is his *own*.'' Such a government is not one that renders all such property insecure through the ''arbitrary seizures of one class of citizens for the service of the rest . . . [or] where arbitrary restrictions, exemptions, and monopolies deny to part of its citizens that free use of their faculties and free choice of their occupations." Madison specifically castigates the polity that would forbid "a manufacturer of linen cloth . . . to bury his own child in a linen shroud, in order to favour his neighbour who manufactures woolen cloth" or that through the imposition of "unequal taxes, oppress[es] one species of property and reward[s] another species" or permits arbitrary taxes to "invade the domestic sanctuaries of the rich," while allowing "excessive taxes [to] grind the faces of the poor." Locke, setting forth the limits under which legislators labor, had said, "They are to govern by *promulgated establish'd Laws,* not to be varied in particular Cases, but to have one Rule for Rich and Poor, for the Favourite at Court, and the Country Man at Plough."[27]

Like Locke, Madison devoted much of his energies to the question of religious liberty. "A Memorial and Remonstrance," which he delivered to the Virginia General Assembly in October 1785 in support of Jefferson's Bill for Religious Liberty, urges: " 'The equal right of every citizen to the free exercise of his Religion according to the dictates of conscience' is held by the same tenure with all our other rights. If we recur to its origin, it is equally the gift of nature." Madison thereby roots his understanding of rights in the venerable laws of nature.

> This right is in its nature an unalienable right. It is unalienable; because the opinions of men, depending only on the evidence contemplated by their own minds, cannot follow the dictates of other men: It is unalienable also, because what is here a right towards men, is a duty towards the Creator. . . . This duty is precedent both in order of time and degree of obligation, to the claims of Civil Society. Before any man can be considered as a member of Civil Society, he must be considered as a subject of the Governor of the Universe.[28]

Acknowledging, as Locke had on his diplomatic jaunt to the Elector of Brandenburg a century earlier, that toleration was the remedy, not the root of religious conflict, Madison thinks government itself "will be best supported by protecting every citizen in the enjoyment of his Religion with the same equal hand which protects his person and his property; by neither invading the equal rights of any Sect, nor suffering any Sect to invade those of another."

Summing it all up, Madison says of a government that would violate "the property which individuals have in their opinions, their religion, their passions, and their faculties—nay more . . . their property in their actual possessions, in the labor that acquires their daily substance. . . . that such a government is not a pattern for the United States."[29] In short, the liberties that flow from the basic faculties and duties of mankind may not be violated. If this great measure of liberty ends in the proliferation of sects, parties, and factions, then it is the prevailing passions and immoderate designs of those parties, not those essential liberties, that must be checked. "The inference to which we are brought is that the *causes* of faction cannot be removed and that relief is only to be sought in the means of controlling its *effects*."[30]

Madison, like Locke, appeals to the reason of mankind to thwart the dangerous passions of mankind. It might happen that distinguished individuals could curry public favor and gain support for their unmerited projects. "The *passions,* therefore, not the *reason* of the public would sit in judgment. But it is the reason, alone, of the public, that ought to control and regulate the government. The passions ought to be controlled and regulated by the government."[31] It is not an easy task, of course. Again and again Madison acknowledges the failure of popular government to safeguard the rights—the property rights—of the minority. "Wherever the real power in a Government lies, there is the danger of oppression," he wrote Jefferson. Since in the American republic power resides with the people, "the invasion of private rights is chiefly to be apprehended, not from acts of Government contrary to the sense of its constituents, but from acts in which the Government is the mere instrument of the major number of the constituents."

The principle upon which Madison's concern is rooted is clearly that of equal protection because, while there appears little danger that, here, the few will abuse the rights of the many, "it is much more to be dreaded that the few will be unnecessarily sacrificed to the many." He steadfastly seeks to render government "sufficiently neutral between the different interests and factions [so as] to control one part of the society from invading the rights of another, and at the same time sufficiently controuled itself, from setting up an interest adverse to that of the whole society."[32]

Madison, in fine, demonstrates a most objective defense of the principle of property, rather than the interests of any special propertied class, as he describes the miscarriage of justice in the states: "Debtors have defrauded their creditors. The landed interest has borne hard on the mercantile interest. The Holders of one species of property have thrown a disproportion of taxes on the holders of another species." Most notably, he urged, "We have seen the mere distinction of colour made in the most enlightened period of time, a ground of the most oppressive dominion ever exercised by man over man."[33]

For educated and literate Americans steeped in eighteenth-century political science and the history of ancient and modern republics, the wild swing of the pendulum toward the pole of democratic excess could come as no surprise; the process was as old as the cycle of history itself. And while the principle of popular government could ensure against the undue influence of minority factions within society, Madison wanted to know what is to be done "when a majority is included in a faction [enabling it] to sacrifice to its ruling passion or interest both the public good and the rights of other citizens"? "To secure the public good and private rights against the danger of such a faction, and at the same time to preserve the spirit and the form of popular government, is then the great object to which our inquiries are directed." In short, "you must first enable the government to control the governed; and in the next place oblige it to control itself."[34]

The solution for Madison lay, first, in building sufficient institutional checks into the frame of government to render it difficult for separate and competing spheres of power (e.g., legislative, executive, and judicial departments) to combine against the general interest, welfare, and rights of the people, and, second, in extending the sphere of politics sufficiently to prevent private factions from combining to effect their selfish schemes of enrichment. This the sheer size of the new nation could accomplish, or so Madison reasoned.

The Foundations of Antifederalism

The Federalist is long on the science of politics but short on the philosophy that would inform such a science (hence the necessity of going to other sources to flesh out Madison's views). Recently, Morton White has attributed the absence of philosophical rigor to the haste with which the papers were written and the immediate and pressing purpose of winning Americans to the side of adoption. Any deeper philosophical argumentation, White is inclined to believe, "might have confused some of Publius's readers while [giving others] the opportunity to engage in . . . irrelevant controversy and logic-chopping."[35] All of this may be so. Another possibility, however, presents itself. This is the possibility that, as in any legal contest, there was generally a good deal that the contending parties were able to stipulate to, i.e., agree upon.

If Federalists and anti-Federalists concurred as to the essential nature—the origins, ends, and limits—of political authority as virtually all patriots had done during the very recent contest with Britain, then the need for such abstract reasoning would have been entirely obviated. Then the entire ratification controversy had only to concern itself with the tendency of the proposed Constitution to promote or undermine what Madison, in *Federalist* 43, considered "the transcendent law of nature and of nature's God," what the unanimous declaration of Congress called the "unalienable rights . . . of life, liberty and the pursuit of happiness.'' This, I believe, was precisely the case. Madison and the Federalists did not have to debate the philosophical fundamentals of government because, for all the divisive acrimony that characterized the ratification contest, on this question the Federalists and anti-Federalists were essentially in accord.

We can begin by acknowledging the fact that many an anti-Federalist readily conceded the excesses of democracy, generally, and the wrongful deprivation of property rights, specifically, perpetrated by the various states under the Articles of Confederation. George Mason and Elbridge Gerry, who would go on to oppose the new frame, both conceded the case in the Convention of 1787.[36] As Cecelia Kenyon has written, the provisions in the Constitution forbidding the states to prevent the due execution of creditors' claims (as discussed earlier) "drew little attention." The foes of the plan "had little to say about these provisions." They were, Patrick Henry said, "founded in good principles." And William Grayson of Virginia, also opposing ratification, said of the provision prohibiting paper money emissions, "It is unanimously wished by every one that it should not be objected to." The Federal Farmer, among the most articulate spokesmen for the anti-Federalist cause, wrote, "Our governments have been new and unsettled, and several legislatures, by making tender, suspension, and paper money laws, have given just cause of uneasiness to creditors."[37]

Beyond this, it is important to recall from the discussion in the preceding chapter that it was that staunch opponent of the Constitution, George Mason (author of the Virginia Bill of Rights), as well as Samuel Adams (frequently quoting Locke verbatim), who worked most ardently to assert and defend the principle of property and the immutable rights of men. What, then, accounts for their profound hostility to the frame of 1787? If Federalist and anti-Federalist could agree on the importance of rendering property secure and on the violations of property rights emanating from the state legislatures, they nonetheless differed on the question of whether the new frame of government could truly protect those very rights (among others) from future encroachments — indeed, whether any species of liberty could be secured under such terms. Would it not be sufficient, they asked, merely to reform the existing articles, strengthening the powers of the confederated Congress? Why the necessity for such a radical reform of American government?

Thus would "Agrippa" (believed to be Massachusetts' James Winthrop) appreciate that "the sober and industrious part of the community should be defended from the rapacity and violence of the vicious and idle. . . . The minority [must be secure] against the usurpation and tyranny of the majority." All that was needed, however, was an amendment to the articles asserting: "It shall be left to every state to make and execute its own laws, except laws impairing contracts, which shall not be made at all.'' In addition Congress could be granted a modest impost to pay for the expense of government and retire the public debt (or the sale of the public lands could be put to that purpose). Finally, to quiet the contentions afflicting the states, the power of regulating commerce between them, and with foreign nations, could also be granted exclusively to Congress.[38]

Why go to so extreme a solution when so little would actually be required to remedy the conditions complained of? Might there be some other motive impelling the Federalist party to overturn the Articles of Confederation thereby unleashing and dramatically expanding the powers of central government? Hadn't the history of mankind and the teachings of the most astute students of politics advised a vigilant suspicion of power and all those who promote it? What in the proposed frame of government could assure power's containment and ward off the universal tendencies of government to consolidate its power, expand its sphere of authority, and endanger the rights and liberties of the people? If the Federalists were focused on the evils emanating from a too weak government, one insufficiently energetic to thwart the *excesses of democracy,* the anti-Federalists were more keenly focused on the universal tendency of governments to exhibit all those evils associated with *aristocratic excess.*

Recalling the Catonic estimate of human nature, the anti-Federalists warned incessantly of the tendency of people to grasp at the strings of power. ''The Experience of all mankind,'' wrote ''Agrippa,'' on 5 February 1788, ''has proved the prevalence of a disposition to use power wantonly.'' Four years earlier in a letter to Elbridge Gerry, Samuel Adams had sternly warned: ''There is a Degree of Watchfulness over all Men possessed of Power or Influence upon which the Liberties of Mankind much depend. It is necessary to guard against the Infirmities of the best as well as the Wickedness of the worst of Men.'' ''Jealousy,'' he concluded, ''is the best Security of public Liberty.'' In much the same spirit, Hugh Hughes, a prominent New York City anti-Federalist wrote: ''From the Conduct of our Church and the Senate, we see how *absolutely requisite* it is, to continually guard against Power; for, when once Bodies of Men, in authority get Possession of, or become invested with, Property or Prerogative, whether it be by Intrigue, Mistake, or chance, they scarcely ever relinquish their Claim, even if founded in Iniquity itself.''[39]

If ''in the history of mankind no perfect government can be found,'' Virginia's Spencer Roane declared on 13 February 1788, ''let it be attributed to the chicane, perfidy and ambition of those who fabricate them; and who are more or less in common with all mankind infected with a *lust for power.*'' And George Clinton, calling himself Cato, soundly warned his fellow New Yorkers: ''You risk much, by indispensably placing trusts of the greatest magnitude, into the hands of individuals whose ambition for power, and aggrandizement will oppress and grind you. . . . rulers in all governments will erect an interest separate from the ruled, which will have a tendency to enslave them."[40]

The Constitution of 1787, Madison's fanciful theories to the contrary notwithstanding, would not check the natural human thirst for power, glory, and riches. The many loopholes in the plan would provide the vehicle and the lawless passions of mankind would surely provide the engine for government growth, consolidation, and corruption. In fact, many anti-Federalists were almost prepared to name names. For Cato, i.e., Clinton, it would be the same cast of characters that had caused his namesakes (i.e., Trenchard and Gordon) so much consternation some sixty years earlier. Writing candidly to Madison on 27 January 1788, Rufus King summed it up this way:

> The Opposition complain that the Lawyers, Judges, Clergymen, Merchants and men of Education are all in Favor of the constitution. . . . [Their view] seems to arise from an Opinion, that is immovable, that some injury is plotted against them, that the system is the production of the Rich and ambitious; that they discern its operation, and that the consequence will be, the establishment of two Orders in the Society, one comprehending the Opulent and Great, the other the poor and illiterate.

Speaking in the Massachusetts Convention at just that time, Amos Singletary also warned: "These lawyers and men of learning and moneyed men, that talk so finely, and gloss over matters so smoothly, to make us poor illiterate people swallow down the pill, expect to be the manager of this Constitution, and get all the power and all the money into their own hands, and then they will swallow up all us little folks, like the great Leviathan. . . . This is what I am afraid of."[41]

"Those furious zealots," wrote "A Federalist" in the *Boston Gazette* on 26 November 1787, "who are for cramming it [the Constitution] down the throats of the people, without allowing them either time or opportunity to scan or weigh it in the balance of their understandings, bear the same marks in their features as those who have been long wishing to erect an aristocracy in THIS COMMONWEALTH." Calling the roll, he continued:

> These consist generally, of the NOBLE order of Cincinnatus, holders of public securities, men of great wealth and expectations of public office, Bankers and Lawyers: those with their train of dependents form the Aristocratick combination. The Lawyers in particular, keep

up an incessant declamation for its adoption; . . . The numerous tribunals to be erected by the new plan of consolidated empire, will find employment for ten times their present numbers; these are the LOAVES AND FISHES for which they hunger.[42]

"Philadelphensis," another Boston anti-Federalist, also exposed the "scheme taken by the despots and their sycophants to bias the public mind in favor of the constitution." He could only curse the "ambitious men . . . whose similitude to each other consisted only in their determination to lord it over their fellow citizens. . . . [They are] unanimous in forming a government that should raise the fortunes and respectability of the well-born few, and oppress the rest." Of the Framers, he injudiciously charged, "They abused this confidence [entrusted to them]; their own private interest, private emollument and hopes of dominion, overcame every consideration of duty, honor and gratitude."[43] You "conquered the enemy," warned "A Farmer and Planter" in the *Baltimore Advertiser* on 1 April 1788, "and the rich men now think to subdue you by their wiles and arts, or make you, or persuade you, to do it yourselves." If you adopt their scheme, "the yoke is fixed on your necks, and you will be undone, perhaps for ever, and your boasted liberty is but a sound."[44] And another patriot, writing as "Centinel," also decried this "government that will give full scope to the magnificent designs of the well-born, [this] government where tyranny may glut its vengeance on the low-born . . . pursuant to the sentiments of that profound, but corrupt politician Machiavel."[45] Speaking of the same orders of men, "Agrippa," cautioned, "Power and high life are their idols, and national funds are necessary to support them."

Richard Henry Lee, who a mere twelve years earlier had introduced the resolution calling for American independence and who could be counted among the most literate and well-read opponents of the Constitution, was somewhat more circumspect. Readily conceding the injustice of the debtor relief measures, he could see the danger to liberty and property emanating from both ends of the social continuum.

One party is composed of little insurgents, men in debt, who want no law, and who want a share of the property of others; these are called levellers, Shaysites, &c. The other party is composed of a few, but more dangerous men, with their servile dependents; these avariciously grasp at all power and property; . . . these are called aristocrats. . . . In 1786, the . . . levellers came forth, invaded the rights of others, and attempted to establish governments according to their wills. Their movements evidently gave encouragement to the other party, which, in 1787, has taken the political field, and with its fashionable dependents, and the tongue and the pen, is endeavouring to establish . . . a politer kind of government.[46]

By what means would "the rich and well-born" effect their scheme to subject and subjugate "the poor and low-born"? With the history of eighteenth-century British politics and the commentary of the Commonwealthman tradition (the warnings of Trenchard and Gordon, Bolingbroke and Burgh, Molesworth, and even Machiavelli) to advise them, the anti-Federalists knew what they could expect. As the Federal Farmer would write: "Should the general government think it politic, as some administration (if not all) probably will, to look for support in a system of influence, the government will take every occasion to multiply laws, and offices to execute them, considering these as so many necessary props for its own support."[47] "A Farmer and a Planter" from Baltimore cautioned: "Should you adopt this new government your taxes will be great, increased to support their . . . servants and retainers, who will be multiplied upon you to keep you in obedience, and collect their duties, taxes, impositions, and excises."[48]

The economic subjection of some for the selfish sake of well-placed others was likewise feared. It was easy for "Agrippa" to imagine the future "limitations of trade, restraints on its freedom, and the alteration of its course, and transfer of the market, all under the pretense of regulation for federal purposes."[49] The anti-Federalists could generally concur with one American, believed to be Franklin, who had written: "Most of the statutes or acts, edicts, arrets and placarts of parliaments . . . for [the] regulating, directing or restraining of trade, have, we think, been either political blunders, or jobs obtained by artful men for private advantage, under pretense of public good." It should be the Americans' aim, "as the first fruits of their independence, to destroy all those commercial restraints which were formerly imposed upon them by European authority, by introducing general and unlimited freedom in every branch of intercourse."[50]

The idea of a civilization open to talent and merit, of a society devoted to the equal protection of human industry and the just enjoyment of the fruits of honest labor, was very much alive in the anti-Federalist mind—as it had been for "Cato" in the age of Walpole.[51] This freedom, wrote "Agrippa," "that every man, whether his capital is large or small, enjoys of entering into any branch that pleases him, rouses a spirit of industry and exertion, that is friendly to commerce. . . . Nothing ought to be done to restrain this spirit." The "spirit of commerce," "Agrippa" said on another occasion, "is the great bond of union among citizens. This furnishes employment for their activity, supplies their mutual wants, defends the rights of property, and producing reciprocal dependencies, renders the whole system harmonious and energetick. Our great object therefore ought to be to encourage this spirit. If we examine the present state of the world we shall find that most of the business is done in the freest states, and that industry decreases in proportion to the rigour of government."[52]

And it was precisely this "rigour of government" that he feared the Constitution would inevitably establish, i.e., "the unlimited right to regulate trade, [which] includes the right of granting exclusive charters." Weighing the dual danger springing from such a power, "Agrippa" concludes: "In most countries of Europe, trade has been more confined by exclusive charters. Exclusive companies are, in trade, pretty much like an aristocracy in government, and produce nearly as bad effects. . . . they always, by the greatness of their capital, have an undue influence on the government."

If this be so "in countries of small extent, they will operate with ten-fold severity upon us, who inhabit an immense tract." If this frame, with all its regulatory powers, is adopted "we shall too have all the intrigues, cabals and bribery practiced, which are usual at elections in Great Britain. We shall see and lament the want of public virtue; and we shall see ourselves bought at a publick market, in order to be sold again to the highest bidder."[53] The demise of liberty in the private sense, given the rapacious passion for power that beats in the human breast, will assure the demise of liberty in the public or republican sense. Both forms of liberty were central components of the anti-Federalist persuasion.

It will not be necessary to rehash all of the features of the Constitution that, from the anti-Federalist perspective, would prove inadequate to the task of containing political power, hence, aristocratic consolidation. Suffice it to say that on the whole, the anti-Federalists were far more mindful of Montesquieu's proscriptions against a republican government extending over a territory as vast as America's. They, much more than the Federalists, heeded the Old Whig precautions, such as making provisions for recall, for sending representatives to Congress under instruction, for periodic rotation of office (i.e., annual elections), for stripping the legislature of any power to alter the time, manner, and place of elections, and, above all, for the necessity of a formal Bill of Rights.

A few things the Constitution did provide for, to the consternation of the anti-Federalists, do deserve some consideration. "My object," wrote "An Old Whig," "is to consider the *undefined, unbounded* and *immense power* which is comprised in the following clause— 'And to make all laws which shall be necessary and proper for carrying into execution the foregoing powers, and all other powers vested by this constitution in the government of the United States; or in any department or offices thereof.' " Under such a clause as this, he stormed, can anything be said to be reserved and kept back from Congress? Can it be said that the Congress have no power but what is expressed? "To make all laws which shall be necessary and proper" — or, in other words, to make all such Laws which the *Congress shall think necessary and proper*—for who shall judge for the Legislature what is necessary and proper? Who shall set themselves above the sovereign?

And in considering the significance of the latter part of the same clause, enabling Congress to make all laws that shall be necessary and proper for carrying into execution "all other powers" (besides those already expressed), the "Old Whig" bitterly remarked: "Was it thought that the foregoing powers might perhaps admit of some restraint, in their construction as to what was necessary and proper to carry them into execution? Or was it deemed right to add still further that they should not be restrained to the powers already named?" Recalling the harsh Declaratory Act of 1766, he concluded: "The British act of Parliament, declaring the power of Parliament to make laws to bind America in all cases whatsoever was not more extensive. For . . . even the British Parliament neither could nor would pass any law in any case in which they did not either deem it necessary and proper to make such a law, or pretend to deem it so."[54]

Given this undefined and unbounded authorization, "Sydney" (New York's Robert Yates) could easily imagine "the general government . . . arrogating to itself the right of interfering in the most minute objects of internal police, and the most trifling domestic concerns of every state." The object of his anxiety, however, was not the "necessary and proper" clause alone. For by this Constitution, the Congress shall have "a power of passing laws 'to provide for the general welfare of the United States,' which [laws] may affect life, liberty and property in every modification . . . unchecked by cautionary reservations and unrestrained by a declaration of any of those rights which the wisdom and prudence of America in the year 1776 held ought to be at all events protected from violation."

By this provision, "Sydney" was led to conclude, "the general government, when completely organized, will absorb all those powers of the state [i.e., New York] which the framers of its constitution had declared should be only exercised by the representatives of the people of the state."[55] And this, "Agrippa," discoursing on the protection of property under the Constitution, was sadly able to confirm: "It is . . . as plain as words can make it, that they have a right to legislate for all kinds of causes respecting property between citizens of different states." And this power "extends to all cases between citizens of the same state," as well:

[This] is evident from the sixth article, which declares all continental laws and treaties to be the *supreme* law of the land, and that all state judges are bound thereby, "anything in the constitution or laws of any state to the contrary notwithstanding." If this is not binding the judges of the separate states in their own office, by continental rules it is perfect nonsense. There is then a complete consolidation of the legislative powers in all cases respecting property.[56]

And if these three clauses (the "necessary and proper," "general welfare," and "supremacy" clauses) gave to the general government a justification for enacting any species of legislation whatsoever, their framers also provided the means of financing and enforcing all future enactments: "The national government," "Centinel" (believed to be Pennsylvania's Samuel Bryan) observed, will "be vested with every species of internal taxation, whatever taxes, duties and excises that they may deem requisite for the general welfare, may be imposed on the citizens of these states." And the collection thereof, "Centinel" caustically added, will "be enforced by the standing army . . . that grand engine of oppression."[57] Melancton Smith, one of New York's leading anti-Federalists, summed up the Catonic fears of many when, speaking before the New York Ratifying Convention, he warned "that power which had both the purse and the sword had the government of the whole country and might extend its power to any and to every object."[58]

In antifederalism, we can clearly discern the unmistakable voice of the eighteenth-century Commonwealthman tradition. The awful fear of power and the terrible estimate of the human passions when whetted by power's corrupting influence form the essential foundation of anti-Federalist invective. At every turn, in nearly every constitutional clause, the anti-Federalists feared and forecast the worst. All of this notwithstanding, in the final analysis they, no less than their Federalist foes, shared the fundamental desire to protect human industry and the enjoyment of its product from the excesses of public power. The two sides differed only in their respective estimates of the Constitution's capacity to so protect the liberty, the property, and the indefeasible rights of the people.

10

The "Triumph" of Antifederalism

Equal Protection and the Bill of Rights

In 1788 antifederalism went down to defeat. The Constitution was ratified, and a year later the great experiment in republicanism got under way. Clearly, the anti-Federalists' worst fears did not come to pass. The experiment did not end in continental consolidation and ruin. Representation was not egregiously restricted, and Congress did not capriciously alter the times and places of elections so as to fill its chambers with its own "corps of dependents." Religious liberty and freedom from arbitrary searches and seizures were not lost, nor were egregious restraints on free speech or a free press imposed, not during Washington's time at least. The rights to a speedy trial and habeas corpus and against self-incrimination did not go out of style. And Americans continued to avail themselves of the right to assemble and petition government for a redress of their grievances.

These important freedoms, it is true, were not especially threatened during the Critical Period (1781–1787). As we have seen, the issue that most perplexed the Framers, aside from interstate animosities, was the want of sufficient political authority to protect the rights of property. Each of the offending state practices was addressed in the 1787 frame. The U.S. Constitution strictly prohibited the states from enacting the species of legislation that had subjected the property and just rights of some to the clamorous and factious demands of others. From here on even a popular or legislative majority, sitting in a statehouse, would be legally barred from sacrificing the few for the sake of the many (the institution of chattel slavery excepted).

As seen in the previous chapter, both sides of the ratification debate perceived the propriety of the prohibitions placed on the state governments. Property was something nearly all Americans wanted to protect. The question on which Federalist and anti-Federalist divided was whether the Constitution contained sufficient safeguards to prevent the national government from infringing on the liberty and property of the people and the precept of equal protection. In fact, the opponents of ratification needed to know that Americans would be protected not just in their property rights, but in their political rights. Liberty, in the classical republican sense, was deemed essential to the preservation of liberty in the private or Lockean sense. In short, Americans needed to be assured that all of the egregious and tyrannical acts of a former king-in-Parliament, so succinctly summarized in the body of Jefferson's Declaration, would never be copied by an American president and an elected Congress.

In this chapter I will argue that although the anti-Federalists were defeated in 1788, the events of the early national period (down to 1792, say) largely vindicated the weighty fears and suspicions they voiced. In the Jeffersonian reaction to the Hamiltonian political economy, we can hear the reinvigorated voice of an antifederalism that was successor to the Spirit of '76, and to a common grandparent: the "Catonic" synthesis of Lockean republicanism that rose in response to Hamilton's chief "instructor," Walpole. Is it any wonder that these founders could be so preoccupied with the "endless cycles of history"?

Antifederalism and the First Congress

In an important sense, the contest over the Constitution continued after its adoption. The ground of battle merely shifted to the proposal calling for a Bill of Rights. The question of appending such a bill to the fundamental frame was, in fact, a legacy of the ratification contest. Several state conventions, upon ratifying the Constitution, stipulated that specific amendments be added in due course. Moreover leading anti-Federalists, such as Richard Henry Lee and Elbridge Gerry, continued to press for substantive amendment of the Constitution, while others moved for adoption of a strong Bill of Rights in the first U.S. Congress. Was the U.S. Constitution, the Bill of Rights included, originally intended to guarantee equal protection, in the broad, Lockean sense discussed earlier, to the citizens of the new nation?

The first proposal for a Bill of Rights was submitted to Congress on 8 June 1789 by James Madison. Originally, Madison had argued against including such a document. He joined Hamilton in arguing against the necessity, indeed the efficacy, of including what, at best, would be but a partial listing of rights. Madison's view was that an expanded republic, housing so many opposing factions of all shapes and sizes, would thwart the schemes of some to subject and subjugate the interests and liberties of others. No single interest would amass sufficient power to effect its private schemes of enrichment when the competing interests that would be adversely affected would enjoy equal representation in the councils of government and could so easily combine in self-defense.

Moreover, Madison reasoned, the Constitution provided for a government that, though national in scope and reach, was strictly federal in the sense of possessing strictly enumerated powers. In *Federalist* 41, he thus took direct aim at those who were alarmed about the "unbounded" and "undefined" power of the federal government to do whatever may be deemed "necessary and proper" to provide for "the general welfare." "No stronger proof," he retorted (in words that would come back to haunt him), "could be given of the distress under which these writers labor for objections, than their stooping to such a misconstruction. . . . For what purpose could the enumeration of particular powers be inserted, if these and all others were meant to be included in the preceding general power? . . . what color can the objection have, when a specification of the objects alluded to by these general terms immediately follows and is not even separated by a longer pause than a semicolon?"[1]

The Bill of Rights as finally adopted was overwhelmingly preoccupied with securing the critical civil rights of the citizens against political encroachment. The body of the Constitution, too, states and protects various civil liberties the Framers deemed crucial to a free government. But what about the principle of equal protection? What constitutional safeguards were afforded to property, industry, contract, and commercial liberty by America's founders? The Fifth Amendment, of course, guarantees that no person would "be deprived of life, liberty and property without due process of law," while the Ninth Amendment affirms that "the Enumeration in the Constitution, of certain rights, shall not be construed to deny or disparage others retained by the people."

After all the invasions of liberty and property recorded in living memory, not to mention the pages of a well-studied history, after the experience with colonial factions, a British king-in-Parliament, and so many state legislators, would statesmen committed to Lockean right be content to distill so vital a principle into two such truncated and obscure legal forms? Could the Framers of the Bill of Rights have believed that these words alone would be sufficient to save such sacred rights from the expansive tendencies exhibited by virtually all central governments at all times? And is it any wonder that so early in the history of the new nation, the Supreme Court jettisoned the natural rights philosophy that constituted the strongest philosophic support for those rights?

In the case of *Calder v. Bull* (1798), in a concurring opinion Justice Iredell set forth the argument that has proved controlling in constitutional jurisprudence. The interpretation of fundamental law, he believed, could not be turned into questions regarding natural justice or natural right, since there is no fixed standard that can determine these. "The ablest and purest men have differed upon the subject; and all that the court could properly say . . . would be, that the legislature (possessed of an equal right of opinion) had passed an act which, in the opinion of the judges, was inconsistent with the abstract principles of natural justice." Acts of legislatures are admissible, as long as they fall "within the general scope of their constitutional power," and "the court cannot pronounce . . . [any act] to be void, merely because it is, in their judgment, contrary to the principles of natural justice." It may be noted that Justice Samuel Chase, who also sat on the High Court and who had signed the Declaration of Independence, did offer "the great first principles of the social compact," i.e., "the general principles of law and reason" a seat at the legal bar in his opinion in the *Calder* case.[2]

Much recent scholarship has been devoted to examining anew the Bill of Rights and its significance for securing Locke's economic liberties against governmental interference. As generally stated, the question is whether the due process clause of the Fifth Amendment was designed to impose a "substantive" test for federal legislation, thereby protecting the rights of property and commerce from many forms of legislative action. Or would this clause merely impose a "procedural" test, thereby granting government a wider latitude for action?[3] In like fashion, scholars have now begun reassessing the importance of the Ninth Amendment in an effort to determine what role it was expected to play in protecting the rights of property against political "encroachment."[4]

I do not wish to delve more deeply into the meaning of these amendments or the debate over their contemporary juridical significance here. Suffice it to say, in the first place, that it was precisely the recent and onerous deprivation of the just rights of property that alarmed Americans and that counseled the need for national political reform. As Madison wrote to Jefferson, it was the "mutability" of the state laws regulating property that, more than anything else, sparked the reformation of 1787. No state at the time was busy imposing press censorship, issuing general writs of assistance, demanding self-incrimination, or inflicting cruel and unusual punishments. In the second place, the leading Framers, certainly Madison but also others such as James Wilson, John Dickinson, and William Livingston, as we have already seen, were firm adherents not merely of property and equal protection, but of the natural rights philosophy, the soil in which these social principles were planted. Many of those who came to oppose ratification, such as George Mason, Richard Henry Lee, and Elbridge Gerry, were equally committed to this philosophy (feeling it was not sufficiently encapsulated in the proposed frame).

Partly on the prompting of Jefferson, partly honoring a campaign pledge made during his congressional election campaign, and also owing to his own changed opinion, Madison introduced a proposed Bill of Rights. Echoing the sentiments that most resolutely rang out at the Revolution, Madison's proposal affirmed "that government is instituted, and ought to be exercised for the benefit of the people; which consists in the enjoyment of life and liberty, with the right of acquiring and using property, and generally of pursuing and obtaining happiness and safety."

He also demanded "that the people have an indubitable, unalienable and indefeasible right to reform or change their government, whenever it be found adverse or inadequate to the purposes of its institution." The rough language that would be spun into the Ninth and Tenth amendments clearly stated that "the exceptions . . . made in favor of particular rights, shall not be construed as to diminish the just importance of other rights retained by the people; or as to enlarge the powers delegated by the constitution; but either as actual limitations of such powers, or as inserted merely for greater caution."[5]

On the same day a flurry of other proposed amendments, those adopted in the ratification conventions of Massachusetts, South Carolina, Virginia, New Hampshire, and New York, were entered into the record. On the whole, the proposals were designed to strictly delimit the authority of the national government, provide for full and fair representation, and guarantee the political and religious rights of individual Americans. In virtually identical language, Massachusetts, Virginia, New Hampshire, and New York sought an express assurance that "Congress do not grant Monopolies or erect any company with exclusive Advantages of Commerce." Each of these states as well rooted its commercial demand in a more fundamental understanding. Reprising the language George Mason incorporated into its own Declaration of Rights, Virginia insisted "that there are certain natural rights of which men, when they form a social compact cannot deprive or divest their posterity, among which are the enjoyment of life and liberty, with the means of acquiring, possessing and protecting property, and pursuing and obtaining happiness and safety."

The New York Convention put it even more succinctly when it stipulated "that the enjoyment of Life, Liberty and the pursuit of Happiness are essential rights which every Government ought to respect and preserve."[6] Even more indicative of these concerns are the various last-minute resolutions, introduced virtually as the final form of the Bill of Rights was being hammered out. The language acknowledging the natural and indefeasible rights of individuals was again repeated, as was the prohibition against the awarding of exclusive "Advantages of Commerce." In addition, the drafters of these articles, led by the gifted and able Richard Henry Lee, wanted it to be asserted "that no man or set of men are entitled to exclusive or separate public emoluments or privileges from the community, but in consideration of public services."

On 24 September 1789 Congress enacted the Bill of Rights as we know it. Writing to Patrick Henry on 27 September 1789, Richard Henry Lee flatly reported, "The English language has been carefully culled to find words feeble in their Nature or doubtful in their meaning!" And echoing Henry's own sentiments, he caustically remarked, "Your observation is perfectly just, that right without power to protect it, is of little avail." And to Francis Lightfoot Lee he wrote of the amendments: "[They are] much mutilated and enfeebled—It is too much the fashion now to look at the rights of the People, as a Miser inspects a Security, to find out a flaw. . . . it is very clear, I think, that a government very different from a free one will take place ere many years are passed."[7] In Congress, Rep. James Jackson of Georgia warned, "There is a maxim in law, and it will apply to bills of rights, that when you enumerate exceptions, that the exceptions operate to the exclusion of all circumstances that are omitted; consequently, unless you except every right from the grant of power, those omitted are inferred to be resigned to the discretion of the government."[8]

The Political Economy of Hamiltonia

Whether the anti-Federalists' fears for the fate of liberty and property sprang from a general Catonic conception of human nature (and the implacable human passion for power and preferment) or from a more historically specific estimate of certain social groupings within their society (e.g., a moneyed or mercantile interest, the war veterans, etc.), those fears and forecasts cannot be dismissed as fanciful or paranoiac delusion. In a serious sense, the American political economy in its first, formative steps was activated by something quite foreign to a conception of equal creation—or equal protection.

From the first, interested parties appealed for special privileges, though always in the name of the general welfare of all Americans. If the Progressive historians interpreted the 1787 frame as a triumph not for people's rights, but for the special interests of various propertied classes, they had ample reason for doing so. No sooner had the ink on Jefferson's parchment Declaration dried than sundry local interests began organizing into continental committees of correspondence. A national interest was indeed forming, as Charles Beard reported:

Before the formation of the constitution, Boston merchants were sending out appeals to other merchants in the several states to join in a national movement for protection; and before the new government went into effect, they were active in stirring up united action among the merchants and manufacturers of the whole country. . . . It cannot be denied that the interests seeking protection were extensive and diversified. This is conclusively shown by the petitions addressed to public bodies, by the number of influential men connected with the movement, and by the rapidity with which the new government under the Constitution responded to their demands.[9]

Within days of its opening session, the House of Representatives received a petition from the businessmen of Baltimore requesting the speedy adoption of a system of tariff measures. Shortly thereafter, similar petitions were delivered to the same body from manufacturers, mechanics, merchants, and shipbuilders in New York, Philadelphia, and Boston. As the Boston petitioners urged:

The happy period having now arrived, when the United States are placed in a new situation when the adoption of the general government gives one sovereign Legislature the sole and exclusive power of laying duties upon imports; your petitioners rejoice at the prospect this affords them . . . and they confidently hope that the encouragement and protection of American manufacturers will claim the earliest attention of the supreme Legislature of the nation.

In much the same fashion, New York's fledgling industrialists eagerly declared, "Your petitioners have long looked forward . . . to the establishment of a government which would have the power to . . . extend a protecting hand to the interests of commerce and the arts."[10] The desired tariff, it must be emphasized, was not conceived as revenue measures designed to defray the costs of government. As the Boston petition urged, "Heavy duties may be laid on such articles as are manufactured by our citizens, humbly conceiving that the impost is not solely considered by Congress as an object of revenue, but in its operation, intended to exclude such importations, and ultimately, establish these several branches of manufacture among themselves."

Just what branches of manufacture could benefit from such protective duties? The Boston petition alone cites: "rope-makers, hatters, pewterers, soap-boilers, and tallow chandlers, wool card-makers, ship-carvers, sailmakers, cabinet makers, coach-makers, tailors, cord-wainers, glue and starch makers, brass-bounders and coppersmiths."[11] Although the first duties levied explicitly for the purpose of encouraging domestic manufacturers were not adopted until 1816, the principle of protectionism was firmly embedded in the nation's first tariff law. The Tariff Act of 1789 had as its objective "the support of the government, the discharge of the debts of the United States and the encouragement and protection of manufacturers."[12] And some domestic economic interests no doubt were encouraged and protected by the modest duties imposed during year one of the experiment in republicanism.

The tariff issue, and more broadly the question of "protectionism," it should be recognized, signifies a momentous shift not only in public policy, but in America's basic philosophy. At issue was not just the sanctity of property or the inviolability of contract; at issue was the precept of equality. Stripped of all inessentials, a protective tariff is little more than a subtle species of special privilege—a form, really, of public assistance. It is a public measure that invariably benefits some individuals ultimately at the expense of others. Who benefited from the tariffs? The class of businessmen commonly called "capitalists," who would be politically "freed" from the rigors of market competition. Who had to pay for those public "benefits"? Consider the southern planters and western farmers who had to sell their produce in a free, politically unprotected market, but who had to pay artificially high prices for the manufactured goods they themselves purchased. Or take the seaport merchant or itinerant trader whose livelihood depended on the free, unrestricted flow of inexpensive European goods, or who exported goods Europeans bought with the foreign exchange earned by the sale of their goods in America. Strictly speaking, the promoters of protectionism saw their government not as a protector, but as a generous *provider*. What they wanted government to provide them with could appropriately be called welfare privilege. And in the office of the nation's first treasury secretary, these "capitalists" had a powerful benefactor.

For Alexander Hamilton, national prosperity and independence were overriding concerns, and they demanded a thriving domestic industry. For him, the interests of manufacturers and the interests of the nation were one and indivisible. With this understanding, Hamilton worked with unparalleled energy to grow America's industrial base. From his powerful position in Washington's cabinet he served as both guardian and tutor to the nation's fledgling political economy. Whatever would advance the cause of American economic growth he would count constitutionally sound. In his arguments, he showed how all interests, not just those of the northern industrialists, would benefit from active government interventions. His plan, he seriously argued, would provide for the greatest good of the greatest number of Americans. Thus he cited as one of the most important advantages of earlier industrialization "the creating, in some instances a new, and securing in all, a more certain and steady demand for the surplus of the soil."[13]

Even granted the benefit to America of industrialization, why was it necessary for government to hasten the prospect? Would not the natural processes of capital formation and the various wants of consumers direct the flow of materials and resources to the most useful enterprises? In a perfect world perhaps. But the world, as Hamilton perceived it, was anything but perfect. "If the system of perfect liberty to industry and commerce were the prevailing system of nations, the arguments which dissuade a country, in the predicament of the United States, from the zealous [i.e., the political] pursuit of manufactures would doubtless have great force. . . . But the system which has been mentioned is far from characterizing the general policy of nations."[14]

Citing the various species of foreign protectionism, Hamilton argues that reciprocity is demanded. Specifically, he names "the bounties, premiums and other artificial encouragements with which foreign nations second the exertions of their own citizens in the branches in which they are to be rivalled." He might also have coined the concept of "dumping." He writes, "It is well known . . . that certain nations grant bounties on the exportations of particular commodities, to enable their own workmen to undersell and supplant all competitors in the countries to which these commodities are sent."[15]

These and other impediments, such as the fear of undertaking new and uncertain ventures and competing with established and well-known enterprises, make it incumbent upon governments to provide sufficient inducements to domestic enterprise. Hamilton, in fact, exhibits no reticence in recommending appropriate palliatives, although, as he certainly appreciated, he would have to step gingerly over the objections of those who yet distrusted public power and who had warned incessantly against it.

The first foray, because the least open to objection, would be the tariff itself. Since the power to impose such duties was explicitly granted to the national legislature, no strong constitutional objection could arise (though they would anyway). Since the duties would also serve as a source of revenue, reducing the need to impose other, more direct taxes, few would be inclined to take issue with them. They were an efficacious means of lending aid and encouragement to domestic industry. McCoy has made the point that Hamilton's reliance on tariffs was restricted and that he much preferred other political tools to advance the cause of commerce. He nonetheless used the acceptance of this form of "subsidy" to great advantage in arguing for various other protectionist devices.[16]

A second such tool for Hamilton was the "pecuniary bounty" (in modern terminology, the ordinary business subsidy). Being the most direct form of encouragement, such bounties would increase the chance of success and so diminish the risks inherent in undertaking new and perhaps untried industrial ventures. In fact agriculture, too, could be encouraged by their aid. By granting agricultural bounties, say, for improving the productivity of farming techniques, the farmer could better compete with foreign agriculture and the manufacturer could reap the harvest of cheap and plentiful produce. And a bounty awarded to the manufacturer on the domestic produce he purchased would relieve his expenses, while at the same time encouraging the purchase of domestic produce and augmenting the farmer's income. The manipulation of commerce through the issuance of bounties would indeed conduce to the general welfare. Unlike the tariff, however, Hamilton knew that the idea of pecuniary bounties would raise great opposition, ethical as well as constitutional. With a keen eye fixed on the much-prized principle of equal protection, he craftily answered: "There is a degree of prejudice against bounties . . . from a supposition that they serve to enrich particular classes at the expense of the community. . . . This source of objection [however] equally lies against other modes of encouragement, which are admitted to be eligible."

If the nation wanted to avoid the granting of special assistance to narrow interests, Hamilton insists, it should have thought more carefully before admitting the tariff into its legal and fundamental framework. Directly addressing the constitutional objections to a broad construction and utterly confounding his old colleague's (i.e., Madison's) rash and dismissive attitude toward those anti-Federalists who saw in the general welfare clause the seed of political consolidation and expansion, Hamilton declared:

> The terms "general welfare" were doubtless intended to signify more [power] than was expressed or imported in those [clauses] which preceded; otherwise numerous exigencies incident to the affairs of a nation would have been left without a provision. The phrase is as comprehensive as any that could have been used. . . . this necessarily embraces a vast variety of particulars, which are susceptible neither of specification nor of definition. . . . It is therefore, of necessity, left to the discretion of the National Legislature to pronounce upon the objects which concern the general welfare, and for which under that description, an appropriation of money is requisite and proper. And there seems to be no . . . doubt, that whatever concerns the general interests of learning, of agriculture, of manufactures, and

of commerce, are within the sphere of the national councils, as far as regards an application of money.

Bounties are to be recommended simply because they "are a species of encouragement more positive and direct than any other, and . . . [have] a more immediate tendency to stimulate . . . new enterprises, increasing the chance of profit and diminishing the risks of loss, in the first attempts."[17] Constitutional niceties aside, the clear standard that prevailed, in the Hamiltonian political economy, was general utility. Hamilton, in fact, went on to recommend an entire panoply of "premiums" — awards granted for specific achievements in the useful arts and crafts, along with "regulations for the inspection of manufactured commodities . . . [that] would insure uniform standards of quality . . . and establish a reputation for the goods of particular domestic industries." He, too, urged his nation to undertake projects to facilitate the transportation of American goods and connect the domestic markets of America.[18]

Just two weeks before Hamilton submitted his "Report on the Subject of Manufactures" to Congress, a Society of Useful Manufactures was incorporated in the state of New Jersey. Hamilton, a principal promoter of the society, had drafted its "Prospectus." Against those who questioned the viability of such a concern, owing "to the dearness of labour and the want of Capital," Hamilton countered, again in strictly utilitarian terms:

> The last objection [the insufficiency of capital to sustain such a venture] disappears in the eye of those who are aware how much may be done by a proper application of the public Debt. Here is the resource which has been hitherto wanted. And while a direction of it to this object may be made a mean of public prosperity and an instrument of profit to adventurers in the enterprise, it, at the same time, affords a prospect of an enhancement of the value of the debt; by giving it a new and additional employment and utility.[19]

Although Hamilton was largely unsuccessful in his efforts to publicly support domestic manufacturing, and although the Society of Useful Manufactures collapsed in the panic and depression of 1792 (an episode that will be discussed shortly), his position in the cabinet enabled him to put into effect his program for funding the public debt, as well as for establishing a Bank of the United States. In the unfolding of these specific policies we can witness the full vindication of the anti-Federalists' worst fears. To appreciate the character and consequences of the Hamiltonian program, however, as well as the moral and practical response that fueled the Jeffersonian reaction to it, the historical record should be examined with some care.

The story begins with the introduction of Hamilton's "Report on the Establishment of Public Credit" in 1790. The plan had two primary objectives: to finance the public debt left over from the revolutionary war (about $50 million held by Congress and another $25 million in outstanding state debt) and to establish the credit of the United States. The latter aim, Hamilton knew, could only be achieved if America honored its fiscal obligations. The report provided for full return of outstanding interest and principal on the debt. New bonds would be issued in lieu of the various certificates that were then circulating; payment would be made in specie, and only current holders of the debt would be paid. No provisions were made for those patriots who originally held certificates of debt, but who had sold them. (Madison, in vain, introduced a resolution designed to compensate the original bondholders in recognition of their patriotic sacrifice.) Finally, the state debt would be funded on a par with the public debt, even though some states had already honored their obligations and would now be taxed to retire debts that other states had failed to honor. The assumption plan was most vehemently resisted, but Hamilton refused to submit the funding legislation alone. Finally, after eight months of debate a compromise was reached primarily between Hamilton, Madison, and Jefferson. The Funding Act of 1790 could be sent to Washington only if the government could be transferred to the Potomac and removed from New York (and the grip of the "moneyed interest").

Aside from the primary objectives voiced by Hamilton, there were others. Once implemented, the funding plan would place vast amounts of capital into the hands of the men who would best know how to employ it—the growing band of financial speculators who, Hamilton believed, would eagerly underwrite America's industrial growth. In addition, the new credit certificates (having the full resources of the government behind them) would serve as a bona fide circulating medium, boosting the money stock and, with it, the pace of business activity. By the same token, assumption of the states' debts would effectively cement the loyalty of the wealthier, more far-sighted citizens to the national government. Being public creditors they would have a keen interest in the federal government's ultimate success.

In fairness, Hamilton appealed to "the established rules of morality and justice" in defending his proposal. These, he urged, "are applicable to nations as well as to individuals. . . . [Both] are bound to keep their promises; to fulfill their engagements [and] to respect the rights of property which others have acquired under contracts with them." In stunning moral tones, he went on: "Without this there is an end of all distinct ideas of right or wrong, justice or injustice, in relation to society or government. There can be no such thing as rights, no such things as property or liberty; . . . [without this] everything must float on the variable and vague opinions of the governing party.''[20]

The funding plan, however, was just a start. If the creation of venture capital was what was needed, then a formidable credit institution, i.e., a bank, was necessary. In December of 1790, Hamilton submitted his historic plan for the creation of a Bank of the United States (BUS). It was to be privately owned and operated, but the federal government would: (1) write the bank's founding charter, (2) subscribe to one-fifth of its stock (amounting to five thousand shares, or $2 million), and (3) enjoy a one-fifth representation on the bank's board of governors. The remaining twenty thousand shares would be offered to the public at $400 per share.

The bank notes, like the public debt certificates, would also serve as a uniform circulating medium. The bank would issue loans to industry and government; in return, it would be understood that all of the resources and powers of the central government would stand squarely behind the bank's success. Initially, the government would float a new loan overseas to pay for its share of the stock subscription. It did so, and in July 1791 the remaining twenty thousand shares went on the block. These were the twin plans for establishing the credit and promoting the industrial growth of the new nation. The results of Hamilton's labors bear examination. The saga begins long before the introduction of Hamilton's two momentous reports and centers around the matter of the public debt. As a result of the long delay in retiring the debt, many original holders of the state and federal securities sold them to pay off debts or raise much-needed money—most often at heavily discounted rates. Northern speculators, realizing that the notes would one day be recalled and seeing the opportunity for vast profits, purchased the bonds (often for as little as five cents on the dollar). On the whole, however, uncertainties kept speculative activity to a minimum.

After 1786, the talk of national political reform increased interest in the debt, and, as James Ferguson reports, by the time the Constitution was ratified, debt stock was selling at about twenty-four cents of par value. By December 1789 (a month before the publication of Hamilton's funding plan) prices climbed to forty-five and fifty cents on the dollar.[21] The burst of speculation triggered at this time exceeded anything that had come before. And yet, it merely represented the take-off stage of what would become a national mania. What sparked the speculative fires? Was it blind gambling on the part of a wealthy minority? Yes and no. Though the lion's share of the eventual profits went to a relatively few speculators, they were not really gambling.

The new nation's capitol in 1790 was closely situated to the nation's young capitalists—both sharing the thoroughfares of lower New York City. It was a cozy arrangement, particularly for those who wanted to play the emerging money markets. Two such individuals were Daniel Parker and Andrew Craigie. In May of 1788, Craigie advised his associate, Parker: "The public debt affords the best field in the world for speculation, but it is a field in which strangers may easily be lost. I know of no way of making safe speculations but by being associated with people who from their official situation know all present and can aid future arrangements wither for or against the funds."[22]

The advice would pay off. But because most of the public debt had already been bought up, new opportunities for profit would have to involve the thorny problem of the states' debt issues. As late as 1790, Craigie, having received inside information regarding the assumption plan, was able to acquire South Carolina notes at seven cents on the dollar. But given the controversy surrounding assumption, the risks were great. Would Hamilton propose full or partial payment? What opposition awaited his plan in Congress? What the speculators needed was a certain someone. He would have to combine an intimate knowledge of public policy with a blinding ambition for fortune and adventure.

Such a man was William Duer. A shrewd and unscrupulous speculator in his own right, Duer was employed as Hamilton's undersecretary. Throughout his tenure in office, William Duer actively engaged in securities trading, both through his own firm of Duer and Flint and on behalf of important foreign interests (e.g., Brissot and Claviere of France and Von Straphorts and Hubbard of Amsterdam). With a complete knowledge of Hamilton's plans and Congress's progress, Duer and his associates were relieved of much of the risk that accompanied public speculation. By the time he left public service, he had essentially embezzled (by obtaining and selling previously redeemed treasury warrants) or lost track of nearly a quarter-of-a-million dollars. Oliver Wolcott, comptroller of the treasury, would discover the shortage, but the government would never recoup the lost fortune.

Though he left the Treasury Department early in 1790, Duer managed to maintain his envied role among New York's speculators. Hamilton, who was not himself a crooked or corrupt public servant and who did not personally profit from his position of public trust, tolerated a great deal where Duer was concerned. As the historian John C. Miller has written, he was willing to grant some measure of latitude to the moneyed interest who, after all, "were men after his own heart."

> Hamilton saw that if capitalism were to prosper, capitalists were indispensable. . . . [He] believed that one of the principle duties of a government dedicated to the general welfare was to foster capitalism

by affording every facility to the accumulation of wealth, and since the United States had few large aggregations of capital, Hamilton thought that the government ought to take an active part in creating wealth and in making sure that it got into the hands of those able to make the best use of it.[23]

Incorporated into Hamilton's financial plans, in fact, were several mechanisms that worked to keep securities prices high and the stock speculators happy. Thus the funding plan contained provisions for a "sinking fund," the invention of Robert Walpole. It was a pool of money, to be used at the secretary's discretion, ostensibly designed to purchase and thereby draw down the national debt. Because it would furnish a greater demand for debt stock, it would also prop up sinking bond prices, assuring public creditors a continued high return on their investments.[24]

In drawing up his proposal for a national bank, Hamilton took a further step toward assuring high bond prices. Anticipating a major outpouring of investor interest in the new project, yet appreciating the scarcity of hard cash, the secretary proposed that the purchase price of each share of bank stock be made with $300 in federal debt certificates and a down payment of $25 specie (on the remaining $100 balance). Since it was anticipated that the bank stock would yield an annual interest of 8 percent (or more), the price, from the investor's point of view, was right provided, that is, he could get his hands on a sufficient amount of debt securities.

As anticipated, the bank plan touched off a wave of furious buying and more, a frantic hunt for available securities. Capturing the excitement of the times, Nathan Schachner writes:

> Since the largest part of the payment could therefore be made only in the certificates, a wild scramble followed for their possession; and, as Hamilton had expected, their price began to soar. But most of the public debt had already fallen into the hands of far-sighted moneyed men. It was therefore necessary to unearth those old certificates of state and national origin which had not yet been converted into the new funds. Once again swift packet boats and expresses raced south to the hinterlands to ferret out the holdings still to be found in isolated communities, where their true value was not known.[25]

Hamilton had been proved right on all counts. The interest generated by the announced sale of bank stock was unprecedented in the nation's history, and that interest sent the prices of federal stock soaring. Of the sale of bank stock, Schachner says:

> On July 4, 1791, at eleven in the morning, the eagerly awaited moment arrived. In Philadelphia, New York, Boston, Baltimore and Charleston, the moneyed men gathered at the offices where the books were held, long before the magic hour. As the clock struck and the books were opened, they rushed forward in a solid mass, clamoring their offers and demanding instant attention. Within half an hour all books were closed. . . . The stock was subscribed and oversubscribed, and double the amount would have been immediately snatched up had it been available.

The spectacular success of the subscription sale set the stage for the next round of speculative frenzy. Within a week, half-shares of the bank "scrip" (issued upon receipt of the down payment and the necessary amount of federal stock) were being traded in the New York securities markets. "The speculation mania, which now rages in the United States for Bank Stock," cried a Boston newspaper, "is unequalled by anything ancient or modern." Writing of his travels to Madison on August 14, Henry Lee reported "one continuous scene of stock gambling; agriculture, commerce and even the fair sex relinquished to make way for unremitted exertion in this favorite pursuit." Throughout July and August the bank scrip rose steadily in price. By mid-August, "the craze had reached its peak. In New York the scrip sold for $280; in Philadelphia it soared to $320. . . . By August 12th the bubble had burst. The scrip fell . . . to $150. On the same toboggan slid the government debt."[26]

Hamilton, true to form, sprang into action. Drawing $150,000 from the sinking fund, he authorized William Seton, cashier of the Bank of New York, to make purchases of federal stock to bolster prices and restore investor confidence. Seton used more than one-third of the funds, $52,000, to relieve William Duer of his overstretched holdings. Prices soon firmed, and by October it was business as usual.

Undaunted by his near brush with financial ruin, the irrepressible Duer resumed his operations, growing bolder (and for a while richer) with each move. Duer's next object of speculation would be the Bank of New York. Though he would eventually gain a corner in the bank stock, he was primarily interested in reaping a windfall by buying and selling the securities at the most propitious moments. From his position in the market, he could circulate rumors, opinions, or "privileged information" to the public thereby influencing trading patterns, while secretly operating from more accurate information. At one point rumors were being spread to the effect that the Bank of New York would soon merge with the Bank of the United States. Such a move could only boost Bank of New York stock. "In his public dealings," Robert Sobel writes, "Duer stated that the BUS-Bank of New York merge was inevitable; privately, he was betting against it. And all the while, he used Craigie, Claviere and the Dutch group to aid in the creation of his private fortune." He might buy up bank scrip with one partner, bidding the prices up with his associates' money, while quietly selling his own shares short.

The wild profits that could be made by trading bank stock fed the speculative fires as nothing else had. Fever turned to frenzy: "Scriptomania," a term coined to describe the frantic dealings in public securities, turned to "Bancomania." And soon the bank boom of 1791 was on. "Duer's activities in Bank of New York stock set the stage for the bancomania," Sobel reports; "talk of incorporating the Million Bank of the State of New York raised the curtain." Its charter provided for an eventual merger with the Bank of New York. "To the average speculator, the meaning was clear: The Bank of New York would merge with the Million Bank, prior to be taken over by the BUS. The shares of all three institutions were bound to rise." The Tammany Bank, capitalized at $200,000 came next, followed by the Merchants Bank, with a capitalization of $100,000. Subscriptions were quickly recorded, and it looked like New York would soon have five banks feeding investment capital into the fledgling economy.

Meanwhile, Duer, buoyed by a string of stock market successes, launched a new project. He would invite interested parties to place their wealth in his hands, offering them as much as 6 percent a month for their faith (and, possibly, their life's savings). The "6% Club," as it came to be called, boasted some of the most prestigious citizens of the day, though it also numbered ordinary merchants, widows, farmers—anyone interested in reaping swift and "certain" financial gains.

All went well, for a while. Then, in March 1792, the bottom fell out. Stock prices tumbled, credit tightened, and Duer, unable to obtain funds to meet his obligations at any rate, crashed. His failure shook New York to its very foundations. "The failure of Mr. Duer," wrote a concerned citizen, "has laid the foundation for others, which affect the community in a manner never experienced in the country before. The fulfillment of individual engagements is not only suspended, but private and public confidence has received such a blow as may eventually stagger the stability of the government." A New York judge, Thomas Jones, echoing the concern, wrote: "Colonel Duer has failed for they say three million dollars, and has taken almost every person in the city, from the richest merchants to even the poorest women and the little shopkeepers. . . . How it will end God only knows; it has put a stop to general business and money is so exceedingly scarce that his runners go about with his printed notes indorsed and signed, but no sum inserted, and if they could find a lender, they give four percent a month and put it in the note."[27]

It was estimated that $7 million was lost in New York, Philadelphia, and Boston alone—and with it, countless jobs and businesses. "New building was suspended, workmen roamed the streets in idleness, and farm produce went begging at any price." As for Duer, on 23 March 1792, he was incarcerated in debtor's prison as was the custom. There he died seven years later. The nation's first financial depression, the "Panic of '92," was considered serious but was not of long duration. On June 18, the *National Gazette* was to report: "The shock at the time was very severe, but of short continuance. Credit is again revived—and prosperity once more approaches in sight."[28]

The Jeffersonian Reaction

Hamilton had conceived of a partnership between business and government, the private sector and the public. Working together, he believed, important industrial projects could be underwritten, needed capital supplied, and men and materials put to work for the benefit of economic growth and expansion. Instead, the political economy he created crashed on the shoals of speculative greed. The experiment failed, and little of any productive use had come of it. The crash of 1792 consumed the various bank projects—as well as the Society of Useful Manufactures, which never got off the ground. Whatever credit and capital were created had fueled the fires of speculation, not productive industrial or commercial growth. As Jefferson himself observed, writing on 29 August 1791: "Ships are lying idle at the wharfs, building are stopped, capital withdrawn from commerce, manufactures, arts and agriculture, to be employed in gambling, and the tide of public prosperity, unparalleled in any country is arrested in its course and suppressed by the rage of getting rich in a day."[29]

For Madison as well, these must have been very dark days, indeed. Writing to Jefferson just six days after the Bank of the United States subscription sale, he sadly reported:

> The plan of the bank gives a moral certainty of gain to the subscribers with scarce a physical possibility of loss. the subscriptions are consequently a mere scramble for so much public plunder which will be engrossed by those already loaded with the spoils of individuals. . . .

It pretty clearly appears in what proportions of the public debt lies in the country, what sort of hands hold it, and by whom the people of the United States are to be governed.

To Henry Lee, Madison wrote the following month, "The stock jobbers will become the pretorian band of the new government, at once its tools and its tyrants; bribed by its largesse, and overawing it by clamors and combinations."[30] It was the prediction another Lee, and so many anti-Federalists, had made from the start. That interested parties, organized as factions, would seek special privileges and emoluments, Madison had no doubt. That they could combine so quickly, in so extended a territory, to defeat all competing parties, at whose expense they would profit—and all under the general welfare provision of the Constitution—this was beyond him. And that all of this would be accomplished by the work of a single, well-positioned public servant, the man with whom he had so arduously collaborated to bring the new government into being, that, perhaps, was the unkindest cut of all.

To counter the dangerous trend Jefferson and Madison mobilized their considerable energies. The compromise they reached with Hamilton, while allowing for the funding and assumption plans, would ultimately sever the seat of power from the seat of speculation and the reach of the moneyed interest. Following the publication of Hamilton's bank plan, both Virginians acted promptly. Revisiting the ground he thought he had fully covered in *Federalist* 41, Madison repudiated Hamilton's construction of the general welfare clause. Taking to the floor of Congress, he warned:

> If Congress can apply money indefinitely to the general welfare, and are the sole and supreme judges of the general welfare, they may take the care of religion into their own hands; they may establish teachers in every State, county, and parish, and pay them out of the public treasury; they may take into their own hands the education of children, establishing in like manner schools throughout the Union, they may undertake the regulation of all roads, other than post roads. In short, everything, from the highest object of State legislation, down to the most minute object of police, would be thrown under the power of congress; for every object I have mentioned would admit the application of money, and might be called, if Congress pleased, provisions for the general welfare.[31]

"To take a single step beyond the boundaries thus specially drawn around the powers of Congress," Jefferson argued in a letter to Washington on the constitutionality of the bank plan, ''is to stake possession of a boundless field of power, no longer susceptible of any definition.'' Conceding that the Constitution authorized the government to ''lay and collect taxes for the purpose of providing for the general welfare,'' he went on to argue that

> the laying of taxes is the *power,* and the general welfare the *purpose* for which the power is to be exercised. they are not to lay taxes *ad libitum* for any purpose they please; but only to pay the debts or provide for the welfare of the Union. In like manner, they are not to do anything they please to provide for the general welfare, but only to lay taxes for that purpose. To consider the latter phrase, not as describing the purpose of the first, but as giving a distinct and independent power to do any act they please, which might be for the good of the Union, would render all the preceding and subsequent enumerations of power completely useless.[32]

Jefferson went on to take a similarly strict construction of the ''necessary and proper'' clause, arguing that if ''conveniency'' were made the test of necessity and ''such a latitude of construction be allowed to this phrase as to give any non-enumerated power, it will go to every one, for there is not one which ingenuity may not torture into a convenience in some instance or other. . . . It would swallow up all the delegated powers and reduce the whole to one power.''[33]

Thus for both Jefferson and Madison, the first line of defense was the constitutional line; in vain, they hoped it would be a line the federal government would not cross. Feeling the need for further action and feeling the sting of the powerful voice raised on behalf of federalism in Fenno's *Gazette of the United States,* Jefferson and Madison saw the need to found a countervailing organ of public opinion. This they did, persuading Madison's schoolmate, Philip Freneau, to come to Philadelphia and edit the new *National Gazette*. They eventually went on to build a triumphant majority party of their own, the Democratic Republican party that, by 1801, would capture the reins of national power. The institution Madison had argued could never be in an extended republic was the only institution these Virginians could rely on to save liberty from the excesses of power.[34]

Pocock, in answering Gordon Wood and exposing the continuing influence exerted by classical republicanism after 1787, pointed precisely to the Jeffersonian reaction to Hamiltonian finance: ''To a quite remarkable degree, the great debate on his [Hamilton's] policies in the 1790's was a replay of Court-Country debates seventy and a hundred years earlier.''[35] He is unquestionably correct. In the first place, the pattern to which the Jeffersonians were responding bore a much closer resemblance to the machinations of Walpole than to, say, the stark assault on liberty waged by Parliament between 1763 and 1776, or the petty contests for spoils in the colonial period, or the desecration of property and contract perpetrated by the several states during the Critical Period. The events that flowed from the South Sea bubble mirror those that followed the adoption of Hamilton's bank plan in nearly every detail. A feeding frenzy of speculation, prompted by the lure of publicly supported enterprises and emoluments and producing little more than financial panic and depression, is the unifying thread.

The Jeffersonian reaction, moreover, parallels the Catonic outcry in at least one critical detail. The revisionists are correct in pointing to the common concern over corruption voiced by both opposition camps. The checks and balances that could be effected only by a separation of executive and legislative powers were uppermost in the minds of Trenchard and Gordon and Jefferson. In conversations with Washington, the secretary of state repeatedly warned of the worrisome effect Hamilton's schemes were having on the independent departments of government. The treasury secretary's plans were not only "withdrawing our citizens from the pursuits of commerce, manufactures, buildings, and other branches of useful industry, to occupy themselves and their capitals in a species of gambling," he told his president they "had introduced [their] poison into the government itself." No, the executive department was not corrupting the legislative department by granting of places, posts, pensions, and public contracts, as Cato had charged Walpole with doing. None of this was necessary. The lure of speculative profits alone had been sufficient to alter the course of legislation and allow "the executive . . . to swallow . . . up the legislative branch." It was open knowledge

> that particular members of the legislature, while those laws were on the carpet, had feathered their nests with paper, had then voted for the laws, and constantly since lent all the energy of their talents, and instrumentality of their offices, to the establishment and enlargement of this system. . . . [In short, it is popularly believed that] there was a squadron devoted to the nod of the Treasury, doing whatever he had directed . . . [and that] a regular system for forming a corps of interested persons, who should be steadily at the orders of the Treasury [was being plotted].[36]

This deep regard for liberty, in the republican sense, however, should not be construed so as to deny or disparage Jefferson's concern for liberty, in the Lockean sense, i.e., in the sense of conceiving of individuals as equally entitled to pursue their lives, acquire, use, and dispose of their property, and enjoy equal protection under law.

Jefferson, as is well known, did extol the virtuous life more easily attainable to the husbandman than to the mechanic. And he found the agrarian manner preferable to the urban and commercial way of life. "Those who labor on the earth," he wrote, "are the chosen people of God . . . whose breasts He has made His peculiar deposit for substantial and genuine virtue." Among all classes of men, he wrote Jay in 1785, "cultivators . . . are the most vigorous, the most independent and the most virtuous."[37] But Jefferson would not let his personal preferences interfere with Americans' free exercise of choice. It was in a letter to G. K. van Hogendorp, written at the same time, that Jefferson volunteered the view that he would have his countrymen "practice neither commerce nor navigation . . . [and] long keep our workmen in Europe." But then he adds: "This is theory only, and a theory which the servants [i.e., governors] of America are not at liberty to follow. Our people have a decided taste for [these commercial forms]. They take this from their mother country; and their servants are in duty bound to calculate all their measures on this dictum: we wish to do it by throwing open all the doors of commerce and knocking off its shackles."[38]

Aware of the navigation policies of the European nations, Jefferson despairingly cautioned, however: "As this cannot be done for others, unless they will do it to us, and there is no great probability that Europe will do this, I suppose we shall be obliged to adopt a system which may shackle them in our ports as they do us in theirs."[39] Personal views aside, Jefferson would give the fullest vent possible to the untrammeled choices and self-directed energies of individuals. With Madison, he would afford greatest latitude to the "diversity in the faculties of men, from which the rights of property originate." And he would steadfastly recognize the right of people to walk in whatever direction their private wills might suggest to them. And all should be protected in the just enjoyment of their property and private rights. As he would write to Du Pont de Nemours in 1816, "I believe that a right to property is founded in our natural wants, in the means with which we are endowed to satisfy these wants, and the right to what we acquire by those means without violating the similar rights of other sensible beings." No one, therefore, "has a right to obstruct another, exercising his faculties innocently for the relief of sensibilities made a part of his nature." Since this pertains to all people as such, he concludes, "the majority oppressing an individual, is guilty of a crime, abuses its strength, and by acting on the law of the strongest breaks up the foundations of society."[40]

John Adams, the Federalist, most eloquently summed up the precept when he said, "It is agreed that the end of all government is the good and ease of the people in a secure enjoyment of their rights, without oppression; but it must be remembered, that the rich are people as well as the poor; that they have rights as well as others; that they have as clear and as sacred a right to their large property as others have to theirs which is smaller; that oppression to them is as possible and as wicked as to others.''

And it is Jefferson the Jeffersonian republican who gave official voice to the sentiment when, in his First Inaugural, he proclaimed: ''Though the will of the majority is in all cases to prevail, that will, to be rightful, must be reasonable; that the minority possess their equal rights, which equal laws must protect, and to violate would be oppression.'' He took the occasion to urge his countrymen and well-wishers to entertain ''a due sense of our equal right to the use of our own faculties, to the acquisitions of our industry . . . resulting not from birth but from our actions.'' From this vision of equal creation, Jefferson reaches a social vision rooted in equal protection: ''A wise and frugal government, which shall restrain men from injuring one another, which shall leave them otherwise free to regulate their own pursuits of industry and improvement, and shall not take from the mouth of labor the bread it has earned. This is the sum of good government.'' And along with moral rectitude and civic virtue, this is also ''necessary to close the circle of our felicity.'' And so he calls upon government to provide ''equal and exact justice to all men, of whatever state or persuasion, religious or political.'' And it should provide all this with ''economy in the public expense, that labor may be lightly burdened.'' And so that public faith be preserved, he called for ''the honest payment of our debts.''[41]

Thomas Jefferson and the Case for Capitalism

The liberalism of Jefferson's republicanism should be manifest. But what precisely are the roots of this liberalism, and in what measure may it be symptomatic of an emerging capitalism? This is an important question suggested by Joyce Appleby. Questioning the republican revisionists' thesis that saw, in Jeffersonianism, the embodiment of continuity with the republican past, Appleby ably argued that Jefferson himself shared the liberal outlook, particularly in his warm regard for laissez faire. Interestingly, she could argue this without any reference to Locke. The classical republican and natural rights philosophies aside, there was another ideology that Appleby found operating on eighteenth-century American culture.[42] Its roots lay in the commercial revolution of the 1690s, which had resulted in a revolution in economic thinking. Left to its own devices, the free, unfettered market would best ''regulat[e] economic life, provid[e] . . . necessary information, encourag[e] . . . long-range planning, and reward . . . ingenuity and efficiency . . . as the desire to enhance purchasing power replaced the traditional propensity of the poor to work only long enough to meet subsistence demands."[43]

This ideological model by Jefferson's day had been distilled in the writings of a Frenchman, Antoine Destutt de Tracy. Tracy authored two works, both of which Jefferson translated into English for his countrymen. And the Virginian regarded the second, *A Treatise on Political Economy* (1817), as nothing less than "the best elementary book on the principles of government" and hoped it would be esteemed "the most precious gift the present age had received." Tracy and Jefferson, Appleby concedes, voiced strong reservations about paper money, bank companies, and public debt (all instruments of modern capitalism). But this does not make classical humanists of either one: "Unlike the Country party critics of England's funded debt, Tracy [and Jefferson] fired at his target with guns newly cast in the *foundry of modern utilitarianism.*" What utility recommended was laissez faire. Summing up the new outlook, Appleby advised: Government "could contribute to progressive economic development by freeing trade and protecting property rights—those of the worker who owns himself and those of the capitalists who set others to work. . . . Free land and free trade spelled progress and prosperity for nations."[44]

Critical here is the utilitarian ethic that Appleby sees as informing both Tracy's and Jefferson's political principles. In *Capitalism and a New Social Order,* her fullest treatment of the new economic ideology, she writes, "The capitalism in my title of course refers to a way of organizing the economy—a particular system for producing and distributing the material goods that sustain and embellish life."[45] Gone are all concerns and conceptions of the immutable and indefeasible rights of man, as presented in Jefferson's *Declaration.* Gone is the absolute, moral basis for determining the origins, ends, and limits of government. In their place emerges a single consideration: the calculus of prudence.

The pressing question, from my standpoint, is this: Would a derivation of the powers of government from Lockean natural right produce the same political architecture as that drawn from the foundry of utility? What practical economic calculation enabled Tracy or Jefferson (or "Cato," who also urged laissez faire) to discount national banks and public debts? What imaginable measure of power could government *not* assume, given enough time and a mind keen to the advantages that could flow from political interventions (such as tariff barriers, monopoly charters, internal improvements, and other industrial encouragements)? "Instrumental, utilitarian, individualistic, egalitarian, abstract and rational," Appleby concluded, "the liberal concept of liberty was everything that the classical republican concept was not.'' Perhaps, but it was many things Locke's concept of liberty was not as well.[46]

Locke, indeed, had contributed to the economic discussion of his day, as we saw much earlier. And his contributions invariably fell on the side of the natural market mechanisms. But in Lockeanism we have an underlying philosophy of right that itself flows more immediately into the precincts of power. Questions of utility are important, and the science of economics is as useful a field for investigation and as pertinent to the well-being of communities as is the science of politics. But by the Lockean view, at least, the "fundamentals of politics," the laws of God and nature are controlling, for they emerge out of a steady view of human nature, a view predicated on the role of reason in human affairs and the responsibility that attaches to a free agent's will and relation to a creator God.

On the surface, it was neither economic utility nor natural right that formed the basis for Jefferson's assault on the Hamiltonian political economy. He reached first for constitutional provisions and went on to emphasize the tendency of Hamilton's politics to corrupt the political process (a concern of classical republicanism). Jefferson did see the government-business partnership as eminently counterproductive. Jefferson shared Locke's distaste for the nonindustrious rich, who consumed themselves in gaming and idleness. None of this could productively contribute to the satisfaction of human want. The pivotal point of contention can be gleaned from Jefferson's practical objections to Hamilton's bank (and the train of events it engendered). Hardly one to advocate legal barriers to the business of banking, Jefferson would write in 1813: "Let us have banks. . . . Let those . . . among us, who have a monied capital, and who prefer employing it in loans rather than otherwise, set up banks, and give cash or national bills for the notes they discount." However, he added, "no one has a natural right to the trade of a money lender, but he who has money to lend."[47] It is when governments whet the appetites of moneyed men with the lure of certain profits that needed capital is diverted from the channels of commerce to the cavernous depths of speculative frenzy.

Again, the evil was not speculation as such. Investments in land, commerce, even joint stock companies were laudable undertakings. Such activities enable the community to increase its store of wealth, Jefferson and his circle believed. But the paper speculation that was so rife at the time drew needed funds out of the productive economy, leaving useful enterprises without sufficient capital. As Jefferson would write later, it is foolish "to believe that legerdemain tricks upon paper can produce as solid wealth as hard labor in the earth. . . . It is an idle dream to believe in a philosopher's stone which is to turn everything into gold, and to redeem man from the original sentence of his Maker, 'in the sweat of his brow shall he eat his bread.' "[48]

All practical calculations notwithstanding, it is clear that Jefferson and Madison, no less than the anti-Federalists, saw in the Hamiltonian political economy an egregious species of special privilege and a commensurate measure of human subjugation. This was the moral element appended to the Jeffersonian critique, and it was rooted in the Lockean precept of equal protection. The rich and well-born were entitled to no exclusive privileges, so long as such privileges could come only at their neighbors' expense.

But what about those honest neighbors, especially in their time of genuine need? The dishonest interests of the rich and well-born aside, ought those genuinely deserving of assistance not receive a helping hand from their public servants? This issue was raised early in the question of "national donations." In 1792 a bill was introduced in Congress to grant bounties to the financially strapped cod fisheries of New England. Two years later, Congress adopted a bill providing $15,000 for the relief of French refugees who had escaped the horrors of a slave insurrection in San Domingo and had found shelter in Baltimore and Philadelphia. In 1796, Congress debated a measure to relieve fire victims in Savannah.

Locke, as many of his contemporaries, had made a careful distinction between the deserving and nondeserving poor. As shown in Chapter 5 he benevolently recommended assistance to the first class, though, as shown in Chapter 6, he objected to the employment of political remedies to relieve that class's distress. The principle of equal protection and the strict ends and limits Locke placed on government precluded any allowance for public "charity." Private charity, the Baconian prospect of material improvement, and the biblical prospect of happier tidings in the afterlife were all Locke could offer the lower ranks.

In America perhaps other forms of relief could be furnished. The Codfisheries Act of February 1792 was adopted into law. Madison voted for it in Congress, and Jefferson authored an essay in support of its adoption.[49] Although predicated on the powers granted Congress under the commerce clause, the implications for the general welfare clause were raised at the time. A single grant of bounties under the general welfare clause, Hugh Williamson of North Carolina (a member of the Convention of 1787) pointed out, will, "in the hands of a good politician . . . supersede every part of our constitution and leave us in the hands of time and chance." Capturing the letter and spirit of equal protection, William Giles of Virginia said even more emphatically, bounties are "nothing more than Governmental thefts committed upon the rights of one part of the community, and an unmerited Governmental munificence to the other." Pointing to the principles of 1776, he warned, "In this country and under this Government, they present an aspect peculiarly dreadful and deformed."

The act for the relief of the French refugees from San Domingo was also enacted by Congress. Congress found constitutional support for the measure not in the general welfare power, but in the debt-paying power. Payments were to be credited against the loans due to the French Republic and would cease should France refuse the condition. On this question, Madison joined Giles in opposition. It would, said Madison, be a dangerous precedent. Nor could Madison "lay his finger on that article of the Federal Constitution which granted a right to Congress of expending on objects of benevolence the money of their constituents." His fellow Virginian, John Nicholas, concurred. "Though to bestow the money of their constituents on an act of charity might be laudable, it was yet beyond their authority."

The third bill, calling for an appropriation of $20,000 for relief of Savannah fire victims, was supported under the general welfare provision of the Constitution, and it was soundly defeated. Congress here heeded Giles's advice: "The House should not attend to what generosity and humanity required but what the Constitution and their duty required." For, as John Nicholas said, "if the General Welfare was to be extended to objects of charity, it was undefined indeed." By 1812, a similar measure, an appropriation of $50,000 for earthquake victims in Caracas, Venezuela, would be enacted into law with "practically no debate in the House or Senate." John C. Calhoun, for one, took his stand in the name of "the sacred cause of distant and oppressed humanity."[50]

Jefferson presumably would have been expected to oppose all such "donations." In the first place, the mere capacity or financial condition that would enable some in society to assist others formed no warrant for public taking. As he wrote in 1816, "To take from one, because it is thought that his own industry and that of his fathers has acquired too much, in order to spare to others, who, or whose fathers have not exercised equal industry and skill, is to violate arbitrarily the first principle of association, the *guarantee* to everyone of a free exercise of his industry, and the fruits acquired by it." But, more deeply, it is Jefferson's resolute sense of the "natural limits of the laws" that militates against the principle of public taking. In yet another formulation that bears a stark resemblance to the philosophy and prose of Locke, Jefferson wrote in 1816:

> Our legislators are not sufficiently apprized of the rightful limits of
> their powers; that their true office is to declare and enforce only our
> natural rights and duties, and to take none of them from us. No man
> has a natural right to commit aggression on the equal rights of an-

other; and that is all from which the laws ought to restrain him; every man is under the natural duty of contributing to the necessities of the society; and this is all the laws should enforce on him; and no man having a natural right to be the judge between himself and another, it is his natural duty to submit to the umpirage of an impartial third. When the laws have declared and enforced all this, they have fulfilled their functions, and the idea is quite unfounded, that on entering into society we give up any natural rights.[51]

But it is not enough to consider the sentiments of a sage in the final years of his life, much less the fine rhetoric prepared for an inaugural celebration. Arguably, what matters more is action—action at the moment it is demanded. Hamilton's financial plans did not whip Jefferson and Madison into a "Catonic" fury. Being political insiders and looking to the long range, they registered their protests and built their party. Their backing of the Codfisheries Act of 1792, not to mention Jefferson's purchase of Louisiana and a grudging endorsement of other worthy national projects (e.g., the Cumberland Road and public education), arguably supports Appleby's case. Such endorsements point to a pragmatic and utilitarian bent of mind, rather than a resolute commitment to philosophic scruple—at least to Locke's. Prudence, rather than principle, as Appleby suggests, would quickly gain ground in the new nation.

But there did arise in Hamilton's time a voice that harked back to the principles of Cato and the philosophy of Locke. Speaking as "A Farmer," George Logan, president of the Germantown Society for Promoting Domestic Manufactures, did raise a "Catonic" hue and cry against the political economy of Hamiltonia.[52] Upon learning the details of Hamilton's plan for a Society of Useful Manufactures, he wrote five letters in fervent opposition to the idea. Logan believed industry could come of age naturally. "The success of American manufactures will not depend on financial calculations, or legislative interference, but on the patronage and encouragement they may receive from patriotic citizens"—their customers. A society, such as the one Hamilton wished government to sponsor, in fact would prove injurious to the promotion of productive manufactures:

> If under a vague undefined idea of supporting the general welfare, congress is permitted to enact partial laws in favour of a few wealthy individuals, and to grant them exclusive privileges in any occupation in which their unbounded avarice may prompt them to engage, such regulations will inevitably destroy the infant manufactures of our

country, and will consign the useful and respectable citizens, personally engaged in them, to contempt and ruin.[53]

"Is it reasonable, is it just," Logan asks, "that a numerous class of citizens, whose knowledge in mechanics and manufactures, not less necessary for the support of their families, than useful to their country, should be sacrificed to a wealthy few, who have no other object in view than to add to their ill-gotten and enormous wealth?" He opposes any measure that would "subvert the principles of that equality, of which freemen ought to be so jealous." A system that "fosters . . . an inequality of fortune," he said, must be "destruct[ive] of the equality of rights." Logan does not really exhibit a familiarity with the Lockean formulations. Interestingly, he quotes Adam Smith to the same effect: "To prohibit a great people from making all that they can of every part of their produce, or of employing their flock and industry in the way that they judge most advantageous to themselves, is a manifest violation of the most sacred rights of mankind."[54]

Logan had a truly strong faith in the natural market order. "Why not," he asked, "adopt a genuine system of policy, founded on the rights of man, and at once remove the evil, by declaring a total freedom of commerce, within the United States?" Rallying to the defense of the agricultural interest, he challenges his northern neighbors. In strong Jeffersonian tones he urges that the cultivators of the soil are "the most numerous, laborious and useful class of citizens." Yet they have never come to government "to solicit partial privileges" for themselves. And he added, "The yeomanry of America only desire what they have a right to *demand*—a free unrestricted sale for the produce of their own industry; and not to have the sacred rights of mankind violated in their persons, by arbitrary laws, prohibiting them from deriving all the advantages they can from every part of the produce of their farms."[55]

George Logan's truly impassioned call for equal protection under law was ultimately not heeded. Before Jefferson's death, the nation would receive the 1824 Inaugural Address of John Quincy Adams, and America would learn how much government could and should do to expand the national economy and make room for the many who could find opportunity and promise in American life. The "American Plan," avidly promoted by John Quincy Adams and Henry Clay, followed closely in Hamilton's train and strayed still further from Lockean right.

The imperial threat had been defeated. The factious spirit that had run rampant in the colonies and then had risen again during the Critical Period (in the several states) had been exposed and rejected. But the principle of privilege had not been vanquished. The quest for privilege and preferment was, as most of the Founders could agree, sewn into the fabric of human nature. The Constitution quieted the clamors of the states. But it could not bar, for long, the pleas for public support. That the pleas came mainly from the "capitalist" class, the "moneyed" interest, should not obscure its character. By the first quarter of the nineteenth century, public works projects on a continental scale—first, roads and canals, later railroads—would be politically promoted, beginning in the several states. Following the Civil War, the principle of protectionism would be encoded into a progressive series of ever more restrictive tariff acts for the benefit of American commerce. Periods of speculation would come and go, and with them the "natural" ups and downs commonly thought to be endemic to the "business cycle." National donations were held in check to a greater extent. The enormous growth of political giving and taking would await world crisis in the twentieth century.

If it was the Framers' intent to provide equal protection for all and to bar special privilege for the few whatever their rank, if America's leading statesmen entertained the Lockean notion that it was every person's *natural right*—and *responsibility*—to provide for his or her own welfare unaided but unimpeded by a protective (hence, intrusive) public agency, then ultimately their victory escaped them. They left the requisite rights and restraints palpably unenumerated, and those principles have been treated as such ever since, as James Jackson of Georgia warned they would be. Perhaps it is as Irving Brant has written:

> [That] in all the world's history, there is nothing to compare with the pledges of human rights and freedom that have been worked into our charter of government at the great moments of national history. . . . It is only at great moments that such advances are possible. Between such moments there is most likely to be, first, a contented coasting on a path made smooth by established rights; then forgetfulness of those rights; finally, a challenge of them fired by passions made dangerous by ignorance. That leads either to loss of liberty or to the restoration of freedom through the resurging spirit of the people.[56]

After the recent commemoration of the nation's bicentennial, it is far from certain whether another such defining moment is quietly or quickly approaching. The contours of American government have certainly grown as crises of varying magnitudes have come and gone.[57] What is the significance of this from a Jeffersonian standpoint?

A theory of utility, such as Appleby attributes to Jeffersonianism, necessarily invites a loose constitutional construction. Consequently, neither Appleby nor Pangle in their analyses of eighteenth-century liberalism could paint a bright line between a "big" and a "little" liberalism, between Cato and Walpole, or Jefferson and Hamilton. In the final analysis, utility can erect no legal barrier against state growth and expansion. The most innocent exception to the absolutism of principle invites with the passage of time the unrelenting power of precedent. On the theory that time changes and so must the law, the principle of utility must passively allow public bodies to determine what will or will not conduce to the general welfare. In time, trade and tariff barriers, commercial privileges and monopoly charters, the terms and conditions of employment, even direct cash grants could all be legislatively determined to be in the public interest. Every such remedy has by now attached itself to American law in response to some series of perceived ills. What is more, an interest group theory of American democracy that seeks to serve the public interest via a never-ending train of concessions to the demands of a welter of disparate individual interests could also answer the demands of utility or democracy.[58]

If it is all "liberalism," or if it is all "capitalism," then how are we to account for the incredible antagonisms that characterized the opposition press in the age of Walpole, or the age of Hamilton? The underlying problem, I wish to suggest, is conceptual. It largely results from a rather unhistorical understanding of the contested issues—a dropping of historical context. Our post-Marxian age confounds the critical distinctions that divided and energized an earlier age. And we too casually integrate, i.e., force, into the same conceptual "bus" the morally separate and unequal political economies of Jefferson and Hamilton, "Cato" and Walpole. For us, it is all of a piece, all a matter of promoting property, economic progress, and "aggressive individualism." We call it the political economy of capitalism. If one favors free enterprise and private property, he or she is taken to favor the interests of the propertied classes and the entire grab bag of state subsidies that have historically "protected" and "promoted" the welfare of the commercial, industrial, and financial communities for the better part of the nation's history. The question is not, is it right, but will it work and do we have the votes? It is democracy at work.

But this is not how the English and American disciples of Locke viewed the world. For them, a just system of political economy, like political science itself, had to proceed from a deeper system of moral philosophy and from the metaphysical makeup of man qua man. For the American Lockeans, it was the moral principle of equal creation, originating in the dictates of nature and right reason and culminating in a precept of equal protection under law, that had to determine the origins, ends, and limits of political authority. Upon such a foundation, the young nation could build the laissez-faire economy enshrined in the Jeffersonian record. For all the reasons already given, however, such a foundation offered no support for the system Hamilton worked so arduously to construct.

Perhaps the Lockean philosophy was inscribed in the Constitution from the start, and perhaps not. (That is not a question I ever hoped to settle.) Whatever the case, it has been my intention merely to record that by 1690, such a philosophy had been made available; that owing to natural circumstance and an imperial crisis, leading Americans by 1776 availed themselves of it; and that largely owing to its neglect in the legislatures of several states down to 1787, that philosophy brought Americans to the doorstep of constitutional reformation by 1789. Embedded in Jeffersonianism, it rose again in opposition to a public policy that had largely lost Locke's moral moorings before succumbing to the corrosive sands of time and sinking into what Appleby could call from the start "the pragmatic interest group politics that became so salient so early in the life of the new nation."[59]

Conclusion: "And from That Equal Creation"

Modern scholarship too hastily identifies the politics of pragmatism, or pluralism, or American-styled capitalism with liberalism, and with Locke. These doctrines may be associated with liberalism, by common usage, but they should not be associated with Locke. The body of belief he bequeathed is not so simple to characterize. It is a complex and comprehensive philosophy of nature and man, an integrated sum of propositions that *only when taken together* define and sanction social and political activity.

For Locke, individuals come into the world with specific needs and with the potential to satisfy those needs through virtuous, i.e., rational and industrious, conduct. By the nature of things and the intent of the creator each individual is deemed accountable and responsible for his or her own welfare and life's choices. God and nature furnish the materials necessary for preservation, but individual initiative, self-mastery, and work are required before the first person can avail himself or herself of the opportunities that nature and providence provide. What one earns by the sweat of one's brow or acquires through voluntary exchange is one's own to keep and enjoy, however much, however little. And while many may meet failure and misfortune in life there is ample space in Locke's moral universe for great acts of human (or Christian) goodness. Locke's egoism is manifestly benignant. He will give encouragement to all forms of social cooperation and philanthropic aid (albeit principally for those in genuine need).

But at maturity individuals must be allowed to exercise their wills and order their actions as they see fit. To help them in attaining a fully human maturity and avoid error, vice, and life's self-inflicted misfortunes, parents and teachers must consider well the task of education (as did Locke). Maturing sons and daughters must be encouraged to diligently and industriously pursue their own chosen ends, but not by indulging any wayward inclination or unchecked passion. That is Hobbes's version of liberty; it is not Locke's.[60] For Locke, to use a well-worn phrase, liberty is not license. True liberty is ordered or structured. It is living a life in conformity with one's most honest and rational estimate of things *as they are!* And reason teaches that all people being similarly endowed and equal one with another, each must be respected in his or her free choices and actions. This moral principle is encapsulated in the doctrine of natural right. As beings of a specific nature, all the work of a common maker, individuals enjoy certain immutable liberties, including those of life, liberty, and property—and the liberty to pursue happiness in peace. And to preserve those natural and inherent rights all are imbued with a corollary right of self-defense, Locke's "executive power."

The stark need for a settled peace and an objective "umpire" to adjudicate claims of criminal or civil injury, i.e., the stark need for government, necessitate a relinquishing of this executive power. By the laws of nature and nature's God it is incumbent on everyone to preserve himself or herself and cooperate for the preservation of all by (1) entering into civil societies and (2) respecting, whether in or out of civil society, the independent wills, acts, and justly acquired goods of others. To secure their rights and uphold the limits of Lockean law, citizens must be ever vigilant against the universal tendency toward moral vice and political corruption. Public virtue is but private virtue's protection. This, indeed, is republicanism's emphasis and lasting contribution. A republican science of politics can furnish additional supports, including the structure and strictures of sovereign law and the institutions necessary to check the rise and spread of corruption. But the republican means furnished, say, by Trenchard and Gordon had to be consistent with the "true, original, extent and end" of government furnished principally by Locke.

Each individual is able to delegate to government only as much of his or her natural liberty as is consistent with the preservation of those essential ends. As no person possesses a right to trespass on the liberties and properties of others, so no government can ever claim to have derived such a measure of power *from the people.* Liberty is thus ordered (i.e., limited) in the political sense as well. The Lockean republic is governed by moral law—not the will of a domineering majority or the factious claims of so many well-organized minorities.[61] From the preeminent principle of equal creation there arises a politically governing precept: equal protection. Equal privileges for all and special privileges for none; such is the essence of Locke's political ethic. What influence did Locke's moral philosophy exert on the founding era?

If a philosophy is not simple, but complex, the same can be said of a nation. It too is not easily sized or summed up. Ultimately, we cannot say of the founding that it definitively was or was not Lockean in nature. It was Lockean, to a very large extent, but *only* to an extent. Locke's essential principles were known to the republic. Equality, Wood has written, was a "weapon to be used not only against . . . superiors, but against any . . . privilege that stood apart from the equal rights of the people. . . . all corporate grants, even when their public purpose was obvious . . . were repugnant to [this spirit of equality]." For this spirit, as one of Wood's Americans said, "does not admit of granting peculiar privileges to any body of men. . . . Equal liberty and equal privileges [in short], are the happy effect of a free government."[62] The revolutionaries understood it, as did leading Federalists, anti-Federalists, and Jeffersonians. At times, at critical times, those noble souls could dominate public affairs, truly shaping the course of human events at the founding.

But throughout the founding era there were those who did not care for or comprehend these philosophic niceties. The spirit of party and faction, indeed any "finagling" ambition, could find expression in the free air of America.[63] In the name of national progress and pride great projects could be underwritten by Republican and Federalist administrations alike. They could be promoted as internal improvements and proposed in the name of the public good, but, invariably, they were good for some (e.g., stock or land speculators) and paid for by others. Publicly supported rail and canal projects or the public sponsorship of banks on the state level, as well as the incessant cry for tariff "protection" on the federal level, attest to the pull of privilege for the quick-witted and well connected. Some might find in all this an innocent utilitarianism, in the Benthamite sense, or the rapacious progress of capitalism, in the Marxian sense, but it really represents the *renunciation* of liberalism—in the Lockean sense. Locke's politics is rooted in immutable right, not political expedience, much less special influence. His is not the type of "pragmatic interest group politics" that Appleby found "so salient so early in the life of the new nation."[64] Nor is it an intellectual opiate, a deceptive and floating superstructure beneath which a base grab for economic advantage can hypocritically hide.

Lamentably, from a Lockean perspective all those developments presaged the decline of virtue in the civic or republican sense, as well. Indeed, it is even possible to speak, in a *Pocockian* sense, of America's own Machiavellian Moment. That was, after all, the pivotal juncture when a republic's very triumph and success set in motion the process of its decline and fall, "when the polis was built up by the very forces that would destroy it."[65] Jefferson glimpsed the moment's arrival early, warning in the revolutionary era that "from the conclusion of this war we shall be going downhill,'' precisely because the citizens of the republic would ''forget themselves, but in the sole faculty of making money.''[66]

The literate elite, those whom Jefferson hoped would form an aristocracy of virtue, increasingly shifted their focus from the political to the commercial. All eyes, the Virginian could have said, were either opened or opening to the *trades* of man. The attention of the educated would now come to rest not on the law of nature and its meaning for politics, but on a science that dismally decreed the laws of economics. Americans' interest in the classical cycles receded, but the modern economic cycles persisted. The connection between government's growth and the economy's periodic plunge might be noticed, but the idea that public policy could efficiently accelerate the quest for prosperity was simply irresistible. As the endemic panics came and went the conclusion grew increasingly clear. The laissez-faire system, built to liberal specification on a base of private property and a ''market'' economy (public inflation, regulation, subsidization, and taxation aside), was inherently weak and unstable. It simply could not furnish the steady and dependable supply of goods or jobs the population demanded, nor could it furnish fairness for all those forced to live by its standard. The theoretical revisions and reformations of liberal democratic capitalism are evident, as are the remedial public programs conceived and created in their wake.[67] And it has been the perceived failures of that mixed political economy, never Lockean or free or attentive to the rule of equality, that have thrust the nation down the path of progressive reform, government growth, and the very utopian ''organic unity'' that Wood thought he saw in the ''Spirit'' of resistance by the close of 1774.

At the height of the Great Depression and in a work fittingly entitled *Jefferson: The Forgotten Man,* Congressman Samuel Pettengill made an insightful observation about the laissez-faire system. I would only paraphrase the long-forgotten Mr. Pettengill and close this way: ''When it is said that *Lockean liberalism* has failed, I must answer we have never permitted it to work.''[68]

Notes

Preface

1. Joyce Oldham Appleby, "The Social Origins of American Revolutionary Ideology," *Journal of American History* 64:4 (March 1978): 937.

Introduction: Locke in America—The State of the Debate

1. Carl L. Becker, *The Declaration of Independence: A Study in the History of Political Ideas* (New York: Vintage, 1942, orig. pub. 1922).
2. Ibid., pp. 27, 79, 72–73.
3. Quoted in ibid., pp. 25–26.
4. Becker notes James Wilson's influential "Considerations on the Nature and Extent of the Legislative Authority of the British Parliament" (1774). Wilson writes: "All men are, by nature, equal and free: no one has a right to any authority over another without his consent; all lawful government is founded in the consent of those who are subject to it; such consent was given with a view to ensure and to increase the happiness of the governed, above what they would enjoy in an independent and unconnected state of nature. The consequence is, that the happiness of the society is the first law of every government" (in Becker, *Declaration of Independence*, p. 128). For Wilson's influence on Jefferson and his countrymen, see Morton White, *The Philosophy of the American Revolution* (New York: Oxford University Press, 1978), esp. pp. 132, 134–36, 227–28, 252, 255–56. See also, Gordon Wood, *The Creation of the American Republic: 1776–1787* (New York: W. W. Norton and Company, 1972), pp. 347–48, 530–31.
5. Becker, *Declaration of Independence*, pp. 105–6, 133.
6. For the significance of Jefferson's substitution of "the Pursuit of Happiness" for Locke's "Property" in the Declaration, see Cecelia Kenyon, "Republicanism and Radicalism in the American Revolution: An Old-Fashioned Interpretation," in Jack P. Greene, ed., *The Reinterpretation of the American Revolution: 1763–1789* (New York: Harper and Row, 1968), pp. 291–320. See also White, *Philosophy of the American Revolution*, esp. pp. 217–20.
7. Emphasizing interests over ideas, Marxist and Progressive historians could view the injuries and usurpations cited in Jefferson's Declaration as so much hysterical hyperbole intended to rally Americans behind the cause of revolution. For recent historical con-

tributions emphasizing the interests of Americans in the founding era, see especially Marc Egnal, "The Pattern of Factional Development in Pennsylvania, New York, and Massachusetts, 1682–1776," in Patricia U. Bonomi, ed., *Party and Political Opposition in Revolutionary America* (Tarrytown, N.Y.: Sleepy Hollow Press, 1980), pp. 43–60, and *A Mighty Empire: The Origins of the American Revolution* (Ithaca, N.Y.: Cornell University Press, 1988). See also the "New Left" historians, including Eric Foner, *Tom Paine and Revolutionary America* (Oxford: Oxford University Press, 1976), Gary Nash, "Artisans and Politics in Eighteenth Century Philadelphia," in Margaret C. Jacob and James R. Jacob, eds., *The Origins of Anglo-American Radicalism* (London: George, Allen and Unwin, 1984), and essays by Foner, Ernst, and Nash in Alfred Young, ed., *The American Revolution: Explanations in the History of American Radicalism* (DeKalb: Northern Illinois University Press, 1976).

8. Louis Hartz, *The Liberal Tradition in America: An Interpretation of American Political Thought since the Revolution* (New York: Harcourt, Brace, World, 1955), pp. 6, 5, 62; emphasis added.

9. Ibid., pp. 60, 61, 65.

10. Ibid., p. 58.

11. Ibid., p. 10. Other consensus studies of the American founding include Clinton Rossiter, *The Political Thought of the American Revolution, Part 3, The Seedtime of the Republic* (New York: Harcourt, Brace and World, 1963), and Daniel Boorstein, *The Lost World of Thomas Jefferson* (New York: Henry Holt, 1948). White, *Philosophy of the American Revolution*, pp. 43–45, 48, 126–27, 233, persuasively argues that Benthamite utilitarianism or pragmatism (which Appleby associates *with*) is antithetical *to* the Lockean or Jeffersonian political ethic.

12. Hartz, *Liberal Tradition*, p. 10.

13. Charles A. Beard, *An Economic Interpretation of the Constitution of the United States* (New York: Macmillan, 1913). For a rejection of the Beardian thesis on Beard's own grounds, see Robert E. Brown, *Charles Beard and the Constitution: A Critical Analysis of "An Economic Interpretation of the Constitution"* (New York: W. W. Norton, 1956), and Forrest McDonald, *We the People: The Economic Origins of the Constitution* (Chicago: University of Chicago Press, 1958). McDonald thus reports that men of various economic backgrounds supported the Constitution while many with much to gain from its adoption (such as public creditors) actually came to oppose it.

14. Brown, *Charles Beard and the Constitution*, p. 3. For Beard's conclusion, see *An Economic Interpretation of the Constitution*, pp. 323–24.

15. Caroline Robbins, *The Eighteenth-Century Commonwealthman: Studies in the Transmission, Development, and Circumstances of English Liberal Thought from the Restoration of Charles II until the War with the Thirteen Colonies* (New York: Atheneum, 1968).

16. Quentin Skinner, *The Foundations of Modern Political Thought*, 2 vols. (Cambridge: Cambridge University Press, 1978).

17. J. G. A. Pocock, "Machiavelli, Harrington, and English Political Ideologies in the Eighteenth Century," in Pocock, ed., *Politics, Language, and Time: Essays on Political Thought and History* (New York: Atheneum, 1973), p. 127.

18. J. G. A. Pocock, "Civic Humanism and its Role in Anglo-American Thought," in *Politics, Language, and Time*, p. 88.

19. Ibid., pp. 86–87.

20. Ibid., p. 88.

21. C. B. Macpherson, *The Political Theory of Possessive Individualism: Hobbes to Locke* (Oxford: Oxford University Press, 1962), pp. 160–93.

22. Pocock, "Machiavelli, Harrington, and English Political Ideologies," pp. 112–14.

23. Ibid., p. 125.

24. Ibid., pp. 130, 136.

25. For a well-developed and quite persuasive argument aimed at decoupling Harrington's civic humanist perspective from the allegedly "neo-Harringtonianism" of Shaftesbury and the exclusion Whigs, see Michael Zuckert, *Natural Rights and the New Republicanism* (Princeton N.J.: Princeton University Press, 1994), chap. 6. Zuckert sees Shaftesbury not so much as the champion of civic virtue, the theoretical defender of the independent citizen whose personality finds fulfillment in the act of political participation, but as a practical political radical fighting to preserve England's ancient liberties against an immediate threat: Stuart Catholicism and absolutism.

26. Ibid., pp. 144–45.

27. J. G. A. Pocock, *The Machiavellian Moment: Florentine Political Thought and the Atlantic Republican Tradition* (Princeton, N.J.: Princeton University Press, 1975), pp. 425, 486.

28. Ibid., p. 502.

29. Ibid., pp. 440, 456, cf. 453–54.

30. Ibid., p. 487. This process is nicely traced in Albert O. Hirschman, *The Passions and the Interests: Political Arguments for Capitalism before Its Triumph* (Princeton, N.J.: Princeton University Press, 1977).

31. Bernard Bailyn, *The Ideological Origins of the American Revolution* (Cambridge, Mass.: Harvard University Press, 1967).

32. Ibid., pp. 77, 28, 43.

33. Wood, *Creation of the American Republic*, pp. 107, 53. For a fuller examination and critical assessment of Wood's classical republican interpretation of the revolutionary period, see Chapter 8. For two very thoughtful studies emphasizing the subtle but significant differences in the concept of republicanism developed by Bailyn, Wood, and Pocock, see Daniel T. Rodgers, "Republicanism: The Career of a Concept," *Journal of American History* 79:1 (June 1992): 17–20, and Michael Zuckert, *Natural Rights and the New Republicanism*, chap. 10. Zuckert is correctly more sympathetic to Bailyn's central theme (liberty against power) than to either Pocock's (self-fulfillment as political participation) or Wood's (the sacrifice of self to the common good).

34. Wood did find, in antifederalism, a continuity of commitment to the classical conception of politics and the sense that society "was a cohesive organic entity with a single homogeneous interest." See *Creation of the American Republic*, pp. 499, cf. p. 418 and chap. 2. For a contrary assessment, see Herbert J. Storing, *What the Antifederalists Were For: The Political Thought of the Opponents of the Constitution* (Chicago: University of Chicago Press, 1981), chap. 3 n.7: "The Antifederalists are liberals . . . in the decisive sense that they see the end of government as the security of individual liberty."

35. Wood, *Creation of the American Republic*, pp. 606–15. For Bailyn's rejection of Wood's discontinuity claim, see Bernard Bailyn, "The Central Themes of the American Revolution," in Stephen J. Kurtz and James H. Hutson, eds., *Essays on the American Revolution* (Chapel Hill: University of North Carolina Press, 1973), pp. 21–26.

36. Wood, *Creation of the American Republic*, pp. 606–7, 614.

37. J. G. A. Pocock, "Virtue and Commerce in the Eighteenth Century," *Journal of Interdisciplinary History* 3 (1972): 119–34. For other treatments emphasizing the continuing influence of republican conceptions and concerns in the early national period, see especially Gerald Stourzh, *Alexander Hamilton and the Idea of Republican Government* (Stanford, Calif.: Stanford University Press, 1970); Lance Banning, *The Jefferson-*

ian Persuasion: Evolution of a Party Ideology (Ithaca, N.Y.: Cornell University Press, 1978), and "Jeffersonian Ideology Revisited: Liberal and Classical Ideas in the New American Republic," *William and Mary Quarterly* 3d ser., 43:1 (1986); Drew R. McCoy, *The Elusive Republic: Political Economy in Jeffersonian America* (Chapel Hill: University of North Carolina Press, 1980); John Murrin, "The Great Inversion, or Court versus Country: A Comparison of the Revolution Settlements in England (1688–1721) and America (1776–1816)," in J. G. A. Pocock, ed., *Three British Revolutions: 1644, 1688, 1776* (Princeton, N.J.: Princeton University Press, 1980). For Murrin, Jeffersonian republicanism triumphed over a liberal Hamiltonianism, on the national level; the court outlook on commerce thereafter retired to the judicial bench and the statehouses: "In this way the Great Inversion became complete. America's Revolution Settlement centralized the Country and decentralized and largely depoliticized the Court" (p. 428).

38. Steven M. Dworetz, *The Unvarnished Doctrine: Locke, Liberalism, and the American Revolution* (Durham, N.C.: Duke University Press, 1990), p. 97. Dworetz, for one, perceives the Lockean/liberal dichotomy to be central to revisionism. "In happily proclaiming the historical triumph (and normative superiority) of civic republicanism over Lockean liberalism, too much has been taken for granted about both. . . . Republicanism . . . is uncritically hailed . . . as the civic humanist alternative to Lockean liberalism, the doctrine of virtue offering ideological salvation for 'the lost soul of American politics.' " See also Leo Strauss, *Natural Right and History* (Chicago: University of Chicago Press, 1953), pp. 202–51, and Macpherson, *Possessive Individualism.* For a critique of the Macphersonian reading of Locke, see Chapter 5.

39. Joyce Appleby, "The Social Origins of American Revolutionary Ideology," *Journal of American History* 64:4 (March 1978): 937. There is, as I shall argue, a confusion over the relation between liberalism and Lockeanism. An "aggressive individualism" that culminates in a "pragmatic interest group politics," which Appleby views as features of liberalism, are and were viewed by many a patriot to be incompatible with the Lockean moral and political ethic. See Chapter 10.

40. Joyce Appleby, *Capitalism and a New Social Order: The Republican Vision of the 1790's* (New York: New York University Press, 1984), p. 22.

41. White, in *Philosophy of the American Revolution*, persuasively argues that Lockeanism and utilitarianism are essentially incompatible.

42. John P. Diggins, *The Lost Soul of American Politics: Virtue, Self-Interest, and the Foundations of Liberalism* (Chicago: University of Chicago Press, 1984), pp. 30, 14, 5 (emphasis added). For his rejection of both the republican revisionist and Marxist reading of the American founding, see "Comrades and Citizens: New Mythologies in American History," *American Political Science Review* 78:1 (March 1984): 614–49.

43. Diggins, *Lost Soul*, p. 97, cf. pp. 340, 80. For Locke as a majority-rule democrat, see Willmoore Kendall, *John Locke and the Doctrine of Majority Rule* (Urbana: University of Illinois Press, 1965), and Bernard Wishy, "John Locke and the Spirit of '76," *Political Science Quarterly* 73 (1958): 413–425.

44. Diggins, *Lost Soul*, pp. 97–98, 80, 83–84. For the thesis that Jefferson and America had adopted not the Lockean or Machiavellian, but the Scottish sentimentalists' model of man and society, see Garry Wills, *Inventing America: Jefferson's Declaration of Independence* (New York: Vintage Books, 1978), *Explaining America: The Federalist* (New York: Doubleday, 1981), and *Cincinnatus: George Washington and the Enlightenment* (New York: Doubleday, 1984). For a very good critique of the Scottish thesis, see Ronald Hamowy, "Jefferson and the Scottish Enlightenment: A Critique of Garry Wills's *Inventing America: Jefferson's Declaration of Independence*," *William and Mary Quarterly* 3d ser., 36 (1979): 503–23.

45. Quoted in Diggins, *Lost Soul,* p. 340.

46. Ibid., p. 17.

47. Thomas L. Pangle, *The Spirit of Modern Republicanism: The Moral Vision of the American Founders and the Philosophy of Locke* (Chicago: University of Chicago Press, 1988); Dworetz, *Unvarnished Doctrine.*

48. Pangle, *Spirit of Modern Republicanism,* pp. 270, 127.

49. Dworetz, *Unvarnished Doctrine,* pp. 70–71.

50. Ibid., p. 70.

51. Paul A. Rahe, *Republics Ancient and Modern: Classical Republicanism and the American Revolution* (Chapel Hill: University of North Carolina Press, 1992), pp. 563–66, 568.

52. Ibid., pp. 552, 551–52, 570.

53. Ibid. For a most useful discussion of virtue, see pp. 748–72. On the need for public education as a vehicle for sustaining republican liberty, see pp. 701–5, 581.

54. Rahe, *Republics Ancient and Modern,* see esp. pp. 582–83. Given the thorny problem of drafting a frame of government and Montesquieu's venerable name and teaching (i.e., republics are suited only to small polities), "It was only natural that American patriots, who had cited [Locke] more than any other writer in the years when they saw need to justify their revolution, should confer similar primacy on [Montesquieu] when America's independence was established and recognized and constitution making had become their principal concern."

55. Ibid., pp. 679–83, 685.

56. Ibid., p. 699.

57. For two recent studies that emphasize the compatibility between republican and Lockean principles, see Alan Craig Houston, *Algernon Sidney and the Republican Heritage in England and America* (Princeton, N.J.: Princeton University Press, 1991), and Michael Zuckert, *Natural Rights and the New Republicanism.* See Chapter 8 for discussion confirming that compatibility.

58. J. G. A. Pocock, "Between Gog and Magog: The Republican Thesis and the Ideologia Americana," *Journal of the History of Ideas* 48:2 (April 1987): 325–46, and Daniel T. Rodgers, "Republicanism: The Career of a Concept," *Journal of American History* 79:1 (June 1992): 11–38.

59. Michael Lienesch, *New Order of the Ages: Time, the Constitution and the Making of Modern American Political Thought* (Princeton, N.J.: Princeton University Press, 1988), p. 8. Quoted in Rodgers, "Republicanism: The Career of a Concept," p. 36.

60. Forrest McDonald, "The Intellectual World of the Founding Fathers," in Forrest McDonald and Ellen Shapiro McDonald, *Requiem: Variations on Eighteenth-Century Themes* (Lawrence: University Press of Kansas, 1988), p. 9. Quoted in Rodgers, "Republicanism: The Career of a Concept," p. 36. Forrest McDonald, *Novus Ordo Seclorum: The Intellectual Origins of the Constitution* (Lawrence: University Press of Kansas, 1985), p. 224. It is also conceivable that the court-country tension could be found within the personality of any number of Americans. For a similar analysis of European Freemasons, see Margaret C. Jacob, *Living the Enlightenment: Freemasonry and Politics in Eighteenth-Century Europe* (New York: Oxford University Press, 1991), p. 54. Jacob's larger argument here nicely examines how an abstract Enlightenment philosophy was lived out in daily practice.

61. Isaac Kramnick, "The 'Great National Discussion': The Discourse of Politics in 1787," *William and Mary Quarterly* 45:1 (January 1988): 4; emphasis added. Kramnick's essays have been collected in *Republicanism and Bourgeois Radicalism: Political Ideol-*

ogy in Late Eighteenth-Century England and America (Ithaca, N.Y.: Cornell University Press, 1990).

62. Rodgers, "Republicanism: The Career of a Concept," pp. 37, 35.

63. Gordon S. Wood, "Ideology and the Origins of Liberal America," *William and Mary Quarterly* 44:3 (July 1987): 634.

64. Banning, *Jeffersonian Persuasion*. For his republican-dominated report on the revolutionary era, see pp. 70–90.

65. See especially McCoy, *Elusive Republic,* and Murrin, "The Great Inversion, or Court versus Country." McCoy, for example, stressed the Jeffersonians' ambivalence toward commercial growth. Supportive of individual industry and economic progress, they nonetheless perceived the threat these developments could pose for the necessary spirit of civic-mindedness and republican liberty.

66. Banning, "Jeffersonian Ideology Revisited," pp. 13, 11. For a very concise statement summing up the opposition between liberalism and republicanism and the reasons for dismissing the notion of Jeffersonianism as solely liberal, ideologically, see p. 16.

67. Lance Banning, "The Republican Interpretation: Retrospect and Prospect," in Milton Klein, Richard D. Brown, and John B. Hench, eds., *The Republican Synthesis Revisited: Essays in Honor of George Athan Billias* (Worcester, Mass.: American Antiquarian Society, 1992), pp. 93–94, 98, 93.

68. Lance Banning, "Some Second Thoughts on Virtue and the Course of Revolutionary Thinking," in Terence Ball and J. G. A. Pocock, eds., *Conceptual Change and the Constitution* (Lawrence: University Press of Kansas, 1988), pp. 198–200, 203. This view is reiterated in Banning, "The Republican Interpretation," pp. 106–8. For late eighteenth-century America's continuing reliance on civic virtue for the maintenance of republican liberty, see also Rahe, *Republics Ancient and Modern,* pp. 748–72. Kramnick, "The 'Great National Discussion,' " p. 22, found "a different language of virtue, one that rejects the assumptions of civic humanism" for "economic productivity and industrious work. . . . The moral and virtuous man was no longer defined by his civic activity but by his economic activity . . . [which while] aimed at private gain . . . still . . . contribute[d] to the public good." Virtue, I shall ultimately argue, was understood and embraced in *both* senses, at once and without contradiction. For Banning's early appreciation of "Cato's" fusion of "opposition thought" and "the theory of a social compact," see *Jeffersonian Persuasion,* pp. 55–56.

69. Banning, "Jeffersonian Ideology Revisited," pp. 11–12: "*Liberalism* is . . . a political philosophy that regards man as possessed of inherent individual rights and the state as existing to protect these rights, deriving its authority from consent. *Classical republicanism* is a term that identif[ies] a mode of thinking about citizenship and the polity . . . [and is] concerned with the individual's participation with others in civic decisions where the needs and powers of those others must be taken into account. . . . Assuming a certain tension between public good and private desires, [classical republicanism] will identify the unrestrained pursuit of purely private interests as incompatible with preservation of a commonwealth."

70. Banning, "The Republican Interpretation," pp. 102–3, 108–9, 113.

71. Ibid., p. 114.

72. Houston, *Algernon Sidney,* esp. pp. 133, 143, 156, 225. See Chapter 8.

73. Rodgers, "Republicanism: The Career of a Concept," p. 34.

74. For a similar appraisal, see Zuckert, *Natural Rights and the New Republicanism*: "These [i.e., the Lockean and republican idioms] were not so much competing traditions . . . but rather modes of political analysis proceeding at different levels and addressing different questions." I fully concur with Zuckert, who writes: The revisionists "have set

in motion false debates and unproductive controversies based on false dichotomies and unproductive categories. . . . Most of what is currently discussed as classical republicanism is political thought at the level of political science; most of what is discussed as liberalism is reflection at the level of political philosophy.''

75. James T. Kloppenberg, ''The Virtues of Liberalism: Christianity, Republicanism, and Ethics in Early American Political Discourse,'' *Journal of American History* 74:1 (June 1987). Kloppenberg's account identifies some of the conflicting values evident within each of three borrowed traditions — the religious, the liberal, and the republican — but ultimately emphasizes the values they manifestly shared, thereby indicating that those disparate traditions *could* be noncontradictorily comprehended by an adventurous and astute nation earnestly seeking to define itself.

76. For a very careful dissection of the separate strands that constitute the republican ''synthesis'' and a critical elucidation of the distinctive characterizations of republicanism as elaborated by Bailyn, Wood, and Pocock, respectively, see Zuckert, *Natural Rights and the New Republicanism,* chap. 6.

Chapter 1. Interpreting Locke's Thought and Assessing Its Influence

1. For a defense of the contextualist methodology, see Quentin Skinner and James Tully, *Meaning and Context: Quentin Skinner and His Critics* (Princeton, N.J.: Princeton University Press, 1988); Quentin Skinner, *The Foundations of Modern Political Thought,* vol. 1, *The Renaissance* (Cambridge: Cambridge University Press, 1978), pp. ix–xv; J. G. A. Pocock, ''Languages and Their Implications: The Transformation of the Study of Political Thought,'' in Pocock, ed., *Politics, Language, and Time: Essays on Political Thought and History* (New York: Atheneum, 1973), and *The Machiavellian Moment: Florentine Political Thought and the Atlantic Republican Tradition* (Princeton, N.J.: Princeton University Press, 1975), esp. pp. 3–82. For a defense of the contextual approach to the reading of Locke, see Richard Ashcraft, *Revolutionary Politics and Locke's ''Two Treatises of Government''* (Princeton, N.J.: Princeton University Press, 1986); Neal Wood, *John Locke and Agrarian Capitalism* (Berkeley: University of California Press, 1984), esp. pp. 1–14; James Tully, *A Discourse on Property: John Locke and His Adversaries* (Cambridge: Cambridge University Press, 1980), pp. ix–x; Thomas A. Horne, *Property Rights and Poverty: Political Argument in Britain, 1605–1834* (Chapel Hill: University of North Carolina Press, 1990), pp. 41–72.

2. Ashcraft, *Revolutionary Politics*; Neal Wood, *John Locke and Agrarian Capitalism* and *The Politics of Locke's Philosophy: A Social Study of ''An Essay concerning Human Understanding''* (Berkeley: University of California Press, 1983); Karen Iverson Vaughn, *John Locke: Economist and Social Scientist* (Chicago: University of Chicago Press, 1980); Quentin Skinner, *The Foundations of Modern Political Thought,* vol. 2, *The Age of Reformation;* Tully, *A Discourse on Property;* Gordon J. Schochet, *Patriarchalism in Political Thought: The Authoritarian Family and Political Speculation and Attitudes, Especially in Seventeenth-Century England* (New York: Basic Books, 1975); G. A. J. Rogers, ''John Locke and the Latitude-men: Ignorance as a Ground of Toleration,'' and John Marshall, ''John Locke and Latitudinarianism,'' in Richard Kroll, Richard Ashcraft, and Perez Zagorin, eds., *Philosophy, Science, and Religion in England: 1640–1700* (Cambridge: Cambridge University Press, 1992). Gordon J. Schochet, ''Radical Politics and Ashcraft's Treatise on Locke,'' *Journal of the History of Ideas* 50:3 (July 1989): 508–9, identifies the same nexus of Lockean intellectual contexts.

3. John Dunn, *The Political Thought of John Locke: An Historical Account of the Argument of the "Two Treatises of Government"* (Cambridge: Cambridge University Press, 1969), p. 103.

4. Ashcraft, *Revolutionary Politics,* p. 5. See also Ashcraft, "Political Theory and the Problem of Ideology," *Journal of Politics* 42:3 (1980): 687–721. Historians, writes Ashcraft, need to move "away from a reliance upon philosophy and assumed definitions towards an historical-sociological approach to political theory . . . [while] recognizing the ways in which one's presuppositions about political theory are structured by the social relationships between political groups in one's own society" (p. 721).

5. Ashcraft, *Revolutionary Politics,* p. 5; emphasis added.

6. Tully, *Meaning and Context,* p. 283. This volume engages Skinner and his critics on the possibility of ever deciphering the meaning of past historical texts.

7. Thomas L. Pangle, *The Spirit of Modern Republicanism: The Moral Vision of the American Founders and the Philosophy of Locke* (Chicago: University of Chicago Press, 1988), p. 395.

8. Ibid., p. 38. For the influence of social and linguistic theory and, specifically, the writings of Clifford Geertz and Thomas Kuhn on the development of paradigmatic "languages" as a tool of historical research (and the researches of Bailyn, Pocock, and Wood), see p. 49. For a much fuller treatment, see Daniel T. Rodgers, "Republicanism: The Career of a Concept," *Journal of Politics* 79:1 (June 1992): 20–23. "For Geertz's converts [Bailyn and Wood] ideology structured the imaginative construction of reality; for Pocock . . . language structured the means and vocabularies by which reality could be described. . . . The need of the moment was for means of investing the ethereal stuff of mind with convincing social power" (pp. 22, 21).

9. John Gough, *John Locke's Political Philosophy: Eight Studies* (Oxford: Clarendon Press, 1973), p. 123. It was, for example, Locke's inconsistent portrait of human nature—men as rational and peaceful, yet so aggressive and violent that they must run from the brutal state of nature into civil society—that led Strauss and Macpherson to dismiss the natural law foundation upon which Locke builds his political theory. See Leo Strauss, *Natural Right and History* (Chicago: University of Chicago Press, 1953), pp. 224–25, and C. B. Macpherson, *The Political Theory of Possessive Individualism: Hobbes to Locke* (Oxford: Oxford University Press, 1962). The inconsistent portrait of human nature led Macpherson to the conclusion that the state of nature and the state of war are identical and that "this is the central contradiction in the explicit postulates on which Locke's political theory is built" (p. 241).

10. Wood, *Locke and Agrarian Capitalism,* p. 93. Charles H. Monson, Jr., "Locke and His Interpreters," in Gordon Schochet, ed., *Life, Liberty, and Property: Essays on Locke's Political Ideas* (Belmont, Calif.: Wadsworth Publishing Company, 1971), pp. 46–47. Gough, *John Locke's Political Philosophy,* p. 123. John Locke, *Two Treatises of Government,* edited with introduction by Peter Laslett (New York: Mentor, 1965), pp. 96–97. Laslett contends that against the confident assertions proffered in Locke's *Two Treatises,* "Locke's chief enterprise in the essay, [is] to portray the character of knowledge by pointing up its limits" (p. 96). That is a small element of his purpose.

11. Thus did Dunn, in *Political Thought of John Locke,* devote three chapters to "The Coherence of a Mind." Neal Wood, *Politics of Locke's Philosophy,* addresses "The Unity of a Mind" in his concluding chapter; and Vaughn, *Locke: Economist and Social Scientist,* purports to see a comprehensive social vision bridging Locke's political and economic writings. Still Wood, *Locke and Agrarian Capitalism* (p. 93), can conclude that while "Locke's thought, in actuality, can be perceived as constituting a whole, . . . the elements are not mutually related in any rigorous logical fashion." Wood and Vaughn both concen-

trate on the economic context that informs Locke's politics, largely discounting the religious and natural law roots so aggressively pursued by Tully and Dunn. Wood writes: "I view the language of natural law primarily as the means adopted by Locke rather than the substance of what he has to say. That substance is in essence the broad economic and social position revealed [in the earlier economic writings]" (p. 50). While he is right when he argues that "to overlook completely this context in favor of that of natural law discourse may very well hinder our understanding of Chapter 5," he fails to grasp that to do the reverse, a la Tully, accomplishes much the same thing.

12. Tully, *A Discourse on Property,* p. 7. On this important epistemological difference between "substances" and "mixed modes and relations," and our greater capacity to know the latter, see also, Ruth Grant, *John Locke's Liberalism* (Chicago: University of Chicago Press, 1987), pp. 12–19, 36.

13. Grant, *John Locke's Liberalism;* Richard Ashcraft, *Locke's "Two Treatises of Government"* (London: Unwin Hyman, 1987), p. 46.

14. These writings include: *A Letter on Toleration* (1689), *Two Treatises on Government* and *An Essay concerning Human Understanding* (1690), *Some Considerations of the Consequences of Lowering the Rate of Interest and Raising the Value of Money* (1691), *Some Thoughts concerning Education* (1695), and *The Reasonableness of Christianity* (1695). I am here presuming, fairly for Locke, I think, that the decision to publish in itself represents an affirmation of one's published views.

15. Locke's writings on the law of nature (which are strongly echoed in his *Essay concerning Human Understanding*), on toleration, and on economic policy, albeit unpublished in his lifetime, date all the way back to the 1660s.

16. Alan Craig Houston, *Algernon Sidney and the Republican Heritage in England and America* (Princeton, N.J.: Princeton University Press, 1991). "Virtually all of the 'republican' principles drawn from Sidney's writings were perfectly compatible with Lockean liberalism. . . . This conclusion casts doubt on the widely held view that there existed a distinct and coherent 'republican' language of politics in revolutionary America that was distinct from and in tension with Lockean liberalism" (pp. 224–25).

17. John Dunn, "The Politics of Locke in England and America in the Eighteenth Century," in John W. Yolton, ed., *John Locke: Problems and Perspectives* (Cambridge: Cambridge University Press, 1969), p. 60.

18. Steven Dworetz, *The Unvarnished Doctrine: Locke, Liberalism, and the American Revolution* (Durham, N.C.: Duke University Press, 1990), pp. 67–68.

Chapter 2. Seventeenth-Century Background: The Threat to Authority

1. Richard Ashcraft, *Revolutionary Politics and Locke's "Two Treatises of Government"* (Princeton, N.J.: Princeton University Press, 1986), pp. 6, 9, 5.

2. I do not mean to suggest that the latitudinarians advocated strict toleration, as would Locke. I use the term in late seventeenth-century terms "casually and variously to mean almost *any kind* of relief from the penalties imposed upon Dissenters from the established church, from indulgence-granted exemption from penal laws, through incorporation into the Church of England by means of comprehension, to statutory legitimation of non-conformity." See Gordon Schochet, "From Persecution to 'Toleration,' " in J. R. Jones, ed., *Liberty Secured?: Britain before and after 1688* (Stanford, Calif.: Stanford University Press, 1992), p. 127.

3. Margaret C. Jacob, *The Newtonians and the English Revolution, 1689–1720* (Ithaca, N.Y.: Cornell University Press, 1976), p. 55. See H. T. Dickinson, *Liberty and Prop-*

erty: Political Ideology in Eighteenth-Century Britain (New York: Holmes and Meier, 1977), p. 15. The elements essential for social order and stability, elements preached in every parish, were "absolute monarchy, divine ordination, indefeasible hereditary succession, non-resistance and passive obedience."

4. Sir Robert Filmore, "Patriarcha" (1680), in Johann P. Summerville, ed., *Patriarcha and Other Writings* (Cambridge: Cambridge University Press, 1991). Written in the 1640s, Filmer's political essays were pressed into service by the court to counter the consent theorists of civil society. Stronger than his positive case for patriarchalism was Filmer's piercing critique of the social contract or populist writers who sought to ground sovereignty in popular, rather than divine will. For a very good summary of Filmer's critique of the contractual or "populist" theory of political society, see Gordon Schochet, *Patriarchalism in Political Thought* (New York: Basic Books, 1975), pp. 115–58. Filmer did publish a large number of shorter essays in the 1640s and 1650s, and the definite consensus is that "Patriarcha" was essentially completed by 1642. On the controversy surrounding the dating of "Patriarcha" see Summerville's introduction, pp. xxxii–xxxiii.

5. Schochet, *Patriarchalism,* pp. 146, 136.

6. Paul Johnson, *A History of the English People* (New York: Harper and Row, 1985), p. 172.

7. Modern feminist authors insist that critical aspects of the patriarchal outlook persisted long after the theory succumbed to contractarianism. See especially Carole Pateman, *The Sexual Contract* (Stanford, Calif.: Stanford University Press, 1988). Thus classical contract theory, though rooted in the claim "that individuals are born free and born equal" and so may not be subjected or subjugated, and while allowing for the marital contract between man and woman, nonetheless assigned only to males the execution of the civil contract and persisted in affirming the authority of men over their wives. Thus did the contract writers turn "a subversive proposition into a defence of civil subjection" (p. 39). On Locke, see especially pp. 52–54. Though Locke, Pateman realizes, afforded the mother a measure of "parental" right over her offspring, along with a right to own property, and even allowed for "a dissoluble marriage contract," he too excluded women from the act of forming civil bonds and endorsed the "Conjugal Power" of the husband (hence feminine subjugation) on the grounds that, in his own words, "generally the Laws of mankind and customs of Nations have ordered it so; and there is, I grant, a Foundation in Nature for it" (p. 52, *First Treatise* [hereafter *FT*], par. 47).

8. Schochet, *Patriarchalism,* pp. 65–66, 74.

9. Ibid., pp. 77–79, 81, 77.

10. Thomas Hobbes, *De Cive*. The idea had widespread appeal and could be found in innumerable discussions. Thus would James Usher, Archbishop of Armagh, remark in *The Power Communicated by God to the Prince, and the Obedience Required of the Subject* (written c. 1644, published in 1661): "A Household is a kind of little Common-wealth, and a Common-wealth a great household. . . . And therefore what in the one a Husband, a Father, and a Master may expect from those who have such relations to him: the like by due proportion, is to have place in the other" (quoted in Schochet, *Patriarchalism, p.* 113).

11. Schochet, *Patriarchalism,* pp. 87, 89–90.

12. Ibid., p. 85.

13. Keith Wrightson, *English Society: 1580–1680* (London: Hutchinson, 1988), p. 186. See also Lawrence Stone, "Social Mobility in England: 1500–1700," in W. B. Owens, ed., *Seventeenth-Century England: A Changing Culture* (London: Ward Lock, 1988), p. 15.

14. Stone, "Social Mobility," p. 209.

15. Pauline Gregg, *Free-Born John: A Biography of John Lilburne* (London: George C. Harran and Company, 1961), p. 39.

16. Ibid., p. 40.

17. Christopher Hill, *The World Turned Upside Down: Radical Ideas during the English Revolution* (New York: Penguin Books, 1972), p. 93.

18. Gregg, *Free-Born John,* p. 40.

19. See R. C. Richardson and G. M. Ridden, eds., *Freedom and the English Revolution: Essays in History and Literature* (Manchester: Manchester University, 1986), p. 3.

20. The more significant Dutch and Huguenot writers included Theodore Beza, Francis Hotman, George Buchanan, Johannes Althusius, and the Catholic Juan de Mariana. For the development of anti-Monarchical theory before Locke, see Quentin Skinner, *The Foundations of Modern Political Thought,* vol. 2, *The Age of Reformation* (Cambridge: Cambridge University Press, 1978). The important natural law writers include Hugo Grotius, Samuel Pufendorf, and Richard Cumberland. See also James Tully, *A Discourse on Property: John Locke and His Adversaries* (Cambridge: Cambridge University Press, 1980); Thomas A. Horne, *Property Rights and Poverty: Political Argument in Britain, 1605–1834* (Chapel Hill: University of North Carolina Press, 1990); and Richard Tuck, *Natural Rights Theories: Their Origins and Development* (Cambridge: Cambridge University Press, 1979). The republican tradition is well captured in J. G. A. Pocock, *The Machiavellian Moment: Florentine Political Thought and the Atlantic Republican Tradition* (Princeton, N.J.: Princeton University Press, 1975). For a wider discussion of Bacon's principles and role in seventeenth-century thought, see Chapter 4.

21. St. Thomas Aquinas, it should not be forgotten, devotes twenty-one questions of his *Summa Theologiae* to the question of happiness and the acts by which men can hope to attain it here and now. St. Thomas Aquinas, *Treatise on Happiness,* ed. and trans. John A. Oesterle (Notre Dame, Ind.: University of Notre Dame Press, 1983).

22. Nicholas Tyacke, "Puritanism, Arminianism and Counter-Revolution," in Owens, ed., *Seventeenth-Century England,* p. 133.

23. Ibid., p. 135.

24. Ibid., pp. 140–42.

25. Wrightson, *English Society,* p. 206.

26. Theodore Calvin Pease, *The Leveller Movement: A Study in the History and Political Theory of the English Great Civil War* (American Historical Association, 1916; reprint, Gloucester, Mass.: Peter Smith, 1965).

27. See especially, Pease, *Leveller Movement,* pp. 74–76, for the arguments against Erastian and Presbyterian hegemony. The leading polemicists, here, were John Goodman, Henry Robinson, and Roger Williams.

28. William Lamont, "Pamphleteering, the Protestant Consensus and the English Revolution," in Richardson and Ridden, *Freedom and the English Revolution,* p. 3.

29. Pease, *Leveller Movement,* pp. 66, 73. For the story of the confrontation between the Erastians in the House of Commons and the Presbyterian divines of the Westminster Assembly, see pp. 76–79.

30. Ibid., pp. 66, 73.

31. Ibid., pp. 179, 185, 189.

32. John Lilburne, *The Freemans Freedom Vindicated* (London, 1646), quoted in Pease, *Leveller Movement,* pp. 139–40. See David McNally, "Locke, Levellers, and Liberty: Property and Democracy in the Thought of the First Whigs," *History of Political Thought* 10:1 (Spring 1989), for an argument aimed at disassociating Locke and Shaftesbury from the goals of the Levellers.

33. Richard Overton, *An Arrow against All Tyrants*, 10 October 1946. Quoted in Pease, *Leveller Movement*, pp. 141–42.

34. Quoted in Conrad Russell, *The Crisis of Parliaments: English History, 1509–1660* (Oxford: Oxford University Press, 1985), pp. 370, 368.

35. Thomas Edwards, *Gangraena*. 26 February 1645, 28 May and 28 December 1646. Quoted in Pease, *Leveller Movement*, p. 121.

36. Quoted in Hill, *World Turned Upside Down*, p. 98.

37. William Walwyn, *The Fountain of Slander Discovered* (1649). Quoted in Pease, *Leveller Movement*, pp. 246–47.

38. Quoted in Russell, *Crisis of Parliaments*, p. 368.

39. Quoted in Hill, *World Turned Upside Down*, pp. 42, 42, 64.

40. Edward Countryman, *The American Revolution* (New York: Hill and Wang, 1985), p. 18.

41. Hill, *World Turned Upside Down*, p. 336. William Penn, *No Cross, No Crown* (1669), quoted in Hill, *World Turned Upside Down*, p. 338. The notion of the "inner light" is developed nowhere more fully and advanced so forcefully as in the writings of John Milton. See especially, *On Christian Doctrine* (1665?). A good discussion of Milton's thought on this point is provided in Basil Willey, *The Seventeenth-Century Background: The Thought of the Age in Relation to Religion and Poetry* (New York: Doubleday Anchor, 1953). "Milton argues that the moral sense, which is the law of God written upon the heart, is the final tribunal—superior even to Scripture itself." Speaking of George Fox and the Quaker's invocation of the "inner light," Willey writes: "The 'inner light' of the Quakers . . . [was one of] the inward certitudes by means of which the century was testing the legacies of antiquity and declaring its spiritual independence," p. 78. For the intransigent individualism to which this idea brought Milton, see Don Wolfe, *Milton in the Puritan Revolution* (New York: Humanities Press, 1963), pp. 60–65.

42. Hill, *World Turned Upside Down*, pp. 189–90.

43. Ibid., pp. 177, 166–67.

44. Ibid., p. 370.

45. Thus could the Leveller manifesto of 14 April 1649 declare: "[We have] never had it in our thoughts to level men's estates, it being the utmost of our aim that . . . every man with as much security as may be enjoy his property." Quoted in Hill, *World Turned Upside Down*, p. 119. But see G. P. Gooch, *English Democratic Ideas in the Seventeenth Century* (New York: Harper Torchbooks, 1959), p. 179, in which the author sees Walwyn as accepting radical, leveling ideas. For a persuasive rebuttal of Gooch's thesis, see Pease, *Leveller Movement*, pp. 255–56, "Walwyn and Communism."

46. Quoted in Hill, *World Turned Upside Down*, pp. 132–33. For Winstanley's body of writings, see G. H. Sabine, ed., *The Works of Gerrard Winstanley* (Ithaca, N.Y.: Cornell University Press, 1941).

47. Quoted in Hill, *World Turned Upside Down*, p. 163.

48. Ibid., p. 330.

49. Quoted in Hill, *World Turned Upside Down*, pp. 117, 115–16, 177.

50. Quoted in Paul Johnson, *A History of the English People* (New York: Harper and Row, 1985), pp. 201–3.

51. Sir Robert Filmer, "The Anarchy of a Limited or Mixed Monarchy" (1680, written 1647), quoted in Schochet, *Patriarchalism*, p. 124.

52. Mark Goldie makes the compelling case that Locke's argument is directed not merely at Filmer's "Patriarcha," but at Anglican royalism generally. Archbishop Sancroft's decision to "launch" "Patriarcha" "as the ideological flagship of Toryism," the best available case for justifying *jure divino* episcopacy and a Bodinian conception of ab-

solute sovereignty, merely caused Locke to narrow his sights on that peculiar target. Goldie, "John Locke and Anglican Royalism," *Political Studies* 31 (1983): 61–85.

53. For Leveller faith in the dignity of man, see Pease, *Leveller Movement,* p. 153. For Locke, see discussion, Chapter 3.

54. Five Mile Act (1665) in Carl Stephenson and Frederick George Marcham, eds., *Sources of English Constitutional History: A Selection of Documents from A.D. 600 to the Present* (New York: Harper and Brothers, 1937), p. 554. Corporation Act (1661) in ibid., p. 543. Act of Uniformity (1662), in ibid., p. 545.

55. For a discussion of Parker's *Discourse* and the Stuart campaign against dissent generally, see Ashcraft, *Revolutionary Politics,* esp. pp. 39–74.

56. Ashcraft, *Revolutionary Politics,* pp. 23, 42.

57. Ibid., p. 72.

58. Ibid., pp. 53–54.

59. Ibid., p. 54.

60. Ibid., pp. 120, 127. Ashcraft provides an encompassing list of those broad issues, including: "the nature of man as a rational being created by God . . . the boundaries between faith and reason, the role of reason with respect to religion, the problem of knowledge and certainty in relation to the diversity of opinions" (p. 127).

61. This uncertainty is underscored by the editors of papers delivered at two recent conferences. See Kroll's introduction in Richard Kroll, Richard Ashcraft, and Perez Zagorin, *Philosophy, Science, and Religion in England: 1640–1700* (Cambridge: Cambridge University Press, 1992), p. 2: "Four days of often intense discussion yielded surprisingly little substantive or methodological agreement about the putative object of our pursuit [i.e., latitudinarianism]." See also Tim Harris's "Introduction: Revising the Restoration," in Tim Harris, Paul Seaward, and Mark Goldie, eds., *The Politics of Religion in Restoration England* (Oxford: Basil Blackwell, 1990), p. 2; John Spurr supports the view in a concluding remark to his "Latitudinarianism and the Restoration Church," *Historical Journal* 31:1 (1988): 82.

62. For the ties between natural theology and Newtonian science, see especially Jacob, *The Newtonians.* See also John Gascoigne, "From Bentley to the Victorians: The Rise and Fall of British Newtonian Natural Theology," *Science in Context* 2:2 (1988): 219–256. For its roots in the Cambridge circle, see John Gascoigne, *Cambridge in the Age of the Enlightenment: Science, Religion and Politics from the Restoration to the French Revolution* (Cambridge: Cambridge University Press, 1989), and W. M. Spellman, *The Latitudinarians and the Church of England, 1660–1700* (Athens: University of Georgia Press, 1993), pp. 11–32. Spurr has questioned the latitudinarians' favorable disposition toward science in " 'Latitudinarianism' and the Restoration Church," pp. 75, 77. Noting that only Glanvill and Wilkins exhibited any deep interest in the new science and that a mere 8 percent of Royal Society fellows were clergymen, he finds in latitudinarianism "not a clique of scientists, rationalists or pro-tolerationists, but a group of like-minded pastors opposed to puritan theology" (p. 77). The interest in "Newtonian natural theology" is a development that dates to the 1690s and a younger generation of moderates. For the seventeenth-century roots of both experimental science and natural theology see discussion of Francis Bacon in Chapter 4.

63. James R. Jacob and Margaret C. Jacob, "The Anglican Origins of Modern Science: The Metaphysical Foundations of the Whig Constitution," *Isis* 71:257 (June 1980): 258.

64. William M. Lamont, *Richard Baxter and the Millennium: Protestant Imperialism and the English Revolution* (Totowa, N.J.: Rowman and Littlefield, 1979), pp. 212–15.

65. See especially Jacob and Jacob, "The Anglican Origins of Modern Science," pp. 251–67; James R. Jacob, *Robert Boyle and the English Revolution* (New York: Burt Franklin, 1977); and Margaret Jacob, *Newtonians.*

66. Gascoigne, "From Bentley to the Victorians," p. 221.

67. See Jacob, *Newtonians,* pp. 64–65. Latitudinarian "matter theory" was expressly used against the Hobbesist and Cartesian view that reduced natural phenomena to bare "matter in motion." For the English virtuosi, "matter had to be dead and lifeless—passive—only then could providence be said to operate and spiritual forces be made dominant: in the natural order and in the affairs of men. If matter moved by its own inherent force, God would be rendered useless and men would pursue their interests unimpeded. If matter was infinite and active and space merely a relative notion, as Descartes would have it, then both space and matter would be eternal and independent of God. The result of such a natural order would be to sanction the Hobbesian world" (pp. 64–65).

68. Gilbert Burnet, *A History of His Own Time* (London, 1839). Quoted in Jacob, *Newtonians,* p. 80.

69. For Locke's relation to the radical community in exile in Holland, following the disclosure of the Rye House Plot, see Ashcraft, *Revolutionary Politics,* pp. 406–520. For the politically conservative character of the latitudinarian, or Low Church, leadership within the clerical Anglicanism, see Jacob, *Newtonians,* especially pp. 72–99.

70. Jacob, *Newtonians,* p. 94. John Spurr, " 'Virtue, Religion and Government': The Anglican Uses of Providence," in Harris et al., eds., *Politics of Religion,* pp. 29–48.

71. John Locke, *A Letter concerning Toleration* (1689), edited with an introduction by Patrick Romanell (Indianapolis, Ind.: Bobbs Merrill, 1958).

72. Richard Ashcraft, "Latitudinarianism and Toleration: Historical Myth versus Political History," in Richard Kroll, Richard Ashcraft, and Perez Zagorin, eds., *Philosophy, Science and Religion in England, 1640–1700* (Cambridge: Cambridge University Press, 1992), p. 155.

73. Ibid., pp. 151–67. Surprisingly, Ashcraft includes Samuel Parker, the arch High Church foe of dissent, among the latitudinarian writers in his *Revolutionary Politics.*

74. Schochet, "From Persecution to 'Toleration,' " pp. 150, 156, and Ashcraft, "Latitudinarianism and Toleration," pp. 151–52.

75. Patrick and Fowler quoted in Spurr, "Latitudinarianism and the Restoration Church," p. 67. The term "latitudinarian" was a mark of derision heaped on the moderate Puritans-turned-Anglicans by Nonconformists *and* the church hierarchy, which suspected and even reviled them for decades to come. Yet, Spurr concludes that "no specifically 'latitudinarian' party or outlook can be distinguished among the Restoration churchmen" (p. 82). For the suspicious and hostile attitude of the High Church toward the moderate wing of Anglicanism, see Spellman, *Latitudinarians and the Church of England,* pp. 34, 138, 140–43. Those who bemoaned "the Church in danger" identified the danger with "the moderate [i.e., latitudinarian] leadership of the 1690's" (p. 142).

76. Simon Patrick's *A Brief Account of the New Sect of Latitude-Men* (1662) and Edward Fowler's *The Principles of Practices of Certain Moderate Divines of the Church of England* (1670) both emphasize the loyalty of the latitude-men to the church. Spurr also emphasizes the moderates' "commitment to her liturgy, ceremonies, doctrines and government." See Spurr, "Latitudinarianism and the Restoration Church," p. 67.

77. On the latitudinarians' emphasis on the wickedness and depravity of human nature after the fall, see especially Spellman, *Latitudinarians and the Church of England,* pp. 54–71.

78. Ashcraft, "Latitudinarianism and Toleration," pp. 157–59, 160.

79. Tillotson, quoted in ibid., p. 164. John Spurr, "Rational Religion in Restoration England," *Journal of the History of Ideas* 49:4 (October 1988): 563–83, argues that the plea for "rational religion" was "the universal disposition of the age," pleaded for by high and low churchmen alike.

80. Ashcraft, "Latitudinarianism and Toleration," p. 167.

81. Ibid., p. 165.

82. Ibid., p. 167.

83. John Marshall, "John Locke and Latitudinarianism," in Kroll et al., *Philosophy, Science, and Religion*, p. 253. Maurice Cranston, *John Locke: A Biography* (Oxford: Oxford University Press, 1985), p. 386.

84. For the expulsion of the latitudinarians from Cambridge and Locke's association with Wilkins's group, see Spellman, *Latitudinarians and the Church of England*, pp. 39–40. For the use of "latitudinarian" as a term of derision employed by their High Church opponents, see Spurr, "Latitudinarianism and the Restoration Church," pp. 62–68. Most resented was the fact that the latitude-men took Puritan ordination during the Interregnum and then joined the Anglican communion at the Restoration to retain their positions within the church. It is Spurr's larger aim to portray the latitudinarians more as faithful sons of the Church of England than as an advanced guard for reason, science, and toleration (an impression that could be gotten from, say, Jacob's *Newtonians*).

85. Cranston, *John Locke*, p. 124.

86. John Locke, *Essays on the Law of Nature*, edited with an introduction by W. von Leyden (Oxford: Clarendon Press, 1954), p. 61.

87. Spellman, *Latitudinarians and the Church of England*, pp. 143, 141.

88. Ibid., pp. 133–35.

89. Cranston, *John Locke*, p. 127.

90. Locke to Richard King, quoted in Marshall, "John Locke and Latitudinarianism," p. 261.

91. Cranston, *John Locke*, p. 357. On Locke's closeness to Newton, see also pp. 264–65, 345, 347, 353, 355, 357–58, 361, 368, 372–74, 396, 439, 462, and 477.

92. Jacob, *Newtonians*, pp. 138–39. See also Gascoigne, "From Bentley to the Victorians," pp. 222–23: The use of Newtonian science was intended "not only to strengthen the position of the established church as a whole but also to consolidate the position of . . . the Low Churchmen in a church which remained deeply divided."

93. Cranston, *John Locke*, p. 127.

94. John Locke, *The Reasonableness of Christianity with a Discourse of Miracles and Part of a Third Letter concerning Toleration*, ed. I. T. Ramsey (Stanford, Calif.: Stanford University Press, 1958), par. 165.

95. Ibid., par. 167.

96. Ibid., pars. 21–22. For the latitudinarians' emphasis on works, their famous attention to moralism, see Spellman, *Latitudinarians and the Church of England*, esp. pp. 115–16, 121. "The acceptance of His grace was not to be achieved without constant attention to the imperatives of strictest Christian morality and reform." For Locke's similarity to the latitudinarians on the question of "faith and works," see Marshall, "John Locke and Latitudinarianism," pp. 258–62. The rigor of Anglican moral life is captured in *The Whole Duty of Man*, a devotional work published in 1658. See John Spurr, *The Restoration Church of England, 1646–1689* (New Haven, Conn.: Yale University Press, 1991), pp. 279–330.

97. Locke, *Reasonableness of Christianity*, par. 1. This theme is developed in Michael P. Zuckert, "John Locke and the Problem of Civil Religion," in Robert H. Horwitz, ed., *The Moral Foundations of the American Republic*, 3d ed. (Charlottesville: University

Press of Virginia, 1986), pp. 181–203. Zuckert points to the ultimate failure of Locke's argument in *Reasonableness of Christianity* to defend the Christian revelation and, therefore, the religious roots of England's political order. See esp. pp. 198–203.

98. Locke, *Reasonableness of Christianity,* par. 241.

99. Ibid.

100. Ibid., par. 242. "Jesus Christ hath given us in the New Testament . . . a full and sufficient rule for our direction, and comfortable to that of reason. But the truth and obligation of its precepts, have their force, and are put past doubt to us, by the evidence of his mission." For a fine discussion of the latitudinarians reliance on "the succor of grace," see Spellman, *Latitudinarians and the Church of England,* pp. 89–111.

101. Spellman, *Latitudinarians and the Church of England,* p. 117; emphasis added. See also Spurr, *Restoration Church of England,* p. 293.

102. John Locke, "Epistle to the Reader," *An Essay concerning Human Understanding,* ed. Alexander Campbell Fraser, 2 vols. (New York: Dover Publications, 1959), p. 1. Hereafter cited as *ECHU.*

103. On the importance of reason and natural religion to demonstrate the veracity of revealed religion, see Spellman, *Latitudinarians and the Church of England,* p. 74, and John Spurr, " 'Rational Religion' in Restoration England," pp. 563–83. Spellman writes: "The debate between defenders of the principle of moral certainty and Catholic infallibilists accelerated after the Restoration, and virtually every one of the moderate churchmen had occasion to enter the fray . . . to vindicate individual freedom in matters of interpretation and to reclaim . . . [the view that salvation] was . . . contingent upon the responsible employment of God-given reason" (p. 78).

104. G. A. J. Rogers, "Locke and the Latitude-men," in Kroll et al., *Philosophy, Science, and Religion,* p. 236. The phrase appears in Locke's *Reasonableness of Christianity,* par. 231.

105. Benjamin Whichcote, *Aphorisms,* quoted in Rogers, "Locke and the Latitudemen," p. 236. Rogers here spells out the latitudinarian lineage of Lockean skepticism.

106. *ECHU,* IV, 17, 21.

107. Ibid., Intro., 1, 4.

108. Ibid., Intro., 6.

109. Jacob, *Newtonians,* p. 37. For the view that many Anglicans who emphasized revealed religion defended their faith in the revealed word of God on rational grounds, see Spurr, "'Rational Religion' in Restoration England." Both in *The Essay concerning Human Understanding* and *The Reasonableness of Christianity* Locke advances a series of rational arguments, all based on sense experience and the testimony of ancient witnesses, for the existence of God and the veracity of the Gospel of Jesus.

110. Simon Patrick, *Agua Genitalis: A Discourse concerning Baptism* (London, 1659), quoted in Jacob, *Newtonians,* p. 42. For the progress of Platonism "From Athens to Cambridge," see James Deotis Roberts, Sr., *From Puritanism to Platonism in Seventeenth Century England* (The Hague: Martinus Nijhoff, 1968), pp. 17–41.

111. For Bacon and God's "revealed" Work, see Chapter 4.

112. Jacob, *Newtonians,* p. 61.

113. Thus Isaac Barrow could preach: "As in the world nature, the parts thereof are so fitted in varieties of size, of quality, of aptitude to motion, that all may stick together, . . . and all co-operate incessantly to the preservation of that common union and harmony which was there intended; so in the world political we observe various propensions and attitudes disposing men to collection and coherence and co-operation in society" (quoted in Jacob, *Newtonians,* p. 62).

114. Ibid., pp. 46–47. For a discussion of the Protestant work ethic, its role in English life, and its relation to Locke's moral theory see Chapter 4.

115. Ibid., pp. 69, 194, 57.

116. Ibid., pp. 57, cf. p. 51. "Monopolies and fixed prices disrupt the providential order; market forces are ultimately more just for they rely on natural forces rather than on the greed of unbridled self-interest" (p. 59). John Gascoigne has questioned Newtonians' commitment to the forward-looking laissez-faire economy in "From Bentley to the Victorians," pp. 224–25.

117. Jacob, *Newtonians,* p. 63. For the role of millenarianism in latitudinarian thought, see especially pp. 100–142.

118. Ashcraft, "Latitudinarianism and Toleration," p. 167.

119. Four editions of the *Essay* appeared between 1690 and 1704 (the year of Locke's death). On the testimony of Leibniz it ranked as "one of the most beautiful and esteemed works of the time." Quoted in the "Prolegomena," John Locke, *ECHU,* pp. xii–xiii.

Chapter 3. The Philosophical Foundations of Locke's Social Thought

1. John Milton, quoted in Christopher Hill, *The Century of Revolution: 1603–1714* (New York: W. W. Norton, 1982), pp. 149–50.

2. Gordon J. Schochet, "From Persecution to 'Toleration,' " in J. R. Jones, ed., *Liberty Secured: Britain before and after 1688* (Stanford, Calif.: Stanford University Press, 1992), pp. 128–30.

3. John Locke, *An Essay concerning Human Understanding,* Alexander Campbell Fraser, ed., 2 vols. (New York: Dover Publications, 1959), IV, 3, 25; II, 23, 10ff; III, 6, 9; IV, 3, 11, 13, 26. Hereafter cited as *ECHU.*

4. Edward Stillingfleet, *A Discourse in Vindication of the Trinity* (1696). Locke subsequently answered his one-time friend in *A Letter to the Bishop of Worcester* (1697). See Maurice Cranston, *John Locke: A Biography* (Oxford: Oxford University Press, 1985), pp. 4l0, 412ff. For the controversy surrounding the nature of substance see R. S. Woolhouse, *Locke* (Minneapolis: University of Minnesota, 1983), pp. 96–103.

5. Locke, *ECHU,* IV, 3, 6: "We have the ideas of *matter* and *thinking,* but possibly shall never be able to know whether matter [in later edition, changed to 'any mere material being'] thinks or no." Stillingfleet's reply came in *A Discourse in Vindication of the Trinity* (1696), and Locke answered in 1697. A useful discussion of this dialogue is provided in Cranston's biography, *John Locke,* pp. 4l0, 412ff. See also, Woolhouse, *Locke,* pp. 96–103, and *ECHU,* 1:107 n. 2 and 2:193 n. 1.

6. Cranston, *John Locke,* p. 127. More recently, G. A. J. Rogers has exposed the influence that epistemological skepticism played in the Cambridge Platonists' own defense of toleration, especially in the writings of Whichcote, More, and Glanvill. He thus draws the parallel between the Cambridge and Lockean outlook on the limits of the understanding and, therefore, the reasonableness of toleration. See G. A. J. Rogers, "Locke and the Latitude-men," in Richard Kroll, Richard Ashcraft, and Perez Zagorin, *Philosophy, Science, and Religion in England: 1640–1700* (Cambridge: Cambridge University Press, 1992), pp. 230–52.

7. Jeremy Taylor, *Discourse of the Liberty of Prophesying* (1647). Cranston, *John Locke,* p. 127. Locke's debt to Chillingworth is acknowledged in a letter to his friend Edward Clarke: "If you would have your son *Reason well,*" he urged, "let him read *Chillingworth*"; quoted in Rogers, "Locke and the Latitude-men," p. 242.

8. Ralph Cudworth, *A Treatise concerning Eternal and Immutable Morality* (1731), in J. B. Schneewind, ed., *Moral Philosophy from Montaigne to Kant: An Anthology,* vol. 1 (Cambridge: Cambridge University Press, 1990), p. 289.

9. C. A. Patrides, *The Cambridge Platonists* (Cambridge, Mass.: Harvard University Press, 1970), p. 37. Or consider Whichcote's formulation: "The Grace of God, to which we owe our Salvation, it doth not only give assistance, recovery, and furtherance to all the Principles of real Righteousness and true Goodness, which do very much need a help . . . because of Man's Fall; but the Grace of God doth its own work besides, it empires the Mind of fond Persuasion, foolish Self-conceit and presumption, and so makes room, gives a Man Capacity to receive from God, both the grace of Assistance, and also makes him capable of Forgiveness" (quoted in Patrides, p. 21). Aside from a valuable introduction, this volume contains an important body of writings by More, Whichcote, Cudworth, and Smith. See also Schneewind, *Moral Philosophy,* p. 276.

10. See Richard Ashcraft, *Locke's "Two Treatises of Government"* (London: Unwin Hyman, 1987). The traditional view, pressed by Aristotle, Hooker, and the Platonists, held that men naturally desired good. "Hobbes radically transformed the nature of the discussion by demolishing the traditional way in which the problem had been structured. There neither was nor could there be any bridge between God's purposes, whatever they were, and human action," pp. 40–41. See also W. M. Spellman, *The Latitudinarians and the Church of England, 1660–1700* (Athens: University of Georgia Press, 1993), p. 124: The latitudinarians' "exaggerated estimation of the power of innate principles to assist in the rehabilitation of the Christian sinner" was growing ever more apparent to the Low Church divines, themselves. "Locke's death warrant for innatism, although angrily contested by contemporaries who worried about its implications for morality, was . . . delivered just in time." The solution lay in the ecclesiastical equivalent of Locke's "plain method," i.e., in plain, unadorned preaching from the Anglican pulpit. On the growing doubt that innate ideas could demonstrate the existence of God, see John Spurr, " 'Rational Religion' in Restoration England," *Journal of the History of Ideas* 49:4 (October 1988): 573.

11. See C. H. Driver, "John Locke," in F. J. C. Hearnshaw, ed., *The Social and Political Ideas of Some English Thinkers of the Augustan Age* (Westport, Conn.: Greenwood Press, 1983, orig. pub. 1923), p. 78: "Locke, the very embodiment of his age, was struggling toward a synthesis of the three great forces which were agitating the age . . . the Cartesian outlook of the philosopher, the experimental method of the scientists, and the utilitarian empiricism he had learnt from Shaftesbury and his contact with practical politics." Driver easily identifies Locke with the latitudinarians as well, noting that "his theory of toleration, indeed, is to a large extent but one corollary drawn from the fundamental Latitudinarian theorem" (p. 74). Also interesting is Driver's claim (without the benefit of Laslett's evidence for dating the *Two Treatises*) that "years before the 1688 episode Locke had reached nearly every one of the positions maintained in his *Civil Government.*" Ultimately, however, unable to correlate Locke's rationalism and empiricism, Driver also believed: "Instead of a system we shall find a rather loose assertion of principles which will more or less cohere, but which leave a great latitude for subsequent deduction and interpretation; and some of which at any rate may be found to be mutually incompatible" (p. 78).

12. *ECHU,* I, 4, 4; cf. I, 3, 12; James Tully, *A Discourse on Property: John Locke and His Adversaries* (Cambridge: Cambridge University Press, 1980), p. 4.

13. *ECHU,* II, 1, 2–9.

14. Ibid., IV, 2, 4.

15. Ibid., IV, 2, 7, 10. Aristotle, centuries earlier, furnished a similar argument for accepting the independent status of the sensory universe. See Aristotle, *Works,* edited with

an introduction by Richard McKeon (New York: Random House, 1941). In the *Physics,* Aristotle thus asserts: "What nature is, then, and the meaning of the terms 'by nature' and 'according to nature' has been stated. *That* nature exists, it would be absurd to try to prove; for it is obvious that there are many things of this kind, and to prove what is obvious by what is not is the mark of a man who is unable to distinguish what is self-evident from what is not. . . . Presumably therefore such persons must be talking about words without any thought to correspond" (bk. 2, chap. 1, par. 193). And Joseph Glanvill also attested to the capacity of our senses to perceive "the realities of things themselves. This is a Principle that we believe firmly; but *cannot prove,* for all proof and reasoning supposeth it" (quoted in Spurr, "'Rational Religion' in Restoration England," p. 577).

16. *ECHU,* II, 8, 5; IV, 3, 18.

17. Locke does develop a doctrine of "substance," positing a corpuscular theory similar to that proffered by Boyle and Newton. Human perception cannot reach this underlying structure of material objects, and so we cannot fathom the real essence, or substance, of things. None of this, however, challenges the basic proposition under discussion here. See *ECHU,* IV, 3, 16, 25; II, 23, 10ff.

18. John Locke, *Essays on the Law of Nature,* (hereafter cited as *ELN*) edited with an introduction by W. von Leyden (Oxford: Clarendon Press, 1954), pp. 153, 48–49. Written early in Locke's career and not previously published, these eight essays bear an important relation to many epistemological doctrines developed in Locke's *Essay concerning Human Understanding.* Here, for example, Locke rejects innate knowledge and upholds the efficacy of reason and sensory experience. On the choice of Locke's arguments for the existence of God, see von Leyden, p. 49: "Locke has singled out the argument from design and the anthropological argument from among the other proofs of God's existence, precisely because these two arguments are derived from sense-experience and, apart from rational inference, require no further proof."

19. *ECHU,* IV, 19, 15.

20. See introductory comments of I. T. Ramsey, ed., John Locke, *The Reasonableness of Christianity with a Discourse of Miracles and Part of "A Third Letter concerning Toleration"* (Stanford, Calif.: Stanford University Press, 1958), pp. 9–16.

21. *ECHU,* II, 2, 3; II, 20, 1; II, 20, 2; cf. II, 21, 43.

22. Ibid., II, 20, 2; II, 20, 5–6.

23. Ibid., II, 20, 14; II, 2, 3.

24. See A. P. Brogan, "John Locke and Utilitarianism," *Ethica* 69 (January 1959): 79–83, and Driver, "John Locke," p. 86.

25. *ECHU,* II, 21, 35, cf. 21; II, 21, 35, 41, 44.

26. Ibid., II, 21, 5, collated from first and second editions by the editor.

27. Ibid., II, 21, 8, 54.

28. Ibid., II, 21, 55, 46. Locke also makes "sociability" to be a natural desire, as had Grotius in *The Laws of War and Peace* (1625). See *ECHU,* III, 1, 1, and *Second Treatise of Government,* par. 77. The idea, of course, goes back to Aristotle. Preservation, for Locke, is also a fundamental and natural inclination.

29. *ECHU,* II, 21, 71 (emphasis added), 47, 53, cf. 57, 45, cf. 59–70.

30. Ibid., II, 21, 52.

31. For the eighteenth century's replacement of "property" with "the pursuit of happiness," and the influence of Burlamaqui on Dickinson, James Wilson, and Jefferson in this development, see Morton White, *The Philosophy of the American Revolution* (Oxford: Oxford University Press, 1978). See Chapter 8.

32. *ECHU,* II, 21, 53.

33. Ruth W. Grant, *John Locke's Liberalism* (Chicago: University of Chicago Press, 1987), p. 44.

34. *ECHU*, II, 21, 54.

35. Ibid., II, 28, 5; emphasis in original. See also, John Locke, "Of Ethica in General," in Lord King, ed., *The Life of John Locke, with Extracts from his Correspondence, Journals, and Commonplace Books* (London, 1829), p. 311. "There is nothing morally good which does not produce pleasure to a man, nor nothing morally evil that does not bring pain to him. . . . For rewards and punishments are the good and evil whereby superiors enforce the observance of their laws; it being impossible to set any other motive or restraint to the actions of a free understanding agent, but the consideration of good or evil; that is, pleasure or pain that will follow from it."

36. *ECHU*, II, 28, 8.

37. Tully, *A Discourse on Property,* pp. 42, 40. See also John Dunn, *The Political Thought of John Locke: An Historical Account of the Argument of the "Two Treatises of Government"* (Cambridge: Cambridge University Press, 1969), p. 24.

38. Locke, *ELN*, p. 187, cf. 153, 157, 183. Locke, further, explains that men's obligations flow "partly from the divine wisdom of the law-maker, and partly from the right which the Creator has over His creation . . . [from their dependence] on his will. . . . [It is, therefore] reasonable that we should do what shall please Him who is omniscient and most wise" (p. 183).

39. Ibid., p. 187. It is worth noting that the sensationalist psychology made famous in the *Essay concerning Human Understanding* is already hard at work in these early *Essays on the Law of Nature*. Reason is a wondrous faculty and can furnish men with a great store of knowledge; but it is not "pure." To raise the understanding, it must process the materials provided by the senses. Thus while "without reason, though actuated by our senses, we scarcely rise to the standard of nature found in brute beasts, . . . without the help and assistance of the senses reason can achieve nothing more than a labourer can working in darkness behind shuttered windows." By Locke's light, "the Foundations . . . on which rests the whole of that knowledge which reason builds up and raises as high as heaven are the objects of sense experience" (*ELN,* p. 149).

40. Ibid., pp. 157, 117, 111.

41. Richard I. Aaron, *John Locke* (Oxford: Clarendon Press, 1971), pp. 256–69; J. W. Gough, *John Locke's Political Philosophy: Eight Studies* (Oxford: Clarendon Press, 1950), pp. 16–17; Driver, "John Locke," pp. 86–87; Ashcraft, *Locke's Two Treatises of Government,* p. 40. Ashcraft, in particular, struggles with the proposition that "it is the rationality of the law that makes it a law." In the end, he rejects it: "In the last analysis . . . Locke never permits any argument advanced by human beings to diminish 'the right which the Creator has over His Creation.' . . . Hence, while Locke's answer is ambiguous, the preponderance of emphasis must be placed upon the voluntarist side of his response." In contrast, see von Leyden, ed., *Essays,* especially pp. 51–52. "After having shown that natural law is binding on man because it is the declaration of God's will, Locke explains that man's rational nature not only indicates to him what are his duties but at the same time constitutes the reason why his duties are binding."

42. Grant, *John Locke's Liberalism,* p. 44.

43. *Essays,* p. 157; emphasis added.

44. Ibid., pp. 113, 199.

45. Ibid., p. 199. Grotius, with whom Locke was well acquainted, in *The Laws of War and Peace* (1625) had already posted such a naturalistic theory of the law of nature, rooting moral law in man's innate sociability.

46. *ECHU,* IV, 3, 18; I, 1, 5; IV, 13, 4; IV, 10, 18; IV, 11, 13.

47. *Essays,* pp. 129, 197; *Second Treatise* (hereafter *ST*), pars. 56, 58, 60, 63, 67, 69; *Some Thoughts concerning Education* (hereafter *STCE*), par. 34; *Essays,* 193, 195; *First Treatise* (hereafter *FT*), 42. For Locke's rendering of the traditional Christian duties (and sins) see *Reasonableness of Christianity,* p. 48.

48. *ECHU,* IV, 17, 1–2.

49. Ibid. II, 21, 52; IV, 17, 24. Cf. *Essays,* p. 157.

50. *ECHU,* IV, 17, 24.

51. Neal Wood, *The Politics of Locke's Philosophy: A Social Study of "An Essay concerning Human Understanding"* (Berkeley: University of California Press, 1983), p. 45. Interestingly, Wood associates the Lockean epistemology with the Protestant work ethic. "The inheritor of the world of knowledge is the industrious cultivator of the vineyard of the intellect. Locke has transformed the physical work-ethic of Protestantism into a morality of mental labor. Mental as well as physical idleness is a sin" (p. 141).

52. *ECHU,* II, 21, 53.

53. John Locke, *Some Thoughts concerning Education* (1695), reprinted in *The Educational Writings of John Locke.* edited with an introduction by John William Adamson (Cambridge: Cambridge University Press, 1922), par. 33; cf. 107, 45.

54. *STCE,* par. 200.

55. John Locke, "Thus I Think," reprinted in Lord King, *The Life of John Locke with Extracts from His Correspondence, Journals, and Commonplace Books* (London, 1829), pp. 306–7.

56. *STCE,* par. 45.

57. *ECHU,* IV, 28, 17.

58. *STCE,* par. 66. Pangle, not incorrectly, appreciates that true "independence" is also a matter of regulating one's own passions. Thomas L. Pangle, *The Spirit of Modern Republicanism: The Moral Vision of the American Founders and the Philosophy of Locke* (Chicago: University of Chicago Press, 1988), p. 266: "Such a person . . . sees that the longing for independence is truly fulfilled through the reasonable regulation of all the passions. Lockean man takes pride in this self-conscious, rational independence. It is here that he finds the source of his dignity." He who is independent is free from irrational passions and opinions.

59. *ECHU,* IV, 20, 18.

60. Ibid., IV, 19, 8.

61. Ibid., IV, 19, 11; IV, 18, 11; IV, 19, 11.

62. Ibid., IV, 19, 2–3.

63. Ibid., IV, 20, 18; IV, 16, 4.

64. Quoted in Cranston, *John Locke,* p. 82.

65. John Locke, *A Letter concerning Toleration* (1689), edited with an introduction by Patrick Romanell (Indianapolis, Ind.: Bobbs Merrill, 1958), pp. 57, 52, 54.

66. *ECHU,* IV, 17, 7.

67. Quoted in *ECHU,* p. 403 n.3.

68. John Locke, *On the Conduct of the Understanding* (1706), reprinted in John William Adamson, *The Educational Writings of John Locke* (Cambridge: Cambridge University Press, 1922), pp. 181–265. In a letter to William Molyneux, dated 10 April 1697, Locke writes of his plan to include this in a future edition of the *Essay* and that it would undoubtedly make up the largest chapter of the work. Molyneux's reply is dated 15 May.

Chapter 4. The Virtue of Industriousness for the Benefit of Life

1. The question of Locke's commitment to private property is still in doubt. See Willmoore Kendall, *John Locke and the Doctrine of Majority Rule* (Urbana: University of Illinois Press, 1965). Property is not truly private if a majority can alter its distribution at will. For a far more fundamental challenge, see James Tully, *A Discourse on Property: John Locke and His Adversaries* (Cambridge: Cambridge University Press, 1980), and Richard Tuck, *Natural Rights Theories: Their Origin and Development* (Cambridge: Cambridge University Press, 1979), pp. 171–73.

2. See Leo Strauss, *Natural Right and History* (Chicago: University of Chicago Press, 1953), pp. 226–27. Strauss dismisses Locke's moral or natural law postulates, since, for Locke, there is "an innate moral right, while there is no natural duty." Men's rights proceed from the innate desire for happiness and aversion to misery, alone. Thus "Locke's moral teaching . . . [may be] taken as the classic doctrine of the 'spirit of capitalism.' . . . [To] accumulate as much . . . wealth as one pleases is . . . by nature just." For a recent endorsement of this view, see Thomas G. West, "Leo Strauss and the American Founding," *Review of Politics* 53:1 (Winter 1991): 160. The fullest treatment of this theme is in C. B. Macpherson, *The Political Theory of Possessive Individualism: Hobbes to Locke* (Oxford: Oxford University Press, 1962).

3. The challenge emerges from the contextual exploration of Locke's relation to seventeenth-century natural law speculation. See especially, Tully, *A Discourse,* Tuck, *Natural Rights Theories,* John Dunn, *The Political Thought of John Locke: An Historical Account of the Argument of the "Two Treatises of Government"* (Cambridge: Cambridge University Press, 1969), and Richard Ashcraft, *Locke's "Two Treatises of Government"* (London: Unwin Hyman, 1987), pp. 35–59. See also discussion in Chapter 5.

4. See Ruth W. Grant, *John Locke's Liberalism* (Chicago: University of Chicago Press, 1987), p. 10. "Some scholars interpret Locke essentially as a progenitor of some political phenomenon found in our own times. They usually identify some negative aspect of life under modern liberal capitalism and look to Locke for its theoretical roots. . . . This . . . tends to distort the reading of that work by viewing it through a prism shaped by our own concerns and our own way of perceiving political problems."

5. C. B. Macpherson, *Possessive Individualism,* p. 228. For his general view regarding Locke's estimate of the laboring classes, see pp. 221–23.

6. Richard Ashcraft, *Revolutionary Politics and Locke's "Two Treatises of Government"* (Princeton, N.J.: Princeton University Press, 1986), and Neal Wood, *John Locke and Agrarian Capitalism* (Berkeley: University of California Press, 1984).

7. Maurice Cranston, *John Locke: A Biography* (Oxford: Oxford University Press, 1985), pp. 184–213, 246–63, 280–311. John Locke, *Two Treatises of Government,* ed., Peter Laslett (New York: Mentor, 1965). See Laslett's Introduction, pp. 43–45.

8. Ashcraft, *Revolutionary Politics,* p. 9.

9. Formerly believed to have been revealed by Shaftesbury, the discovery of the secret treaty has recently and persuasively been attributed to Ralph Montagu. See Jonathan Scott, *Algernon Sidney and the Restoration Crisis: 1677–1683* (Cambridge: Cambridge University Press, 1991).

10. Ashcraft, *Revolutionary Politics,* pp. 202–3.

11. Ibid., pp. 191–92, cf. p. 120: "As a defense against popery, arbitrary power, and tyranny, and as a means for insuring the advance of trade and the protection of civil liberties, toleration was the keystone of Shaftesbury's political theory."

12. Ibid., p. 120. On the composition, contents, and consequences of the "Letter," see pp. 117–23. Upon its being publicly burned by the common hangman on 10 November 1675, Locke left England, remaining in France for the next three years.

13. Ibid., pp. 264, 281. Gordon Schochet, "Radical Politics and Ashcraft's Treatise on Locke," *Journal of the History of Ideas* 50:3 (July 1989): 505, takes exception to Ashcraft's insistence that by "the people" Locke literally meant the "lowest social classes" (i.e., all white males). Schochet insists on confining the category to the "proto-bourgeois[ie]," conceding that Locke had more than "the conventional, aristocratic landowning class" in mind. Lois G. Schwoerer, "Locke, Lockean Ideas, and the Glorious Revolution," *Journal of the History of Ideas* 51:4 (October 1990): 535, also takes Schochet's more restrictive view, defining Locke's "people" as "all adult males who had some stake in society, men (such as artisans and tradesmen) who were outside conventional social and political elite groups." Against Ashcraft, Schwoerer situates Locke more in the mainstream than on the radical fringe, by 1689.

14. Ashcraft, *Revolutionary Politics,* p. 251. In *The Anarchy of a Limited or Mixed Monarchy* (1680), Filmer reprises the debate between Ireton and the Levellers at Putney, arguing that the popular consent theory posed a far graver danger to property than could any English king. To avoid the dreaded monarchy, "we shall run into the liberty of having as many kings as there be men in the world . . . [and in truth] every man would notwithstanding his political compact, be left with natural liberty, which is the mischief the pleaders for natural liberty do pretend they would avoid" (reprinted in *Patriarcha and Other Writings,* Johann P. Sommerville, ed. [Cambridge: Cambridge University Press, 1991], p. 141.

15. Ibid., p. 264; emphasis added. See p. 280 n.202, for a list of scholars who follow Macpherson's basic formulation.

16. For a fuller treatment of this shared vocabulary, see Richard Ashcraft, "Revolutionary Politics and Locke's 'Two Treatises of Government': Radicalism and Lockean Political Theory," *Political Theory* 8:4 (1980): 429–86.

17. Wood, *John Locke and Agrarian Capitalism,* p. 13.

18. Ibid., p. 60. John Locke, *Second Treatise,* par. 37, in John Locke's *Two Treatises of Government,* Peter Laslett, ed. (New York: Mentor Books, 1965): "In the wild and uncultivated waste of America left to Nature, without any improvement, tillage or husbandry, [will] a thousand acres . . . yield the needy and wretched inhabitants as many conveniences of life as ten acres of equally fertile land does in Devonshire where they are well cultivated?"

19. See Mildred Campbell, *The English Yeoman under Elizabeth and the Early Stuarts* (New Haven, Conn.: Yale University Press, 1942), pp. 376ff. Quoted in Wood, *John Locke and Agrarian Capitalism,* p. 60.

20. Wood, *John Locke and Agrarian Capitalism,* p. 23.

21. Ibid., pp. 25, 22, 26.

22. Ibid., p. 113.

23. Cranston, *John Locke,* p. 107.

24. Ibid., p. 119.

25. Laslett, ed., *Two Treatises,* Introduction, pp. 56–57. Wood acknowledges Locke's commercial investments, but nonetheless insists on his narrow, agrarian reading of Locke (Wood, *John Locke and Agrarian Capitalism,* p. 20).

26. Laslett, ed., *Two Treatises,* pp. 56–57.

27. Locke, *Second Treatise* (hereafter *ST*), par. 6.

28. Locke, *Essays on the Law of Nature,* ed. W. von Leyden (Oxford: Clarendon Press, 1954), p. 157.

29. Locke, *First Treatise* (hereafter *FT*), par. 6. See also John Locke, *A Letter concerning Toleration,* ed. Patrick Romanell (Indianapolis, Ind.: Bobbs Merrill, 1955), p. 47: "But besides their souls, which are immortal, men have also their temporal lives here on earth; the state whereof being frail and fleeting, and the duration uncertain, they have need of several outward conveniences to the support thereof, which are to be procured or preserved by pains and industry. For those things that are necessary to the comfortable support of our lives are not the spontaneous products of nature, nor do [they] offer themselves fit and prepared for our use."

30. *ST,* par. 35.

31. John Locke, *An Essay concerning Human Understanding,* ed. Alexander Campbell Fraser, 2 vols. (New York: Dover Publications, 1959), I, 1, 5; IV, 12, 12. Hereafter cited as *ECHU.*

32. Neal Wood, *The Politics of Locke's Philosophy: A Social Study of "An Essay concerning Human Understanding"* (Berkeley: University of California Press, 1983), pp. 126–27.

33. Wood, *John Locke and Agrarian Capitalism,* p. 46.

34. John Locke, *Some Considerations of the Consequences of the Lowering of Interest and Raising the Value of Money* (1691), reprinted in J. R. McCulloch, *Principles of Political Economy: With Sketch of the Rise and Progress of the Science* (London: Ward, Lock and Company, 1825), pp. 220–75. Opposing the legal lowering of interest, Locke finds it neither prudent nor just to "give to Richard what is Peter's due, for no other reason, but because one was borrower, and the other lender" (p. 225).

35. For Locke's attitude toward the various economic interests, see Karen Iversen Vaughn, *John Locke: Economist and Social Scientist* (Chicago: University of Chicago Press, 1980).

36. Locke, *Some Considerations,* p. 269.

37. Besides the "idleness" and "extravagance" evidenced by those of the landed and commercial classes, Locke objects to these middlemen shopkeepers for depriving manufacturers of capital needed for reinvestment. See Locke, *Some Considerations,* p. 238.

38. Ibid., pp. 268–69.

39. The two classic studies of this subject are Max Weber, *The Protestant Ethic and the Spirit of Capitalism: The Relationships between Religion and the Economic and Social Life in Modern Culture* (New York: Charles Scribner's Sons, 1958), and R. H. Tawney, *Religion and the Rise of Capitalism: A Historical Study* (New York: Penguin, 1947).

40. Tawney, *Religion and the Rise of Capitalism,* p. 167.

41. Ibid., pp. 177, 176, Richard Steele, *The Tradesman's Calling; Being a Discourse concerning the Nature, Necessity, Choices of a Calling, etc.* (1684), quoted in Tawney, *Religion and the Rise of Capitalism,* pp. 200, 191.

42. Ames *De Conscientia,* quoted in Tawney, *Religion and the Rise of Capitalism,* p. 180. See also pp. 179–89 for a discussion of the moral restraints on acquisitiveness down to the 1670s. Enclosure and usury are still held suspect and guidance on the setting of a "just price" freely provided.

43. Ibid., pp. 182ff.; see also pp. 210–26 on "The New Medicine for Poverty." Locke exhibits a similarly harsh attitude toward the poor in his 1696 memorandum on "Reform of the Poor Laws," reprinted in Peter Gay, ed., *The Enlightenment: A Comprehensive Anthology* (New York: Simon and Schuster, 1973), pp. 99–107.

44. Tawney, *Religion and the Rise of Capitalism,* p. 200. "Convinced that character is all and circumstances nothing, he sees in the poverty of those who fall by the way not a misfortune to be pitied and relieved, but a moral failing to be condemned" (p. 191).

45. Richard Steele, *The Tradesman's Calling,* in Tawney, *Religion and the Rise of Capitalism,* pp. 200–205.

46. Ibid., p. 203.

47. Ibid., pp. 206, 188. "In their emphasis on the moral duty of untiring activity, on work as an end in itself, on the evils of luxury and extravagance, on foresight and thrift, on moderation and self-discipline and rational calculation, they had created an ideal of Christian conduct, which canonized as an ethical principle the efficiency which economic theorists were preaching as a specific for social disorders" (Hill, *World Turned Upside Down,* p. 177).

48. Ibid., p. 215.

49. Ibid., p. 214. While Dunn's more recent efforts to link Locke to the Protestant ethic in *Political Thought of John Locke* comport well with Tawney's early analysis, there will be a serious tension between Tawney's liberalism and the restraints on acquisitiveness as developed not just by Dunn, but especially by Tully. See discussion in Chapter 5.

50. *ECHU,* IV, 12, 12.

51. Basil Willey, *The Seventeenth-Century Background: The Thought of the Age in Relation to Religion and Poetry* (New York: Doubleday Anchor, 1953), pp. 39–40.

52. Ibid., pp. 30, 35.

53. Francis Bacon, *The Great Instauration,* quoted in Norman F. Cantor and Peter L. Klein, eds., *Bacon and Descartes: Seventeenth-Century Rationalism* (Blaisdell, Mass.: Blaisdell Publishing Company, 1969), pp. 25, 24.

54. Ibid., p. 24.

55. Ibid., p. 28.

56. Ibid., p. 30.

57. Ibid.

58. Francis Bacon, *Nova Organon,* in Cantor and Klein, *Bacon and Descartes,* p. 40.

59. Jacob Brownowski and Bruce Mazlish, *The Western Intellectual Tradition* (New York: Harper Torchbooks, 1960), p. 182.

60. Ibid., p. 187.

61. Wood, *Politics of Locke's Philosophy,* p. 77.

62. Margaret C. Jacob, *The Cultural Meaning of the Scientific Revolution* (New York: Alfred A. Knopf, 1988), pp. 84–85.

63. Wood, *Politics of Locke's Philosophy,* p. 77.

64. J. R. Jacob, *Robert Boyle and the English Revolution* (New York: Burt Franklin, 1977), esp. pp. 144–58.

65. Thomas L. Pangle, *The Spirit of Modern Republicanism: The Moral Vision of the American Founders and the Philosophy of Locke* (Chicago: University of Chicago Press, 1988), pp. 270–71.

Chapter 5. A Benignant Egoism: John Locke's Social Ethic

1. C. B. Macpherson, *The Political Theory of Possessive Individualism: Hobbes to Locke* (Oxford: Oxford University Press, 1962), pp. 194–262. For a very well-crafted rejection of the idea that Locke believed that individuals are or ought to behave as socially isolated atoms, see Ruth W. Grant, "Locke's Political Anthropology and Lockean Individualism," *Journal of Politics* 50:1 (February 1988): 42–63.

2. James Tully, *A Discourse on Property: John Locke and His Adversaries* (Cambridge: Cambridge University Press, 1980).

3. For the importance of Sir Edward Coke to the development of American constitutional law, see Edward S. Corwin, *The Higher Law Background of American Constitutional Law* (Ithaca, N.Y.: Cornell University Press, 1955, orig. pub. 1928).

4. Tully, *A Discourse,* pp. 6–7.

5. John Locke, *First Treatise* (hereafter *FT*), reprinted in Peter Laslett, ed., John Locke, *Two Treatises of Government* (New York: Mentor Books, 1965), par. 126.

6. Robert Nozick, *Anarchy, State, and Utopia* (Oxford: Basil Blackwell, 1974), p. 9.

7. Tully, *A Discourse,* pp. 6–7.

8. Richard Ashcraft, *Revolutionary Politics and Locke's "Two Treatises of Government"* (Princeton, N.J.: Princeton University Press, 1986), p. 251. "The Whigs needed some means of reconciling the language of equality, natural rights, and the view that all property was originally given to mankind 'in common' with a justification of individual property rights in order to defend themselves against the accusation of a design to level men's estates, which the Tories repeatedly hurled at them in their exclusion sermons and pamphlets."

9. Gordon J. Schochet, *Patriarchalism in Political Thought: The Authoritarian Family and Political Speculation and Attitudes Especially in Seventeenth-Century England* (New York: Basic Books, 1975), p. 122.

10. Hugo Grotius, *The Laws of War and Peace* (London, 1738), pp. 145–46.

11. Thomas A. Horne, *Property Rights and Poverty: Political Argument in Britain, 1605–1834* (Chapel Hill: University of North Carolina Press, 1990), pp. 14–15.

12. Sir Robert Filmer, *Observations concerning the Originall of Government* (1652), quoted in Schochet, *Patriarchalism,* p. 125.

13. Filmer, *Anarchy of a Limited or Mixed Monarchy* (London, 1648), quoted in ibid., p. 123.

14. Filmer, "Patriarcha," p. 65, quoted in Schochet, p. 129.

15. Horne, *Property Rights and Poverty,* p. 20. For a brief but useful discussion of "inclusive rights," see pp. 3–8. Horne's work explores the coherence between the early modern concern with exclusive and inclusive rights and today's debate that pits property rights against welfare rights. See Tully, *A Discourse,* pp. 67–68, 75–77.

16. Samuel Pufendorf, *Of the Law of Nature and Nations* (1672), in Horne, *Property Rights and Poverty,* p. 34.

17. Ibid., pp. 364, 34–35.

18. Pufendorf, p. 207, in Horne, *Property Rights and Poverty,* p. 36.

19. John Locke, *Second Treatise* (hereafter *ST*), reprinted in Peter Laslett, ed., John Locke, *Two Treatises of Government* (New York: Mentor Books, 1965), par. 6.

20. Ibid., pars. 25, 29.

21. Ibid., par. 33; cf. pars. 31, 37.

22. Ibid., par. 27: "Though the Earth and all inferior Creatures be common to all Men, yet every Man has a *Property* in his own *Person*. This no Body has any Right to but himself. The *Labour* of his Body, and the *Work* of his Hands, we may say are his. Whatsoever then he removes out of the State that Nature hath provided, and left it in, he hath mixed his *Labour* with, and joyned to it something that is his own, and thereby makes it his *Property*." The central importance of labor, as opposed to mere "seizing," was already suggested by Pufendorf, though not stressed. On this, see Horne, *Property Rights and Poverty,* p. 51. The idea was made even more explicit by another natural law writer, Matthew Hale. See Richard Tuck, *Natural Rights Theories: Their Origins and Development* (Cambridge: Cambridge University Press, 1979), p. 164.

23. *ST,* par. 32.

24. Ibid., par. 36; emphasis in original.

25. *ST*, par. 50. "Men have agreed to disproportionate and unequal Possession of the Earth, they having by a tacit and voluntary consent found out a way, how a man may fairly possess more land than he himself can use the product of, by receiving in exchange for the overplus, Gold and Silver, which may be hoarded up without injury to any one, these metalls not spoileing or decaying in the hands of the possessor." See Horne, *Property Rights and Poverty*, p. 53.

26. Macpherson, *Possessive Individualism*, p. 221.

27. Ashcraft believes that it is at precisely the moment that individuals consented to use money, and therefore enlarge their possessions, that the natural law basis of property was overthrown. People may still claim a right to their property, but that conventional right is superseded by the needy, whose natural law right to preservation is, at all times, controlling. See Richard Ashcraft, *Locke's "Two Treatises of Government"* (London: Unwin Hyman, 1987), pp. 138–43. But, for Locke, the right to enlarge one's possessions, following the agreement to accept money as a medium of exchange, is natural, not conventional. Another important move made by Locke is worth noting. Earlier natural law writers placed great weight on the actual historical contracts that began the civil state. Thus although posting an absolutist doctrine regarding property and political power, the principle of "interpretive charity" allowed Grotius to surmise that the original compact-crafters may well have sanctioned resistance to authority or property redistribution under certain extreme conditions. This led Tuck to speak of Grotius's theory as "janus-faced" (*Natural Rights Theories*, pp. 79–80). It also allowed Filmer to ridicule the idea of ever locating the time, let alone the terms, of the signing ceremony. Locke eluded this Filmerian challenge by substituting "consent" for "contract." As Schochet explains: "Consent represented the personal and contemporary manner in which individuals could claim the same freedom that had belonged to their fathers before them. . . . [For Locke] men were not obligated because they lived under a government that had begun in voluntary association but because some, by acts of their own, had personally consented (however tacitly) . . . to be bound by a just authority that did not violate its trust" (*Patriarchalism*, p. 252). For Locke's rejection of this "genetic" brand of political thinking, see pp. 259–64.

28. John Dunn, *The Political Thought of John Locke: An Historical Account of the Argument of the "Two Treatises of Government"* (Cambridge: Cambridge University Press, 1969), p. 216.

29. Tully, *A Discourse*, p. 143.

30. Ibid., p. 150. I shall take up Locke's relation to an emergent capitalism in the following chapter.

31. Tuck, *Natural Rights Theories*, p. 172.

32. Locke, *ST*, par. 134.

33. Ashcraft, *Locke's "Two Treatises of Government*," pp. 46–47.

34. Leo Strauss, *Natural Right and History* (Chicago: University of Chicago Press, 1953), pp. 208–9. Locke, Strauss believed, took a page of strategy from Jesus, who "perplexed his meaning . . . [so that he could do] the work which he came to do." Strauss came to this conclusion after carefully discrediting Locke's own natural law teaching. For Locke, law, to *be* law, must be promulgated and known and backed by sanctions. Seeing the traditional sanction as inner conscience and finding Locke's sanction to be the mundane "executive power" individuals possess to punish the law's transgression, Strauss finds no sanction in Locke's natural law teaching. Nor can he find any satisfactory promulgation of the law, since it depends upon men's use of reason. But since the warlike conditions existing in the state of nature are inimical to the leisure needed to develop reason and since Locke himself concedes in the *Reasonableness* that "the greatest part of

mankind want leisure or capacity for demonstration'' long after men form their civil bonds, Strauss's Locke cannot defend his natural law argument on his own terms. There is a natural law, Strauss concludes, only it is the empirical law all men naturally follow to seek happiness. This brings Strauss to his major interpretive conclusion: ''The desire for happiness and the pursuit of happiness have the character of an absolute right, of a natural right. . . . [There is, then,] an innate natural right, while there is no natural duty. . . . [And since] the right of nature is innate, whereas the law of nature is not, the right of nature is more fundamental than the law of nature and is the foundation of the law of nature'' (pp. 222, 224–25, 215, 226–27).

For a remarkably similar treatment of Locke's natural law enterprise, resting primarily on a careful exegesis of Locke's *Essays on the Law of Nature,* see Michael Zuckert, *Natural Rights and the New Republicanism* (Princeton N.J.: Princeton University Press, 1994), chap. 7. Zuckert also sees reason as a tool woefully inadequate to promulgate natural law; sees Locke's teaching as requiring a firm sanction in an afterlife yet finds no proof of the soul's immortality; and sees Locke's theory as wholly voluntarist, requiring a lawgiver, yet espies no adequate proof of God's existence in the *Essays.* Clearly echoing Strauss, Zuckert finds that there are ''rights'' in nature *without* there being any laws of nature, as such. ''Morality . . . is in the service of natural right and derivative from it, rather than primary and underived'' (pp. 472–73).

The origin of these ''rights of nature'' is self-interest, although Zuckert allows for a ''long-term self-interest'' that counsels concern for the common good and the entering into social compacts. ''Such compacts may establish . . . moral limits on human actions, limits which may look very like the precepts of the traditional natural law, but they do not prove the existence of a law of nature at all, . . . and issue from no principle of nature whatsoever'' (p. 471). The ''workmanship model,'' critical to the natural law discourse that Zuckert's Locke has repudiated is replaced with a ''self-ownership'' principle, which Locke nowhere philosophically defends. The doctrine of natural right thus assumes the character not of natural properties inherent in the human personality, but, really, a convenient fantasy necessary for the peace and prosperity of civil society. Ultimately, the lines between Hobbes and Locke become blurred to the point of indistinction. And Locke is not a theorist of human morality, but of utilitarian expediency. ''From the keeping of this law peace arises, concord, friendship, freedom from punishments, security, the possession of our own property, and, to embrace all these in a single word, happiness.'' With Strauss, Zuckert interprets Locke's effort to be largely ''deceptive . . . but the reason for his deception is not far to seek. . . . Whatever its defects, the natural law tradition has something crucial to say, and Locke does not want to demolish its hold on the minds of his compatriots.''

Had Zuckert filled in the necessary gaps contained in Locke's unpublished *Essays on the Law of Nature* with a careful reading of the *Essay concerning Human Understanding* (remarkably, it is barely brought up) he might have more readily discerned how Locke in fact did derive natural rights from a resolute, if novel, interpretation of natural law (see Chapter 2).

35. Thomas Hobbes, *Leviathan,* C. B. Macpherson, ed. (New York: Penguin Books, 1971), pp. 185–86.

36. Tully, *A Discourse,* p. 49. Locke indeed writes of all men ''sharing in one community of nature'' (*ST,* 6), reasoning that ''all men alike are friends of one another and so bound together by common interests'' (John Lock, *Essays on the Law of Nature* [hereafter *ELN*], ed. W. von Leyden [Oxford: Oxford University Press, 1954], p. 163) and so form ''a common bond whereby human kind is united into one fellowship and society'' (*ST,* 172). On this point, see Ashcraft, *Locke's Two Treatises,* pp. 99–111. ''Locke assumes

that the communal objectives of natural law are supported by a sense of community shared by those who enforce its commands'' (p. 109).

37. Locke, *Essays*, p. 207.

38. Locke, manuscript of 1677, quoted in Tully, *A Discourse*, p. 47.

39. Tully, *A Discourse*, p. 40.

40. *ST,* par. 6. See also, Ashcraft, *Locke's Two Treatises*, p. 108. Locke not only believes that ''the preservation of all mankind . . . [is] the true principle to regulate our religion, politics, and morality by'' (John Locke, *Some Thoughts concerning Education* [hereafter *STCE*], par. 116, reprinted in John William Anderson, ed., *The Educational Writings of John Locke* [Cambridge: Cambridge University Press, 1922], pp. 22–170), he also believes that this belief is a constitutive element of human consciousness in the state of nature. It is the ability of individuals to act on the basis of such a belief that ensures that the precepts of natural law can, *in any degree,* be enforced in that state (*ST,* 11, 134–35, 159, 171, 182–83).

41. Tully, *A Discourse*, p. 104.

42. Ibid., pp. 122, 124, 132.

43. Ibid., pp. 133, 124–25.

44. Ibid., p. 147; emphasis added.

45. Ibid., p. 150, *ST,* par. 46, Tully, *A Discourse*, pp. 147, 150. *STCE*, par. 110.

46. Tully, *A Discourse*, p. 154.

47. *ST,* par. 129.

48. Ibid., par. 138

49. Tully, *A Discourse*, pp. 165, 170.

50. Ibid., p. 170. As we have seen, several natural law writers before Locke who explicitly accepted charity or distributive social policies in civil society did spell out the forms and mechanisms of assistance they wished to adopt.

51. See Ashcraft, *Revolutionary Politics*, p. 115. Shaftesbury had been a signatory to the Treaty of Dover (1670), in which France and England joined in common cause against the Dutch. By 1773, an earlier treaty that had been agreed to by the French and English monarchs came to Shaftesbury's attention. Its terms were something altogether different. Ashcraft writes: ''The first Treaty of Dover had been a highly secretive affair, and for good reason. That document contained clauses in which Charles II promised to declare his adherence to the Roman Catholic religion. Payment of å200,000 and assignment of 6,000 French troops by Louis XIV were to assist the English king in . . . this grand conversion.''

52. *ST,* par. 194.

53. This precisely points to the importance of situating a text (and its author) within the widest possible number of appropriate contextual settings to verify (or falsify) a scholar's interpretive findings (see Chapter 1). A brief examination of another interpretive reading of Locke on property, one that is closer to Macpherson's Locke than to Tully's, should help emphasize the value of this contextual cross-checking. Textually situating Locke's chapter on property within the preceding and following chapters that describe the relations between master and slave, parent and child, husband and wife, and magistrate and subject, respectively, Zuckert, *Natural Rights and the New Republicanism,* concludes that Locke's purpose here is to explain ''how master-servant relations arise, and what they are in contrast to the political relation''—even if, as Zuckert admits, Locke ''does not make the 'master-servant' relation explicitly thematic in [chapter five] as he does in the chapters devoted to [the other relations]'' and even though Locke stated his aim quite clearly: ''to shew, how men might come to have a property in several parts of that which God gave to mankind in common, and that whtout any express compact of all the commoners'' (*ST,* par. 25). Pointing again to Locke's deceptive literary practice (see n. 34 above), Zuckert

reasons: "Locke chooses not to emphasize . . . his true destination . . . [i.e., exposing] the end result of the process whereby some are dispossessed and thus relegated to the role of 'day labourer,' but rather the conundrum of how the originally common could become private at all. As Laslett rightly emphasized, Locke has set his problem up in terms of his on-going confrontation with Filmer, on the one hand, and Grotius on the other." But Locke's veracity and stated intent need not be challenged; for as Ashcraft rightly emphasized, that particular "conundrum" lay at the ideological heart of Shaftesbury's political mission. In exposing the manifest weakness of Grotius's populist/contractarian theory, Filmer was able to drive home his own natural law doctrine, thereby rendering the lives and estates of every Englishman the property of a divinely appointed absolute monarch. The relation between master and servant aside, Locke in building his own theory of property had to fulfill the Grotian project while avoiding the Filmerian trap.

54. *ST,* par. 26.

55. Ashcraft, *Revolutionary Politics,* p. 218; *ST,* par. 36, 39, 51, 107.

56. *ST,* pars. 33, 46, cf. 60.

57. Ibid., pars. 131, 137, cf. 171.

58. Tully, *A Discourse,* p. 149.

59. *ST,* par. 37.

60. Ibid., pars. 40, 44.

61. Tully, *A Discourse,* p. 250.

62. Ibid., p. 251.

63. *ST,* par. 33.

64. Ibid., par. 34.

65. W. von Leyden, "John Locke and Natural Law," in Gordon Schochet, ed., *Life, Liberty, and Property: Essays on Locke's Political Ideas* (Belmont, Calif.: Wadsworth Publishing Company, 1971), p. 25.

66. *ST,* par. 6.

67. Tully, *A Discourse,* 162–63. "Locke redescribes the natural end of political society as the public good. . . . In his definition of political power, Locke places the regulation of property as the means to an end of the public good. . . . Locke uses the public good as a distributive principle. Since the public good is the natural end of preservation as it applies to political society, it is equivalent to the good of preservation of each. . . . [As Locke himself writes:] 'the end of Government it self . . . is the publick good and preservation of Property' " (*ST,* par. 239).

68. Tully, *A Discourse,* p. 63. On this point, see Dunn, *Political Thought of John Locke,* p. 218. "[What] defines human life [for Locke] is a set of duties and a right to promote happiness in any way compatible with these duties."

69. John Locke, *An Essay concerning Human Understanding,* ed. Alexander Campbell Fraser, 2 vols. (New York: Dover Publications, 1959), II, 21, 57; emphasis added. Hereafter cited as *ECHU.* In his considerations "On the Reform of the Poor Laws" (1697) Locke emphasized the responsibility he placed on the poor for their plight. Attributing the spread of pauperism to "the relaxation of discipline and corruption of manners," he urged a policy of firmness. Expressing more sympathy for "the burden that lies upon the industrious for maintaining the poor" than for those "begging drones, who live unnecessarily upon other people's labour," he urges an unyielding compliance with the Act of Settlement (preventing migrancy) and other laws against them. See John Locke, "On the Reform of the Poor Laws" (1697), in Peter Gay, ed., *The Enlightenment: A Comprehensive Anthology* (New York: Simon and Schuster, 1973), pp. 99–107. For an alternative interpretation, emphasizing the "charity" expressed by Locke in these reforms, see Horne, *Property Rights and Poverty,* pp. 64–65. However harsh the proposals might appear, "pre-

venting vagrancy, relieving distress, and maintaining social stability were the goals . . . [that] can be seen in Locke's plan.''

70. *ST*, par. 85; emphasis added.

71. John Locke, *Some Considerations of the Consequences of Lowering the Rate of Interest and Raising the Value of Money* (1691), in J. R. McCulloch, *Principles of Political Economy: With Sketch of the Rise and Progress of the Science* (London: Ward, Lock and Company, 1825), p. 268.

72. In Chapter 6, I shall take up Macpherson's contention, in *Possessive Individualism,* pp. 233–34, that not being able to appropriate and therefore not being fully rational, the laboring classes enjoyed no political rights in Locke's natural law theory. Locke's harsh attitude toward the idle poor was, of course, typical of his age and was shared by the latitudinarians. See Gertrude Himmelfarb, *The Idea of Poverty: England in the Early Industrial Age* (New York: Vintage Books, 1983), pp. 23–41.

73. Ashcraft, *Revolutionary Politics,* pp. 159–60.

74. Neal Wood, *The Politics of Locke's Philosophy: A Social Study of "An Essay concerning Human Understanding"* (Berkeley: University of California Press, 1983), p. 177.

75. Macpherson, *Possessive Individualism,* pp. 233–34. Believing he had placed Locke's thought in a proper historical context, Macpherson was able to ascribe to him a sanction for such exploitation: ''The working class was regarded not as citizens but as a body of actual and potential labour available for the purposes of the nation. . . . the common assumption was that the labouring class was something that was to be managed by the state to make it productive of national gain'' (p. 228).

76. As early as 1918, Sterling Lamprecht, in *The Moral and Political Philosophy of John Locke* (New York: Columbia University Press, 1918), p. 132, perceived that for Locke, ''mankind has from the very earliest times possessed social instincts and a social nature. He [Locke] contrasted political life, not with an anti-social life (as Hobbes did), but with a social life in which the social welfare was very imperfectly attained.'' See notes 31, 32, and 33 for the statements of Tuck, Ashcraft, and Horne. Dunn also perceives the social and communal nature of human action. My complaint is that all the recent commentators have gone too far in asserting the moral duties that flow from the ''communal'' character of human relations.

77. *ECHU*, III, 1, 1.

78. Locke, *FT*, par. 42. For what is, perhaps, Locke's strongest language enjoining the biblical duty of charity, see Locke, *The Reasonableness of Christianity with a Discourse of Miracles and Part of a Third Letter concerning Toleration,* ed. I. T. Ramsey (Stanford, Calif.: Stanford University Press, 1958), par. 226.

79. Emphasis added. ''Venditio'' has been reprinted in John Dunn, ''Justice and the Interpretation of Locke's Political Theory,'' *Political Studies* 16:1 (1968): 68–87. For the relevance of this piece to Locke's capitalism see Chapter 6.

80. Quoted in Maurice Cranston, *John Locke: A Biography* (Oxford: Oxford University Press, 1985), p. 426. The distinction drawn by Locke between the ''deserving'' and ''nondeserving'' poor reflects the attitude of the latitudinarians, generally. See Margaret C. Jacob, *The Newtonians and the English Revolution, 1689–1720* (Ithaca, N.Y.: Cornell University Press, 1976), p. 55.

81. *STCE*, par. 109.

82. Ibid., par. 110, p. 86.

83. Ibid.

84. Ibid.

85. Lance Banning, ''Jeffersonian Ideology Revisited: Liberal and Classical Ideas in the New American Republic,'' *William and Mary Quarterly* 3d. ser., 43:1 (1986): 11–12.

Robert H. Horwitz, "John Locke and the Preservation of Liberty: A Perennial Problem of Civic Education," in Robert H. Horwitz, ed., *The Moral Foundations of the American Republic* (Charlottesville: University Press of Virginia, 1986), pp. 136–64. The dichotomy between liberalism and republicanism is not as neat as many have attempted to make it.

86. Horwitz, "Locke and the Preservation of Liberty," p. 164, very appropriately asks, "If Locke's teaching on education for civic virtue and its relationship to the stability of the regime is sound, then must we not ponder its implications for our quasi-Lockean political order in the United States?"

87. See discussion in Chapters 3 and 4.

Chapter 6. The True, Original, Extent, and End of Civil Government

1. John Locke, "Some Thoughts concerning Reading and Study for a Gentleman," in *The Works of John Locke,* 10 vols. (London, 1823), 3: 296. John Locke, *Wisdom* (1672) quoted in Laslett's Introduction to John Locke's, *Two Treatises of Government,* ed. Peter Laslett (New York: Mentor, 1965), p. 47. On this point, see James Tully, *A Discourse on Property: John Locke and His Adversaries* (Cambridge: Cambridge University Press, 1980), pp. 28–29; Richard Ashcraft, *Locke's "Two Treatises of Government"* (London: Unwin Hyman, 1987), pp. 50–51; Ruth W. Grant, *John Locke's Liberalism* (Chicago: University of Chicago Press, 1987), pp. 21–24. Locke, in "Some Thoughts . . . for a Gentleman," recommends the study of ancient republican writers, such as Livy and Cicero.

2. In particular, the conceptions we commonly associate with the "republican" discourse of Machiavelli, Harrington, and the neo-Harringtonians can be appended to the fundamentals carefully developed by Locke. As I show in Chapter 8, Lockean liberalism and "republicanism" can be mutually accommodating, a point that is confirmed in Alan Craig Houston, *Algernon Sidney and the Republican Heritage in England and America* (Princeton, N.J.: Princeton University Press, 1991). Houston makes it clear that Sidney's republican principles are raised on what essentially is a Lockean foundation. For Locke's and Sidney's accord on the fundamentals of government, see esp. pp. 130–34, 143, 156, and 200 (where the principle of "equal protection" finds clear voice). For a virtually identical discussion of this critical distinction between the fundamentals and the science of politics and, therefore, of the compatibility between the Lockean and republican "languages," see Michael Zuckert, *Natural Rights and the New Republicanism* (Princeton N.J.: Princeton University Press, 1994), chap. 10.

3. C. B. Macpherson, *The Political Theory of Possessive Individualism: Hobbes to Locke* (Oxford: Oxford University Press, 1962), pp. 250–51, 256.

4. Ibid., p. 256.

5. John Locke, *Second Treatise* (hereafter *ST*), pars. 129, 120, reprinted in Peter Laslett, ed., John Locke, *Two Treatises of Government* (New York: Mentor Books, 1965).

6. Ibid., par. 120.

7. Ibid., pars. 95–98. See Willmoore Kendall, *John Locke and the Doctrine of Majority Rule* (Urbana: University of Illinois Press, 1965). Kendall was among the first to emphasize that "Locke's treatment of the right of property . . . is predicated throughout upon assumptions which are collectivist in the extreme." He writes: The individual's "rights (including his rights of property) are merely those vouchsafed to him by the positive law of his society" (pp. 71, 104). In Kendall's analysis, ultimate sovereignty is lodged in the hands of the majority—and nowhere else: "The inalienable rights of the individual are . . . such rights as may be compatible with the public good of his society, and . . . that public good is merely that which the 'opinion' and 'humour' of the people

designate as good . . . [and] the inalienable rights of the individual prove to be merely those which the majority of the people have not yet seen fit to withdraw" (p. 113). For a rebuttal of this view, see discussion of majority will in this chapter.

8. For Locke's defense of the state of nature as a historical condition, see *ST,* 100–110. The approach taken here, with respect to the state of nature, is similar to that found in Hans Aarsleff, "The State of Nature and the Nature of Man in Locke," in John Yolton, ed., *John Locke: Problems and Perspectives* (Cambridge: Cambridge University Press, 1969), pp. 99–136. See also Grant, *John Locke's Liberalism,* esp. p. 66. "The state of nature may incidentally be an imagined picture of the historical beginnings of mankind or a useful construct for highlighting the basis for an purposes of political life, but essentially it is a logical necessity."

9. Locke, *ST,* par. 11.

10. Ibid., par. 4.

11. Ibid., par. 6.

12. Ibid., par. 65.

13. Ibid., par. 7. Both the "executive power" and the "appropriation power" are corollaries of the fundamental right to preservation. Zuckert, *Natural Rights and the New Republicanism,* captures the idea well: "The appropriating power of labor is in effect equivalent to the executive power of the law of nature, a necessary inference from our fundamental right to life" (chap. 9).

14. *ST,* par. 65.

15. Ibid., par. 63; emphasis in original.

16. John Locke, *A Letter concerning Toleration* (1689), edited with an introduction by Patrick Romanell (Indianapolis, Ind.: Bobbs Merrill, 1958), p. 18.

17. Macpherson, *Possessive Individualism,* p. 241. See also Zuckert, *Natural Rights and the New Republicanism,* chap. 8: "The violent and unacceptable character of the state of nature follows as much from the use of rightful as from unlawful force. . . . under the conditions of the state of nature, the difference between the two becomes exceedingly difficult to ascertain. . . . [Thus] given all the force used in the state of nature, it is not so clear how different Locke's version of the natural condition is from Hobbes'."

18. *ST,* par. 13.

19. Ibid., par. 129.

20. Ibid., pars. 131, 129.

21. Ibid., par. 130.

22. Ibid., pars. 96, 98, 99.

23. Ibid., par. 140.

24. Ibid., par. 124 (emphasis in original); cf. 94, 95, 116, 127, 131.

25. Ibid., par. 134.

26. Ibid.; emphasis in original.

27. Ibid., par. 116.

28. Ibid., par. 135.

29. Ibid., par. 131.

30. Ibid.

31. Ibid., par. 6.

32. Ibid., par. 135, cf. 138.

33. Locke, *A Letter concerning Toleration,* pp. 30, 32, 49.

34. Ibid., p. 24.

35. Ibid., p. 41.

36. Tully, *A Discourse on Property,* pp. 140, 143, 149, 145, 149 (cf. Perry Anderson, *Lineages of the Absolutist State* [London: New Left Books, 1977]).

37. John Locke, *Some Considerations of the Consequences of the Lowering of Interest and Raising the Value of Money* (1691) in J. R. McCulloch, *Principles of Political Economy: With Sketch of the Rise and Progress of the Science* (London: Ward, Lock and Company, 1825), pp. 220–75. See this chapter for further discussion of Locke's economic ideas. See also Karen Iversen Vaughn, *John Locke: Economist and Social Scientist* (Chicago: University of Chicago Press, 1980), and William Letwin, *The Origins of Scientific Economics* (Garden City, N.Y.: Anchor Books, 1965), pp. 158–95.

38. Werner Sombart, *The Quintessence of Capitalism* (New York, 1915).

39. See, for example, Frances Fox Piven and Richard A. Cloward, *Regulating the Poor: The Functions of Public Welfare* (New York: Vintage, 1971), and Edward S. Greenberg, *Understanding Modern Government: The Rise and Decline of the American Political Economy* (New York: John Wiley and Son, 1979).

40. Locke, *Some Considerations*, p. 225.

41. Vaughn, *Locke: Economist and Social Scientist*, pp. 106–7. Vaughn's emphasis here is on Locke's treatment of "natural law" in the scientific, rather than the religious, sense. Locke, qua empiricist, wants to fathom the principles that drive the market and the impact of public regulations that thwart those natural market propensities. On the major questions that came up for consideration in his day, Locke came down on the side of political noninterference. As Vaughn concludes, "The government is limited in its ability to control economic phenomena both practically and morally: practically in that any attempt to legislate contrary to economic laws is doomed to the failure of unexpected, adverse consequences, and morally in that governments should not pass laws which contradict natural laws" (p. 118).

42. Sir Josiah Child, *Brief Observations concerning Trade and the Interest on Money*, 3d ed. (London, 1668).

43. To be sure, Locke did not base his argument for an unregulated interest rate on considerations of natural law and the rights of property. He couched his argument in essentially prudential terms. This, however, should not be surprising. The Lockean fundamentals of government formed no part of the revolutionary settlement and would have had little persuasive power in the policy debates of the 1690s. The question, however, being of very great concern to Locke (see letter of Lady Masham in Maurice Cranston's *John Locke: A Biography* [Oxford: Oxford University Press, 1985], pp. 351–52), he entered the fray making his case in just those terms.

44. For a very good discussion of the issues involved in the recoinage debate, see Joyce Oldham Appleby, *Economic Thought and Ideology in Seventeenth-Century England* (Princeton, N.J.: Princeton University Press, 1978), pp. 217–41. See also Peter Laslett, "John Locke, the Great Recoinage, and the Origins of the Board of Trade, 1695–1698," *William and Mary Quarterly* 14 (July 1957): 370–92.

45. Appleby, *Economic Thought and Ideology*, p. 221; emphasis added. Appleby concludes: "Upon this ground the father of empiricism built the gold standard edifice that was to stand for the next two centuries." See Locke's *Some Considerations*, p. 278: The depreciation of money "will rob all creditors of . . . their quit-rents for ever; and in all other rents, as far as their former contracts reach . . . of their yearly income."

46. Appleby, *Economic Thought and Ideology*, pp. 236, 39, cf. 254.

47. Ibid., p. 254. On the origins of English mercantilist policy, she writes: "The first appearance in England of anything that could be called mercantilism—that is, a body of public law directed toward state economic goals—emerged at the beginning of the eighteenth century under the sponsorship of landlords and manufacturers rather than that of the merchants from whom its name is derived" (pp. 250–51). See Letwin, *Origins of Scientific Economics*, esp. p. 194. Seizing on Locke's recommendations, namely, the suppres-

sion of the Irish woolen industry and what he regards as Locke's "repeated insistence in the *Considerations* that the Government must regulate trade in order to assure a proper balance of trade," Letwin decides that Locke was "very much an advocate of government intervention in economic affairs." For an answer to Letwin, see Vaughn, *Locke: Economist and Social Scientist*, esp. pp. 122–23.

48. Appleby, *Economic Thought and Ideology*, pp. 258–59. "The liberals conceived of a commercial society built upon an economic meritocracy and uniform market responses, a competitive model rendered safe to them by their own commercial aptitude. . . . The economic model of Locke and the landed Whig magnates who made the critical decisions for English economic development rested upon the sanctity of the silver standard and the notion of balancing trade accounts, ideas replete with political meaning." Thus Locke, in his *Some Considerations*, states that bringing in more wealth from abroad, "being the only concernment of the kingdom, in reference to its wealth, is apt to be supposed by us without doors to be the only care of Parliament." He attributes to "mismanaged government" the loss of specie.

49. Neal Wood, *John Locke and Agrarian Capitalism* (Berkeley: University of California Press, 1984), and David McNally, "Locke, Levellers, and Liberty: Property and Democracy in the Thought of the First Whigs," *History of Political Thought* 10:1 (Spring 1989): 17–40.

50. Appleby, *Economic Thought and Ideology*, p. 271.

51. Ibid., p. 277.

52. Ibid.

53. Locke, *Some Considerations*, p. 268.

54. Ibid., p. 256.

55. Ibid., p. 289; cf. p. 241.

56. Locke, *Some Considerations*, p. 273. See also p. 238: "We may see what injury the lowering of interest is like to do us, by hindering trade, when it shall either make the foreigner call home his money, or your own people backward to lend, the reward not being judged proportionable to the risque."

57. Locke, *Some Considerations*, pp. 243–44. "It being evident therefore that he that has skill in traffick, but has not money enough to exercise it . . . has [as] much reason to pay use for that money, as he, who having skill in husbandry, but no land of his own to employ it in. . . . it follows, that borrowing money upon interest for its use is not only, by the necessity of affairs, and the constitution of human society, unavoidable to some men; but that also to receive profit for the loan of money, is as equitable and lawful, as receiving rent for land."

58. Ibid., pp. 225–26.

59. Ibid., p. 268.

60. Ibid., pp. 255–56, 269.

61. *ST*, par. 87.

62. Ibid., par. 85, emphasis added.

63. Ibid., par. 142. The reader should not be left with the impression that Locke's political theory, even on the limited issue with which I have been concerned, is without blemish or blatant contradiction. Locke's teaching may be most severely faulted with respect to his argument for, and personal investments in, slavery. Besides investing in the Africa Company, he helped draft the *Fundamental Constitutions of Carolina* (1669), serving as secretary on the board of the Lords Proprietor for that colony. That constitution provided, among other things, that every freeman "shall have absolute power and authority over his negro slaves." See discussion in Laslett, *Two Treatises*, par. 24, pp. 325–26. As Grant rightly points out, even if a slave was to be taken in a "just war," there would be little justice in selling his or her children into bondage. See Grant's *John Locke's Lib-*

eralism, p. 68 n.22. Locke's theory, if intended to sanction the colonial slave trade, as Seliger argued, could do so only by denying its own deepest premises. See Martin Seliger, "Locke, Liberalism, and Nationalism," in Yolton, *John Locke,* p. 28.

64. It is necessary to add that such a philosophic system is only as strong as the number of claims of truth (especially of fundamental truths) it can verify. For example, such a system may contain a systematic set of propositions in all the pertinent fields of philosophical speculation. Its politics may indeed logically flow from its ethics, and its ethics from its theory of knowledge and metaphysics. But that entire system may rest on a set of metaphysical premises that are bizarre, that defy all "common sense" and sensory experience, and that received little attention, elaboration, or proof. The strength, i.e., the veraciy, of such a system would surely be in doubt, whatever the logical rigor of its subsequently developed doctrines. I should add that I have nowhere sought to argue that Locke's system of thought is a "strong" one in this sense or that he has proven his philosophical case entire.

Chapter 7. Eighteenth-Century Background: Locke in America

1. Martyn P. Thompson, "The Reception of Locke's 'Two Treatises of Government': 1690–1706," *Political Studies* 24:2 (June 1976): 184–91; Jeffrey Nelson, "Unlocking Locke's Legacy: A Comment," *Political Studies* 26 (1978): 101–8; J. P. Kenyon, *Revolution Principles: The Politics of Party, 1689–1720* (Cambridge: Cambridge University Press, 1977); H. T. Dickinson, *Liberty and Property: Political Ideology in Eighteenth-Century Britain* (New York: Holmes and Meier, 1977); J. H. Plumb, *The Growth of Political Stability in England: 1675–1725* (London: Macmillan, 1967); Richard Ashcraft, *Revolutionary Politics and Locke's "Two Treatises of Government"* (Princeton, N.J.: Princeton University Press, 1986), esp. pp. 551–601.

No element of Locke's radical resistance theory was employed by the convention Parliament to justify William's ascension to the throne, and, as Ashcraft persuasively argues, Locke himself grew increasingly frustrated by the proceedings and proclamations that transferred power to the new king. Although Locke's defense of private property would eventually be taken up by the court Whigs, notable Tories such as Charles Leslie, William Sherlock, and Offspring Blackall attacked Locke's radical theory. In sum, Locke's political work was either not relevant to the technicalities of governing an established polity or considered too incendiary to preserve the peace of Britain (if, for example, adopted by seekers of Irish independence).

2. John Dunn, "The Politics of Locke in England and America in the Eighteenth Century," in John Yolton, ed., *John Locke: Problems and Perspectives* (Cambridge: Cambridge University Press, 1969).

3. Ibid., pp. 70–71. See also Jay Fliegelman, *Prodigals and Pilgrims: The American Revolution against Patriarchal Authority, 1750–1800* (Cambridge: Cambridge University Press, 1982), p. 38.

4. Dunn, "The Politics of Locke," p. 72.

5. Ibid., pp. 70, 77, 65, 60.

6. Ibid., pp. 78–79. Benjamin Rush, quoted in Dunn, "The Politics of Locke in England and America," p. 78.

7. Bernard Bailyn, "Political Experience and Enlightenment Ideas in Eighteenth-Century America," in Jack P. Greene, ed., *The Reinterpretation of the American Revolution: 1763–1789* (New York: Harper and Row, 1968), pp. 277–90.

8. John Locke, *First Treatise* (hereafter *FT*), in Peter Laslett, ed., *John Locke's* "Two Treatises of Government" (New York: Mentor Books, 1965), pars. 87–98, 111, 112, 119.

9. Bailyn, "Political Experience," p. 284.

10. Jefferson's rough draft of the Declaration accused the king of "waging cruel war against human nature itself, violating it's [*sic*] most sacred rights of life & liberty in the persons of a distant people who never offended him; captivating & carrying them into slavery in another hemisphere." This language, of course, was stricken from the adopted draft. Bernard Bailyn, *The Ideological Origins of the American Revolution* (Cambridge, Mass.: Harvard University Press, 1967), pp. 232–46, traces the rise of antislavery sentiment to the revolutionary principles themselves. "No one had set out to question the institution of chattel slavery, but by 1776 it had come under severe attack by writers following out the logic of Revolutionary thought" (p. 232). Jefferson, Madison, Benjamin Rush, James Otis, John Dickinson, and Samuel Hopkins all worked and wrote against the institution, and the first antislavery society was founded in 1775 in Philadelphia. For the progress of abolitionist views, see Alice Dana Adams, *The Neglected Period of Anti-Slavery in America, 1808–1831* (Gloucester, Mass.: Peter Smith, 1964).

11. Isaac Kramnick, "Republican Revisionism Revisited," *American Historical Review* 87:3 (1982): 629–64. Kramnick points to the debt that the late eighteenth-century radicals owed to Locke and their self-conscious embrace of his fundamental political teaching. For Locke's statement, see John Locke, *Second Treatise* (hereafter *ST*), in Peter Laslett, ed., John Locke, *Two Treatises of Government* (New York: Mentor Books, 1965), 157–58.

12. Bailyn, "Political Experience," p. 285.

13. Ibid., p. 287; emphasis added.

14. Patricia U. Bonomi, *Under the Cope of Heaven: Religion, Society, and Politics in Colonial America* (Oxford: Oxford University Press, 1986). Thus up to 1765, more "sermons, devotional writings, catechisms, pious legends and theological treatises . . . [were] published than were writings on political science, history, and law combined, and even during the Revolutionary era devotional works comprised the largest single classification. Moreover this reflected the reading of all ranks" (p. 4). See also Ellis Sandoz, *A Government of Laws: Political Theory, Religion, and the American Founding* (Baton Rouge: Louisiana State University Press, 1990).

15. Bonomi, *Under the Cope of Heaven*, p. 21.

16. Ibid., p. 23.

17. Ibid., p. 32.

18. Vernon L. Parrington, *Main Currents in American Thought*, vol. 1, *The Colonial Mind* (New York: Harcourt, Brace and World, 1927), pp. 20, 24–25. Cambridge Platform (1648), reprinted in Henry Steele Commager, *Documents of American History* (New York: Appleton-Century-Crofts, 1958), pp. 29–31.

19. Parrington, *Main Currents*, 1:32, 33–34, 31.

20. John Cotton, quoted in ibid., pp. 35–36.

21. John Winthrop, "Little Speech on Liberty" (1645), reprinted in Alpheus Thomas Mason, *Free Government in the Making: Readings in American Political Thought* (New York: Oxford University Press, 1965), pp. 60–61.

22. Roger Williams, "A Reply to the Aforesaid Answer of Mr. Cotton, in a Conference between Truth and Peace," in ibid., p. 66. For "The Bloudy Tenent of Persecution for Cause of Conscience Discussed" (1644), and John Cotton's response, see pp. 63–65.

23. Williams, "The Bloudy Tenent," quoted in Parrington, *Main Currents*, 1:63, 70.

24. Charter of Rhode Island and Providence Plantations (1663); reprinted in Bernard Schwartz, ed., *The Roots of the Bill of Rights*, 5 vols. (New York: Chelsea House Publishers, 1980), 1:95–96.

25. Parrington, *Main Currents*, 1:65.

26. The writings of John Wise, according to Parrington, "stirred the mind of New England profoundly. What [Jonathan] Edwards did later for the doctrinal side of Congregationalism, John Wise did for the institutional." See *Main Currents,* 1:121. See also Bonomi, *Under the Cope of Heaven*, pp. 63–64.

27. John Wise, *A Vindication of the Government of New England Churches*, reprinted in Mason, *Free Government*, p. 71. Wise, *A Vindication*, quoted in Parrington, *Main Currents*, 1:123.

28. John Wise, *A Vindication*, in Mason, *Free Government*, pp. 68–71.

29. Ibid., pp. 73–74.

30. Bonomi, *Under the Cope of Heaven*, pp. 64–66.

31. Ibid., pp. 72–85. The "open and democratic forms" and "collective proprietorship over church affairs posed a firm barrier . . . [to] clerical . . . control. Pastors had to strike a delicate balance between their sacerdotal responsibilities and the opinions of a congregation upon whose affections and financial support they were dependent" (p. 80).

32. William Penn, *Pennsylvania Frame of Government* (1682), reprinted in Schwartz, *Roots of the Bill of Rights*, p. 143. Quoted in Bonomi, *Under the Cope of Heaven*, p. 36. Penn, "Preface" to *Pennsylvania Frame of Government*, pp. 163, 132. William Penn, "England's Present Interest Considered" (1675), ibid., pp. 158–59. *Pennsylvania Frame* in Schwartz, p. 140.

33. Quoted in Caroline Robbins, "William Penn, 1689–1702: Eclipse, Frustration, and Achievement," in Richard S. Dunn and Mary Maples Dunn, eds., *The World of William Penn* (Philadelphia: University of Pennsylvania Press, 1986), p. 78.

34. Bonomi, *Under the Cope of Heaven*, pp. 80, 84.

35. Perry Miller, "Solomon Stoddard, 1643–1729," *Harvard Theological Review* 34 (1941): 298. Quoted in C. C. Goen, *Revivalism and Separatism in New England, 1740–1800* (Middletown, Conn.: Wesleyan University Press, 1987), p. 5.

36. Against the views of Perry Miller and Rossiter, who believed the awakening was confined to the lower orders of society, see Edwin S. Gaustad, "Society and the Great Awakening in New England" (1954), in Abraham S. Eisenstadt, ed., *American History: Recent Interpretations*, bk. 1 (New York: Thomas E. Crowell, 1969), pp. 125–34, and Goen, *Revivalism and Separatism*, pp. 8–35.

37. Charles Chauncy, "Civil Magistrates Must Be Just: Ruling in the Fear of God" (1747), reprinted in Ellis Sandoz, ed., *Political Sermons of the Founding Era: 1730–1805* (Indianapolis, Ind.: Liberty Press, 1991), p. 158.

38. Jonathan Edwards, *Narrative of Surprising Conversions* (1737), quoted in Goen, *Revivalism and Separatism*, pp. 13–14. For Jonathan Edwards, see Parrington, *Main Currents*, 1:151–65.

39. Goen, *Revivalism and Separatism*, p. 17.

40. Account of Benjamin Trumbull, *A Complete History of Connecticut* (New Haven, 1818), quoted in ibid., p. 18.

41. Ibid., p. 25.

42. Charles Hartsborn Maxson, *The Great Awakening in the Middle Colonies* (Chicago, 1920), quoted in Goen, *Revivalism and Separatism*, p. 17.

43. Goen, *Revivalism and Separatism*, p. 28. For a discussion of Hume's insightful finding that religious "enthusiasm" tends to inspire self-confidence and independence and render believers "free from the yoke of ecclesiastics," see Paul A. Rahe, *Republics*

Ancient and Modern: Classical Republicanism and the American Revolution (Chapel Hill: University of North Carolina Press, 1992), pp. 550–51.

44. Bonomi, *Under the Cope of Heaven*, p. 139.

45. Ibid., pp. 147, 158–60.

46. Ibid., p. 160. This judgment is confirmed by Goen: "The revival he [Whitefield] fostered encouraged men to criticize entrenched conservatism and eventually to revolt against constituted authority, and thus sharpened the sensibilities that led to the Declaration of Independence. Not without reason has the Great Awakening been called 'our national conversion' " (*Revivalism and Separatism*, p. 28).

47. Quoted in Bonomi, *Under the Cope of Heaven*, p. 156.

48. Elisha Williams, "The Essential Rights and Liberties of Protestants" (Boston, 1774), reprinted in Sandoz, *Political Sermons*, p. 62. Dunn, "The Politics of Locke in England and America," p. 73, writes: "In William's dazzling assault . . . [on] authority . . . Locke's notions of toleration were fused with a brilliant presentation of his theory of government, and a doctrine of startling originality appeared." But if one grasps the full structure of Locke's philosophy, one easily perceives how unoriginal William's argument actually is. It was *Locke* who fused religious and civil liberty, rooting both in the fundamental character of rational nature and its need for liberty per se.

49. Claude Newlin, *Philosophy and Religion in Colonial America* (New York: Philosophical Library, 1962), p. 31. Cotton Mather, *The Christian Philosopher* (1721), quoted in Newlin, pp. 33–35; emphasis in original.

50. Benjamin Coleman, "A Humble Discourse on the Incomprehensibleness of God" (1715) and "God Deals with Us as Rational Creatures" (1723), quoted in Newlin, *Philosophy and Religion*, pp. 42–43.

51. John White, *New England's Lamentations* (1734), quoted in Newlin, *Philosophy and Religion*, p. 64. Samuel Johnson, *The Necessity of Revealed Religion*, in Newlin, p. 62.

52. Ibid., p. 74.

53. Ibid., p. 90. For a careful summary of Edwards's theory of the emotions as they relate to religion, see pp. 94–102.

54. Ibid., p. 87.

55. Charles Chauncy, *Seasonable Thoughts on the State of Religion in New England*, quoted in ibid., pp. 91, 94. Chauncy's post-Revolution views on the benevolence of God were developed in *The Mystery Hid from Ages and Generations, or, The Salvation of All Men* (1784), and his repudiation of the doctrine of human depravity and original sin, in *Five Dissertations on the Scripture Account of the Fall* (1785).

56. Ebenezer Gay, *Natural Religion as Distinguished from Revealed* (1759), quoted in Newlin, *Philosophy and Religion*, p. 199.

57. Gad Hitchcock, *Natural Religion Aided by Revelation and Perfected by Christianity* (1779). Quoted in Newlin, ibid.

58. Bonomi, *Under the Cope of Heaven*, pp. 97–98.

59. Goen, *Revivalism and Separatism*, p. 25.

60. Ibid., p. 105.

61. Samuel Johnson, *A System of Morality* (1746), quoted in Newlin, *Philosophy and Religion*, p. 112.

62. Ibid., p. 118.

63. Ibid., p. 114.

64. Ibid., pp. 120–21.

65. Ibid., p. 120.

66. Ibid., pp. 123–24, 132.

67. Carl Van Doren, *Benjamin Franklin* (New York: Viking Press, 1938), p. 193.

68. The career of Phillip Doddridge, in particular, attests to the ease with which latitudinarian and Dissenter could join in common cause. Himself a Dissenter, Doddridge was encouraged to enter the ministry by the latitudinarian Samuel Clarke.

69. Jay Fliegelman, *Prodigals and Pilgrims*. The author follows Mott in defining an American "bestseller" as a work with sales in excess of twenty thousand copies (representing 1 percent of the population). See Frank Luther Mott, *The Golden Multitudes: The Story of Bestsellers in the United States* (New York: Macmillan, 1947).

70. Fliegelman, *Prodigals and Pilgrims*, p. 33.

71. Ibid., p. 40.

72. Gordon S. Wood, *The Radicalism of the American Revolution: How a Revolution Transformed a Monarchical Society into a Democratic One unlike Any That Had Ever Existed* (New York: Alfred A. Knopf, 1992), pp. 11–94.

73. Newlin, *Philosophy and Religion*, pp. 112–19.

74. Henry Steele Commager, *The Empire of Reason: How Europe Invented and America Realized the Enlightenment* (Garden City, N.Y.: Anchor Press, 1977), p. xii. For key Enlightenment ideas, as expounded by Franklin, Jefferson, John Adams, Madison, and Hamilton, see Adrienne Koch, *The American Enlightenment: The Shaping of the American Experiment and a Free Society as Revealed in the Thoughts and Writings of our Major Philosopher-Statesmen* (New York: George Braziller, 1965). See also Henry E. May, *The Enlightenment in America* (Oxford: Oxford University Press, 1976), and Ernest Cassara, *The Enlightenment in America* (New York: University Press of America, 1988). For the French influence see Paul Merrill Spurlin, *The French Enlightenment in America: Essays on the Times of the Founding Fathers* (Athens: University of Georgia Press, 1984).

75. William S. Sachs and Ari Hoogenboom, *The Enterprising Colonials: Society on the Eve of the Revolution* (Chicago: Argonaut Publishers, 1965), p. 79.

76. "Franklin to My Friend, A. B.," in Benjamin Franklin, *The Autobiography and Other Writings*, ed. Jesse Lemisch (New York: New American Library, 1961), p. 143. Cf. "The Way to Wealth," pp. 145–51. For Franklin's emphasis on moral self-improvement and his "arduous project of arriving at moral perfection," see pp. 65–71.

77. Sachs and Hoogenboom, *Enterprising Colonials*, pp. 79, 85. A far more detailed analysis of the colonial economy is contained in Robert A. East, *Business Enterprise in the American Revolutionary Era* (Gloucester, Mass.: Peter Smith, 1964). For the enthusiasm toward and growth of American enterprise, see Joseph Gies and Frances Gies, *The Ingenious Yankees: The Men, Ideas, and Machines That Transformed a Nation, 1776–1876* (New York: Thomas E. Crowell, 1976), pp. 1–84; John Chamberlain, *The Enterprising Americans: A Business History of the United States* (New York: Harper and Row, 1963); James Blaine Walker, *The Epic of American Industry* (New York: Harper and Brothers, 1949), pp. 1–39. For a concise enumeration of the rapidly emerging colonial industries, see Louis M. Hacker et al., *The United States: A Graphic History* (New York: Modern Age Books, 1937), pp. 18ff. See also John J. McCusker and Russell R. Menard, *The Economy of British America* (Chapel Hill: University of North Carolina Press, 1985).

78. See Sachs and Hoogenboom, *Enterprising Colonials*, p. 81. For moral and even legal restraints on extravagance, especially as they relate to sumptuary laws, see Forrest McDonald, *Novus Ordo Seclorum: The Intellectual Origins of the Constitution* (Lawrence: University Press of Kansas, 1985), pp. 15–16, 88–90, 173, 288.

79. Lord Bacon, quoted in Paul Johnson, *A History of the English People* (New York: Harper and Row, 1985), pp. 205-6.

80. Bailyn, "Political Experience and Enlightenment ideas," p. 287.

81. Jack P. Greene, *Pursuits of Happiness: The Social Development of Early Modern British Colonies and the Formation of American Culture* (Chapel Hill: University of North Carolina Press, 1988), p. 195. Although he treats the theme of equality in his discussion of the postrevolutionary period, Gordon Wood also sees this stark pattern of social transformation in America. See *Radicalism of the American Revolution,* esp. pp. 232–43.

82. Quoted in Douglas North, ed., *The Growth of the American Economy to 1860* (New York: Harper Torchbooks, 1968), p. 141.

83. Clarence L. Ver Steeg, *The Formative Years: 1607–1763* (New York: Hill and Wang, 1964), p. 221.

84. J. Hector St. John de Crevecoeur, "What Is an American?" in *Letters from an American Farmer and Sketches of Eighteenth-Century America* (1782), ed. Albert E. Stone (New York: Penguin, 1981), pp. 81–83. For a useful biography, see Gay Wilson Allen and Roger Asselineau, *St. John de Crevecoeur: The Life of an American Farmer* (New York: Viking Press, 1987). Francis Grund, quoted in Douglas Miller, *The Birth of Modern America: 1820–1850* (New York: Bobbs Merrill, 1970), p. 31. Other visitors reported much the same thing, though not with such characteristic flair. See William Cobbett, *Journal of a Year's Residence* (1817), in Walter Allen, *Transatlantic Crossings: American Visitors to Britain and British Visitors to America in the Nineteenth Century* (London: Heinemann, 1971), pp. 164–67. See also Basil Hall, "Travels in North America" (1828), in ibid., pp. 170–74. See also the comments of Matthew Carey, *Essay on Wages* (1829), Horatio Greenough in Douglas Miller, *The Birth of Modern America,* pp. 40, 30. No one, of course, better captured the exuberant pace of American life, along with its pitfalls and problems, than Alexis de Tocqueville in *Democracy in America,* ed. Andrew Hacker (New York: Washington Square Press, 1964). For his view on the themes developed in this chapter, see especially "How Equality Suggests to the Americans the Idea of the Infinite Perfectibility of Man" (pp. 141–43), "That the Americans Combat the Effects of Individualism by Free Institutions" (pp. 176–80), "Of the Use Which Americans Make of Public Associations in Civil Life" (pp. 181–85), "How the Americans Combat Individualism by the Principle of Enlightened Self-Interest" (pp. 195–98), "Of the Taste for Physical Well-Being in America" (pp. 199–201), "How the Taste for Physical Gratification is United in America to Love of Freedom and Attention to Public Affairs" (pp. 209–12), and "What Causes Almost All Americans to Follow Industrial Callings" (p. 213).

85. Wood, *Radicalism of the American Revolution,* p. 7.

86. Jefferson to Peter Carr, 10 August 1787, in Gordon C. Lee, ed., *Crusade against Ignorance: Thomas Jefferson on Education* (New York: Teachers College, Columbia University, 1961), p. 146. Elihu Palmer, quoted in Leonard Peikoff, *The Ominous Parallels: The End of Freedom in America* (New York: Stein and Day, 1982), p. 109.

Chapter 8. The Spirit of '76

1. Edward Countryman, *The American Revolution* (New York: Hill and Wang, 1985), pp. 48–49: "The act managed to offend everyone. The rich, the poor, producers, consumers, the powerful, the powerless, people of commerce, people of the fields, old people making their wills, young people planning to marry, pious people going to church, ribald people going to the tavern, all of them would feel it."

2. Bernard Bailyn, *The Ideological Origins of the American Revolution* (Cambridge, Mass.: Harvard University Press, 1967), pp. 77, 28.

3. Ibid., p. 43.

4. For a virtually identical estimate see Michael Zuckert, *Natural Rights and the New Republicanism* (Princeton N.J.: Princeton University Press, 1994). "Cato was a source from whom both the English and the Americans of the eighteenth century learned Lockean politics. Cato's creators are important because they built the new republicanism on the foundation supplied by Locke, but incorporated in their work the older Whig political science. Trenchard and Gordon thus fused into a coherent whole two lines of thought which had proceeded in partial independence of each other previously, Whig political science and Lockean political philosophy."

5. As I indicated in Chapter 6 n.2, Sidney's *Discourses concerning Government,* like *Cato's Letters,* is a comprehensive Lockean-republican synthesis. See Alan Craig Houston, *Algernon Sidney and the Republican Heritage in England and America* (Princeton, N.J.: Princeton University Press, 1991). See discussion this chapter.

6. John Trenchard and Thomas Gordon, *Cato's Letters, 1620–1623,* 4 vols. (New York: Russell and Russell, 1969), reprinted from 1733 edition. For its influence on America, see Bailyn, *Ideological Origins,* esp. pp. 34–36, 43, 45; Lawrence H. Leder, *Liberty and Authority: Early American Political Ideology, 1689–1763* (New York: W. W. Norton, 1968), p. 25; Clinton Rossiter, *The Political Thought of the American Revolution, Part 3, Seedtime of the Republic* (New York: Harcourt, Brace and World, 1963), pp. 67–68.

7. Bailyn, *Ideological Origins,* pp. 46, 51.

8. Trenchard and Gordon, *Cato's Letters,* vol. 1, no. 30, p. 257, "Cautions against the Natural Encroachments of Power" (17 June 1721).

9. Ibid., vol. 1, no. 33, pp. 257, 259, 260–61 (17 June 1721).

10. Ibid., vol. 1, no. 25, p. 184 (15 April 1721), "Considerations on the Destructive Spirit of Arbitrary Power. With the Blessings of Liberty and our own Constitution."

11. Ibid., vol. 1, no. 18, pp. 121–22 (25 February 1720), "The Terrible Tendency of Public Corruption to Ruin a State . . . applied to our own."

12. Ibid., vol. 3, no. 70, p. 14 (17 March 1721).

13. Ibid., vol. 2, no. 60, p. 230 (6 January 1721), "All Government proved to be instituted by Men, and only to intend the general Good of Men."

14. Contrast Montesquieu's congratulatory rendering of England's "mixed constitution" in *The Spirit of the Laws* (1748) and the ebullient self-congratulatory air of Augustan times with the picture of British politics in Bernard Bailyn, *The Origins of American Politics* (New York: Vintage Books, 1967), pp. 14–31.

15. Bailyn, *Origins of American Politics,* p. 24.

16. Shepard Bancroft Clough and Charles Woolsey Cole, *Economic History of Europe* (Boston: D. C. Heath, 1941), pp. 288, 280.

17. *Cato's Letters,* vol. 3, no. 91, p. 206 (25 August 1722), "How Exclusive Companies influence and hurt our Government."

18. Ibid., pp. 203, 206.

19. Ibid., vol. 1, no. 20, pp. 140–41 (11 March 1720).

20. Clough and Cole, *Economic History of Europe,* p. 301.

21. *Cato's Letters,* vol. 3, no. 91, p. 211.

22. Ibid., vol. 3, no. 69, p. 10 (10 March 1721), "Address to the Freeholders, &c. about the Choice of their Representatives."

23. Henry St. John Viscount Bolingbroke, *The Craftsman,* quoted in Bailyn, *Origins of American Politics,* p. 4.

24. Bailyn, *Origins of American Politics,* pp. 38, 39, 53, and *Ideological Origins,* p. 54.

25. Bailyn, *Ideological Origins,* p. 86. Most popular was James Burgh's *Britain's Remembrancer: or, The Danger Not Over . . .* (London: 1746). Burgh rails against "our

degenerate times and corrupt nation," "luxury and irreligion . . . venality, perjury, faction . . . gluttony . . . gaming . . . [and] self-murders." Quoted in Bailyn, *Ideological Origins*, p. 86.

26. John Dickinson, "London Letters," in Bailyn, *Ideological Origins*, p. 90. For Franklin's and the Carrolls' thoughts, see pp. 89, 91–92.

27. Gordon Wood, *The Creation of the American Republic* (New York: W. W. Norton, 1972). For Wood's treatment of America's perception of British corruption and its impact on the interpretation of Parliament's acts after 1763, see pp. 28–43.

28. Ibid., pp. 107–8, 110–12. On colonial factions, see p. 76. The significance of factions, for the republican, and Lockean, perspective, is critical and will be taken up in this chapter.

29. Ibid., pp. 107, 53.

30. Ibid., pp. 55, 59, 117.

31. The preponderance of controversy has surrounded the extent to which America actually remained loyal to republicanism in the years following independence. I discuss the critical and constitutional periods of American history in Chapter 9.

32. John Dickinson, "Letters from a Farmer in Pennsylvania," quoted in Merrill Jensen, *Tracts of the American Revolution, 1763–1776* (Indianapolis, Ind.: Bobbs Merrill, 1967), pp. 128–32. "London Letters," quoted in Bailyn, *Ideological Origins*, p. 90; "An Address to the Committee of Correspondence in Barbados," quoted in Cecelia Kenyon, "Republicanism and Radicalism in the American Revolution: An Old-Fashioned Interpretation," in Sidney Fine and Gerald S. Brown, eds., *The American Past: Conflicting Interpretations of the Great Issues* (New York: Macmillan, 1976), pp. 156–57 n.13.

33. Samuel West, "On the Right to Rebel against Governors" (Boston, 1776), in Charles S. Hyneman and Donald S. Lutz, *American Political Writing during the Founding Era: 1760–1805*, 2 vols. (Indianapolis, Ind.: Liberty Press, 1983), 1:410–17.

34. Abraham Williams, "An Election Sermon" (Boston, 1762), in Hyneman and Lutz, *American Political Writing*, 1:7–8. In same volume, see also Simeon Howard, "A Sermon Preached to the Ancient and Honorable Artillery Company in Boston" (Boston, 1773), p. 187: "In a State of nature, or where men are under no civil government, God has given to every one liberty to pursue his own happiness in whatever way, and by whatever means he pleases, without asking the consent or consulting the inclination of any other man, provided he keeps within the bounds of the law of nature. Within these bounds, he may govern his actions, and dispose of his property and person, as he thinks proper." Also, Samuel West, "On the Right to Rebel against Governors" (Boston, 1776), pp. 413–17. Or, see John Alman, "A Constitutional Answer to the Rev. Mr. John Wesley's Calm Address to the American Colonies," (London, 1775), in Ellis Sandoz, ed., *Political Sermons of the American Founding Era: 1730–1805* (Indianapolis, Ind.: Liberty Press, 1991). For the revival of interest in Locke's influence on American thought, see Stephen Botein, "Religion and Politics in Revolutionary New-England: Natural Rights Reconsidered," in Patricia U. Bonomi, ed., *Party and Political Opposition in Revolutionary America* (Tarrytown, N.Y.: Sleepy Hollow Press, 1980), pp. 13–34. In same, see comment by Stanley N. Katz, pp. 35–42. For earlier treatment, see Leder, *Liberty and Authority*. And see especially Steven M. Dworetz, *The Unvarnished Doctrine: Locke, Liberalism, and the American Revolution* (Durham, N.C.: Duke University Press, 1990).

35. John Adams's notes on Otis's protest are reprinted in Max Beloff, ed., *The Debate on the American Revolution, 1761–1783* (London: Adam and Charles Black, 1972), p. 45. For a very good discussion of the legal traditions and arguments involved in the contest against parliamentary supremacy, see Edward Corwin, *The "Higher Law" Background of American Constitutional Law* (Ithaca, N.Y.: Cornell University Press, 1955).

36. James Otis, "The Rights of the British Colonies Asserted and Proved" (*Boston Gazette,* 23 July 1764), in Max Beloff, *Debate on the American Revolution,* p. 63. With respect to James Otis's popularity, see Jensen, *Tracts of the American Revolution,* p. xxii. Otis "became the darling of the populace of Boston, which elected him to the legislature in 1761. Thereafter he usually dominated the Boston town meeting, and was one of the most vocal members of the House of Representatives."

37. Beloff, *The Debate on the American Revolution,* pp. 64, 67–68, 48–49, 54–55.

38. "The Massachusetts Circular Letter of 1768," reprinted in Henry Steele Commager, *Documents of American History,* 2 vols. in 1 book (New York: Appleton-Century-Crofts, 1958), 1:66.

39. Jensen, *Tracts of the American Revolution,* p. 1. Document reprinted on pp. 233–55.

40. "Declarations and Resolves of the First Continental Congress," reprinted in Commager, *Documents of American History* 1:83; "Address of the Continental Congress to the Inhabitants of Canada," reprinted in ibid., p. 91.

41. The Virginia and Massachusetts Bills of Rights are reprinted in Commager, *Documents* 1:103–4 and 107–10, respectively.

42. Philip Greven, *The Protestant Temperament: Patterns of Child Rearing, Religious Experience, and the Self in Early America* (Chicago: University of Chicago Press, 1977), pp. 352, 357. Greven, like Wood, sees the Revolution in utopian terms, something that demanded "the total annihilation of self-interest and selfishness, [and] the hope for a new birth that . . . [would] transform . . . a life of sin and of corruption into a life of grace, selflessness and purity" (pp. 354–55).

43. The Massachusetts Bills of Rights, reprinted in Commager, *Documents* 1:108.

44. Despite the poor reception accorded to Locke's anonymously published *Two Treatises,* Locke's political ideas were able to penetrate eighteenth-century British culture through the publication of several works. Three editions of essentially the same pamphlet, in fact, appeared in 1690, 1709, and 1710. Variously titled *Political Aphorisms, Vox Populi, Vox Dei,* and *The Judgment of Whole Kingdoms and Nations,* they contained ideas and language directly taken, without ascription, from John Locke's political text. Among "the best-selling pamphlets of the eighteenth-century," Ashcraft and Goldsmith report, these works enabled "not only Lockean principles, but also actual phrases taken from the *Two Treatises* [to] enter . . . into the political consciousness of many Englishmen." See Richard Ashcraft and M. M. Goldsmith, "Locke, Revolution Principles, and the Formation of Whig Ideology," *Historical Journal* 26:4 (1983): 789, 793. For a very useful discussion of further sources that could disseminate Locke's natural rights/resistance views and meld them into the Whiggish common law tradition, see Zuckert, *Natural Rights and the New Republicanism,* chap. 10.

45. *Cato's Letters,* vol. 2, no. 60, p. 227; no. 59, p. 210; no. 67, p. 304.

46. Ibid., vol. 2, no. 67, p. 304; no. 62, p. 252; no. 62, p. 248.

47. Ibid., vol. 2, no. 62, p. 252; vol. 2, no. 108, p. 24 (emphasis added).

48. Ibid., vol. 1, no. 11, p. 66; no. 55, p. 169; no. 62, pp. 243–44; no. 60, p. 228; no. 11, p. 66.

49. The failure of scholars to sufficiently differentiate the fundamental premises of the left and right opposition parties (their common views on corruption and the Constitution aside) has obscured Locke's influence for the radical perspective. For a good contrast, see Herbert M. Atherton, *Political Prints in the Age of Hogarth* (Oxford: Clarendon Press, 1974), esp. chaps. 5 and 6. See also, Ronald Hamowy, "Cato's Letters, John Locke, and the Republican Paradigm," in Edward J. Harpham, ed., *John Locke's "Two Treatises of*

Government'': *New Interpretations* (Lawrence: University Press of Kansas, 1992), pp. 148–72.

50. On the explosion of the British public debt across the eighteenth century and its failure to drive the nation to bankruptcy and ruin (as "Cato," Bolingbroke, and the opposition insisted it would), see Lord Macaulay's *History of England* (1855), extensively quoted in Clough and Cole, *Economic History of Europe*, pp. 288–91. "At every stage in the growth of that debt it has been seriously asserted by wise men that bankruptcy and ruin were at hand. Yet still the debt went on growing and still bankruptcy and ruin were as remote as ever'' (pp. 288-89).

51. Isaac Kramnick, "English Middle Class Radicalism in the Eighteenth Century,'' *Literature of Liberty: A Review of Contemporary Liberal Thought* 3:2 (1980): 5–48, and "Republican Revisionism Revisited,'' *American Historical Review* 87:3 (June 1982): 629–64. Kramnick's writings on the subject appear in *Republicanism and Bourgeois Radicalism: Political Ideology in Late Eighteenth-Century England and America* (Ithaca, N.Y.: Cornell University Press, 1990). As Kramnick urged, the demand for "a full and fair representation,'' so integral to the republican tradition, was a Lockean political requisite as well. See John Locke, *Second Treatise* (hereafter *ST*), reprinted in Peter Laslett, ed., John Locke, *Two Treatises of Government* (New York: Mentor Books, 1965), pars. 157–58.

52. See Eric Foner, *Tom Paine and Revolutionary America* (Oxford: Oxford University Press, 1976), pp. 9–19.

53. For Locke's influence on the English radicals and their connections and correspondence with important Americans during the revolutionary period and beyond, see also Colin Bonwick, *English Radicals and the American Revolution* (Chapel Hill: University of North Carolina Press, 1977). Bonwick's larger story is of the inspiration the American Revolution afforded the English Dissenters. For America's keen interest in English politics, see especially Pauline Maier, "John Wilkes and American Disillusionment,'' *William and Mary Quarterly* 3d ser., 20:3 (July 1963): 373–95. In Parliament's imperious treatment of Wilkes, repeatedly elected but refused a seat there, the Americans found more evidence of constitutional corruption.

54. Houston, *Algernon Sidney,* pp. 102–3.

55. Sidney, *Discourses,* quoted in Houston, *Algernon Sidney,* p. 115. Houston, it should be noted, finds innumerable points separating Sidney and Locke as well. In particular, where Sidney begins with a resolute belief in people's inherent freedom (in the four senses discussed), Locke ties that freedom to a natural law conception rooted in the model of man as God's special creation, pp. 103–8, 114.

56. Zuckert, *Natural Rights and the New Republicanism,* chap. 10.

57. Ibid. Zuckert indeed cites a host of the Catonic texts, already cited, that demonstrate Locke's unmistakable imprint on Trenchard and Gordon's thought.

58. *Cato's Letters,* vol. 2, no. 45, p. 85. Quoted in Zuckert, chap. 10.

59. For a compelling expose of Americans' manifest fear of the corrupting effects of wealth and luxury, see esp. Wood, *Creation of the American Republic,* pp. 416–24.

60. Ibid., pp. 59, 58.

61. Stephen Hopkins, "An Essay on the Trade of the Northern Colonies'' (6 and 13 February 1764), in Jensen, *Tracts of the American Revolution,* pp. 3–18. Hopkins was expressly speaking for the merchants of Newport and Providence, who, themselves, were responding to an alarm sounded by Boston's merchants in the "State of Trade'' (1763). Hopkins "Essay,'' Jensen reports, was reprinted in the *Boston Evening Post,* the *New York Mercury,* the *Newport Mercury,* the *Pennsylvania Journal,* and published in London as a pamphlet. For a careful summary of Americans' economic grievances against Parliament,

see Thomas Jefferson, *A Summary View of the Rights of British America* (1774), in same volume, pp. 256–76. On the egregious practices of customs officials and British judges and their impact on commerce, generally, and on individual merchants, in particular, see Henry Laurens, *Extracts from the Proceedings of the Court of Vice-Admiralty,* reprinted in Jensen, *Tracts of the American Revolution,* pp. 185–207.

62. Bonomi, *Under the Cope of Heaven,* p. 206. Adams to Dr. J. Morse, 2 December 1815, quoted in Patricia U. Bonomi, *Under the Cope of Heaven: Religion, Society, and Politics in Colonial America* (Oxford: Oxford University Press, 1986), p. 200. Cf. pp. 199–209. See also, Bailyn, *Ideological Origins,* pp. 95–98.

63. Houston, *Algernon Sidney,* p. 166, corroborates the idea: "Civic virtue did not grow out of the renunciation of private interests, but rather out of the recognition that the vast majority of private interests are encompassed in, indeed are part and parcel of, the public interest. To put the point somewhat baldly, self-interest was the strongest possible foundation for civic virtue."

64. Zuckert's view of Locke differs from my own on this point. Quite correctly he perceives Locke's beings not as mere bourgeois appropriators, but as individuals "able to give shape and form to their lives, able to suspend their desires and act on reason. . . . [They are] free, self-directing beings." But that is as far as Zuckert's Locke apparently goes. "Cato's importance," consists in his appending a civic side to the Lockean personality. "Civil and political freedom, even at the risk of life, is the necessary completion or fulfillment of the Lockean philosophy of the self. Cato's importance lies in part in bringing this side of Locke forcefully into the fore." "Cato" thus effects a "real rapprochement" between Locke and an "older moral sensibility" (chap. 10). However, as I pointed out earlier, neither in his writing nor in his life's record did Locke betray a deficiency of civic valor. To that extent Zuckert overstates Cato's achievement by understating Locke's.

65. *Cato's Letters,* vol, 3, no. 89, pp. 192–93.

66. John Dickinson's "Letters from a Farmer in Pennsylvania," reprinted in Jensen, *Tracts of the American Revolution,* pp. 134, 138, 160–61, 132.

67. Edmund Burke, "Speech in Support of Resolutions for Conciliation with the American Colonies" (22 March 1775), in Elliott R. Barkan, ed., *Edmund Burke on the American Revolution: Selected Speeches and Letters* (New York: Harper Torchbooks, 1966), p. 86.

68. Quoted in Claude Newlin, *Philosophy and Religion in Colonial America* (New York: Philosophical Library, 1962), p. 114; For Locke's similar view, see Locke, *An Essay concerning Human Understanding,* ed. Alexander Campbell Fraser, 2 vols. (New York: Dover Publications, 1959), III, 1, 1.

69. In Newlin, *Philosophy and Religion,* p. 114.

70. Benjamin Franklin, *The Autobiography and Other Writings,* ed. Jesse Lemisch (New York: New American Library, 1961), p. 86.

71. See Ralph Lerner, *The Thinking Revolutionary: Principle and Practice in the New Republic* (Ithaca, N.Y.: Cornell University Press, 1987), p. 30. "The first act of discrimination . . . [for] the student of past thought when confronting those thousands of individuals of whose doings and speeches some record remains . . . [consists of] noting which of those historical actors were held in special regard or notoriety by contemporaries."

72. Bailyn, *Ideological Origins,* p. 123.

73. Thomas L. Pangle, *The Spirit of Modern Republicanism: The Moral Vision of the American Founders and the Philosophy of Locke* (Chicago: University of Chicago Press, 1988), p. 33.

74. Thomas Bradbury, *The Ass, or, the Serpent* (Boston, 1768), in Bailyn, *Ideological Origins,* pp. 130–31 (emphasis added). John Dickinson, "Two Letters on the Tea Tax,"

quoted in Vernon Parrington, *Main Currents in American Thought,* vol. 1, *The Colonial Mind* (New York: Harcourt, Brace and World, 1927), pp. 233–34. Thomas Jefferson, "Rough Draft of the Declaration," reprinted in Henry Steele Commager and Richard B. Morris, eds., *The Spirit of '76: The Story of the American Revolution as Told by Participants,* 2 vols. (Indianapolis, Ind.: Bobbs Merrill, 1958), 1:316 (emphasis added). Jefferson, *A Summary View of the Rights of British America* (1774), in Jensen, *Tracts of the American Revolution,* p. 275 (emphasis added). Samuel Adams, *A State of the Rights of the Colonists,* in Jensen, p. 239 (emphasis in original). See John Locke, *Second Treatise,* par. 142.

75. James Otis, *Boston Gazette,* 11 January 1762, quoted in Gary Nash, "Social Change and Prerevolutionary Urban Radicalism," in Alfred F. Young, ed., *The American Revolution: Explorations in the History of American Radicalism* (DeKalb: Northern Illinois University Press, 1976), p. 26.

76. Wood, *Creation of the American Republic,* p. 64.

77. Ibid., p. 54; emphasis added.

78. Quoted in ibid., pp. 71, 74.

79. Bailyn, *Origins of American Politics,* pp. 182, 183.

80. Ibid., pp. 107–8.

81. William S. Sachs and Ari Hoogenboom, *The Enterprising Colonials: Society on the Eve of the Revolution* (Chicago: Argonaut, 1965), p. 56.

82. Bailyn, *Origins of American Politics,* p. 125.

83. For a rather different approach to colonial factionalism and the origins of the American Revolution, see Marc Egnal, "The Pattern of Factional Development in Pennsylvania, New York, and Massachusetts, 1682–1776," in Patricia U. Bonomi, ed., *Party and Political Opposition in Revolutionary America* (Tarrytown, N.Y.: Sleepy Hollow Press, 1980), pp. 43–60; see also Egnal, *A Mighty Empire: The Origins of the American Revolution* (Ithaca, N.Y.: Cornell University Press, 1988). For Egnal, factions divided over the question of expansionism. Those who were for American glory and growth generally supported the Revolution (and later the Constitution); those who were not, did not.

84. Milton M. Klein, ed., *The Independent Reflector, or Essays on Sundry Important Subjects More Particularly Adapted to the Province of New York* (Cambridge, Mass.: Belknap Press of Harvard University Press, 1963). Expressly patterned after Trenchard and Gordon's influential series, *The Independent Whig,* it consisted of some fifty-two essays penned, principally, by New York's William Livingston, William Smith, Jr., and John Morin Scott. For the authors' debt to Trenchard and Gordon, see pp. 450–52.

85. Ibid., pp. 215, 216.

86. Ibid., "Of Patriotism" (5 May 1753), pp. 215–19; "Of Party Divisions" (22 February 1753), p. 148.

87. Ibid., "Of the Waste of Life" (25 October 1753), p. 407.

88. Ibid., "The Different Effects of an Absolute and a Limited Monarchy" (21 December 1752), pp. 78, 79–80.

89. Ibid., "A Discant on the Origin, Nature, Use, and Abuse of Civil Government" (12 July 1753), p. 288.

90. Ibid., "Further Reflections on the Doctrines of Passive Obedience and Non-Resistance" (23 August 1753), pp. 330–32. The editor, while acknowledging such precursors as John Wise and Jonathan Mayhew, considers Livingston's views "to be the first public expression in the colonies of the right of resistance . . . rooted exclusively in a natural rights philosophy and expounded within a purely secular and legalistic framework . . . [and] one of the clearest and most forceful assertions of the Lockean theory of government" (pp. 290–91 n.3).

91. Ibid., p. 143.

92. Sachs and Hoogenboom, *Enterprising Colonials,* p. 83.

93. Gary Nash, "Artisans and Politics in Eighteenth Century Philadelphia," in Margaret C. Jacob and James R. Jacob, eds., *The Origins of Anglo-American Radicalism* (London: George, Allen and Unwin, 1984), p. 178. See also Gary Nash, "Social Change and the Growth of Prerevolutionary Urban Radicalism," in Young, *American Revolution.* See, in same volume, Joseph Ernst's essay, pp. 159–86.

94. Nash, "Artisans and Politics," p. 177.

95. Eric Foner, "Tom Paine's Republic: Radical Ideology and Social Change," in Young, *American Revolution,* p. 217. See also Foner, *Tom Paine and Revolutionary America.*

96. For the limits of "equal protection" afforded Americans and the protests against slavery and religious intolerance, see Bailyn, *Ideological Origins,* pp. 230–72. See also, in Young, *American Revolution,* essays by Francis Jennings, Ira Berlin, and Joan Hoff Wilson on "The Indians' Revolution," "The Revolution in Black Life," and "Women and the American Revolution," respectively. For an assessment of Jefferson's attitudes see Joyce Oldham Appleby, *Without Resolution: The Jeffersonian Tensions in American Nationalism* (Oxford: Clarendon Press, 1992).

97. Jefferson to Benjamin Rush, 1800. Quoted in Saul K. Padover, *Thomas Jefferson on Democracy* (New York: Mentor, 1939), p. 108.

98. John Dickinson, *Farmer's Letters: An Address to the Committee of Correspondence in Barbados* (Philadelphia, 1766), quoted in Cecelia Kenyon, "Republicanism and Radicalism in the American Revolution," in Fine and Brown, eds., *American Past,* pp. 156–57 n.13. Kenyon appropriately concludes: "Dickinson is here clearly placing happiness as a right logically prior to property, and even to liberty, which stand in relation to it as means to end." Others, such as James Wilson, did likewise. And "Jefferson [in the Declaration] gave official sanction to these views" (p. 157 n.13).

99. Morton White, *The Philosophy of the American Revolution* (New York: Oxford University Press, 1978), pp. 182–83, 219–20 (emphasis added), 215, 216, 217, 220.

100. Daniel Leonard, "Letter of Massachusettensis," 23 January 1775, quoted in Parrington, *Main Currents,* 1:217. Jonathan Boucher, *A View of the Causes and Consequences of the American Revolution* (London, 1797) in Parrington, pp. 220, 222.

101. For the continued importance of family and community bonds in the founding era, despite the strong emphasis on industry, see Jack P. Greene, *Pursuits of Happiness: The Social Development of Early Modern British Colonies and the Formation of American Culture* (Chapel Hill: University of North Carolina Press, 1988), pp. 196–98.

102. John Adams, *Dissertation on the Canon and the Feudal Law,* quoted in Houston, *Algernon Sidney,* p. 237.

Chapter 9. The Constitution of '87

1. Rush, quoted in John Dunn, "The Politics of Locke in England and America in the Eighteenth Century," in John Yolton, ed., *John Locke: Problems and Perspectives* (Cambridge: Cambridge University Press, 1969), p. 78.

2. Ibid., pp. 78–80.

3. John P. Diggins, *The Lost Soul of American Politics: Virtue, Self-Interest, and the Foundations of Liberalism* (Chicago: University of Chicago Press, 1984), pp. 80, 83–84.

4. Matthew Carey, ed., *The Debates of the General Assembly of Pennsylvania* (Philadelphia, 1786), and various essays of *The Philadelphia, Pa. Packet,* quoted in Gor-

don S. Wood, *The Creation of the American Republic* (New York: W. W. Norton, 1972), pp. 401–2.

5. Charles A. Beard, *An Economic Interpretation of the Constitution of the United States* (New York: Macmillan, 1913), p. 48; James E. Ferguson, *The Power of the Purse: A History of American Public Finance, 1776–1790* (Chapel Hill: University of North Carolina Press, 1961), p. 337; Jackson T. Main, *The Antifederalists: Critics of the Constitution, 1781–88* (Chapel Hill: University of North Carolina Press, 1961), pp. 177–78; Merrill Jensen, *The New Nation: A History of the United States during the Confederation, 1781–89* (New York: Alfred A. Knopf, 1965), pp. 348–49; Forrest McDonald, *Novus Ordo Seclorum: The Intellectual Origins of the Constitution* (Lawrence: University Press of Kansas, 1985), pp. 175–77.

6. See especially, Jensen, *New Nation*, pp. 256, 339–40, 423–24.

7. Wood, *Creation of the American Republic*, pp. 393, 406, 414.

8. John C. Miller, *Alexander Hamilton and the Growth of the New Nation* (New York: Harper and Row, 1959), pp. 291, 135, 282. James Madison, Alexander Hamilton, and John Jay, *The Federalist Papers*, ed. Clinton Rossiter (New York: New American Library, 1961), no. 22.

9. On the importance of retiring the debt owed to public creditors see especially James Madison, "Address to the States, by the United States in Congress Assembled" (26 April 1783), reprinted in Marvin Meyers, ed., *The Mind of the Founder: Sources of the Political Thought of James Madison* (Indianapolis, Ind.: Bobbs Merrill, 1973), pp. 23–32. If the burden of public debt is not borne with dispatch, "the last and fairest experiment in favor of the rights of human nature will be . . . insulted and silenced by the votaries of tyranny and usurpation" (p. 32).

10. Quoted in Wood, *Creation of the American Republic*, p. 416.

11. Ibid., p. 407.

12. John Locke, *Second Treatise* (hereafter *ST*), reprinted in Peter Laslett, ed., John Locke, *Two Treatises of Government* (New York: Mentor Books, 1965), pars. 47–49, 48.

13. Quoted in Wood, *Creation of the American Republic*, pp. 404–6, 411. Papers of American Museum, vol. 1, p. 118, quoted in Beard, *An Economic Interpretation of the Constitution*, p. 181.

14. Wood, *Creation of the American Republic*, p. 412. See also McDonald, *Novus Ordo Seclorum*, pp. 177–78. "The general impression of what Shays' rebellion had been about was fabricated by Henry Knox."

15. Quoted in Beard, *An Economic Interpretation of the Constitution*, pp. 182–83.

16. Madison, quoted in Beard, *An Economic Interpretation of the Constitution*, p. 178. For Madison's own concern over the multiplicity and mutability of the laws of the states, see "The Vices of the System" (April 1787), reprinted in Meyers, *Mind of the Founder*, pp. 87–88.

17. Beard, *An Economic Interpretation of the Constitution*, pp. 182–83.

18. J. P. Diggins, *The Lost Soul of American Politics: Virtue, Self-Interest, and the Foundations of Liberalism* (Chicago: University of Chicago Press, 1984), pp. 349, 351, 352, 359.

19. *Federalist* no. 49, p. 315; no. 63, p. 384.

20. McDonald, *Novus Ordo Seclorum*, pp. 219–24, and *We the People: The Economic Origins of the Constitution* (Chicago: University of Chicago Press, 1958), pp. 38–92. For a rejection of the Beardian thesis, see also Robert E. Brown, *Charles Beard and the Constitution: A Critical Analysis of "An Economic Interpretation of the Constitution"* (New York: W. W. Norton, 1956).

21. See especially, Wood, *Creation of the American Republic,* pp. 416–18.

22. Gordon Wood has recently remarked on this important distinction. See *The Radicalism of the American Revolution: How a Revolution Transformed a Monarchical Society into a Democratic One unlike Any That Had Ever Existed* (New York: Alfred A. Knopf, 1992), p. 5.

23. Madison in *Federalist* no. 10, pp. 79–80.

24. Locke, *ST,* par. 63.

25. Ibid., par. 6.

26. Madison, *National Gazette* (29 March 1792), reprinted in Meyers, *Mind of the Founder,* pp. 243–45.

27. Ibid.; Locke, *ST,* par. 142.

28. Madison, "A Memorial and Remonstrance," reprinted in Meyers, *Mind of the Founder,* pp. 11, 9, 13.

29. Madison, *National Gazette* (29 March 1792), reprinted in Meyers, *Mind of the Founder,* pp. 243–46. For a very similar treatment of the philosophical underpinnings of *The Federalist,* see Morton White, *Philosophy, The Federalist, and the Constitution* (New York: Oxford University Press, 1989), pp. 25–37.

30. Madison, *Federalist* no. 10, p. 80.

31. Ibid., no. 49, p. 317.

32. Madison to Jefferson, 17 October 1788, in Wood, *Creation of the American Republic,* pp. 410, 413. Madison, "Vices of the Political System of the United States" (April 1787), reprinted in Meyers, *The Mind of the Founder,* p. 91.

33. Meyers, *The Mind of the Founder,* p. 77.

34. Madison, *Federalist* 10, p. 80.

35. White, *Philosophy, The Federalist, and the Constitution,* p. 26.

36. James Madison, *Notes of Debates in the Federal Convention of 1787,* ed. Adrienne Koch (New York: Norton, 1966), pp. 39, 40.

37. Cecelia Kenyon, ed., *The Antifederalists* (Indianapolis, Ind.: Bobbs Merrill, 1975), p. lxxxviii. "Letters from a Federal Farmer," in Paul L. Ford, *Pamphlets on the Constitution* (New York: Da Capo Press, 1968), p. 283.

38. Quoted in Ford, *Pamphlets,* p. 117; in Kenyon, *Antifederalists,* p. 156.

39. "Agrippa's" letter, addressed to the Massachusetts ratifying convention, *National Gazette,* 5 February 1788, reprinted in Kenyon, *Antifederalists,* p. 154; Samuel Adams to Elbridge Gerry (1784), reprinted in Main, *Antifederalists,* p. 9. Hugh Hughes, in same, p. 10.

40. Spencer Roane, "Letters of a Plain Dealer (13 February 1788) in Paul Leicester Ford, *Essays on the Constitution* (Brooklyn, N.Y.: Historical Printing Club, 1892), p. 391 (emphasis added); George Clinton, "The Letters of 'Cato,' " reprinted in Ford, *Essays,* p. 257.

41. King to Madison (27 January 1788) in *Documentary History of the Constitution of the United States* (Washington, 1894–1905), vol. 5, p. 459; Amos Singletary, "Address to Massachusetts Ratifying Convention" (January–February 1788), quoted in Saul K. Padover, *The Living U.S. Constitution* (New York: NAL, 1953), p. 34. On the interests aligned on the side of ratification, see Cathy D. Matson and Peter S. Onuf, *A Union of Interests: Political and Economic Thought in Revolutionary America* (Lawrence: University Press of Kansas, 1990). The authors argue that it was the Federalists' genius to associate the new union with rapid commercial development, thereby appealing "to the many optimistic and enterprising Americans who hoped to reap the rewards of independence" (p. 2).

42. "A Federalist," *Boston Gazette,* 26 November 1787, in Morton Borden, ed., *The Antifederalist Papers* (Detroit: Michigan University Press, 1965), pp. 108–9.

43. "The Letters of Philadelphensis," *The Independent Gazetteer* (Philadelphia), in Kenyon, *Antifederalists,* p. 81.

44. "A Farmer and Planter" *Baltimore Advertiser,* 1 April 1788, in Borden, *Antifederalist Papers,* pp. 108–9.

45. "Centinel," in Ford, *Essays,* p. 89.

46. Richard Henry Lee, "Letters from a Federal Farmer," quoted in Vernon L. Parrington, *Main Currents in American Thought,* vol. 1, *The Colonial Mind* (New York: Harcourt, Brace and World, 1927), p. 295.

47. Richard Henry Lee, "Letters from a Federal Farmer" (10 October 1787), reprinted in Kenyon, *Antifederalists,* p. 224.

48. "A Farmer and Planter," in Borden, *Antifederalist Papers,* p. 109.

49. "Agrippa" in Ford, *Essays,* p. 54.

50. *Pennsylvania Gazette,* 17 November 1784, quoted in Jensen, *New Nation,* pp. 282, 283.

51. For a confirmation of this opinion, see especially Herbert J. Storing, *What the Antifederalists Were For: The Political Thought of the Opponents of the Constitution* (Chicago: University of Chicago Press, 1981), pp. 20, 21, and 87 n.6.

52. "Agrippa," in Ford, *Essays,* pp. 109, 55. For a good discussion of the beneficial effects of an unfettered commerce, as portrayed in the literature of the very popular Connecticut Wits (John Trumbull, David Humphreys, Timothy Dwight, and especially Joel Barlow), see William C. Dowling, *Poetry and Ideology in Revolutionary Connecticut* (Athens: University of Georgia Press, 1990), pp. 85–86, 95–97, 101–5, 123–25.

53. "Agrippa," in Ford, *Essays,* pp. 109, 71, 104.

54. "An Old Whig," quoted in Borden, *Antifederalist Papers,* pp. 131–32.

55. "Sidney," in ibid., p. 130.

56. "Agrippa," in Ford, *Essays,* pp. 96–97.

57. "Centinel" (5 October 1787), in Kenyon, *Antifederalists,* p. 8.

58. Melancton Smith, in New York Ratifying Convention, in Alfred Young, *The Debate over the Constitution: 1787–1789* (Chicago: Rand McNally, 1965), p. 25.

Chapter 10. The "Triumph" of Antifederalism

1. James Madison, *The Federalist Papers,* ed. Clinton Rossiter (New York: New American Library, 1961), no. 41, pp. 262–63.

2. Quoted in Bernard Siegan, *Economic Liberties and the Constitution* (Chicago: University of Chicago Press, 1980), pp. 33–34. It is Siegan's aim, here, to argue that the Framers did intend to effect "substantive," and not just "procedural," protection to the economic liberties underpinning a Lockean social order.

3. See especially Siegan's developed argument in *Economic Liberties.* For a very good summary of the high points in the constitutional conflict between "substantive" due process and "procedural" due process, as it has related to the Fifth Amendment's guarantee of "life, liberty and property," see William Letwin, "Economic Due Process in the American Constitution and the Rule of Law," in Robert L. Cunningham, ed., *Liberty and the Rule of Law* (College Station: Texas A&M University Press, 1979), pp. 22–73. A most engaging colloquy on the subject of the Framers' intentions is contained in Robert A. Licht, ed., *The Framers and Fundamental Rights* (Washington, D.C.: American Enterprise Institute Press, 1991); see especially the essays by Judith A. Best, Lino A. Graglia,

Thomas L. Pangle, and Mark Tushnet. For a series of essays generally tending to discount or restrain the scope of economic liberty designed into the Constitution by the Framers see Ellen Frankel Paul and Howard Dickman, eds., *Liberty, Property, and the Foundations of the American Constitution* (Albany: State University of New York Press, 1989).

4. By far the fullest treatment of Ninth Amendment scholarship is provided in Randy E. Barnett, *The Rights Retained by the People: The History and Meaning of the Ninth Amendment* (Fairfax, Va.: George Mason University Press, 1989). Barnett argues that this amendment, insofar as it was of Madison's design, should be viewed as broadly protective of liberty in the full Lockean sense.

5. Madison's resolution to Congress on a bill of rights, in Helen E. Veit, Kenneth R. Bowling, and Charlene Bangs Bickford, *Creating the Bill of Rights: The Documentary Record from the First Federal Congress* (Baltimore, Md.: Johns Hopkins University Press, 1991), pp. 11–15.

6. Ibid., pp. 14, 16, 17, 21.

7. Ibid., pp. 42–43, "Additional Articles of Amendment" (7 and 8 September 1789). Richard Henry Lee to Patrick Henry (27 September 1789), to Francis Lightfoot Lee (13 September 1789), pp. 299, 294.

8. James Jackson, speech to Congress, in ibid., p. 87.

9. Charles A. Beard, *An Economic Interpretation of the Constitution of the United States* (New York: Macmillan, 1913), pp. 45, 48–49.

10. Ibid., pp. 42–44.

11. Ibid., pp. 44–45, 46.

12. Reprinted in Sidney Ratner, ed., *The Tariff in American History* (New York: D. Van Nostrand Company, 1972), p. 91.

13. Alexander Hamilton, "Report on Manufactures" (1791), reprinted in Jacob E. Cooke, ed., *The Reports of Alexander Hamilton* (New York: Harper and Row, 1964), pp. 115–205. "It is evident that the exertions of the husbandman will be steady or fluctuating, vigorous or feeble, in proportion to the steadiness or fluctuation . . . of the markets on which he must depend for the vent of the surplus which may be produced by his labor. . . . This idea of an extensive domestic market for the surplus produce of the soil, is of the first consequence. . . . To secure such a market, there is no other expedient than to promote manufacturing establishments" (pp. 133–35). On Hamilton's program and the Madisonian response, see Drew R. McCoy, *The Elusive Republic: Political Economy in Jeffersonian America* (Chapel Hill: University of North Carolina Press, 1980), p. 134. For the debate over the importance and advisability of industrializing per se, see Michael Brewster Folsom and Steven D. Lubar, eds., *The Philosophy of Manufactures: Early Debates over Industrialization in the United States* (Cambridge, Mass.: MIT Press, 1982).

14. See Hamilton, "Report on Manufactures," in Cooke, *Reports*, pp. 137–38.

15. Ibid., p. 141.

16. McCoy, *Elusive Republic*, p. 151.

17. Hamilton, "Report on the Subject of Manufactures," in Cooke, *Reports*, pp. 171–72, 168–69.

18. Ibid., pp. 173–78.

19. Alexander Hamilton, "Prospectus of the Society for Establishing Useful Manufactures" (1791), in Folsom and Lubar, *Philosophy of Manufactures*, pp. 97–98.

20. Alexander Hamilton, "Report on the Establishment of Public Credit," in Douglas C. North and Robert Paul Thomas, *The Growth of the American Economy to 1860* (New York: Harper and Row, 1968), p. 159.

21. James E. Ferguson, *The Power of the Purse: A History of American Public Finance, 1776–1790* (Chapel Hill: University of North Carolina Press, 1961), pp. 323–35, 256.

22. Robert Sobel, *Panic on Wall Street: A History of America's Financial Disasters* (New York: Collier, 1968), pp. 13–14. Craigie to Parker (May 1790) quoted in Nathan Schachner, *The Founding Fathers* (New York: A. S. Barnes, 1970), p. 86.

23. John C. Miller, *Alexander Hamilton and the Growth of the New Nation* (New York: Harper and Row, 1959), pp. 232–33.

24. See Donald F. Swanson and Andrew P. Trout, "Alexander Hamilton's Hidden Sinking Fund," *William and Mary Quarterly* 3d ser., 49:1 (January 1992): 108–16.

25. Schachner, *Founding Fathers,* p. 181.

26. Ibid., pp. 179, 181, 182.

27. Sobel, *Panic on Wall Street,* pp. 23–24, 27–28.

28. Schachner, *Founding Fathers,* p. 216; Sobel, *Panic on Wall Street,* p. 30.

29. Jefferson to Edward Rutledge, 29 August 1791, quoted in Schachner, *Founding Fathers,* p. 182.

30. Madison to Jefferson, 10 July 1791, quoted in ibid., p. 264. Madison to Richard Henry Lee, 8 August 1791, in ibid., p. 181.

31. Madison in Congress, quoted in Adrienne Koch, *Jefferson and Madison: The Great Collaboration* (Oxford: Oxford University Press, 1950), p. 129.

32. Jefferson to Washington, 15 February 1791, in Frederick C. Prescott, ed., *Alexander Hamilton and Thomas Jefferson: Representative Selections* (New York: American Book Company, 1934), p. 307.

33. Ibid., p. 308.

34. For a general study of the press reaction to Hamilton, see Donald H. Stewart, *The Opposition Press of the Federalist Period* (Albany: State University of New York Press, 1969), pp. 33–114. I thank the late Saul Padover for pointing out the irony of Madison's relying on a *majority party* to restore constitutional balance in the young republic.

35. J. G. A. Pocock, "Virtue and Commerce in the Eighteenth Century," *Journal of Interdisciplinary History* 3 (1972): 131.

36. Franklin B. Sawvel, ed., *The Anas of Thomas Jefferson* (New York: Da Capo Press, 1970), pp. 54, 91, 55, 91. An account, dated 4 February 1818, discusses the stormy period of Hamilton's stewardship at Treasury. Hamilton, Sawvel concludes, regarded "corruption" as much a blessing as the public debt. He "was not only a monarchist, but for a monarchy bottomed on corruption" (p. 36).

37. Thomas Jefferson, *Notes on the State of Virginia,* ed. William Peden (New York: W. W. Norton, 1982). See especially, "Query XIX," "The present state of manufacturers, commerce, interior and exterior trade" Jefferson to Jay (23 August 1785) reprinted in Folsom and Lubar, *Philosophy of Manufactures,* p. 20. For Jefferson's stunning repudiation of the views voiced in the *Notes on Virginia,* owing largely to the unsettling circumstances of 1816, see Jefferson to Benjamin Austin, reprinted in Folsom and Lubar, pp. 30–32.

38. Thomas Jefferson to G. K. van Hogendorp (13 October 1785), reprinted in Folsom and Lubar, *Philosophy of Manufactures,* pp. 20–22. See Jefferson to John Jay (23 August 1785), pp. 20–21.

39. Ibid.

40. Jefferson to Du Pont de Nemours (1816) in Saul K. Padover, ed., *Thomas Jefferson on Democracy* (New York: Mentor Books, 1939), p. 18.

41. John Adams, quoted in Vernon Parrington, *Main Currents in American Thought,* vol. 1, *The Colonial Mind* (New York: Harcourt, Brace and World, 1927), p. 322. Thomas

Jefferson, "Inaugural Address" (4 March 1801), reprinted in Saul K. Padover, *The Complete Jefferson* (New York: Duell Sloan and Pearce, 1943), pp. 384–86.

42. On a deeper theoretical level, Appleby was properly rejecting the "ideological school's" simplicity of vision. See especially "Republicanism and Ideology," *William and Mary Quarterly* 3d ser., 37:4 (Fall 1985): 462, 469, and "Republicanism in Old and New Contexts," *William and Mary Quarterly* 3d ser., 43:1 (January 1986): 28–29. In perceiving individuals to be conceptually tied to a singular ideological outlook (i.e., classical republicanism), revisionism diminished "drastically the independence of the word and the autonomy of the author." The republican writers rejected the progressive's claim that men are moved solely by their interests, only to endorse the deeper claim that men are not free, but *determined* — trapped, if not by their interests then by their ideas: "Where the decision-making individual once stood at the center of our analysis of politics, ideology has pushed to the fore the social forces that presumably have shaped the consciousness of the individuals we study." It was this deeper determinism that Appleby was determined to resist: "In pluralistic, uncensored, literate societies, the ideological predispositions of human beings have an opposite effect. Instead of insuring social solidarity, competing ideologies thwart it."

43. Joyce Appleby, "The Social Origins of American Revolutionary Ideology," *Journal of American History* 64:4 (March 1978): 941, 942, 948. See also *Economic Thought and Ideology in Seventeenth-Century England* (Princeton, N.J.: Princeton University Press, 1978). On the relation of theory to daily practice, as evidenced in the phenomenal rise of if not all, at least the "middling ranks" of men, see Harold Perkins, "The Social Causes of the British Industrial Revolution," *Transactions of the Royal Society* (1968): 135–36.

44. Joyce Oldham Appleby, "What Is Still American in the Political Philosophy of Thomas Jefferson?" *William and Mary Quarterly* 3d ser., 34:2 (April 1982): 300, 301.

45. Joyce Oldham Appleby, *Capitalism and a New Social Order: The Republican Vision of the 1790's* (New York: New York University Press, 1984), p. 22.

46. Ibid., p. 21. For a clear argument soundly distancing Locke and Jefferson from the politics of utilitarianism, see Morton White, *The Philosophy of the American Revolution* (New York: Oxford University Press, 1978), pp. 41–52, 233, on Locke and Jefferson, respectively.

47. Jefferson to J. W. Eppes (1813) in Padover, *Jefferson on Democracy*, p. 77.

48. On Jefferson's distinction between productive and destructive forms of speculation, see Sobel, *Panic on Wall Street*, p. 12. Jefferson to Colonel Yancy (1816) in Padover, *Jefferson on Democracy*, p. 78.

49. See Jefferson, "Report on Cod and Whale Fisheries" (1 February 1791), reprinted in Padover, *The Complete Jefferson*, pp. 320–41. For a brief history of this and the San Domingo relief measure, see Charles Warren, *Congress as Santa Clause, or National Donations and the General Welfare Clause of the Constitution* (New York: Arno Press, 1978), pp. 15–19.

50. Hugh Williamson, William Giles, John Nicholas, speeches in Congress, quoted in Warren, *Congress as Santa Clause*, pp. 15–19. On the Caracas earthquake relief measure, see pp. 19–20.

51. Thomas Jefferson, "Prospectus on Political Economy," reprinted in Padover, *The Complete Jefferson*, p. 372; Jefferson to F. W. Gilmer (1816) in Padover, *Jefferson on Democracy*, pp. 17–18.

52. "A Farmer" (George Logan), "Five Letters addressed to the Yeomanry of the United States, containing some observations on the dangerous scheme of governor Duer and mr. Secretary Hamilton, to establish national manufactories" (September–October

1792), reprinted in Folsom and Lubar, *Philosophy of Manufactures,* pp. 107, 106, 105, 104, 109, 110.

53. Ibid., pp. 107, 106.

54. Ibid., pp., 105, 104.

55. Ibid., pp. 109, 110.

56. Irving Brant, *The Bill of Rights: Its Origin and Meaning* (New York: Bobbs Merrill, 1965), p. 4.

57. For a view that sees the American state building as successive pragmatic adjustments to recurring crises, see Robert Higgs, *Crisis and Leviathan: Critical Episodes in the Growth of American Government* (Oxford: Oxford University Press, 1987).

58. For the Madisonian roots of modern interest group liberalism, see Theodore Lowi, *The End of Liberalism: The Second Republic of the United States* (New York: W. W. Norton, 1979), pp. 22–60. "Since the days of Madison the pluralist view has been that there is nothing to fear from government so long as many factions compete for its favor. Modern pluralism turned the Madisonian position from negative to positive; that is, government is good because many factions do compete for its favor. . . . In such a manner pluralist theory became the handmaiden of interest-group liberalism, and interest-group liberalism became the handmaiden of modern American positive national statehood, and the First Republic became the Second Republic." (pp. 35, 55).

59. Appleby, "Social Origins of American Revolutionary Ideology," p. 937.

60. The point has been ably stated by James T. Kloppenberg, "The Virtues of Liberalism: Christianity, Republicanism, and Ethics in Early American Political Discourse," *Journal of American History* 74:1 (June 1987): 16: "[Locke's] belief in a natural law discernible by reason led him to condemn the unregulated pursuit of self-interest that Hobbes considered natural and that later writers who celebrated a market economy sanctioned."

61. See Lowi, *End of Liberalism.*

62. Gordon Wood, *The Creation of the American Republic: 1776–1787* (New York: W. W. Norton, 1972), p. 401. Anonymous American quoted by Wood.

63. Nathan Miller, *The Founding Finaglers and Other Scoundrels in a Fascinating History of Corruption in America from Jamestown to Teapot Dome* (New York: David McKay Company, 1976).

64. Appleby, "Social Origins of American Revolutionary Ideology," p. 937.

65. J. G. A. Pocock, *The Machiavellian Moment: Florentine Political Thought and the Atlantic Republican Tradition* (Princeton, N.J.: Princeton University Press, 1975), p. 499; cf. p. 500.

66. Jefferson, quoted in Paul A. Rahe, *Republics Ancient and Modern: Classical Republicanism and the American Revolution* (Chapel Hill: University of North Carolina Press, 1992), p. 767.

67. For two very telling critiques of liberalism that detail the progressive theoretical and historical reforms it has adopted in the face of its weaknesses, see C. B. Macpherson, *The Life and Times of Liberal Democracy* (Oxford: Oxford University Press, 1977), and Harold Schultz, ed., *English Liberalism and the State: Individualism or Collectivism?* (Lexington, Mass.: D. C. Heath, 1972).

68. Samuel Pettengill, *Jefferson: The Forgotten Man* (New York: America's Future, 1938).

Bibliography

Aaron, Richard I. *John Locke*. Oxford: Clarendon Press, 1971.

Aarsleff, Hans. "The State of Nature and the Nature of Man in Locke." In *John Locke: Problems and Perspectives,* edited by John Yolton, pp. 99–136. Cambridge: Cambridge University Press, 1969.

Adair, Douglass. "That Politics May Be Reduced to a Science: David Hume, James Madison, and the Tenth Federalist." In *The American Past: Conflicting Interpretations of the Great Issues,* vol. 1, edited by Sidney Fine and Gerald S. Brown, pp. 228–41. New York: Macmillan, 1957.

Adams, Alice Dana. *The Neglected Period of Anti-Slavery in America, 1808–1831.* Gloucester, Mass.: Peter Smith, 1964.

Allen, Gay Wilson, and Roger Asselineau. *St. John de Crevecoeur: The Life of an American Farmer.* New York: Viking Press, 1987.

Allen, Walter. *Transatlantic Crossings: American Visitors to Britain and British Visitors to America in the Nineteenth Century.* London: Heinemann, 1971.

Anderson, Perry. *Lineages of the Absolutist State.* London: New Left Books, 1977.

Appleby, Joyce Oldham. *Capitalism and a New Social Order: The Republican Vision of the 1790's.* New York: New York University Press, 1984.

_____. *Economic Thought and Ideology in Seventeenth-Century England.* Princeton, N.J.: Princeton University Press, 1978.

_____. "Republicanism and Ideology," *William and Mary Quarterly* 3d ser., 37:4 (Fall 1985): 461–73.

_____. "Republicanism in Old and New Contexts." *William and Mary Quarterly* 3d ser., 43:1 (January 1986): 20–34.

_____. "The Social Origins of American Revolutionary Ideology." *Journal of American History* 64:4 (March 1978): 935–58.

_____. "What Is Still American in the Political Philosophy of Thomas Jefferson?" *William and Mary Quarterly* 3d ser., 34:2 (April 1982): 287–309.

Aquinas, St. Thomas. *Treatise on Happiness.* Edited by John A. Oesterle. Notre Dame, Ind.: University of Notre Dame Press, 1983.

Aristotle. *Works.* Edited by Richard McKeon. New York: Random House, 1941.

Ashcraft, Richard. *Locke's "Two Treatises of Government."* London: Unwin Hyman, 1987.

_____. "Political Theory and the Problem of Ideology." *Journal of Politics* 42:3 (1980): 687–721.

_____. *Revolutionary Politics and Locke's "Two Treatises of Government."* Princeton, N.J.: Princeton University Press, 1986.

_____. "Revolutionary Politics and Locke's 'Two Treatises of Government': Radicalism and Lockean Political Theory." *Political Theory* 8:4 (1980): 429–86.

_____. "Simple Objections and Complex Reality: Theorizing Political Radicalism in Seventeenth-Century England." *Political Studies* 40 (1992): 99–115.

Ashcraft, Richard, and M. M. Goldsmith. "Locke, Revolution Principles, and the Formation of Whig Ideology." *Historical Journal* 26:4 (1983): 773–800.

Atherton, Herbert M. *Political Prints in the Age of Hogarth.* Oxford: Clarendon Press, 1974.

Bailyn, Bernard. "The Central Themes of the American Revolution." In *Essays on the American Revolution,* edited by Stephen J. Kurtz and James H. Hutson, pp. 3–31. Chapel Hill: University of North Carolina Press, 1973.

_____. *The Ideological Origins of the American Revolution.* Cambridge, Mass.: Harvard University Press, 1967.

_____. *The Origins of American Politics.* New York: Vintage Books, 1967.

_____. "Political Experience and Enlightenment Ideas in Eighteenth-Century America." In *American History: Recent Interpretations,* vol. 1, *To 1877,* edited by Abraham S. Eisenstadt, pp. 135–49. New York: Thomas E. Crowell, 1969.

Bailyn, Bernard, ed. *Pamphlets of the American Revolution, 1750–1776.* Cambridge, Mass.: Belknap Press of Harvard University Press, 1965.

Ball, Terence, and J. G. A. Pocock, eds. *Conceptual Change and the Constitution.* Lawrence: University Press of Kansas, 1988.

Banning, Lance. "James Madison and the Nationalists, 1780–1783." *William and Mary Quarterly* 40 (1983): 227–55.

_____. "Jeffersonian Ideology Revisited: Liberal and Classical Ideas in the New American Republic." *William and Mary Quarterly* 3d ser., 43:1 (1986): 3–19.

_____. *The Jeffersonian Persuasion: Evolution of a Party Ideology.* Ithaca, N.Y.: Cornell University Press, 1978.

_____. "The Republican Interpretation: Retrospect and Prospect." In *The Republican Synthesis Revisited: Essays in Honor of George Athan Billias,* edited by Milton M. Klein, Richard D. Brown, and John B. Hench, pp. 91–118. Worcester, Mass.: American Antiquarian Society, 1992.

_____. "Some Second Thoughts on Virtue and the Course of Revolutionary Thinking." In *Conceptual Change and the Constitution,* edited by Terence Ball and J. G. A. Pocock, pp. 194–212. Lawrence: University Press of Kansas, 1988.

_____. "Virginia: Sectionalism and the General Good." In *Ratifying the Constitution,* edited by Michael Allen Gillespie and Michael Lienesch, pp. 261–99. Lawrence: University Press of Kansas, 1989.

Barkan, Elliott R., ed. *Edmund Burke on the American Revolution: Selected Speeches and Letters.* New York: Harper Torchbooks, 1966.

Barnett, Randy E. *The Rights Retained by the People: The History and Meaning of the Ninth Amendment.* Fairfax, Va.: George Mason University Press, 1989.

Beard, Charles A. *An Economic Interpretation of the Constitution of the United States.* New York: Macmillan, 1913.

Becker, Carl. *The Declaration of Independence: A Study in the History of Political Ideas.* New York: Vintage Books, 1942.

Beloff, Max, ed. *The Debate on the American Revolution, 1761–1783.* London: Adam and Charles Black, 1972.

Billington, Ray Allen, ed. *The Reinterpretation of American History: Essays in Honor of John Edwin Pomfret*. New York: W. W. Norton, 1968.

Bonomi, Patricia U. *Under the Cope of Heaven: Religion, Society, and Politics in Colonial America*. Oxford: Oxford University Press, 1986.

Bonomi, Patricia U., ed. *Party and Political Opposition in Revolutionary America*. Tarrytown, N.Y.: Sleepy Hollow Press, 1980.

Bonwick, Colin. *English Radicals and the American Revolution*. Chapel Hill: University of North Carolina Press, 1977.

Boorstin, Daniel. *The Lost World of Thomas Jefferson*. New York: Henry Holt, 1948.

Borden, Morton, ed. *The Antifederalist Papers*. Detroit: Michigan University Press, 1965.

Boucher, Jonathan. *A View of the Causes and Consequences of the American Revolution*. London, 1797.

Brant, Irving. *The Bill of Rights: Its Origin and Meaning*. New York: Bobbs Merrill, 1965.

Brogan, A. P. "John Locke and Utilitarianism." *Ethica* 69 (January 1959): 79–93.

Brown, Robert E. *Charles Beard and the Constitution: A Critical Analysis of "An Economic Interpretation of the Constitution."* New York: W. W. Norton, 1956.

Brownowski, Jacob, and Bruce Mazlish. *The Western Intellectual Tradition*. New York: Harper Torchbooks, 1960.

Burgh, James. *Britain's Remembrancer: or, The Danger Not Over*. London, 1746.

Burnet, Gilbert. *A History of His Own Time*. London, 1839.

Campbell, Mildred. *The English Yeoman under Elizabeth and the Early Stuarts*. New Haven, Conn.: Yale University Press, 1942.

Cantor, Norman F., and Peter L. Klein. *Bacon and Descartes: Seventeenth-Century Rationalism*. Blaisdell, Mass.: Blaisdell Publishing Company, 1969.

Cantor, Norman F., and Michael S. Werthman. *The English Tradition: Modern Studies in English History*. New York: Macmillan, 1967.

Carey, Matthew, ed. *The Debates of the General Assembly of Pennsylvania*. Philadelphia, 1786.

Carswell, John. "The Advent of Whiggery." In *The English Tradition,* edited by Norman F. Cantor and Michael S. Wertham, pp. 362–68. New York: Macmillan, 1967.

Cassara, Ernest. *The Enlightenment in America*. New York: University Press of America, 1988.

Chamberlain, John. *The Enterprising Americans: A Business History of the United States*. New York: Harper and Row, 1963.

Chauncy, Charles. "Civil Magistrates Must Be Just: Ruling in the Fear of God." 1747. In *Political Sermons of the Founding Era: 1730–1805,* edited by Ellis Sandoz, pp. 137–78. Indianapolis, Ind.: Liberty Press, 1991.

Child, Sir Josiah. *Brief Observations concerning Trade and the Interest on Money*. London, 1668. 3d ed. 1690.

Clough, Shepard Bancroft, and Charles Woolsey Cole. *Economic History of Europe*. Boston: D. C. Heath, 1941.

Coleman, Benjamin. *A Humble Discourse on the Incomprehensibleness of God*. Boston, 1715.

Commager, Henry Steele. *Documents of American History,* 2 vols. in 1 book. New York: Appleton-Century-Crofts, 1958.

———. *The Empire of Reason: How Europe Invented and America Realized the Enlightenment*. Garden City, N.Y.: Anchor Press, 1977.

Commager, Henry Steele, and Richard B. Morris, eds. *The Spirit of '76: The Story of the American Revolution as Told by Participants*. 2 vols. Indianapolis, Ind.: Bobbs Merrill, 1958.

Cooke, Jacob E., ed. *The Reports of Alexander Hamilton*. New York: Harper and Row, 1964.

Cooper, Thomas. *Some Information Respecting America*. 1794. Reprint, New York: Augustus M. Kelley, 1969.

Corwin, Edward S. *The "Higher Law" Background of American Constitutional Law*. Ithaca, N.Y.: Cornell University Press, 1955.

Countryman, Edward. *The American Revolution*. New York: Hill and Wang, 1985.

Cranston, Maurice. *John Locke: A Biography*. Oxford: Oxford University Press, 1985.

Crevecoeur, J. Hector St. John de. *Letters from an American Farmer and Sketches of Eighteenth-Century America*. 1782. Edited by Albert E. Stone. New York: Penguin, 1981.

Cudworth, Ralph. *A Treatise concerning Eternal and Immutable Morality*. London, 1731.

Cunningham, Noble E., Jr. *In Pursuit of Reason: The Life of Thomas Jefferson*. Baton Rouge: Louisiana State University Press, 1987.

Cunningham, Robert L., ed. *Liberty and the Rule of Law*. College Station: Texas A&M University Press, 1979.

DeNovo, John A., ed. *Selected Readings in American History*, vol. 1, *Main Themes to 1877*. New York: Charles Scribner's Sons, 1969.

Dickinson, H. T. *Liberty and Property: Political Ideology in Eighteenth-Century Britain*. New York: Holmes and Meier, 1977.

Diggins, John P. "Comrades and Citizens: New Mythologies in American History." *American Political Science Review* 78:1 (March 1984): 614–49.

_____. *The Lost Soul of American Politics: Virtue, Self-Interest, and the Foundations of Liberalism*. Chicago: University of Chicago Press, 1984.

Doren, Carl Van. *Benjamin Franklin*. New York: Viking Press, 1938.

Dowling, William C. *Poetry and Ideology in Revolutionary Connecticut*. Athens: University of Georgia Press, 1990.

Driver, C. H. "John Locke." In *The Social and Political Ideas of Some English Thinkers of the Augustan Age,* edited by F. J. C. Hearnshaw, pp. 69–96. Westport, Conn.: Greenwood Press, 1983.

Dunn, John. "Justice and the Interpretation of Locke's Political Theory." *Political Studies* 16:1 (1968): 68–87.

_____. *The Political Thought of John Locke: An Historical Account of the Argument of the "Two Treatises of Government."* Cambridge: Cambridge University Press, 1969.

_____. "The Politics of Locke in England and America in the Eighteenth Century." In *John Locke: Problems and Perspectives,* edited by John Yolton, pp. 45–80. Cambridge: Cambridge University Press, 1969.

Dworetz, Steven M. *The Unvarnished Doctrine: Locke, Liberalism, and the American Revolution*. Durham, N.C.: Duke University Press, 1990.

East, Robert A. *Business Enterprise in the American Revolutionary Era*. Gloucester, Mass.: Peter Smith, 1964.

Egnal, Marc. *A Mighty Empire: The Origins of the American Revolution*. Ithaca, N.Y.: Cornell University Press, 1988.

_____. "The Pattern of Factional Development in Pennsylvania, New York, and Massachusetts, 1682–1776." In *Party and Political Opposition in Revolutionary America,* edited by Patricia U. Bonomi, pp. 43–60. Tarrytown, N.Y.: Sleepy Hollow Press, 1980.

Ernst, Joseph. "Ideology and an Economic Interpretation of the Revolution." In *The American Revolution: Explanations in the History of American Radicalism*, edited by Alfred F. Young, pp. 159–86. Dekalb: Northern Illinois University Press, 1976.

Ernst, Joseph, and Marc Egnal. "An Economic Interpretation of the American Revolution." *William and Mary Quarterly* 3d ser., 29 (1972): 3–32.

Farrand, Max, ed. *The Records of the Federal Convention of 1787*. 4 vols. New Haven, Conn.: Yale University Press, 1966.

Ferguson, James E. *The Power of the Purse: A History of American Public Finance, 1776–1790*. Chapel Hill: University of North Carolina Press, 1961.

Filmer, Sir Robert. *Anarchy of a Limited or Mixed Monarchy*. Reprinted in *Patriarcha and Other Writings*, edited by Johann P. Sommerville, pp. 131–71. Cambridge: Cambridge University Press, 1991.

_____. *Observations Concerning the Originall of Government*. Reprinted in *Patriarcha and Other Writings*, edited by Johann P. Sommerville, pp. 184–234. Cambridge: Cambridge University Press, 1991.

_____. "Patriarcha." Reprinted in *Patriarcha and Other Writings*, edited by Johann P. Sommerville, pp. 1–68. Cambridge: Cambridge University Press, 1991.

Fine, Sidney, and Gerald S. Brown, eds. *The American Past: Conflicting Interpretations of the Great Issues*, vol. 1. New York: Macmillan, 1957.

Fliegelman, Jay. *Prodigals and Pilgrims: The American Revolution against Patriarchal Authority, 1750–1800*. Cambridge: Cambridge University Press, 1982.

Folsom, Michael Brewster, and Steven D. Lubar, eds. *The Philosophy of Manufactures: Early Debates over Industrialization in the United States*. Cambridge, Mass.: MIT Press, 1982.

Foner, Eric. *Tom Paine and Revolutionary America*. Oxford: Oxford University Press, 1976.

_____. "Tom Paine's Republic: Radical Ideology and Social Change." In *The American Revolution*, edited by Alfred F. Young, pp. 187–232. Dekalb: Northern Illinois University Press, 1976.

_____. "Why Is There No Socialism in the United States?" *History Workshop* 17 (Spring 1984): 57–80.

Ford, Paul L. *Essays on the Constitution*. Brooklyn, N.Y.: Historical Printing Club, 1892.

_____. *Pamphlets on the Constitution*. New York: Da Capo Press, 1968.

Fowler, Edward. *The Principles and Practices of Certain Moderate Divines of the Church of England*. London, 1670.

Franklin, Benjamin. *The Autobiography and Other Writings*. Edited by I. Jesse Lemisch. New York: New American Library, 1961.

Gascoigne, John. *Cambridge in the Age of the Enlightenment: Science, Religion, and Politics from the Restoration to the French Revolution*. Cambridge: Cambridge University Press, 1989.

_____. "From Bentley to the Victorians: The Rise and Fall of British Newtonian Natural Theology." *Science in Context* 2:2 (1988): 219–56. Gaustad, Edwin Scott. *A Religious History of America*. New York: HarperCollins, 1990.

_____. "Society and the Great Awakening in New England." In *American History*, edited by Abraham S. Eisenstadt, pp. 125–34. New York: Thomas E. Crowell, 1969.

Gay, Ebenezer. *Natural Religion as Distinguished from Revealed*. Boston, 1759.

Gay, Peter, ed. *The Enlightenment: A Comprehensive Anthology*. New York: Simon and Schuster, 1973.

Gies, Joseph, and Frances Gies. *The Ingenious Yankees: The Men, Ideas, and Machines That Transformed a Nation, 1776–1876*. New York: Thomas E. Crowell, 1976.

Gilje, Paul A., and Howard B. Rock, eds. *Keepers of the Revolution: New Yorkers at Work in the Early Republic*. Ithaca, N.Y.: Cornell University Press, 1992.

Gillespie, Allen, and Michael Lienesch, eds. *Ratifying the Constitution*. Lawrence: University Press of Kansas, 1989.

Goen, C. C. *Revivalism and Separatism in New England, 1740–1800*. Middletown, Conn.: Wesleyan University Press, 1987.

Goldie, Mark. "Danby, the Bishops, and the Whigs." In *The Politics of Religion in Restoration England,* edited by Tim Harris, Paul Seaward, and Mark Goldie, pp. 75–106. Oxford: Basil Blackwell, 1990.

_____. "John Locke and Anglican Royalism." *Political Studies* 31 (1983): 61–85.

Gooch, G. P. *English Democratic Ideas in the Seventeenth Century.* New York: Harper Torchbooks, 1959.

Gough, John. *John Locke's Political Philosophy: Eight Studies*. Oxford: Clarendon Press, 1950.

Grant, Ruth W. *John Locke's Liberalism*. Chicago: University of Chicago Press, 1987.

_____. "Locke's Political Anthropology and Lockean Individualism." *Journal of Politics* 50:1 (February 1988): 42–63.

Greenberg, Edward S. *Understanding Modern Government: The Rise and Decline of the American Political Economy*. New York: John Wiley and Son, 1979.

Greene, Jack P., ed. *The Reinterpretation of the American Revolution: 1763–1789*. New York: Harper and Row, 1968.

Greene, Jack P. "Changing Interpretations of Early American Politics." In *The Reinterpretation of American History,* edited by Ray Allen Billington, pp. 151–84. New York: W. W. Norton, 1968.

_____. *Pursuits of Happiness: The Social Development of Early Modern British Colonies and the Formation of American Culture*. Chapel Hill: University of North Carolina Press, 1988.

Gregg, Pauline. *Free-Born John: A Biography of John Lilburne*. London: George C. Harran and Company, 1961.

Greven, Philip. *The Protestant Temperament: Patterns of Child Rearing, Religious Experience, and the Self in Early America*. Chicago: University of Chicago Press, 1977.

Grob, Gerald N., and George Athan Billias, eds. *Interpretations of American History: Patterns and Perspectives*. New York: Free Press, 1972.

Grotius, Hugo. *The Law of War and Peace,* translated by F. W. Kelsey. New York: Bobbs Merrill, 1925.

Hacker, Louis M., et al. *The United States: A Graphic History*. New York: Modern Age Books, 1937.

Haller, William. "The Emergence of Religious Individualism." In *The English Tradition,* edited by Norman F. Cantor and Michael S. Werthman, pp. 325–31. New York: Macmillan, 1967.

Haller, William, and Godfrey Davies, eds. *The Leveller Tracts: 1647–1653*. Gloucester, Mass.: Peter Smith, 1964.

Hamowy, Ronald. "Cato's Letters, John Locke, and the Republican Paradigm." In *John Locke's "Two Treatises of Government": New Interpretations,* edited by Edward J. Harpham, pp. 148–72. Lawrence: University Press of Kansas, 1992.

_____. "Jefferson and the Scottish Enlightenment: A Critique of Garry Wills's *Inventing America: Jefferson's Declaration of Independence*." *William and Mary Quarterly* 3d ser., 36 (1979): 502–23.

Harpham, Edward, ed. *John Locke's "Two Treatises of Government": New Interpretations*. Lawrence: University Press of Kansas, 1992.

Harris, Tim, Paul Seaward, and Mark Goldie. "Revising the Restoration." In *The Politics of Religion in Restoration England,* edited by Tim Harris, Paul Seaward, and Mark Goldie, pp. 1–28. Oxford: Basil Blackwell, 1990.

Hartz, Louis. *The Liberal Tradition in America: An Interpretation of American Political Thought since the Revolution.* New York: Harcourt, Brace, World, 1955.

Higgs, Robert. *Crisis and Leviathan: Critical Episodes in the Growth of American Government.* Oxford: Oxford University Press, 1987.

Hill, Christopher. *The Century of Revolution: 1603–1714.* New York: W. W. Norton, 1982.

———. *Some Intellectual Consequences of the English Revolution.* Madison: University of Wisconsin Press, 1980.

———. *The World Turned Upside Down: Radical Ideas during the English Revolution.* New York: Penguin Books, 1972.

Himmelfarb, Gertrude. *The Idea of Poverty: England in the Early Industrial Age.* New York: Vintage Books, 1983.

Hirshman, Albert O. *The Passions and the Interests: Political Arguments for Capitalism before Its Triumph.* Princeton, N.J.: Princeton University Press, 1977.

Hitchcock, Gad. *Natural Religion Aided by Revelation and Perfected by Christianity.* Boston, 1779.

Hobbes, Thomas. *Leviathan.* Edited by C. B. Macpherson. New York: Penguin Books, 1971.

Horne, Thomas A. *Property Rights and Poverty: Political Argument in Britain, 1605–1834.* Chapel Hill: University of North Carolina Press, 1990.

Horton, John, and Susan Mendus, eds. *John Locke: A Letter concerning Toleration.* London: Routledge, 1991.

Horwitz, Robert H. "John Locke and the Preservation of Liberty: A Perennial Problem of Civic Education." In *The Moral Foundations of the American Republic,* edited by Robert H. Horwitz, pp. 138–64. Charlottesville: University Press of Virginia, 1986.

Houston, Alan Craig. *Algernon Sidney and the Republican Heritage in England and America.* Princeton, N.J.: Princeton University Press, 1991.

Hyneman, Charles S., and Donald S. Lutz. *American Political Writing during the Founding Era: 1760–1805.* 2 vols. Indianapolis, Ind.: Liberty Press, 1983.

Jacob, J. R. *Robert Boyle and the English Revolution.* New York: Burt Franklin, 1977.

Jacob, James R., and Margaret C. Jacob. "The Anglican Origins of Modern Science: The Metaphysical Foundations of the Whig Constitution." *Isis* 71 (June 1980): 251–67.

Jacob, Margaret C. *The Cultural Meaning of the Scientific Revolution.* New York: Alfred A. Knopf, 1988.

———. *Living the Enlightenment: Freemasonry and Politics in Eighteenth-Century Europe.* New York: Oxford University Press, 1991.

———. *The Newtonians and the English Revolution, 1689–1720.* Ithaca, N.Y.: Cornell University Press, 1976.

———. *The Radical Enlightenment: Pantheists, Freemasons, and Republicans.* London: George, Allen and Unwin, 1981.

Jacob, Margaret C., and James R. Jacob, eds. *The Origins of Anglo-American Radicalism.* London: George, Allen and Unwin, 1984.

Jefferson, Thomas. *Notes on the State of Virginia.* Edited by William Peden. New York: W. W. Norton, 1982.

Jensen, Merrill. *The New Nation: A History of the United States during the Confederation, 1781–89.* New York: Alfred A. Knopf, 1965.

———. *Tracts of the American Revolution, 1763–1776.* Indianapolis, Ind.: Bobbs Merrill, 1967.

Johnson, Paul. *A History of the English People*. New York: Harper and Row, 1985.

Kendall, Willmoore. *John Locke and the Doctrine of Majority Rule*. Urbana: University of Illinois Press, 1965.

Kenyon, Cecelia. "Republicanism and Radicalism in the American Revolution: An Old-Fashioned Interpretation." In *The American Past: Conflicting Interpretations of the Great Issues,* edited by Sidney Fine and Gerald S. Brown, pp. 140–64. New York: Macmillan, 1976.

Kenyon, Cecelia, ed. *The Antifederalists*. Indianapolis, Ind.: Bobbs Merrill, 1975.

Kenyon, J. P. *Revolution Principles: The Politics of Party, 1689–1720*. Cambridge: Cambridge University Press, 1977.

Klein, Milton M., Richard D. Brown, and John B. Hench, eds. *The Republican Synthesis Revisited: Essays in Honor of George Athan Billias*. Worcester, Mass.: American Antiquarian Society, 1992.

Kloppenberg, James T. "The Virtues of Liberalism: Christianity, Republicanism, and Ethics in Early American Political Discourse." *Journal of American History* 74:1 (June 1987): 9–33.

Koch, Adrienne. *The American Enlightenment: The Shaping of the American Experiment and a Free Society as Revealed in the Thoughts and Writings of Our Major Philosopher-Statesmen*. New York: George Braziller, 1965.

————. *Jefferson and Madison: The Great Collaboration*. Oxford: Oxford University Press, 1950.

————. *The Philosophy of Thomas Jefferson*. Chicago: Quadrangle Books, 1964.

Kramnick, Isaac. *Bolingbroke and His Circle: The Politics of Nostalgia in the Age of Walpole*. Cambridge, Mass.: Harvard University Press, 1968.

————. "English Middle Class Radicalism in the Eighteenth Century." *Literature of Liberty: A Review of Contemporary Liberal Thought* 3:2 (1980): 5–48.

————. "The 'Great National Discussion': The Discourse of Politics in 1787." *William and Mary Quarterly* 3d ser., 45:1 (January 1988): 3–32.

————. *Republicanism and Bourgeois Radicalism: Political Ideology in Late Eighteenth-Century England and America*. Ithaca, N.Y.: Cornell University Press, 1990.

————. "Republican Revisionism Revisited." *American Historical Review* 87:3 (June 1982): 629–64.

Lamont, William. "Pamphleteering, the Protestant Consensus and the English Revolution." In *Freedom and the English Revolution,* edited by R. C. Richardson and G. M. Ridden, pp. 72–92. Manchester: Manchester University, 1986.

————. *Richard Baxter and the Millennium: Protestant Imperialism and the English Revolution*. Totowa, N.J.: Rowman and Littlefield, 1979.

Lamprecht, Sterling. *The Moral and Political Philosophy of John Locke*. New York: Columbia University Press, 1918.

Laslett, Peter. "John Locke, the Great Recoinage, and the Origins of the Board of Trade, 1695–1698." *William and Mary Quarterly* 3d ser., 14 (July 1957): 370–92.

Leder, Lawrence H. *Liberty and Authority: Early American Political Ideology, 1689–1763*. New York: W. W. Norton, 1968.

Lerner, Ralph. *The Thinking Revolutionary: Principle and Practice in the New Republic*. Ithaca, N.Y.: Cornell University Press, 1987.

Letwin, William. *The Origins of Scientific Economics*. Garden City, N.Y.: Anchor Books, 1965.

Letwin, William, ed. *A Documentary History of American Economic Policy since 1789*. New York. W. W. Norton, 1972.

Licht, Robert A., ed. *The Framers and Fundamental Rights*. Washington, D.C.: American Enterprise Institute Press, 1991.

Lilburne, John. *The Freemans Freedom Vindicated*. London, 1646.

Livingston, William, William Smith, Jr., and John Morin Scott. *The Independent Reflector, or Essays on Sundry Important Subjects More Particularly Adapted to the Province of New York*. Edited by Milton M. Klein. Cambridge, Mass.: Belknap Press of Harvard University Press, 1963.

Locke, John. *An Essay concerning Human Understanding*. 2 vols. Edited by Alexander Campbell Fraser. New York: Dover Publications, 1959.

_____. *Essays on the Law of Nature*. Edited by W. von Leyden. Oxford: Clarendon Press, 1954.

_____. *A Letter concerning Toleration*. 1689. Edited by Patrick Romanell. Indianapolis, Ind.: Bobbs Merrill, 1955.

_____. "Of Ethica in General." In *The Life of John Locke with Extracts from his Correspondence, Journals, and Commonplace Books*, edited by Lord King, pp. 308–22. London, 1829.

_____. *On the Conduct of the Understanding*. 1706. Reprinted in John William Adamson, ed., *The Educational Writings of John Locke*, pp. 181–265. Cambridge: Cambridge University Press, 1922.

_____. *The Reasonableness of Christianity with a Discourse of Miracles and Part of a Third Letter concerning Toleration*. Edited by I. T. Ramsey. Stanford, Calif.: Stanford University Press, 1958.

_____. "Reform of the Poor Laws," 1697. In *The Enlightenment: A Comprehensive Anthology*, edited by Peter Gay, pp. 99–107. New York: Simon and Schuster, 1973.

_____. *Some Considerations on the Consequences of Lowering the Rate of Interest and Raising the Value of Money*. 1691. Reprinted in J. R. McCulloch, *Principles of Political Economy: With Sketch of the Rise and Progress of the Science*, pp. 220–300. London: Ward, Lock and Co., 1825.

_____. *Some Thoughts concerning Education*. London, 1695. Reprinted in John William Adamson, ed., *The Educational Writings of John Locke*, pp. 22–178. Cambridge: Cambridge University Press, 1922.

_____. *Two Treatises of Government*. 1690. Edited with an Introduction by Peter Laslett. New York: Mentor, 1965.

_____. "Venditio." Reprinted in John Dunn, "Justice and the Interpretation of Locke's Political Theory." *Political Studies* 16:1 (1968): 68–87.

_____. *The Works of John Locke*. 10 vols. London, 1823.

Lowi, Theodore. *The End of Liberalism: The Second Republic of the United States*. New York: W. W. Norton, 1979.

Lutz, Donald. "The Relative Influence of European Writers on Late Eighteenth-Century American Political Thought." *American Political Science Review* 78 (1984): 189–97.

McConnell, Grand. *Private Power and American Democracy*. New York: Vintage, 1966.

McCusker, John J., and Russell R. Menard. *The Economy of British America*. Chapel Hill: University of North Carolina Press, 1985.

McDonald, Forrest. *E Pluribus Unum: The Formation of the American Republic, 1776–1790*. Indianapolis, Ind.: Liberty Press, 1979.

_____. *Novus Ordo Seclorum: The Intellectual Origins of the Constitution*. Lawrence: University Press of Kansas, 1985.

_____. *We the People: The Economic Origins of the Constitution*. Chicago: University of Chicago Press, 1958.

Mace, George. *Locke, Hobbes, and The Federalist Papers: An Essay on the Genesis of the American Political Heritage.* Carbondale: Southern Illinois University Press, 1979.

McMichael, Jack R., and Barbara Taft, eds. *The Writings of William Walwyn.* Athens: University of Georgia Press, 1989.

McNally, David. "Locke, Levellers, and Liberty: Property and Democracy in the Thought of the First Whigs." *History of Political Thought* 10:1 (Spring 1989): 17–40.

Macpherson, C. B. *The Life and Times of Liberal Democracy.* Oxford: Oxford University Press, 1977.

_____. *The Political Theory of Possessive Individualism: Hobbes to Locke.* Oxford: Oxford University Press, 1962.

_____. "The Social Bearing of Locke's Political Theory." In *Life, Liberty, and Property,* edited by Gordon Schochet, pp. 60–85. Belmont, Calif.: Wadsworth, 1971.

_____. "The Structure of Seventeenth-Century Political Theory." In Norman F. Cantor and Michael S. Werthman, *The English Tradition,* pp. 341–46. New York: Macmillan, 1967.

Madison, James. *Notes of Debates in the Federal Convention of 1787.* Edited by Adrienne Koch. New York: Norton, 1966.

Madison, James, Alexander Hamilton, and John Jay. *The Federalist Papers.* Edited by Clinton Rossiter. New York: New American Library, 1961.

Maier, Pauline. "John Wilkes and American Disillusionment." *William and Mary Quarterly* 3d ser., 20:3 (July 1963): 373–95.

Main, Jackson T. *The Antifederalists: Critics of the Constitution, 1781–88.* Chapel Hill: University of North Carolina Press, 1961.

Marshall, John. "John Locke and Latitudinarianism." In *Philosophy, Science, and Religion in England: 1640–1700,* edited by Richard Kroll, Richard Ashcraft, and Perez Zagorin, pp. 253–82. Cambridge: Cambridge University Press, 1992.

Martin, James Kirby, ed. *Interpreting Colonial America: Selected Readings.* New York: Harper and Row, 1973.

Mason, Alpheus Thomas. *Free Government in the Making: Readings in American Political Thought.* New York: Oxford University Press, 1965.

Mather, Cotton. *The Christian Philosopher.* Boston, 1771.

Matson, Cathy D., and Peter S. Onuf. *A Union of Interests: Political and Economic Thought in Revolutionary America.* Lawrence: University Press of Kansas, 1990.

Maxson, Charles Hartsborn. *The Great Awakening in the Middle Colonies.* Chicago: University of Chicago Press, 1920.

May, Henry E. *The Enlightenment in America.* Oxford: Oxford University Press, 1976.

Meyers, Marvin, ed. *The Mind of the Founder: Sources of the Political Thought of James Madison.* Indianapolis, Ind.: Bobbs Merrill, 1973.

Miller, Douglas. *The Birth of Modern America: 1820–1850.* New York: Bobbs Merrill, 1970.

Miller, John C. *Alexander Hamilton and the Growth of the New Nation.* New York: Harper and Row, 1959.

Miller, Nathan. *The Founding Finaglers and Other Scoundrels in a Fascinating History of Corruption in America from Jamestown to Teapot Dome.* New York: David McKay Company, 1976.

Miller, Perry. "Solomon Stoddard, 1643–1729." *Harvard Theological Review* 34 (1941): 277–320.

Monson, Charles H., Jr. "Locke and His Interpreters." In *Life, Liberty, and Property,* edited by Gordon Schochet, pp. 33–48. Belmont, Calif.: Wadsworth, 1971.

Morgan, Edmund S. "The Puritan Ethic and the American Revolution." *William and Mary Quarterly* 3d ser., 24 (1967): 3–43.

Morgan, Edmund S., and Helen Morgan. *The Stamp Act Congress: Prologue to Revolution.* New York: Macmillan, 1962.

Mott, Frank Luther. *The Golden Multitudes: The Story of Bestsellers in the United States.* New York: Macmillan, 1947.

Murrin, John. "The Great Inversion, or Court versus Country: A Comparison of the Revolution Settlements in England (1688–1721) and America (1776–1816)." In *Three British Revolutions: 1644, 1688, 1776,* edited by J. G. A. Pocock, pp. 368–453. Princeton, N.J.: Princeton University Press, 1980.

Nash, Gary. "Artisans and Politics in Eighteenth Century Philadelphia." In *The Origins of Anglo-American Radicalism,* edited by Margaret E. Jacob and James R. Jacob, pp. 162–82. London: George, Allen and Unwin, 1984.

———. "Social Change and the Growth of Prerevolutionary Radicalism." In *The American Revolution,* edited by Alfred Young, pp. 3–36. Dekalb: Northern Illinois University Press, 1976.

Nelson, Jeffrey. "Unlocking Locke's Legacy: A Comment." *Political Studies* 26 (1978): 101–8.

Newlin, Claude. *Philosophy and Religion in Colonial America.* New York: Philosophical Library, 1962.

North, Douglas, ed. *The Growth of the American Economy to 1860.* New York: Harper Torchbooks, 1968.

Nozick, Robert. *Anarchy, State, and Utopia.* Oxford: Basil Blackwell, 1974.

Orren, Karen. *Belated Feudalism: Labor, the Law, and Liberal Development in the United States.* Cambridge: Cambridge University Press, 1991.

Otis, James. "The Rights of the British Colonies Asserted and Proved." *Boston Gazette,* 23 July 1764.

Overton, Richard. *An Arrow against All Tyrants.* London, 1946.

Pachter, Marc, and Frances Wein. *Abroad in America: Visitors to the New Nation, 1776–1914.* Reading, Mass.: Addison-Wesley, 1976.

Padover, Saul K. *The Complete Jefferson.* New York: Duell Sloan and Pearce, 1943.

———. *The Living U.S. Constitution.* New York: NAL, 1953.

———. *Thomas Jefferson on Democracy.* New York: Mentor Books, 1939.

Padover, Saul K., ed. *The Complete Madison: His Basic Writings.* Millwood, N.Y.: Harper and Brothers, 1953.

Pangle, Thomas L. *The Spirit of Modern Republicanism: The Moral Vision of the American Founders and the Philosophy of Locke.* Chicago: University of Chicago Press, 1988.

Parrington, Vernon L. *Main Currents in American Thought,* vol. 1, *The Colonial Mind.* New York: Harcourt, Brace and World, 1927.

Pateman, Carole. *The Sexual Contract.* Stanford, Calif.: Stanford University Press, 1988.

Patrick, Simon. *Agua Genitalis: A Discourse concerning Baptism.* London, 1659.

———. *A Brief Account of the New Sect of Latitude-Men.* London, 1662.

Patrides, C. A. *The Cambridge Platonists.* Cambridge, Mass.: Harvard University Press, 1970.

Patterson, Bennett B. *The Forgotten Ninth Amendment: A Call for Legislative and Judicial Recognition of Rights under Social Conditions of Today.* Indianapolis, Ind.: Bobbs Merrill, 1955.

Paul, Ellen Frankel, and Howard Dickman, eds. *Liberty, Property, and the Foundations of the American Constitution.* Albany: State University of New York Press, 1989.

Pease, Theodore Calvin. *The Leveller Movement: A Study in the History and Political Theory of the English Great Civil War*. Reprint, Gloucester, Mass.: Peter Smith, 1965.

Peikoff, Leonard. *The Ominous Parallels: The End of Freedom in America*. New York: Stein and Day, 1982.

Penn, William. *No Cross, No Crown*. London, 1669.

_____. *Pennsylvania Frame of Government*. Reprinted in Bernard Schwartz, *The Roots of the Bill of Rights*, vol. 1, pp. 132-44. New York: Chelsea House Publishers, 1980.

Perkins, Harold. "The Social Causes of the British Industrial Revolution." *Transactions of the Royal Society* (1968): 132–44.

Petegorsky, David W. *Left-Wing Democracy in the English Civil War: A Study of the Social Philosophy of Gerrard Winstanley*. New York: Haskell House, 1972.

Pettengill, Samuel. *Jefferson: The Forgotten Man*. New York: America's Future, 1938.

Piven, Francis Fox, and Richard A. Cloward. *Regulating the Poor: The Functions of Public Welfare*. New York: Vintage Books, 1971.

Plumb, J. H. *The Growth of Political Stability in England, 1675–1725*. London: Macmillan, 1967.

Pocock, J. G. A. "Between Gog and Magog: The Republican Thesis and the Ideologia Americana." *Journal of the History of Ideas* 48:2 (April--June 1987): 325–46.

_____. "Civic Humanism and Its Role in Anglo-American Thought." In J. G. A. Pocock, ed., *Politics, Language, and Time: Essays on Political Thought and History*, pp. 80–103. New York: Atheneum, 1973.

_____. *The Machiavellian Moment: Florentine Political Thought and the Atlantic Republican Tradition*. Princeton, N.J.: Princeton University Press, 1975.

_____. "Machiavelli, Harrington, and English Political Ideologies in the Eighteenth Century." In J. G. A. Pocock, ed., *Politics, Language, and Time*, pp. 104–47.

_____. "Virtue and Commerce in the Eighteenth Century." *Journal of Interdisciplinary History* 3 (1972): 119–34.

Post, David M. "Jeffersonian Revisions of Locke: Education, Property-Rights, and Liberty." *Journal of the History of Ideas* 47:1 (1986): 147–57.

Prescott, Frederick C., ed. *Alexander Hamilton and Thomas Jefferson: Representative Selections*. New York: American Book Company, 1934.

Pufendorf, Samuel. *Of the Law of Nature and Nations*. Amsterdam, 1672.

Rahe, Paul A. *Republics Ancient and Modern: Classical Republicanism and the American Revolution*. Chapel Hill: University of North Carolina Press, 1992.

Richardson, R. C., and G. M. Ridden, eds. *Freedom and the English Revolution: Essays in History and Literature*. Manchester: Manchester, Eng.: Manchester University, 1986.

Robbins, Caroline. *The Eighteenth-Century Commonwealthman: Studies in the Transmission, Development, and Circumstances of English Liberal Thought from the Restoration of Charles II until the War with the Thirteen Colonies*. New York: Atheneum, 1968.

_____. "William Penn, 1689–1702: Eclipse, Frustration, and Achievement." In *The World of William Penn*, edited by Richard S. Dunn and Mary Maples Dunn, pp. 71–84. Philadelphia: University of Pennsylvania Press, 1986.

Roberts, James Deotis. *From Puritanism to Platonism in Seventeenth Century England*. The Hague: Martinus Nijhoff, 1968.

Rogers, G. A. J. "John Locke and the Latitude-men: Ignorance as a Ground of Toleration." In *Philosophy, Science, and Religion in England: 1640–1700*, edited by Richard Kroll, Richard Ashcraft, and Perez Zagorin, pp. 230–52. Cambridge: Cambridge University Press, 1992.

Rossiter, Clinton. *The Political Thought of the American Revolution, Part 3, Seedtime of the Republic.* New York: Harcourt, Brace and World, 1963.

Russell, Conrad. *The Crisis of Parliaments: English History, 1509–1660.* Oxford: Oxford University Press, 1985.

Rutland, Robert Allen. *The Birth of the Bill of Rights, 1776–1791.* Chapel Hill: University of North Carolina Press, 1955.

Ryan, Alan. "Locke and the Dictatorship of the Bourgeoisie." In *Life, Liberty, and Property,* edited by Gordon Schochet, pp. 86–106. Belmont, Calif.: Wadsworth, 1971.

Sabine, G. H., ed. *The Works of Gerrard Winstanley.* Ithaca, N.Y.: Cornell University Press, 1941.

Sachs, William S., and Ari Hoogenboom. *The Enterprising Colonials: Society on the Eve of the Revolution.* Chicago: Argonaut, 1965.

Sandoz, Ellis. *A Government of Laws: Political Theory, Religion, and the American Founding.* Baton Rouge: Louisiana State University Press, 1990.

———. *Political Sermons of the American Founding Era: 1730–1805.* Indianapolis, Ind.: Liberty Press, 1991.

Sawvel, Franklin B., ed. *The Anas of Thomas Jefferson.* New York: Da Capo Press, 1970.

Schachner, Nathan. *The Founding Fathers.* New York: A. S. Barnes, 1970.

Schneewind, J. B. *Moral Philosophy from Montaigne to Kant: An Anthology.* 2 vols. Cambridge: Cambridge University Press, 1990.

Schochet, Gordon J., ed. *Life, Liberty, and Property: Essays on Locke's Political Ideas.* Belmont, Calif.: Wadsworth, 1971.

Schochet, Gordon J. "From Persecution to Toleration." In *Liberty Secured? Britain before and after 1688,* edited by J. R. Jones, pp. 122–57. Stanford, Calif.: Stanford University Press, 1992.

———. *Patriarchalism in Political Thought: The Authoritarian Family and Political Speculation and Attitudes, Especially in Seventeenth-Century England.* New York: Basic Books, 1975.

———. "Radical Politics and Ashcraft's Treatise on Locke." *Journal of the History of Ideas* 50:3 (July 1989): 491–510.

Schultz, Harold J., ed. *English Liberalism and the State: Individualism or Collectivism?* Lexington, Mass.: D. C. Heath, 1972.

Schwartz, Bernard. *The Roots of the Bill of Rights.* 5 vols. New York: Chelsea House Publishers, 1980.

Schwoerer, Lois G. "Locke, Lockean Ideas, and the Glorious Revolution." *Journal of the History of Ideas* 51:4 (October 1990): 531–48.

Seliger, Martin. "Locke, Liberalism, and Nationalism." In *John Locke: Problems and Perspectives,* edited by John Yolton, pp. 19–33. Cambridge: Cambridge University Press, 1969.

Shaw, Peter. *American Patriots and the Rituals of Revolution.* Cambridge, Mass.: Harvard University Press, 1981.

Siegan, Bernard. *Economic Liberties and the Constitution.* Chicago: University of Chicago Press, 1980.

Skinner, Quentin. *The Foundations of Modern Political Thought.* 2 vols. Cambridge: Cambridge University Press, 1978.

Sobel, Robert. *Panic on Wall Street: A History of America's Financial Disasters.* New York: Collier, 1968.

Soderlund, Jean R., ed. *William Penn and the Founding of Pennsylvania, 1680–1684: A Documentary History.* Philadelphia: University of Pennsylvania Press, 1983.

Spellman, W. M. *John Locke and the Problem of Depravity.* Oxford: Clarendon Press, 1988.

———. *The Latitudinarians and the Church of England, 1660–1700.* Athens: University of Georgia Press, 1993.

Spurlin, Paul Merrill. *The French Enlightenment in America: Essays on the Times of the Founding Fathers.* Athens: University of Georgia Press, 1984.

Spurr, John. "Latitudinarianism and the Restoration Church." *Historical Journal* 31:1 (1988): 61–82.

———. "Rational Religion in Restoration England." *Journal of the History of Ideas* 49:4 (October 1988): 563–84.

Steele, Richard. *The Tradesman's Calling; Being a Discourse Concerning the Nature, Necessity, Choices of a Calling, etc.* London, 1684.

Stephenson, Carl, and Frederick George Marcham, eds. *Sources of English Constitutional History: A Selection of Documents from A.D. 600 to the Present.* New York: Harper and Brothers, 1937.

Stewart, Donald H. *The Opposition Press of the Federalist Period.* Albany: State University of New York Press, 1969.

Stillingfleet, Edward. *A Discourse in Vindication of the Trinity.* London, 1696.

Stone, Lawrence. "Social Mobility in England: 1500–1700." In *Seventeenth-Century England: A Changing Culture,* edited by W. B. Owens, pp. 7–23. London: Ward Lock, 1988.

Storing, Herbert J. *What the Antifederalists Were For: The Political Thought of the Opponents of the Constitution.* Chicago: University of Chicago Press, 1981.

Stourzh, Gerald. *Alexander Hamilton and the Idea of Republican Government.* Stanford, Calif.: Stanford University Press, 1970.

Strauss, Leo. "Locke and the Modern Theory of Natural Right." In *Life, Liberty, and Property,* edited by Gordon Schochet, pp. 26–32. Belmont, Calif.: Wadsworth, 1971.

———. *Natural Right and History.* Chicago: University of Chicago Press, 1953.

Swanson, Donald F., and Andrew P. Trout. "Alexander Hamilton's Hidden Sinking Fund." *William and Mary Quarterly* 3d ser., 49:1 (January 1992): 108–16.

Tawney, R. H. *Religion and the Rise of Capitalism: A Historical Study.* New York: Penguin Books, 1947.

Taylor, Jeremy. *Discourse of the Liberty of Prophesying.* London, 1647.

Thompson, E. P. "The Moral Economy of the English Crowd in the Eighteenth Century." *Past and Present* 50 (February 1971): 76–136.

Thompson, Martyn P. "The Reception of Locke's 'Two Treatises of Government': 1690–1706." *Political Studies* 24:2 (June 1976): 184–91.

Tocqueville, Alexis de. *Democracy in America.* Edited by Andrew Hacker. New York: Washington Square Press, 1964.

Trenchard, John, and Thomas Gordon. *Cato's Letters. 1620–1623.* 4 vols. in 2 books. New York: Russell and Russell, 1969.

Trumbull, Benjamin. *A Complete History of Connecticut.* New Haven, 1818.

Tuck, Richard. *Natural Rights Theories: Their Origins and Development.* Cambridge: Cambridge University Press, 1979.

Tully, James. *A Discourse on Property: John Locke and His Adversaries.* Cambridge: Cambridge University Press, 1980.

Tully, James, and Quentin Skinner. *Meaning and Context: Quentin Skinner and His Critics.* Princeton, N.J.: Princeton University Press, 1988.

Tyacke, Nicholas. "Puritanism, Arminianism, and Counter-Revolution." In *Seventeenth-Century England: A Changing Culture,* edited by W. B. Owens, pp. 130–45. London: Ward Lock, 1988.

Usher, James. *The Power Communicated by God to the Prince and the Obedience Required of the Subject.* London, 1644.

Vaughn, Karen Iversen. *John Locke: Economist and Social Scientist.* Chicago: University of Chicago Press, 1980.

Veit, Helen E., Kenneth R. Bowling, and Charlene Bangs Bickford. *Creating the Bill of Rights: The Documentary Record from the First Federal Congress.* Baltimore, Md.: Johns Hopkins University Press, 1991.

Ver Steeg, Clarence L. *The Formative Years: 1607–1763.* New York: Hill and Wang, 1964.

von Leyden, W. "John Locke and Natural Law." In *Life, Liberty, and Property: Essays on Locke's Political Ideas,* edited by Gordon Schochet, pp. 12–25. Belmont, Calif.: Wadsworth Publishing Company, 1971.

Walker, James Blaine. *The Epic of American Industry.* New York: Harper and Brothers, 1949.

Walwyn, William. *The Fountain of Slander Discovered.* London, 1649.

Warren, Charles. *Congress as Santa Clause, or National Donations and the General Welfare Clause of the Constitution.* New York: Arno Press, 1978.

Weber, Max. *The Protestant Ethic and the Spirit of Capitalism: The Relationships between Religion and the Economic and Social Life in Modern Culture.* New York: Charles Scribner's Sons, 1958.

Weslager, C. A. *The Stamp Act Congress: With an Exact Copy of the Complete Journal.* Newark: University of Delaware Press, 1976.

West, Thomas G. "Leo Strauss and the American Founding." *Review of Politics* 53:1 (Winter 1991): 157–72.

White, Morton. *The Philosophy of the American Revolution.* New York: Oxford University Press, 1978.

_____. *Philosophy, The Federalist, and the Constitution.* New York: Oxford University Press, 1989.

Wiley, Basil. *The Seventeenth-Century Background: The Thought of the Age in Relation to Religion and Poetry.* New York: Doubleday Anchor, 1953.

Williams, Elisha. "The Essential Rights and Liberties of Protestants." Boston, 1774.

Williams, Roger. "The Bloudy Tenent of Persecution for Cause of Conscience Discussed," 1644. Reprinted in Alpheus Thomas Mason, *Free Government in the Making,* pp. 63–65. New York: Oxford University Press, 1965.

Wills, Garry. *Cincinnatus: George Washington and the Enlightenment.* New York: Doubleday, 1984.

_____. *Explaining America: The Federalist.* New York: Doubleday, 1981.

_____. *Inventing America: Jefferson's Declaration of Independence.* New York: Vintage Books, 1978.

Wilson, James. "Considerations on the Nature and Extent of the Legislative Authority of the British Parliament." Philadelphia, 1774.

Winthrop, John. "Little Speech on Liberty," 1645. Reprinted in Alpheus Thomas Mason, *Free Government in the Making,* pp. 60–61. New York: Oxford University Press, 1965.

Wise, John. *A Vindication of the Government of New England Churches.* Reprinted in Alpheus Thomas Mason, *Free Government in the Making,* pp. 68–71. New York: Oxford University Press, 1965.

Wishy, Bernard. "John Locke and the Spirit of '76." *Political Science Quarterly* 73:3 (1958): 413–25.

Wollstonecraft, Mary. *Vindication of the Rights of Woman*. Edited by Miriam Brody Kramnick. New York: Pelican Classics, 1975.

Wood, Gordon S. *The Creation of the American Republic: 1776–1787*. New York: W. W. Norton and Company, 1972.

_____. *The Radicalism of the American Revolution: How a Revolution Transformed a Monarchical Society into a Democratic One Unlike Any That Had Ever Existed*. New York: Alfred A. Knopf, 1992.

Wood, Neal. *John Locke and Agrarian Capitalism*. Berkeley: University of California Press, 1984.

_____. *The Politics of Locke's Philosophy: A Social Study of "An Essay concerning Human Understanding."* Berkeley: University of California Press, 1983.

Woolhouse, R. S. *Locke*. Minneapolis: University of Minnesota Press, 1983.

Wooton, David. "John Locke and Richard Ashcraft's 'Revolutionary Politics.' " *Political Studies* 40 (1992): 79–98.

Wrightson, Keith. *English Society: 1580–1680*. London: Hutchinson, 1988.

Yolton, Jean S., and John S. Yolton. "Locke's Suggestion of Thinking Matter and Some Eighteenth-Century Portuguese Reactions." *Journal of the History of Ideas* 45:2 (April 1984): 303–7.

Yolton, John W. *John Locke and the Way of Ideas*. Oxford: Oxford University Press, 1956.

Young, Alfred. *The Debate over the Constitution: 1787–1789*. Chicago: Rand McNally, 1965.

Young, Alfred, ed. *The American Revolution: Explorations in the History of American Radicalism*. Dekalb: Northern Illinois University Press, 1976.

Zuckert, Michael. "John Locke and the Problem of Civil Religion." In *The Moral Foundations of the American Republic,* edited by Robert H. Horwitz, pp. 181–203. Charlottesville: University Press of Virginia, 1986.

_____. *Natural Rights and the New Republicanism*. Princeton, N.J.: Princeton University Press, 1994.

Index